COMICS BUYER'S GUIDE

Marvel Comics

Checklist & Price Guide

1961 to Present

Edited by Don & Maggie Thompson

Published by

**krause
publications**

700 E. State Street • Iola, WI 54990-0001
Telephone: 715/445-2214

Library of Congress Catalog Number: 93-77551
ISBN: 0-87341-245-1
Printed in the United States of America

Contents

Acknowledgments 4
Foreword by Stan Lee 5
Introduction 7
    Including games, watches, and Crunch 'n Munch
A Brief History of Marvel Comics 11
    Marvel year-by-year 1961-1993
Novelties 28
    1966 Topps Marvel Flyers; PVC figures
Cards 29
Color Collectibles 33
Press Posters 92
For Your Reference 94
Books: Epic 95
    Hardcovers, trade paperbacks, mass-market paperbacks
Books: Marvel 96
    Hardcovers, trade paperbacks, mass-market paperbacks
Books: Marvel/Nelson; Marvel/Berkeley;
    Marvel/Grandreams 101
Comic Books: Epic 103
Comic Books: Marvel 110
Comic Books: Marvel UK 250
Comic Books: Marvel/Nelson;
    Marvel/Razorline; Star 259

Acknowledgments

So many people have helped to provide information for this edition that we know as we write this sentence that we are bound to miss a few. To those we apologize — as we thank them.

Thanks to Cliff Biggers for input on pricing and title additions to our listings.

Thanks to Gary Guzzo for providing information and help right from the start — and, moreover, to the kind Marvel folk whose services he used to provide the information he didn't have at hand.

Thanks to Don Butler and Peter Sanderson, both of whom came through with perspectives and hard information.

Thanks to Paul Curtis for fan-club information.

Thanks to the behind-the-scenes people at Marvel who saw to it that so many neat things reached us, the public — and were there to collect.

Thanks to licensees who also helped, especially SkyBox and Comic Images.

Thanks to our own behind-the-scenes people, including computer guru Steve Duberstein, photographer Ross Hubbard, designer Allen West, designer Patsy Morrison, and editorial staffers Brent Frankenhoff and Julie Stuempfig. There are lots more (Greg Loescher, Mary Sieber, Pat Klug, and Barb Lefeber among them), but we've got to be brief so we can get this project out the door to make room for the next one.

Thanks to the countless creators who have made Marvel that well-known House of Ideas — from the days of Jack Kirby, Steve Ditko, Dick Ayers, and so many, many others right up to today and beyond.

Finally, thanks to Stan Lee for his foreword — and, of course, for his part in making this all possible and downright necessary.

Don and Maggie Thompson, Iola, Wisconsin, November 12, 1993

Foreword

By Stan Lee

Hi, Heroes!

Wouldja believe I threw away countless copies of the first issue of *Fantastic Four*? Not only *The FF*, but *Spider-Man, The Hulk,* and all the rest of them.

And it wasn't just me. Practically the whole brain-dead Bullpen did the same thing.

You see, when Marvel was just abornin', back in the early '60s, there were no such things as price guides to comics. Those poor, seemingly valueless little mags were just read and tossed away. Nobody knew, or even suspected, that one day they would appreciate in value faster than most stocks on Wall Street!

Since I was one of those fenderheads who never saved any items from those grand and glorious early days of comics, imagine how I now feel, when I see the value which the collectors' market puts on even the most trivial old-time comic-book artifacts.

Of course, I get a big kick out of many of the rare old Marvel collectibles. One of my favorites is the original MMMS membership kit. For those of you who weren't with us then, those now-hallowed initials stood for The Merry Marvel Marching Society, the fan club to end all fan clubs. I still remember wanting to give our merry marchers something special in their membership kits, so I got most of the gang together (our bullpen being a lot smaller in the '60s than it is today) and marched them all to a recording studio, where we ad-libbed a special message to all our club members. Artie Simek, our top letterer at the time, played a brief but ear-splitting harmonica solo as his contribution to the record's hilarity, while Jolly Jack and I traded gags so corny that not even Irving Forbush would have said them with a straight face, and so it went, with Jolly Solly Brodsky, Fabulous Flo Steinberg, and most of our other talk-show-host-wannabes contributing to what was undoubtedly the wackiest record of all time. The records were stamped out on disks of vinyl, which was the only material we could afford, and given away free with each membership. Since they were totally amateurish and certifiably insane, what could be more natural than for those few remaining records to be prized collectors' items today?

But what of the future? We've got a zillion new grand and goofy schemes coming your way, though here's one that is probably the most original: We're going to make it possible for you to get a special book into which you can paste each installment of the daily and Sunday *Spider-Man* newspaper strip. This strip, which starts in early December, will be the same story as the three-part mini-series which will appear in Spidey's own mag, running through the December, January, and February issues, featuring The Hobgoblin and The Beast. But — though both the newspaper strip and the three-issue comic book will feature the same plot line, the incidents themselves will be varied and seen in different perspectives, since they'll each be told from a different viewpoint. Since this concept

is brand new and somewhat daring, not to mention indescribably complicated, it may well become one of the biggest collectors' items of all!

Oh, I just remembered — getting back to the good ol' MMMS, some of you may be aware that we later formed a second fan club called FOOM. (And I'm certain you've already guessed that those time-honored initials stand for Friends Of Ol' Marvel!) I can't quite remember what that particular membership kit consisted of, but I'm sure it was something equally freaky and far-out. I mean, hey, this is Marvel, right?

And now, for those of you who are sulking in the corner because you missed out on all those never-to-be-repeated opportunities for fame and glory, all is not yet lost. Out of the kindness of our hearts (and the greed of our wallets) we've formed the wacky and wondrous Agents of WAM, our newest and perhaps most totally incomprehensible (and therefore most desirable) fan club yet! Yea, truly — today, WAM! Tomorrow, the pages of *Comics Buyer's Guide to Marvel Comics*!

Just think how exciting it is. As the years go by, so many of the things we did become more and more valuable in the collectors' market — and so many of the things we're *about* to do will probably become equally valuable in the years to come.

I guess the trick is to save everything!

As a matter of fact, that may just solve a little mystery that's been bugging me. Now, at last, I can guess why so many artists and writers are renting warehouses!

Happy collecting, Frantic Ones!

Excelsior!

Stan Lee

Introduction

By Don and Maggie Thompson

There is a yearning to hold onto a project until it is perfect, until all the information is in, until nothing is left for future researchers.

When writers give in to this yearning, Parkinson's Law takes over, as work expands to fill the time alloted.

What seems a simple project turns inevitably into an eternity-consuming job, and it is never released. Meanwhile, an *imperfect* research project is published, additions and corrections are supplied by readers, an updated, more nearly perfect version is published, and more and more information is more and more widely available.

We had hoped to provide a list of two editions of Marvel Slurpee Cups. We had hoped to provide a section on Marvel Fan Clubs with a listing of what each had provided as collectibles. (Members of Wild Agents of Marvel, today's fan club, for example, received a number of mailings; there are even variant membership cards.)

We had hoped to provide current prices being asked for material released in England.

We had hoped to provide lots and lots of pictures. We *took* lots and lots of pictures but were quickly faced with the choice of making the type of a convenient size or of running pictures — and we opted for large, clear type. (Even then, we ended up shrinking some of the type to try to cram more in.)

On the other hand, we crammed a lot of material in this volume that has never been accumulated in one spot before. And we hope you'll join us in gathering more information — especially of the large number of Comic Images card sets we could *not* get data on.

We'll be running material as we get it in our bi-monthly *Comics Buyer's Guide Price Guide*, 700 East State Street, Iola, Wisconsin 54990. And, of course, we'll do our best to get it in the next version of this book, too.

Let us hear from you. (And let us know how you like our checklist format. It's designed so that you can use it in a number of ways, from simply crossing out boxes for items you have — to filling in those boxes with condition designations (e.g., "G" for a good-condition copy) or a count of the number of copies of the issue you have.

And here's additional information:

Brent Frankenhoff offers the following summary of some of the games that can be collected. (Not only will some of these games be hard to find in years to come; working equipment on which to play them will be hard to find — and tips on playing the games may be virtually impossible to locate.)

In the 1980s the home video game market had its first surge with such units as the Atari 2600, Mattel's Intellivision, and others, along with the first personal computer boom. Although Marvel licensing was not as widely seen then in the home video game market as it has been more recently with Nintendo and Sega, several games were produced.

In 1980, Bandai America introduced two hand-held video games featuring Spider-Man and The Hulk. *Spider-Man Rescue* allowed up to two players to help Spider-Man rescue his friend, while *Hulk Escapes* let up to two players help The Hulk elude his enemies.

At least two cartridges were released for use with the Atari 2600. One of the cartridges pitted Spider-Man against The Green Goblin, while the other, *G.I. Joe: Cobra Strike*, let players choose whether to play the part of the Joe team or Cobra Commander. Both cartridges were manufactured by Parker Brothers.

With personal computers from Apple, Commodore, Atari, and Radio Shack, as well as other manufacturers, enjoying immense popularity, and predictions indicating a personal computer in every home by the 1990s, Marvel began looking into developing adventure games featuring its characters in 1983. Scott Adams' Adventure International, a company that produced some of the first computer adventure games, was eventually hired and developed the Questprobe series which began in the mid-'80s. Three games were produced in the series, featuring Spider-Man, The Hulk, The Thing, and The Human Torch. The storyline, which was also covered in *Questprobe* comics, involved each character's search for mystic gems.

Other Marvel-related computer games from the 1980s included *G.I. Joe* from Epyx, *The Transformers* from Activision, and several games from Paragon software, a division of MicroProse Software Inc. *Dr. Doom's Revenge* sent Spider-Man and Captain America into Doom's Latverian castle in an attempt to stop the launch of a nuclear missile. Another game in the series, *X-Men: Madness in Murderworld*, chronicled the mutants' attempts to escape from Arcade's Murderworld. Both games were packaged with a Marvel comic book that served as an introduction to the game.

Paragon also produced a Spider-Man adventure game in 1990 which allowed players to outwit Mysterio and rescue Mary Jane from him. The company also adapted the *Uncanny X-Men* storyline "Fall of the Mutants" from *Uncanny X-Men* #225-227. (Players chose a team of five X-Men to restore the balance between Order and Chaos and defeat Freedom Force.) A Punisher adventure game was also produced by the company and later adapted for use with the Nintendo Entertainment System by LJN Ltd. (Frank Castle sought vengeance for the murder of his family from The Kingpin, and on the way battled such villains as Colonel Kliegg, Hitman, Sijo, and Jigsaw.)

In the 1990s, Marvel has returned to the video cartridge market with a number of games for the various Nintendo and Sega game systems and both *X-Men* and *Captain America and the Avengers* arcade units. Most of the cartridges feature Spider-Man or the X-Men, although *Captain America and the Avengers* has been adapted for home use, and several other Marvel characters have had their own games.

Among the first games for the Nintendo Entertainment System (NES) was *The Uncanny X-Men*, produced by LJN. (Players took the part of Professor Xavier and sent various members of the team on missions to defeat evil mutants.) The first LJN-produced X-Men game for Sega Genesis also included appearances by members of Excalibur and several mutant enemies including Magneto, Sabretooth, and Juggernaut. Wolverine

also had his own solo LJN adventure; he battled Sabretooth and Magneto, receiving help from Havok, Jubilee, and Psylocke.

Spider-Man has had three games produced for the Nintendo Game Boy by LJN. In the first, Spider-Man faced a threat similar to his solo adventure from Paragon Software with Mysterio kidnapping Mary Jane. The Hobgoblin and The Scorpion were among the enemies faced in the game. The second game put him face-to-face with Carnage and Venom, and in the third the Spider Slayers attacked.

Sega Genesis players also helped Spider-Man fight crime, and the first Spider-Man game for the Sega CD unit pitted Spider-Man against The Kingpin, Electro, Hobgoblin, and Venom in a race to save New York City from nuclear armageddon. At one point in the game, Spider-Man was trapped inside a giant pinball machine.

Spider-Man and members of the X-Men teamed up in *Arcade's Revenge* for the Super Nintendo Entertainment System and Sega Genesis. Members of The X-Men appearing in the game included Wolverine, Cyclops, Storm, and Gambit. The game was a joint effort between LJN and Acclaim Entertainment's Flying Edge division.

Captain America and the Avengers adapted the Data East arcade game of the same name for the Sega Genesis and the NES and allowed players to become Captain America or Hawkeye and battle The Red Skull, Ultron, The Mandarin, and other enemies in a quest to find Iron Man and The Vision. The cartridge was packaged with a collector's pin.

The Silver Surfer was featured in a game for the NES by Arcadia Systems Inc. with the Surfer charged with the task of repelling an interdimensional invasion.

Taxan came out with a G.I. Joe video game for the NES in the spring of 1991, with players choosing from five different team members to send on three-person missions. Capcom also produced a G.I. Joe NES adventure, *G.I. Joe: The Atlantis Factor*, in which the Joe team discovered that Cobra Commander, whom they thought they had destroyed at the end of a previous adventure, had been revived by an ancient power source from Atlantis.

Many games have been adapted for systems other than the ones listed here, and this is only an indication of some of the Marvel games available for collecting.

Finally, information continues to come into the office even as we prepare to send this book to press. We conclude the introduction with two such listings. (As throughout the book, of course, "NVE" means "No Value Established."):

1993 Character Time X-Men

Produced by California-based Character Time, these cards were produced and packaged with X-Men watches, which were made to honor the 30th Anniversary of the X-Men. A total of 5,000 watches (and sets of cards) were produced and were available initially through mail-order only for around $65, which included one watch and a card. The total package was elaborate, up to and including the box in which the watch came and the watch container within the box. Cards were unnumbered; backs featured a reproduction of a scene from one of the comic books (for instance, a Jack Kirby Cyclops/Marvel Girl Iceman panel on the back of The Original X-Men, Neal Adams Cyclops on the back

of the Cyclops card, and John Byrne's Jean Grey on the back of Dark Phoenix). The artist listed here produced the card front only.

1993 Character Time X-Men

	Card	
Complete set (6)		NVE
Common card		NVE

#	Card	M
❑ xx	Cable (Ted McKeever)	NVE
❑ xx	Cyclops (Dave Dorman)	NVE
❑ xx	Dark Phoenix (Jim Steranko)	NVE
❑ xx	Original X-Men (Ken Steacy)	NVE
❑ xx	Professor Xavier (Bill Sienkiewicz)	NVE
❑ xx	Wolverine (Andy Kubert, Joe Kubert)	NVE

1993 Crunch 'n Munch Marvel Super-Heroes

As part of a year-long promotion, one of six unnumbered cards featuring Marvel super-hero characters was issued in each box of Franklin Crunch 'n Munch. The six-card set featured five heroes (backs included biographical notes) and one super-heroes card (which included information on the first appearances of each of the five characters in the set). Cards sported full-color fronts and backs and were printed on thin cardboard.

An on-box offer allowed collectors to send in three proofs of purchase and $2.95 to get a Marvel Master Vision poster featuring more than 25 of the Marvel super-heroes signed by artists Ron Lim, Terry Austin, and Paul Mounts.

1993 Crunch 'n Munch Marvel Super-Heroes

Complete set (6)	6.00
Each card	1.00
Poster	5.00

#	Card	M
❑ xx	Cage	1.00
❑ xx	Hulk	1.25
❑ xx	Storm	1.00
❑ xx	Spider-Man	1.25
❑ xx	Wolverine	1.00
❑ xx	Team card	1.25

A Brief History of Marvel Comics

By Peter Sanderson

Today Marvel Comics is the largest comic-book publisher on the North American continent, and its enormous "universe" of characters has spread from its home medium into movies, television, comic strips, video games, and more. Its audience ranges from small children to middle-aged adults. Yet only 33 years ago Marvel was no more than a single magazine casting about for a new direction in a market believed to consist solely of children. Marvel went on to transform the super-hero comic book and its audience and has continued as the principal influence on the widest-selling adventure comics to this day.

*The company now known as Marvel has actually existed for well over 50 years under a variety of names, most notably Timely Comics during the "Golden Age" of the 1940s. It was in 1939, the year after Superman's debut, that its first super-hero comic book, **Marvel Comics** #1, featuring the original Human Torch and Prince Namor the Sub-Mariner, was published. Already there was something different about this particular publisher. Carl Burgos's Torch was not truly "Human," but an android, and Bill Everett's Sub-Mariner started out by attacking humanity for its depredations against his undersea race.*

*Two years later the team of Joe Simon and Jack Kirby created Timely's most famous Golden Age hero, Captain America, a living embodiment of patriotic fervor in a time of war. It was as author of a text story in **Captain America Comics** that the teen-age Stan Lee made his comic-book debut.*

There were many other Timely super-heroes — the original Angel and Vision, Miss America, The Whizzer — but apart from its three aforementioned stars, the company's characters did not capture the public imagination the way the heroes of Superman's National Comics (now known as DC) or the original Captain Marvel's Fawcett did.

By 1951 the public's enthusiasm even for those heroes had virtually died. An attempted revival of Captain America, The Torch, and Namor swiftly failed, as did Stan Lee's Arthurian saga The Black Knight. The company that would become Marvel worked instead in other genres, such as

"girls' comics" like **Patsy Walker** and **Millie the Model**, Westerns like **Kid Colt** and **Rawhide Kid**, and Cold War intrigue in **The Yellow Claw.** (All of these characters would resurface in the "Marvel Age of Comics.")

By the beginning of the 1960s Stan Lee and a handful of artists, notably Jack Kirby and Steve Ditko, were devoting themselves to science-fiction comics, which, in practice, meant stories about enormous monsters with names like Googam, Son of Goom, and Spragg the Living Hill.

Over at National, however, editor Julius Schwartz had scored great success by revamping and reviving super-heroes from the Golden Age, beginning with The Flash in 1956. The high sales of Schwartz's super-hero team comic book **Justice League of America** led publisher Martin Goodman to ask his own editor Stan Lee to create a counterpart for their company.

Deeply dissatisfied with his comics career, Lee decided to take the opportunity to create a super-hero team comic book that he himself would want to read, one with believable characterizations and in which the fantasy elements were firmly grounded in a recognizable reality. He decided to name this projected new line of comics "Marvel," after Timely's first super-hero comic book, and thus it began.

1961

This was the year that the Marvel revolution started with but a single issue of a single magazine: *Fantastic Four* #1, cover-dated November 1961, by Stan Lee and Jack Kirby. It was not a complete break with the past. After all, the most prominent figure on the cover was a monster who was not unlike Fin Fang Foom and his ilk. But the stories inside were replete with innovations. The Fantastic Four did not wear masks or have secret identities. They lived in a recognizably real and contemporary world, complete with a Cold War and space race. Unlike preceding super-hero groups, The FF were not simply a team, but a kind of family, united by love but often shaken by disagreements and tensions. Perhaps most shockingly, one of the four, Ben Grimm, was not the usual handsome leading man, but had been transformed into a grotesque monster, riven by self-loathing. The idea that to be different from ordinary people could make one an outcast, that a great gift of power could also become a dire curse, was startlingly new to a genre in which super-heroes were traditionally universally acclaimed and free from any reason for despair. And this was only the beginning.

1962

The year began with Lee and Kirby building astonishingly fast on the groundwork laid down in *FF* #1. The next issue, cover-dated January 1962, introduced Marvel's first alien race, the Skrulls, who used their shape-changing powers to frame The Fantastic Four as criminals. Thus Lee and Kirby concocted a story that first showed how the public

would turn super-heroes into celebrities in the "real world," but would hunt them down out of fear and jealousy if given any cause for suspicion.

The Fantastic Four managed to clear their names, but fate would not prove so kind to another Lee and Kirby creation, The Incredible Hulk, who made his debut in his own short-lived, six-issue series in May. Like Ben Grimm, Bruce Banner was transformed by nuclear radiation into a monster, but Banner became a physical reincarnation of the dangerously vicious dark side of his own repressed personality turned violently loose to be hunted down by society.

The last of the three revolutionary series was inaugurated by Stan Lee and Steve Ditko in August in the fifteenth and last issue of *Amazing Fantasy*, the even more Amazing Spider-Man. Its hero was Peter Parker, a high-school student, as nerdy as Clark Kent only pretended to be, who gained super-human powers through sheer accident. But Spider-Man was no god in human guise like Superman, nor, despite his youth, was he a mere "kid sidekick." Spider-Man became the Everyman as super-hero, misunderstood by society, isolated even from those he loved, beset by the common tribulations of life and his own neuroses, yet managing from time to time to rise above it all in triumph.

In this very busy year, Lee and Kirby also introduced Henry Pym, "The Man in the Ant Hill" in *Tales to Astonish*, who became the costumed hero Ant-Man later that year. They reinterpreted Norse myths for the contemporary comics medium with the mighty Thor, beginning in *Journey into Mystery* #83. In recognition of the forebear of the Marvel style, they brought back The Sub-Mariner, who launched a new war on the human race in *Fantastic Four* #4. Then, in the very next issue, they introduced The Fantastic Four's greatest opponent, Doctor Doom, a villain of grandeur such as had never before been seen in super-hero comics and that has still yet to be equaled.

1963

Another of the essential elements of Marvel Comics' success was the concept of the Marvel Universe. In past decades super-heroes from various series had met regularly in such magazines as *All-Star* and *Justice League* from DC. But at Marvel crossovers were not restricted to certain comic books but became a regular occurrence, strengthening the readers' sense that the characters not only were published by the same company but also lived in the same fictional reality. Hence, in the first issue of *The Amazing Spider-Man*, the title character asked The Fantastic Four if he could get a job with them. That same month The Fantastic Four would head west in their own series to combat The Hulk.

Meanwhile, new characters continued to appear every month. Stan Lee, Larry Lieber, and Don Heck introduced inventor Tony Stark and his armored identity of Iron Man in *Tales of Suspense* #39, and the tireless Kirby took over the art with the following issue. Lee and Kirby brought their brands of characterization and adventure to the war genre with

Sgt. Fury and His Howling Commandos. Henry Pym gained a crime-fighting partner, The Wasp, and a new identity, Giant-Man.

Spider-Man artist Steve Ditko demonstrated a very different side of his talents by co-creating Doctor Strange in *Strange Tales* with Stan Lee, in which Ditko's unique depictions of occult entities and surreal worlds would make him a comics legend.

Lee and Kirby finally created a Marvel version of Justice League with *The Avengers*, teaming many of their new super-hero creations, beginning with a September cover date.

That same month saw the premiere of a series that was less popular at the time but would one day become Marvel's best seller: *The X-Men*, with original members Professor X, Cyclops, Marvel Girl (Jean Grey), The Beast, The Angel, and Iceman. In making their latest group of alienated, misunderstood super-heroes members of a race of mutants, Lee and Kirby had hit upon a concept that would strike a chord with generations of comics readers still to come.

It is amazing that so few individuals could sustain such a high level of creativity over these few years. Other memorable characters who first appeared in 1963 include Magneto, The Impossible Man, J. Jonah Jameson, The Watcher, The Vulture, Nightmare, Doctor Octopus, The Sandman, Kang (in his Rama-Tut guise), The Molecule Man, and The Lizard.

Lee, Kirby, and Ditko must have felt they had more than enough work for themselves, since only one major new Marvel comic book was launched this year: *Daredevil*, co-created by Stan Lee and Namor's Bill Everett, with the art soon being taken over by E.C. Comics giant Wally Wood.

The biggest news of 1964, however, was surely the return of Marvel's greatest Golden Age hero, Captain America, who was found frozen in suspended animation in *Avengers* #4. Cap quickly became the central figure of the team and won his own Lee-Kirby series, sharing the "split book" *Tales of Suspense* with Iron Man beginning with issue #59. The Hulk, meanwhile, took over half of *Tales to Astonish*, beginning with issue #60, now with Ditko as his artist.

Other major Marvel characters appearing for the first time in 1964 included Quicksilver, The Scarlet Witch, Hawkeye, and The Black Widow, (all of whom started out as villains), Iron Man's arch-foe The Mandarin, the original Green Goblin, Electro, Mysterio, Kraven the Hunter, Kang (this time as himself), Dormammu, Clea, and The Avengers' butler Jarvis. Wonder Man started his sole 1960s appearance, in *Avengers* #9, as the team's enemy but died after saving their lives. It would be well over a decade before he was brought back to life by later writers.

Halfway through the '60s came a big year for romance at Marvel. It was rare that an established comic-book character's life changed up until then; no one seriously believed that Superman would ever marry Lois Lane. But in 1965 Lee and Kirby changed the rules of the game once more with the wedding of Mister Fantastic and The Invisible Girl in *Fantastic Four Annual* #3, which was also the first *en masse* crossover involving virtually all extant Marvel heroes and villains.

This was also the year that Peter Parker entered college and met his first true love, Gwen Stacy, as well as his future friend — and enemy — Harry Osborn. Peter's future wife, Mary Jane Watson, also first appeared in *Amazing Spider-Man* #25 — but with her face concealed.

Lee and Kirby introduced a new modern version of the jungle lord Ka-Zar into *X-Men* #9 and re-introduced Captain America's nemesis, The Red Skull, in *Tales of Suspense*. Daredevil got the costume he would wear for nearly three more decades in issue #7, and The Sub-Mariner received his first modern day series in *Tales to Astonish* #70, by Stan Lee and "Adam Austin," the then-secret identity of another Silver Age Marvel great, Gene Colan.

Kirby left *The Avengers* with issue #16 but not before he and Lee did the unexpected once again. The original members all quit, leaving Captain America in charge of a new team of reformed villains: Hawkeye, Quicksilver, and The Scarlet Witch.

Kirby's artwork was now quickly reaching its peak period of power and dynamism that would last into the 1970s, and he and Lee collaborated on stories that remain classics to this day, such as "The Trial of the Gods" in *Thor* and the introduction of The Inhumans in *Fantastic Four*.

In Kirby's last run of *X-Men* issues, he and Lee created The Juggernaut and finally crystallized the theme of humanity's persecution of mutants through the introduction of The Sentinels in #14.

Surprisingly, Lee and Kirby crossbred war comics with the new craze for James Bond-style spies and came up with *Nick Fury, Agent of S.H.I.E.L.D.*, which began in *Strange Tales* #135.

This year is marked by a passing of much of the Old Guard of the early Silver Age and their replacement by a new wave of talent.

The most significant departure was that of Steve Ditko from Marvel, although not before doing the "Master Planner" storyline, featuring perhaps his most famous sequence of art, in which a trapped Spider-Man frees himself in a single supreme effort. Ditko's re-

placement was John Romita Sr., who earlier that year had taken over *Daredevil* from Wally Wood. Romita made a memorable *Spider-Man* debut with a two-parter at last revealing the true identity of The Green Goblin. Not stopping there, Lee and Romita also finally revealed the face of Mary Jane Watson in issue #42. "Adam Austin" was unmasked as Gene Colan, now drawing both *Daredevil* and *Iron Man*. (In another name change, *Journey into Mystery* became *Thor*.)

Marvel's first major writer after Stan Lee, Roy Thomas, took over as writer of both *The X-Men* and *The Avengers* this year, and Jim Steranko began doing finishes over Kirby layouts on *S.H.I.E.L.D.*

In the midst of all these changes Stan Lee and Jack Kirby produced the stories generally believed to be the peak of their collaboration: *Fantastic Four* #48-51. The first three make up the classic "Galactus Trilogy," which pitted The Fantastic Four against the ultimate menace and introduced Kirby's own creation, The Silver Surfer, the angel-like alien who discovers the meaning and worth of humanity. Immediately following came "This Man, This Monster," a character study of a nameless man that is, perhaps, Lee and Kirby's masterpiece.

Were all of this not enough, 1966 saw the creation of Marvel's first black super-hero, The Black Panther, and another classic Lee-Kirby trilogy, in which Captain America faced a Red Skull armed with the all-powerful Cosmic Cube.

This was Marvel's finest year. The company has produced many more comic books in subsequent years, but never any that were superior to the best of 1966.

1967

After all of this, 1967 must suffer by comparison, but there was still a great deal to appreciate. Gil Kane came to Marvel on both *Hulk* and *Captain America,* while John Buscema returned to comics with superb work with Roy Thomas on *The Avengers*. Lee and Kirby were still amazing their fans with a seemingly inexhaustible stream of new concepts in *Fantastic Four*, including the alien Kree and the artificially created being "Him," known in later years as Adam Warlock. Another great Marvel villain, The Kingpin, made his first appearance in *Amazing Spider-Man* #50. Steranko awed readers with his dazzling work writing and drawing *S.H.I.E.L.D.*, and Lee and Colan's enthusiasm was infectious, as they concocted a thrilling but underappreciated series of high adventures all year long for Daredevil. Finally, Marvel launched *Not Brand Ecch* ("Brand Ecch" being Stan Lee's pet name for the stodgy DC Comics of that time), which carried on the style of Harvey Kurtzman's early *Mad Magazine* in parodies of Marvel's own heroes.

1968

So far Marvel was producing only a relative handful of super-hero titles (although Lee and Kirby's workloads were still enough to make one gasp). 1968 was the year of Marvel's first great expansion, as each of the "split" comics — *Astonish, Suspense,* and *Strange Tales* — became two, resulting in *Captain America* (by Lee and Kirby), *Doctor Strange* (Thomas and Colan), *The Incredible Hulk* (eventually Lee and Herb Trimpe), *Iron Man* (Archie Goodwin and George Tuska), *Nick Fury, Agent of S.H.I.E.L.D.* (Steranko), and *Sub-Mariner* (Thomas and Buscema). The Silver Surfer, who became something of a '60s icon, also received his own comic book by Lee and Buscema, as did a new character with a name borrowed from a classic Golden Age hero: Captain Marvel.

Marvel also made its first foray into the field of black-and-white magazines, with the original *Spectacular Spider-Man,* which lasted a mere two issues.

1968 also saw Lee and Kirby continuing to break new ground when The Invisible Girl gave birth to Franklin Richards in *Fantastic Four Annual* #6. Roy Thomas created modern versions of Timely heroes The Black Knight and The Vision in *Avengers,* and Ultron, Mephisto, and Annihilus first reared their evil heads.

1969

By now new talent was beginning to enter the Marvel Bullpen, as Neal Adams began an extraordinary series of *X-Men* stories with Roy Thomas, and Barry Smith (later known as Barry Windsor-Smith) drew Stan Lee's final issues of *Daredevil.*

Marvel's first African-American hero, The Falcon, began his career in the pages of *Captain America,* while a somewhat less notable black hero, Brother Voodoo, made his debut in a revived *Strange Tales.* Thomas and Gil Kane revised Captain Marvel, giving him a new costume and powers.

Unfortunately, it appeared that Marvel had expanded a little too much and too fast: Both *Doctor Strange* and *S.H.I.E.L.D.* came to their ends, although several new incarnations awaited them in coming years.

1970

Appropriately enough, the last year of Marvel's first decade was marked by endings. The most important of these was Jack Kirby's departure from Marvel to write and draw *The New Gods* and other new creations for DC. Hence, this year was his last on *The Fantastic Four* and *Thor,* the two series he had co-plotted (or perhaps often entirely plotted) and drawn for so many years, and the first *Silver Surfer* series came to an end with two Kirby issues.

Today's readers may find it incredible, but, despite the widespread acclaim for the Thomas-Adams issues, it was too late to save *The X-Men* from cancellation. No one could see in 1970 what it was destined to become a mere five years hence.

Marvel launched two more short-lived split comics: *Amazing Adventures* starring The Inhumans (initially by Kirby) and The Black Widow, and *Astonishing Tales* with Ka-Zar (first drawn by Kirby, then by Barry Smith) and Doctor Doom (with eerie art by Wally Wood in the early issues).

But 1970 also brought with it a great new beginning with the first issue of *Conan the Barbarian* by Roy Thomas and Barry Smith. Robert E. Howard's warrior hero from the pulp magazines of the 1930s had only recently been revived in paperback collections, but it was through Thomas's remarkable comic-book version over the next decade that Conan finally achieved real fame, to the point at which many magazine and newspaper articles about the movie versions assumed the character had originated in comic books.

Marvel's first and greatest surge of creativity came to an end with the exit of Jack Kirby. Stan Lee began to devote himself more to his business duties, and 1971 saw his final issues of both *The Fantastic Four* and *Thor*. He continued on *Amazing Spider-Man,* however, and made headlines with a three-part story, drawn by Gil Kane, dealing with the dangers of addictive drugs, which was published over the opposition of the Comics Code Authority. The storyline's success prompted the first step in the increasing liberalization of the Code, leading to the far greater freedom of expression in comics that readers no doubt take for granted today.

Some tend to characterize the 1970s as a low period for Marvel creatively. It has been observed that, except for *Spectacular Spider-Man*, no title introduced in the 1970s has been continuously published to the present day.

But the 1970s saw the arrival of the first great wave of comic-book fans from the 1960s turned writers and artists — Gerry Conway, Len Wein, Marv Wolfman, Steve Englehart, Steve Gerber, Don McGregor, Jim Starlin, Howard Chaykin, Doug Moench, Walt Simonson, Chris Claremont, and John Byrne, among many others — many of whom regarded comic books as a medium of personal expression, an artform whose full potential had yet to be reached. The '70s were the years in which Marvel experimented in many new directions, in which some of the most interesting work appeared in "peripheral" series, and in which concepts were created — like The Ghost Rider, Punisher, and the "new" X-Men — that would become major phenomena in succeeding decades.

The greatest event of 1971 was the beginning of The Avengers' most memorable storyline, the clash of two galactic empires in the original Kree-Skrull War by Roy Thomas, John Buscema, Neal Adams, and others. Other noteworthy events of that year include the first appearance of The Hulk's beloved alien queen Jarella in an issue plotted by Har-

Ian Ellison, the debuts of The Squadron Supreme in *Avengers*, Doc Samson in *Hulk*, Morbius the Living Vampire in *Amazing Spider-Man*, and The Defenders in *Marvel Feature #1*. The first issue of the black-and-white magazine *Savage Tales* introduced Marvel's own shambling swamp creature, The Man-Thing, and another Howard hero won his own series in *Kull the Conqueror*.

1972

This was the year that the New Guard fully took over, with Roy Thomas succeeding Stan Lee as editor-in-chief, and Lee handing the writing of *Amazing Spider-Man* over to Gerry Conway. Steve Englehart, meanwhile, began his long, innovative run on *Captain America and The Falcon*.

As a further move towards prominently featuring African-American heroes, Marvel started *Luke Cage, Hero for Hire*. That same year Marvel finally launched Spider-Man in a successful companion series, *Marvel Team-Up*, The Beast took over *Amazing Adventures*, and Adam Warlock and The Defenders received their own series. Marvel's attempt to start a number of comic books centering on heroines, including *The Cat* and *Shanna the She-Devil*, however, proved short-lived.

The big news of 1972, however, was Marvel's new expansion into color horror comics, thanks to a relaxation of the Comics Code's restrictions against them. The first was *Tomb of Dracula*, which would achieve classic status under the team of Marv Wolfman, Gene Colan, and Tom Palmer. It was soon followed by *Werewolf by Night*.

Finally, in a welcome nod to the past, Bill Everett returned for a final stint on his creation *Sub-Mariner*, during which he created Namor's cousin, the future New Warrior Namorita.

1973

Marvel's move into horror gained momentum quickly this year, starting with *The Monster of Frankenstein* with superb artwork by Mike Ploog. The series, unfortunately, would not last long, but *Ghost Rider*, featuring the original Rider, John Blaze, would cycle on for a decade to come.

There was also an entire new line of black-and-white horror magazines, wholly free from Code restrictions, including *Dracula Lives, Monsters Unleashed, Vampire Tales*, and *Tales of the Zombie*. The Man-Thing now appeared in *Fear*, and an old-time Marvel monster, It, the Living Colossus, took over *Astonishing Tales*.

Jim Starlin's villainous creation Thanos first appeared in *Iron Man* and then moved over to the *Captain Marvel* series, as Starlin took over as its writer-artist. This same year Don McGregor began his classic work on the *War of the Worlds* (later known as *Killraven*) series in *Amazing Adventures* and the "Panther's Rage" storyline in *Jungle Action*.

Then, at year's end, Steve Gerber introduced a "throwaway" character into one of his more bizarre storylines in *Fear* #19; that character's name was Howard the Duck.

This year The Punisher inaugurated his war on crime in *Amazing Spider-Man* #129. As for Spider-Man himself, he began starring in a comic book for beginning readers, *Spidey Super Stories,* produced by Marvel in cooperation with PBS's program *The Electric Company.* Man-Thing and Ka-Zar won their own titles, as did The Thing with *Marvel Two-in-One,* and Doctor Strange returned in a new series with extraordinary work by Steve Englehart, Frank Brunner, and Gene Colan.

Marvel was now trying its hand at another new genre, the kung fu thrillers as popularized by Bruce Lee, through the adventures of Shang-Chi as chronicled by Englehart and later Doug Moench in *Master of Kung Fu.* Shang-Chi was also the lead in a new black-and-white magazine, *Deadly Hands of Kung Fu,* which was soon joined by another, *The Savage Sword of Conan.*

Oh, yes, and Len Wein and Herb Trimpe came up with a hot-tempered, rather short character named Wolverine in *Incredible Hulk* #180.

At first glance Marvel's creativity might seem to be running low in 1975. What can one say about the year that gave us *Skull the Slayer* and *The Champions?* Well, it also launched Hellstorm in his first series, *The Son of Satan.* Roy Thomas paid tribute to Timely's wartime comics with *The Invaders,* excitingly illustrated by Frank Robbins.

But, most importantly, 1975 was the year that two events occurred that foreshadowed super-hero comics as we know them today. Len Wein and Dave Cockrum unveiled a brand new team of X-Men in *Giant-Size X-Men* #1. And over in a new martial arts series, *Iron Fist,* up-and-coming writer Chris Claremont began his collaboration with the equally up-and-coming penciller John Byrne. History was being made.

But at the time people inside and outside the comics industry were paying considerably more attention to Howard the Duck, whose unexpected popularity quickly resulted in his own title, written by Steve Gerber and drawn by Frank Brunner, followed by Gene Colan. Despite the infamously unsuccessful movie version made later, Gerber's original "Howard" stories remain brilliantly written works of satire to this day.

Gerber also experimented this year with the enigmatic *Omega the Unknown,* and Marv Wolfman and Sal Buscema created future New Warrior Nova, who also starred in his

own series. *Spectacular Spider-Man* returned as a new monthly four-color comic book, and the original version of Marvel's speculative *What If?* first appeared.

Unexpectedly, Jack Kirby had returned to Marvel, this time both writing and drawing *Captain America* and a new series based on the film *2001*, in which he introduced the human robot Machine Man the following year. Kirby's most impressive work on his return, though, was his creation of the epic storyline of *The Eternals.*

Chris Claremont joined *The X-Men*'s creative team with the first regular issue of the new series, and he and artist Dave Cockrum rapidly made it the cutting edge of super-hero adventure comics, culminating that year with the first appearance of Phoenix in #101.

Over the last decade and a half Marvel had become DC's only serious rival, but the two companies buried the hatchets in 1976 long enough to produce the *Superman vs. Spider-Man* tabloid comic book, the first of a series of four crossovers between their respective universes.

Marvel was now becoming more interested in adapting outside properties and scored an impressive coup, when Roy Thomas persuaded the company to secure the comics rights to a then little-known science-fiction film still months away from release. Its name: *Star Wars*. 1977 also brought Marvel's entertaining, if short-lived, series plunking Godzilla down in the middle of the Marvel Universe.

Joining the barbarian comic books was *Red Sonja* #1, starring the female warrior who was Conan's sometime rival and ally, and a new effort was made to create a comic book starring a female super-hero with *Ms. Marvel.*

Jack Kirby took over *Jungle Action,* which was renamed after its star, *The Black Panther.* Meanwhile, The Hulk got his own black-and-white magazine, *The Rampaging Hulk,* with dynamic artwork by Walter Simonson and Doug Moench's handling of the lead character's personality that anticipated The Hulk of more recent times.

In response to its accelerating popularity, the new *X-Men* series went monthly, and by year's end Dave Cockrum ceded the role of penciller to John Byrne, who started out with the epic conclusion to the first Phoenix storyline in issue #108.

Kirby's *2001* was renamed after Machine Man, who had become the star of the comic book, but it would be Steve Ditko who saw this series to its conclusion. Kirby created one last series for Marvel, the prehistoric adventure *Devil Dinosaur,* before leaving the company for the final time.

Marvel was winding down its interest in starting series over the next several years. The original Spider-Woman made her debut in her own comic book in April. *The Rampaging Hulk* became the full-color magazine *The Hulk!* in response to the new TV show's success. Its original back-up may have been the most intriguing of 1978's new series: Howard Chaykin's 1930s swashbuckling adventure *Dominic Fortune.*

1979

The end of the 1970s brought with it the beginning of another of the formative influences on present-day adventure comics, as Frank Miller started pencilling *Daredevil* with #158. Meanwhile, his future collaborator, Bill Sienkiewicz, was making his own debut as artist of the new *Moon Knight* series in the back of *The Hulk!*

This year saw a new trend at Marvel: comic books based on toys, namely *Rom* and *The Micronauts,* whose early issues boasted stunning artwork by Michael Golden. In another nod to Japanese influences, Marvel also brought us the gigantic robots known as the *Shogun Warriors.*

Another trend, though, was finally reaching its end: Neither the black-and-white magazine versions of *Howard the Duck* nor *Tomb of Dracula* would last long. Of all the black-and-whites, only *Savage Sword of Conan* would continue into the present.

1980

The beginning of the '80s brought with it much that was new to Marvel. After a long series of editors-in-chief who eventually left to pursue writing — Roy Thomas, Len Wein, Marv Wolfman, Gerry Conway, and Archie Goodwin — Marvel finally found one who stayed for a long time and left an indelible mark. It was Jim Shooter who established the editorial system at Marvel that permitted both far greater expansion of the line and, for good or ill, much stronger editorial direction over the comic books' contents.

Furthermore, in response to the growing proliferation of creator-owned titles in the newly expanding direct-sales market, Marvel inaugurated its own line of creator-owned material, beginning with the anthology magazine *Epic Illustrated,* originally edited by Rick Marschall.

Moon Knight and The She-Hulk both received their own titles in 1980, but the landmark story of the year was unquestionably the Claremont and Byrne Dark Phoenix saga in *Uncanny X-Men,* culminating with the controversial death of Phoenix in #137.

1981

Claremont and Byrne may have even topped "Dark Phoenix" with the startling "Days of Future Past" in *Uncanny X-Men* #141-142, whose repercussions are still affecting Mar-

vel storylines today. Soon after, though, John Byrne left *X-Men* to strike out on his own as a writer-artist on *Fantastic Four*.

Similarly, Frank Miller began writing as well as drawing *Daredevil,* introducing the female assassin Elektra in his first solo issue, #168. Miller's blend of *film noir* and super-heroics, his dynamic action sequences, and his ability to evoke near-tragic moods would influence the many "grim and gritty" comics to come.

Marvel still demonstrated little interest in creating new series, although 1981 did bring the forgettable *Dazzler* and Bruce Jones's and Brent Anderson's unusual reinterpretation of *Ka-Zar the Savage*.

By 1982, however, the increasing expansion of the direct-sales market led Marvel to experiment with new formats. Jim Starlin wrote and drew Marvel's first graphic novel, *The Death of Captain Marvel,* and he was also responsible for *Dreadstar,* the first individual creator-owned comic book from Marvel's Epic department, now headed by Archie Goodwin. Al Milgrom, meanwhile, was in charge of the new *Marvel Fanfare,* an anthology title produced on slick paper especially for the new collector's market.

Rather than start ongoing series, Marvel turned its hand to producing "limited series" such as the first *Hercules* and *Vision and The Scarlet Witch* series, as well as *Contest of Champions,* the first limited series to feature a team-up of most of Marvel's starring heroes.

From a creative point of view, however, the most important 1982 limited series was *Wolverine* by Chris Claremont and Frank Miller, which solidly defined the Canadian mutant's personality as we now know it.

The X-Men's success still continued to mount, leading to the creation of a companion series to The X-Men, *The New Mutants.* Some months later, John Byrne started another X-Men spinoff, *Alpha Flight.* Indeed, within the next 10 years Marvel would publish as many "mutant" comic books per month as it had super-hero comic books in the 1960s.

1983 also saw the start of a contemporary classic, Walter Simonson's witty, dramatic, and action-packed run on *The Mighty Thor,* beginning with the introduction of Beta Ray Bill in issue #337.

With more than 20 years' worth of stories and characters making up the complex and interwoven saga of the Marvel super-heroes, the time had come to begin keeping records of it all, and, thus, in 1983 Mark Gruenwald initiated the original *Official Handbook of the Marvel Universe,* which has been in constant need of updates ever since.

Limited series continued to proliferate, most notably including Roger Stern and Bob Hall's *West Coast Avengers* and Chris Claremont and Al Milgrom's *Kitty Pryde and Wolverine.* The year's biggest news, however, was *Marvel Super Heroes Secret Wars,* the first "event" limited series crossing over into virtually all the others. (It also introduced the alien "black costume" that eventually became part of Venom.)

Chris Claremont and Bill Siekiewicz joined forces on a conceptually and visually dazzling year of issues of *The New Mutants.* 1984 also saw the debut of *Power Pack,* a charming series (originated by Louise Simonson and June Brigman) about a family of children who gained super-powers. In a short number of years, though, the market's tastes would grow too "grim and gritty" for such a comic book to exist.

Inevitably the great commercial success of the first *Secret Wars* led to its sequel, *Secret Wars II.* Spider-Man won his third series, *Web of Spider-Man,* and The West Coast Avengers received their own ongoing series, written by the newly returned Steve Englehart. The Epic line continued to grow and this year picked up one of modern comics' funniest series, *Sergio Aragons' Groo the Wanderer.* Perhaps the most notable of the year's limited series were Mark Gruenwald's *Squadron Supreme* and *Longshot,* which introduced Marvel fans to the stunning artwork of Arthur Adams.

Jim Shooter came up with an appealing idea: to start a new comics universe from scratch, "the world outside your window," in which super-heroes were just beginning to appear. These new characters would be handled more realistically: They would not necessarily devote their lives to crime-fighting or wear costumes, for example. Perhaps it was the decision to avoid so many sure-fire fantasy elements that was to blame. In any event the New Universe comics, including Shooter's own *Star Brand,* were all commercial failures and vanished long ago.

More significant events were taking place in the regular Marvel line. Although until now he was often treated (not without reason) as a villain, The Punisher began his real rise to stardom with his 1986 limited series, written by Steven Grant and pencilled by Mike Zeck.

Frank Miller returned to the Daredevil mythos, writing the astonishingly dramatic "Born Again" storyline in DD's own series, drawn by David Mazzucchelli and collabo-

rating with Bill Sienkiewicz on the surrealistic black comedy-adventure *Elektra: Assassin* for Epic.

John Byrne wrote and drew a brief but memorable run on *The Incredible Hulk,* including the long-delayed wedding of Bruce Banner and Betty Ross. And another future New Mutant, Firestar, starred in a limited series by Tom DeFalco and Mary Wilshire.

As the '80s began to draw to a close, Marvel went through a period of transition, with Tom DeFalco succeeding Shooter as editor-in-chief. The Silver Surfer began his current series under the creative team of Steve Englehart and Marshall Rogers, while Captain Britain and other characters from Marvel's United Kingdom comics were introduced to an American readership in the first *Excalibur Special Edition.* (The regular *Excalibur* comics series would start the following year.) Little remarked upon at the time was the arrival on *The Incredible Hulk* of two men who would be among comics' leading talents of the '90s: Peter David and Todd McFarlane.

Here was still another relatively quiet year. Doctor Strange began his current series, and Steve Ditko took on his last Marvel series to date, *Speedball.* The biggest new project was the launch of the bi-weekly anthology series (and Wolverine starring vehicle) *Marvel Comics Presents.*

John Byrne returned from revamping Superman for DC to take over *West Coast Avengers* and break down the fourth wall with his exuberantly comedic *Sensational She-Hulk.* Mark Gruenwald began the cosmic adventures of Quasar. Most significant for the future of comics, however, was the name of the artist of the very last issue of *X-Men* cover-dated in the '80s: Jim Lee, future co-founder of Image Comics.

By the '90s the direct-sales market supplanted the newsstand as the driving force behind comic-book sales. Marvel was aiming its new product directly at the booming collectors' market, as well as revamping old character concepts to suit a new audience. The new versions of Deathlok and, especially, The Ghost Rider proved far more popular than their predecessors. The artists who would form Image were fast developing their styles on Marvel books, with Jim Lee on *Uncanny X-Men,* Todd McFarlane scripting and illus-

trating a fourth *Spider-Man* title, and Jim Valentino as writer-artist on the revived *Guardians of the Galaxy*. Yet another, Rob Liefeld, was slowly but surely making *The New Mutants* over into his own image, introducing Cable in issue #86. Now members of the "Old Guard," John Byrne created a new *Namor* series and Frank Miller finished his disturbing graphic novel *Elektra Lives Again*. Another new star, Fabian Nicieza, made a stir with the debut of *The New Warriors* and his dark *Nomad* limited series.

1991

Marvel's greatest expansion ever now truly began gathering force. The signal event this year was the departure of Chris Claremont, after 16 years, from the mutant titles, contributing to their near-total makeover. Liefeld started *The New Mutants* over as *X-Force*, Peter David took over writing an entirely different *X-Factor*, and Jim Lee now both plotted and pencilled a new *X-Men* series. New characters Darkhawk and Sleepwalker first appeared in their own titles, while long-time Avenger Wonder Man finally won his own series. Jim Starlin created the first of his crossover limited series, *The Infinity Gauntlet*, and Marvel licensed a new outside property, *Barbie*.

1992

And now the explosion began. With new hands-on corporate ownership Marvel was out to create as many new comic books every year as it could. This year brought: the "Big Guns" line including *Cage, Punisher War Zone, Silver Sable*, and *Terror, Inc*; the horror-oriented "Midnight Sons" line with *Spirits of Vengeance, Morbius, Nightstalkers*, and *Darkhold*; the Marvel Universe of the future, featuring *Spider-Man 2099, Ravage 2099, Punisher 2099*, and *Doom 2099*; and even an invasion of titles from Marvel's United Kingdom division, such as *Death's Head II* and *Motormouth*. Jim Starlin created *Warlock and The Infinity Watch* and the *Infinity War* crossover series, and the Kree-Shi'ar War swept through the Avengers-related titles. In addition, there were the aptly titled *Slapstick* and *X-Men Adventures* — with the latter adapting episodes of the wildly successful new animated *X-Men* television series.

1993

Today, in the year this is written, the deluge of Marvel comics continues. Now headed by Carl Potts, Epic has come out with the action-oriented *Heavy Hitters* line. Marvel is also publishing horror author Clive Barker's own *Razorline* of super-heroes. New characters, both heroes like Cable, Night Thrasher, and Thunderstrike and villains like Venom and Deadpool, are starring in their own series, while old-timers like Hellstorm and The Defenders are reworked for new publications.

Marvel creators from the past continue in Starlin's *Infinity Crusade* and Miller's *Daredevil: The Man without Fear*, and The X-Men get yet another spin-off in *X-Men 2099*. Even the quarterly "giant" format of the '70s is reborn with such series as *Spider-Man Unlimited*, *X-Men Unlimited*, and *Fantastic Four Unlimited*.

Still further expansion seems likely for the foreseeable future. From a small, alternative company of the 1960s Marvel has grown into a giant to which most other comics companies must react, either through imitation or rebellion.

Although the art of the comics medium has evolved and matured at some other companies in ways Marvel has not chosen to follow, it is at Marvel that the new styles and trends of the most popular comics of today originated and developed. Despite surging competition, Marvel remains the dominant force in American comics.

Novelties

1966 TOPPS MARVEL FLYERS

This series of 12 flyers, originally sold for a dime apiece in 1966, depicted 12 of Marvel's popular heroes. Flyers came in three pieces — the "arms" of the character were put in the middle of the body section, while another section, depicting part of a cape, for example, was used as the tail section. This was Topps' first association with Marvel. The envelope containing the flyers was opaque and showed the Human Torch, and it was impossible to determine which figure a buyer would receive. A list of all the characters in the series appeared on the wrapper.

Complete set (12)	500.00		xx	Hulk	40.00
Each flyer	40.00		xx	Human Torch	40.00
Unassembled flyers	NVE		xx	Iron Man	40.00
# Flyer	Ex		xx	Spider-Man	40.00
xx Angel	40.00		xx	Sub-Mariner	40.00
xx Captain America	40.00		xx	Thing	40.00
xx Daredevil	40.00		xx	Thor	40.00
xx Dr. Doom	40.00		xx	Wasp	40.00

PVC FIGURES

Series I (1989)

#	Figure
1	Spider-Man
2	Captain America
3	Wolverine
4	Punisher

Series I (1990)

#	Figure
5	Thor
6	Iron Man
7	Thing
8	Nightcrawler
9	Hobgoblin
10	Dr. Doom

Series II (1990)

11	Hulk (gray)
12	Wolverine II
13	Daredevil
14	Colossus
15	Scarlet Witch
16	Vision

Series III (1990)

#	Figure
17	Storm
18	Cyclops
19	She-Hulk
20	Silver Surfer
21	Mr. Fantastic
22	Captain Britain
23	Black Panther
24	Marvel Girl

Series I (1991)

#	Figure
25	Spider-Man II
26	Dr. Strange
27	Archangel
28	Rogue
29	Lizard
30	Havok

Series II (1991)

#	Figure
31	Thing

(continued)

#	Figure
32	Magneto
33	Ghost Rider

Series III (1991)

#	Figure
34	Wolverine III
35	Storm II
36	Cable
37	Gambit
38	Xmas Spider-Man
39	Xmas Hulk

Series I (1992)

#	Figure
40	Thanos
41	Dr. Octopus
42	Sabretooth
43	Venom
44	Punisher
45	Ghost Rider
46	Wolverine
47	Silver Surfer

Cards:
An Introduction

By Don Butler

This value list/checklist is intended only as a brief overview on the range and variety of Marvel-related card sets.

Because of the difficulty in tracking down many of the sets — including the early Comic Images sets and most of the non-"mainstream" sets (1979 Drake's Incredible Hulk, for example), we have concentrated on the easy-to-find sets in this edition. We hope future editions will include a card-by-card listing.

Information is fairly complete on some of the better-known early Marvel sets, later Comic Images sets, and the Impel/SkyBox line of cards.

The first Marvel cards sprang up only a few years after the company had begun, which can be viewed in two ways: The competition among card companies (Fleer, Topps, Philadelphia Gum) was as aggressive as it had ever been, and each firm was looking for a hot kids' property. It's also a testament to how quickly Marvel broke into the entertainment field.

The approach to practically every Marvel comics-related set (until Impel and Comic Images picked up the license) was to take a standard pose of the character — in the case of the mid-1970s Topps sets, using the character pose from the upper left cover box of any title — and writing a funny caption. Topps had great success in the late 1950s and all through the 1960s with this approach to its humorous card sets; it seemed to work for the Marvel cards.

SkyBox was founded in 1989 as Impel Marketing Inc. and entered the trading-card world with the introduction of NBA Hoops. In 1990, the company introduced its Marvel Universe line; in April 1992 it changed its name to SkyBox.

When Impel received the Marvel Universe license and Comic Images was allowed to produce cards of individual titles, the approach to the cards changed. Realizing how seriously readers took their comics, both companies emphasized storylines and characters.

When Marvel bought Fleer in July 1992, that marked the end of the card relationships with Comic Images and SkyBox. Beginning in January 1994, Fleer will be the exclusive Marvel card licensee.

SkyBox Cards

1990 Impel Marvel I promo cards

A total of 20 sample cards were issued in randomly collated five-card cello packs. The key differences between these cards and the "real cards" in the series are some numerical differences and some slight variations in copy on the back and in the name banners on the front of some cards ("The Hulk" instead of "Hulk"). To date, no complete set has been reported.

1990 Impel Marvel I promo cards

Complete set (20) .... NVE
Each card .... NVE

#	Card	M
❑ xx	The Hulk	NVE
❑ 6	The Thing	NVE
❑ 8	Cyclops	NVE
❑ 29	Spider-Man	NVE
❑ 32	Silver Surfer 32	NVE
❑ 39	She-Hulk	NVE
❑ 57	Sabretooth	NVE
❑ 60	Doctor Doom	NVE
❑ 62	Enchantress	NVE
❑ 63	Magneto	NVE
❑ 78	Mephisto	NVE
❑ 82	Ghost Rider	NVE
❑ 83	Deathlok	NVE
❑ 87	The Thing vs. The Hulk	NVE
❑ 89	Fantastic Four vs. Doctor Doom	NVE
❑ 96	Silver Surfer vs. Mephisto	NVE
❑ 100	X-Men vs. Magneto	NVE
❑ 125	Amazing Fantasy #15	NVE
❑ 136	Fantastic Four	NVE
❑ 139	X-Men	NVE

1989 Impel Marvel Series I

Cards were released in wax packs and in "tin" factory sets. Five different holograms were randomly packed.

1989 Impel Marvel Series I

Complete set (no holograms) (162) 35.00
Complete set (with holograms) (167) 150.00
Complete Premium set (167) 275.00
Complete hologram set (5) 50.00
Common card 25
Common hologram 10.50

#	Card	M
❑ 1	Captain America (Tom Morgan)	.10
❑ 2	Spider-Man: black costume (Ron Frenz, Joe Rubenstein)	.50
❑ 3	Hulk: green (Tom Morgan)	.20
❑ 4	Daredevil (Mark Bagley, Tom Morgan	.10
❑ 5	Nick Fury (Tom Morgan)	.05
❑ 6	Thing (Tom Morgan)	.10
❑ 7	Professor X (Sal Buscema, Joe Sinnott	.05
❑ 8	Cyclops (Tom Morgan)	.05
❑ 9	Marvel Girl (Mark Bagley, Tom Morgan)	.05
❑ 10	Wolverine: second costume (Jim Lee, Tom Morgan)	.75
❑ 11	Phoenix (Mark Bagley, Joe Rubenstein)	.25
❑ 12	Power Man (Mark Bagley, Tom Morgan)	.05
❑ 13	Dazzler (Tom Morgan)	.05
❑ 14	Dagger (Mark Bagley, Tom Morgan)	.05
❑ 15	Quasar (Paul Ryan, Joe Rubenstein)	.05
❑ 16	Namor (Tom Morgan)	.25
❑ 17	Hulk: gray (Art Adams)	.10
❑ 18	Thor (Tom Morgan)	.10
❑ 19	Mr. Fantastic (Tom Morgan)	.05

❑ 20 Black Panther (Paul Ryan, Joe Rubenstein) .05

❑ 21 Archangel (Mark Bagley, Tom Morgan) .20

❑ 22 Iceman (Tom Morgan) .05

❑ 23 Wolverine: yellow costume (Jim Lee, Tom Morgan) .75

❑ 24 Storm (Mike Manley) .05

❑ 25 Shadowcat (Art Adams) .05

❑ 26 Moon Knight (Paul Ryan, Mike Manley) .10

❑ 27 Lockheed (Mark Bagley, Tom Morgan) .05

❑ 28 Aunt May (Ron Frenz, Joe Rubenstein) .05

❑ 29 Spider-Man: red & blue suit (Tom Morgan) .50

❑ 30 Cosmic Spider-Man (Sal Buscma, Joe Sinnott) .50

❑ 31 Captain America & motorcycle (Paul Ryan, Joe Rubenstein) .05

❑ 32 Silver Surfer (Tom Morgan) .75

❑ 33 Human Torch (Tom Morgan) .05

❑ 34 Dr. Strange (Tom Morgan) .05

❑ 35 Havok (Mark Bagley, Tom Morgan) .10

❑ 36 Colossus (Mike Manley) .10

❑ 37 Wolverine: Patch costume (Jim Lee, Tom Morgan) 1.00

❑ 38 Nightcrawler (Tom Morgan) .05

❑ 39 She-Hulk (Tom Morgan) .10

❑ 40 Captain Britain (Mark Bagley, Tom Morgan) .10

❑ 41 Rogue (Mike Manley) .05

❑ 42 Iron Man (Paul Ryan, Joe Rubenstein) .20

❑ 43 Invisible Woman (Ron Frenz, Joe Rubenstein) .05

❑ 44 Punisher & Van (Mark Bagley, Tom Morgan) .50

❑ 45 Longshot (Art Adams) .30

❑ 46 Beast (Mike Manley) .05

❑ 47 Punisher (Tom Morgan) .50

❑ 48 Storm: punk look (Jim Lee, Tom Morgan) .05

❑ 49 Elektra (Mark Bagley, Tom Morgan) .10

❑ 50 Cloak (Mark Bagley, Tom Morgan) .05

❑ 51 Red Skull (Paul Ryan, Joe Rubenstein) .05

❑ 52 Kingpin (Ron Frenz, Joe Rubenstein) .05

❑ 53 Baron Zemo (Paul Ryan, Joe Rubenstein) .05

❑ 54 Loki (Ron Frenz, Joe Rubenstein) .05

❑ 55 Juggernaut (Tom Morgan) .05

❑ 56 Nightmare (Art Adams) .05

❑ 57 Sabretooth (Tom Morgan) .50

❑ 58 Electro (Ron Frenz, Joe Rubenstein) .05

❑ 59 Dr. Octopus (Ron Frenz, Joe Rubenstein) .05

❑ 60 Dr. Doom (Tom Morgan) .15

❑ 61 Ultron (Paul Ryan, Mike Manley) .05

❑ 62 Enchantress (Tom Morgan) .05

❑ 63 Magneto (Tom Morgan) .10

❑ 64 Bullseye (Mark Bagley, Tom Morgan) .05

❑ 65 Mr. Sinister (Mark Bagley, Tom Morgan) .10

❑ 66 Sandman (Ron Frenz, Joe Rubenstein) .10

❑ 67 Lizard (Mark Bagley, Tom Morgan) .05

❑ 68 Mole Man (Tom Morgan) .05

❑ 69 Dormammu (Art Adams) .05

❑ 70 Leader (Sal Buscema,
       Joe Sinnott)   .10
❑ 71 Blob (Art Adams)   .05
❑ 72 Black Cat (Ron Frenz,
       Joe Rubenstein)   .05
❑ 73 Venom (Mark Bagley,
       Tom Morgan)   .75
❑ 74 Green Goblin (Ron Frenz,
       Joe Rubenstein)   .10
❑ 75 Galactus (Ron Frenz,
       Joe Rubenstein)   .05
❑ 76 Mandarin (Paul Ryan,
       Joe Rubenstein)   .05
❑ 77 High Evolutionary (Ron Frenz,
       Joe Rubenstein   .05
❑ 78 Mephisto (Tom Morgan)   .05
❑ 79 Thanos (Paul Ryan,
       Joe Rubenstein)   .75
❑ 80 Apocalypse (Art Adams)   .20
❑ 81 Guardians of the Galaxy
       (Mark Bagley, Bob McLeod   .15
❑ 82 Ghost Rider (Tom Morgan)   .90
❑ 83 Deathlok (Tom Morgan)   .60
❑ 84 New Warriors (Mark Bagley,
       Bob McLeod)   .50
❑ 85 Foolkiller (Mark Bagley, Tom
       Morgan)   .50
❑ 86 Nomad (Mark Bagley, Bob
       McLeod)   .20
❑ 87 Thing vs. Hulk (Tom Morgan) .10
❑ 88 Fantastic Four vs. Galactus
       (Ron Frenz, Jim Sanders III)   .10
❑ 89 Fantastic Four vs. Dr. Doom
       (Tom Morgan)   .05
❑ 90 Thor vs. Surtur (Ron Frenz,
       Jim Sanders III)   .10
❑ 91 First Kree-Skrull War (Paul
       Ryan, Mike Manley)   .05
❑ 92 Spider-Man vs. Kraven
       (Sal Buscema, Joe Sinnott)   .10

❑ 93 Spider-Man vs. Dr. Octopus
       (Ron Frenz, Jim Sanders III)   .10
❑ 94 Daredevil vs. Bullseye
       (Mark Bagley, Bob McLeod)   .05
❑ 95 Daredevil vs. Kingpin
       (Mark Bagley, Bob McLeod)   .05
❑ 96 Silver Surfer vs. Mephisto
       (Tom Morgan)   .10
❑ 97 Capt. America vs. Red Skull
       (Art Adams)   .05
❑ 98 Dark Phoenix (Mark Bagley,
       Jim Sanders III)   .05
❑ 99 X-Men vs. Avengers
       (Mark Bagley, Jim Sanders III) .20
❑100 X-Men vs. Magneto
       (Tom Morgan)   .20
❑101 Fantastic Four vs. X-Men
       (Mark Bagley, Jim Sanders III) .20
❑102 Fall of the Mutants
       (Mark Bagley, Jim Sanders III) .10
❑103 Evolutionary War (Paul Ryan,
       Mike Manley)   .05
❑104 Atlantis Attacks (Paul Ryan,
       Mike Manley)   .05
❑105 Acts of Vengeance (Paul Ryan,
       Mike Manley)   .05
❑106 Spider-Man vs. Venom
       (Mark Bagley, Bob McLeod)   .50
❑107 Fury vs. Hydra (Mark Bagley,
       Jim Sanders III)   .05
❑108 Armor Wars I (Paul Ryan,
       Mike Manley)   .05
❑109 Daredevil vs. Wolverine
       (Mark Bagley, Joe Rubenstein .50
❑110 Daredevil vs. Punisher
       (Mark Bagley, Joe Rubenstein .50
❑111 Spider-Man vs. Green Goblin
       (Mark Bagley, Joe Rubenstein .10
❑112 Spider-Man vs. Hobgoblin
       (Sal Buscema, Joe Sinnott)   .10

The "Marvel Age of Comics" began without a "Marvel" logo. (Note its absence on **The Fantastic Four** #1.) Distribution on early issues was spotty, and success of a character was iffy. (This incarnation of **The Incredible Hulk** ran only six issues before it folded as a failure. This version of **X-Men** eventually went entirely to reprints.) Some super-heroes appeared as featured, ongoing characters but didn't have their own titles. Today, early Marvel super-hero issues command high prices.

Through the decades Marvel has produced comics, some have become hard to find, some were never widely distributed to collectors, and some were not widely collected when they were first released. In some cases, later collectors drove up prices on these hard-to-find items; in other cases, prices remain low but the comics are hard to find. In the early '90s, novelty printing processes attracted many collectors, some of whom bought in large quantities.

Publications of Marvel stories have appeared in a number of formats. Sometimes, sizes varied widely; here you see a "normal" comic book with size shown in relation to a "treasury" size and the 1966 "Marvel Mini-Books," perhaps the smallest comic books ever printed. There were novels written about Marvel characters, tie-ins to TV shows of Marvel characters, and more.

Marvel has offered different specials for its devotees over the years. The first was The Merry Marvel Marching Society (MMMS); the record in the first kit offered was **Voices of the Marvel Bullpen** and in this **Scream along with Marvel**. The second was Marvelmania. The third was Friends Of Old Marvel (FOOM). The fourth is the current fan club, Wild Agents of Marvel. Marvel completists will find a number of small-circulation oddities in their mailboxes, if they have a WAM membership.

What **won't** you find detailed checklists for in this book? A lot of these items, for starters (although there is a listing for the Topps Marvel Flyers). Toys, cups, videos, banks, and pins, pins, pins are only some of the Marvel collectibles for which listings are still being compiled. Some of the pins are giveaways of cheap metal or plastic, used as promotional items for conventions. Some are cloisonne designs produced by pin makers.

Marvel cards have been many, and even some card makers do not provide complete lists. In addition, Marvel itself began to produce its own "trading" cards of its staffers in 1991 with portraits on the front and space for an autograph on the back. In recent card sets, besides traditional trading card images, "gimmick" "chase" cards are usual-ly included.

❑113 Hulk vs. Spider-Man
Art Adams) .20

❑114 Hulk vs. Wolverine (Sal
Buscema,Joe Sinnott) .75

❑115 Capt. America vs. Wolverine
(Mark Bagley, Bob McLeod) .50

❑116 Silver Surfer vs. Thanos (Mark
Bagley, Joe Rubenstein) .50

❑117 X-Factor vs. Apocalypse
(Mark Bagley, Joe Rubenstein .15

❑118 X-Men vs. Freedom Force
(Mark Bagley, Jim Sanders III) .15

❑119 Wolverine vs. Sabretooth
(Mark Bagley, Joe Rubenstein .75

❑120 X-Men in Savage Land
(Mark Bagley, Jim Sanders III) .10

❑121 Iron Man vs. Titanium Man
(Mark Bagley, Joe Rubenstein .05

❑122 Thor vs. Loki (Ron Frenz,
Jim Sanders III) .05

❑123 Fantastic Four #1
(reproduction art) .05

❑124 X-Men #1 (reproduction art) .05

❑125 Amazing Fantasy #15
(reproduction art) .10

❑126 The Punisher #1
(reproduction art) .10

❑127 Avengers #1 (reproduction art) .20

❑128 Journey into Mystery #83
(reproduction art) .05

❑129 Amazing Spider-Man #129
(reproduction art) .20

❑130 Avengers #1 (reproduction art) .05

❑131 Amazing Spider-Man #1
(reproduction art) .10

❑132 Giant-Size X-Men #1
(reproduction art) ..10

❑133 Wolverine L.S. #1
(reproduction art) .20

❑134 Hulk #181 (reproduction art) .20

❑135 Tales of Suspense #39
(reproduction art) .05

❑136 Avengers #4 (reproduction art) .05

❑137 Fantastic Four (Tom Morgan) .05

❑138 Avengers (Paul Ryan,
Mike Manley) .05

❑139 X-Men (Mark Bagley,
Jim Sanders III) .50

❑140 X-Men: from Annual #9
(Tom Morgan) .50

❑141 Cloak & Dagger (Sal
Buscema, Joe Sinnott) .05

❑142 New Mutants (Sal Buscema,
Joe Sinnott) .25

❑143 X-Factor (Mark Bagley,
Jim Sanders III) .25

❑144 Excalibur (Mark Bagley,
Jim Sanders III) .20

❑145 Brotherhood of Evil Mutants
(Mark Bagley, Jim Sanders III) .05

❑146 Sinister Six (Mark Bagley,
Jim Sanders III) .05

❑147 Hellfire Club (Mark Bagley,
Jim Sanders III) .05

❑148 Alpha Flight (Mark Bagley,
Jim Sanders III) .10

❑149 SMP: Spider-Man
(John Romita) .10

❑150 SMP: Dr. Doom (John Romita) .05

❑151 SMP: Dr. Octopus
(John Romita) .05

❑152 SMP: Hulk (John Romita) .10

❑153 SMP: Silver Surfer
(John Romita) .10

❑154 SMP: Thor (John Romita) .05

❑155 SMP: Punisher (John Romita) .25

❑156 SMP: Magneto (John Romita) .05

❑157 SMP: Captain America
(John Romita) .05

❏158 SMP: Dr. Strange
　　　 (John Romita)　　　　　　.05

❏159 SMP: Iron Man (John Romita) .05

❏160 SMP: Wolverine
　　　 (John Romita)　　　　　　.25

❏161 Stan Lee (Arnie Sawyer)　 1.25

❏162 Checklist　　　　　　　　.10

1989 Impel Marvel I holograms

Cards were randomly inserted into Marvel Series I packs.

1989 Marvel I holograms

Complete set (M) (132)................... 75.00

Common card (M).............................15

#	Card	M
❏M1	Cosmic Spider-Man	10.00
❏M2	Magneto	10.00
❏M3	Silver Surfer	15.00
❏M4	Wolverine	17.00
❏M5	Spider-Man vs. Green Goblin	10.00

1992 Impel Marvel Universe Series II promos

Five sample cards were packed in five-card cello packs. The key differences are in the colors, which are not as bright as the final product (the color of the Spider-Man card, in particular, is bad and incomplete).

1992 SkyBox Marvel II promo cards

Complete set (5)............................... NVE

Each card .... NVE

#	Card	M
❏ 1	Spider-Man	NVE
❏ 45	Silver Surfer	NVE
❏ 51	Cyclops	NVE
❏ 57	Magneto	NVE
❏124	Fantastic Four vs. Doctor Doom	NVE

1992 Impel Marvel Series II

Following Impel's successful first release, cards were released in wax packs in mid-1991.

1991 Impel Marvel Series II

Complete set (162)..........................20.00

Common card................................... .05

#	Card	M
❏ 1	Spider-Man (Erik Larsen)	.25
❏ 2	Daredevil (John Romita Jr., Al Williamson)	.05
❏ 3	Thing (Erik Larsen)	.05
❏ 4	Marvel Girl (Art Adams)	.05
❏ 5	Phoenix (Steve Lightle)	.05
❏ 6	Namor (Paul Ryan, Terry Austin)	.15
❏ 7	Mr. Fantastic (Paul Ryan, Terry Austin)	.05
❏ 8	Iceman (Lee Weeks)	.05
❏ 9	Shadowcat (Ron Lim, Jim Sanders)	.05
❏ 10	Human Torch (Paul Ryan, Terry Austin)	.05
❏ 11	Nightcrawler (Paul Ryan, Terry Austin)	.05
❏ 12	Captain Britain (Paul Ryan, Terry Austin)	.10
❏ 13	Iron Man (Art Adams)	.10
❏ 14	Punisher (Erik Larsen)	.50
❏ 15	Cable (Tom Morgan)	1.00
❏ 16	Deathlok (Art Adams)	.40
❏ 17	Gambit (Jim Lee, Terry Austin)	.20
❏ 18	Psylocke Ron Lim, Jim Sanders)	.20
❏ 19	Vision (Paul Ryan, Terry Austin)	.05
❏ 20	Hawkeye (Paul Ryan, Terry Austin)	.05
❏ 21	Silver Sable (Ron Frenz, Jim Sanders)	.20

❑ 22 Night Thrasher (Mark Bagley, Joe Sinnott) .15

❑ 23 Puck (Mark Bagley, Joe Sinnott) .05

❑ 24 Union Jack (Mark Bagley, Mike Manley) .05

❑ 25 Quicksilver (Paul Ryan, Terry Austin) .05

❑ 26 Scarlet Witch (Paul Ryan, Terry Austin) .05

❑ 27 Havok (Jim Lee, Terry Austin) .10

❑ 28 Iron Fist (Mark Bagley, Mike Manley) .10

❑ 29 Adam Warlock (Art Adams) .50

❑ 30 Wonder Man (Paul Ryan, Terry Austin) .05

❑ 31 Sasquatch (Erik Larsen) .10

❑ 32 Firestar (Art Adams) .05

❑ 33 Death's Head (Art Adams) .75

❑ 34 Speedball (Art Adams) .15

❑ 35 U.S. Agent (Paul Ryan, Terry Austin) .05

❑ 36 Banshee (Lee Weeks) .05

❑ 37 Meggan (Art Adams) .15

❑ 38 Jubilee Mike Manley) .10

❑ 39 Ghost Rider (Art Adams) .50

❑ 40 Beast (Erik Larsen) .05

❑ 41 Invisible Woman (Paul Ryan, Terry Austin) .05

❑ 42 Rogue (Art Adams) .05

❑ 43 She-Hulk (Art Adams) .10

❑ 44 Dr. Strange (Art Adams) .15

❑ 45 Silver Surfer (Paul Ryan, Terry Austin) .40

❑ 46 Storm (Art Adams) .05

❑ 47 Archangel (Mark Bagley, Jim Sanders) .10

❑ 48 Thor (Ron Frenz, Jim Sanders) .10

❑ 49 Quasar (Paul Ryan, Terry Austin) .05

❑ 50 Wolverine (Art Adams) .50

❑ 51 Cyclops (Ron Lim, Jim Sanders) .05

❑ 52 Nick Fury (Bret Blevins) .05

❑ 53 Hulk (Art Adams) .25

❑ 54 Captain America (Art Adams) .10

❑ 55 Kingpin (Erik Larsen) .05

❑ 56 Sabretooth (Jim Lee, Terry Austin) .25

❑ 57 Magneto (Ron Lim, Jim Sanders) .10

❑ 58 Venom (Lee Weeks) .50

❑ 59 Galactus (Art Adams) .05

❑ 60 Mandarin (Lee Weeks) .05

❑ 61 Chameleon (Lee Weeks) .05

❑ 62 Super-Skrull (Ron Lim, Jim Sanders) .05

❑ 63 Grim Reaper (Paul Ryan, Terry Austin) .05

❑ 64 Mojo (Mike Manley) .15

❑ 65 Fin Fang Foom (Art Adams) .05

❑ 66 Jigsaw (Mark Bagley, Mike Manley) .10

❑ 67 Tombstone (Lee Weeks) .05

❑ 68 Ulik (Art Adams) .05

❑ 69 Baron Strucker (Mark Bagley, Mike Manley) .05

❑ 70 Mysterio (Steve Lightle) .05

❑ 71 Sauron (Art Adams) .10

❑ 72 Annihilus (Art Adams) .05

❑ 73 Rhino (Erik Larsen) .05

❑ 74 Absorbing Man (Art Adams) .05

❑ 75 Dr. Octopus (Erik Larsen) .05

❑ 76 Baron Mordo (Mike Manley) .05

❑ 77 Saracen (Mark Bagley, Mike Manley) .05

❑ 78 Nebula (Paul Ryan, Terry Austin) .10

❏ 79 Puma (Lee Weeks)   .10
❏ 80 Deathwatch (Mark Bagley, Joe
       Sinnott)   .10
❏ 81 Kang (Mike Manley)   .05
❏ 82 Blackout (Mark Bagley,
       Mike Manley)   .05
❏ 83 Calypso (Bret Blevins)   .15
❏ 84 Ultron (Art Adams)   .10
❏ 85 Thanos (Art Adams)   .50
❏ 86 Hobgoblin (Erik Larsen)   .25
❏ 87 Lizard (Erik Larsen)   .10
❏ 88 Dr. Doom (Art Adams)   .10
❏ 89 Loki (Ron Frenz, Jim Sanders).05
❏ 90 Red Skull (Ron Lim, Jim
       Sanders)   .05
❏ 91 Spider-Man vs. Venom (Mark
       Bagley, Joe Sinnott)   .50
❏ 92 Fantastic Four vs. Skrulls
       (Ron Lim, Jim Sanders)   .05
❏ 93 Wolverine vs. Sabretooth
       (Mark Bagley, Jim Sanders)   .50
❏ 94 Silver Surfer vs. Galactus
       (Ron Lim, Jim Sanders)   .20
❏ 95 Daredevil vs. Elektra
       (Art Adams)   .05
❏ 96 Avengers vs. Kang (Steve
       Lightle)   .05
❏ 97 Human Torch vs. Sub-Mariner
       (Mark Bagley, Joe Sinnott)   .10
❏ 98 Spider-Man vs. Hobgoblin
       (Mike Manley)   .25
❏ 99 Captain America vs. Baron
       Zemo (Art Adams)   .05
❏100 Punisher vs. Jigsaw (Mark
       Bagley, Joe Sinnott)   .25
❏101 X-Factor vs. Apocalypse (Ron
       Lim, Jim Sanders)   .10
❏102 Punisher vs. Kingpin (Mark
       Bagley, Joe Sinnott)   .25
❏103 Thing vs. Hulk (Art Adams)   .20

❏104 Daredevil vs. Bullseye   .05
❏105 Spider-Man vs. Doctor
       Octopus (Erik Larsen)   .10
❏106 X-Men vs. Sentinels (Mark
       Bagley, Jim Sanders)   .25
❏107 Fantastic Four vs. Galactus
       (Steve Lightle)   .05
❏108 Wolverine vs. Hulk (Erik
       Larsen)   .50
❏109 Ghost Rider vs. Deathwatch
       (Mark Bagley, Mike Manley)   .40
❏110 Dr. Strange vs. Baron Mordo
       (Lee Weeks)   .05
❏111 Fury vs. Strucker (Steve
       Lightle)   .05
❏112 Spider-Man vs. Lizard
       (Steve Lightle)   .10
❏113 Silver Surfer vs. Thanos
       (Ron Lim, Jim Sanders)   .50
❏114 Avengers vs. Ultron (Mark
       Bagley, Mike Manley)   .05
❏115 Captain America vs. Red Skull
       (Ron Lim, Jim Sanders)   .05
❏116 Daredevil vs. Punisher
       (Lee Weeks)   .25
❏117 X-Men vs. Marauders
       (Steve Lightle)   .25
❏118 Iron Man vs. Mandarin
       (John Romita Jr.,
       Al Williamson)   .10
❏119 Hulk vs. Leader (Lee Weeks) .25
❏120 Thor vs. Loki (Art Adams)   .05
❏121 Spider-Man vs. J. Jonah
       Jameson (John Romita)   .10
❏122 Thor vs. Ulik (Art Adams)   .05
❏123 Silver Surfer vs. Mephisto
       (Ron Lim)   .25
❏124 Fantastic Four vs. Dr. Doom
       (Ron Lim, Jim Sanders)   .10

❏125 X-Men vs. Magneto (Lee Weeks) .15

❏126 Daredevil vs. Kingpin (John Romita Jr., Al Williamson) .05

❏127 Capt. America's shield (Ron Lim, Jim Sanders) .05

❏128 Thor's hammer (Ron Frenz, Jim Sanders) .05

❏129 Daredevil's billy club (John Romita Jr., Al Williamson) .05

❏130 Ultimate Nullifier (Ron Lim, Jim Sanders) .05

❏131 Spidey's web shooters (John Romita) .10

❏132 Punisher's arsenal (Lee Weeks) .25

❏133 Iron Man's armor (John Romita Jr., Al Williamson) .05

❏134 Infinity Gauntlet (Ron Lim, Jim Sanders) .25

❏135 Quasar's quantum bands (Mike Manley) .05

❏136 Dr. Octopus' arms (John Romita) .05

❏137 Mandarin's rings (Mark Bagley, Jim Sanders) .05

❏138 Wolverine's claws (Jim Lee, Terry Austin) .20

❏139 Captain Marvel (Mark Bagley, Mike Manley) .05

❏140 Bucky (Mark Bagley, Mike Manley) .05

❏141 Green Goblin (John Romita) .10

❏142 Original Ghost Rider (Bob Budiansky, Terry Austin) .40

❏143 Kraven (Steve Lightle) .10

❏144 Dark Phoenix (Bret Blevins) .10

❏145 Darkhawk (Mike Manley) .50

❏146 Sleepwalker (Bret Blevins) .25

❏147 Rage (Paul Ryan, Terry Austin) .15

❏148 X-Force (Tom Morgan) 1.50

❏149 New Fantastic Four (Art Adams) .60

❏150 Fantastic Four (Art Adams) .05

❏151 Avengers (Paul Ryan, Terry Austin) .05

❏152 Avengers West Coast (Paul Ryan, Terry Austin) .05

❏153 X-Men (Mark Bagley, Mike Manley) .25

❏154 X-Factor (Mark Bagley, Jim Sanders) .20

❏155 Excalibur (Mark Bagley, Mike Manley) .10

❏156 New Warriors (Mark Bagley, Joe Sinnott) .20

❏157 Masters of Evil (Mark Bagley, Mike Manley) .05

❏158 Marauders (Mark Bagley, Mike Manley) .15

❏159 Strength/Speed .10

❏160 Agility/Stamina .10

❏161 Durability/Intelligence .10

❏162 Checklist .10

1991 Impel Marvel II holograms

Cards were randomly inserted into Marvel Series II packs.

1992 Marvel II holograms

Complete set (5)..............................30.00

Common hologram............................7.00

#	Card	M
❏ M1	Spider-Man (Art Adams)	10.00
❏ M2	Doctor Doom (Art Adams)	10.00
❏ M3	Punisher (Lee Weeks)	15.00
❏ M4	Fantastic Four vs. Mole Man (Art Adams)	7.00
❏ M5	Hulk (Art Adams)	10.00

1992 SkyBox Marvel Universe Series III promos

Three sample cards were packed in three-card cello packs. The only difference between the promo cards and regular-issue cards is "prototype" was stamped in black ink across the backs. In addition, a Venom hologram from Marvel 3 was run as a sample in Capital City's catalog *Advance Comics*; it had a completely different, promotional back.

1992 SkyBox Marvel III promo cards

Complete set (3) .... NVE
Each card .... NVE

#	Card	M
❑ 1	Spider-Man	NVE
❑ 34	Invisible Woman	NVE
❑ 37	Captain America	NVE
❑ xx	Venom	NVE

1992 SkyBox Marvel Series III

Cards were released in wax packs. Five different holograms were randomly packed. Cards were arranged in subsets: Super-Heroes (1-70), Team-Ups (71-100, Super-Villains (101-140), Rookies (141-149), Cosmic Beings (150-160), Origins (161-170), Teams (171-183), Wars (184-191), and Milestones (192-200).

1989 SkyBox Marvel Series III

Complete set (no holograms) (200) 14.00
Common card .... .05

#	Card	M
❑ 1	Spider-Man (Erik Larsen)	.20
❑ 2	Quasar (Greg Capullo, Harry Candelario)	.05
❑ 3	Sleepwalker (Bret Blevins)	.05
❑ 4	Gambit (Lee Weeks)	.15
❑ 5	Cannonball (Ron Lim, Terry Austin)	.05
❑ 6	Beast (Javier Saltares)	.05
❑ 7	Quicksilver (Ron Lim, Al Milgrom)	.05
❑ 8	Weapon Omega (Tom Morgan)	.05
❑ 9	Dr. Strange (Sam Kieth)	.15
❑ 10	Major Victory (Jim Valentino)	.05
❑ 11	Phoenix (Kevin Maguire)	.05
❑ 12	Black Widow (Lee Weeks)	.05
❑ 13	Hulk (Kirk Jarvinen, Jimmy Palmiotti)	.15
❑ 14	Sunfire (Jeff Johnson, Terry Austin)	.05
❑ 15	Silver Surfer (Ron Lim, Terry Austin)	.25
❑ 16	She-Hulk (Marc Silvestri)	.10
❑ 17	Captain Britain (Javier Saltares)	.10
❑ 18	Cage (Dwayne Turner)	.15
❑ 19	Domino (Bret Blevins)	.10
❑ 20	Daredevil (Lee Weeks)	.05
❑ 21	Morbius (Ron Wagner)	.30
❑ 22	Nightcrawler (Sam Kieth)	.05
❑ 23	Black Panther (Dwayne Turner)	.05
❑ 24	Ant-Man (Paul Ryan, Terry Austin)	.05
❑ 25	Ghost Rider (Mark Texeira)	.15
❑ 26	Darkhawk (Mike Manley)	.10
❑ 27	Iceman (Lee Weeks)	.05
❑ 28	Punisher (John Romita Jr.)	.15
❑ 29	Wolfsbane (Ron Lim)	.05
❑ 30	Storm (Lee Weeks)	.05
❑ 31	Wonder Man (Jeff Johnson, Terry Austin)	.05
❑ 32	Moon Knight (Dwayne Turner)	.05
❑ 33	Mr. Fantastic (Paul Ryan, Terry Austin)	.05
❑ 34	Invisible Woman (Paul Ryan, Terry Austin)	.05

❏ 35 Shadowcat (Mike Manley) .05
❏ 36 Warlock (Ron Lim, Terry
Austin) .20
❏ 37 Captain America (Ron Lim,
Terry Austin) .05
❏ 38 Wolverine (Marc Silvestri) .25
❏ 39 Namor (Erik Larsen) .20
❏ 40 Nick Fury (Lee Weeks) .05
❏ 41 Professor X (Karl Alstaetter,
Jim Lee) .05
❏ 42 Shatterstar (Ron Lim,
Terry Austin) .05
❏ 43 Multiple Man (Ron Lim,
Al Milgrom) .05
❏ 44 Blaze (Mark Texeira) .15
❏ 45 Deathlok (Denys Cowan) .10
❏ 46 Colossus (Michael Bair) .05
❏ 47 Meggan (Javier Saltares) .10
❏ 48 Thor (Ron Frenz) .05
❏ 49 Namorita (Kevin Maguire,
Terry Austin) .15
❏ 50 Cable (Mark Texeira) .35
❏ 51 Psylocke (Paul Ryan,
Terry Austin)* .15
❏ 52 Warpath (Mark Texeira) .10
❏ 53 Nomad (Samuel Clarke
Hawbaker) .05
❏ 54 Polaris (Ron Lim, Terry Austin).10
❏ 55 Charlie-27 (Jim Valentino) .10
❏ 56 Thing (Paul Ryan, Terry
Austin) .05
❏ 57 Longshot (Ron Lim, Terry
Austin) .10
❏ 58 Human Torch (Paul Ryan, Terry
Austin) .05
❏ 59 Night Thrasher (Alex Saviuk,
Brad Vancata) .10
❏ 60 Siryn (Alex Saviuk, Brad
Vancata) .05
❏ 61 Nova (Erik Larsen) .05

❏ 62 Iron Man (Paul Ryan,
Terry Austin) .05
❏ 63 Archangel (Marc Silvestri, Harry
Candelario) .10
❏ 64 Rogue (Marc Silvestri) .05
❏ 65 Silver Sable (Ron Frenz) .15
❏ 66 Jean Grey (Marc Silvestri, Harry
Candelario) .05
❏ 67 Feral (Kevin Maguire,
Terry Austin) .05
❏ 68 Cyclops (Lee Weeks) .05
❏ 69 Starhawk (Jim Valentino) .10
❏ 70 Havok (Joe Madureira, Harry
Candelario) .10
❏ 71 Spider-Man & Human Torch
(Sal Buscema) .05
❏ 72 Spider-Man & Ghost Rider
(Javier Saltares) .10
❏ 73 Spider-Man & Punisher (John
Romita Jr.) .15
❏ 74 Spider-Man & Wolverine (John
Romita Jr.) .15
❏ 75 Wolverine & Captain America
(Lee Weeks) .15
❏ 76 Wolverine & Hulk (Kevin
Maguire, Terry Austin) .20
❏ 77 Wolverine & Cable (Tom
Morgan) .20
❏ 78 Dr. Doom & Magneto
(Paul Ryan, Terry Austin) .05
❏ 79 Ghost Rider & Blaze (Mark
Texeira) .10
❏ 80 Captain America & Nomad
(Ron Lim, Terry Austin) .05
❏ 81 Spider-Man & Darkhawk (Alex
Saviuk, Keith Williams) .10
❏ 82 Human Torch & Iceman (Paul
Ryan, Terry Austin) .05
❏ 83 Captain America & USAgent
(Ron Lim, Terry Austin) .05

❏ 84 Wolverine & Daredevil (Lee Weeks) .10
❏ 85 Vision & Scarlet Witch (Bret Blevins) .05
❏ 86 Punisher & Deathlok (Mike Manley) .10
❏ 87 Thor Corps (Ron Frenz, Joe Sinnott) .05
❏ 88 Wolverine, Punisher & Ghost Rider (Mike Harris) .20
❏ 89 Wonder Man & Beast (Jeff Johnson, Terry Austin) .05
❏ 90 Ghost Rider & Daredevil (Mark Texeira) .10
❏ 91 Wolverine & Havok (Walt Simonson) .10
❏ 92 Punisher & Daredevil (John Romita Jr.) .10
❏ 92 Daredevil & Black Widow (Lee Weeks) .05
❏ 94 Punisher & Captain America (Mike Harris .10
❏ 95 Spider-Man & Sleepwalker (Bret Blevins) .10
❏ 96 Power Man & Iron Fist (Dwayne Turner) .05
❏ 97 Spider-Man & Daredevil (Mike Harris) .10
❏ 98 Hulk & Thing (Paul Ryan, Terry Austin) .10
❏ 99 Red Skull & Baron Zemo (Ron Lim, Terry Austin) .05
❏ 100 Juggernaut & Black Tom Cassidy (Paul Ryan, Terry Austin) .05
❏ 101 Abomination (Kirk Jarvinen, Jimmy Palmiotti) .05
❏ 102 Zodiak (Mark Texeira) .05
❏ 103 Apocalypse (Walt Simonson) .10
❏ 104 Sphinx (Alex Saviuk, Brad Vancata) .05

❏ 105 Destroyer (Ron Frenz) .05
❏ 106 Red Skull (Ron Lim, Terry Austin) .05
❏ 107 Puppet Master (Paul Ryan, Terry Austin) .05
❏ 108 Venom (Erik Larsen) .40
❏ 109 Diablo (Tom Morgan) .05
❏ 110 The Rose (Alex Saviuk, Brad Vancata) .05
❏ 111 Dr. Doom (Paul Ryan, Terry Austin) .05
❏ 112 Magneto (Kirk Jarvinen, Brad Vancata) .05
❏ 113 Necrom (Denys Cowan) .05
❏ 114 Green Goblin (Sal Buscema) .05
❏ 115 Dracula (Ron Wagner) .25
❏ 116 Sauron (Mark Texeira) .05
❏ 117 Cyber (Sam Kieth) .05
❏ 118 Mephisto (Ron Frenz) .05
❏ 119 Mad Thinker (Paul Ryan, Terry Austin) .05
❏ 120 Carnage (Ron Lim, Terry Austin) .60
❏ 121 Hobgoblin (Alex Saviuk, Terry Austin) .10
❏ 122 Gideon (Richard Case) .05
❏ 123 White Queen (Mike Harris) .05
❏ 124 Omega Red (Jeff Johnson, Terry Austin) .05
❏ 125 Maelstrom (Greg Capullo, Henry Candelario .05
❏ 126 Thanos (Ron Lim, Terry Austin) .25
❏ 127 Zarrko (Ron Frenz) .05
❏ 128 Magus (Ron Lim, Terry Austin).15
❏ 129 Sabretooth (Marc Silvestri) .15
❏ 130 Kingpin (Lee Weeks) .05
❏ 131 Silvermane (Alex Saviuk, Brad Vancata) .05
❏ 132 Cardiac (Erik Larsen) .05

❏133 Blackheart (Bret Blevins) .05

❏134 Terrax (Jeff Johnson, Terry Austin) .05

❏135 Mr. Sinister (Walt Simonson) .10

❏136 Slug (Ron Lim, Terry Austin) .05

❏137 Hate-Monger (Mike Manley) .05

❏138 Crossbones (Ron Lim, Terry Austin) .05

❏139 Shiva (Marc Silvestri) .05

❏140 Blackout (Mark Texeira) .05

❏141 Pantheon (Kirk Jarvinen, Jimmy Palmiotti) .10

❏142 Slapstick (James Fry) .05

❏143 Cerise (Denys Cowan) .05

❏144 Darkhold Redeemers (Richard Case) .15

❏145 Strong Guy (Ron Lim) .10

❏146 Bishop (Karl Alstaetter, Jim Lee) .15

❏147 Silhouette (Bret Blevins) .05

❏148 Kylun (Denys Cowan) .05

❏149 Talon (Jim Valentino) .05

❏150 Collector (Mark Texeira) .05

❏151 Galactus (Tom Morgan) .05

❏152 Watcher (Paul Ryan, Terry Austin) .05

❏153 Living Tribunal (Paul Ryan, Terry Austin) .05

❏154 Ego (Paul Ryan, Terry Austin) .05

❏155 Eternity (Paul Ryan, Terry Austin) .05

❏156 Celestials (Ron Frenz) .05

❏157 Death (Paul Ryan, Terry Austin) .05

❏158 Stranger (Paul Ryan, Terry Austin) .05

❏159 In-Betweener (Ron Lim, Terry Austin) .05

❏160 Epoch (Greg Capullo, Henry Candelario) .05

❏161 Hulk (Sal Buscema) .10

❏162 Spider-Man (Alex Saviuk, Brad Vancata) .10

❏163 Silver Surfer (Ron Lim) .10

❏164 Wolverine (Tom Morgan) .15

❏165 Iron Man (John Romita) .05

❏166 Captain America (John Romita) .05

❏167 Ghost Rider (Mark Texeira) .10

❏168 Daredevil (John Romita) .05

❏169 Thor (Ron Frenz) .05

❏170 Fantastic Four (Paul Ryan, Terry Austin) .05

❏171 Avengers (Steve Epting) .05

❏172 X-Force (Karl Alstaetter, Jim Lee) .10

❏173 X-Factor (Ron Lim, Al Milgrom) .10

❏174 New Warriors (Paul Ryan, Terry Austin) .05

❏175 Alpha Flight (Tom Morgan) .05

❏176 Avengers West Coast (Tom Morgan) .05

❏177 Nightstalkers (Mark Texeira) .10

❏178 Guardians Of The Galaxy (Jim Valentino) .10

❏179 X-Men Gold (Kirk Jarvinen, Brad Vancata) .10

❏180 Excalibur (Tom Morgan) .05

❏181 Fantastic Four (Paul Ryan, Terry Austin) .05

❏182 X-Men Blue (Kirk Jarvinen, Brad Vancata) .10

❏183 Serpent Society (Ron Lim, Jimmy Palmiotti) .05

❏184 X-Tinction Agenda (Kirk Jarvinen, Jimmy Palmiotti) .10

❏185 Evolutionary War (Kirk Jarvinen, Brad Vancata) .05

❑186 Operation Galactic Storm
(Steve Epting) .05

❑187 Secret Wars (Steve Epting) .10

❑188 Inferno (Kirk Jarvinen, Jimmy
Palmiotti) .05

❑189 Infinity Gauntlet (Ron Lim,
Jimmy Palmiotti) .10

❑190 Kree/Skrull War (Ron Lim,
Jimmy Palmiotti) .05

❑191 Atlantis Attacks (Ron Lim,
Jimmy Palmiotti) .05

❑192 I Married A Skrull (Paul
Ryan, Terry Austin) .05

❑193 Days Of Future Past (Bret
Blevins) .10

❑194 All Hulks Unite (Kirk
Jarvinen, Brad Vancata) .10

❑195 Dark Phoenix Saga (Bret
Blevins) .05

❑196 The Coming Of Galactus (Steve
Epting) .05

❑197 Death of Gwen Stacy (John
Romita) .05

❑198 Fall Of The Kingpin (Lee
Weeks) .05

❑199 Wedding of Spider-Man
(Paul Ryan, Terry Austin) .10

❑200 Checklist .05

1992 Impel Marvel III holograms

Five different holograms were randomly packed.

1992 Impel Marvel III holograms

Complete hologram set (5) 30.00
Common hologram 4.00

#	Card	M
❑ H1	Hulk (Sam Kieth)	5.00
❑ H2	Thing (Walt Simonson)	4.00
❑ H3	Wolverine (Kirk Jarvinen, Brad Vancata)	6.00
❑ H4	Venom (Ron Lim)	8.00
❑ H5	Ghost Rider (Lee Weeks)	5.00

1993 SkyBox Marvel Universe Series IV promos

Two sample cards were created by SkyBox for this series. The Deathlok card with CBG stamp on the back was available only in the June/July issue of *Comics Buyer's Guide Price Guide*. Each card had promotional copy on the back instead of regular card backs.

1993 SkyBox Marvel IV promo cards

Complete set (2) .... NVE
Each card .... NVE

#	Card	M
❑ xx	Deathlok	NVE
❑ xx	Silver Sable	NVE

1993 SkyBox Marvel Universe Series IV

This set was organized into "regional groupings" — in other words, characters who shared common environments. Subsets included: West Coast (1-9), Avengers Mansion (10-18), Gritty Urban (19-27), High-Tech (28-36), New Warriors HQ 937-45), Extradimensional (46-54), Spider-Man — New York City (55-63), Gothic — Midnight Sons (64-72), X-Mansion (73-81), Post-apocalyptic (82-90), U.K.-Canada-Washington, D.C. (91-99), Outer Space (100-108), Four Freedoms Plaza (109-117), Marvel U.K. (118-126), Alien Races (127-135), Unsolved Mysteries (136-144), and Famous Battles (145-180). Cards were released in packs only in June 1993.

1993 SkyBox Marvel IV

Complete set (180) 16.00
Each card 10

#	Card	M
❑ 1	War Machine (Jeff Johnson, Sam De La Rosa)	.20

❑	2	Iron Man (Jeff Johnson, Sam De La Rosa)	.10
❑	3	USAgent (Jeff Johnson, Sam De La Rosa)	.15
❑	4	Scarlet Witch (Jeff Johnson, Sam De La Rosa)	.10
❑	5	Spider-Woman (Jeff Johnson, Sam De La Rosa)	.10
❑	6	Wonder Man (Jeff Johnson, SamDe La Rosa)	.10
❑	7	Splice (Jeff Johnson, Sam De La Rosa)	.15
❑	8	Namor (Jeff Johnson, Sam De LaRosa)	.10
❑	9	Tiger Shark (Jeff Johnson, Sam De La Rosa)	.10
❑	10	Red Skull (Ron Frenz, Tom Palmer)	.10
❑	11	Bloodaxe (Ron Frenz, Tom Palmer)	.10
❑	12	Black Widow (Ron Frenz, Tom Palmer)	.10
❑	13	Hercules (Ron Frenz, Tom Palmer)	.10
❑	14	Black Knight (Ron Frenz, Tom Palmer)	.10
❑	15	Crystal (Ron Frenz, Tom Palmer)	.10
❑	16	Proctor (Ron Frenz, Tom Palmer)	.10
❑	17	Thunderstrike (Ron Frenz, Tom Palmer)	.15
❑	18	Captain America (Ron Frenz, Tom Palmer)	.10
❑	19	Cage (Lee Weeks)	.10
❑	20	Punisher (Lee Weeks)	.30
❑	21	Hardcore (Lee Weeks)	.10
❑	22	Terror Inc. (Lee Weeks)	.10
❑	23	Iron Fist (Lee Weeks)	.15
❑	24	Nomad (Lee Weeks)	.10
❑	25	She-Hulk (Lee Weeks)	.10
❑	26	Falcon (Lee Weeks)	.10
❑	27	Scarecrow (Lee Weeks)	.10
❑	28	Deathlok (Steven Butler)	.20
❑	29	Siege (Steven Butler)	.15
❑	30	Moses Magnum (Steven Butler)	.10
❑	31	Silver Sable (Steven Butler)	.15
❑	32	Wild Pack (Steven Butler)	.10
❑	33	Moon Knight (Steven Butler)	.10
❑	34	Deadzone (Steven Butler)	.10
❑	35	Hulk (Steven Butler)	.20
❑	36	Doc Samson (Steven Butler)	.15
❑	37	Darkhawk (Darick Robertson, Larry Mahlstedt)	.10
❑	38	Firestar (Darick Robertson, Larry Mahlstedt)	.15
❑	39	Speedball (Darick Robertson, Larry Mahlstedt)	.10
❑	40	Night Thrasher (Darick Robertson, Larry Mahlstedt)	.15
❑	41	Nova (Darick Robertson, Larry Mahlstedt)	.20
❑	42	Turbo (Darick Robertson, Larry Mahlstedt)	.10
❑	43	Rage (Darick Robertson, Larry Mahlstedt)	.10
❑	44	Namorita (Darick Robertson, Larry Mahlstedt)	.20
❑	45	Cardinal (Darick Robertson, Larry Mahlstedt)	.10
❑	46	Sleepwalker (Steve Lightle)	.10
❑	47	Cobweb (Steve Lightle)	.10
❑	48	Dr. Strange (Steve Lightle)	.10
❑	49	Dormammu (Steve Lightle)	.10
❑	50	Hellstorm (Steve Lightle)	.20
❑	51	Blackheart (Steve Lightle)	.10
❑	52	Thor (Steve Lightle)	.10
❑	53	Loki (Steve Lightle)	.10

❑ 54	Beta Ray Bill (Steve Lightle)	.20
❑ 55	Spider-Man (Ron Lim, Terry Austin)	.10
❑ 56	Venom (Ron Lim, Terry Austin)	.40
❑ 57	Carnage (Ron Lim, Terry Austin)	.65
❑ 58	Hobgoblin (Ron Lim, Terry Austin)	.30
❑ 59	Demogoblin (Ron Lim, Terry Austin)	.25
❑ 60	Cardiac (Ron Lim, Terry Austin)	.10
❑ 61	Rhino (Ron Lim, Terry Austin)	.10
❑ 62	Daredevil (Ron Lim, Terry Austin)	.10
❑ 63	Shock (Ron Lim, Terry Austin)	.10
❑ 64	Ghost Rider (Michael Bair)	.15
❑ 65	Blaze (Michael Bair)	.15
❑ 66	Redeemers (Michael Bair)	.15
❑ 67	Morbius (Michael Bair)	.15
❑ 68	Nightstalkers (Michael Bair)	.10
❑ 69	Lilith (Michael Bair)	.15
❑ 70	Deathwatch (Michael Bair)	.10
❑ 71	Basilisk (Michael Bair)	.10
❑ 72	Heart Attack (Michael Bair)	.10
❑ 73	Magneto (Art Thibert)	.20
❑ 74	Storm (Art Thibert)	.10
❑ 75	Wolverine (Art Thibert)	.30
❑ 76	Bishop (Art Thibert)	.20
❑ 77	Cyclops (Art Thibert)	.10
❑ 78	Beast (Art Thibert)	.15
❑ 79	Gambit (Art Thibert)	.15
❑ 80	Rogue (Art Thibert)	.10
❑ 81	Archangel (Art Thibert)	.15
❑ 82	Sabretooth (Joe Madureira, Mark Farmer)	.30
❑ 84	Shatterstar (Joe Madureira, Mark Farmer)	.15
❑ 85	Deadpool (Joe Madureira, Mark Farmer)	.15
❑ 86	Slayback (Joe Madureira, Mark Farmer)	.15
❑ 87	Stryfe (Joe Madureira, Mark Farmer)	.15
❑ 88	Mr. Sinister (Joe Madureira, Mark Farmer)	.15
❑ 89	Apocalypse (Joe Madureira, Mark Farmer)	.15
❑ 90	Cannonball (Joe Madureira, Mark Farmer)	.10
❑ 91	Captain Britain (Brandon Peterson, Dan Panosian)	.15
❑ 92	Nightcrawler (Brandon Peterson, Dan Panosian)	.10
❑ 93	Phoenix (Brandon Peterson, Dan Panosian)	.15
❑ 94	Micromax (Brandon Peterson, Dan Panosian)	.20
❑ 95	Guardian (Brandon Peterson, Dan Panosian)	.10
❑ 96	Wildheart (Brandon Peterson, Dan Panosian)	.10
❑ 97	Strong Guy (Brandon Peterson, Dan Panosian)	.20
❑ 98	Psylocke (Brandon Peterson, Dan Panosian)	.15
❑ 99	Havok (Brandon Peterson, Dan Panosian)	.20
❑100	Galactus (Ron Lim, Tom Christopher)	.10
❑101	Warlock (Ron Lim, Tom Christopher)	.15
❑102	Drax (Ron Lim, Tom Christopher)	.15
❑103	Starhawk (Ron Lim, Tom Christopher)	.10
❑104	Quasar (Ron Lim, Tom Christopher)	.10

❏105 Silver Surfer (Ron Lim, Tom Christopher) .20

❏106 Thanos (Ron Lim, Tom Christopher) .25

❏107 Morg (Ron Lim, Tom Christopher) .10

❏108 Goddess (Ron Lim, Tom Christopher) .10

❏109 Mr. Fantastic (Mike Manley) .10

❏110 Invisible Woman (Mike Manley) .10

❏111 Thing (Mike Manley) .10

❏112 Human Torch (Mike Manley) .10

❏113 Dr. Doom (Mike Manley) .10

❏114 Klaw (Mike Manley) .10

❏115 Molecule Man (Mike Manley) .10

❏116 Occulus (Mike Manley) .10

❏117 Lyja (Mike Manley) .10

❏118 Death's Head 2 (Liam Sharp, Andy Lanning) .25

❏119 Bloodseed (Liam Sharp, Andy Lanning) .20

❏120 Motormouth & Killpower (Liam Sharp, Andy Lanning) .20

❏121 Dark Angel (Liam Sharp, Andy Lanning) .15

❏122 Warheads (Liam Sharp, Andy Lanning) .15

❏123 Black Axe (Liam Sharp, Andy Lanning) .15

❏124 MysTech Board (Liam Sharp, Andy Lanning) .15

❏125 Death Metal (Liam Sharp, Andy Lanning) .15

❏126 Wild Thing (Liam Sharp, Andy Lanning) .15

❏127 Kree (Tom Morgan) .10

❏128 Brood (Tom Morgan) .10

❏129 Asgardians (Tom Morgan) .10

❏130 Rigellians (Tom Morgan) .10

❏131 Skrulls (Tom Morgan) .10

❏132 Badoon (Tom Morgan) .10

❏133 Ovoids (Tom Morgan) .10

❏134 Shi'ar (Tom Morgan) .10

❏135 Titans (Tom Morgan) .10

❏136 Origin of Wolverine (George Perez) .25

❏137 Origin of Cable (George Perez) .25

❏138 Darkhawk's Helmet (Ian Akin) .10

❏139 Origins of Ghost Rider (Pat Broderick, Bruce Patterson) .15

❏140 Who betrays the X-Men? (Kirk Jarvinen, Brad Vancata) .15

❏141 Face of Dr. Doom (Pat Broderick, Bruce Patterson) .10

❏142 Sixth Member of the Infinity Watch (Art Nichols, Al Vey) .10

❏143 Spidey's Parents (Alex Saviuk, Joe Rubinstein) .10

❏144 Origins of Nightcrawler (Kirk Jarvinen, (Brad Vancata) .10

❏145 Spidey vs. Carnage (Alex Saviuk, Joe Rubinstein) .35

❏146 Cable vs. Stryfe (Pat Broderick, Bruce (Patterson) .35

❏147 Ghost Rider vs. Lilith (Geof Isherwood, Jimmy Palmiotti) .15

❏148 Silver Surfer vs. Morg (Pat Olliffe, Mark McKenna) .15

❏149 Wolverine vs. Sabretooth (Kirk Jarvinen, Brad Vancata) .25

❏150 Thor vs. Loki (George Perez) .10

❏151 War Machine (Pat Broderick, Bruce (Patterson) .10

❏152 Spider-Man vs. Venom (Alex Saviuk, Joe Rubinstein) .25

❏153 Punisher vs. Thorn (Geof Isherwood, Jimmy Palmiotti) .15

❑154 X-Cutioner's Song (Kirk Jarvinen, Brad Vancata) .20

❑155 Spider-Man vs. Sinister Six (Alex Saviuk, (Joe Rubinstein) .10

❑156 Infinity War (Kirk Jarvinen, Brad Vancata) .10

❑157 Spirits of Venom (Alex Saviuk, Joe Rubinstein) .10

❑158 Hulk vs. Leader (Kirk Jarvinen, Brad Vancata) .10

❑159 Ghost Rider vs. Blackout (Pat Broderick, Bruce Patterson) .15

❑160 Dr. Strange vs. Dormammu (Geof Isherwood, Jimmy Palmiotti) .10

❑161 Wolverine vs. Cyber (Kirk Jarvinen, Brad Vancata) .20

❑162 Captain America vs. Crossbones (Pat Olliffe, Mark McKenna) .10

❑163 Punisher vs. Jigsaw (Art Nichols, Al Vey) .20

❑164 Wolverine vs. Venom (Kirk Jarvinen, Brad Vancata) .20

❑165 Spider-Man vs. Juggernaut (Alex Saviuk, Joe Rubinstein) .10

❑166 Darkhawk vs. Evilhawk (Pat Broderick, Bruce Patterson) .10

❑167 X-Force vs. Brotherhood of Evil Mutants (Art Nichols, Al Vey) .15

❑168 Daredevil vs. Typhoid Mary (Geof Isherwood, Jim Palmiotti) .10

❑169 Spider-Man vs. Kingpin (Alex Saviuk, Joe Rubinstein) .10

❑170 Thor vs. Bloodaxe (Geof Isherwood, Jimmy Palmiotti) .10

❑171 Warlock vs. Man-Beast (Pat Olliffe, Mark McKenna) .10

❑172 Ghost Rider vs. Blaze (Pat Broderick, Bruce Patterson) .15

❑173 Green Hulk vs. Gray Hulk (Kirk Jarvinen, Brad Vancata) .10

❑174 Fantastic Four vs. Secret Defenders (Kirk Jarvinen, Brad Vancata) .10

❑175 Spider-Man vs. Cardiac (Alex Saviuk, Joe Rubinstein) .10

❑176 Punisher vs. Ghost Rider (Art Nichols, Al Vey) .15

❑177 Wolverine vs. Omega Red (Kirk Jarvinen, Brad Vancata) .15

❑178 Cable vs. Deadpool (Art Nichols, Al Vey) .20

❑179 Hulk vs. X-Factor (Kirk Jarvinen,Brad Vancata) .15

❑180 Checklist .10

1993 Marvel IV inserts

These cards were randomly issued in foil packs. The insert sets include nine foil-stamped Marvel 2099 cards and one Spider-Man Super 3-D card. The 3-D card was much harder to find than the other nine.

1993 SkyBox Marvel IV inserts

Complete insert set 85.00
Complete foil-stamped set (9) 60.00
Common foil-stamped card 5.00

#	Card	M
❑ F1	Spider-Man 2099 (Rick Leonardi, Al Williamson)	8.00
❑ F2	Punisher 2099 (Rick Leonardi, Al Williamson)	7.00
❑ F3	Ravage 2099 (Rick Leonardi, Al Williamson)	5.00
❑ F4	Doom 2099 (Rick Leonardi, Al Williamson)	5.00
❑ F5	Fearmaster (Rick Leonardi, Al Williamson)	5.00

	#	Card	
❑	F6	Dethstryk (Rick Leonardi, Al Williamson)	5.00
❑	F7	Tiger Wylde (Rick Leonardi, Al Williamson)	5.00
❑	F8	The Specialist (Rick Leonardi, Al Williamson)	5.00
❑	F9	Vulture (Rick Leonardi, Al Williamson)	6.00
❑	3D1	Spider-Man vs. Venom (Bret Blevins)	20.00

1992 SkyBox X-Men Series I promos

A total of five promo cards were packed in five-card cello packs. The backs were slightly different in terms of the rations, and the "X" logo on the front was not as clear as it appeared on the final cards. In addition, the Magneto hologram appeared in Capital City's catalog *Advance Comics*; it had a completely different promotional back.

1992 SkyBox X-Men I promo cards

Complete set (6) .... NVE
Each card .... NVE

	#	Card	M
❑	2	Wolverine	NVE
❑	14	Storm	NVE
❑	17	X-Men	NVE
❑	19	Cable	NVE
❑	41	Magneto	NVE
❑	xx	Magneto hologram	NVE

1992 SkyBox

Uncanny X-Men Series I

Cards were released in wax packs. The set was also available as a tin factory set. All cards were pencilled and inked by Jim Lee.

1991 SkyBox Uncanny X-Men Series I

Complete set (100) 12.00
Complete factory set (100) 60.00
Common card .... .10

	#	Card	M
❑	1	Beast	.10
❑	2	Wolverine	.50
❑	3	Havok	.10
❑	4	Iceman	.10
❑	5	Phoenix	.10
❑	6	Nightcrawler	.10
❑	7	Cannonball	.10
❑	8	Wolfsbane	.10
❑	9	Siryn	.10
❑	10	Lockheed	.10
❑	11	Professor X	.10
❑	12	Psylocke	.20
❑	13	Domino	.15
❑	14	Storm	.10
❑	15	Meggan	.20
❑	16	Feral	.10
❑	17	Cyclops	.10
❑	18	Gambit	.25
❑	19	Cable	.60
❑	20	Archangel	.20
❑	21	Banshee	.10
❑	22	Shadowcat	.10
❑	23	Kylun	.15
❑	24	Jean Grey	.10
❑	25	Colossus	.10
❑	26	Warpath	.10
❑	27	Polaris	.15
❑	28	Boom Boom	.10
❑	29	Jubilee	.15
❑	30	Shatterstar	.10
❑	31	Strong Guy	.15
❑	32	Captain Britain	.15
❑	33	Forge	.10
❑	34	Madrox	.10
❑	35	Quicksilver	.10
❑	36	Rogue	.10
❑	37	Widget	.10
❑	38	Bishop	.20
❑	39	Maverick	.10

❑ 40	Cerise	.10
❑ 41	Magneto	.10
❑ 42	Mr. Sinister	.15
❑ 43	Deadpool	.10
❑ 44	Proteus	.10
❑ 45	Mojo 2	.20
❑ 46	Juggernaut	.10
❑ 47	Sentinels	.15
❑ 48	Gideon	.10
❑ 49	Masque	.10
❑ 50	Shiva	.10
❑ 51	Apocalypse	.15
❑ 52	Sabretooth	.50
❑ 53	Mojo	.15
❑ 54	Caliban	.10
❑ 55	Gatecrasher	.10
❑ 56	Brood	.10
❑ 57	Blob	.10
❑ 58	Stryfe	.25
❑ 59	Warwolves	.10
❑ 60	Omega Red	.10
❑ 61	Black Tom	.10
❑ 62	Mystique	.10
❑ 63	Sauron	.10
❑ 64	Satyrayne	.10
❑ 65	Toad	.10
❑ 66	Shadow King	.10
❑ 67	White Queen	.10
❑ 68	Mastermind	.10
❑ 69	Deathbird	.10
❑ 70	Lady Deathstrike	.10
❑ 71	X-Men Gold	.15
❑ 72	X-Men Blue	.15
❑ 73	X-Factor	.15
❑ 74	X-Force	.15
❑ 75	Excalibur	.10
❑ 76	Hellfire Club	.10
❑ 77	Mutant Liberation Front	.10
❑ 78	Brotherhood of Evil Mutants	.10
❑ 79	Upstarts	.10

❑ 80	Technet	.10
❑ 81	Sunspot	.10
❑ 82	Dark Phoenix	.10
❑ 83	Longshot	.15
❑ 84	Magik	.10
❑ 85	Dazzler	.10
❑ 86	Starjammers	.10
❑ 87	Imperial Guard	.10
❑ 88	Lilandra	.10
❑ 89	Weird Happenings Organization	.10
❑ 90	Roma	.10
❑ 91	Danger Room	.10
❑ 92	Danger Room	.10
❑ 93	Danger Room	.10
❑ 94	Danger Room	.10
❑ 95	Danger Room	.10
❑ 96	Danger Room	.10
❑ 97	Danger Room	.10
❑ 98	Danger Room	.10
❑ 99	Danger Room	.10
❑ 100	Checklist	.10

1992 Impel X-Men
Series I holograms

Cards were randomly issued in Series I packs.

1992 Impel X-Men I holograms

Complete set (5).............................17.00

Common hologram............................2.00

#	Card	M
❑ H1	Wolverine	4.50
❑ H2	Cable	5.00
❑ H3	Gambit	3.00
❑ H4	Magneto	2.00
❑ H5	X-Men	3.00

1993 SkyBox X-Men II promo cards

Complete set (2)............................. NVE

Each card .... NVE

#	Card	M
☐ xx	Juggernaut (Comic Book Collector)	NVE
☐ xx	Juggernaut (promo)	NVE

1993 SkyBox
Uncanny X-Men II

Cards were released in six-card packs in February 1993. The set featured original art by Marvel's X-Men artists and was divided into several subsets: Heroes (1-36), Arch-Enemies (37-54), Villains (55-81), Teams (82-90), and Animated TV Series (91-99). The Arch-Enemies subset was offered in a multi-card puzzle format. Backs included additional art, a DNA analysis of powers, and personal file notes.

1993 SkyBox
Marvel X-Men Series II

Complete set (100) 11.00
Common card .... .10

#	Card	M
☐ 1	Archangel (Brandon Peterson, Jimmy Palmiotti)	.15
☐ 2	Beast (Andy Kubert, Mark Pennington)	.10
☐ 3	Bishop (Brandon Peterson, Jimmy Palmiotti)	.10
☐ 4	Boomer (Greg Capullo, Jimmy Palmiotti)	.10
☐ 5	Cable (Greg Capullo, Jimmy Palmiotti)	.40
☐ 6	Cannonball (Greg Capullo, Jimmy Palmiotti)	.10
☐ 7	Captain Britain (Alan Davis, Mark Farmer)	.10
☐ 8	Cerise (Alan Davis, Mark Farmer)	.10
☐ 9	Colossus (Brandon Peterson, Jimmy Palmiotti)	.10
☐ 10	Cyclops	.10
☐ 11	Domino	.10
☐ 12	Gambit	.20
☐ 13	Jean Grey (Brandon Peterson, Jimmy Palmiotti)	.10
☐ 14	Havok (Joe Quesada, Joe Rubenstein)	.10
☐ 15	Iceman (Brandon Peterson, Jimmy Palmiotti)	.10
☐ 16	Jubilee (Andy Kubert, Mark Pennington)	.10
☐ 17	Kylun (Alan Davis, Mark Farmer)	.10
☐ 18	Meggan (Alan Davis, Mark Farmer)	.15
☐ 19	Multiple Man (Joe Quesada, Joe Rubenstein)	.10
☐ 20	Nightcrawler (Alan Davis, Mark Farmer)	.10
☐ 21	Phoenix (Alan Davis, Mark Farmer)	.10
☐ 22	Polaris (Joe Quesada, Joe Rubenstein)	.10
☐ 23	Professor X (Brandon Peterson, Mark Farmer)	.10
☐ 24	Psylocke (Andy Kubert, Mark Pennington)	.15
☐ 25	Quicksilver (Joe Quesada, Joe Rubenstein)	.10
☐ 26	Rictor (Greg Capullo, Jimmy Palmiotti)	.10
☐ 27	Rogue (Andy Kubert, Mark Pennington)	.10
☐ 28	Shadowcat (Alan Davis, Mark Farmer)	.10
☐ 29	Shatterstar (Greg Capullo, Jimmy Palmiotti)	.10
☐ 30	Siryn (Greg Capullo, Jimmy Palmiotti)	.10
☐ 31	Storm (Brandon Peterson, Jimmy Palmiotti)	.10

❑ 32 Strong Guy (Joe Quesada, Joe Rubenstein) .15

❑ 33 Sunspot (Greg Capullo, Jimmy Palmiotti) .10

❑ 34 Warpath (Greg Capullo, Jimmy Palmiotti) .10

❑ 35 Wolfsbane (Joe Quesada, Joe Rubenstein) .10

❑ 36 Wolverine (Andy Kubert, Mark Pennington) .50

❑ 37 Archangel vs. Apolcalypse (Brandon Peterson, Mark Farmer) .15

❑ 38 Apocalypse vs. Archangel (Brandon Peterson, Mark Farmer) .15

❑ 39 X-Men vs. Magneto & Acolytes (Brandon Peterson, Mark Farmer) .15

❑ 40 Bishop vs. Fitzroy (Brandon Peterson, Al Milgrom) .15

❑ 41 Fitzroy vs. Bishop (Brandon Peterson, Al Milgrom) .15

❑ 42 Magneto & Acolytes vs. X-Men (Brandon Peterson, Al Milgrom) .15

❑ 43 Cable vs. Stryfe (Art Thibert) .20

❑ 44 Stryfe vs. Cable (Art Thibert) .20

❑ 45 Acolytes & Magneto vs. X-Men (Brandon Peterson Mark Farmer) .15

❑ 46 Storm vs. Mystique (Brandon Peterson,z Al Milgrom) .10

❑ 47 Mystique vs. Storm (Brandon Peterson, Al Milgrom) .10

❑ 48 X-Factor vs. Mr. Sinister (Joe Quesada, Joe Rubenstein) .15

❑ 49 Wolverine vs. Omega Red (Brandon Peterson, Mark Farmer) .20

❑ 50 Omega Red vs. Wolverine (Brandon Peterson, Mark Farmer) .20

❑ 51 Mr. Sinister vs. X-Factor (Joe Quesada, Joe Rubenstein) .15

❑ 52 Wolverine vs. Sabretooth (Brandon Peterson, Mark Farmer) .25

❑ 53 Sabretooth vs. Wolverine (Brandon Peterson, Mark Farmer) .25

❑ 54 Nasty Boys vs. X-Factor (Joe Quesada, Joe Rubenstein) .10

❑ 55 Arcade (Joe Madureira, Art Thibert) .10

❑ 56 Black Queen (Mark Pacella, Dan Panosian) .10

❑ 57 Black Tom (Mark Pacella, Dan Panosian) .10

❑ 58 Blob (Mark Pacella, Art Thibert) .10

❑ 59 Jamie Braddock .10

❑ 60 The Brood (Brandon Peterson, Jimmy Palmiotti) .10

❑ 61 Callisto (Joe Madureira, Art Thibert) .10

❑ 62 Deadpool (Joe Madureira, Art Thibert) .10

❑ 63 Deathbird (Brandon Peterson, Jimmy Palmiotti) .10

❑ 64 Fenris (Art Thibert) .10

❑ 65 Gideon (Art Thibert) .10

❏ 66 Juggernaut (Mark Pacella,
      Art Thibert)   .10

❏ 67 Lady Deathstrike (Joe Madureira,
      Art Thibert)   .10

❏ 68 Mastermind (Mark Pacella,
      Dan Panosian)   .10

❏ 69 Mojo (Joe Madureira,
      Art Thibert)   .10

❏ 70 Phantazia (Mark Pacella,
      Dan Panosian)   .10

❏ 71 Pyro (Mark Pacella,
      Dan Panosian)   .10

❏ 72 Sat-Yr-9 (Alan Davis,
      Mark Farmer)   .10

❏ 73 Sauron (Mark Pacella,
      Art Thibert)   .10

❏ 74 The Sentinels (Joe Madureira,
      Art Thibert)   .15

❏ 75 Shinobi (Mark Pacella,
      Dan Panosian)   .10

❏ 76 Hazard (Art Thibert)   .10

❏ 77 Siena Blaze (Mark Pacella,
      Dan Panosian)   .10

❏ 78 Silver Fox (Mark Pacella,
      Dan Panosian)   .10

❏ 79 Toad (Mark Pacella,
      Art Thibert)   .10

❏ 80 Tolliver (Art Thibert)   .10

❏ 81 White Queen (Brandon Peterson,
      Jimmy Palmiotti)   .10

❏ 82 Excalibur (Alan Davis,
      Mark Farmer)   .15

❏ 83 X-Factor (Joe Quesada,
      Joe Rubenstein)   .15

❏ 84 X-Force (Greg Capullo,
      Jimmy Palmiotti)   .15

❏ 85 X-Men: Blue Team (Andy Kubert,
      Mark Pennington)   .15

❏ 86 X-Men: Gold Team (Brandon
      Peterson, Mark Farmer)   .15

❏ 87 Evil Mutants (Mark Pacella,
      Dan Panosian)   .10

❏ 88 Dark Riders (Mark Pacella,
      Dan Panosian)   .10

❏ 89 Mutant Liberation Front
      (Art Thibert)   .10

❏ 90 Six Pack (Art Thibert)   .10

❏ 91 Sabretooth Unleashed!
      (animation art)   .15

❏ 92 The Sentinels Strike!
      (animation art)   .10

❏ 93 Persuasion, Gambit-Style
      (animation art)   .10

❏ 94 Rogue and Storm in Action!
      (animation art)   .10

❏ 95 Jubilee's Fireworks
      (animation art)   .10

❏ 96 Beast Hangs Out
      (animation art)   .10

❏ 97 The Power of Professor X
      (animation art)   .10

❏ 98 The Claws of Wolverine
      (animation art)   .15

❏ 99 The Fury of Storm
      (animation art)   .10

❏100 Checklist   .10

1993 SkyBox
X-Men II inserts

   SkyBox introduced three levels of bonus cards randomly packed in X-Men II packs: nine foil-stamped cards, three full-color holograms, and a 3-D card.

1993 SkyBox X-Men II inserts

Complete set (13)..............................65.00

Complete foil-stamped set set
(G1-G9) 27.00

Common foil-stamped insert 3.00

Complete hologram set (H1-HX)I 25.00

Common hologram..............................5.00

#	Card	M
❏ G1	Cable (Greg Capullo, Jimmy Palmiotti)	4.00
❏ G2	Cyclops (Andy Kubert, Mark Pennington)	3.00
❏ G3	Juggernaut (Mark Pacella, Art Thibert)	3.00
❏ G4	Magneto (Brandon Peterson, Mark Farmer)	3.00
❏ G5	Professor X (Brandon Peterson, Mark Farmer)	3.00
❏ G6	Rogue (Andy Kubert, Mark Pennington)	3.00
❏ G7	The Sentinels (Joe Madureira, Art Thibert)	3.00
❏ G8	Storm (Brandon Peterson, Jimmy Palmiotti)	3.00
❏ G9	Wolverine (Andy Kubert, Mark Pennington)	4.00
❏ H1	Cable (Art Thibert)	6.00
❏ H2	Magneto (Art Thibert)	5.00
❏ H3	Storm (Art Thibert)	5.00
❏ HX	Wolverine 3-D (sculpture)	20.00

1992 SkyBox Marvel Masterpieces promo cards

Six sample cards were created for this series. Three had two versions and were issued in publications that appeared in July and August 1992: Spider-Man (one with "PROTOTYPE" and regular back, one with promotional copy that appeared in *Previews*, the Diamond distributor catalog); Wolverine (two versions: one with "PROTOTYPE" and regular back; one with promotional copy that appeared in *Up and Coming*, the Friendly Frank's distributor catalog); Psylocke (with promotional back; appeared in *Wizard*); Silver Surfer (with promotional back; appeared in the September/October 1992 issue of *Comics Buyer's Guide Price Guide*); Hulk (two versions: one with "PROTOTYPE" and regular back; one with promotional copy which appeared in *Marvel Age*); Captain America (with promotional back; appeared in *Scoreboard*, the distributor catalog from Heroes World). Card fronts appeared in the regular series.

1992 SkyBox Marvel Masterpieces promo cards

Complete set (6)	NVE
Each card	NVE

#	Card	M
❏ xx	Captain America	NVE
❏ xx	Hulk (promo)	NVE
❏ xx	Hulk (Marvel Age)	NVE
❏ xx	Psylocke	NVE
❏ xx	Silver Surfer	NVE
❏ xx	Spider-Man (promo)	NVE
❏ xx	Spider-Man (Previews)	NVE
❏ xx	Wolverine (promo)	NVE
❏ xx	Wolverine (Up and Coming)	NVE

1992 SkyBox Marvel Masterpieces

Cards were released in packs in November 1992. Art for all cards was by long-time cover artist Joe Jusko, who painted all 105 paintings in 120 days between April and July 1992. A total of 17,500 cases were produced; five hologram cards were randomly packed. Cards were sold in six-card foil packs with a suggested retail price of 99¢ each.

1992 SkyBox Marvel Masterpieces

Complete set (36)	24.00
Complete hologram set (B1-B5)	25.00
Common card	.20
Common hologram	4.00

#	Card	M
❏ 1	Blob	.20
❏ 2	Blaze	.35
❏ 3	Black Widow	.20
❏ 4	Black Panther	.20
❏ 5	Black Cat	.20
❏ 6	Bishop	.50
❏ 7	Beast	.35
❏ 8	Archangel	.35
❏ 9	Apocalype	.35
❏ 10	Adam Warlock	1.00
❏ 11	Darkhawk	.35
❏ 12	Daredevil	.20
❏ 13	Cyclops	.20
❏ 14	Colossus	.20
❏ 15	Captain Britain	.35
❏ 16	Captain America	.20
❏ 17	Cage	.20
❏ 18	Cable	1.50
❏ 19	Bullseye	.20
❏ 20	Dazzler	.20
❏ 21	Enchantress	.20
❏ 22	Elektra	.20
❏ 23	Electro	.20
❏ 24	Dr. Strange	.50
❏ 25	Dr. Octopus	.20
❏ 26	Dr. Doom	.35
❏ 27	Dormammu	.20
❏ 28	Deathlok	.50
❏ 29	Gambit	.50
❏ 30	Galactus	.20
❏ 31	Human Torch	.20
❏ 32	Hulk	.50
❏ 33	Hobgoblin	.50
❏ 34	Hawkeye	.20
❏ 35	Havok	.35
❏ 36	Green Goblin	.20
❏ 37	Ghost Rider	.50
❏ 38	Iron Man	.35
❏ 39	Invisible Woman	.20
❏ 40	Iceman	.20
❏ 41	Lizard	.20
❏ 42	Leader	.20
❏ 43	Kingpin	.20
❏ 44	Kang	.20
❏ 45	Juggernaut	.20
❏ 46	Jean Grey	.20
❏ 47	Mandarin	.20
❏ 48	Major Victory	.20
❏ 49	Magneto	.35
❏ 50	Loki	.20
❏ 51	Moon Knight	.20
❏ 52	Mole Man	.20
❏ 53	Mojo	.35
❏ 54	Mephisto	.20
❏ 55	Meggan	.35
❏ 56	Namorita	.35
❏ 57	Namor	.50
❏ 58	Mr. Sinister	.35
❏ 59	Mr. Fantastic	.20
❏ 60	Morbius	.50
❏ 61	Nightmare	.20
❏ 62	Nightcrawler	.20
❏ 63	Night Thrasher	.35
❏ 64	Nick Fury	.20
❏ 65	Psylocke	.35
❏ 66	Professor X	.20
❏ 67	Phoenix	.20
❏ 68	Nova	.20
❏ 69	Northstar	.20
❏ 70	Nomad	.20
❏ 71	Quicksilver	.20
❏ 72	Quasar	.20
❏ 73	Punisher	.75
❏ 74	Shatterstar	.20
❏ 75	Shadowcat	.20
❏ 76	Sauron	.20
❏ 77	Sandman	.20
❏ 78	Sabretooth	1.00
❏ 79	Rogue	.20

❑ 80	Red Skull	.20
❑ 81	Silver Sable	.50
❑ 82	She-Hulk	.35
❑ 83	Thanos	1.00
❑ 84	Super Skrull	.20
❑ 85	Strong Guy	.35
❑ 86	Storm	.20
❑ 87	Spider-Man	.50
❑ 88	Speedball	.35
❑ 89	Sleepwalker	.35
❑ 90	Silver Surfer	.50
❑ 91	Thing	.20
❑ 92	Thor	.20
❑ 93	Wonder Man	.20
❑ 94	Wolverine	1.00
❑ 95	White Queen	.20
❑ 96	Weapon Omega	.35
❑ 97	Venom	1.50
❑ 98	Ultron	.20
❑ 99	Tombstone	.20
❑100	Checklist	.20

1992 SkyBox Marvel Masterpieces holograms

Cards were randomly inserted in foil packs.

1992 SkyBox Marvel Masterpieces holograms

Complete set (5).............................	35.00
Common hologram............................	4.00

#	Card	M
❑ B1	Thing vs. Hulk	4.00
❑ B2	Silver Surfer vs. Thanos	7.50
❑ B3	Wolverine vs. Sabretooth	7.50
❑ B4	Spider-Man vs. Venom	10.00
❑ B5	Captain America vs. Red Skull	4.00

1993 Marvel Masterpieces II

Cards were released in October 1993. Like the first Marvel Masterpieces series, the total print run was 17,500 cases.

1993 Marvel Masterpieces II checklist

❑	1	Hulk (Bill Sienkiewicz)
❑	2	Human Torch (Jim Steranko)
❑	3	Thor (Lou Harrison)
❑	4	Iron Man (Julie Bell)
❑	5	Spider-Man (Michael Kaluta)
❑	6	Wolverine (Bill Sienklewicz)
❑	7	Cyclops (Joe Phillips)
❑	8	Doctor Strange (Mike Kaluta)
❑	9	Namor (Jim Steranko)
❑	10	Storm (Michael Kaluta)
❑	11	Silver Surfer (Julie Bell)
❑	12	Vison (Joe Jusko)
❑	13	Ghost Rider (Bill Sienklewicz)
❑	14	Thing (George Prez)
❑	15	Captain America (Jim Steranko)
❑	16	Archangel (Joe Phillips)
❑	17	Beast (George Prez)
❑	18	Cable (Dan Brereton)
❑	19	Carnage (Joe Jusko)
❑	20	Hulk 2099 (Dave Dorman)
❑	21	Doctor Doom (Glenn Fabry)
❑	22	Daredevil (Tristan Shane)
❑	23	Iron Fist (Joe Jusko)
❑	24	Psylocke (Julie Bell)
❑	25	Morbius (Brian Stelfreeze)
❑	26	Punisher (Mike Zeck/Phil Zimelman)
❑	27	Rogue (Brian Stelfreeze)
❑	28	Sabretooth (Bill Sienklewicz)
❑	29	Forge (Joe Jusko)
❑	30	She-Hulk (Joe Jusko)
❑	31	Gambit (Joe Phillips)
❑	32	U.S. Agent (Frank Spinks)
❑	33	Spiker-Woman (Tristan Shane)
❑	34	Stryfe (Joe Jusko)
❑	35	Thanos (Ray Lago)
❑	36	Blade (Tom Palmer)
❑	37	Adam Warlock (Ray Lago)
❑	38	Colossus (Julie Bell)

- ❏ 39 Magneto (Jimmy Palmiotti)
- ❏ 40 Vulture (Bill Sienklewicz)
- ❏ 41 Spider-Man (2099)
- ❏ 42 Punisher 2099 (Joe Jusko)
- ❏ 43 Doom 2099 (Joe Jusko)
- ❏ 44 Ravage 2099 (Joe Jusko)
- ❏ 45 Venom (Dave Dorman)
- ❏ 46 Domino (Joe Jusko)
- ❏ 47 Annihilus (Glenn Fabry)
- ❏ 48 Rhino (Bret Blevins)
- ❏ 49 Puma (Joe Phillips)
- ❏ 50 Cannonball (Joe Jusko)
- ❏ 51 Polaris (Dan Lawlis)
- ❏ 52 Longshot (Joe Phillips)
- ❏ 53 Cyber (Joe Jusko)
- ❏ 54 Omega Red (Bret Blevins)
- ❏ 55 Deadpool (Joe Jusko)
- ❏ 56 Kingpin (John Romita Sr.)
- ❏ 57 Bishop (Brian Stelfreeze)
- ❏ 58 Absorbing Man (Dave Dorman)
- ❏ 59 Darkhawk (Ken Steady)
- ❏ 60 Mystique (Brian Stelfreeze)
- ❏ 61 Abomination (Joe Phillips)
- ❏ 62 Wasp (John Estes)
- ❏ 63 Scorpion (Bret Blevins)
- ❏ 64 Captain Britain (Joe Phillips)
- ❏ 65 Black Knight (Tom Palmer)
- ❏ 66 Sasquatch (Brian Stelfreeze)
- ❏ 67 Black Widow (Joe Chlodo)
- ❏ 68 Typhoid Mary (Bret Blevins)
- ❏ 69 War Machine (Joe Jusko)
- ❏ 70 Hawkeye (Ray Lago)
- ❏ 71 Deathlok (Dan Brereton)
- ❏ 72 Nightcrawler (Kent Williams)
- ❏ 73 Thunderstrike (Joe Jusko)
- ❏ 74 Vengeance (Tristan Shane)
- ❏ 75 Jean Grey (Carl Potts)
- ❏ 76 Shatterstar (Lou Harrison)
- ❏ 77 Beta Ray Bill (Joe Phillips)
- ❏ 78 Night Thrasher (Bret Blevins)
- ❏ 79 Red Skull (Mike Zeck/Phil Zimelman)
- ❏ 80 Lilith (Kent Williams)
- ❏ 81 Falcon (Kent Williams)
- ❏ 82 Hercules (Ray Lago)
- ❏ 83 Nova (Ray Lago)
- ❏ 84 Havok (Joe Phillips)
- ❏ 85 Phoenix (Lou Harrison)
- ❏ 86 Crystal (Bret Blevins)
- ❏ 87 Drax (Lou Harrison)
- ❏ 88 Terrax (Glenn Fabry)
- ❏ 89 Vulture 2099 (Kent Williams)
- ❏ 90 Checklist

X-Men 2099 chase cards subset

- ❏ S1 Meanstreak (Bob Larkin)
- ❏ S2 Cerebra (Bob Larkin)
- ❏ S3 Krystalin (Bob Larkin)
- ❏ S4 Metalhead (Bob Larkin)
- ❏ S5 Serpentina (Bob Larkin)
- ❏ S6 Bloodhawk (Bob Larkin)
- ❏ S7 Skullfire (Bob Larkin)
- ❏ S8 Xi'an (Bob Larkin)

1966 Donruss Marvel Super-Heroes

Originally available for 5¢ per pack, this was the first in a line of "funny Marvel super-hero" cards. Each card featured a comic-book panel with a humorous word balloon or caption; roughly a quarter of the cards had empty speech balloons for kids to fill in their own sayings. When put together, backs formed a puzzle featuring the Marvel characters; cards are numbered on the front and are grouped by super-hero.

1966 Donruss Marvel Super-Heroes

Complete set (66) 160.00

Each card 2.50

#	Card	NM
	Captain America	
❏ 1	I love these class parties!	2.50

❑ 2 But lady, the subscription only costs $3.98! 2.50

❑ 3 (Fill in caption) 2.50

❑ 4 You're going to love our steam room! 2.50

❑ 5 I told you to keep those pigeons out of my yard! 2.50

❑ 6 These class parties give me a headache! 2.50

❑ 7 (Fill in caption) 2.50

❑ 8 You and your fire sales! 2.50

❑ 9 Don't go to pieces over the crabgrass! 2.50

❑ 10 (Fill in caption) 2.50

❑ 11 I got it for 362 books of stamps! 2.50

Iron Man

❑ 12 "Get the lead out!" 2.50

❑ 13 I hate these toy kits! 2.50

❑ 14 Do you have iron deficiency anemia? 2.50

❑ 15 (Fill in caption) 2.50

❑ 16 To get your atom smasher, send in 5 box tops and $1,000,000! 2.50

❑ 17 And you said, "Add a little more lighter fluid!" 2.50

❑ 18 (Fill in caption) 2.50

❑ 19 Please, I'd rather do it myself. 2.50

❑ 20 (Fill in caption) 2.50

❑ 21 That chick really puts me in orbit! 2.50

❑ 22 When did you first notice those stomach pains? 2.50

Daredevil

❑ 23 But Halloween is next week! 2.50

❑ 24 Let Hurts put you in the driver's seat! 2.50

❑ 25 (Fill in caption) 2.50

❑ 26 I'm sorry, I'm tied up this evening! 2.50

❑ 27 With these trading stamps you can get anything! 2.50

❑ 28 He still thinks he's in the circus! 2.50

❑ 29 Wait till I turn the antenna! 2.50

❑ 30 (Fill in caption) 2.50

❑ 31 I didn't know you had a game room! 2.50

❑ 32 How's this for a finish? 2.50

❑ 33 (Fill in caption) 2.50

Spider-Man

❑ 34 Next time I'll fly the kite! 2.50

❑ 35 Next time you change the tire! 2.50

❑ 36 (Fill in caption) 2.50

❑ 37 Just what I needed, a bug bomb! 2.50

❑ 38 What'ya mean, 50 cents extra for gift wrapping! 2.50

❑ 39 I made a "Before And After" commercial 2.50

❑ 40 This fly paper is rough on the hair! 2.50

❑ 41 Just fixing a little! 2.50

❑ 42 I meant, hang up the phone! 2.50

❑ 43 Those kids and those Build-It Yourself A-Bomb kits! 2.50

❑ 44 (Fill in caption) 2.50

Hulk

❑ 45 (Fill in caption) 2.50

❑ 46 These PTA meetings drive me crazy! 2.50

❑ 47 OK, so you're the Green Giant! 2.50

❑ 48 When I was an 82-lb. weakling... 2.50

❑ 49 Come on out and play! 2.50

❏ 50 But I wanted an A-bomb for Christmas! 2.50

❏ 51 Let's go swimming, buddy! 2.50

❏ 52 From now on, take your coffee breaks with the rest of the guests! 2.50

❏ 53 This will really curl your hair! 2.50

❏ 54 Watch that first step! 2.50

❏ 55 I don't believe I've met you guys!

Thor

❏ 56 She's always hiding the soap! 2.50

❏ 57 I'd rather fight, but I don't smoke! 2.50

❏ 58 The peasants are always throwing rocks! 2.50

❏ 59 I don't care if you do have "We Tried Harder" buttons! 2.50

❏ 60 Just who does your hair? 2.50

❏ 61 I get 8 shaves from each blade of Koo-coo! 2.50

❏ 62 I think the trouble is in the fuel pump! 2.50

❏ 63 No, I don't want any Scout cookies! 2.50

❏ 64 We try harder — we're only No. Two! 2.50

❏ 65 (Fill in caption) 2.50

❏ 66 (Fill in caption) 2.50

1967 Philadelphia Gum Marvel Super Hero Stickers

This 55-sticker set depicts various Marvel heroes in dramatic poses with humorous speech bubbles. Backs are blank, but the stickers are numbered on the front. Note: Stickers are often found miscut. Packs originally sold for a nickel.

1967 Philadelphia Gum Marvel Super Hero Stickers

Complete set (55) 350.00

Each sticker 6.00

#	Card	NM
❏ 1	Human Torch (I must get that roof fixed!)	6.00
❏ 2	Human Torch (How do you like your hamburgers?)	6.00
❏ 3	Daredevil (It might have been easier to take the elevator!)	6.00
❏ 4	Thor (That's right, this big! But it got away!)	6.00
❏ 5	Hulk (My father can lick your father!)	6.00
❏ 6	Hulk (But I though you took the garbage out!)	6.00
❏ 7	Thing (It's clobberin' time!)	6.00
❏ 8	Thing (No fair using water guns!)	6.00
❏ 9	Human Torch (I wish I'd used that sun tan lotion!)	6.00
❏ 10	Iron Man (What if I am a high school drop-out?)	6.00
❏ 11	Daredevil (Taxi!)	6.00
❏ 12	Spider-Man (Some web-shooter!)	6.00
❏ 13	Thor (You sent for a carpenter?)	6.00
❏ 14	Sub-Mariner (I'm the only wash and-wear hero in town!)	6.00
❏ 15	Sub-Mariner (Yipe! That water's cold!)	6.00
❏ 16	Human Torch (Butterfingers!)	6.00
❏ 17	Thing (Stop talking while I'm interrupting!)	6.00
❏ 18	Dardevil (Now where did I leave my clothes?)	6.00
❏ 19	Thor (Why yes, I do set my hair myself!)	6.00
❏ 20	Thing (I'm not fat, I'm just short for my width!)	6.00

❑ 21 Spider-Man (Aren't we a little too old to play leapfrog, Herman?)   6.00

❑ 22 Hulk (Which hand has the choco late candy?)   6.00

❑ 23 Daredevil (Who moved the trapeze?)   6.00

❑ 24 Dr. Strange (All I get is nag, nag, nag!)   6.00

❑ 25 Thing (That dry skin cream is just no good!)   6.00

❑ 26 Sub-Mariner (Who stole my pants?)   6.00

❑ 27 Daredevil (Darn! Missed the bus again!)   6.00

❑ 28 Iron Man (Well, there goes my last roll of caps!)   6.00

❑ 29 Spider-Man (But mother, I'm too old for dance lessons!)   6.00

❑ 30 Hulk (What do you mean you don't have my shoe size?)   6.00

❑ 31 Hulk (Who used up the hot water?)   6.00

❑ 32 Thing (Clyde! How you've changed!)   6.00

❑ 33 Iron Man (Ouch! Bwang!)   6.00

❑ 34 Dr. Strange (If you can't beat 'em call 'em names!)   6.00

❑ 35 Captain America (No, lady, this isn't your trash can lid!)   6.00

❑ 36 Thing (I may not be brave, but I'm handsome!)   6.00

❑ 37 Iron Man (Let's see, now — what's good for rust?)   6.00

❑ 38 Hulk (This is the last time I'll babysit!)   6.00

❑ 39 Spider-Man (I must have made a wrong turn!)   6.00

❑ 40 Iron Man (My work is so secret, even I don't know what I'm doing!)   6.00

❑ 41 Thor (Turn that air conditioner off!)   6.00

❑ 42 Spider-Man (Smile! Later today you won't feel like it!)   6.00

❑ 43 Spider-Man (May I leave the room?)   6.00

❑ 44 Iron Man (They just don't make chains the way they used to!)6.00

❑ 45 Hulk (Rah! Rah! Team!)   6.00

❑ 46 Sub-Mariner (Which way is the men's locker room?)   6.00

❑ 47 Hulk (The dance is tonight! Why isn't my suit ready?)   6.00

❑ 48 Hulk (One, two, cha cha cha!)   6.00

❑ 49 Spider-Man (Hey, lady, you dropped your package!)   6.00

❑ 50 Captain America (Regular aspirin just isn't enough!)   6.00

❑ 51 Thing (We're the new singing group — Him, Her and It!)   6.00

❑ 52 Thor (One more word out of you, Charlie, and you get it!) 6.00

❑ 53 Captain America (Jaywalker!)6.00

❑ 54 Captain America (May I take two giant steps?)   6.00

❑ 55 Human Torch (Don't you call me a slob!)   6.00

1975 Topps Comic Book Heroes stickers

These sticker-cards were issued in wax packs with a piece of gum in 1975. The stickers featured die-cut action poses of Marvel characters combined with a humorous speech bubble. Backs either contained a piece to a puzzle (Fantastic Four) or a checklist. It's believed an initial set

was tested, then was issued nationally. Stickers are unnumbered and are listed here in the order in which they appeared on the checklist.

1975 Topps Comic Book Heroes stickers

Complete set (40) 200.00
Each sticker 4.50

#	Card	M
❑ xx	The Falcon (You bet your bird!)	4.50
❑ xx	The Thing 1 (It's clobberin' time!)	4.50
❑ xx	Frankenstein's Monster (Maybe it's my breath!)	4.50
❑ xx	Shang-Chi, Master of Kung Fu (All aspirin is not alike!)	4.50
❑ xx	Dr. Strange (Darn those house calls!)	4.50
❑ xx	Dracula 1 (Sure doesn't taste like tomato juice!)	4.50
❑ xx	Human Torch 1 (Tan, don't burn!)	4.50
❑ xx	Daredevil (Badness makes me see red!)	4.50
❑ xx	Iron Man (Fight rust!)	4.50
❑ xx	Werewolf	4.50
❑ xx	Thor 1 (Support your local Thunder God!)	4.50
❑ xx	Sub-Mariner (Don't pollute my waters!)	4.50
❑ xx	Hawkeye (Annie Oakley I Ain't!)	4.50
❑ xx	Captain Marvel (Fly the friendly skies of United!)	4.50
❑ xx	Ghost Rider (Peter Fonda look out!)	4.50
❑ xx	The Living Mummy (Which hand has the M&Ms?)	4.50
❑ xx	Morbius, the Living Vampire (Which way to the blood bank?)	4.50
❑ xx	Ka-Zar (Be kind to animals — or else!)	4.50
❑ xx	Spider-Man 1 (Who'd you expect? Little Miss Muffet?)	4.50
❑ xx	Captain America 1 (I'm a Yankee Doodle Dandy!)	4.50
❑ xx	Conan (Trick or treat!)	4.50
❑ xx	Kull (These pants don't fit!)	4.50
❑ xx	Dr. Doom (I'm dressed to kill!)	4.50
❑ xx	The Son of Satan (The devil made me do it!)	4.50
❑ xx	Spider-Man 2 (You drive me up a wall!)	4.50
❑ xx	Dracula 2 (Flying drives me bats!)	4.50
❑ xx	Human Torch 2 (When you're hot, you're hot!)	4.50
❑ xx	Thor 2 (Who said blondes have more fun?)	4.50
❑ xx	Hulk 2 (Green power!)	4.50
❑ xx	The Thing 2 (I'm going to pieces!)	4.50
❑ xx	Captain America 2 (Look ma, no cavities!)	4.50
❑ xx	Dr. Octopus (I'm just a well-armed crook!)	4.50
❑ xx	The Valkyrie	4.50
❑ xx	Mr. Fantastic (I'm the long arm of the law!)	4.50
❑ xx	Medusa (Darn that cheap hairspray!)	4.50
❑ xx	Black Widow (I'm Natasha, fly me to Miami!)	4.50
❑ xx	Iron Fist (Kung fooey!)	4.50
❑ xx	Man-Thing (I dropped the soap in the shower!)	4.50
❑ xx	Hulk 2 (Green power!)	4.50

❏ xx   Luke Cage (I was a 98-pound
      weakling!)   4.50

1976 Topps Marvel Super Heroes stickers

This 40-card set was a follow-up to the successful 1975 edition. Backs either contain either a checklist or one of nine puzzle pieces which form the cover to *Conan the Barbarian* #1. As with the previous set, stickers are die cut and feature a Marvel character in an action pose with a humorous speech bubble. Interestingly, many of the poses seem to be taken from the upper left corner of the character's comic book. Stickers are unnumbered and are listed here in the order in which they appeared on the checklist.

1976 Marvel Super-Heroes

Complete set (40 stickers,
9 cards)... 135.00
Each sticker...................................... 3.50
Each card 2.00

#	Card	M
❏ xx	Hulk (Help cure athlete's feet!)	
		3.50
❏ xx	Warlock (Stop me if you heard this before...)	3.50
❏ xx	Kid Colt (I am not kidding around!)	3.50
❏ xx	Iron Man (Quick — anyone have an oil can?)	3.50
❏ xx	Goliath (Wanna hear a tall story?)	3.50
❏ xx	Deathlok (I'm the seven million dollar man!)	3.50
❏ xx	Capt. America (I've got to stand this way or my pants fall down!)	3.50
❏ xx	Spider-Man (Insects scare me silly!)	3.50

❏ xx	Iceman (I'll never eat another frozen dinner!)	3.50
❏ xx	Dr. Strange (Did anyone see a flying sorcerer?)	3.50
❏ xx	Silver Surfer (You'll take a shine to me!)	3.50
❏ xx	Thing (Who said I'm a falling rock zone?)	3.50
❏ xx	Human Torch (Who called me a hothead?)	3.50
❏ xx	Howard the Duck (I'm going quackers!)	3.50
❏ xx	Daredevil (See no evil!)	3.50
❏ xx	Loki (Who says I'm bull-headed?)	
		3.50
❏ xx	Sgt. Fury (War makes me fighting mad!)	3.50
❏ xx	The Watcher (Hiya kids! Hiya! Hiya Hiya!)	3.50
❏ xx	Luke Cage (Like my denture work?)	3.50
❏ xx	Tigra (Cat food for dinner again?)	
		3.50
❏ xx	Thor (Don't make me Thor!)	3.50
❏ xx	Red Sonja (My sword gives six extra shaves!)	3.50
❏ xx	Dr. Doom (Anyone out there have a can opener?)	3.50
❏ xx	Conan (Hold the pickle — or else!)	3.50
❏ xx	Son of Stan (Waiter, bring me a clean fork!)	3.50
❏ xx	The Vision (Who stole my yo-yo?)	
		3.50
❏ xx	Red Skull (What makes you think I'm angry?)	3.50
❏ xx	Peter Parker (Peter Parker picked a peck of pickled peppers!)	3.50
❏ xx	Killraven (I'll teach you to make fun of my hair-do!)	3.50

❑ xx Galactus (No, I'm not the
         Mad Hatter!)   3.50

❑ xx Cyclops (I'm a sight for
         sore eyes!)   3.50

❑ xx Black Goliath (Bowling
         sure is fun!)   3.50

❑ xx Punisher (Oh boy! I win the
         kewpie doll!)   3.50

❑ xx Dracula (So this is how
         you do The Hustle!)   3.50

❑ xx Blade (I'm a real cut-up!)   3.50

❑ xx Hercules (Look, I have a
         hang-nail!)   3.50

❑ xx Bucky (How'd you like
         a knuckle sandwich?)   3.50

❑ xx Invisible Girl (I use
         vanishing cream!)   3.50

❑ xx Volstagg (Fat is beautiful!)   3.50

❑ xx Angel (I'm heading south for
         the winter!)   3.50

1978 Topps Marvel Comics

Topps issued this set of comics panels in 1978 — a comic strip was wrapped around a stick of sugar-free gum, with the display advertising on the outside and the strip on the inside. Each strip was generally three panels long, and the bottom portion featured "Dr. Strange's Fortunes." Because most strips suffered some tearing damage when they were opened, strips are generally graded in Excellent condition. The strips are numbered; the description here includes the character featured in the panel. Thanks to the popularity of the TV show, the Hulk is featured on more than a third of the strips.

1979 Topps Marvel Comics

Complete set (34) 85.00

Each panel 2.50

#	Card	Ex
❑ 1	Sub-Mariner	2.50
❑ 2	Dr. Strange	2.50
❑ 3	Hulk	2.50
❑ 4	Silver Surfer	2.50
❑ 5	Hulk	2.50
❑ 6	Hulk	2.50
❑ 7	Iron Man	2.50
❑ 8	Sub-Mariner	2.50
❑ 9	Fantastic Four	2.50
❑ 10	Spider-Man	2.50
❑ 11	Spider-Man	2.50
❑ 12	Hulk	2.50
❑ 13	Fantastic Four	2.50
❑ 14	Iron Man	2.50
❑ 15	Thor	2.50
❑ 16	Hulk	2.50
❑ 17	Hulk	2.50
❑ 18	Iron Man	2.50
❑ 19	Iron Man	2.50
❑ 20	Fantastic Four	2.50
❑ 21	Hulk	2.50
❑ 22	Captain America	2.50
❑ 23	Iron Man	2.50
❑ 24	Hulk	2.50
❑ 25	Iron Man	2.50
❑ 26	Sub-Mariner	2.50
❑ 27	Hulk	2.50
❑ 28	Sub-Mariner	2.50
❑ 29	Hulk	2.50
❑ 30	Hulk	2.50
❑ 31	Hulk	2.50
❑ 32	Spider-Man	2.50
❑ 33	Fantastic Four	2.50
❑ 34	The Thing	2.50

1979 Topps Marvel Comics

The panels are almost identical to those issued the previous year except: the indicia targeting the panels from 1979; the line underneath "Dr. Strange's Fortunes"

indicating the panel number in the set; the size of the set (33 panels this year, down one from the previous year); and the fact the panels were not part of the wrapper (and, in fact, were only 5¢ apiece, compared to 20¢ the previous year). Panels are identical between the two sets (except panels #8, 19, and 33, which feature the Thing twice and Sub-Mariner once), but two #20s were printed, while no #30 was issued.

1978 Topps Marvel Comics

Complete set (33)............................ 70.00
Each panel... 1.50

#	Card	Ex
❑ 1	Sub-Mariner	1.50
❑ 2	Doctor Strange	1.50
❑ 3	Hulk	1.50
❑ 4	Silver Surfer	1.50
❑ 5	Hulk	1.50
❑ 6	Hulk	1.50
❑ 7	Iron Man	1.50
❑ 8	The Thing	1.50
❑ 9	Fantastic Four	1.50
❑ 10	Spider-Man	1.50
❑ 11	Spider-Man	1.50
❑ 12	Hulk	1.50
❑ 13	Fantastic Four	1.50
❑ 14	Iron Man	1.50
❑ 15	Thor	1.50
❑ 16	Hulk	1.50
❑ 17	Hulk	1.50
❑ 18	Iron Man	1.50
❑ 19	Sub-Mariner	1.50
❑ 20	Fantastic Four	1.50
❑ 20	Hulk	1.50
❑ 21	Hulk	1.50
❑ 22	Captain America	1.50
❑ 23	Iron Man	1.50
❑ 24	Hulk	1.50
❑ 25	Iron Man	1.50
❑ 26	Sub-Mariner	1.50
❑ 27	Hulk	1.50
❑ 28	Sub-Mariner	1.50
❑ 29	Hulk	1.50
❑ 31	Hulk	1.50
❑ 32	Spider-Man	1.50
❑ 33	The Thing	1.50

1979 Topps Incredible Hulk (TV)

The series featured scenes from the TV series that starred Lou Ferrigno and Bill Bixby in the late 1970s. Cards featured green borders; the backs of 10 of the cards were "TV Facts" about the making of the show, while the other 78 cards had puzzle pieces that created four different puzzles. Each pack contained seven cards and one of 22 stickers. (Each pack cost 15¢ at the time.) Interestingly, Topps used both varieties of the Hulk logo: The stylized version of the logo which began in the mid-100 run of the comic book was used as poster ads, while the "block" version used originally (and currently featured) on the comic book was used on packs and display boxes.

1979 Topps Incredible Hulk

Complete set (88)............................13.00
Each card 25

#	Card	M
❑ 1	No Power To Save Her!	
❑ 2	Experiment: Perilous!	.25
❑ 3	Unearthly Seizure	.25
❑ 4	Birth Of The Beast Man	.25
❑ 5	This Man...This Monster!	.25
❑ 6	Friend...of Fiend?	.25
❑ 7	The Hand Of Fear	.25
❑ 8	The Creature's Plan	.25
❑ 9	Power Of The Brute	.25
❑ 10	To Rescue A Child	.25

❑ 11	The Make-Shift Bridge	.25
❑ 12	The Creature...Shot!	.25
❑ 13	Fury Of The Hulk	.25
❑ 14	The Charging Terror	.25
❑ 15	The Monster Strikes!	.25
❑ 16	In The Clutches Of Horror!	.25
❑ 17	The Incredible Man Monster	.25
❑ 18	Prehistoric Mutant	.25
❑ 19	Portrait Of A Monster	.25
❑ 20	Horror In The Woods	.25
❑ 21	Stirrings Within The Beast	.25
❑ 22	The Pawn Of Destiny	.25
❑ 23	Monstrous Reflection	.25
❑ 24	Metamorphosis	.25
❑ 25	Inside The Hyperbaric Chamber	.25
❑ 26	Engine Of Destruction	.25
❑ 27	No Walls Can Hold Him!	.25
❑ 28	The Creature Is Loose!	.25
❑ 29	Living Nightmare	.25
❑ 30	The Abomination	.25
❑ 31	Modified Hulk Make-Up	.25
❑ 32	Back From Beyond	.25
❑ 33	Ferrigno In Character	.25
❑ 34	Filming The Episode "Married"	.25
❑ 35	The Flame And The Fury	.25
❑ 36	The Inferno	.25
❑ 37	Death Of Dr. Marks	.25
❑ 38	The Hulk Strikes Back!	.25
❑ 39	Nightmare At The Ranch	.25
❑ 40	Has The Hulk Met His Match?	.25
❑ 41	Battle Of The Behemoths	.25
❑ 42	Monster In The Mansion	.25
❑ 43	No Escaped From The Brute	.25
❑ 44	A Titan In Times Square	.25
❑ 45	Manhattan Mayhem	.25
❑ 46	The Beast Bursts Through	.25
❑ 47	The 747 Affair	.25
❑ 48	Stranger At The Door	.25
❑ 49	Face Of Fear	.25
❑ 50	The Dark Journey Back	.25
❑ 51	Bringing In A 747	.25
❑ 52	"No! It Can't Happen Now!"	.25
❑ 53	Caught In Mid-Transformation!	.25
❑ 54	Banner's Titanic Struggle!	.25
❑ 55	Suppressing The Demon Within Him	.25
❑ 56	Creature In The Pilot's Seat	.25
❑ 57	Monster At The Controls	.25
❑ 58	Panic In The Cockpit	.25
❑ 59	Greetings From Our Captain!	.25
❑ 61	Racing Through The Airliner	.25
❑ 62	Stan Lee's Creation...The Hulk.	.25
❑ 63	Creature On The Runway!	.25
❑ 64	Nobody Fences In The Hulk!	.25
❑ 65	David Banner Confronts...Himself!	.25
❑ 66	Hope Through Hypnotherapy	.25
❑ 67	A Man Possessed	.25
❑ 68	The Raging Spirit	.25
❑ 69	The Humanoid Appears	.25
❑ 70	Tower Of Strength	.25
❑ 71	No Longer Human	.25
❑ 72	The Captive Creature	.25
❑ 73	The Tranquilizing Gas	.25
❑ 74	The Two Faces Of Dr. Banner	.25
❑ 75	Nothing Can Stop The Hulk!	.25
❑ 76	Netting The Hulk	.25
❑ 77	Sensing Danger	.25
❑ 78	The Capture	.25
❑ 79	David Banner's Wedding Day	.25
❑ 80	The Recurring Dream	.25
❑ 81	The Force Inside Banner	.25
❑ 82	Demon With A Soul	.25
❑ 83	The Mindless Primitive	.25
❑ 84	Mightiest Creature On Earth	.25
❑ 85	The Monster Within Us All!	.25
❑ 86	Being Of Fantastic Proportions.	.25
❑ 87	Victim Of Gamma Radiation	.25
❑ 88	Eyes Of David Banner	.25

1979 Topps Incredible Hulk stickers

Stickers were issued one per pack of Incredible Hulk cards. Photos were framed inside a TV set.

1979 Topps Incredible Hulk stickers

Complete set (22) 4.00
Each sticker .... .25

#	Card	M
❏ 1	Modified Hulk Make-Up	.25
❏ 2	Metamorphosis	.25
❏ 3	Hope Through Hypnotherapy	.25
❏ 4	The Hulk Strikes Back!	.25
❏ 5	The Monster Within Us All	.25
❏ 6	Manhattan Mayhem	.25
❏ 7	Portrait Of A Monster	.25
❏ 8	Mightiest Creature On Earth	.25
❏ 9	Suppressing The Demon Within Him	.25
❏ 10	The Monster Strikes!	.25
❏ 11	This Man...This Monster!	.25
❏ 12	The Creature...Shot!	.25
❏ 13	Racing Through The Airliner	.25
❏ 14	The Incredible Man Monster	.25
❏ 15	Friend...Or Fiend?	.25
❏ 16	Ferrigno In Character	.25
❏ 17	In The Clutches Of Horror!	.25
❏ 18	A Titan In Times Square	.25
❏ 19	Has The Hulk Met His Match?	.25
❏ 20	Pawn Of Destiny	.25
❏ 21	Experiment: Perilous!	.25
❏ 22	The Mindless Primitive	.25

Comic Images
Card Timeline
1987

January: Marvel Universe 90-card series.

April: Marvel Series I 75-sticker set and album.

September: Colossal Conflicts 90-card set.

1988

February: Wolverine Trivia 50-card series

April: Punisher 50-card series.

June: Conan 50-card series. This is one of the most difficult to find of all Comic Images card sets.

October: Heroic Origins 90-card series. This series told the origin of many Marvel heroes.

1989

April: Todd McFarlane I 45-card series. Cards featured work from McFarlane's stint on *Amazing Spider-Man*.

May: Mike Zeck 45-card series.

August: John Byrne 45-card series.

October: Arthur Adams 45-card series.

November: Excalibur 45-card series.

1990

January: X-Men Covers I 90-card series.

February: Wolverine Untamed 75-sticker set.

March: Spider-Man Team-Up 45-card series. This set included items from the *Marvel Team-Up* series.

May: Captain America 50th Anniversary 45-card series.

June: Punisher Papers 75-sticker set.

July: Jim Lee I 45-card series. This set included Lee's work on *Uncanny X-Men* and *Alpha Flight*.

August: Todd McFarlane II 45-card series.

September: Ghost Rider I 45-card series.

November: X-Men Covers II 45-card series.

1991

January: Spider-Man "Webs" 75-sticker set.

February: Wolverine from Then 'til Now I 45-card set.

March: Jim Lee II 45-card series.

May: Incredible Hulk 90-card series. This included artwork and covers from the Dale Keown-Peter David run on *Incredible Hulk*.

June: X-Force Beginning of the End 90-card series.

July: Marvel First Covers Serties II 100-card series. This was a follow-up to the Fantasy Trading Card Co.'s 1984 set.

August: X-Men 90-card series.

September: X-Force autographed 91-card series.

1992

January: Spider-Man I "McFarlane-Era" 90-card series and six prisms. This set included artwork from McFarlane's run on 16 issues of *Spider-Man*.

April: Ghost Rider II Spirit of Vengeance 80-card series and 10 glow-in-the-dark cards.

June: Spider-Man II 30th Anniversary 90-card set and six prisms. This set includes covers and art from 30 years of *Amazing Spider-Man*.

July: Wolverine from Then 'til Now II 90-card series and six prisms.

September: Punisher Guts & Gunpowder 90-card series, three prisms, and three scratch 'n sniff gunpowder cards.

November: Silver Surfer 72-card all-prism series.

1988 Comic Images Heroic Origins

Billed as the fourth in a series of origins of Marvel Universe characters, these cards were released in wax packs in October 1988.

1988 Comic Images Heroic Origins

Complete set (90) 20.00

Each card .... .25

#	Card	M
❑ 1	Alpha Flight	.25
❑ 2	Avengers	.25
❑ 3	Battlestar	.25
❑ 4	Beast	.25
❑ 5	Black Knight	.25
❑ 6	Black Panther	.25
❑ 7	Box	.25
❑ 8	Cannonball	.25
❑ 9	The Captain	.25
❑ 10	Captain America	.25
❑ 11	Captain Britain	.25
❑ 12	Captain Marvel	.25
❑ 13	Cloak	.25
❑ 14	Colossus	.25
❑ 15	Counterweight	.25
❑ 16	Crystal	.25
❑ 17	Cyclops	.25
❑ 18	Dagger	.25
❑ 19	Daredevil	.25
❑ 20	Dazzler	.25
❑ 21	Death	.25
❑ 22	Destroyer	.25
❑ 23	Dr. Druid	.25
❑ 24	Dr. Pym	.25
❑ 25	Dr. Strange	.25
❑ 26	Elektra	.25
❑ 27	Excaliber	.25
❑ 28	Falcon	.25
❑ 29	Fantastic Four	.25
❑ 30	Forge	.25
❑ 31	Galactus	.25
❑ 32	Goblyn	.25
❑ 33	Havok	.25
❑ 34	Hawkeye	.25

❑ 35	Hulk	.25	❑ 75	Tattletale	.25
❑ 36	Human Torch	.25	❑ 76	Thing	.25
❑ 37	Iceman	.25	❑ 77	Thor	.25
❑ 38	Invisible Girl	.25	❑ 78	Tigra	.25
❑ 39	Iron Man	.25	❑ 79	Vindicator	.25
❑ 40	Kingpin	.25	❑ 80	Vision	.25
❑ 41	Longshot	.25	❑ 81	Warlock	.25
❑ 42	Madelyn Pryor	.25	❑ 82	Wasp	.25
❑ 43	Magik	.25	❑ 83	Watcher	.25
❑ 44	Magneto	.25	❑ 84	W.C. Avengers	.25
❑ 45	Marvel Girl	.25	❑ 85	Wolfsbane	.25
❑ 46	Mary Jane Parker	.25	❑ 86	Wolverine	.25
❑ 47	Meggan	.25	❑ 87	Wonder Man	.25
❑ 48	Mirage	.25	❑ 88	X-Factor	.25
❑ 49	Mr. Fantastic	.25	❑ 89	X-Men	.25
❑ 50	Ms. Marvel	.25	❑ 90	Checklist	.25
❑ 51	Mockingbird	.25			
❑ 52	Molecula	.25			
❑ 53	Moon Knight	.25			
❑ 54	New Mutants	.25			
❑ 55	Nightcrawler	.25			
❑ 56	Nomad	.25			
❑ 57	Nova	.25			
❑ 58	Phoenix II	.25			
❑ 59	Power Pack	.25			
❑ 60	Professor X	.25			
❑ 61	Psylocke	.25			
❑ 62	Punisher	.25			
❑ 63	Purple Girl	.25			
❑ 64	Rogue	.25			
❑ 65	Sasquatch	.25			
❑ 66	Scarlet Witch	.25			
❑ 67	Shadowcat	.25			
❑ 68	She-Hulk	.25			
❑ 69	Silver Surfer	.25			
❑ 70	Spider-Man	.25			
❑ 71	Starstreak	.25			
❑ 72	Storm	.25			
❑ 73	Sub-Mariner	.25			
❑ 74	Sunspot	.25			

1988 Comic Images The Punisher I

This first series of Punisher cards, released only in wax packs in April 1988, featured panels and covers from the first 25 or so issues of *The Punisher*.

1988 Comic Images Punisher I

Complete set (50)............................20.00
Each card 25

#	Card	M
❑ 1	Checklist	.40
❑ 2	Circle of Blood	.40
❑ 3	The Files	.40
❑ 4	Attacked	.40
❑ 5	Jigsaw	.40
❑ 6	Prepare to Escape	.40
❑ 7	Saved	.40
❑ 8	Prison Break	.40
❑ 9	Plan Two	.40
❑ 10	The Offer	.40
❑ 11	Forced Revenge	.40
❑ 12	Back to the War	.40
❑ 13	Get Kingpin	.40
❑ 14	The Trap	.40
❑ 15	BOOM!	.40

❏ 16	Rescued	.40
❏ 17	Alaric	.40
❏ 18	Set Up	.40
❏ 19	Ambushed	.40
❏ 20	Face to Face	.40
❏ 21	Angela's Secret	.40
❏ 22	Slaughterday	.40
❏ 23	Santiago	.40
❏ 24	The New Driver	.40
❏ 25	Don't Snivel	.40
❏ 26	You're Not Mob	.40
❏ 27	Lookalike	.40
❏ 28	One Down	.40
❏ 29	Hello Marcus	.40
❏ 30	Angela?!	.40
❏ 31	Not You, Too!	.40
❏ 32	Final Solution	.40
❏ 33	Surprise Visit	.40
❏ 34	Dead Aide	.40
❏ 35	Packing it in	.40
❏ 36	Drive On	.40
❏ 37	Jigsaw or Punisher	.40
❏ 38	Showdown	.40
❏ 39	Come with Me	.40
❏ 40	Down the Hatch	.40
❏ 41	In the Chamber	.40
❏ 42	Final Solution II	.40
❏ 43	Strategy Time	.40
❏ 44	Vapor Lock	.40
❏ 45	Breakout	.40
❏ 46	Strike Back	.40
❏ 47	Off Guard	.40
❏ 48	Do it, Or Else	.40
❏ 49	Enough, Tony	.40
❏ 50	Do Nothing	.40

1988 Comic Images Wolverine

This 50-card set was released in wax packs only in February 1988.

1988 Comic Images Wolverine I

Complete set (50)............................15.00
Each card .... .30

#	Card	M
❏ 1	Challenge	.30
❏ 2	Masks	.30
❏ 3	Confrontation	.30
❏ 4	What the	.30
❏ 5	Juggernaut	.30
❏ 6	Savage Land	.30
❏ 7	Trio	.30
❏ 8	Attraction	.30
❏ 9	Sewer Rat	.30
❏ 10	Tag	.30
❏ 11	Back Off	.30
❏ 12	Come On	.30
❏ 13	Co-Leaders	.30
❏ 14	Solitude	.30
❏ 15	Eye to Eye	.30
❏ 16	Stalker	.30
❏ 17	Re-Match	.30
❏ 18	Lemme at 'Em	.30
❏ 19	Whoosh!	.30
❏ 20	Deadly Intent	.30
❏ 21	Primal Scream	.30
❏ 22	Howdy	.30
❏ 23	Classic Wolvie	.30
❏ 24	Ready	.30
❏ 25	At Odds	.30
❏ 26	Surprise	.30
❏ 27	Battleground	.30
❏ 28	Eat Adamantium	.30
❏ 29	Outta My Face	.30
❏ 30	Weapon X	.30
❏ 31	Slash	.30
❏ 32	Dropping In	.30
❏ 33	New Beginning	.30
❏ 34	Reborn	.30
❏ 35	Dead End	.30
❏ 36	Tables Are Turned	.30

❏ 37	Dream	.30
❏ 38	Nightmare	.30
❏ 39	Binge	.30
❏ 40	Kitty 'n Me	.30
❏ 41	Greetings	.30
❏ 42	Blizzard	.30
❏ 43	Snikt!	.30
❏ 44	Saved	.30
❏ 45	Pain In The Neck	.30
❏ 46	Eternal Foe	.30
❏ 47	Reluctant Duo	.30
❏ 48	I'm Home	.30
❏ 49	Teammates	.30
❏ 50	Checklist	.30

1989 Comic Images Excalibur

This series, released in November 1989, featured 45 cards depicting panels and covers from the first several issues of *Excalibur.*

1989 Comic Images Excalibur

Complete set (45) 15.00
Each card .... .25

#	Card	M
❏ 1	Checklist	.25
❏ 2	Goblin Princess	.25
❏ 3	Daydreaming	.25
❏ 4	Trouble	.25
❏ 5	Widget	.25
❏ 6	Excalibur	.25
❏ 7	Psychic Attack	.25
❏ 8	Gate Crasher	.25
❏ 9	Whoops	.25
❏ 10	Captain Britain	.25
❏ 11	Lockheed	.25
❏ 12	Meggan	.25
❏ 13	Concern	.25
❏ 14	Ready	.25
❏ 15	Stalking	.25
❏ 16	One Kiss	.25
❏ 17	Take That!	.25
❏ 18	Warlord	.25
❏ 19	Surrounded	.25
❏ 20	Free-e-e	.25
❏ 21	Britains	.25
❏ 22	Changeling	.25
❏ 23	Agony	.25
❏ 24	Scatterbrain	.25
❏ 25	Angry	.25
❏ 26	Ghouls	.25
❏ 27	Phoenix	.25
❏ 28	Shadowcat	.25
❏ 29	Warwolves	.25
❏ 30	Til Death	.25
❏ 31	Exploding	.25
❏ 32	Restrained	.25
❏ 33	Crazy Gang	.25
❏ 34	Nightcrawler	.25
❏ 35	Arcade	.25
❏ 36	Sobering	.25
❏ 37	Saturnyne	.25
❏ 38	Nightmare	.25
❏ 39	Juggernaut	.25
❏ 40	King Arthur	.25
❏ 41	Stop!	.25
❏ 42	Slashed	.25
❏ 43	Tea Party	.25
❏ 44	Bodybag	.25
❏ 45	Enough!	.25

1989 Comic Images Todd McFarlane I

Complete set (90) 12.00
Each card .... .15

#	Card	M
❏ 1	The Beginning	.15
❏ 2	Uptown	.15
❏ 3	Arachknight	.15
❏ 4	Arise	.15
❏ 5	Married Life	.15
❏ 6	The Lizard	.15
❏ 7	Friendly, Neighborhood . . .	.15
❏ 8	Connors	.15

❑ 9	A Spider	.15
❑ 10	Spider-Sense	.15
❑ 11	Attacked	.15
❑ 12	Poison	.15
❑ 13	Fatality	.15
❑ 14	Alone	.15
❑ 15	Resurrection	.15
❑ 16	The Hunter	.15
❑ 17	Rooftop	.15
❑ 18	Trashed	.15
❑ 19	Dazed	.15
❑ 20	The Past	.15
❑ 21	Drugged	.15
❑ 22	Kraven	.15
❑ 23	The Witch	.15
❑ 24	Once Again	.15
❑ 25	Explosion	.15
❑ 26	Crawling Out	.15
❑ 27	Voodoo	.15
❑ 28	Last Time	.15
❑ 29	Death	.15
❑ 30	Home	.15
❑ 31	Another Time	.15
❑ 32	Dark Days	.15
❑ 33	Hobogoblin	.15
❑ 34	Headng Out	.15
❑ 35	Tuning In	.15
❑ 36	Ghost Rider	.15
❑ 37	The Kid	.15
❑ 38	Team-up	.15
❑ 39	Busting In	.15
❑ 40	Spirit of Vengeance	.15
❑ 41	Ready	.15
❑ 42	Fire Creature	.15
❑ 43	Stop This	.15
❑ 44	Perceptions	.15
❑ 45	Folklore	.15
❑ 46	Hanging Out	.15
❑ 47	J.J. Jameson	.15
❑ 48	Murder	.15
❑ 49	Wolverine	.15
❑ 50	The Mystery	.15
❑ 51	Got'cha	.15
❑ 52	The Hunter	.15
❑ 53	The Myth	.15
❑ 54	Investigation	.15
❑ 55	Shot	.15
❑ 56	Into The Woods	.15
❑ 57	Wounded	.15
❑ 58	Wendigo	.15
❑ 59	Primal	.15
❑ 60	Time To Go	.15
❑ 61	Crime Fighters	.15
❑ 62	Evidence	.15
❑ 63	Parker	.15
❑ 64	Hurt	.15
❑ 65	The Bullet	.15
❑ 66	Pondering	.15
❑ 67	Together	.15
❑ 68	Stay Here	.15
❑ 69	Masked	.15
❑ 70	Trapped	.15
❑ 71	Set-up	.15
❑ 72	Sub-City	.15
❑ 73	Keever	.15
❑ 74	Web-Swinger	.15
❑ 75	Black Costume	.15
❑ 76	Morbius	.15
❑ 77	Spotted	.15
❑ 78	Vampire	.15
❑ 79	Down Under	.15
❑ 80	Too Many	.15
❑ 81	Male Bonding	.15
❑ 82	Mouthful	.15
❑ 83	Bad Ones	.15
❑ 84	I'm Gone	.15
❑ 85	X-Force	.15
❑ 86	Juggernaut	.15
❑ 87	Young Ones	.15
❑ 88	Cable	.15

| ☐ | 89 | Join Together | .15 |
| ☐ | 90 | Checklist | .15 |

1989 Comic Images Todd McFarlane I

This 45-card series was released in wax packs in April 1989. Card art features panels and covers primarily from McFarlane's stint on *The Amazing Spider-Man*.

1989 Comic Images Todd McFarlane I

Complete set (45) 18.00

Each card .... .40

#	Card	M
☐ 1	Friends	.40
☐ 2	Jump for Joy	.40
☐ 3	Venom	.40
☐ 4	Snikt	.40
☐ 5	Oh, Yeah	.40
☐ 6	Savage	.40
☐ 7	The Leader	.40
☐ 8	Spidey	.40
☐ 9	X-Factor	.40
☐ 10	Price of Fame	.40
☐ 11	Chance	.40
☐ 12	Thing	.40
☐ 13	The Prowler	.40
☐ 14	Don't Cry	.40
☐ 15	Lizard	.40
☐ 16	Who, Me?	.40
☐ 17	Taskmaster	.40
☐ 18	Busted	.40
☐ 19	Silver Sable	.40
☐ 20	Sandman	.40
☐ 21	Out of the Fire . . .	.40
☐ 22	Green Goblin	.40
☐ 23	Hobgoblin	.40
☐ 24	The Black Fox	.40
☐ 25	There's No Key?!	.40
☐ 26	Ho Ho Ho	.40
☐ 27	Hey, Tiger	.40
☐ 28	Aargh	.40
☐ 29	The Chameleon	.40
☐ 30	Killer Shrike	.40
☐ 31	Peter	.40
☐ 32	Mary Jane	.40
☐ 33	Jolly Jonah	.40
☐ 34	Styx & Stone	.40
☐ 35	Smile	.40
☐ 36	Wolverine	.40
☐ 37	Mysterio	.40
☐ 38	Down and Out	.40
☐ 39	Humbug	.40
☐ 40	Black Cat	.40
☐ 41	Next	.40
☐ 42	Hydro-Man	.40
☐ 43	Buddies	.40
☐ 44	Web Swinging	.40
☐ 45	Checklist	.40

1990 Comic Images Jim Lee

This 45-card series was released in wax packs in July 1990. Cards featured work from his first Marvel assignment, *Alpha Flight*, as well as X-Men work.

1990 Comic Images Jim Lee

Complete set (45) 8.00

Each card .... .20

#	Card	M
☐ 1	Surprise!	.20
☐ 2	Beast	.20
☐ 3	Two against . . .	.20
☐ 4	Dreamqueen	.20
☐ 5	Puck	.20
☐ 6	Blast Off!	.20
☐ 7	Purple Man	.20
☐ 8	Sub-Mariner	.20
☐ 9	Double Take!	.20
☐ 10	To the death!	.20
☐ 11	African Saga	.20
☐ 12	Gator fight	.20
☐ 13	Survival	.20
☐ 14	Shot!	.20
☐ 15	Black Widow	.20

	#	Card	M
❏	16	Bushwacker	.20
❏	17	Stay Back!	.20
❏	18	Teamwork	.20
❏	19	J.J. Jameson	.20
❏	20	Vacation	.20
❏	21	Jet ski	.20
❏	22	Aloha!	.20
❏	23	Armory	.20
❏	24	Mandarin	.20
❏	25	Here I am!	.20
❏	26	Lady Mandarin	.20
❏	27	Meditation	.20
❏	28	Banshee	.20
❏	29	Jean Grey	.20
❏	30	Animal Rage	.20
❏	31	It's My Turn!	.20
❏	32	Night stalker	.20
❏	33	Youth	.20
❏	34	Logan & Reed	.20
❏	35	Hulk	.20
❏	36	Blackheart	.20
❏	37	Ghost Rider	.20
❏	38	Harriers	.20
❏	39	Trio	.20
❏	40	Quasar	.20
❏	41	Wild Child	.20
❏	42	Caught	.20
❏	43	Vindicator	.20
❏	44	Fight back!	.20
❏	45	Checklist	.20

1990 Comic Images Spider-Man Team-Up

This 45-card series was released in March 1990 and featured artwork from the pages of *Marvel Team-Up*.

1990 Comic Images Spider-Man Team-Up

Complete set (45) 15.00
Each card .... .35

	#	Card	M
❏	1	Dazzler	.35
❏	2	Doc Samson	.35
❏	3	Nighthawk	.35
❏	4	Wolverine	.35
❏	5	Fantastic Four	.35
❏	6	Classic X-Men	.35
❏	7	Hulk	.35
❏	8	Ms. Marvel	.35
❏	9	Iron Man	.35
❏	10	Captain Britain	.35
❏	11	Stranglehold!	.35
❏	12	Nightcrawler	.35
❏	13	Havok	.35
❏	14	Angel	.35
❏	15	Crashing in!	.35
❏	16	Iron Fist	.35
❏	17	Ya missed!	.35
❏	18	Dr. Strange	.35
❏	19	Paladin	.35
❏	20	Man-Thing	.35
❏	21	Power Man	.35
❏	22	Together	.35
❏	23	Santa	.35
❏	24	Blackcat	.35
❏	25	Captain America	.35
❏	26	Human Torch	.35
❏	27	Prowler	.35
❏	28	Silver Sable	.35
❏	29	The Beast	.35
❏	30	Against the Wall	.35
❏	31	Sandman	.35
❏	32	Tigra	.35
❏	33	Iceman	.35
❏	34	Johnny Storm	.35
❏	35	Falcon	.35
❏	36	Frankenstein's Monster	.35
❏	37	Rematch	.35
❏	38	Targeted	.35
❏	39	Thor	.35

	#	Card	M
❑	40	Hercules	.35
❑	41	Busting in!	.35
❑	42	Man-Wolf	.35
❑	43	Iron Man	.35
❑	44	Sub-Mariner	.35
❑	45	Checklist	.35

1991 Comic Images Marvel First Covers II

This 100-card set, which was a follow-up to the FTCC Marvel First Covers set, included 100 additional covers. Cards were released in wax packs only.

1991 Comic Images Marvel First Covers II

Complete set (100) 12.00
Each card .... .15

	#	Card	M
❑	1	Beware	.15
❑	2	Curse of Dracula	.15
❑	3	Spectacular Spider Man	.15
❑	4	The Human Fly	.15
❑	5	Marvel No Prize Book	.15
❑	6	Contest of Champons	.15
❑	7	Hercules	.15
❑	8	Wolverine	.15
❑	9	Vision and Scarlet Witch	.15
❑	10	X-Men at the State Fair	.15
❑	11	Marvel Age	.15
❑	12	Obnoxio the Clown	.15
❑	13	The Saga of Crystar	.15
❑	14	Hawykeye	.15
❑	15	Cloak and Dagger	.15
❑	16	Peter Porker	.15
❑	17	The Falcon	.15
❑	18	Magik	.15
❑	19	The Jack of Hearts	.15
❑	20	X-Men and Micronauts	.15
❑	21	Secret Wars	.15
❑	22	Power Pack	.15
❑	23	West Coast Avengers	.15
❑	24	Machine Man	.15
❑	25	Web of Spider-Man	.15
❑	26	Moon Knight	.15
❑	27	Cloak and Dagger	.15
❑	28	Secret Wars II	.15
❑	29	Captain Marvel	.15
❑	30	Longshot	.15
❑	31	Squadron Supreme	.15
❑	32	Vision and Scarlet Witch	.15
❑	33	Nightcrawler	.15
❑	34	Marvel Universe	.15
❑	35	X-Men and Alpha Flight	.15
❑	36	The Punisher	.15
❑	37	X-Factor	.15
❑	38	Classic X-Men	.15
❑	39	Strikeforce Morituri	.15
❑	40	The Nam	.15
❑	41	The Comet Man	.15
❑	42	Fallen Angels	.15
❑	43	Strange Tales	.15
❑	44	X-Men vs. The Avengers	.15
❑	45	Silver Surfer	.15
❑	46	The Punisher	.15
❑	47	Hawkeye and Mockingbird	.15
❑	48	Wolverine	.15
❑	49	Spellbound	.15
❑	50	Nick Fury vs. S.H.I.E.L.D.	.15
❑	51	Black Panther	.15
❑	52	What The?!	.15
❑	53	Wolfpack	.15
❑	54	Excalibur	.15
❑	55	X-Terminators	.15
❑	56	Sub-Mariner	.15
❑	57	Punisher War Journal	.15
❑	58	Wolverine	.15
❑	59	Semper Fi	.15
❑	60	Fred Hemeck	.15
❑	61	What If	.15
❑	62	Solarman	.15
❑	63	Damage Control	.15

❏ 64	She Hulk	.15
❏ 65	Spector Moon Knight	.15
❏ 66	Nth Man	.15
❏ 67	Nick Fury	.15
❏ 68	Power Pachyderms	.15
❏ 69	The Wolverine Saga	.15
❏ 70	Quasar	.15
❏ 71	Shadow Masters	.15
❏ 72	The War	.15
❏ 73	Damage Control Vol. II	.15
❏ 74	Open Space	.15
❏ 75	Punisher: No Escape	.15
❏ 76	The Thanos Quest	.15
❏ 77	Starjammers	.15
❏ 78	Namor	.15
❏ 79	Human Torch	.15
❏ 80	Ghost Rider	.15
❏ 81	Spring Special	.15
❏ 82	Black Knight	.15
❏ 83	Guardians of the Galaxy	.15
❏ 84	Deathlok	.15
❏ 85	The New Warriors	.15
❏ 86	The Punisher Armory	.15
❏ 87	Spider-Man	.15
❏ 88	Fool Killer	.15
❏ 89	Nomad	.15
❏ 90	Panther's Prey	.15
❏ 91	Punisher: P.O.V.	.15
❏ 92	Darkhawk	.15
❏ 93	Nighcat	.15
❏ 94	Sweet Sixteen	.15
❏ 95	Foes of Spider-Man	.15
❏ 96	Damage Control Vol. III	.15
❏ 97	Sleepwalker	.15
❏ 98	Deathlok	.15
❏ 99	Infinity Gauntlet	.15
❏ 100	Checklist	.15

1991 Comic Images Incredible Hulk

Released in May 1991, this 90-card series recapped events in *The Incredible Hulk* during the Peter David/Dale Keown run; art is taken from covers and interior art from those comic books. The set includes guest appearances from Wolverine, The Leader, Madman, The Freedom Force, Namor, Dr. Strange, Betty Banner, Doc Samson, The Super Skrull, Rick Jones, and members of The Pantheon. It also includes the transformation from The Gray Hulk to The Green Hulk. All art on card fronts is by Dale Keown.

1991 Comic Images Incredible Hulk

Complete set (90) 9.00
Each card .... .10

#	Card	M
❏ 1	Transformation	.10
❏ 2	I'm Grey	.10
❏ 3	Wolverine	.10
❏ 4	Poisoned	.10
❏ 5	What's Wrong	.10
❏ 6	The Lader	.10
❏ 7	Madman	.10
❏ 8	Too Weak	.10
❏ 9	Phil	.10
❏ 10	Antidote	.10
❏ 11	Freedom Force	.10
❏ 12	Discovered	.10
❏ 13	Abused?	.10
❏ 14	Mystique	.10
❏ 15	Pyro	.10
❏ 16	Commando	.10
❏ 17	Blob	.10
❏ 18	Defenders	.10
❏ 19	New York	.10
❏ 20	Unknown	.10
❏ 21	Inside	.10
❏ 22	Argue	.10
❏ 23	Grabbed	.10
❏ 24	Darkness	.10
❏ 25	Dark Hulk	.10

❑	26	Take Over	.10	❑	66	Stay Back	.10
❑	27	Namor	.10	❑	67	Battle	.10
❑	28	Dr. Strange	.10	❑	68	Put Me Down	.10
❑	29	Revived	.10	❑	69	In the Middle	.10
❑	30	Betty	.10	❑	70	Stop It	.10
❑	31	Speeding	.10	❑	71	Who's Inside	.10
❑	32	He's Back...	.10	❑	72	Monster!	.10
❑	33	...And Green	.10	❑	73	Let's Go	.10
❑	34	Shocked	.10	❑	74	Escape	.10
❑	35	Rejoined	.10	❑	75	Murderer	.10
❑	36	I Get It!	.10	❑	76	Mom	.10
❑	37	No-o-o!	.10	❑	77	Graveyard	.10
❑	38	Skinned	.10	❑	78	You Did It	.10
❑	39	Doc Samson	.10	❑	79	Father	.10
❑	40	Tank You	.10	❑	80	Resolved	.10
❑	41	Come on	.10	❑	81	New Hulk	.10
❑	42	Mouthful	.10	❑	82	Barkeep	.10
❑	43	Not You!	.10	❑	83	Ajax	.10
❑	44	Rick Jones	.10	❑	84	Ulysses	.10
❑	45	The Thing?	.10	❑	85	Atalanta	.10
❑	46	Now Listen	.10	❑	86	Hector	.10
❑	47	Thugs	.10	❑	87	Achilles	.10
❑	48	To Sleep	.10	❑	88	Rebound	.10
❑	49	Rick's Past	.10	❑	89	Oh Yeah!	.10
❑	50	Tortured	.10	❑	90	Checklist	.10
❑	51	Super Skrull	.10				
❑	52	On Board	.10				
❑	53	Skrull	.10				
❑	54	Locked Up	.10				
❑	55	Stretch	.10				
❑	56	Fight On	.10				
❑	57	On Fire	.10				
❑	58	Captain	.10				
❑	59	Invisible	.10				
❑	60	Marlo	.10				
❑	61	Conflict	.10				
❑	62	Going Home	.10				
❑	63	Prometheus	.10				
❑	64	Agamemnon	.10				
❑	65	Help Me!	.10				

1991 Comic Images Jim Lee II

This 45-card series was released in March 1991 and included Lee's art featuring Marvel characters.

1991 Comic Images Jim Lee II

Complete set (45) 8.00

Each card 20

#		Card	M
❑	1	Punisher	.20
❑	2	Suvivalist	.20
❑	3	Hang On!	.20
❑	4	Carno	.20
❑	5	Biker	.20
❑	6	The Blade	.20
❑	7	Armory II	.20

❑	8	The Pest	.20
❑	9	Rules. . .	.20
❑	10	Microchip	.20
❑	11	Dr. Doom	.20
❑	12	Moonknight	.20
❑	13	Kingpin	.20
❑	14	Hercules	.20
❑	15	Bushwacker	.20
❑	16	Black Panther	.20
❑	17	Heroes	.20
❑	18	Magik	.20
❑	19	Nightcat	.20
❑	20	Brother Voodoo	.20
❑	21	Black Widow	.20
❑	22	Speedball	.20
❑	23	Captain America	.20
❑	24	Wolverine	.20
❑	25	Struggle	.20
❑	26	Rage	.20
❑	27	I'm Ready	.20
❑	28	Three of Us	.20
❑	29	Deathstrike	.20
❑	30	Lien	.20
❑	31	Hounds	.20
❑	32	Oprhan Maker	.20
❑	33	Magneto	.20
❑	34	Four of Us	.20
❑	35	Beast	.20
❑	36	Hevok	.20
❑	37	Hodge	.20
❑	38	X-Tinction	.20
❑	39	Psylocke	.20
❑	40	Dual	.20
❑	41	Cable	.20
❑	42	Savage Land	.20
❑	43	Storm	.20
❑	44	Glory Days	.20
❑	45	Checklist	.20

1991 Comics Images Wolverine I

Subtitled From Then 'Til Now I, this series featured panels and covers focusing on Wolverine from early *X-Men* to recent mini-series. Cards were released in wax packs in February 1991.

1991 Comic Images Wolverine I

Complete set (45)............................15.00
Each card 30

	#	Card	M
❑	1	Wolverine	.30
❑	2	Wendigo	.30
❑	3	Spider-Man	.30
❑	4	Bloodlust	.30
❑	5	Attacked	.30
❑	6	Come On	.30
❑	7	Android	.30
❑	8	The Blues	.30
❑	9	Pull Me Up	.30
❑	10	Blood	.30
❑	11	Four of Us	.30
❑	12	Brood	.30
❑	13	New Worriors	.30
❑	14	Patch	.30
❑	15	The Team	.30
❑	16	Hulk	.30
❑	17	Come On	.30
❑	18	Ghost Rider	.30
❑	19	Cable	.30
❑	20	Logan	.30
❑	21	Meltdown	.30
❑	22	Gotcha	.30
❑	23	A-A-A-HI	.30
❑	24	The Beast	.30
❑	25	Webbed	.30
❑	26	Metamorphosis	.30
❑	27	Crucified	.30
❑	28	Buried	.30
❑	29	Deathstrike	.30
❑	30	Surrounded	.30

❑ 31	Mad as . . .	.30	
❑ 32	Werewolf	.30	
❑ 33	In the Dark	.30	
❑ 34	Trio	.30	
❑ 35	X-Men	.30	
❑ 36	Jubilee	.30	
❑ 37	Hodge	.30	
❑ 38	X-tinction	.30	
❑ 39	Archangel	.30	
❑ 40	Help Me	.30	
❑ 41	Weapon X	.30	
❑ 42	Sedated	.30	
❑ 43	Rage	.30	
❑ 44	Massacre	.30	
❑ 45	Checklist	.30	

1991 Comic Images X-Men

This 90-card series, released in wax packs in August 1991, featured characters and storylines from the X-Men comic books.

1991 Comic Images X-Men

Complete set (90) 12.00

Each card .... .15

Y	#	Card	M
❑	1	The X-Men	.10
❑	2	The Reavers	.10
❑	3	The Mandarin	.10
❑	4	Betsy	.10
❑	5	Slaymaster	.10
❑	6	Lady Mandarin	.10
❑	7	Patch	.10
❑	8	Accommodation	.10
❑	9	The Beast	.10
❑	10	Games	.10
❑	11	My Turn	.10
❑	12	#1 Fan	.10
❑	13	Harrjers	.10
❑	14	Magistrates	.10
❑	15	Lian	.10
❑	16	Storm	.10

❑ 17	Gambit	.10	
❑ 18	Nanny	.10	
❑ 19	Oprhanmaker	.10	
❑ 20	Partners	.10	
❑ 21	Together Again	.10	
❑ 22	Captain America	.10	
❑ 23	Friend	.10	
❑ 24	My Turf	.10	
❑ 25	Black Widow	.10	
❑ 26	To the Rescue	.10	
❑ 27	Coflict	.10	
❑ 28	Cyborgs	.10	
❑ 29	Ms. Marvel	.10	
❑ 30	Savage Land	.10	
❑ 31	Shadow King	.10	
❑ 32	Drained	.10	
❑ 33	Magneto	.10	
❑ 34	First Strike	.10	
❑ 35	Danger Room	.10	
❑ 36	Our Turn	.10	
❑ 37	Pathfinders	.10	
❑ 38	Strikeforce	.10	
❑ 39	Flight	.10	
❑ 40	Powerless	.10	
❑ 41	Warlock	.10	
❑ 42	Take 'em Out	.10	
❑ 43	Psylocke	.10	
❑ 44	Cameron	.10	
❑ 45	Havok	.10	
❑ 46	Mutate #20	.10	
❑ 47	On Trial	.10	
❑ 48	Hodge	.10	
❑ 49	Cable	.10	
❑ 50	Match	.10	
❑ 51	Restored	.10	
❑ 52	Final Strike	.10	
❑ 53	What's Next?	.10	
❑ 54	Allies	.10	
❑ 55	Assault	.10	
❑ 56	Zaladane	.10	

❑ 57	Teleported	.10
❑ 58	Deathbird	.10
❑ 59	Starjammers	.10
❑ 60	Imperial Fleet	.10
❑ 61	Manacle	.10
❑ 62	Fair Game	.10
❑ 63	Lilandra	.10
❑ 64	Conquered	.10
❑ 65	Rejoined	.10
❑ 66	Airborne	.10
❑ 67	Revenge	.10
❑ 68	Brainchild	.10
❑ 69	Draining	.10
❑ 70	Repowered	.10
❑ 71	Mentor?	.10
❑ 72	The Dungeons	.10
❑ 73	My Wings!	.10
❑ 74	Execution	.10
❑ 75	We're Back	.10
❑ 76	War Skrull	.10
❑ 77	Aboard	.10
❑ 78	In Space	.10
❑ 79	Remember Us	.10
❑ 80	One-One-One	.10
❑ 81	Professor X	.10
❑ 82	Colossus	.10
❑ 83	Testing	.10
❑ 84	Old Times	.10
❑ 85	Whoa!	.10
❑ 86	Watch It	.10
❑ 87	On the Move	.10
❑ 88	Homosuperiors	.10
❑ 89	Omega Red	.10
❑ 90	Checklist	.10

1992 Comics Images Ghost Rider II

Released in April 1992, Ghost Rider II: Spirits of Vengeance was a 90-card series released in wax packs. Much of the art and text was taken from the first several issues of *Ghost Rider/Blaze: Spirits of Vengeance* series issued by Marvel in 1992. The final 10 cards in the set are glow-in-the-dark cards, numbered G1-G10; cards were randomly issued in packs and are generally included in hand-collated sets.

1992 Comic Images Ghost Rider II

Complete set (90).............................. 9.00
Each card .... .10
Glow-in-the-dark card......................... .25

#	Card	M
❑ 1	Blood Signs	.10
❑ 2	Zodiak	.10
❑ 3	Possessed	.10
❑ 4	Asleep	.10
❑ 5	Zarathos	.10
❑ 6	Dr. Strange	.10
❑ 7	Captured	.10
❑ 8,	Snowblind	.10
❑ 9	Johnny Blaze	.10
❑ 10	The Original	.10
❑ 11	Old Times	.10
❑ 12	Control	.10
❑ 13	Freedom	.10
❑ 14	Confrontation	.10
❑ 15	Hellfire!	.10
❑ 16	Shot!	.10
❑ 17	Wounded	.10
❑ 18	No Escape	.10
❑ 19	Stop It!	.10
❑ 20	Scarred	.10
❑ 21	Exhausted	.10
❑ 22	Team-up	.10
❑ 23	Hobgoblin	.10
❑ 24	Spider-Man	.10
❑ 25	Fire Power	.10
❑ 26	Styge	.10
❑ 27	Bare Bones	.10
❑ 28	In Between	.10
❑ 29	Suicide	.10

- ❑ 30 Mephisto .10
- ❑ 31 Death .10
- ❑ 32 Punishment .10
- ❑ 33 Penance Stare .10
- ❑ 34 Ningas .10
- ❑ 35 Buried .10
- ❑ 36 Deathwatch .10
- ❑ 37 Hag and Troll .10
- ❑ 38 Final Conflict .10
- ❑ 39 You Will Die .10
- ❑ 40 Revenge .10
- ❑ 41 Dan's Death .10
- ❑ 42 Nightmare .10
- ❑ 43 New Orleans .10
- ❑ 44 Frenzy .10
- ❑ 45 Wolverine .10
- ❑ 46 Cable .10
- ❑ 47 Hearts of Darkness .10
- ❑ 48 Blackheart .10
- ❑ 49 Sleepwalker .10
- ❑ 50 Deathlock .10
- ❑ 51 Moon Knight .10
- ❑ 52 Daredevil .10
- ❑ 53 Fear .10
- ❑ 54 Fantastic Four? .10
- ❑ 55 Four of Us .10
- ❑ 56 The Midnight Sons .10
- ❑ 57 Lilith's Motive .10
- ❑ 58 Lilith .10
- ❑ 59 Morbius .10
- ❑ 60 Duo .10
- ❑ 61 Nighstalkers .10
- ❑ 62 Mistaken I.D. .10
- ❑ 63 Darkhold .10
- ❑ 64 Spirits of Vengeance .10
- ❑ 65 Partners .10
- ❑ 66 Teacher .10
- ❑ 67 Vendetta .10
- ❑ 68 First Mission .10
- ❑ 69 Demon? .10
- ❑ 70 Transformation .10
- ❑ 71 Emblem .10
- ❑ 72 The Chain .10
- ❑ 73 Powers and Abilities .10
- ❑ 74 Pain .10
- ❑ 75 Taking a Human Life .10
- ❑ 76 First Series .10
- ❑ 77 The Start .10
- ❑ 78 The Champions .10
- ❑ 79 Restarted .10
- ❑ 80 Checklist .10
- ❑ G1 Illuminating .25
- ❑ G2 Morbius .25
- ❑ G3 My Arsenal .25
- ❑ G4 Power Source .25
- ❑ G5 Wolverine .25
- ❑ G6 The Flames .25
- ❑ G7 Punisher .25
- ❑ G8 Hot Air .25
- ❑ G9 Cable .25
- ❑ G10 Grin and Bear It .25

1992 Comic Images Silver Surfer

Comic Images' last Marvel-licensed set was a 72-card all-prism Silver Surfer set released in November 1992.

1992 Comic Images Silver Surfer

Complete set (72)............................20.00

Each card 30

	#	Card	M
❑	1	First Issue	.30
❑	2	Galactus	.30
❑	3	Zenn-La	.30
❑	4	The Herald	.30
❑	5	Cosmic Energy	.30
❑	6	Silver Surfer	.30
❑	7	Morals	.30
❑	8	In the Beginning	.30
❑	9	The Watcher	.30
❑	10	Fantastic Four	.30
❑	11	Betrayed	.30

❑ 12	Confined	.30
❑ 13	Presence	.30
❑ 14	Dr. Doom	.30
❑ 15	Mephisto	.30
❑ 16	Home	.30
❑ 17	Demon	.30
❑ 18	Nova	.30
❑ 19	Unchangeable	.30
❑ 20	The Hulk	.30
❑ 21	Doctor Strange	.30
❑ 22	Sub-Mariner	.30
❑ 23	Life Energies	.30
❑ 24	Firelord	.30
❑ 25	The Stranger	.30
❑ 26	Inhumans	.30
❑ 27	Celestrials	.30
❑ 28	Eternity	.30
❑ 29	Infinity	.30
❑ 30	Hyperspace	.30
❑ 31	In-Betweener	.30
❑ 32	Living Tribunal	.30
❑ 33	Jack of Hearts	.30
❑ 34	Mentor	.30
❑ 35	Starfox	.30
❑ 36	Thor	.30
❑ 37	Humans	.30
❑ 38	Captain Marvel	.30
❑ 39	Thanos	.30
❑ 40	Death	.30
❑ 41	Destroyer	.30
❑ 42	Judgment	.30
❑ 43	Deathwish	.30
❑ 44	Infinity Gauntlet	.30
❑ 45	Genocide	.30
❑ 46	Drax	.30
❑ 47	Partners	.30
❑ 48	Soul Gem	.30
❑ 49	Inmates	.30
❑ 50	Escape	.30
❑ 51	Lord of Evil	.30

❑ 52	Control	.30
❑ 53	Infinity Watch	.30
❑ 54	Philosopher	.30
❑ 55	Peace	.30
❑ 56	Mantis	.30
❑ 57	Champion	.30
❑ 58	Ego	.30
❑ 59	Quasar	.30
❑ 60	Skrulls	.30
❑ 61	Super Skrull	.30
❑ 62	Guilt	.30
❑ 63	Inner Self	.30
❑ 64	Darkside	.30
❑ 65	Two Halves	.30
❑ 66	Infinity War	.30
❑ 67	Another	.30
❑ 68	Morg	.30
❑ 69	Casualty	.30
❑ 70	Heralds	.30
❑ 71	Resurrection	.30
❑ 72	Checklist	.30

1992 Comic Images Spider-Man McFarlane Era I

Released in January 1992, this series — released in wax packs only — featured art from McFarlane's stint on *Spider-Man* #1-#16.

1992 Comic Images Spider-Man II: 30th Anniversary

This series, released only in wax packs in June 1992, was a 90-card set with six randomly packed prism cards. The set features covers, interiors, and promotional pieces from the entire run of *Amazing Spider-Man* and includes art by Steve Ditko, John Romita and Todd McFarlane.

1992 Comic Images Spider-Man II

Complete set (90)............................10.00

Each card .... .10

#	Card	M
❑ 1	September 1962	.10
❑ 2	6 Years Old	.10
❑ 3	The Exhibition	.10
❑ 4	Human Spider	.10
❑ 5	Reflexes	.10
❑ 6	Wall Climber	.10
❑ 7	Spider-Sense	.10
❑ 8	Web-Shooters	.10
❑ 9	Web Fluid	.10
❑ 10	Equipment	.10
❑ 11	Wrestling	.10
❑ 12	Irony	.10
❑ 13	A Hero Is Born	.10
❑ 14	Amazing Spider-Man	.10
❑ 15	The Chameleon	.10
❑ 16	J.J. Jameson	.10
❑ 17	Bad Press	.10
❑ 18	John Jameson	.10
❑ 19	Fantastic Four	.10
❑ 20	Shutter-Bug	.10
❑ 21	Duel to the Death	.10
❑ 22	The Vulture	.10
❑ 23	The Tinkerer	.10
❑ 24	Doctor Octopus	.10
❑ 25	First Defeat	.10
❑ 26	Sandman	.10
❑ 27	Doctor Doom	.10
❑ 28	The Lizard	.10
❑ 29	Four Eyes	.10
❑ 30	Electro	.10
❑ 31	Betty Brant	.10
❑ 32	The Enforcers	.10
❑ 33	Mysterio	.10
❑ 34	Green Goblin	.10
❑ 35	Break-Up	.10
❑ 36	Big Shoes	.10
❑ 37	The Hulk	.10
❑ 38	Kraven	.10
❑ 39	The Ringmaster	.10
❑ 40	Daredevil	.10
❑ 41	Sinister Six	.10
❑ 42	The Scorpion	.10
❑ 43	Spider-Slayer	.10
❑ 44	Molten Man	.10
❑ 45	The Rhino	.10
❑ 46	The Test	.10
❑ 47	The X-Men	.10
❑ 48	The Shocker	.10
❑ 49	Captain Stacy	.10
❑ 50	The Prowler	.10
❑ 51	Drug Abuse	.10
❑ 52	Morbius	.10
❑ 53	Man-Wolf	.10
❑ 54	Gwen Stacy	.10
❑ 55	Gwen's Death	.10
❑ 56	Green Goblin's Death	.10
❑ 57	The Jackal	.10
❑ 58	The Punisher	.10
❑ 59	Vigilante	.10
❑ 60	Seeing Green	.10
❑ 61	Black Cat	.10
❑ 62	The Burglar	.10
❑ 63	Hydro-Man	.10
❑ 64	Hobgoblin	.10
❑ 65	Kingpin	.10
❑ 66	Secret Wars	.10
❑ 67	The Suit	.10
❑ 68	Bad Luck	.10
❑ 69	The Rose	.10
❑ 70	The Symbiote	.10
❑ 71	The Avengers	.10
❑ 72	Venom	.10
❑ 73	Unmasked	.10
❑ 74	Marriage	.10
❑ 75	Buried Alive	.10
❑ 76	Vermin	.10
❑ 77	Universal Powers	.10
❑ 78	Captured	.10
❑ 79	Issue #300	.10

❏ 80	Silver Sable	.10
❏ 81	Arrogance	.10
❏ 82	Spider-Man #1	.10
❏ 83	Heroes	.10
❏ 84	Spawn	.10
❏ 85	New Rose	.10
❏ 86	New Warriors	.10
❏ 87	Soul of the Hunter	.10
❏ 88	Parents	.10
❏ 89	Spider-Man 2099	.10
❏ 90	Checklist	.10

1992 Comic Images Wolverine:
From Then 'Til Now

This series, released in wax packs only in July 1992, consisted of 90 cards and six randomly issued prisms. The set featured a history of Wolverine and featured panels by such artists as John Byrne, John Buscema, and Jim Lee.

1992 Comic Images Wolverine:
From Then 'Til Now

Complete set (90) 9.00
Each card .... .10

#	Card	M
❏ 1	Wolverine	.10
❏ 2	Change	.10
❏ 3	Mutation	.10
❏ 4	Fox-Like	.10
❏ 5	Aging	.10
❏ 6	S.H.I.E.L.D.	.10
❏ 7	Logan	.10
❏ 8	Project X	.10
❏ 9	The Professor	.10
❏ 10	Dr. A.B. Cornelius	.10
❏ 11	Wild Beast	.10
❏ 12	Helmet	.10
❏ 13	I Like Him	.10
❏ 14	Shiva	.10
❏ 15	Triggers	.10
❏ 16	Mutant Powers	.10
❏ 17	Ferocious	.10
❏ 18	Adamantium	.10
❏ 19	Claws	.10
❏ 20	Hunting	.10
❏ 21	Berser	.10
❏ 22	Discipline	.10
❏ 23	Wild Beast	.10
❏ 24	Animalistic	.10
❏ 25	Department H	.10
❏ 26	First Mission	.10
❏ 27	First Defeat	.10
❏ 28	Weapon Alpha	.10
❏ 29	In Search Of	.10
❏ 30	New X-Men	.10
❏ 31	Krakoa	.10
❏ 32	Teammates	.10
❏ 33	Just Kidding	.10
❏ 34	Resentment	.10
❏ 35	Magneto	.10
❏ 36	Costume	.10
❏ 37	Phoenix	.10
❏ 38	Mariko	.10
❏ 39	Alpha Flight	.10
❏ 40	Hellfire Club	.10
❏ 41	Slice and Dice	.10
❏ 42	Old Ties	.10
❏ 43	Disgrace	.10
❏ 44	New Threats	.10
❏ 45	The Brood	.10
❏ 46	Mutant Massacre	.10
❏ 47	Fastball Special	.10
❏ 48	Vindicator	.10
❏ 49	Mutant Massacre	.10
❏ 50	Grey Hulk	.10
❏ 51	Resurrection	.10
❏ 52	Patch	.10
❏ 53	Genosha	.10
❏ 54	Donald Pierce	.10
❏ 55	Reavers	.10
❏ 56	Jubilation Lee	.10

❑	57	1941	.10
❑	58	The X-Men	.10
❑	59	Psylocke	.10
❑	60	Gambit	.10
❑	61	Popularity	.10
❑	62	Cable	.10
❑	63	Scorpio	.10
❑	64	Appeal	.10
❑	65	Lady Deathstrike	.10
❑	66	Cylia	.10
❑	67	Punisher	.10
❑	68	Buried Alive	.10
❑	69	Deadly Imitator	.10
❑	70	Elsie Dee	.10
❑	71	Matsuo	.10
❑	72	Flashback	.10
❑	73	Maverick	.10
❑	74	Resurrected	.10
❑	75	Omega Red	.10
❑	76	Carbonadium	.10
❑	77	Honor	.10
❑	78	Sabretooth	.10
❑	79	Silver Fox	.10
❑	80	Reiko	.10
❑	81	Heavy Metal	.10
❑	82	Escape	.10
❑	83	Barbaric	.10
❑	84	Rip and Tear	.10
❑	85	Ghost Rider	.10
❑	86	Cyber	.10
❑	87	Venom	.10
❑	88	The End?	.10
❑	89	The Future?	.10
❑	90	Checklist	.10

1992 Comic Images
Wolverine "From Then 'Til Now" II

Issued in July 1992, this 90-card set featured more artwork and text on Wolverine.

1992 Comic Images Wolverine II

Complete set (90)............................10.00
Common card...................................10

#		Card	M
❑	1	Wolverine	.10
❑	2	Change	.10
❑	3	Mutation	.10
❑	4	Fox-Like	.10
❑	5	Aging	.10
❑	6	S.H.I.E.L.D.	.10
❑	7	Logan	.10
❑	8	Project X	.10
❑	9	The Professor	.10
❑	10	Dr. A.B. Cornelius	.10
❑	11	Wild Beast	.10
❑	12	Helmet	.10
❑	13	I Like Him	.10
❑	14	Shiva	.10
❑	15	Triggers	.10
❑	16	Mutant Powers	.10
❑	17	Ferocious	.10
❑	18	Adamantium	.10
❑	19	Claws	.10
❑	20	Hunting	.10
❑	21	Berserk	.10
❑	22	Discipline	.10
❑	23	Wild Beast	.10
❑	24	Animalistic	.10
❑	25	Department H	.10
❑	26	First Mission	.10
❑	27	First Defeat	.10
❑	28	Weapon Alpha	.10
❑	29	In Search Of	.10
❑	30	New X-Men	.10
❑	31	Krakoa	.10
❑	32	Teammates	.10
❑	33	Just Kidding	.10
❑	34	Resentment	.10
❑	35	Magneto	.10
❑	36	Costume	.10

	#		
❑	37	Phoenix	.10
❑	38	Mariko	.10
❑	39	Alpha Flight	.10
❑	40	Hellfire Club	.10
❑	41	Slice and Dice	.10
❑	42	Old Ties	.10
❑	43	Disgrace	.10
❑	44	New Threads	.10
❑	45	The Brood	.10
❑	46	Shadowcat	.10
❑	47	Fastball Special	.10
❑	48	Vindicator	.10
❑	49	Mutant Massacre	.10
❑	50	Grey Hulk	.10
❑	51	Resurrecton	.10
❑	52	Patch	.10
❑	53	Genosha	.10
❑	54	Donald Pierce	.10
❑	55	Reavers	.10
❑	56	Jubilation Lee	.10
❑	57	1941	.10
❑	58	The X-Men	.10
❑	59	Psylocke	.10
❑	60	Gambit	.10
❑	61	Popularity	.10
❑	62	Cable	.10
❑	63	Scorpio	.10
❑	64	Appeal	.10
❑	65	Lady Deathstrike	.10
❑	66	Cylla	.10
❑	67	Punisher	.10
❑	68	Buried Alive	.10
❑	69	Deadly Imitator	.10
❑	70	Elsie Dee	.10
❑	71	Matsuo	.10
❑	72	Flashback	.10
❑	73	Maverick	.10
❑	74	Resurrected	.10
❑	75	Omega Red	.10
❑	76	Carbonadium	.10
❑	77	Honor	.10
❑	78	Sabretooth	.10
❑	79	Silver Fox	.10
❑	80	Reiko	.10
❑	81	Heavy Metal	.10
❑	82	Escape	.10
❑	83	Barbaric	.10
❑	84	Rip and Tear	.10
❑	85	Ghost Rider	.10
❑	86	Cyber	.10
❑	87	Venom	.10
❑	88	The End?	.10
❑	89	The Future?	.10
❑	90	Checklist	.10

1992 Comic Images Wolverine II prisms

Prisms were randomly inserted in Wolverine II packs.

1992 Comic Images Wolverine II prisms

Complete set (6) 30.00

Each prism 5.00

	#	Prism	M
❑	1		.10
❑	2		5.00
❑	3		5.00
❑	4		5.00
❑	5		5.00
❑	6		5.00

Press Posters

No.	Poster	Subject	Artist	Price	Date
1	X-Men	"Sentinels"	Guice/Wiacek	3.95	
2	Alpha Flight	"Big Puck"	Byrne	3.95	
3	Dr. Strange	"Conjuring"	Nowlan	3.95	
4	Spider-Man		John Romita	3.95	
5	New Mutants	"Collage"	Sienkiewicq	3.95	
6	Fantastic Four	"Family Portrait"	Bryne	3.95	
7	Avengers	"East & West"	Milgrom/Hall	3.95	
8	Cloak & Dagger		Leonardi/Austin	3.95	
9	Dreadstar		Starlin	3.95	9/84
10	Hulk	"Face"	Bob Larkin	3.95	1/85
11	X-Men Women	"Poolside"	Carl Potts	3.95	1/85
12	She-Hulk	"Walkman"	Bryne	3.95	1/85
13	Spider-Man	"Old & New"	Ron Frenq	3.95	1/85
14	White Queen	"Sulty"	Mary Wilshire	3.95	6/85
15	Punisher I	"Dodging Bullets"	Zeck	3.95	6/85
16	Daredevil	"Cityscape"	Miller/Janson	3.95	6/85
17	X-Men	"Reprint of Poster #1"	Guice/Wiacek	3.95	6/85
18	Secret Wars	"Beyonder"	Wilson/Leialoha	3.95	10/85
19	Star Comics	"Montage"	Warren Kremer	3.95	10/85
20	Wolverine	"Montage"	Leonardi/Austin	3.95	10/85
21	Alien Legion	"Recruit Poster"	Cirocco	3.95	10/85
22	Thor	"Big Ship"	Jusko	3.95	5/86
23	Silver Surfer	"Comet"	Pollard/Coffey	3.95	5/86
24	Dark Phoenix	"Montage"	Leonardi/Austin	3.95	5/86
25	X-Factor	"Cover of issue #1"	Simonson	3.95	5/86
26	New Universe	"Montage"	Sienkiewicq	3.95	8/86
27	Marvel's 25th		Gammil/Rubenstein	3.95	8/86
28	Punisher II		Zeck	4.95	3/87
29	Wolverine	"Cover to TPB"	Miller	4.95	3/87
30	Elektra	"Elektra Assassin"	Sienkiewicq	4.95	
31	Cloak & Dagger II		Carl Potts	4.95	
32	Storm I	"Old & New"	Larkin	4.95	
33	Magik		Kaluta	4.95	
34	Captain America		Zeck/Zimelman	4.95	
35	Scarlet Witch		P. Craig Russell	4.95	
36	X-Men		Art Adams	4.95	
37	Black Cat		Jusko	4.95	
38	Punisher III	"Target"	Zeck	4.95	
39	Silver Surfer		Murh	4.95	
40	Daredevil II		Mazzuchelli	4.95	5/88
41	Spider-Man IV		McFarlane	4.95	5/88
42	Thor II		Frenz/Horne	4.95	5/88
43	Iron Man I		Zeck/Zimelman	4.95	5/88
44	Marvel Universe		Hannigan/Rubinstein	14.95	5/88
45	Nick Fury	"Shield"	Steranko	4.95	8/88
46	Excalibur		Davis/Neary	4.95	8/88
47	She-Hulk	"Muscle Beach"	Jusko	4.95	8/88
48	Hulk/Wolverine	"Reflecting Claws"	McFarlane	4.95	8/88
49	Power Pack		Brigman/P.C. Russe	4.95	12/88
50	Silver Surfer		Moebius	4.95	12/88
51	Groo The Wanderer		Aragones	4.95	12/88
52	Wolverine III		Kent Williams	4.95	12/88
53	X-Factor II		Walt Simonson	4.95	1/89
54	Punisher IV		Zeck/Zimelman	4.95	1/89
55	Rogue		Cindy Martin	4.95	1/89
56	Wolverine IV		Art Adams	4.95	1/89
57	Wolvie/Cap		Zeck	4.95	4/89
58	Hulk II		McFarlane	4.95	4/89
59	Silver Surfer		Buscema/Jusko	4.95	4/89
60	Thor III		Vallejo	4.95	4/89
61	Elektra II	"Elektra Lives"	Sienkiewicq	4.95	9/89
62	Punisher IV	"Movie Poster"	Brent Anderson	4.95	9/89
63	Mutants		Art Adams	4.95	9/89
64	Spider-Man V		Jusko	4.95	9/89
65	Marshall Law		Kevin O'Neill	4.95	11/89
66	Avengers II	"Avengers Assemble"	Paul Ryan	4.95	11/89
67	Wolverine/N. Fury		Chaykin	4.95	11/89
68	Iron Man II		Moebius	4.95	11/89
69	Spider-Man VI	"Upside-Down"	Romita Sr	4.95	2/90
70	Sub-Mariner		Scott Hampton	4.95	2/90
71	Punisher VII	"Holding Pistols"	Zeck	4.95	2/90
72	Daredevil III		Moebius	4.95	2/90
73	Wolverine V		Chaykin	4.95	5/90
74	She-Hulk III		Chiodo	4.95	5/90
75	Spider-Man VII		McFarlane	4.95	8/90
76	Major Grubert		Moebius	4.95	8/90
77	Fantastic Four		Mignola	4.95	8/90
78	Captain America	"50th Anniversary"	Zeck	4.95	8/90
79	Punisher IX		Jusko	4.95	8/90
80	Electra III		Moebius	4.95	8/90
81	Dracula		J. Muth	4.95	10/90

	#	Title	Note	Artist	Price	Date
☐	82	Hellraiser	"Pinhead"	Bolton	4.95	10/901
☐	83	Storm II		Vess	4.95	10/90
☐	84	Wolverine VI		Moebius	4.95	10/90
☐	85	X-Men Triptych I		Jim Lee/S. Williams	5.95	12/90
☐	86	X-Men Triptych II		Jim Lee/S. Williams	5.95	12/90
☐	87	X-Men Triptych III		Jim Lee/S. Williams	5.95	12/90
☐	88	Black Widow		Chiodo	5.95	2/91
☐	89	Marvel Universe II		E. Larsen	5.95	2/91
☐	90	Punisher X	"Graphitti"	Zeck/Zimelman	5.95	2/91
☐	91	Spider-Man VIII		Moebius	5.95	2/91
☐	92	Deathlok I		Jusko	5.95	5/91
☐	93	Wolverine VI		Blevins	5.95	5/91
☐	94	Surfer/Galactus	"Neon"	Jim Lee/S. Williams	5.95	5/91
☐	95	Thing		Moebius	5.95	5/91
☐	?	Mary Jane Door	"taken from MI"	Jusko	12.95	7/91
☐	96	X-Men III	"Cover to #275"	Jim Lee/S. Williams	5.95	8/91
☐	97	Thing vs Hulk		Matt Wagner	5.95	8/91
☐	98	Captain America		Jusko	5.95	8/91
☐	99	Punisher XI		Moebius	5.95	8/91
☐	?	Marvel/DC	"Diptych"	Byrne	5.95	11/91
☐	100	Wolverine VII		Sam Kieth	5.95	12/91
☐	101	Wolv/Pun/Gr		Romita Jr./Wright	5.95	12/91
☐	102	Spider-Man VII	"Cityscape"	Leonardi/Williamson	5.95	12/91
☐	103	DD & Elektra		Kent Williams	5.95	12/91
☐	104	Guard. Galaxy		Valentino		
☐	105	Iron Man	"Suits of Armor"	Layton	4.95	2/92
☐	106	Ghost Rider	"Fluorescent"	Texeira	4.95	2/92
☐	107	Dr. Strange	"Skulls"	Plunkett	4.95	2/92
☐	108	X-Men	"Grounded"	Lee/Williams	4.95	2/92
☐	109	Thor Corps		Frenz/Milgrom	4.59	5/92
☐	110	Infinity War		Lim/Austin	4.95	5/92
☐	111	Spider-Man	"30th Anniversary"	Steacy	4.95	5/92
☐	112	Wolv./Cable		Mignola	4.95	5/92
☐	113	X-Men: A	"Villains Gallery"	Lee/Willams	4.95	7/92
☐	114	X-Men: B	"Original X-Men"	Lee/Willams	4.95	7/92
☐	115	X-Men: C	"Things To Come"	Lee/Williams	4.95	7/92
☐	116	X-Men: D	"Time Off"	Lee/Williams	4.95	7/92
☐	117	Ghost Rider		Seinkewicq	4.95	8/92
☐	118	Guardians		Valentino/Liefield	4.95	8/92
☐	119	Punisher XII	"With Gun"	Jusko	4.95	8/92
☐	120	Wolverine	"Scuba"	Steacy	4.95	8/92
☐	121	X-Men	"Vertical Door"	Lee/Williams	15.95	9/92
☐	122	Ghost Rider	"Midnight Sons"	Kubert/Kubert	15.95	10/92
☐	123	X-Men	"Horizontal Door"	Lee/Williams	15.95	11/92
☐	124	Excalibur		Davis/Farmer	4.95	10/92
☐	125	Spidey 2099	"Present & Future"	Leonardi/Williamson	4.95	19/92
☐	126	Hulk	"Fist"	Larkin	4.95	10/92
☐	127	Psylocke	"Swimsuit"	Lee/Wright	4.95	10/92
☐	128	Marvel Universe	"Part 1 of 2"	Various	5.95	11/92
☐	129	Marvel Universe	"Part 2 of 2"	Various	5.95	11/92
☐	130	X-Men	"Tryptich"	Lee/Williams	15.95	12/92
☐	131	X-Men	"Swimsuit"	Portacio/Williams	4.95	12/92
☐	132	Spidey vs Venom		Chido	4.95	12/92
☐	133	Ghost Rider		Bret Blevins	4.95	12/92
☐	134	Death's Head II		Liam Sharpe	4.95	12/92
☐	135	Silver Sable		Chido	4.95	3/93
☐	136	Punisher (reprint)	"PUN X:Graffiti" (rep)	Zeck/Zimelman	4.95	3/93
☐	137	Cable		Thiebert	4.95	3/93
☐	138	Wolverine		Quesada/Palmiotti	4.95	3/93
☐	139	Ghost Rider		Texeira	4.95	5/93
☐	140	Wolv. vs Sabre		Chido		5/93
☐	141	Carn/Spidey/Venom		Bagley/Emberlin		5/93
☐	142	Hulk	"Swimsuit"	Keown/Farmer		5/93
☐	143	Deadpool I		Madureira/Farmer		7/93
☐	144	Magneto I		Lee/Williams		7/93
☐	145	Spidey/Mary Jane	"Swimsuit"	Duursema		7/93
☐	146	Infinity Crusade		Starlin		7/93
☐	147	Wolverine		Beachum		9/93
☐	148	Avengers	"30th Anniversary"			9/93
☐	149	Storm				9/93
☐	150	New Warriors		D. Robertson		11/93
☐	151	Punisher XIII		Beachum		11/93
☐	152	X-Men		Larkin		11/93
☐	153	Venom		Adam Kubert/Steacy		11/93
☐	154	Gr/Mid Sons				1/94
☐	155	Wolv & Sabre		Chiodo		1/94
☐	156	Spidey/Silver Sable				1/94
☐	157	Spidey/DD				1/94
☐	158	Spidey				3/94
☐	159	Gr/Pun				3/94
☐	160	Gr/Pun		Steven Butler		3/94
☐	161	Gr/Pun				3/94
☐	162	Gr/Pun				3/95
☐	163	X-Men/Spidey/Wolverine		Texeira		5/94
☐	164	X-Men/Spidey/Venom (1/2 & 1/2)				5/94
☐	165	X-Men/Spidey				5/94

For Your Reference:

Grading Guide

Theoretically, given a set of grading rules, determining condition of a comic book should be simple. Unfortunately, flaws vary from item to item, and it can be difficult to pin one label on a particular issue. In no way is anyone bound to follow this or any other standard, but all are welcome to use this as a service which can clarify collecting terms.

Mint This is a perfect comic book. Its cover has full luster, with its edges sharp and its pages like new. There are no signs of wear or aging. It is not imperfectly printed nor markedly off-center. "Mint" means just what it says.

Fine This comic book's cover is worn but flat and clean with no defacement. There is no cover writing or tape repair. Stress lines around the staples and more rounded corners are permitted. It is a good-looking issue at first glance.

Good This is a complete but very worn comic book. Creases, minor tears, rolled spine, and cover flaking are permissable — but there is no tape or browned pages. Older Golden Age comics often come in this condition.

Fair This comic book may have a soiled, slightly damaged cover, badly rolled spine, cover flaking, corners gone, tears, and the like. It is an issue with multiple problems but it is intact. Tape may be present.

Using this book: *You will note that we list four prices for most titles: the original price, the price in good condition, in fine condition, and near-mint condition. You will also note that a formula was used to determine the prices between near-mint and good; a truly mint issue would be valued at 120% of the near-mint price — but truly mint copies are seldom found, especially of early issues. You will also note there are parts of the guide which do not list values — or, in some cases, original price. If information was not available by press time, no approximations or guesses were included. We welcome additional information.*

Abbreviations
Creators

AA	Alfredo Alcala	
AAd	Art Adams	
AM	Al Milgrom	
AMo	Alan Moore	
AW	Al Williamson	
BA	Brent Anderson	
BEv	Bill Everett	
BG	Butch Guice	
BH	Bob Hall	
BL	Bob Layton	
BMc	Bob McLeod	
BS	Barry Smith	
BSz	Bill Sienkiewicz	
BT	Bryan Talbot	
BWi	Bob Wiacek	
BWr	Berni Wrightson	
CI	Carmine Infantino	
CR	P. Craig Russell	
CV	Charles Vess	
DA	Dan Adkins	
DC	Dave Cockrum	
DaG	Dave Gibbons	
DG	Dick Giordano	
DGr	Dan Green	
DH	Don Heck	
DP	Don Perlin	
DS	Dan Spiegle	
EL	Erik Larsen	
FB	Frank Brunner	
FH	Fred Hembeck	
FM	Frank Miller	
FMc	Frank McLaughlin	
FR	Frank Robbins	
FS	Frank Springer	
FT	Frank Thorne	
GC	Gene Colan	
GD	Gene Day	
GK	Gil Kane	
GM	Gray Morrow	
GP	George Perez	
GT	George Tuska	

HC	Howard Chaykin
HK	Harvey Kurtzman
HT	Herb Trimpe
JB	John Buscema
JBy	John Byrne
JCr	Johnny Craig
JK	Jack Kirby
JKu	Joe Kubert
JLee	Jim Lee
JOy	Jerry Ordway
JR	John Romita
JR2	John Romita Jr.
JSa	Joe Staton
JSe	John Severin
JSh	Jim Sherman
JSn	Jim Starlin
JSo	Jim Steranko
JSt	Joe Sinnott
KG	Keith Giffen
KGa	Kerry Gammill
KJ	Klaus Janson
KN	Kevin Nowlan
KP	Keith Pollard
LMc	Luke McDonnell
MG	Michael Golden
MGr	Mike Grell
MGu	Mike Gustovich
MK	Mike Kaluta
MP	Mike Ploog
MR	Marshall Rogers
MW	Matt Wagner
MZ	Mike Zeck
NA	Neal Adams
NG	Neil Gaiman
NR	Nestor Redondo
PB	Pat Broderick
PG	Paul Gulacy
PS	Paul Smith
RA	Ross Andru
RB	Rich Buckler
RHo	Richard Howell

RL	Rob Liefeld
RT	Romeo Tanghal
SA	Sergio Aragones
SB	Sal Buscema
SD	Steve Ditko
S&K	Simon & Kirby
SRB	Stephen R. Bissette
TA	Terry Austin
TD	Tony DeZuniga
TMc	Todd McFarlane
TP	Tom Palmer
TS	Tom Sutton
TY	Tom Yeates
VM	Val Mayerik
WP	Wendy Pini
WS	Walter Simonson
WW	Wally Wood

Other Abbreviations

A	Appearance of
C	Cameo of
(c)	cover
D	Death of
I	Introduction of
(i)	inks
J	Joining of
L	Leaving of
M or W	Wedding of
N	New costume
nn	no number
O	Origin of
(p)	pencils
R	Revival of
rep.	reprint
SpM	Spider-Man
Thg	Thing
tpb	trade paperback
V	versus
1	first appearance of

Books

	ORIG.	GOOD	FINE	N-MINT

EPIC

67 SECONDS
| | 15.95 | 3.19 | 9.57 | 15.95 |

AKIRA BOOK 1

AKIRA BOOK 2

AKIRA BOOK 3

AKIRA BOOK 4

AKIRA BOOK 5
| | 14.95 | 2.99 | 8.97 | 14.95 |

AKIRA BOOK 6
| | 14.95 | 2.99 | 8.97 | 14.95 |

AKIRA BOOK 7
| | 14.95 | 2.99 | 8.97 | 14.95 |

AKIRA BOOK 8
| | 16.95 | 3.39 | 10.17 | 16.95 |

ALIEN LEGION: GRIMROD
| | 5.95 | 1.19 | 3.57 | 5.95 |

ART OF MOEBIUS, THE
| tpb | 14.95 | 2.99 | 8.97 | 14.95 |

BLOOD: A TALE
| tpb | 15.95 | 3.19 | 9.57 | 15.95 |

BLOODLINES: A TALE FROM THE HEART OF AFRICA
| | 5.95 | 1.19 | 3.57 | 5.95 |

BLUEBERRY 1: CHIHUAHUA PEARL
| | 12.95 | 2.59 | 7.77 | 12.95 |

BLUEBERRY 2: BALLAD FOR A COFFIN
| | 14.95 | 2.99 | 8.97 | 14.95 |

BLUEBERRY 3: ANGEL FACE
| | 12.95 | 2.59 | 7.77 | 12.95 |

BLUEBERRY 4: THE GREAT TRIBE
| | 12.95 | 2.59 | 7.77 | 12.95 |

BLUEBERRY 5: THE END OF THE TRAIL
| | 12.95 | 3.39 | 10.17 | 12.95 |

CLIVE BARKER'S HELLRAISER POSTERBOOK
| 1 BSz | 4.95 | 0.99 | 2.97 | 4.95 |

CRIME & PUNISHMENT: MARSHAL LAW TAKES MANHATTAN
| | 4.95 | 0.99 | 2.97 | 4.95 |

ELEKTRA: ASSASSIN
| tpb | 12.95 | 2.59 | 7.77 | 12.95 |

ESPERS
| tpb | 9.95 | 1.99 | 5.97 | 9.95 |

EVERYMAN, THE
| | 4.50 | 0.90 | 2.70 | 4.50 |

HARVEY KURTZMAN'S STRANGE ADVENTURES
| hardcover | 19.95 | 3.99 | 11.97 | 19.95 |

HEARTS AND MINDS
| | 8.95 | 1.79 | 5.37 | 8.95 |

INCAL 1, THE
| | 10.95 | 2.19 | 6.57 | 10.95 |

INCAL 2, THE
| | 10.95 | 2.59 | 7.77 | 10.95 |

INCAL 3, THE
| | 10.95 | 2.19 | 6.57 | 10.95 |

IRON MAN: CRASH
| | 12.95 | 2.59 | 7.77 | 12.95 |

JHEREG
| | 8.95 | 1.79 | 5.37 | 8.95 |

LAST OF THE DRAGONS
| | 6.95 | 1.39 | 4.17 | 6.95 |

LIEUTENANT BLUEBERRY: GENERAL GOLDEN MANE
| | 14.95 | 2.99 | 8.97 | 14.95 |

MARSHAL LAW: FEAR AND LOATHING
| tpb | 14.95 | 2.99 | 8.97 | 14.95 |

MOEBIUS 1: UPON A STAR
| | 9.95 | 1.99 | 5.97 | 9.95 |
| (2nd printing) | 9.95 | 1.99 | 5.97 | 9.95 |

MOEBIUS 2: ARZACH
| | 9.95 | 1.99 | 5.97 | 9.95 |

MOEBIUS 3: AIRTIGHT GARAGE
| | 12.95 | 2.59 | 7.77 | 12.95 |

MOEBIUS 4: THE LONG TOMORROW
| | 9.95 | 1.99 | 5.97 | 9.95 |

MOEBIUS 5: THE GARDENS OF AEDENA
| | 9.95 | 1.99 | 5.97 | 9.95 |

MOEBIUS 6: PHARAGONESIA
| | 9.95 | 1.99 | 5.97 | 9.95 |

MOEBIUS 7: THE GODDESS
| | 12.95 | 2.59 | 7.77 | 12.95 |

MOONSHADOW
| tpb | 18.95 | 3.79 | 11.37 | 18.95 |

NEUROMANCER
| | 8.95 | 1.79 | 5.37 | 8.95 |

PUNISHER: RETURN TO BIG NOTHING, THE
| hc | 16.95 | 3.39 | 10.17 | 16.95 |

SEVEN BLOCK
| tpb | 4.50 | 0.90 | 2.70 | 4.50 |

	ORIG.	GOOD	FINE	N-MINT
SILVER SURFER, THE				
☐ hc, Moebius 19.95	3.99	11.97	19.95
SIX FROM SIRUS				
☐ tpb PG 8.95	1.79	5.37	8.95
SOMEPLACE STRANGE				
☐ 6.95	1.39	4.17	6.95
TALES FROM THE HEART OF AFRICA: THE TEMPORARY NATIVES				
☐ 3.95	0.79	2.37	3.95

MARVEL

	ORIG.	GOOD	FINE	N-MINT
ABSLOM DAAK-DALEK KILLER				
☐ 8.95	1.79	5.37	8.95
AGENT, THE				
☐ 9.95	1.99	5.97	9.95
ALADDIN EFFECT				
☐ (MGN #16)........................ 5.95	1.19	3.57	5.95
ALF BOOKSHELF EDITION				
☐ 1 r: #1-3 .... 4.95	0.99	2.97	4.95
ALIEN LEGION: A GREY DAY TO DIE				
☐ 5.95	1.19	3.57	5.95
AMAZING SPIDER-MAN				
☐ (Simon & Schuster Fireside tpb)...................... 3.95	0.79	2.37	3.95
AMAZING SPIDER-MAN MASTERWORKs VOLUME 1				
☐ tpb reprint, SD 12.95	2.59	7.77	12.95
AMAZING SPIDER-MAN, THE				
☐ (Pocket Books 1977) 1.95	0.39	1.17	NVE
☐ 1 (Pocket Books 1980; strip reprints)..................... 2.50	0.50	1.50	NVE
☐ 2 (Pocket Books 1978) 1.95	0.39	1.17	NVE
☐ 2 (Pocket Books 1980; strip reprints)..................... 2.50	0.50	1.50	NVE
☐ 3 (Pocket Books 1978) 2.25	0.45	1.35	NVE
AMAZING SPIDER-MAN: FEARFUL SYMMETRY: KRAVEN'S LAST HUNT				
☐ tpb................................ 15.95	3.19	9.57	15.95
AMAZING SPIDER-MAN: HOOKY				
☐ 5.95	1.39	4.17	5.95
AMAZING SPIDER-MAN: PARALLEL LIVES				
☐ 8.95	1.79	5.37	8.95
AMAZING SPIDER-MAN: SAGA OF THE ALIEN COSTUME, THE				
☐ 1 tpb................................ 9.95	1.99	5.97	9.95
AMAZING SPIDER-MAN: SPIRITS OF THE DEAD				
☐ 18.95	3.79	11.37	18.95
AMAZING SPIDER-MAN: THE DEATH OF JEAN DE WOLFF				
☐ tpb................................ 10.95	2.19	6.57	10.95

	ORIG.	GOOD	FINE	N-MINT
AMAZING SPIDER-MAN: THE ORIGIN OF THE HOBGOBLIN				
☐ tpb................................ 14.95	2.99	8.97	14.95
AMAZING SPIDER-MAN: THE WEDDING				
☐ tpb................................ 15.95	3.19	9.57	15.95
ARENA				
☐ 5.95	1.19	3.57	5.95
AVENGERS, THE				
☐ (Lancer 1982).................... 1.75	2.00	6.00	10.00
AVENGERS-EMPEROR DOOM				
☐ 5.95	1.19	3.57	5.95
AVENGERS: DEATHTRAP, THE VAULT				
☐ (also published as Venom: Deathtrap-the Vault)........... 9.95	1.99	5.97	9.95
AX				
☐ 5.95	1.19	3.57	5.95
BATTLESTAR GALACTICA				
☐ (Ace 1978) 1.95	0.39	1.17	NVE
BATTLESTAR GALACTICA, VOLUME II				
☐ (Ace 1979) 2.25	0.45	1.35	NVE
BEST OF MARVEL COMICS, VOLUME ONE				
☐ hc, padded covers, no price listed			
BEST OF SPIDER-MAN				
☐ (newspaper strips, Ballantine Books tpb).......................... 9.95	1.99	5.97	9.95
BLACK WIDOW: THE COLDEST WAR				
☐ 9.95	1.99	5.97	9.95
BLADE RUNNER				
☐ (Marvel 1982)................... 1.75	0.35	1.05	NVE
BOYS' RANCH				
☐ 39.95	7.99	23.97	39.95
BRING ON THE BAD GUYS: ORIGINS OF THE MARVEL COMICS VILLAINS				
☐ (Fireside)........................... 6.95	1.39	4.17	6.95
BULLWINKLE AND ROCKY				
☐ tpb, collection 4.95	0.99	2.97	4.95
CABLE AND THE NEW MUTANTS				
☐ tpb................................ 15.95	3.19	9.57	15.95
CAPTAIN AMERICA				
☐ (Pocket Books 1979)......... 2.25	0.45	1.35	NVE
CAPTAIN AMERICA: SENTINEL OF LIBERTY				
☐ (Fireside)............................			
CAPTAIN AMERICA: THE CLASSIC YEARS				
☐ hc, two volumes, slipcased 75.00	15.00	45.00	75.00
CAPTAIN AMERICA: WAR AND REMEMBRANCE				
☐ tpb JBy 12.95	2.59	7.77	12.95
CAPTAIN BRITAIN				
☐ 1 tpb................................ 9.95	1.99	5.97	9.95
CLOAK AND DAGGER IN PREDATOR AND PREY				
☐ 5.95	1.19	3.57	5.95

	ORIG.	GOOD	FINE	N-MINT
CONAN OF THE ISLES				
❑	8.95	1.79	5.37	8.95
CONAN THE REAVER				
❑	6.50	1.30	3.90	6.50
CONAN THE ROGUE				
❑	9.95	1.99	5.97	9.95
CONAN, VOLUME 1				
❑ (Ace 1978)	1.95	1.20	3.60	6.00
CONAN, VOLUME 2				
❑ (Ace 1978)	1.95	1.20	3.60	6.00
CONAN, VOLUME 3				
❑ (Ace 1978)	1.95	1.20	3.60	6.00
CONAN, VOLUME 4				
❑ (Ace 1978)	1.95	1.20	3.60	6.00
CONAN, VOLUME 5				
❑ (Ace 1978)	2.25	1.20	3.60	6.00
CONAN, VOLUME 6				
❑ (Ace 1978)	2.25	1.20	3.60	6.00
CONAN-THE MOVIE				
❑ (Marvel 1982)	1.75	0.35	1.05	NVE
CONAN: THE HORN OF AZOTH				
❑	8.95	1.79	5.37	8.95
CONAN: THE RAVAGERS OUT OF TIME				
❑	9.95	1.99	5.97	9.95
CONAN: THE SKULL OF SET				
❑	8.95	1.79	5.37	8.95
CONAN: THE WITCH QUEEN OF ACHERON				
❑ (MGN #19)	6.50	1.39	4.17	6.95
DAREDEVIL AND THE PUNISHER				
❑ "Child's Play" pb	4.95	0.99	2.97	4.95
DAREDEVIL IN LOVE AND WAR				
❑ tpb	6.95	1.39	4.17	6.95
DAREDEVIL/BLACK WIDOW: ABATTOIR				
❑	14.95	2.99	8.97	14.95
DAREDEVIL: BORN AGAIN				
❑ tpb	9.95	1.99	5.97	9.95
DAREDEVIL: MARKED FOR DEATH				
❑ tpb FM, KJ reprint	9.95	1.99	5.97	9.95
DAZZLER: THE MOVIE				
❑ (MGN #12)	6.95	1.39	4.17	6.95
DEATH OF CAPTAIN MARVEL				
❑ (MGN #1)	5.95	6.00	18.00	30.00
DOCTOR STRANGE				
❑ 1 (Pocket Books 1979)	2.25	0.45	1.35	NVE
❑ 2 (Pocket Books 1979)	2.25	0.45	1.35	NVE

	ORIG.	GOOD	FINE	N-MINT
DOCTOR STRANGE AND DOCTOR DOOM: TRIUMPH AND TRAGEDY				
❑ hc	17.95	5.00	15.00	25.00
DOCTOR STRANGE: MASTER OF THE MYSTIC ARTS				
❑ (Fireside)	3.95	0.79	2.37	3.95
DOCTOR STRANGE: SHAMBALLA				
❑	5.95	1.39	4.17	6.95
DOCTOR WHO-VOYAGER				
❑	8.95	1.79	5.37	8.95
DRACULA: A SYMPHONY IN MOONLIGHT AND NIGHTMARES				
❑	7.95	3.00	9.00	15.00
DREADSTAR				
❑ (MGN #3)	4.95	1.80	5.40	9.00
DREAMWALKER				
❑	6.95	1.39	4.17	6.95
ELRIC: THE DREAMING CITY				
❑ (MGN #2)	5.95	2.00	6.00	10.00
EXCALIBUR SPECIAL: SWORD IS DRAWN				
❑ 1 1st printing	3.25	3.60	10.80	18.00
❑ 1 2nd printing	3.50	1.00	3.00	5.00
❑ 1 3rd printing	3.50	0.70	2.10	3.50
EXCALIBUR SPECIAL: XX CROSSING				
❑ X-Men	2.50	0.50	1.50	2.50
EXCALIBUR: AIR APPARENT				
❑	4.95	0.99	2.97	4.95
EXCALIBUR: MOJO MAYHEM				
❑ 1 AAd/TA	4.50	1.20	3.60	6.00
EXCALIBUR: THE POSSESSION				
❑	2.95	0.59	1.77	2.95
FANTASTIC FOUR				
❑ (Fireside)	3.95	0.79	2.37	3.95
FANTASTIC FOUR RETURN, THE				
❑ (Lancer)	0.50	2.40	7.20	12.00
FANTASTIC FOUR VS. THE X-MEN				
❑ tpb	9.95	1.99	5.97	9.95
FANTASTIC FOUR, THE				
❑ (Lancer)	0.50			
❑ (Pocket 1979)	1.95	0.39	1.17	NVE
❑ (Marvel)	1.75	0.35	1.05	NVE
FANTASTIC FOUR: MONSTERS UNLEASHED				
❑ tpb AAd reprint	5.95	1.19	3.57	5.95
FANTASTIC FOUR: THE SECRET STORY OF MARVEL'S COSMIC QUARTET				
❑ (Ideals)	2.95	0.59	1.77	2.95
FANTASTIC FOUR: THE TRIAL OF GALACTUS				
❑ 1 tpb, JBy	12.95	2.59	7.77	12.95
FIGHTING AMERICAN				
❑ hc, JS/JK	35.95	7.19	21.57	35.95
FUTURIANS				
❑ (MGN #9)	6.95	1.39	4.17	6.95

	ORIG.	GOOD	FINE	N-MINT
G.I. JOE SPECIAL MISSIONS				
❑ tpb.................................6.95	1.39	4.17	6.95
GHOST RIDER/ WOLVERINE/ PUNISHER: HEARTS OF DARKNESS				
❑ squarebound.....................4.95	0.99	2.97	4.95
GREENBERG THE VAMPIRE				
❑ (MGN #20).........................6.96	1.39	4.18	6.96
HEARTBURST				
❑ (MGN #10).........................4.95	1.19	3.57	5.95
HERCULES PRINCE OF POWER: FULL CIRCLE				
❑ 6.95	1.39	4.17	6.95
HERCULES, PRINCE OF POWER				
❑ tpb, BL............................5.95	1.19	3.57	5.95
HERE COMES...DAREDEVIL				
❑ (Lancer)...........................0.50	2.40	7.20	12.00
INCREDIBLE HULK				
❑ (Fireside).........................7.95	1.59	4.77	7.95
INCREDIBLE HULK AND THE THING: THE BIG CHANCE				
❑ 29.....................................5.95	1.19	3.57	5.95
INCREDIBLE HULK VOLUME 2, THE				
❑ (Tempo, newspaper				
strips)................................1.95	0.39	1.17	1.95
INCREDIBLE HULK, THE				
❑ (Lancer)...........................0.50			
❑ (Tempo, newspaper				
strips)................................1.75	0.35	1.05	1.75
❑ (Pocket)...........................1.95	0.39	1.17	1.95
❑ (Marvel)...........................2.50	0.50	1.50	2.50
❑ 2 (Pocket)........................1.95	0.39	1.17	1.95
INCREDIBLE HULK: A MAN-BRUTE BERSERK!, THE				
❑ (Tor).................................3.50	0.70	2.10	3.50
INFINITY GAUNTLET				
❑ tpb.................................19.95	3.99	11.97	19.95
INHUMANS				
❑ 7.95	1.59	4.77	7.95
IRON MAN: ARMOR WARS				
❑ tpb reprint.....................12.95	2.59	7.77	12.95
KA-ZAR: GUNS OF THE SAVAGE LAND				
❑ 8.95	1.79	5.37	8.95
KILLRAVEN				
❑ (MGN #7).........................5.95	1.39	4.17	5.95
KULL: THE VALE OF SHADOW				
❑ 6.95	1.39	4.17	6.95
LIFE AND TIMES OF DEATH'S HEAD				
❑ tpb.................................12.95	2.59	7.77	12.95
LIFE OF CAPTAIN MARVEL				
❑ tpb.................................14.95	2.99	8.97	14.95
MACHINE MAN (1984-1985)				
❑ tpb HT/BS.........................6.95	1.39	4.17	6.95

	ORIG.	GOOD	FINE	N-MINT
MARADA THE SHE-WOLF				
❑ 5.95	1.39	4.17	5.95
MARVEL COMICS				
❑ 1 hc reprint....................17.95	3.59	10.77	17.95
MARVEL MASTERWORKS				
❑ 1 Spider-Man..................29.95	7.00	21.00	35.00
❑ 2 Fantastic Four..............29.95	7.00	21.00	35.00
❑ 3 X-Men...........................29.95	8.00	24.00	40.00
❑ 4 Avengers......................29.95	6.40	19.20	32.00
❑ 5 Spider-Man...................29.95	6.40	19.20	32.00
❑ 6 Fantastic Four..............29.95	6.40	19.20	32.00
❑ 7 X-Men...........................29.95	7.00	21.00	35.00
❑ 8 Hulk..............................24.95	5.99	17.97	29.95
❑ 9 Avengers......................29.95	5.99	17.97	29.95
❑ 10 Spider-Man.................29.95	5.99	17.97	29.95
❑ 11 X-Men.........................29.95	5.99	17.97	29.95
❑ 12 X-Men.........................29.95	5.99	17.97	29.95
❑ 13 Fantastic Four.............34.95	6.99	20.97	34.95
❑ 14 Capt. America.............34.95	6.99	20.97	34.95
❑ 15 Surfer.........................34.95	6.99	20.97	34.95
❑ 16 Spider-Man.................34.95	6.99	20.97	34.95
❑ 17 Daredevil....................34.95	6.99	20.97	34.95
❑ 18 Thor............................34.95	6.99	20.97	34.95
❑ 19 Silver Surfer...............44.95	8.99	26.97	44.95
❑ 20 Iron Man.....................34.95	6.99	20.97	34.95
❑ 21 Fantastic Four.............34.95	6.99	20.97	34.95
❑ 22 Spider-Man.................34.95	6.99	20.97	34.95
❑ 23 Doctor Strange...........39.95	7.99	23.97	39.95
MARVEL MAZES TO DRIVE YOU MAD!				
❑ (Fireside)..........................2.95	0.59	1.77	2.95
MARVEL NOVEL SERIES (Pocket Books; not comics)				
❑ 1 (Incredible Hulk: Stalker				
from the Stars)...................1.75	0.35	1.05	1.75
❑ 2 (Amazing Spider-Man:				
Mayhem in Manhattan)......1.75	0.35	1.05	1.75
❑ 3 (Incredible Hulk: Cry				
of the Beast).....................1.75	0.35	1.05	1.75
❑ 4 (Captain America:				
Holocaust for Hire)............1.95	0.39	1.17	1.95
❑ 5 (Fantastic Four:				
Doomsday).......................1.95	0.39	1.17	1.95
❑ 6 (Iron Man: And Call				
My Killer...Modok!).............1.95	0.39	1.17	1.95
❑ 7 (Doctor Strange:				
Nightmare).......................1.95	0.39	1.17	1.95
❑ 8 (Spider-Man:				
Crime Campaign)..............1.95	0.39	1.17	1.95
❑ 9 (The Marvel Superheroes)				
(short stories)....................1.95	0.39	1.17	1.95
❑ 10 (Avengers: The Man Who				
Stole Tomorrow)................1.95	0.39	1.17	1.95
❑ 11 (Hulk and Spider-Man:				
Murdermoon)....................1.95	0.39	1.17	1.95

	ORIG.	GOOD	FINE	N-MINT
MARVEL SUPER HEROES SECRET WARS				
❏ tpb.................... 19.95	3.99	11.97	19.95
MARVEL'S GREATEST SUPERHERO BATTLES				
❏ (Fireside) 6.95	2.40	7.20	12.00
MARVEL: FIVE FABULOUS DECADES OF THE WORLD'S GREATEST COMICS				
❏ (Abrams).............................			
MIGHTY MARVEL COMICS STRENGTH AND FITNESS BOOK				
❏ (Fireside) 3.95	0.79	2.37	3.95
MIGHTY MARVEL FUN BOOK				
❏ 3 (Fireside) 2.95	0.59	1.77	2.95
❏ 4 (Fireside) 2.95	0.59	1.77	2.95
❏ 5 (Fireside) 2.95	0.59	1.77	2.95
MIGHTY MARVEL SUPERHEROES FUN BOOK				
❏ (Fireside) 2.95	0.59	1.77	2.95
❏ 2 (Fireside) 2.95	0.59	1.77	2.95
MIGHTY MARVEL TEAM-UP THRILLERS				
❏ tpb.................... 5.95	1.19	3.57	5.95
MIGHTY THOR!, THE				
❏ (Lancer) 0.50			
MIGHTY THOR: ALONE AGAINST THE CELESTIALS				
❏ tpb.................... 5.95	1.19	3.57	5.95
MIGHTY THOR: BALLAD OF BETA RAY BILL				
❏ tpb, WS............................ 8.95	1.79	5.37	8.95
MIGHTY THOR: I, WHOM THE GODS WOULD DESTROY				
❏	5.95	1.19	3.57	5.95
MONSTER MASTERWORKS				
❏ tpb, JK, SD, BEv............. 12.95	2.59	7.77	12.95
MOON KNIGHT: DIVIDED WE FALL				
❏	4.95	0.99	2.97	4.95
NAM, THE				
❏ 1 .... 4.95	1.39	4.17	4.95
❏ 2 .... 6.95	1.39	4.17	6.95
❏ 3 .... 6.95	1.39	4.17	6.95
NEW FANTASTIC FOUR: MONSTERS UNLEASHED				
❏ tpb.................... 5.95	1.19	3.57	5.95
NEW MUTANTS				
❏ (MGN #4, O:New Mutants)............................ 4.95	2.50	7.50	12.50
NEW MUTANTS: THE DEMON BEAR SAGA				
❏ tpb.................... 8.95	1.79	5.37	8.95
NEW WARRIORS: BEGINNINGS				
❏ tpb.................... 12.95	2.59	7.77	12.95
NICK FURY VS. S.H.I.E.L.D.				
❏ tpb.................... 15.95	3.19	9.57	15.95
NIGHT RAVEN: HOUSE OF CARDS				
❏ tpb.................... 5.95	1.19	3.57	5.95

	ORIG.	GOOD	FINE	N-MINT
NOTHING CAN STOP THE JUGGERNAUT				
❏ tpb, Spider-Man 3.95	0.79	2.37	3.95
OFFICIAL HANDBOOK OF THE MARVEL UNIVERSE (trade paperbacks)				
❏ 1 ....6.95	1.39	4.17	6.95
❏ 2 ....6.95	1.39	4.17	6.95
❏ 3 ....6.95	1.39	4.17	6.95
❏ 4 ....6.95	1.39	4.17	6.95
❏ 5 ....6.95	1.39	4.17	6.95
❏ 6 ....6.95	1.39	4.17	6.95
❏ 7 ....6.95	1.39	4.17	6.95
❏ 8 ....6.95	1.39	4.17	6.95
❏ 9 ....6.95	1.39	4.17	6.95
❏ 10 ....6.95	1.39	4.17	6.95
ORIGINS OF MARVEL COMICS				
❏ (Fireside) hc (First ed.)....10.95	5.00	15.00	25.00
❏ (Fireside) tpb (First ed.) 6.95	4.00	12.00	20.00
POWER OF IRON MAN, THE				
❏ tpb....................6.95	1.39	4.17	6.95
POWER PACK ORIGIN ALBUM				
❏ tpb, O:Power Pack...........7.95	1.59	4.77	7.95
POWER PACK/CLOAK AND DAGGER: SHELTER FROM THE STORM				
❏	7.95	1.59	4.77	7.95
PUNISHER				
❏ tpb 7.95	1.59	4.77	7.95
PUNISHER BOOK ONE				
❏ pb 9.95	1.99	5.97	9.95
PUNISHER/BLACK WIDOW: SPINNING DOOMSDAY'S WEB				
❏ graphic novel....................9.95	1.99	5.97	9.95
PUNISHER/WOLVERINE AFRICAN SAGA				
❏ tpb reprint........................5.95	1.19	3.57	5.95
PUNISHER: AN EYE FOR AN EYE				
❏ tpb 9.95	1.99	5.97	9.95
PUNISHER: ASSASSIN'S GUILD				
❏	6.95	1.39	4.17	6.95
PUNISHER: BLOOD ON THE MOORS				
❏ hc 16.95	3.39	10.17	16.95
PUNISHER: BLOODLINES				
❏	5.95	1.19	3.57	5.95
PUNISHER: CIRCLE OF BLOOD, THE				
❏ tpb 7.95	1.59	4.77	7.95
PUNISHER: DIE HARD IN THE BIG EASY				
❏ tpb 4.95	0.99	2.97	4.95
PUNISHER: INTRUDER				
❏ hc 14.95	2.99	8.97	14.95
❏ pb 9.95	1.99	5.97	9.95
PUNISHER: KINGDOM COME				
❏ hc 16.95	3.39	10.17	16.95
PUNISHER: NO ESCAPE				
❏	4.95	0.99	2.97	4.95

	ORIG.	GOOD	FINE	N-MINT
PUNISHER: RETURN TO BIG NOTHING				
☐ (published in hardcover as an Epic Graphic Novel)....	12.95	2.59	7.77	12.95
PUNISHER: THE PRIZE				
☐	4.95	0.99	2.97	4.95
RAVEN BANNER				
☐ (MGN #15, C.Vess)	5.95	1.19	3.57	5.95
REN & STIMPY SHOW, THE				
☐ tpb....................	12.95	2.59	7.77	12.95
REVENGE OF THE LIVING MONOLITH				
☐ (MGN #17)........................	6.95	1.39	4.17	6.95
RIO RIDES AGAIN				
☐	9.95	1.99	5.97	9.95
RISE OF THE MIDNIGHT SONS				
☐ tpb....................	19.95	3.99	11.97	19.95
ROGER RABBIT: THE RESURRECTION OF DOOM				
☐	8.95	1.79	5.37	8.95
SAILOR'S STORY, A				
☐	5.95	1.19	3.57	5.95
SAILOR'S STORY: WINDS, DREAMS, AND DRAGONS, A				
☐	6.95	1.39	4.17	6.95
SAVAGE LAND, THE				
☐ tpb MG,DC,TA,JBu...........	5.95	1.19	3.57	5.95
SENSATIONAL SHE-HULK				
☐ (MGN #18, J. Byrne).........	6.95	1.39	4.17	6.95
SENSATIONAL SPIDER-MAN, THE				
☐ tpb, FM	5.95	1.19	3.57	5.95
SHADOW: HITLER'S ASTROLOGER, THE				
☐ hc.....................	12.95	2.59	7.77	12.95
SILVER SURFER				
☐ (Fireside, 1978) (original graphic novel by Stan Lee & Jack Kirby)	4.95	10.00	30.00	50.00
SILVER SURFER: JUDGMENT DAY				
☐ hc.....................	14.95	2.99	8.97	14.95
SILVER SURFER: REBIRTH OF THANOS				
☐ tpb.....................	12.95	2.59	7.77	12.95
SILVER SURFER: THE COMING OF GALACTUS				
☐ reprint	5.95	1.19	3.57	5.95
SILVER SURFER: THE ENSLAVERS				
☐ hc.....................	16.95	3.39	10.17	16.95
SON OF ORIGINS OF MARVEL COMICS				
☐ (Fireside)	6.95	4.00	12.00	20.00
SPIDER-MAN VS. VENOM				
☐ tpb TMc............................	9.95	1.99	5.97	9.95
SPIDER-MAN, PUNISHER, SABRE-TOOTH: DESIGNER GENES				
☐	8.95	1.79	5.37	8.95
SPIDER-MAN/DR. STRANGE: THE WAY TO DUSTY DEATH				
☐ graphic novel	6.95	1.39	4.17	6.95
SPIDER-MAN: CARNAGE				
☐ tpb..................................	6.95	1.39	4.17	6.95
SPIDER-MAN: FEAR ITSELF				
☐	12.95	2.59	7.77	12.95
SPIDER-MAN: FEARFUL SYMMETRY				
☐ hc....................	19.95	3.99	11.97	19.95
☐ paperbound....................	15.95	3.19	9.57	15.95
SPIDER-MAN: HIS GREATEST TEAM-UP BATTLES				
☐ newsstand pb....................	2.50	0.50	1.50	2.50
SPIDER-MAN: THE ASSASSIN NATION PLOT				
☐ tpb, TMc	14.95	2.99	8.97	14.95
SPIDER-MAN: THE COSMIC ADVENTURES				
☐ tpb	19.95	3.99	11.97	19.95
SPIDER-MAN: THE SECRET STORY OF MARVEL'S WORLD-FAMOUS WALL-CRAWLER				
☐ (Ideals)	2.95	0.59	1.77	2.95
SPIDER-MAN: VENOM RETURNS				
☐ tpb	12.95	2.59	7.77	12.95
SPIDER-WOMAN				
☐ (Pocket newsstand pb)	2.50	0.50	1.50	2.50
SQUADRON SUPREME: DEATH OF A UNIVERSE				
☐	9.95	1.99	5.97	9.95
STAR SLAMMERS				
☐ (MGN #6, W. Simonson)....5.95		1.39	4.17	6.95
STAR TREK				
☐ (Marvel newsstand pb)......	2.50	0.50	1.50	2.50
STAR WARS				
☐ (Del Rey newsstand pb)...	1.50	0.30	0.90	1.50
STAR WARS (newsstand pb)				
☐ (Marvel)...........................	2.50	0.50	1.50	2.50
☐ 2 (Marvel)..........................	1.75	0.35	1.05	1.75
STAR WARS: RETURN OF THE JEDI				
☐ (Marvel newsstand pb)......	2.50	0.50	1.50	2.50
STAR WARS: THE EMPIRE STRIKES BACK				
☐ (Marvel newsstand pb)......	2.50	0.50	1.50	2.50
STARSTRUCK				
☐ (MGN #13)	6.95	1.39	4.17	6.95
SUPER BOXERS				
☐ (MGN #8)	5.95	1.39	4.17	5.95
SUPERHERO WOMEN, THE				
☐ (Fireside)...........................	6.95	1.39	4.17	6.95
SUPERMAN AND SPIDER-MAN				
☐ (Warner newsstand pb).....	2.50	0.50	1.50	2.50
SWORDS OF SWASHBUCKLERS				
☐ (MGN #14)	5.95	1.19	3.57	5.95
THING: PEGASUS PROJECT				
☐ pb JBy,GP........................	6.95	1.39	4.17	6.95
TRANSFORMERS UNIVERSE, THE				
☐ tpb..................................	5.95	1.19	3.57	5.95

	ORIG.	GOOD	FINE	N-MINT
UNCANNY X-MEN MASTERWORKS, THE				
❏ tpb.................. 12.95		2.59	7.77	12.95
UNCANNY X-MEN, THE				
❏ tpb.................. 6.95		1.39	4.17	6.95
❏ (Tor newsstand pb)... 2.95		0.59	1.77	2.95
UNCANNY X-MEN: DAYS OF FUTURE PAST				
❏ 1 rep. JBy,TA.................. 3.95		0.79	2.37	3.95
VENOM: DEATHTRAP-THE VAULT				
❏ tpb (also published as Avengers,				
Death Trap: the Vault) 6.95		1.39	4.17	6.95
VERY BEST OF MARVEL COMICS, THE				
❏ tpb.................. 12.95		2.59	7.77	12.95
VOID INDIGO				
❏ (MGN #11)......... 4.95		2.00	6.00	10.00
WEAPON X				
❏ BWS, hc reprint 19.95		3.99	11.97	19.95
WHO FRAMED ROGER RABBIT?				
❏ movie adaptation 6.95		1.39	4.17	6.95
WILLOW				
❏ movie adaptation 6.95		1.39	4.17	6.95
WILLOW: THE ILLUSTRATED VERSION				
❏ (Del Rey newsstand pb) ... 4.95		0.99	2.97	4.95
WOLFPACK				
❏	7.95	1.59	4.77	7.95
WOLVERINE (paperbacks)				
❏ 1 edition 4.95		2.00	6.00	10.00
❏ 2 edition, FM..... 5.95		1.20	3.60	6.00
WOLVERINE BATTLES THE INCREDIBLE HULK				
❏ tpb.................. 4.95		0.99	2.97	4.95
WOLVERINE/NICK FURY: THE SCORPIO CONNECTION				
❏ hc.................. 16.95		3.39	10.17	16.95
❏ pb.................. 12.95		2.59	7.77	12.95
WOLVERINE: BLOODLUST				
❏	4.95	0.99	2.97	4.95
WOLVERINE: INNER FURY				
❏	5.95	1.19	3.57	5.95
WOLVERINE: RAHNE OF TERRA				
❏ tpb.................. 5.95		1.19	3.57	5.95

	ORIG.	GOOD	FINE	N-MINT
WOLVERINE: SAVE THE TIGER!				
❏ 1 .... 2.95		0.59	1.77	2.95
WOLVERINE: THE JUNGLE ADVENTURE				
❏ 1 .... 4.50		0.90	2.70	4.50
X-FACTOR: PRISONER OF LOVE				
❏	4.95	0.99	2.97	4.95
X-FORCE AND SPIDER-MAN: SABOTAGE				
❏ TMc, RL 6.95		1.39	4.17	6.95
X-MEN ANIMATION SPECIAL: THE PRYDE OF THE X-MEN				
❏	10.95	2.19	6.57	10.95
X-MEN VS. THE AVENGERS				
❏ tpb.................. 12.95		2.59	7.77	12.95
X-MEN, THE				
❏ (Marvel newsstand pb)...... 1.75		0.35	1.05	1.75
X-MEN: DAYS OF FUTURE PRESENT				
❏ tpb.................. 14.95		2.99	8.97	14.95
X-MEN: GOD LOVES, MAN KILLS				
❏ (MGN #5) 5.95		3.20	9.60	16.00
X-MEN: THE ASGARDIAN WARS				
❏ tpb, AAd 14.95		2.99	8.97	14.95

MARVEL/NELSON

	ORIG.	GOOD	FINE	N-MINT
PILGRIM'S PROGRESS, THE				
❏ adaptation 9.99		2.00	5.99	9.99

MARVEL/BERKLEY

	ORIG.	GOOD	FINE	N-MINT
DUNE				
❏ (movie adaptation) 3.95		0.79	2.37	3.95

MARVEL/GRANDREAMS

	ORIG.	GOOD	FINE	N-MINT
CAPTAIN AMERICA				
❏ hc.................. 3.95		0.79	2.37	3.95
HULK ANNUAL				
❏ hc.................. 3.95		0.79	2.37	3.95
SPIDER-MAN ANNUAL				
❏ hc.................. 3.95		0.79	2.37	3.95
X-MEN				
❏ hc.................. 3.95		0.79	2.37	3.95

Comic Books

	ORIG.	GOOD	FINE	N-MINT

EPIC

A1

		ORIG.	GOOD	FINE	N-MINT
❏	1	5.95	1.19	3.57	5.95
❏	2	5.95	1.19	3.57	5.95
❏	3	5.95	1.19	3.57	5.95
❏	4	5.95	1.19	3.57	5.95

AIRTIGHT GARAGE

		ORIG.	GOOD	FINE	N-MINT
❏	1 Moebius	2.50	0.50	1.50	2.50
❏	2 Moebius	2.50	0.50	1.50	2.50
❏	3 Moebius	2.50	0.50	1.50	2.50
❏	4 Moebius	2.50	0.50	1.50	2.50

AKIRA

		ORIG.	GOOD	FINE	N-MINT
❏	1 1st printing		4.00	12.00	20.00
❏	1 2nd printing		1.00	3.00	5.00
❏	2 1st printing		2.40	7.20	12.00
❏	2 2nd printing		0.70	2.10	3.50
❏	3		2.00	6.00	10.00
❏	4		2.00	6.00	10.00
❏	5		2.00	6.00	10.00
❏	6		1.60	4.80	8.00
❏	7		1.60	4.80	8.00
❏	8		1.60	4.80	8.00
❏	9		1.60	4.80	8.00
❏	10		1.60	4.80	8.00
❏	11		1.20	3.60	6.00
❏	12		1.20	3.60	6.00
❏	13		1.20	3.60	6.00
❏	14		1.20	3.60	6.00
❏	15		1.20	3.60	6.00
❏	16		1.20	3.60	6.00
❏	17		1.20	3.60	6.00
❏	18		1.20	3.60	6.00
❏	19		1.20	3.60	6.00
❏	20		1.20	3.60	6.00
❏	21		0.90	2.70	4.50
❏	22		0.90	2.70	4.50
❏	23		0.90	2.70	4.50
❏	24		0.90	2.70	4.50
❏	25		0.90	2.70	4.50
❏	26		0.90	2.70	4.50
❏	27		0.90	2.70	4.50
❏	28		0.90	2.70	4.50
❏	29		0.90	2.70	4.50
❏	30		0.90	2.70	4.50
❏	31		0.79	2.37	3.95
❏	32		0.79	2.37	3.95
❏	33		0.79	2.37	3.95

ALIEN LEGION

		ORIG.	GOOD	FINE	N-MINT
❏	1 TA	2.00	0.80	2.40	4.00
❏	2	1.50	0.60	1.80	3.00

		ORIG.	GOOD	FINE	N-MINT
❏	3	1.50	0.60	1.80	3.00
❏	4	1.50	0.60	1.80	3.00
❏	5	1.50	0.60	1.80	3.00
❏	6	1.50	0.40	1.20	2.00
❏	7	1.50	0.40	1.20	2.00
❏	8	1.50	0.40	1.20	2.00
❏	9	1.50	0.40	1.20	2.00
❏	10	1.50	0.40	1.20	2.00
❏	11	1.50	0.40	1.20	2.00
❏	12	1.50	0.40	1.20	2.00
❏	13	1.50	0.40	1.20	2.00
❏	14	1.50	0.40	1.20	2.00
❏	15	1.50	0.40	1.20	2.00
❏	16	1.50	0.40	1.20	2.00
❏	17	1.50	0.40	1.20	2.00
❏	18	1.75	0.40	1.20	2.00
❏	19	1.75	0.40	1.20	2.00
❏	20	1.75	0.40	1.20	2.00

ALIEN LEGION (Volume Two)

		ORIG.	GOOD	FINE	N-MINT
❏	1	1.25	0.40	1.20	2.00
❏	2	1.25	0.25	0.75	1.25
❏	3	1.25	0.25	0.75	1.25
❏	4	1.25	0.25	0.75	1.25
❏	5	1.25	0.25	0.75	1.25
❏	6	1.25	0.25	0.75	1.25
❏	7	1.25	0.25	0.75	1.25
❏	8	1.50	0.30	0.90	1.50
❏	9	1.50	0.30	0.90	1.50
❏	10	1.50	0.30	0.90	1.50
❏	11	1.50	0.30	0.90	1.50
❏	12	1.50	0.30	0.90	1.50
❏	13	1.50	0.30	0.90	1.50
❏	14	1.50	0.30	0.90	1.50
❏	15	1.50	0.30	0.90	1.50
❏	16	1.50	0.30	0.90	1.50
❏	17	1.50	0.30	0.90	1.50
❏	18	1.50	0.30	0.90	1.50

ALIEN LEGION: ON THE EDGE

		ORIG.	GOOD	FINE	N-MINT
❏	1	4.50	0.90	2.70	4.50
❏	2	4.50	0.90	2.70	4.50
❏	3	4.50	0.90	2.70	4.50

ALIEN LEGION: ONE PLANET AT A TIME

		ORIG.	GOOD	FINE	N-MINT
❏	1	4.95	0.99	2.97	4.95
❏	2	4.95	0.99	2.97	4.95
❏	3	4.95	0.99	2.97	4.95

ALIEN LEGION: TENANTS OF HELL

		ORIG.	GOOD	FINE	N-MINT
❏	1	4.50	0.90	2.70	4.50
❏	2	4.50	0.90	2.70	4.50

ATOMIC AGE

		ORIG.	GOOD	FINE	N-MINT
❏	1		0.90	2.70	4.50

	ORIG.	GOOD	FINE	N-MINT
❏ 2		0.90	2.70	4.50
❏ 3		0.90	2.70	4.50
❏ 4		0.90	2.70	4.50

BLACK DRAGON

	ORIG.	GOOD	FINE	N-MINT
❏ 1		0.60	1.80	3.00
❏ 2		0.40	1.20	2.00
❏ 3		0.40	1.20	2.00
❏ 4		0.40	1.20	2.00
❏ 5		0.40	1.20	2.00
❏ 6		0.40	1.20	2.00

BLOOD: A TALE

	ORIG.	GOOD	FINE	N-MINT
❏ 1	3.25	1.00	3.00	5.00
❏ 2	3.25	0.80	2.40	4.00
❏ 3	3.25	0.80	2.40	4.00
❏ 4	3.25	0.80	2.40	4.00

BOZZ CHRONICLES

	ORIG.	GOOD	FINE	N-MINT
❏ 1	1.50	0.30	0.90	1.50
❏ 2	1.50	0.30	0.90	1.50
❏ 3	1.50	0.30	0.90	1.50
❏ 4	1.50	0.30	0.90	1.50
❏ 5	1.50	0.30	0.90	1.50
❏ 6	1.50	0.30	0.90	1.50

CADILLACS & DINOSAURS

	ORIG.	GOOD	FINE	N-MINT
❏ 1	2.50	0.50	1.50	2.50
❏ 2	2.50	0.50	1.50	2.50
❏ 3	2.50	0.50	1.50	2.50
❏ 4	2.50	0.50	1.50	2.50
❏ 5	2.50	0.50	1.50	2.50
❏ 6	2.50	0.50	1.50	2.50

CAPTAIN CONFEDERACY

	ORIG.	GOOD	FINE	N-MINT
❏ 1	1.95	0.39	1.17	1.95
❏ 2	1.95	0.39	1.17	1.95
❏ 3	1.95	0.39	1.17	1.95
❏ 4	1.95	0.39	1.17	1.95

CAR WARRIORS

	ORIG.	GOOD	FINE	N-MINT
❏ 1	2.25	0.45	1.35	2.25
❏ 2	2.25	0.45	1.35	2.25
❏ 3	2.25	0.45	1.35	2.25
❏ 4	2.25	0.45	1.35	2.25

CLIVE BARKER'S BOOK OF THE DAMNED

	ORIG.	GOOD	FINE	N-MINT
❏ 1	4.95	0.99	2.97	4.95
❏ 2	4.95	0.99	2.97	4.95
❏ 3	4.95	0.99	2.97	4.95
❏ 4	4.95	0.99	2.97	4.95

CLIVE BARKER'S BOOK OF THE DAMNED II

	ORIG.	GOOD	FINE	N-MINT
❏	4.95	0.99	2.97	4.95

CLIVE BARKER'S BOOK OF THE DAMNED III

	ORIG.	GOOD	FINE	N-MINT
❏	4.95	0.99	2.97	4.95

CLIVE BARKER'S HELLRAISER

	ORIG.	GOOD	FINE	N-MINT
❏ 1	4.95	2.00	6.00	10.00
❏ 2	4.95	1.20	3.60	6.00
❏ 3	4.95	1.20	3.60	6.00
❏ 4	4.95	1.20	3.60	6.00

	ORIG.	GOOD	FINE	N-MINT
❏ 5	5.95	1.19	3.57	5.95
❏ 6	5.95	1.19	3.57	5.95
❏ 7	5.95	1.19	3.57	5.95
❏ 8	5.95	1.19	3.57	5.95
❏ 9	5.95	1.19	3.57	5.95
❏ 10	4.50	0.90	2.70	4.50
❏ 11	4.50	0.90	2.70	4.50
❏ 12	4.50	0.90	2.70	4.50
❏ 13	4.95	0.99	2.97	4.95
❏ 14	4.95	0.99	2.97	4.95
❏ 15	4.95	0.99	2.97	4.95
❏ 16 NG	4.95	0.99	2.97	4.95
❏ 17 NG	4.95	0.99	2.97	4.95
❏ 18 NG	4.95	0.99	2.97	4.95
❏ 19 NG	4.95	0.99	2.97	4.95
❏ 20 NG	4.95	0.99	2.97	4.95

CLIVE BARKER'S HELLRAISER DARK HOLIDAY SPECIAL

	ORIG.	GOOD	FINE	N-MINT
❏ 1	4.95	0.99	2.97	4.95

CLIVE BARKER'S HELLRAISER SUMMER SPECIAL

	ORIG.	GOOD	FINE	N-MINT
❏ 1	5.95	1.19	3.57	5.95

CLIVE BARKER'S NIGHTBREED

	ORIG.	GOOD	FINE	N-MINT
❏ 1	1.95	0.80	2.40	4.00
❏ 2	1.95	0.60	1.80	3.00
❏ 3	1.95	0.60	1.80	3.00
❏ 4	1.95	0.60	1.80	3.00
❏ 5	2.25	0.45	1.35	2.25
❏ 6	2.25	0.45	1.35	2.25
❏ 7	2.25	0.45	1.35	2.25
❏ 8	2.25	0.45	1.35	2.25
❏ 9	2.25	0.45	1.35	2.25
❏ 10	2.25	0.45	1.35	2.25
❏ 11	2.25	0.45	1.35	2.25
❏ 12	2.25	0.45	1.35	2.25
❏ 13 Rawhead Rex	2.25	0.45	1.35	2.25
❏ 14	2.25	0.45	1.35	2.25
❏ 15	2.25	0.45	1.35	2.25
❏ 16	2.25	0.45	1.35	2.25
❏ 17	2.25	0.45	1.35	2.25
❏ 18	2.25	0.45	1.35	2.25
❏ 19	2.25	0.45	1.35	2.25
❏ 20	2.50	0.50	1.50	2.50
❏ 21	2.50	0.50	1.50	2.50
❏ 22	2.50	0.50	1.50	2.50
❏ 23	2.50	0.50	1.50	2.50
❏ 24	2.50	0.50	1.50	2.50
❏ 25	2.50	0.50	1.50	2.50

COYOTE

	ORIG.	GOOD	FINE	N-MINT
❏ 1	1.50	0.30	0.90	1.50
❏ 2	1.50	0.30	0.90	1.50
❏ 3	1.50	0.30	0.90	1.50
❏ 4	1.50	0.30	0.90	1.50
❏ 5	1.50	0.30	0.90	1.50
❏ 6	1.50	0.30	0.90	1.50

	ORIG.	GOOD	FINE	N-MINT
7	1.50	0.30	0.90	1.50
8	1.50	0.30	0.90	1.50
9	1.50	0.30	0.90	1.50
10	1.50	0.30	0.90	1.50
11 TMc	1.50	0.80	2.40	4.00
12 TMc	1.50	0.80	2.40	4.00
13 TMc	1.50	0.80	2.40	4.00
14 A:Badger	1.50	1.60	4.80	8.00
15	1.50	0.30	0.90	1.50
16	1.50	0.30	0.90	1.50

CRASH RYAN

	ORIG.	GOOD	FINE	N-MINT
1	1.50	0.30	0.90	1.50
2	1.50	0.30	0.90	1.50
3	1.50	0.30	0.90	1.50
4	1.50	0.30	0.90	1.50

CRITICAL MASS

	ORIG.	GOOD	FINE	N-MINT
1 BSz,GM	4.95	0.99	2.97	4.95
2	4.95	0.99	2.97	4.95
3	4.95	0.99	2.97	4.95
4	4.95	0.99	2.97	4.95
5	4.95	0.99	2.97	4.95
6	4.95	0.99	2.97	4.95
7	5.95	1.19	3.57	5.95

DINOSAURS: A CELEBRATION

	ORIG.	GOOD	FINE	N-MINT
1 Horns and heavy armor	4.95	0.99	2.97	4.95
2 Bone heads and Duck-bills	4.95	0.99	2.97	4.95
3 Egg stealers and Earth shakers	4.95	0.99	2.97	4.95
4 Terrible claws and tyrants	4.95	0.99	2.97	4.95

DOCTOR ZERO

	ORIG.	GOOD	FINE	N-MINT
1 BSz(c)	1.25	0.30	0.90	1.50
2 BSz(c)	1.25	0.30	0.90	1.50
3	1.25	0.30	0.90	1.50
4	1.50	0.30	0.90	1.50
5	1.50	0.30	0.90	1.50
6	1.50	0.30	0.90	1.50
7	1.50	0.30	0.90	1.50
8	1.50	0.30	0.90	1.50

DRAGON LINES

	ORIG.	GOOD	FINE	N-MINT
1 embossed cover	2.50	0.50	1.50	2.50
2	1.95	0.39	1.17	1.95
3	1.95	0.39	1.17	1.95
4	1.95	0.39	1.17	1.95

DREADLANDS

	ORIG.	GOOD	FINE	N-MINT
1	3.95	0.79	2.37	3.95
2	3.95	0.79	2.37	3.95
3	3.95	0.79	2.37	3.95
4	3.95	0.79	2.37	3.95

DREADSTAR

	ORIG.	GOOD	FINE	N-MINT
1 JSn	1.50	1.00	3.00	5.00
2 JSn, Willow	1.50	0.60	1.80	3.00

	ORIG.	GOOD	FINE	N-MINT
3 JSn, Lord Papal	1.50	0.50	1.50	2.50
4 JSn	1.50	0.45	1.35	2.25
5 JSn	1.50	0.45	1.35	2.25
6 JSn	1.50	0.40	1.20	2.00
7 JSn	1.50	0.40	1.20	2.00
8 JSn	1.50	0.40	1.20	2.00
9 JSn	1.50	0.40	1.20	2.00
10 JSn	1.50	0.40	1.20	2.00
11 JSn	1.50	0.40	1.20	2.00
12 JSn	1.50	0.40	1.20	2.00
13 JSn	1.50	0.40	1.20	2.00
14 JSn	1.50	0.40	1.20	2.00
15 JSn	1.50	0.40	1.20	2.00
16 JSn	1.50	0.30	0.90	1.50
17 JSn	1.50	0.30	0.90	1.50
18 JSn	1.50	0.30	0.90	1.50
19 JSn	1.50	0.30	0.90	1.50
20 JSn	1.50	0.35	1.05	1.75
21 JSn	1.50	0.35	1.05	1.75
22 JSn	1.50	0.35	1.05	1.75
23 JSn	1.50	0.35	1.05	1.75
24 JSn	1.50	0.35	1.05	1.75
25 JSn (moves to First)	1.50	0.35	1.05	1.75

DREADSTAR & COMPANY

	ORIG.	GOOD	FINE	N-MINT
1 reprints	0.75	0.20	0.60	1.00
2 reprints	0.75	0.20	0.60	1.00
3 reprints	0.75	0.20	0.60	1.00
4 reprints	0.75	0.20	0.60	1.00
5 reprints	0.75	0.20	0.60	1.00
6 reprints	0.75	0.20	0.60	1.00

DREADSTAR ANNUAL

	ORIG.	GOOD	FINE	N-MINT
1 JSn	2.00	0.60	1.80	3.00

ELEKTRA: ASSASSIN

	ORIG.	GOOD	FINE	N-MINT
1 FM,BSz	1.50	1.60	4.80	8.00
2 FM,BSz	1.50	1.20	3.60	6.00
3 FM,BSz	1.50	1.20	3.60	6.00
4 FM,BSz	1.50	1.20	3.60	6.00
5 FM,BSz	1.50	1.20	3.60	6.00
6 FM,BSz	1.50	1.20	3.60	6.00
7 FM,BSz	1.75	1.20	3.60	6.00
8 FM,BSz	1.75	1.20	3.60	6.00

ELFQUEST

	ORIG.	GOOD	FINE	N-MINT
1 WP	0.75	1.00	3.00	5.00
2 WP	0.75	0.60	1.80	3.00
3 WP	0.75	0.60	1.80	3.00
4 WP	0.75	0.60	1.80	3.00
5 WP	0.75	0.60	1.80	3.00
6 WP	0.75	0.40	1.20	2.00
7 WP	0.75	0.40	1.20	2.00
8 WP	0.75	0.40	1.20	2.00
9 WP	0.75	0.40	1.20	2.00
10 WP	0.75	0.40	1.20	2.00
11 WP	0.75	0.40	1.20	2.00
12 WP	0.75	0.40	1.20	2.00

	ORIG.	GOOD	FINE	N-MINT
13 WP	0.75	0.40	1.20	2.00
14 WP	0.75	0.40	1.20	2.00
15 WP	0.75	0.40	1.20	2.00
16 WP	0.75	0.40	1.20	2.00
17 WP	0.75	0.40	1.20	2.00
18 WP	0.75	0.40	1.20	2.00
19 WP	0.75	0.40	1.20	2.00
20 WP	0.75	0.40	1.20	2.00
21 WP	0.75	0.40	1.20	2.00
22 WP	1.00	0.40	1.20	2.00
23 WP	1.00	0.40	1.20	2.00
24 WP	1.00	0.40	1.20	2.00
25 WP	1.00	0.40	1.20	2.00
26 WP	1.00	0.40	1.20	2.00
27 WP	1.00	0.40	1.20	2.00
28 WP	1.00	0.40	1.20	2.00
29 WP	1.00	0.40	1.20	2.00
30 WP	1.00	0.40	1.20	2.00
31 WP	1.00	0.40	1.20	2.00
32 WP	1.00	0.40	1.20	2.00

ELSEWHERE PRINCE, THE

	ORIG.	GOOD	FINE	N-MINT
1 Moebius	1.95	0.39	1.17	1.95
2 Moebius	1.95	0.39	1.17	1.95
3 Moebius	1.95	0.39	1.17	1.95
4 Moebius	1.95	0.39	1.17	1.95
5 Moebius	1.95	0.39	1.17	1.95
6 Moebius	1.95	0.39	1.17	1.95

EPIC

	ORIG.	GOOD	FINE	N-MINT
1	4.95	0.99	2.97	4.95
2	4.95	0.99	2.97	4.95
3	4.95	0.99	2.97	4.95
4	4.95	0.99	2.97	4.95

EPIC ILLUSTRATED

	ORIG.	GOOD	FINE	N-MINT
1 (magazine)	2.00	0.40	1.20	2.00
2 (magazine)	2.00	0.40	1.20	2.00
3 (magazine)	2.00	0.40	1.20	2.00
4 (magazine)	2.00	0.40	1.20	2.00
5 (magazine)	2.00	0.40	1.20	2.00
6 (magazine)	2.00	0.40	1.20	2.00
7 (magazine)	2.00	0.40	1.20	2.00
8 (magazine)	2.00	0.40	1.20	2.00
9 (magazine)	2.00	0.40	1.20	2.00
10 (magazine)	2.00	0.40	1.20	2.00
11 (magazine)	2.50	0.50	1.50	2.50
12 (magazine)	2.50	0.50	1.50	2.50
13 (magazine)	2.50	0.50	1.50	2.50
14 (magazine)	2.50	0.50	1.50	2.50
15 (magazine)	2.50	0.50	1.50	2.50
16 (magazine)	2.50	0.50	1.50	2.50
17 (magazine)	2.50	0.50	1.50	2.50
18 (magazine)	2.50	0.50	1.50	2.50
19 (magazine)	2.50	0.50	1.50	2.50
20 (magazine)	2.50	0.50	1.50	2.50
21 (magazine)	2.50	0.50	1.50	2.50
22 (magazine)	2.50	0.50	1.50	2.50
23 (magazine)	2.50	0.50	1.50	2.50
24 (magazine)	2.50	0.50	1.50	2.50
25 (magazine)	2.50	0.50	1.50	2.50
26 (magazine)	2.50	0.50	1.50	2.50
27 (magazine)	2.50	0.50	1.50	2.50
28 (magazine)	2.50	0.50	1.50	2.50
29 (magazine)	2.50	0.50	1.50	2.50
30 (magazine)	2.50	0.50	1.50	2.50
31 (magazine)	2.50	0.50	1.50	2.50
32 (magazine)	2.50	0.50	1.50	2.50
33 (magazine)	2.50	0.50	1.50	2.50
34 (magazine)	2.50	0.50	1.50	2.50
35 (magazine)	2.50	0.50	1.50	2.50
36 (magazine)	2.50	0.50	1.50	2.50

EPIC LITE

	ORIG.	GOOD	FINE	N-MINT
1	3.95	0.79	2.37	3.95

FAFHRD AND THE GRAY MOUSER

	ORIG.	GOOD	FINE	N-MINT
1 MM, AW	4.50	0.90	2.70	4.50
2 MM, AW	4.50	0.90	2.70	4.50
3 MM, AW	4.50	0.90	2.70	4.50
4 MM, AW	4.50	0.90	2.70	4.50

FAREWELL TO WEAPONS

	ORIG.	GOOD	FINE	N-MINT
nn	2.25	0.45	1.35	2.25

FEUD

	ORIG.	GOOD	FINE	N-MINT
1 embossed cover	2.50	0.50	1.50	2.50
2	1.95	0.39	1.17	1.95
3	1.95	0.39	1.17	1.95

GROO CHRONICLES, THE

	ORIG.	GOOD	FINE	N-MINT
1 SA, reprints	3.50	0.70	2.10	3.50
2 SA, reprints	3.50	0.70	2.10	3.50
3 SA, reprints	3.50	0.70	2.10	3.50
4 SA, reprints	3.50	0.70	2.10	3.50
5 SA, reprints	3.50	0.70	2.10	3.50
6 SA, reprints	3.50	0.70	2.10	3.50

GROO THE WANDERER
(see Sergio Aragones' Groo the Wanderer)

HAVOK & WOLVERINE: MELTDOWN

	ORIG.	GOOD	FINE	N-MINT
1	3.50	2.80	8.40	14.00
2	3.50	2.40	7.20	12.00
3	3.50	2.00	6.00	10.00
4	3.50	2.00	6.00	10.00

HELLRAISER III: HELL ON EARTH

	ORIG.	GOOD	FINE	N-MINT
1 movie	4.95	0.99	2.97	4.95

HELLRAISER/NIGHTBREED: JIHAD

	ORIG.	GOOD	FINE	N-MINT
1	4.50	0.90	2.70	4.50
2	4.50	0.90	2.70	4.50

HOLLYWOOD SUPERSTARS

	ORIG.	GOOD	FINE	N-MINT
1 DS	2.95	0.59	1.77	2.95
2 DS	2.25	0.45	1.35	2.25
3 DS	2.25	0.45	1.35	2.25
4 DS	2.25	0.45	1.35	2.25
5 DS	2.25	0.45	1.35	2.25

	ORIG.	GOOD	FINE	N-MINT
IDOL				
1	2.95	0.59	1.77	2.95
2	2.95	0.59	1.77	2.95
3	2.95	0.59	1.77	2.95
INTERFACE				
1	1.95	0.39	1.17	1.95
2	1.95	0.39	1.17	1.95
3	1.95	0.39	1.17	1.95
4	1.95	0.39	1.17	1.95
5	1.95	0.39	1.17	1.95
6	2.25	0.45	1.35	2.25
7	2.25	0.45	1.35	2.25
8	2.25	0.45	1.35	2.25
JOE KUBERT'S TOR				
1 large size	5.95	1.19	3.57	5.95
2 large size	5.95	1.19	3.57	5.95
LANCE BARNES: POST NUKE DICK				
1	2.50	0.50	1.50	2.50
2	2.50	0.50	1.50	2.50
3	2.50	0.50	1.50	2.50
4	2.50	0.50	1.50	2.50
LAST AMERICAN, THE				
1	2.25	0.45	1.35	2.25
2	2.25	0.45	1.35	2.25
3	2.25	0.45	1.35	2.25
4	2.25	0.45	1.35	2.25
LAWDOG				
1 embossed cover	2.50	0.50	1.50	2.50
2	1.95	0.39	1.17	1.95
3	1.95	0.39	1.17	1.95
4	1.95	0.39	1.17	1.95
5	1.95	0.39	1.17	1.95
LIGHT AND DARKNESS WAR, THE				
1	1.95	0.39	1.17	1.95
2	1.95	0.39	1.17	1.95
3	1.95	0.39	1.17	1.95
4	1.95	0.39	1.17	1.95
5	1.95	0.39	1.17	1.95
6	1.95	0.39	1.17	1.95
MARSHAL LAW				
1	1.95	0.80	2.40	4.00
2	1.95	0.50	1.50	2.50
3	1.95	0.50	1.50	2.50
4	1.95	0.50	1.50	2.50
5	1.95	0.50	1.50	2.50
6	1.95	0.50	1.50	2.50
MEMORIES				
1 Japanese, b&w	2.50	0.50	1.50	2.50
METROPOL				
1	2.95	0.59	1.77	2.95
2	2.95	0.59	1.77	2.95
3	2.95	0.59	1.77	2.95
4	2.95	0.59	1.77	2.95

	ORIG.	GOOD	FINE	N-MINT
5	2.95	0.59	1.77	2.95
6	2.95	0.59	1.77	2.95
7	2.95	0.59	1.77	2.95
8	2.95	0.59	1.77	2.95
9	2.95	0.59	1.77	2.95
10	2.95	0.59	1.77	2.95
11	2.95	0.59	1.77	2.95
12	2.95	0.59	1.77	2.95
METROPOL A.D.				
1	3.50	0.70	2.10	3.50
2	3.50	0.70	2.10	3.50
3	3.50	0.70	2.10	3.50
MIDNIGHT MEN				
1 HC, embossed foil cover	2.50	0.50	1.50	2.50
2 HC	1.95	0.39	1.17	1.95
3 HC	1.95	0.39	1.17	1.95
4 HC	1.95	0.39	1.17	1.95
MOONSHADOW				
1	1.50	1.40	4.20	7.00
2	1.50	0.80	2.40	4.00
3	1.50	0.80	2.40	4.00
4	1.50	0.80	2.40	4.00
5	1.50	0.80	2.40	4.00
6	1.50	0.50	1.50	2.50
7	1.50	0.50	1.50	2.50
8	1.50	0.50	1.50	2.50
9	1.50	0.50	1.50	2.50
10	1.50	0.50	1.50	2.50
11	1.50	0.50	1.50	2.50
12	1.75	0.60	1.80	3.00
MUTATIS				
1	2.25	0.45	1.35	2.25
2	2.25	0.45	1.35	2.25
3	2.25	0.45	1.35	2.25
NEW ADVENTURES OF CHOLLY AND FLYTRAP				
1	2.50	0.50	1.50	2.50
2	2.50	0.50	1.50	2.50
3	2.50	0.50	1.50	2.50
OFFCASTES				
1 embossed cover	2.50	0.50	1.50	2.50
2	1.95	0.39	1.17	1.95
3	1.95	0.39	1.17	1.95
OLYMPIANS, THE				
1	3.95	0.79	2.37	3.95
2	3.95	0.79	2.37	3.95
ONE, THE				
1	1.50	0.40	1.20	2.00
2	1.50	0.40	1.20	2.00
3	1.50	0.40	1.20	2.00
4	1.50	0.40	1.20	2.00
5	1.50	0.40	1.20	2.00
6	1.50	0.40	1.20	2.00

	ORIG.	GOOD	FINE	N-MINT
ONYX OVERLORD				
☐ 1 Moebius	2.75	0.55	1.65	2.75
☐ 2	2.75	0.55	1.65	2.75
☐ 3	2.75	0.55	1.65	2.75
☐ 4	2.75	0.55	1.65	2.75
PLASTIC FORKS				
☐ 1	4.95	0.99	2.97	4.95
☐ 2	4.95	0.99	2.97	4.95
☐ 3	4.95	0.99	2.97	4.95
☐ 4	4.95	0.99	2.97	4.95
☐ 5	4.95	0.99	2.97	4.95
POWER LINE				
☐ 1	1.25	0.25	0.75	1.25
☐ 2	1.25	0.25	0.75	1.25
☐ 3	1.25	0.25	0.75	1.25
☐ 4	1.50	0.30	0.90	1.50
☐ 5	1.50	0.30	0.90	1.50
☐ 6	1.50	0.30	0.90	1.50
☐ 7	1.50	0.30	0.90	1.50
☐ 8	1.50	0.30	0.90	1.50
PSYCHONAUTS				
☐ 1	4.95	0.99	2.97	4.95
SAM & MAX FREELANCE POLICE SPECIAL COLOR COLLECTION				
☐ nn, 1992	4.95	0.99	2.97	4.95
SAM & MAX, FREELANCE POLICE				
☐ nn, 1992	2.25	0.45	1.35	2.25
SAMURAI CAT				
☐ 1	2.25	0.45	1.35	2.25
☐ 2	2.25	0.45	1.35	2.25
☐ 3	2.25	0.45	1.35	2.25
SERGIO ARAGONES' GROO THE WANDERER				
☐ 1 SA	0.75	3.60	10.80	18.00
☐ 2 SA	0.75	2.40	7.20	12.00
☐ 3 SA	0.75	2.00	6.00	10.00
☐ 4 SA	0.75	2.00	6.00	10.00
☐ 5 SA	0.75	2.00	6.00	10.00
☐ 6 SA	0.75	1.40	4.20	7.00
☐ 7 SA	0.75	1.40	4.20	7.00
☐ 8 SA	0.75	1.40	4.20	7.00
☐ 9 SA	0.75	1.40	4.20	7.00
☐ 10 SA	0.75	1.40	4.20	7.00
☐ 11 SA	0.75	1.40	4.20	7.00
☐ 12 SA	0.75	1.40	4.20	7.00
☐ 13 SA	0.75	1.40	4.20	7.00
☐ 14 SA	0.75	1.40	4.20	7.00
☐ 15 SA	0.75	1.40	4.20	7.00
☐ 16 SA	0.75	1.40	4.20	7.00
☐ 17 SA	0.75	1.40	4.20	7.00
☐ 18 SA	0.75	1.40	4.20	7.00
☐ 19 SA	0.75	1.40	4.20	7.00
☐ 20 SA	0.75	1.40	4.20	7.00
☐ 21 SA	0.75	1.20	3.60	6.00
☐ 22 SA	0.75	1.20	3.60	6.00

	ORIG.	GOOD	FINE	N-MINT
☐ 23 SA	0.75	1.20	3.60	6.00
☐ 24 SA	0.75	1.20	3.60	6.00
☐ 25 SA	0.75	1.20	3.60	6.00
☐ 26 SA	0.75	1.20	3.60	6.00
☐ 27 SA	1.00	1.20	3.60	6.00
☐ 28 SA	1.00	1.20	3.60	6.00
☐ 29 SA	1.00	1.60	4.80	8.00
☐ 30 SA	1.00	1.40	4.20	7.00
☐ 31 SA	1.00	1.00	3.00	5.00
☐ 32 SA	1.00	1.00	3.00	5.00
☐ 33 SA	1.00	1.00	3.00	5.00
☐ 34 SA	1.00	1.00	3.00	5.00
☐ 35 SA	1.00	1.00	3.00	5.00
☐ 36 SA	1.00	1.00	3.00	5.00
☐ 37 SA	1.00	1.00	3.00	5.00
☐ 38 SA	1.00	1.00	3.00	5.00
☐ 39 SA	1.00	1.00	3.00	5.00
☐ 40 SA	1.00	1.00	3.00	5.00
☐ 41 SA	1.00	1.00	3.00	5.00
☐ 42 SA	1.00	1.00	3.00	5.00
☐ 43 SA	1.00	1.00	3.00	5.00
☐ 44 SA	1.00	1.00	3.00	5.00
☐ 45 SA	1.00	1.00	3.00	5.00
☐ 46 SA	1.00	1.00	3.00	5.00
☐ 47 SA	1.00	1.00	3.00	5.00
☐ 48 SA	1.00	1.00	3.00	5.00
☐ 49 SA A:Chakaal	1.00	1.00	3.00	5.00
☐ 50 SA A:Chakaal	1.00	1.00	3.00	5.00
☐ 51 SA A:Chakaal	1.00	0.40	1.20	2.00
☐ 52 SA A:Chakaal	1.00	0.40	1.20	2.00
☐ 53 SA A:Chakaal	1.00	0.40	1.20	2.00
☐ 54 SA	1.00	0.40	1.20	2.00
☐ 55 SA	1.00	0.40	1.20	2.00
☐ 56 SA	1.00	0.40	1.20	2.00
☐ 57 SA	1.00	0.40	1.20	2.00
☐ 58 SA	1.00	0.40	1.20	2.00
☐ 59 SA	1.00	0.40	1.20	2.00
☐ 60 SA	1.00	0.40	1.20	2.00
☐ 61 SA	1.00	0.40	1.20	2.00
☐ 62 SA	1.00	0.40	1.20	2.00
☐ 63 SA	1.00	0.40	1.20	2.00
☐ 64 SA	1.00	0.20	0.60	1.00
☐ 65 SA	1.00	0.20	0.60	1.00
☐ 66 SA	1.00	0.20	0.60	1.00
☐ 67 SA	1.00	0.20	0.60	1.00
☐ 68 SA	1.00	0.20	0.60	1.00
☐ 69 SA	1.00	0.20	0.60	1.00
☐ 70 SA	1.00	0.20	0.60	1.00
☐ 71 SA	1.00	0.20	0.60	1.00
☐ 72 SA	1.00	0.20	0.60	1.00
☐ 73 SA	1.00	0.20	0.60	1.00
☐ 74 SA	1.00	0.20	0.60	1.00
☐ 75 SA	1.00	0.20	0.60	1.00
☐ 76 SA	1.00	0.20	0.60	1.00
☐ 77 SA	1.00	0.20	0.60	1.00

	ORIG.	GOOD	FINE	N-MINT
❏ 78 SA bookburners	1.00	0.20	0.60	1.00
❏ 79 SA	1.00	0.20	0.60	1.00
❏ 80 SA 1:Thaiis	1.00	0.20	0.60	1.00
❏ 81 SA Thaiis	1.00	0.20	0.60	1.00
❏ 82 SA Thaiis	1.00	0.20	0.60	1.00
❏ 83 SA Thaiis	1.00	0.20	0.60	1.00
❏ 84 SA	1.00	0.20	0.60	1.00
❏ 85 SA	1.00	0.20	0.60	1.00
❏ 86 SA	1.25	0.25	0.75	1.25
❏ 87 SA direct sale	2.25	0.45	1.35	2.25
❏ 88 SA direct sale	2.25	0.45	1.35	2.25
❏ 89 SA direct sale	2.25	0.45	1.35	2.25
❏ 90	2.25	0.45	1.35	2.25
❏ 91	2.25	0.45	1.35	2.25
❏ 92	2.25	0.45	1.35	2.25
❏ 93	2.25	0.45	1.35	2.25
❏ 94	2.25	0.45	1.35	2.25
❏ 95	2.25	0.45	1.35	2.25
❏ 96	2.25	0.45	1.35	2.25
❏ 97	2.25	0.45	1.35	2.25
❏ 98	2.25	0.45	1.35	2.25
❏ 99	2.25	0.45	1.35	2.25
❏ 100 Groo learns to read	2.95	0.59	1.77	2.95
❏ 101	2.25	0.45	1.35	2.25
❏ 102	2.25	0.45	1.35	2.25
❏ 103	2.25	0.45	1.35	2.25
❏ 104	2.25	0.45	1.35	2.25
❏ 105	2.25	0.45	1.35	2.25

SILVER SURFER, THE (1988)

	ORIG.	GOOD	FINE	N-MINT
❏ 1 Moebius	1.00	0.60	1.80	3.00
❏ 2 Moebius	1.00	0.40	1.20	2.00

SISTERHOOD OF STEEL

	ORIG.	GOOD	FINE	N-MINT
❏ 1	1.50	0.30	0.90	1.50
❏ 2	1.50	0.30	0.90	1.50
❏ 3	1.50	0.30	0.90	1.50
❏ 4	1.50	0.30	0.90	1.50
❏ 5	1.50	0.30	0.90	1.50
❏ 6	1.50	0.30	0.90	1.50
❏ 7	1.50	0.30	0.90	1.50
❏ 8	1.50	0.30	0.90	1.50

SIX FROM SIRUS

	ORIG.	GOOD	FINE	N-MINT
❏ 1 PG	1.50	0.40	1.20	2.00
❏ 2 PG	1.50	0.40	1.20	2.00
❏ 3 PG	1.50	0.40	1.20	2.00
❏ 4 PG	1.50	0.40	1.20	2.00

SIX FROM SIRUS II

	ORIG.	GOOD	FINE	N-MINT
❏ 1	1.75	0.35	1.05	1.75
❏ 2	1.75	0.35	1.05	1.75
❏ 3	1.75	0.35	1.05	1.75
❏ 4	1.75	0.35	1.05	1.75

SLEEZE BROTHERS, THE (1989-90)

	ORIG.	GOOD	FINE	N-MINT
❏ 1	1.75	0.35	1.05	1.75
❏ 2	1.75	0.35	1.05	1.75
❏ 3	1.75	0.35	1.05	1.75
❏ 4	1.75	0.35	1.05	1.75
❏ 5	1.75	0.35	1.05	1.75
❏ 6	1.75	0.35	1.05	1.75

SLEEZE BROTHERS, THE (1991)

	ORIG.	GOOD	FINE	N-MINT
❏ nn	3.95	0.79	2.37	3.95

SPYKE

	ORIG.	GOOD	FINE	N-MINT
❏ 1 embossed cover	2.50	0.50	1.50	2.50
❏ 2	1.95	0.39	1.17	1.95
❏ 3	1.95	0.39	1.17	1.95

ST. GEORGE

	ORIG.	GOOD	FINE	N-MINT
❏ 1	1.25	0.25	0.75	1.25
❏ 2	1.25	0.25	0.75	1.25
❏ 3	1.50	0.30	0.90	1.50
❏ 4	1.50	0.30	0.90	1.50
❏ 5	1.50	0.30	0.90	1.50
❏ 6	1.50	0.30	0.90	1.50
❏ 7	1.50	0.30	0.90	1.50
❏ 8	1.50	0.30	0.90	1.50

STALKERS

	ORIG.	GOOD	FINE	N-MINT
❏ 1	1.50	0.30	0.90	1.50
❏ 2	1.50	0.30	0.90	1.50
❏ 3	1.50	0.30	0.90	1.50
❏ 4	1.50	0.30	0.90	1.50
❏ 5	1.50	0.30	0.90	1.50
❏ 6	1.50	0.30	0.90	1.50
❏ 7	1.50	0.30	0.90	1.50
❏ 8	1.50	0.30	0.90	1.50
❏ 9	1.50	0.30	0.90	1.50
❏ 10	1.50	0.30	0.90	1.50
❏ 11	1.50	0.30	0.90	1.50
❏ 12	1.50	0.30	0.90	1.50

STARSTRUCK

	ORIG.	GOOD	FINE	N-MINT
❏ 1 MK	1.50	0.30	0.90	1.50
❏ 2 MK	1.50	0.30	0.90	1.50
❏ 3 MK	1.50	0.30	0.90	1.50
❏ 4 MK	1.50	0.30	0.90	1.50
❏ 5 MK	1.50	0.30	0.90	1.50
❏ 6 MK	1.50	0.30	0.90	1.50

STEELGRIP STARKEY

	ORIG.	GOOD	FINE	N-MINT
❏ 1	1.50	0.30	0.90	1.50
❏ 2	1.50	0.30	0.90	1.50
❏ 3	1.50	0.30	0.90	1.50
❏ 4	1.50	0.30	0.90	1.50
❏ 5	1.50	0.30	0.90	1.50
❏ 6	1.75	0.35	1.05	1.75

STRAY TOASTERS

	ORIG.	GOOD	FINE	N-MINT
❏ 1 BSz	3.50	0.70	2.10	3.50
❏ 2 BSz	3.50	0.70	2.10	3.50
❏ 3 BSz	3.50	0.70	2.10	3.50
❏ 4 BSz	3.50	0.70	2.10	3.50

SWORDS OF THE SWASHBUCKLERS

	ORIG.	GOOD	FINE	N-MINT
❏ 1	1.50	0.40	1.20	2.00
❏ 2	1.50	0.30	0.90	1.50

Top-right of second column (continued entries before SLEEZE BROTHERS 1991):

	ORIG.	GOOD	FINE	N-MINT
❏ 4	1.75	0.35	1.05	1.75
❏ 5	1.75	0.35	1.05	1.75
❏ 6	1.75	0.35	1.05	1.75

	ORIG.	GOOD	FINE	N-MINT
3	1.50	0.30	0.90	1.50
4	1.50	0.30	0.90	1.50
5	1.50	0.30	0.90	1.50
6	1.50	0.30	0.90	1.50
7	1.50	0.30	0.90	1.50
8	1.50	0.30	0.90	1.50
9	1.50	0.30	0.90	1.50
10	1.50	0.30	0.90	1.50
11	1.50	0.30	0.90	1.50
12	1.75	0.35	1.05	1.75

TEKWORLD

	ORIG.	GOOD	FINE	N-MINT
1	1.75	0.60	1.80	3.00
2	1.75	0.50	1.50	2.50
3	1.75	0.40	1.20	2.00
4	1.75	0.40	1.20	2.00
5	1.75	0.40	1.20	2.00
6	1.75	0.35	1.05	1.75
7	1.75	0.35	1.05	1.75
8	1.75	0.35	1.05	1.75
9	1.75	0.35	1.05	1.75
10	1.75	0.35	1.05	1.75
11	1.75	0.35	1.05	1.75
12	1.75	0.35	1.05	1.75
13	1.75	0.35	1.05	1.75

TIMESPIRITS

	ORIG.	GOOD	FINE	N-MINT
1	1.50	0.30	0.90	1.50
2	1.50	0.30	0.90	1.50
3	1.50	0.30	0.90	1.50
4	1.50	0.30	0.90	1.50
5	1.50	0.30	0.90	1.50
6	1.50	0.30	0.90	1.50
7	1.50	0.30	0.90	1.50
8	1.50	0.30	0.90	1.50

TOMB OF DRACULA

	ORIG.	GOOD	FINE	N-MINT
1 GC,AW	4.95	0.99	2.97	4.95
2 GC,AW	4.95	0.99	2.97	4.95
3 GC,AW	4.95	0.99	2.97	4.95
4 GC,AW	4.95	0.99	2.97	4.95

TOMORROW KNIGHTS

	ORIG.	GOOD	FINE	N-MINT
1	1.95	0.39	1.17	1.95
2	1.50	0.30	0.90	1.50
3	1.50	0.30	0.90	1.50
4	1.50	0.30	0.90	1.50
5	1.50	0.30	0.90	1.50
6	1.50	0.30	0.90	1.50

TRANSMUTATION OF IKE GARUDA, THE

	ORIG.	GOOD	FINE	N-MINT
1	3.95	0.79	2.37	3.95
2	3.95	0.79	2.37	3.95

TROUBLE WITH GIRLS

	ORIG.	GOOD	FINE	N-MINT
1 embossed cover	2.50	0.50	1.50	2.50
2	1.95	0.39	1.17	1.95
3	1.95	0.39	1.17	1.95
4	1.95	0.39	1.17	1.95

UNTAMED

	ORIG.	GOOD	FINE	N-MINT
1 embossed cover	2.50	0.50	1.50	2.50
2	1.95	0.39	1.17	1.95

VIDEO JACK

	ORIG.	GOOD	FINE	N-MINT
1 KG	1.25	0.25	0.75	1.25
2 KG	1.25	0.25	0.75	1.25
3 KG	1.25	0.25	0.75	1.25
4 KG	1.25	0.25	0.75	1.25
5 KG	1.25	0.25	0.75	1.25
6 KG	1.25	0.25	0.75	1.25
6 KG,FH,JS,WS		0.25	0.75	

VOID INDIGO

	ORIG.	GOOD	FINE	N-MINT
1 VM	1.50	0.70	2.10	3.50
2 VM	1.50	0.70	2.10	3.50

WEAVEWORLD

	ORIG.	GOOD	FINE	N-MINT
1 Clive Barker	4.95	0.99	2.97	4.95
2 Clive Barker	4.95	0.99	2.97	4.95
3 Clive Barker	4.95	0.99	2.97	4.95

WILD CARDS

	ORIG.	GOOD	FINE	N-MINT
1	4.50	0.90	2.70	4.50
2	4.50	0.90	2.70	4.50
3	4.50	0.90	2.70	4.50
4	4.50	0.90	2.70	4.50

MARVEL

2001

	ORIG.	GOOD	FINE	N-MINT
1 JK	0.30			
2 JK	0.30			
3 JK	0.30			
4 JK	0.30			
5 JK	0.30			
6 JK	0.30			
7 JK	0.30			
8 JK	0.30			
9 JK	0.30			
10 JK	0.30			

2010

	ORIG.	GOOD	FINE	N-MINT
1 movie	0.75	0.20	0.60	1.00
2 movie	0.75	0.20	0.60	1.00

2099 UNLIMITED

	ORIG.	GOOD	FINE	N-MINT
1	3.95	1.00	3.00	5.00
2	3.95	0.79	2.37	3.95

ADVENTURE INTO FEAR (see Fear)

ADVENTURES IN READING STARRING: THE AMAZING SPIDER-MAN

	ORIG.	GOOD	FINE	N-MINT
1 giveaway		0.20	0.60	1.00

ADVENTURES OF CAPTAIN AMERICA

	ORIG.	GOOD	FINE	N-MINT
1 O:Capt. America	4.95	1.20	3.60	6.00
2 O:Capt. America	4.95	0.99	2.97	4.95
3 O:Capt. America	4.95	0.99	2.97	4.95
4 O:Capt. America	4.95	0.99	2.97	4.95

	ORIG.	GOOD	FINE	N-MINT

ADVENTURES OF KOOL-AID MAN

	ORIG.	GOOD	FINE	N-MINT
nn, giveaway		0.20	0.60	1.00

ADVENTURES OF QUIK BUNNY

	ORIG.	GOOD	FINE	N-MINT
nn, giveaway				

ADVENTURES OF THE THING

	ORIG.	GOOD	FINE	N-MINT
1 reprint	1.25	0.25	0.75	1.25
2 reprint	1.25	0.25	0.75	1.25
3 reprint	1.25	0.25	0.75	1.25
4 reprint	1.25	0.25	0.75	1.25

AIR RAIDERS (Was Star Comic)

	ORIG.	GOOD	FINE	N-MINT
3	1.00	0.20	0.60	1.00
4	1.00	0.20	0.60	1.00
5	1.00	0.20	0.60	1.00

ALF

	ORIG.	GOOD	FINE	N-MINT
1 TV series	1.00	1.00	3.00	5.00
2	1.00	0.50	1.50	2.50
3	1.00	0.50	1.50	2.50
4	1.00	0.30	0.90	1.50
5	1.00	0.30	0.90	1.50
6	1.00	0.20	0.60	1.00
7	1.00	0.20	0.60	1.00
8	1.00	0.20	0.60	1.00
9	1.00	0.20	0.60	1.00
10	1.00	0.20	0.60	1.00
11	1.00	0.20	0.60	1.00
12	1.00	0.20	0.60	1.00
13	1.00	0.20	0.60	1.00
14	1.00	0.20	0.60	1.00
15	1.00	0.20	0.60	1.00
16	1.00	0.20	0.60	1.00
17	1.00	0.20	0.60	1.00
18	1.00	0.20	0.60	1.00
19	1.00	0.20	0.60	1.00
20	1.00	0.20	0.60	1.00
21	1.00	0.20	0.60	1.00
22 X-Men parody	1.00	0.20	0.60	1.00
23	1.00	0.20	0.60	1.00
24	1.00	0.20	0.60	1.00
25	1.00	0.20	0.60	1.00
26	1.00	0.20	0.60	1.00
27	1.00	0.20	0.60	1.00
28	1.00	0.20	0.60	1.00
29 "3-D" cover	1.00	0.20	0.60	1.00
30	1.00	0.20	0.60	1.00
31	1.00	0.20	0.60	1.00
32	1.00	0.20	0.60	1.00
33	1.00	0.20	0.60	1.00
34	1.00	0.20	0.60	1.00
35	1.00	0.20	0.60	1.00
36	1.00	0.20	0.60	1.00
37	1.00	0.20	0.60	1.00
38	1.00	0.20	0.60	1.00
39	1.00	0.20	0.60	1.00
40	1.00	0.20	0.60	1.00

	ORIG.	GOOD	FINE	N-MINT
41	1.00	0.20	0.60	1.00
42	1.00	0.20	0.60	1.00
43	1.00	0.20	0.60	1.00
44 X-Men parody	1.00	0.20	0.60	1.00
45	1.00	0.20	0.60	1.00
46	1.00	0.20	0.60	1.00
47	1.00	0.20	0.60	1.00
48	1.00	0.20	0.60	1.00
49	1.00	0.20	0.60	1.00
50	1.75	0.35	1.05	1.75

ALF ANNUAL

	ORIG.	GOOD	FINE	N-MINT
1 Evolutionary War	1.75	0.35	1.05	1.75
2 BSz(c)	2.00	0.40	1.20	2.00
3 TMNT parody	2.00	0.40	1.20	2.00

ALF COMICS MAGAZINE

	ORIG.	GOOD	FINE	N-MINT
1 digest	1.50	0.30	0.90	1.50
2 digest	1.50	0.30	0.90	1.50

ALF HOLIDAY SPECIAL

	ORIG.	GOOD	FINE	N-MINT
1	1.75	0.35	1.05	1.75
2	2.00	0.40	1.20	2.00

ALF SPRING SPECIAL

	ORIG.	GOOD	FINE	N-MINT
1	1.75	0.35	1.05	1.75

ALL ABOUT COLLECTING COMIC BOOKS

	ORIG.	GOOD	FINE	N-MINT
giveaway		0.20	0.60	1.00

ALPHA FLIGHT

	ORIG.	GOOD	FINE	N-MINT
1 JBy, 1:Puck, Marrina	1.00	1.20	3.60	6.00
2 JBy	0.60	0.70	2.10	3.50
3 JBy	0.60	0.60	1.80	3.00
4 JBy	0.60	0.60	1.80	3.00
5 JBy	0.60	0.60	1.80	3.00
6 JBy	0.60	0.60	1.80	3.00
7 JBy	0.60	0.60	1.80	3.00
8 JBy	0.60	0.50	1.50	2.50
9 JBy	0.60	0.50	1.50	2.50
10 JBy	0.60	0.50	1.50	2.50
11 JBy	0.60	0.50	1.50	2.50
12 JBy D:Guardian	0.60	0.50	1.50	2.50
13 Wolverine	0.60	2.20	6.60	11.00
14	0.60	0.35	1.05	1.75
15	0.60	0.35	1.05	1.75
16	0.60	0.35	1.05	1.75
17 JByA:Wolverine	0.60	2.00	6.00	10.00
18 JBy	0.60	0.50	1.50	2.50
19 JBy, 1:Talisman	0.60	0.50	1.50	2.50
20 JBy	0.60	0.50	1.50	2.50
21 JBy	0.65	0.50	1.50	2.50
22 JBy	0.65	0.50	1.50	2.50
23 JBy	0.65	0.50	1.50	2.50
24 JBy	1.25	0.50	1.50	2.50
25 JBy	0.65	0.50	1.50	2.50
26 JBy	0.65	0.50	1.50	2.50
27 JBy	0.65	0.50	1.50	2.50
28 JBy Secret Wars II	0.65	0.50	1.50	2.50
29	0.65	0.50	1.50	2.50

	ORIG.	GOOD	FINE	N-MINT
30	0.65	0.50	1.50	2.50
31	0.75	0.50	1.50	2.50
32	0.75	0.50	1.50	2.50
33 Wolverine	0.75	1.60	4.80	8.00
34 Wolverine	0.75	1.60	4.80	8.00
35	0.75	0.40	1.20	2.00
36	0.75	0.40	1.20	2.00
37	0.75	0.40	1.20	2.00
38	0.75	0.40	1.20	2.00
39	0.75	0.40	1.20	2.00
40	0.75	0.40	1.20	2.00
41	0.75	0.40	1.20	2.00
42	0.75	0.40	1.20	2.00
43	0.75	0.40	1.20	2.00
44	0.75	0.40	1.20	2.00
45	0.75	0.40	1.20	2.00
46	0.75	0.40	1.20	2.00
47	0.75	0.40	1.20	2.00
48	0.75	0.40	1.20	2.00
49	0.75	0.40	1.20	2.00
50	1.25	0.50	1.50	2.50
51 JL (first Marvel)	0.75	3.00	9.00	15.00
52 Wolverine	1.00	1.60	4.80	8.00
53 Wolverine	1.00	1.60	4.80	8.00
54	1.00	0.80	2.40	4.00
55	1.00	0.80	2.40	4.00
56	1.00	0.80	2.40	4.00
57	1.00	0.80	2.40	4.00
58	1.00	0.80	2.40	4.00
59	1.00	0.80	2.40	4.00
60	1.25	0.80	2.40	4.00
61	1.25	0.40	1.20	2.00
62	1.25	0.40	1.20	2.00
63	1.25	0.40	1.20	2.00
64	1.25	0.40	1.20	2.00
65	1.50	0.40	1.20	2.00
66	1.50	0.40	1.20	2.00
67	1.50	0.40	1.20	2.00
68	1.50	0.40	1.20	2.00
69	1.50	0.40	1.20	2.00
70	1.50	0.40	1.20	2.00
71	1.50	0.40	1.20	2.00
72	1.50	0.40	1.20	2.00
73	1.50	0.40	1.20	2.00
74	1.50	0.40	1.20	2.00
75	1.95	0.39	1.17	1.95
76	1.50	0.30	0.90	1.50
77	1.95	0.39	1.17	1.95
78	1.50	0.30	0.90	1.50
79 Vengeance	1.50	0.50	1.50	2.50
80 Vengeance	1.50	0.50	1.50	2.50
81	1.50	0.30	0.90	1.50
82	1.50	0.30	0.90	1.50
83	1.50	0.30	0.90	1.50
84	1.50	0.30	0.90	1.50

	ORIG.	GOOD	FINE	N-MINT
85	1.50	0.30	0.90	1.50
86	1.50	0.30	0.90	1.50
87 Wolverine	1.50	1.20	3.60	6.00
88 Wolverine	1.50	0.80	2.40	4.00
89 Guardian returns, Wolverine	1.50	0.80	2.40	4.00
90	1.50	0.60	1.80	3.00
91 Dr. Doom	1.50	0.30	0.90	1.50
92	1.50	0.30	0.90	1.50
93	1.50	0.30	0.90	1.50
94 Fantastic 4	1.50	0.30	0.90	1.50
95	1.50	0.30	0.90	1.50
96	1.50	0.30	0.90	1.50
97	1.50	0.30	0.90	1.50
98	1.50	0.30	0.90	1.50
99	1.50	0.30	0.90	1.50
100	2.00	0.40	1.20	2.00
101	1.50	0.30	0.90	1.50
102	1.50	0.30	0.90	1.50
103	1.50	0.30	0.90	1.50
104	1.50	0.30	0.90	1.50
105	1.75	0.35	1.05	1.75
106 Northstar admits he's gay, 1st printing	1.75	3.00	9.00	15.00
106 2nd printing	1.75	0.80	2.40	4.00
107	1.75	0.35	1.05	1.75
108	1.75	0.35	1.05	1.75
109	1.75	0.35	1.05	1.75
110	1.75	0.35	1.05	1.75
111	1.75	0.35	1.05	1.75
112	1.75	0.35	1.05	1.75
113	1.75	0.35	1.05	1.75
114	1.75	0.35	1.05	1.75
115	1.75	0.35	1.05	1.75
116	1.75	0.35	1.05	1.75
117	1.75	0.35	1.05	1.75
118	1.75	0.35	1.05	1.75
119	1.75	0.35	1.05	1.75
120 with poster	2.25	0.45	1.35	2.25
121	1.75	0.35	1.05	1.75
122	1.75	0.35	1.05	1.75
123	1.75	0.35	1.05	1.75
124	1.75	0.35	1.05	1.75
125	1.75	0.35	1.05	1.75

ALPHA FLIGHT ANNUAL

	ORIG.	GOOD	FINE	N-MINT
1	1.25	0.25	0.75	1.25
2	1.25	0.25	0.75	1.25

ALPHA FLIGHT SPECIAL

	ORIG.	GOOD	FINE	N-MINT
nn (1992)	2.50	0.50	1.50	2.50

ALPHA FLIGHT SPECIAL (1991)

	ORIG.	GOOD	FINE	N-MINT
1 reprint	1.50	0.30	0.90	1.50
2 reprint	1.50	0.30	0.90	1.50
3 reprint	1.50	0.30	0.90	1.50
4 reprint	2.00	0.40	1.20	2.00

	ORIG.	GOOD	FINE	N-MINT
AMAZING ADVENTURES				
❑ 1 JK/JB, Inhumans 0.15		3.20	9.60	16.00
❑ 1 squarebound 0.15		0.99	2.97	4.95
❑ 2 .... 0.15		1.20	3.60	6.00
❑ 3 .... 0.15		1.20	3.60	6.00
❑ 4 .... 0.15		1.20	3.60	6.00
❑ 5 NA 0.15		1.20	3.60	6.00
❑ 6 NA 0.15		1.20	3.60	6.00
❑ 7 NA 0.15		1.20	3.60	6.00
❑ 8 NA 0.15		1.60	4.80	8.00
❑ 9 .... 0.20		1.00	3.00	5.00
❑ 10 .... 0.20		1.00	3.00	5.00
❑ 11 O:new Beast 0.20		3.60	10.80	18.00
❑ 12 .... 0.20		2.00	6.00	10.00
❑ 13 .... 0.20		2.00	6.00	10.00
❑ 14 .... 0.20		2.00	6.00	10.00
❑ 15 .... 0.20		2.00	6.00	10.00
❑ 16 .... 0.20		2.00	6.00	10.00
❑ 17 .... 0.20		2.00	6.00	10.00
❑ 18 HC/NA, I:Killraven 0.20		3.00	9.00	15.00
❑ 19 Killraven 0.20		0.80	2.40	4.00
❑ 20 Killraven 0.20		0.80	2.40	4.00
❑ 21 Killraven 0.20		0.80	2.40	4.00
❑ 22 Killraven 0.20		0.80	2.40	4.00
❑ 23 Killraven 0.20		0.80	2.40	4.00
❑ 24 Killraven 0.25		0.80	2.40	4.00
❑ 25 Killraven 0.25		0.80	2.40	4.00
❑ 26 Killraven 0.25		0.80	2.40	4.00
❑ 27 CR/JSn, Killraven 0.25		0.80	2.40	4.00
❑ 28 CR, Killraven 0.25		0.40	1.20	2.00
❑ 29 CR, Killraven 0.25		0.40	1.20	2.00
❑ 30 CR, Killraven 0.25		0.40	1.20	2.00
❑ 31 CR, Killraven 0.25		0.40	1.20	2.00
❑ 32 CR, Killraven 0.25		0.25	0.75	1.25
❑ 33 CR, Killraven 0.25		0.25	0.75	1.25
❑ 34 CR, Killraven 0.25		0.25	0.75	1.25
❑ 35 CR, Killraven 0.25		0.40	1.20	2.00
❑ 36 CR, Killraven 0.25		0.40	1.20	2.00
❑ 37 CR, O:Old Skull 0.25		0.25	0.75	1.25
❑ 38 CR, Killraven 0.30		0.40	1.20	2.00
❑ 39 CR, Killraven 0.30		0.40	1.20	2.00
AMAZING ADVENTURES (1988)				
❑ 1 .... 4.95		0.99	2.97	4.95
AMAZING ADVENTURES (2nd series)				
❑ 1 rep. X-Men #1 .... 0.40		0.25	0.75	1.25
❑ 2 all X-Men rep. 0.40		0.20	0.60	1.00
❑ 3 all X-Men rep.		0.20	0.60	1.00
❑ 4 all X-Men rep.		0.20	0.60	1.00
❑ 5 all X-Men rep.		0.20	0.60	1.00
❑ 6 all X-Men rep.		0.20	0.60	1.00
❑ 7 all X-Men rep.		0.20	0.60	1.00
❑ 8 all X-Men rep.		0.20	0.60	1.00
❑ 9 all X-Men rep.		0.20	0.60	1.00
❑ 10 all X-Men rep.		0.20	0.60	1.00

	ORIG.	GOOD	FINE	N-MINT
❑ 11 all X-Men rep. 0.50		0.20	0.60	1.00
❑ 12 all X-Men rep. 0.50		0.20	0.60	1.00
❑ 13 all X-Men rep. 0.50		0.20	0.60	1.00
❑ 14 all X-Men rep. 0.50		0.20	0.60	1.00
AMAZING FANTASY				
❑ 15 SD, 1&O:Spider-Man ... 0.12		2000.00	6000.00	10000.00
AMAZING HIGH ADVENTURE				
❑ 1 .... 2.00		0.50	1.50	2.50
❑ 2 .... 2.00		0.40	1.20	2.00
❑ 3 .... 2.00		0.40	1.20	2.00
❑ 4 .... 2.00		0.40	1.20	2.00
❑ 5 .... 2.00		0.40	1.20	2.00
AMAZING SPIDER-MAN				
❑ 1 SD, O:Spider-Man 0.12		1800.00	5400.00	9000.00
❑ 2 SD, 1:Vulture 0.12		400.00	1200.00	2000.00
❑ 3 SD, 1:Dr. Octopus 0.12		240.00	720.00	1200.00
❑ 4 SD, 1:Sandman 0.12		160.00	480.00	800.00
❑ 5 .... 0.12		130.00	390.00	650.00
❑ 6 SD 0.12		120.00	360.00	600.00
❑ 7 SD 0.12		80.00	240.00	400.00
❑ 8 SD 0.12		80.00	240.00	400.00
❑ 9 SD 0.12		80.00	240.00	400.00
❑ 10 SD 0.12		80.00	240.00	400.00
❑ 11 SD 0.12		52.00	156.00	260.00
❑ 12 SD 0.12		52.00	156.00	260.00
❑ 13 .... 0.12		60.00	180.00	300.00
❑ 14 SD, 1:Green Goblin 0.12		200.00	600.00	1000.00
❑ 15 SD, 1:Kraven 0.12		52.00	156.00	260.00
❑ 16 .... 0.12		32.00	96.00	160.00
❑ 17 Green Goblin 0.12		60.00	180.00	300.00
❑ 18 SD 0.12		32.00	96.00	160.00
❑ 19 SD 0.12		32.00	96.00	160.00
❑ 20 SD, 1&O:Scorpion 0.12		32.00	96.00	160.00
❑ 21 SD 0.12		24.00	72.00	120.00
❑ 22 SD 0.12		24.00	72.00	120.00
❑ 23 SD 0.12		33.00	99.00	165.00
❑ 24 SD 0.12		24.00	72.00	120.00
❑ 25 SD 0.12		24.00	72.00	120.00
❑ 26 SD 0.12		24.00	72.00	120.00
❑ 27 SD 0.12		24.00	72.00	120.00
❑ 28 SD 0.12		24.00	72.00	120.00
❑ 29 SD 0.12		24.00	72.00	120.00
❑ 30 SD 0.12		24.00	72.00	120.00
❑ 31 SD 0.12		20.00	60.00	100.00
❑ 32 SD 0.12		20.00	60.00	100.00
❑ 33 SD 0.12		20.00	60.00	100.00
❑ 34 SD 0.12		20.00	60.00	100.00
❑ 35 SD 0.12		20.00	60.00	100.00
❑ 36 SD 0.12		20.00	60.00	100.00
❑ 37 SD 0.12		20.00	60.00	100.00
❑ 38 SD 0.12		20.00	60.00	100.00
❑ 39 Green Goblin 0.12		24.00	72.00	120.00
❑ 40 JR 0.12		30.00	90.00	150.00
❑ 41 JR 0.12		10.00	30.00	50.00

	ORIG.	GOOD	FINE	N-MINT
42 JR	0.12	10.00	30.00	50.00
43 JR	0.12	10.00	30.00	50.00
44 JR	0.12	10.00	30.00	50.00
45 JR	0.12	10.00	30.00	50.00
46 JR	0.12	10.00	30.00	50.00
47 JR	0.12	10.00	30.00	50.00
48 JR	0.12	10.00	30.00	50.00
49 JR	0.12	10.00	30.00	50.00
50 JR, 1:Kingpin	0.12	40.00	120.00	200.00
51	0.12	20.00	60.00	100.00
52	0.12	6.40	19.20	32.00
53	0.12	6.40	19.20	32.00
54	0.12	6.40	19.20	32.00
55	0.12	6.40	19.20	32.00
56	0.12	6.40	19.20	32.00
57	0.12	6.40	19.20	32.00
58	0.12	6.40	19.20	32.00
59	0.12	6.40	19.20	32.00
60	0.12	6.40	19.20	32.00
61	0.12	6.40	19.20	32.00
62	0.12	5.60	16.80	28.00
63	0.12	5.60	16.80	28.00
64	0.12	5.60	16.80	28.00
65	0.12	5.60	16.80	28.00
66	0.12	5.60	16.80	28.00
67	0.12	5.60	16.80	28.00
68	0.12	5.60	16.80	28.00
69	0.12	5.60	16.80	28.00
70	0.12	5.60	16.80	28.00
71	0.12	5.60	16.80	28.00
72	0.12	5.60	16.80	28.00
73	0.12	5.60	16.80	28.00
74	0.12	5.60	16.80	28.00
75	0.15	5.60	16.80	28.00
76	0.15	5.60	16.80	28.00
77	0.15	5.60	16.80	28.00
78	0.15	5.60	16.80	28.00
79	0.15	5.60	16.80	28.00
80	0.15	5.60	16.80	28.00
81	0.15	5.60	16.80	28.00
82	0.15	4.00	12.00	20.00
83	0.15	4.00	12.00	20.00
84	0.15	4.00	12.00	20.00
85	0.15	4.00	12.00	20.00
86	0.15	4.00	12.00	20.00
87	0.15	4.00	12.00	20.00
88	0.15	4.00	12.00	20.00
89	0.15	4.00	12.00	20.00
90 A:Dr. Octopus	0.15	6.00	18.00	30.00
91	0.15	4.00	12.00	20.00
92	0.15	4.00	12.00	20.00
93	0.15	4.00	12.00	20.00
94 JR/SB, A:Beetle	0.15	6.00	18.00	30.00
95 JR/SB	0.15	4.00	12.00	20.00
96	0.15	8.00	24.00	40.00

	ORIG.	GOOD	FINE	N-MINT
97	0.15	8.00	24.00	40.00
98	0.15	8.00	24.00	40.00
99 A:Johnny Carson	0.15	4.00	12.00	20.00
100 A:Green Goblin	0.15	20.00	60.00	100.00
101 GK, A:Morbius	0.15	30.00	90.00	150.00
101 1:Morbius, reprint	1.75	0.35	1.05	1.75
102 GK, A:Morbius	0.25	18.00	54.00	90.00
103	0.20	3.00	9.00	15.00
104	0.20	3.00	9.00	15.00
105	0.20	3.00	9.00	15.00
106	0.20	3.00	9.00	15.00
107	0.20	3.00	9.00	15.00
108	0.20	3.00	9.00	15.00
109	0.20	3.00	9.00	15.00
110	0.20	3.00	9.00	15.00
111	0.20	3.00	9.00	15.00
112	0.20	3.00	9.00	15.00
113 JR/JSn	0.20	3.00	9.00	15.00
114 JR/JSn	0.20	3.00	9.00	15.00
115 JR	0.20	2.80	8.40	14.00
116 JR	0.20	2.80	8.40	14.00
117 JR	0.20	2.80	8.40	14.00
118 JR	0.20	2.80	8.40	14.00
119 Hulk	0.20	3.20	9.60	16.00
120 Hulk	0.20	2.80	8.40	14.00
121 A:Green Goblin	0.20	24.00	72.00	120.00
122 A:Green Goblin	0.20	24.00	72.00	120.00
123 Power Man	0.20	3.60	10.80	18.00
124	0.20	2.80	8.40	14.00
125	0.20	2.80	8.40	14.00
126	0.20	2.80	8.40	14.00
127	0.20	2.80	8.40	14.00
128	0.20	2.80	8.40	14.00
129 RA, 1:Punisher	0.20	70.00	210.00	350.00
130	0.20	2.80	8.40	14.00
131	0.20	2.80	8.40	14.00
132	0.25	2.80	8.40	14.00
133	0.25	2.80	8.40	14.00
134 Punisher cameo	0.25	8.00	24.00	40.00
135 Punisher	0.25	9.00	27.00	45.00
136 Green Goblin	0.25	8.00	24.00	40.00
137	0.25	2.80	8.40	14.00
138	0.25	2.80	8.40	14.00
139	0.25	2.80	8.40	14.00
140	0.25	2.80	8.40	14.00
141	0.25	2.80	8.40	14.00
142	0.25	2.80	8.40	14.00
143	0.25	2.80	8.40	14.00
144	0.25	2.80	8.40	14.00
145	0.25	2.80	8.40	14.00
146	0.25	2.80	8.40	14.00
147	0.25	2.80	8.40	14.00
148	0.25	2.80	8.40	14.00
149	0.25	2.80	8.40	14.00
150	0.25	2.80	8.40	14.00

	ORIG.	GOOD	FINE	N-MINT
151	0.25	2.40	7.20	12.00
152	0.25	2.40	7.20	12.00
153	0.25	2.40	7.20	12.00
154	0.25	2.40	7.20	12.00
155	0.25	2.40	7.20	12.00
156	0.25	2.40	7.20	12.00
157	0.25	2.40	7.20	12.00
158	0.25	2.40	7.20	12.00
159	0.25	2.40	7.20	12.00
160	0.30	2.40	7.20	12.00
161 A:Nightcrawler	0.30	4.80	14.40	24.00
162 A:Punisher	0.30	8.00	24.00	40.00
163	0.30	1.60	4.80	8.00
164	0.30	1.60	4.80	8.00
165	0.30	1.60	4.80	8.00
166	0.30	1.60	4.80	8.00
167	0.30	1.60	4.80	8.00
168	0.30	1.60	4.80	8.00
169	0.30	1.60	4.80	8.00
170	0.30	1.60	4.80	8.00
171	0.30	1.60	4.80	8.00
172	0.30	1.60	4.80	8.00
173	0.30	1.60	4.80	8.00
174	0.35	4.00	12.00	20.00
175	0.35	4.00	12.00	20.00
176	0.35	1.60	4.80	8.00
177	0.35	1.60	4.80	8.00
178	0.35	1.60	4.80	8.00
179	0.35	1.60	4.80	8.00
180	0.35	1.60	4.80	8.00
181	0.35	1.40	4.20	7.00
182	0.35	1.40	4.20	7.00
183	0.35	1.40	4.20	7.00
184	0.35	1.40	4.20	7.00
185	0.35	1.40	4.20	7.00
186	0.35	1.40	4.20	7.00
187	0.35	1.40	4.20	7.00
188	0.35	1.40	4.20	7.00
189 JB, A:Man-Wolf	0.35	1.40	4.20	7.00
190 JB, A:Man-Wolf	0.35	1.40	4.20	7.00
191	0.35	1.40	4.20	7.00
192	0.40	1.40	4.20	7.00
193	0.40	1.40	4.20	7.00
194 1:Black Cat	0.40	1.40	4.20	7.00
195	0.40	1.40	4.20	7.00
196	0.40	1.40	4.20	7.00
197	0.40	1.40	4.20	7.00
198	0.40	1.40	4.20	7.00
199	0.40	1.40	4.20	7.00
200 RP, O:Spider-Man	0.75	6.00	18.00	30.00
201 RP, A:Punisher	0.40	5.00	15.00	25.00
202 RP, A:Punisher	0.40	5.00	15.00	25.00
203 RP, A:Dazzler	0.40	1.00	3.00	5.00
204 A:Black Cat	0.40	1.00	3.00	5.00
205 A:Black Cat	0.40	1.00	3.00	5.00
206	0.40	1.00	3.00	5.00
207	0.40	1.00	3.00	5.00
208	0.50	1.00	3.00	5.00
209	0.50	1.00	3.00	5.00
210	0.50	1.00	3.00	5.00
211	0.50	1.00	3.00	5.00
212	0.50	1.00	3.00	5.00
213	0.50	1.00	3.00	5.00
214	0.50	1.00	3.00	5.00
215	0.50	1.00	3.00	5.00
216	0.50	1.00	3.00	5.00
217	0.50	1.00	3.00	5.00
218	0.50	1.00	3.00	5.00
219	0.50	1.00	3.00	5.00
220 A:Moon Knight	0.50	1.00	3.00	5.00
221	0.50	1.00	3.00	5.00
222	0.50	1.00	3.00	5.00
223	0.50	1.00	3.00	5.00
224	0.60	1.00	3.00	5.00
225	0.60	1.00	3.00	5.00
226 JR2, Black Cat	0.60	1.00	3.00	5.00
227 JR2, Black Cat	0.60	1.00	3.00	5.00
228 JR2	0.60	1.00	3.00	5.00
229 JR2	0.60	1.00	3.00	5.00
230 JR2	0.60	1.00	3.00	5.00
231 JR2	0.60	1.00	3.00	5.00
232 JR2	0.60	1.00	3.00	5.00
233 JR2	0.60	1.00	3.00	5.00
234	0.60	1.00	3.00	5.00
235	0.60	1.00	3.00	5.00
236	0.60	1.00	3.00	5.00
237	0.60	1.00	3.00	5.00
238 1:Hobgoblin	0.60	10.00	30.00	50.00
239	0.60	4.80	14.40	24.00
240	0.60	1.00	3.00	5.00
241	0.60	1.00	3.00	5.00
242	0.60	1.00	3.00	5.00
243	0.60	1.00	3.00	5.00
244	0.60	1.60	4.80	8.00
245	0.60	1.60	4.80	8.00
246	0.60	1.00	3.00	5.00
247	0.60	1.00	3.00	5.00
248	0.60	1.00	3.00	5.00
249	0.60	1.60	4.80	8.00
250	0.60	2.00	6.00	10.00
251	0.60	1.60	4.80	8.00
252 new costume	0.60	3.60	10.80	18.00
253 Rose	0.60	2.40	7.20	12.00
254	0.60	1.20	3.60	6.00
255	0.60	1.20	3.60	6.00
256	0.60	1.20	3.60	6.00
257	0.60	1.20	3.60	6.00
258	0.60	1.20	3.60	6.00
259	0.60	1.20	3.60	6.00
260	0.60	1.20	3.60	6.00

	ORIG.	GOOD	FINE	N-MINT
261	0.60	1.20	3.60	6.00
262	0.60	1.20	3.60	6.00
263	0.65	1.00	3.00	5.00
264	0.65	1.00	3.00	5.00
265 1:Silver Sable	0.65	3.20	9.60	16.00
265 2nd printing	1.25	0.25	0.75	1.25
266	0.65	1.00	3.00	5.00
267	0.65	1.00	3.00	5.00
268 Secret Wars II	0.65	1.00	3.00	5.00
269	0.65	1.00	3.00	5.00
270	0.65	1.00	3.00	5.00
271	0.65	1.00	3.00	5.00
272	0.65	1.00	3.00	5.00
273 Secret Wars II	0.75	2.00	6.00	10.00
274 Secret Wars II	0.75	1.00	3.00	5.00
275 O:Spider-Man	1.25	1.60	4.80	8.00
276	0.75	0.80	2.40	4.00
277	0.75	0.80	2.40	4.00
278	0.75	0.50	1.50	2.50
279	0.75	0.80	2.40	4.00
280	0.75	0.80	2.40	4.00
281	0.75	0.80	2.40	4.00
282	0.75	0.80	2.40	4.00
283	0.75	0.80	2.40	4.00
284 A:Punisher	0.75	3.00	9.00	15.00
285 Punisher	0.75	4.00	12.00	20.00
286	0.75	1.60	4.80	8.00
287 Erik Larsen	0.75	2.40	7.20	12.00
288	0.75	1.60	4.80	8.00
289 Hobgoblin unmasked	1.25	5.60	16.80	28.00
290 proposal	0.75	1.40	4.20	7.00
291	0.75	1.20	3.60	6.00
292	0.75	1.20	3.60	6.00
293 V:Kraven	0.75	2.00	6.00	10.00
294 V:Kraven	0.75	2.00	6.00	10.00
295 BSz(c)	0.75	1.00	3.00	5.00
296 V:Dr. Octopus	0.75	1.00	3.00	5.00
297 V:Dr. Octopus	0.75	1.00	3.00	5.00
298 TMc	0.75	8.00	24.00	40.00
299 TMc	0.75	7.20	21.60	36.00
300 TMc	1.50	15.00	45.00	75.00
301 TMc	1.00	4.00	12.00	20.00
302 TMc	1.00	4.00	12.00	20.00
303 TMc	1.00	4.00	12.00	20.00
304 TMc	1.00	4.00	12.00	20.00
305 TMc	1.00	4.00	12.00	20.00
306 TMc	1.00	3.00	9.00	15.00
307 TMc	1.00	3.00	9.00	15.00
308 TMc	1.00	3.00	9.00	15.00
309 TMc	1.00	3.00	9.00	15.00
310 TMc	1.00	3.00	9.00	15.00
311 TMc Inferno	1.00	2.40	7.20	12.00
312 TMc Inferno	1.00	2.40	7.20	12.00
313 TMc Inferno	1.00	2.40	7.20	12.00
314 TMc	1.00	2.40	7.20	12.00

	ORIG.	GOOD	FINE	N-MINT
315 TMc	1.00	2.40	7.20	12.00
316 TMc	1.00	3.60	10.80	18.00
317 TMc	1.00	3.20	9.60	16.00
318 TMc	1.00	3.20	9.60	16.00
319 TMc	1.00	2.40	7.20	12.00
320 TMc	1.00	2.00	6.00	10.00
321 TMc	1.00	2.00	6.00	10.00
322 TMc	1.00	2.00	6.00	10.00
323 TMc	1.00	2.00	6.00	10.00
324 TMc(c)	1.00	2.00	6.00	10.00
325 TMc	1.00	2.00	6.00	10.00
326 vengeance	1.00	1.00	3.00	5.00
327 vengeance, cosmic Spider-Man	1.00	1.20	3.60	6.00
328 TMc vengeance, Hulk	1.00	2.40	7.20	12.00
329 vengeance	1.00	1.60	4.80	8.00
330 Punisher	1.00	1.60	4.80	8.00
331 Punisher	1.00	1.60	4.80	8.00
332 Venom	1.00	2.00	6.00	10.00
333 Venom	1.00	2.00	6.00	10.00
334 Sinister Six	1.00	1.00	3.00	5.00
335 Sinister Six	1.00	0.60	1.80	3.00
336 Sinister Six	1.00	0.40	1.20	2.00
337 Sinister Six	1.00	0.40	1.20	2.00
338 Sinister Six	1.00	0.40	1.20	2.00
339 Sinister Six	1.00	0.40	1.20	2.00
340	1.00	0.40	1.20	2.00
341 Powerless	1.00	0.40	1.20	2.00
342 Powerless	1.00	0.40	1.20	2.00
343	1.00	0.40	1.20	2.00
344 Carnage(?)	1.00	2.40	7.20	12.00
345 Carnage	1.00	3.00	9.00	15.00
346 Venom	1.00	1.60	4.80	8.00
347 Venom	1.00	1.60	4.80	8.00
348 Avengers	1.00	0.40	1.20	2.00
349	1.00	0.40	1.20	2.00
350 V:Dr. Doom	1.50	0.60	1.80	3.00
351	1.00	0.30	0.90	1.50
352	1.00	0.30	0.90	1.50
353	1.00	0.30	0.90	1.50
354	1.00	0.30	0.90	1.50
355 Punisher, Moon Knight, others	1.00	0.30	0.90	1.50
356 Punisher, Moon Knight, others	1.00	0.30	0.90	1.50
357 Punisher, Moon Knight, others	1.00	0.30	0.90	1.50
358 Punisher, Moon Knight, others	1.00	0.30	0.90	1.50
359	1.25	0.30	0.90	1.50
360	1.25	0.30	0.90	1.50
361 Carnage	1.25	4.00	12.00	20.00
361 2nd printing	1.25	0.80	2.40	4.00
362 Carnage	1.25	2.00	6.00	10.00
362 2nd printing	1.25	0.25	0.75	1.25

	ORIG.	GOOD	FINE	N-MINT
363 Carnage	1.25	1.20	3.60	6.00
364	1.25	0.25	0.75	1.25
365 hologram cover	3.95	0.79	2.37	3.95
366	1.25	0.25	0.75	1.25
367	1.25	0.25	0.75	1.25
368	1.25	0.25	0.75	1.25
369	1.25	0.25	0.75	1.25
370	1.25	0.25	0.75	1.25
371	1.25	0.25	0.75	1.25
372	1.25	0.25	0.75	1.25
373	1.25	0.25	0.75	1.25
374	1.25	0.25	0.75	1.25
375 foil cover	1.25	0.79	2.37	3.95
376	1.25	0.25	0.75	1.25
377	1.25	0.25	0.75	1.25
378 Maximum Carnage	1.25	0.25	0.75	1.25
379 Maximum Carnage	1.25	0.25	0.75	1.25
380 Maximum Carnage	1.25	0.25	0.75	1.25
381 Hulk	1.25	0.25	0.75	1.25
382	1.25	0.25	0.75	1.25

AMAZING SPIDER-MAN 30TH ANNIVERSARY POSTER MAGAZINE

	3.95	0.79	2.37	3.95

AMAZING SPIDER-MAN ANNUAL/SPECIAL

	ORIG.	GOOD	FINE	N-MINT
1 SD, 1:Sinister Six	0.25	72.00	216.00	360.00
2 SD, reprint	0.25	30.00	90.00	150.00
3	0.25	14.00	42.00	70.00
4	0.25	12.00	36.00	60.00
5 JR, A:Red Skull	0.25	7.00	21.00	35.00
5 (Peter's Parents)	0.25	13.00	39.00	65.00
6 reprint	0.25	2.00	6.00	10.00
7 reprint	0.25	2.00	6.00	10.00
8 reprint	0.25	2.00	6.00	10.00
9 reprint	0.35	1.60	4.80	8.00
10 GK, A:Human Fly	0.50	1.60	4.80	8.00
11	0.50	1.60	4.80	8.00
12 reprint	0.60	1.20	3.60	6.00
13 JBy/TA	0.75	1.20	3.60	6.00
14 FM	0.75	2.40	7.20	12.00
15 FM, Punisher	0.75	6.00	18.00	30.00
16 1:new Captain Marvel	1.00	1.00	3.00	5.00
17	1.00	0.80	2.40	4.00
18	1.00	0.80	2.40	4.00
19	1.25	0.80	2.40	4.00
20	1.25	0.80	2.40	4.00
21 W:SM direct-sale	1.25	1.40	4.20	7.00
21 W:SM newsstand	1.25	1.40	4.20	7.00
22 Evolutionary War, 1:Speedball, A:Daredevil	1.75	1.40	4.20	7.00
23 Atlantis Attacks	2.00	0.80	2.40	4.00
24 GK, SD, Ant-Man	2.00	0.60	1.80	3.00
25 Vibranium Vendetta	2.00	0.40	1.20	2.00
26	2.25	0.45	1.35	2.25
27 trading card	2.95	0.59	1.77	2.95

AMAZING SPIDER-MAN GIVEAWAYS

	ORIG.	GOOD	FINE	N-MINT
nn, child abuse, with New Mutants				
nn, Crisis at Cape Canaveral				
nn, Spider-Man vs. Dr. Octopus				
1 (two different, both #1)				

AMAZING SPIDER-MAN MANAGING MATERIALS

nn giveaway		0.20	0.60	1.00

AMAZING SPIDER-MAN VS. THE PRODIGY!, THE

Planned Parenthood giveaway, miniature				

AMAZING SPIDER-MAN: CHAOS IN CALGARY

4	1.50	0.30	0.90	1.50

AMAZING SPIDER-MAN: DOUBLE TROUBLE!

2	1.50	0.30	0.90	1.50

AMAZING SPIDER-MAN: HIT AND RUN!

3	1.50	0.30	0.90	1.50

AMAZING SPIDER-MAN: SKATING ON THIN ICE!

1	1.50	0.30	0.90	1.50

AMAZING SPIDER-MAN: SOUL OF THE HUNTER

nn	5.95	1.19	3.57	5.95

AMAZING SPIDER-MAN: THE BIRTH OF A SUPER HERO!, THE

small reprint; was attached to Eye magazine				

AN AMERICAN TAIL: FIEVEL GOES WEST

1 movie	1.00	0.20	0.60	1.00
2 movie	1.00	0.20	0.60	1.00
3 movie	1.00	0.20	0.60	1.00

ANNIE

1 movie story	0.60	0.20	0.60	1.00
2 movie story	0.60	0.20	0.60	1.00

ASTONISHING TALES

1 JK/WW, Ka-Zar, Dr. Doom	0.15	3.60	10.80	18.00
2 JK/WW, Ka-Zar/Dr. Doom	0.15 / 2.40	7.20	12.00	
3 Ka-Zar, Dr. Doom	0.15	3.00	9.00	15.00
4 Ka-Zar, Dr. Doom	0.15	3.00	9.00	15.00
5 Ka-Zar, Dr. Doom	0.15	3.00	9.00	15.00
6 Ka-Zar, Dr. Doom	0.15	3.00	9.00	15.00
7 Ka-Zar/Dr. Doom	0.15	2.00	6.00	10.00
8 Ka-Zar/Dr. Doom	0.25	2.00	6.00	10.00
9 Ka-Zar/Dr. Doom	0.20	2.00	6.00	10.00
10 SB/BS, Ka-Zar/Dr. Doom	0.20	1.60	4.80	8.00
11	0.20	1.20	3.60	6.00
12	0.20	1.20	3.60	6.00
13	0.20	0.60	1.80	3.00
14	0.20	0.60	1.80	3.00
15	0.20	0.60	1.80	3.00
16	0.20	0.60	1.80	3.00
17	0.20	0.60	1.80	3.00
18	0.20	0.60	1.80	3.00
19	0.20	0.60	1.80	3.00
20	0.20	0.60	1.80	3.00

	ORIG.	GOOD	FINE	N-MINT
☐ 21	0.20	0.60	1.80	3.00
☐ 22	0.20	0.60	1.80	3.00
☐ 23	0.20	0.60	1.80	3.00
☐ 24	0.25	0.60	1.80	3.00
☐ 25 RB, O:Deathlok	0.25	18.00	54.00	90.00
☐ 26 Deathlok	0.25	7.00	21.00	35.00
☐ 27 Deathlok	0.25	6.00	18.00	30.00
☐ 28 Deathlok	0.25	6.00	18.00	30.00
☐ 29 1:Guardians of Galaxy				
	0.25	5.20	15.60	26.00
☐ 30 RB/KP Deathlok	0.25	3.20	9.60	16.00
☐ 31 Deathlok	0.25	3.20	9.60	16.00
☐ 32 Deathlok	0.25	3.20	9.60	16.00
☐ 33 Deathlok	0.25	3.20	9.60	16.00
☐ 34 Deathlok	0.25	3.20	9.60	16.00
☐ 35 Deathlok	0.25	3.20	9.60	16.00
☐ 36 Deathlok	0.25	3.20	9.60	16.00

AVENGERS

	ORIG.	GOOD	FINE	N-MINT
☐ 1 JK, origin	0.12	360.00	1080.00	1800.00
☐ 2 JK, Space Phantom	0.12	90.00	270.00	450.00
☐ 3 JK,	0.12	70.00	210.00	350.00
☐ 4 JK, Capt. America	0.12	160.00	480.00	800.00
☐ 5 JK, Hulk leaves	0.12	30.00	90.00	150.00
☐ 6 JK	0.12	30.00	90.00	150.00
☐ 7 JK	0.12	30.00	90.00	150.00
☐ 8 JK	0.12	30.00	90.00	150.00
☐ 9 JK, D:Wonder Man	0.12	36.00	108.00	180.00
☐ 10 JK, I:Hercules	0.12	28.00	84.00	140.00
☐ 11 JK, Spider-Man	0.12	18.00	54.00	90.00
☐ 12 JK	0.12	18.00	54.00	90.00
☐ 13 JK	0.12	18.00	54.00	90.00
☐ 14 JK	0.12	18.00	54.00	90.00
☐ 15 JK	0.12	18.00	54.00	90.00
☐ 16 JK	0.12	15.00	45.00	75.00
☐ 17 JK	0.12	10.00	30.00	50.00
☐ 18 JK	0.12	10.00	30.00	50.00
☐ 19 JK	0.12	10.00	30.00	50.00
☐ 20 JK/DH	0.12	7.00	21.00	35.00
☐ 21 JK/DH	0.12	7.00	21.00	35.00
☐ 22 JK/DH	0.12	7.00	21.00	35.00
☐ 23 JK/DH	0.12	6.00	18.00	30.00
☐ 24 JK/DH	0.12	6.00	18.00	30.00
☐ 25 JK/DH	0.12	6.00	18.00	30.00
☐ 26 JK/DH	0.12	6.00	18.00	30.00
☐ 27 JK/DH	0.12	6.00	18.00	30.00
☐ 28 JK/DH	0.12	6.00	18.00	30.00
☐ 29 JK/DH	0.12	6.00	18.00	30.00
☐ 30 JK/DH	0.12	6.00	18.00	30.00
☐ 31 JK/DH	0.12	6.00	18.00	30.00
☐ 32	0.12	4.00	12.00	20.00
☐ 33	0.12	4.00	12.00	20.00
☐ 34	0.12	4.00	12.00	20.00
☐ 35	0.12	4.00	12.00	20.00
☐ 36	0.12	4.00	12.00	20.00
☐ 37	0.12	4.00	12.00	20.00

	ORIG.	GOOD	FINE	N-MINT
☐ 38	0.12	4.00	12.00	20.00
☐ 39	0.12	4.00	12.00	20.00
☐ 40	0.12	4.00	12.00	20.00
☐ 41	0.12	2.40	7.20	12.00
☐ 42	0.12	2.40	7.20	12.00
☐ 43	0.12	2.40	7.20	12.00
☐ 44	0.12	2.40	7.20	12.00
☐ 45	0.12	2.40	7.20	12.00
☐ 46	0.12	2.40	7.20	12.00
☐ 47	0.12	2.40	7.20	12.00
☐ 48	0.12	2.40	7.20	12.00
☐ 49	0.12	2.40	7.20	12.00
☐ 50	0.12	2.40	7.20	12.00
☐ 51	0.12	2.40	7.20	12.00
☐ 52	0.12	2.40	7.20	12.00
☐ 53 JB, X-Men	0.12	3.00	9.00	15.00
☐ 54 JB	0.12	2.40	7.20	12.00
☐ 55 JB	0.12	2.40	7.20	12.00
☐ 56 JB	0.12	2.40	7.20	12.00
☐ 57 JB, 1:Vision	0.12	8.00	24.00	40.00
☐ 58 JB, O:Vision	0.12	6.00	18.00	30.00
☐ 59 JB	0.12	2.00	6.00	10.00
☐ 60 JB	0.12	2.00	6.00	10.00
☐ 61 JB	0.12	2.00	6.00	10.00
☐ 62	0.12	2.00	6.00	10.00
☐ 63	0.12	2.00	6.00	10.00
☐ 64	0.12	2.00	6.00	10.00
☐ 65	0.12	2.00	6.00	10.00
☐ 66 BS	0.15	2.80	8.40	14.00
☐ 67 BS	0.15	2.80	8.40	14.00
☐ 68	0.15	2.00	6.00	10.00
☐ 69	0.15	2.00	6.00	10.00
☐ 70	0.15	2.00	6.00	10.00
☐ 71 SB/SB, 1:Invaders	0.15	2.40	7.20	12.00
☐ 72	0.15	2.00	6.00	10.00
☐ 73	0.15	2.00	6.00	10.00
☐ 74	0.15	2.00	6.00	10.00
☐ 75	0.15	2.00	6.00	10.00
☐ 76	0.15	2.00	6.00	10.00
☐ 77	0.15	2.00	6.00	10.00
☐ 78	0.15	2.00	6.00	10.00
☐ 79	0.15	2.00	6.00	10.00
☐ 80	0.15	2.00	6.00	10.00
☐ 81	0.15	2.00	6.00	10.00
☐ 82	0.15	2.00	6.00	10.00
☐ 83 JB, 1:Valkyrie	0.15	2.00	6.00	10.00
☐ 84 JB	0.15	1.60	4.80	8.00
☐ 85 JB	0.15	1.60	4.80	8.00
☐ 86 JB	0.15	1.60	4.80	8.00
☐ 87 O:Black Panther	0.15	1.60	4.80	8.00
☐ 88 SB	0.15	1.60	4.80	8.00
☐ 89 SB	0.15	1.60	4.80	8.00
☐ 90 SB	0.15	1.60	4.80	8.00
☐ 91 SB	0.15	1.60	4.80	8.00
☐ 92 SB, NA(c)	0.15	1.60	4.80	8.00

	ORIG.	GOOD	FINE	N-MINT
❑ 93 NA	0.25	8.00	24.00	40.00
❑ 94 NA, 52 pages	0.20	4.80	14.40	24.00
❑ 95 NA	0.20	4.00	12.00	20.00
❑ 96 NA	0.20	4.00	12.00	20.00
❑ 97 SB/BEv/GK	0.20	2.40	7.20	12.00
❑ 98 BS	0.20	3.00	9.00	15.00
❑ 99 BS	0.20	3.00	9.00	15.00
❑ 100 BS	0.20	6.00	18.00	30.00
❑ 101	0.20	1.20	3.60	6.00
❑ 102	0.20	1.20	3.60	6.00
❑ 103	0.20	1.20	3.60	6.00
❑ 104	0.20	1.20	3.60	6.00
❑ 105	0.20	1.20	3.60	6.00
❑ 106	0.20	1.20	3.60	6.00
❑ 107 JS, DC	0.20	1.20	3.60	6.00
❑ 108	0.20	1.20	3.60	6.00
❑ 109	0.20	1.20	3.60	6.00
❑ 110 DH, X-Men	0.20	2.40	7.20	12.00
❑ 111 DH, X-Men	0.20	2.40	7.20	12.00
❑ 112 DH, 1:Mantis	0.20	1.60	4.80	8.00
❑ 113 Silver Surfer	0.20	1.60	4.80	8.00
❑ 114 Silver Surfer	0.20	1.60	4.80	8.00
❑ 115 Silver Surfer	0.20	1.60	4.80	8.00
❑ 116 Silver Surfer	0.20	1.60	4.80	8.00
❑ 117 Silver Surfer	0.20	1.60	4.80	8.00
❑ 118 Silver Surfer	0.20	1.60	4.80	8.00
❑ 119 Silver Surfer	0.20	1.60	4.80	8.00
❑ 120 DH/JSn	0.20	1.00	3.00	5.00
❑ 121	0.20	1.00	3.00	5.00
❑ 122	0.20	1.00	3.00	5.00
❑ 123	0.25	1.00	3.00	5.00
❑ 124	0.25	1.00	3.00	5.00
❑ 125	0.25	1.00	3.00	5.00
❑ 126	0.25	1.00	3.00	5.00
❑ 127	0.25	1.00	3.00	5.00
❑ 128	0.25	1.00	3.00	5.00
❑ 129	0.25	1.00	3.00	5.00
❑ 130	0.25	1.00	3.00	5.00
❑ 131 SB	0.25	1.00	3.00	5.00
❑ 132 SB	0.25	1.00	3.00	5.00
❑ 133 SB	0.25	1.00	3.00	5.00
❑ 134	0.25	1.00	3.00	5.00
❑ 135	0.25	1.00	3.00	5.00
❑ 136	0.25	1.00	3.00	5.00
❑ 137	0.25	1.00	3.00	5.00
❑ 138	0.25	1.00	3.00	5.00
❑ 139	0.25	1.00	3.00	5.00
❑ 140	0.25	1.00	3.00	5.00
❑ 141	0.25	1.00	3.00	5.00
❑ 142	0.25	0.80	2.40	4.00
❑ 143	0.25	0.80	2.40	4.00
❑ 144	0.25	0.80	2.40	4.00
❑ 145	0.25	0.80	2.40	4.00
❑ 146	0.25	0.80	2.40	4.00
❑ 147	0.25	0.80	2.40	4.00

	ORIG.	GOOD	FINE	N-MINT
❑ 148	0.25	0.80	2.40	4.00
❑ 149	0.25	0.80	2.40	4.00
❑ 150 GP	0.25	0.80	2.40	4.00
❑ 151	0.30	0.80	2.40	4.00
❑ 152	0.30	0.80	2.40	4.00
❑ 153	0.30	0.80	2.40	4.00
❑ 154	0.30	0.80	2.40	4.00
❑ 155	0.30	0.80	2.40	4.00
❑ 156	0.30	0.80	2.40	4.00
❑ 157	0.30	0.80	2.40	4.00
❑ 158	0.30	0.80	2.40	4.00
❑ 159	0.30	0.80	2.40	4.00
❑ 160	0.30	0.80	2.40	4.00
❑ 161 JBy/GP	0.30	0.60	1.80	3.00
❑ 162 JBy/GP	0.30	0.60	1.80	3.00
❑ 163 JBy/GP	0.30	0.60	1.80	3.00
❑ 164 JBy/GP	0.30	1.10	3.30	5.50
❑ 165 JBy	0.35	1.10	3.30	5.50
❑ 166 JBy	0.35	1.10	3.30	5.50
❑ 167	0.35	0.60	1.80	3.00
❑ 168	0.35	0.60	1.80	3.00
❑ 169	0.35	0.60	1.80	3.00
❑ 170	0.35	0.60	1.80	3.00
❑ 171	0.35	0.60	1.80	3.00
❑ 172	0.35	0.60	1.80	3.00
❑ 173	0.35	0.60	1.80	3.00
❑ 174	0.35	0.60	1.80	3.00
❑ 175	0.35	0.60	1.80	3.00
❑ 176	0.35	0.60	1.80	3.00
❑ 177	0.35	0.60	1.80	3.00
❑ 178	0.35	0.60	1.80	3.00
❑ 179	0.35	0.60	1.80	3.00
❑ 180	0.35	0.60	1.80	3.00
❑ 181 JBy/GP/TA, new team				
	0.35	1.00	3.00	5.00
❑ 182	0.35	0.60	1.80	3.00
❑ 183	0.40	0.60	1.80	3.00
❑ 184	0.40	0.60	1.80	3.00
❑ 185	0.40	0.60	1.80	3.00
❑ 186	0.40	0.60	1.80	3.00
❑ 187	0.40	0.60	1.80	3.00
❑ 188	0.40	0.60	1.80	3.00
❑ 189	0.40	0.60	1.80	3.00
❑ 190 JBy, Daredevil	0.40	0.70	2.10	3.50
❑ 191 JBy/GP	0.40	0.60	1.80	3.00
❑ 192	0.40	0.30	0.90	1.50
❑ 193	0.40	0.30	0.90	1.50
❑ 194	0.40	0.30	0.90	1.50
❑ 195	0.40	0.30	0.90	1.50
❑ 196	0.40	0.30	0.90	1.50
❑ 197	0.40	0.30	0.90	1.50
❑ 198	0.40	0.30	0.90	1.50
❑ 199	0.50	0.30	0.90	1.50
❑ 200 GP L:Ms. Marvel	0.75	0.60	1.80	3.00
❑ 201	0.50	0.40	1.20	2.00

	ORIG.	GOOD	FINE	N-MINT		ORIG.	GOOD	FINE	N-MINT
202	0.50	0.40	1.20	2.00	256	0.65	0.40	1.20	2.00
203	0.50	0.40	1.20	2.00	257	0.65	0.40	1.20	2.00
204	0.50	0.40	1.20	2.00	258	0.65	0.40	1.20	2.00
205	0.50	0.40	1.20	2.00	259	0.65	0.40	1.20	2.00
206	0.50	0.40	1.20	2.00	260 Secret Wars II	0.65	0.40	1.20	2.00
207	0.50	0.40	1.20	2.00	261 Secret Wars II	0.65	0.40	1.20	2.00
208	0.50	0.40	1.20	2.00	262	0.65	0.40	1.20	2.00
209	0.50	0.40	1.20	2.00	263 X-Factor	0.65	0.80	2.40	4.00
210	0.50	0.40	1.20	2.00	264	0.75	0.40	1.20	2.00
211 GC/DG, Moon Knight, Dazzler					265 Secret Wars II	0.75	0.40	1.20	2.00
	0.50	0.40	1.20	2.00	266 Secret Wars II	0.75	0.40	1.20	2.00
212	0.50	0.40	1.20	2.00	267	0.75	0.40	1.20	2.00
213	0.50	0.40	1.20	2.00	268	0.75	0.40	1.20	2.00
214	0.50	0.40	1.20	2.00	269	0.75	0.40	1.20	2.00
215	0.60	0.40	1.20	2.00	270	0.75	0.40	1.20	2.00
216	0.60	0.40	1.20	2.00	271	0.75	0.40	1.20	2.00
217	0.60	0.40	1.20	2.00	272	0.75	0.40	1.20	2.00
218	0.60	0.40	1.20	2.00	273	0.75	0.40	1.20	2.00
219	0.60	0.40	1.20	2.00	274	0.75	0.40	1.20	2.00
220	0.60	0.40	1.20	2.00	275	0.75	0.40	1.20	2.00
221 Wolverine	0.60	1.00	3.00	5.00	276	0.75	0.40	1.20	2.00
222	0.60	0.40	1.20	2.00	277	0.75	0.40	1.20	2.00
223	0.60	0.40	1.20	2.00	278	0.75	0.40	1.20	2.00
224	0.60	0.40	1.20	2.00	279	0.75	0.40	1.20	2.00
225	0.60	0.40	1.20	2.00	280	0.75	0.40	1.20	2.00
226	0.60	0.40	1.20	2.00	281	0.75	0.40	1.20	2.00
227	0.60	0.40	1.20	2.00	282	0.75	0.40	1.20	2.00
228	0.60	0.40	1.20	2.00	283	0.75	0.40	1.20	2.00
229	0.60	0.40	1.20	2.00	284	0.75	0.40	1.20	2.00
230	0.60	0.40	1.20	2.00	285	0.75	0.40	1.20	2.00
231	0.60	0.40	1.20	2.00	286	0.75	0.40	1.20	2.00
232	0.60	0.40	1.20	2.00	287	0.75	0.40	1.20	2.00
233	0.60	0.40	1.20	2.00	288	0.75	0.40	1.20	2.00
234	0.60	0.40	1.20	2.00	289	0.75	0.40	1.20	2.00
235	0.60	0.40	1.20	2.00	290	0.75	0.40	1.20	2.00
236	0.60	0.40	1.20	2.00	291	1.00	0.40	1.20	2.00
237	0.60	0.40	1.20	2.00	292	1.00	0.40	1.20	2.00
238	0.60	0.40	1.20	2.00	293 D:Marrina	1.00	0.40	1.20	2.00
239	0.60	0.40	1.20	2.00	294 L:Capt. Marvel	1.00	0.40	1.20	2.00
240	0.60	0.40	1.20	2.00	295	1.00	0.40	1.20	2.00
241	0.60	0.40	1.20	2.00	296	1.00	0.40	1.20	2.00
242	0.60	0.40	1.20	2.00	297 L:Thor, L:Black Knight, L:She-Hulk, D:Dr. Druid				
243	0.60	0.40	1.20	2.00		1.00	0.40	1.20	2.00
244	0.60	0.40	1.20	2.00	298 Inferno	1.00	0.40	1.20	2.00
245	0.60	0.40	1.20	2.00	299 Inferno	1.00	0.40	1.20	2.00
246	0.60	0.40	1.20	2.00	300 new team, Inferno	1.75	0.40	1.20	2.00
247	0.60	0.40	1.20	2.00	301	1.00	0.40	1.20	2.00
248	0.60	0.40	1.20	2.00	302	1.00	0.40	1.20	2.00
249	0.60	0.40	1.20	2.00	303	1.00	0.40	1.20	2.00
250	1.00	0.40	1.20	2.00	304	1.00	0.40	1.20	2.00
251	0.60	0.40	1.20	2.00	305 JBy(c)	1.00	0.30	0.90	1.50
252	0.60	0.40	1.20	2.00	306	1.00	0.30	0.90	1.50
253	0.60	0.40	1.20	2.00	307	1.00	0.30	0.90	1.50
254	0.65	0.40	1.20	2.00	308	1.00	0.30	0.90	1.50
255	0.65	0.40	1.20	2.00	309	1.00	0.30	0.90	1.50

	ORIG.	GOOD	FINE	N-MINT
☐ 310	1.00	0.30	0.90	1.50
☐ 311 Acts of Vengeance	1.00	0.30	0.90	1.50
☐ 312 Acts of Vengeance	1.00	0.30	0.90	1.50
☐ 313 Acts of Vengeance	1.00	0.30	0.90	1.50
☐ 314 Spider-Man	1.00	0.40	1.20	2.00
☐ 315 Spider-Man	1.00	0.40	1.20	2.00
☐ 316 Spider-Man	1.00	0.40	1.20	2.00
☐ 317 Spider-Man	1.00	0.40	1.20	2.00
☐ 318 Spider-Man	1.00	0.40	1.20	2.00
☐ 319 Crossing Line	1.00	0.30	0.90	1.50
☐ 320 Crossing Line	1.00	0.30	0.90	1.50
☐ 321 Crossing Line	1.00	0.30	0.90	1.50
☐ 322 Crossing Line	1.00	0.30	0.90	1.50
☐ 323 Crossing Line	1.00	0.30	0.90	1.50
☐ 324 Crossing Line	1.00	0.30	0.90	1.50
☐ 325	1.00	0.20	0.60	1.00
☐ 326	1.00	1.00	3.00	5.00
☐ 327	1.00	0.20	0.60	1.00
☐ 328 O:Rage	1.00	0.60	1.80	3.00
☐ 329	1.00	0.30	0.90	1.50
☐ 330	1.00	0.30	0.90	1.50
☐ 331	1.00	0.30	0.90	1.50
☐ 332	1.00	0.30	0.90	1.50
☐ 333	1.00	0.30	0.90	1.50
☐ 334	1.00	0.30	0.90	1.50
☐ 335	1.00	0.30	0.90	1.50
☐ 336	1.00	0.30	0.90	1.50
☐ 337	1.00	0.30	0.90	1.50
☐ 338	1.00	0.30	0.90	1.50
☐ 339	1.00	0.30	0.90	1.50
☐ 340	1.00	0.30	0.90	1.50
☐ 341	1.00	0.30	0.90	1.50
☐ 342	1.00	0.30	0.90	1.50
☐ 343	1.00	0.30	0.90	1.50
☐ 344	1.25	0.30	0.90	1.50
☐ 345 Galactic Storm	1.25	0.30	0.90	1.50
☐ 346 Galactic Storm	1.25	0.30	0.90	1.50
☐ 347 Storm ends	1.75	0.35	1.05	1.75
☐ 348	1.25	0.25	0.75	1.25
☐ 349	1.25	0.25	0.75	1.25
☐ 350	2.50	0.50	1.50	2.50
☐ 351	1.25	0.25	0.75	1.25
☐ 352	1.25	0.25	0.75	1.25
☐ 353	1.25	0.25	0.75	1.25
☐ 354	1.25	0.25	0.75	1.25
☐ 355	1.25	0.25	0.75	1.25
☐ 356	1.25	0.25	0.75	1.25
☐ 357	1.25	0.25	0.75	1.25
☐ 358	1.25	0.25	0.75	1.25
☐ 359	1.25	0.25	0.75	1.25
☐ 360 foil cover	2.95	0.80	2.40	4.00
☐ 361	1.25	0.25	0.75	1.25
☐ 362	1.25	0.25	0.75	1.25
☐ 363 silver embossed cover				
	2.95	0.59	1.77	2.95

	ORIG.	GOOD	FINE	N-MINT
☐ 364	1.25	0.25	0.75	1.25
☐ 365	1.25	0.25	0.75	1.25

AVENGERS ANNUAL

	ORIG.	GOOD	FINE	N-MINT
☐ 1 DH	0.25	7.20	21.60	36.00
☐ 2	0.25	3.00	9.00	15.00
☐ 3	0.25	3.00	9.00	15.00
☐ 4 reprint	0.25	0.60	1.80	3.00
☐ 5 reprint	0.25	0.60	1.80	3.00
☐ 6 GP	0.50	0.50	1.50	2.50
☐ 7 JSn, Warlock	0.60	1.50	4.50	7.50
☐ 8 GP	0.60	0.60	1.80	3.00
☐ 9 DN	0.60	0.60	1.80	3.00
☐ 10 MG, X-Men	0.75	0.60	1.80	3.00
☐ 11	1.00	0.20	0.60	1.00
☐ 12	1.00	0.20	0.60	1.00
☐ 13 JBy	1.00	0.30	0.90	1.50
☐ 14 JBy	1.25	0.30	0.90	1.50
☐ 15	1.25	0.25	0.75	1.25
☐ 16	1.25	0.25	0.75	1.25
☐ 17 Evolutionary War	1.75	0.40	1.20	2.00
☐ 18 Atlantis Attacks	2.00	0.60	1.80	3.00
☐ 19 Terminus	2.00	0.40	1.20	2.00
☐ 20 Subterranean Wars	2.00	0.40	1.20	2.00
☐ 21	2.25	0.45	1.35	2.25
☐ 22 trading card	2.95	0.59	1.77	2.95

AVENGERS SPOTLIGHT (was Solo Avengers)

	ORIG.	GOOD	FINE	N-MINT
☐ 21	0.75	0.20	0.60	1.00
☐ 22	1.00	0.20	0.60	1.00
☐ 23	1.00	0.20	0.60	1.00
☐ 24	1.00	0.20	0.60	1.00
☐ 25	1.00	0.20	0.60	1.00
☐ 26 Acts of Vengeance	1.00	0.20	0.60	1.00
☐ 27 Acts of Vengeance	1.00	0.20	0.60	1.00
☐ 28 Acts of Vengeance	1.00	0.20	0.60	1.00
☐ 29 Acts of Vengeance	1.00	0.20	0.60	1.00
☐ 30 new Hawkeye costume	1.00	0.20	0.60	1.00
☐ 31	1.00	0.20	0.60	1.00
☐ 32	1.00	0.20	0.60	1.00
☐ 33	1.00	0.20	0.60	1.00
☐ 34	1.00	0.20	0.60	1.00
☐ 35	1.00	0.20	0.60	1.00
☐ 36	1.00	0.20	0.60	1.00
☐ 37	1.00	0.20	0.60	1.00
☐ 38	1.00	0.20	0.60	1.00
☐ 39	1.00	0.20	0.60	1.00
☐ 40	1.00	0.20	0.60	1.00

AVENGERS WEST COAST
(was West Coast Avengers)

	ORIG.	GOOD	FINE	N-MINT
☐ 48	1.00	0.20	0.60	1.00
☐ 49	1.00	0.20	0.60	1.00
☐ 50 Golden Age Human Torch returns				
	1.00	0.20	0.60	1.00
☐ 51	1.00	0.20	0.60	1.00
☐ 52	1.00	0.20	0.60	1.00

	ORIG.	GOOD	FINE	N-MINT
53 Acts of Vengeance 1.00	0.20	0.60	1.00
54 Acts of Vengeance 1.00	0.20	0.60	1.00
55 Acts of Vengeance 1.00	0.20	0.60	1.00
56 JBy............................ 1.00	0.20	0.60	1.00
57 JBy............................ 1.00	0.20	0.60	1.00
58 .... 1.00	0.20	0.60	1.00
59 .... 1.00	0.20	0.60	1.00
60 .... 1.00	0.20	0.60	1.00
61 .... 1.00	0.20	0.60	1.00
62 .... 1.00	0.20	0.60	1.00
63 .... 1.00	0.20	0.60	1.00
64 .... 1.00	0.20	0.60	1.00
65 .... 1.00	0.20	0.60	1.00
66 .... 1.00	0.20	0.60	1.00
67 .... 1.00	0.20	0.60	1.00
68 .... 1.00	0.20	0.60	1.00
69 .... 1.00	0.20	0.60	1.00
70 .... 1.00	0.20	0.60	1.00
71 .... 1.00	0.20	0.60	1.00
72 .... 1.00	0.20	0.60	1.00
73 .... 1.00	0.20	0.60	1.00
74 .... 1.00	0.20	0.60	1.00
75 .... 1.50	0.30	0.90	1.50
76 .... 1.00	0.20	0.60	1.00
77 .... 1.00	0.20	0.60	1.00
78 .... 1.00	0.20	0.60	1.00
79 .... 1.25	0.25	0.75	1.25
80 Galactic Storm 1.25	0.25	0.75	1.25
81 Galactic Storm 1.25	0.25	0.75	1.25
82 Galactic Storm 1.25	0.25	0.75	1.25
83 .... 1.25	0.25	0.75	1.25
84 O:Spider Woman 1.25	0.25	0.75	1.25
85 .... 1.25	0.25	0.75	1.25
86 .... 1.25	0.25	0.75	1.25
87 .... 1.25	0.25	0.75	1.25
88 .... 1.25	0.25	0.75	1.25
89 .... 1.25	0.25	0.75	1.25
90 .... 1.25	0.25	0.75	1.25
91 .... 1.25	0.25	0.75	1.25
92 .... 1.25	0.25	0.75	1.25
93 .... 1.25	0.25	0.75	1.25
94 .... 1.25	0.25	0.75	1.25
95 .... 1.25	0.25	0.75	1.25
96 .... 1.25	0.25	0.75	1.25
97 .... 1.25	0.25	0.75	1.25
98 .... 1.25	0.25	0.75	1.25
99 .... 1.25	0.25	0.75	1.25

AVENGERS WEST COAST ANNUAL
(was West Coast Avengers Annual)

	ORIG.	GOOD	FINE	N-MINT
4 Atlantis Attacks 2.00	0.40	1.20	2.00
5 Terminus Factor 2.00	0.40	1.20	2.00
6 Subterranean Wars 2.00	0.40	1.20	2.00
7 .... 2.25	0.45	1.35	2.25
8 trading card.................. 2.95	0.59	1.77	2.95

	ORIG.	GOOD	FINE	N-MINT
AVENGERS: THE TERMINATOR OBJECTIVE			
1 foil cover...................... 2.50	0.50	1.50	2.50

BALDER THE BRAVE

	ORIG.	GOOD	FINE	N-MINT
1 .... 0.75	0.40	1.20	2.00
2 .... 0.75	0.20	0.60	1.00
3 .... 0.75	0.20	0.60	1.00
4 .... 0.75	0.20	0.60	1.00

BARBIE

	ORIG.	GOOD	FINE	N-MINT
1 with door hanger 1.00	1.20	3.60	6.00
1 with membership card.... 1.00	1.20	3.60	6.00
2 .... 1.00	0.60	1.80	3.00
3 .... 1.00	0.40	1.20	2.00
4 .... 1.00	0.40	1.20	2.00
5 .... 1.00	0.40	1.20	2.00
6 .... 1.00	0.40	1.20	2.00
7 .... 1.00	0.40	1.20	2.00
8 .... 1.00	0.40	1.20	2.00
9 .... 1.00	0.40	1.20	2.00
10 .... 1.00	0.40	1.20	2.00
11 .... 1.00	0.40	1.20	2.00
12 .... 1.00	0.40	1.20	2.00
13 .... 1.00	0.40	1.20	2.00
14 .... 1.25	0.40	1.20	2.00
15 .... 1.25	0.40	1.20	2.00
16 .... 1.25	0.40	1.20	2.00
17 .... 1.25	0.40	1.20	2.00
18 .... 1.25	0.40	1.20	2.00
19 .... 1.25	0.40	1.20	2.00
20 .... 1.25	0.40	1.20	2.00
21 .... 1.25	0.25	0.75	1.25
22 .... 1.25	0.25	0.75	1.25
23 .... 1.25	0.25	0.75	1.25
24 .... 1.25	0.25	0.75	1.25
25 .... 1.25	0.25	0.75	1.25
26 .... 1.25	0.25	0.75	1.25
27 .... 1.25	0.25	0.75	1.25
28 .... 1.25	0.25	0.75	1.25
29 .... 1.25	0.25	0.75	1.25
30 .... 1.25	0.25	0.75	1.25
31 .... 1.25	0.25	0.75	1.25
32 .... 1.25	0.25	0.75	1.25
33 .... 1.25	0.25	0.75	1.25
34 .... 1.25	0.25	0.75	1.25

BARBIE FASHION

	ORIG.	GOOD	FINE	N-MINT
1 with doorknob hanger 1.00	1.00	3.00	5.00
2 .... 1.00	0.60	1.80	3.00
3 .... 1.00	0.40	1.20	2.00
4 .... 1.00	0.40	1.20	2.00
5 .... 1.00	0.40	1.20	2.00
6 .... 1.00	0.40	1.20	2.00
7 .... 1.00	0.40	1.20	2.00
8 .... 1.00	0.40	1.20	2.00
9 .... 1.00	0.40	1.20	2.00
10 .... 1.00	0.40	1.20	2.00

	ORIG.	GOOD	FINE	N-MINT
11	1.00	0.40	1.20	2.00
12	1.00	0.40	1.20	2.00
13	1.00	0.40	1.20	2.00
14	1.00	0.40	1.20	2.00
15	1.00	0.40	1.20	2.00
16	1.00	0.40	1.20	2.00
17	1.00	0.40	1.20	2.00
18	1.00	0.40	1.20	2.00
19	1.00	0.40	1.20	2.00
20	1.00	0.40	1.20	2.00
21	1.25	0.25	0.75	1.25
22	1.25	0.25	0.75	1.25
23	1.25	0.25	0.75	1.25
24	1.25	0.25	0.75	1.25
25	1.25	0.25	0.75	1.25
26	1.25	0.25	0.75	1.25
27	1.25	0.25	0.75	1.25
28	1.25	0.25	0.75	1.25
29	1.25	0.25	0.75	1.25
30	1.25	0.25	0.75	1.25
31	1.25	0.25	0.75	1.25
32	1.25	0.25	0.75	1.25
33	1.25	0.25	0.75	1.25

BATTLE TIDE II

	ORIG.	GOOD	FINE	N-MINT
3	1.75	0.35	1.05	1.75

BATTLESTAR: GALACTICA

	ORIG.	GOOD	FINE	N-MINT
1	0.35	0.60	1.80	3.00
2	0.35	0.40	1.20	2.00
3	0.40	0.30	0.90	1.50
4	0.40	0.30	0.90	1.50
5	0.40	0.30	0.90	1.50
6	0.40	0.30	0.90	1.50
7	0.40	0.30	0.90	1.50
8	0.40	0.30	0.90	1.50
9	0.40	0.30	0.90	1.50
10	0.40	0.30	0.90	1.50
11	0.40	0.20	0.60	1.00
12	0.40	0.20	0.60	1.00
13	0.40	0.20	0.60	1.00
14	0.40	0.20	0.60	1.00
15	0.40	0.20	0.60	1.00
16	0.40	0.20	0.60	1.00
17	0.40	0.20	0.60	1.00
18	0.40	0.20	0.60	1.00
19	0.50	0.20	0.60	1.00
20	0.50	0.20	0.60	1.00
21	0.50	0.20	0.60	1.00
22	0.50	0.20	0.60	1.00
23	0.50	0.20	0.60	1.00

BATTLETIDE

	ORIG.	GOOD	FINE	N-MINT
1 Death's Head II, Killpower	1.75	0.35	1.05	1.75
2	1.75	0.35	1.05	1.75
3	1.75	0.35	1.05	1.75
4	1.75	0.35	1.05	1.75

BATTLETIDE II

	ORIG.	GOOD	FINE	N-MINT
1	2.95	0.59	1.77	2.95
2	1.75	0.35	1.05	1.75

BEAUTY AND THE BEAST

	ORIG.	GOOD	FINE	N-MINT
1 DP	0.75	0.30	0.90	1.50
2 DP	0.75	0.20	0.60	1.00
3 DP	0.75	0.20	0.60	1.00
4 DP	0.75	0.20	0.60	1.00

BILL & TED'S EXCELLENT COMIC BOOK

	ORIG.	GOOD	FINE	N-MINT
1	1.00	0.20	0.60	1.00
2	1.00	0.20	0.60	1.00
3	1.25	0.25	0.75	1.25
4	1.25	0.25	0.75	1.25
5	1.25	0.25	0.75	1.25
6	1.25	0.25	0.75	1.25
7	1.25	0.25	0.75	1.25
8	1.25	0.25	0.75	1.25
9	1.25	0.25	0.75	1.25
10	1.25	0.25	0.75	1.25
11	1.25	0.25	0.75	1.25
12	1.25	0.25	0.75	1.25

BIZARRE ADVENTURES

	ORIG.	GOOD	FINE	N-MINT
34 (was b&w magazine)	2.00	0.40	1.20	2.00

BIZARRE ADVENTURES (b&w magazine)

	ORIG.	GOOD	FINE	N-MINT
25 (was Marvel Preview) Black Widow	1.25	0.25	0.75	1.25
26 Kull	1.25	0.25	0.75	1.25
27 X-Men	1.25	0.25	0.75	1.25
28 Elektra	1.50	0.30	0.90	1.50
29 Stephen King	1.50	0.30	0.90	1.50
30 Paradox	1.50	0.30	0.90	1.50
31	1.50	0.30	0.90	1.50
32 Thor	1.50	0.30	0.90	1.50
33 (becomes comic book) Dracula, Zombie	1.50	0.30	0.90	1.50

BLACK AXE

	ORIG.	GOOD	FINE	N-MINT
1	1.75	0.35	1.05	1.75
2	1.75	0.35	1.05	1.75
3	1.75	0.35	1.05	1.75
4	1.75	0.35	1.05	1.75
5	1.75	0.35	1.05	1.75
6	1.75	0.35	1.05	1.75

BLACK KNIGHT

	ORIG.	GOOD	FINE	N-MINT
1 O:Black Knight	1.50	0.30	0.90	1.50
2 Capt. Britain	1.50	0.30	0.90	1.50
3 Dr. Strange, 1:new Valkyrie	1.50	0.30	0.90	1.50
4 Dr. Strange, Valkyrie	1.50	0.30	0.90	1.50

BLACK PANTHER (1976-1978)

	ORIG.	GOOD	FINE	N-MINT
1	0.30	2.00	6.00	10.00
2	0.30	1.20	3.60	6.00

	ORIG.	GOOD	FINE	N-MINT
❏ 3	0.30	1.00	3.00	5.00
❏ 4	0.30	1.00	3.00	5.00
❏ 5	0.30	1.00	3.00	5.00
❏ 6	0.35	0.80	2.40	4.00
❏ 7	0.35	0.80	2.40	4.00
❏ 8	0.35	0.80	2.40	4.00
❏ 9	0.35	0.80	2.40	4.00
❏ 10	0.35	0.80	2.40	4.00
❏ 11	0.35	0.60	1.80	3.00
❏ 12	0.35	0.60	1.80	3.00
❏ 13	0.35	0.60	1.80	3.00
❏ 14	0.35	0.60	1.80	3.00
❏ 15	0.35	0.60	1.80	3.00

BLACK PANTHER (mini-series)

	ORIG.	GOOD	FINE	N-MINT
❏ 1	1.25	0.25	0.75	1.25
❏ 2	1.25	0.25	0.75	1.25
❏ 3	1.25	0.25	0.75	1.25
❏ 4	1.25	0.25	0.75	1.25

BLACK PANTHER: PANTHER'S PREY

	ORIG.	GOOD	FINE	N-MINT
❏ 1	4.95	0.99	2.97	4.95
❏ 2	4.95	0.99	2.97	4.95
❏ 3	4.95	0.99	2.97	4.95
❏ 4	4.95	0.99	2.97	4.95

BLADE RUNNER

	ORIG.	GOOD	FINE	N-MINT
❏ 1 AW movie	0.60	0.20	0.60	1.00
❏ 2 AW movie	0.60	0.20	0.60	1.00

BLIP

	ORIG.	GOOD	FINE	N-MINT
❏ 1 video game mag. in comic-book format/size	1.00	0.20	0.60	1.00
❏ 2	1.00	0.20	0.60	1.00
❏ 3	1.00	0.20	0.60	1.00
❏ 4	1.00	0.20	0.60	1.00
❏ 5	1.00	0.20	0.60	1.00
❏ 6	1.00	0.20	0.60	1.00

BLOODSEED

	ORIG.	GOOD	FINE	N-MINT
❏ 1	1.95	0.39	1.17	1.95

BRUTE FORCE

	ORIG.	GOOD	FINE	N-MINT
❏ 1 O:Brute Force	1.00	0.20	0.60	1.00
❏ 2	1.00	0.20	0.60	1.00
❏ 3	1.00	0.20	0.60	1.00
❏ 4	1.00	0.20	0.60	1.00

BUCK ROGERS

	ORIG.	GOOD	FINE	N-MINT
❏ (giant movie edition)	1.50	0.30	0.90	1.50

BUCKAROO BANZAI

	ORIG.	GOOD	FINE	N-MINT
❏ 1 movie	0.75	0.20	0.60	1.00
❏ 2 movie	0.75	0.20	0.60	1.00

BULLWINKLE AND ROCKY (was Star Comic)

	ORIG.	GOOD	FINE	N-MINT
❏ 3	1.00	0.20	0.60	1.00
❏ 4	1.00	0.20	0.60	1.00
❏ 5	1.00	0.20	0.60	1.00
❏ 6	1.00	0.20	0.60	1.00
❏ 7	1.00	0.20	0.60	1.00

	ORIG.	GOOD	FINE	N-MINT
❏ 8	1.00	0.20	0.60	1.00
❏ 9	1.00	0.20	0.60	1.00

CABLE (mini-series)

	ORIG.	GOOD	FINE	N-MINT
❏ 1	2.50	1.20	3.60	6.00
❏ 1 autographed by John Romita Jr., with certificate		4.00	12.00	20.00
❏ 2 autographed by John Romita Jr., with certificate		4.00	12.00	20.00
❏ 2	2.50	0.80	2.40	4.00
❏ 3	2.00	0.40	1.20	2.00

CABLE (ongoing series, 1993-)

	ORIG.	GOOD	FINE	N-MINT
❏ 1 foil cover	3.50	0.70	2.10	3.50
❏ 2	2.00	0.40	1.20	2.00
❏ 3	2.00	0.40	1.20	2.00
❏ 4	2.00	0.40	1.20	2.00

CAGE

	ORIG.	GOOD	FINE	N-MINT
❏ 1	1.50	0.30	0.90	1.50
❏ 2	1.25	0.25	0.75	1.25
❏ 3 Punisher	1.25	0.25	0.75	1.25
❏ 4 Punisher	1.25	0.25	0.75	1.25
❏ 5	1.25	0.25	0.75	1.25
❏ 6	1.25	0.25	0.75	1.25
❏ 7	1.25	0.25	0.75	1.25
❏ 8	1.25	0.25	0.75	1.25
❏ 9	1.25	0.25	0.75	1.25
❏ 10	1.25	0.25	0.75	1.25
❏ 11	1.25	0.25	0.75	1.25
❏ 12 Iron Fist	1.75	0.35	1.05	1.75
❏ 13	1.25	0.25	0.75	1.25
❏ 14	1.25	0.25	0.75	1.25
❏ 15	1.25	0.25	0.75	1.25
❏ 16	1.25	0.25	0.75	1.25
❏ 17	1.25	0.25	0.75	1.25
❏ 18	1.25	0.25	0.75	1.25
❏ 19	1.25	0.25	0.75	1.25

CAMP CANDY

	ORIG.	GOOD	FINE	N-MINT
❏ 1	1.00	0.20	0.60	1.00
❏ 2	1.00	0.20	0.60	1.00
❏ 3	1.00	0.20	0.60	1.00
❏ 4	1.00	0.20	0.60	1.00
❏ 5	1.00	0.20	0.60	1.00
❏ 6	1.00	0.20	0.60	1.00
❏ 7	1.00	0.20	0.60	1.00

CAPTAIN AMERICA (was Tales of Suspense)

	ORIG.	GOOD	FINE	N-MINT
❏ 100 JK, A:Avengers	0.12	60.00	180.00	300.00
❏ 101 JK, I:4th Sleeper	0.12	13.00	39.00	65.00
❏ 102 JK	0.12	4.80	14.40	24.00
❏ 103 JK	0.12	4.80	14.40	24.00
❏ 104 JK	0.12	4.80	14.40	24.00
❏ 105 JK	0.12	4.80	14.40	24.00
❏ 106 JK	0.12	4.80	14.40	24.00
❏ 107 JK	0.12	4.80	14.40	24.00
❏ 108 JK	0.12	4.80	14.40	24.00
❏ 109 JK, O:retold	0.12	7.00	21.00	35.00

	ORIG.	GOOD	FINE	N-MINT		ORIG.	GOOD	FINE	N-MINT
❏ 110 JSo	0.12	8.80	26.40	44.00	❏ 164	0.20	1.00	3.00	5.00
❏ 111 JSo	0.12	8.80	26.40	44.00	❏ 165	0.20	1.00	3.00	5.00
❏ 112 JK/GT, album	0.12	2.00	6.00	10.00	❏ 166	0.20	1.00	3.00	5.00
❏ 113 JSo, Avengers	0.12	8.80	26.40	44.00	❏ 167	0.20	1.00	3.00	5.00
❏ 114	0.12	2.00	6.00	10.00	❏ 168	0.20	1.00	3.00	5.00
❏ 115	0.12	2.00	6.00	10.00	❏ 169	0.20	1.00	3.00	5.00
❏ 116	0.15	2.00	6.00	10.00	❏ 170	0.20	1.00	3.00	5.00
❏ 117 GC/JSt, I:Falcon	0.15	2.40	7.20	12.00	❏ 171	0.20	1.00	3.00	5.00
❏ 118 GC/JSt, A:Falcon	0.15	1.50	4.50	7.50	❏ 172 SB	0.20	1.60	4.80	8.00
❏ 119 GC/JSt, A:Falcon	0.15	1.50	4.50	7.50	❏ 173 SB X-Men	0.25	2.00	6.00	10.00
❏ 120 GC/JSt, A:Falcon	0.15	1.50	4.50	7.50	❏ 174 SB X-Men	0.25	2.00	6.00	10.00
❏ 121 GC	0.15	1.20	3.60	6.00	❏ 175 SB X-Men	0.25	2.00	6.00	10.00
❏ 122 GC	0.15	1.20	3.60	6.00	❏ 176 SB	0.25	1.60	4.80	8.00
❏ 123 GC	0.15	1.20	3.60	6.00	❏ 177 SB	0.25	0.80	2.40	4.00
❏ 124 GC	0.15	1.20	3.60	6.00	❏ 178 SB	0.25	0.80	2.40	4.00
❏ 125 GC	0.15	1.20	3.60	6.00	❏ 179 SB	0.25	0.80	2.40	4.00
❏ 126 GC	0.15	1.20	3.60	6.00	❏ 180 SB	0.25	0.80	2.40	4.00
❏ 127 GC	0.15	1.20	3.60	6.00	❏ 181	0.25	0.80	2.40	4.00
❏ 128 GC	0.15	1.20	3.60	6.00	❏ 182	0.25	0.80	2.40	4.00
❏ 129 GC	0.15	1.20	3.60	6.00	❏ 183	0.25	2.00	6.00	10.00
❏ 130 GC	0.15	1.20	3.60	6.00	❏ 184	0.25	0.80	2.40	4.00
❏ 131 GC	0.15	1.20	3.60	6.00	❏ 185	0.25	0.80	2.40	4.00
❏ 132 GC	0.15	1.20	3.60	6.00	❏ 186	0.25	0.80	2.40	4.00
❏ 133 GC	0.15	1.20	3.60	6.00	❏ 187	0.25	0.80	2.40	4.00
❏ 134 GC	0.15	1.20	3.60	6.00	❏ 188	0.25	0.80	2.40	4.00
❏ 135 GC	0.15	1.20	3.60	6.00	❏ 189	0.25	0.80	2.40	4.00
❏ 136 GC	0.15	1.20	3.60	6.00	❏ 190	0.25	0.80	2.40	4.00
❏ 137 GC/BEv, A:Spider-Man					❏ 191	0.25	0.80	2.40	4.00
	0.15	3.00	9.00	15.00	❏ 192	0.25	0.80	2.40	4.00
❏ 138 JR, A:Spider-Man	0.15	2.40	7.20	12.00	❏ 193 JK	0.25	0.80	2.40	4.00
❏ 139	0.15	1.00	3.00	5.00	❏ 194 JK	0.25	0.80	2.40	4.00
❏ 140	0.15	1.00	3.00	5.00	❏ 195 JK	0.25	0.80	2.40	4.00
❏ 141	0.15	1.00	3.00	5.00	❏ 196 JK	0.25	0.80	2.40	4.00
❏ 142	0.15	1.00	3.00	5.00	❏ 197 JK	0.25	0.80	2.40	4.00
❏ 143	0.25	1.00	3.00	5.00	❏ 198 JK	0.25	0.80	2.40	4.00
❏ 144	0.20	1.00	3.00	5.00	❏ 199 JK	0.25	0.80	2.40	4.00
❏ 145	0.20	1.00	3.00	5.00	❏ 200 JK	0.25	1.20	3.60	6.00
❏ 146	0.20	1.00	3.00	5.00	❏ 201	0.30	1.00	3.00	5.00
❏ 147	0.20	1.00	3.00	5.00	❏ 202	0.30	1.00	3.00	5.00
❏ 148	0.20	1.00	3.00	5.00	❏ 203	0.30	1.00	3.00	5.00
❏ 149	0.20	1.00	3.00	5.00	❏ 204	0.30	1.00	3.00	5.00
❏ 150	0.20	1.00	3.00	5.00	❏ 205	0.30	1.00	3.00	5.00
❏ 151	0.20	1.00	3.00	5.00	❏ 206	0.30	1.00	3.00	5.00
❏ 152	0.20	1.00	3.00	5.00	❏ 207	0.30	1.00	3.00	5.00
❏ 153	0.20	1.00	3.00	5.00	❏ 208	0.30	1.00	3.00	5.00
❏ 154	0.20	1.60	4.80	8.00	❏ 209	0.30	1.00	3.00	5.00
❏ 155	0.20	1.00	3.00	5.00	❏ 210	0.30	1.00	3.00	5.00
❏ 156	0.20	1.00	3.00	5.00	❏ 211	0.30	1.00	3.00	5.00
❏ 157	0.20	1.00	3.00	5.00	❏ 212	0.30	1.00	3.00	5.00
❏ 158	0.20	1.00	3.00	5.00	❏ 213	0.30	1.00	3.00	5.00
❏ 159	0.20	1.00	3.00	5.00	❏ 214	0.30	1.00	3.00	5.00
❏ 160	0.20	1.00	3.00	5.00	❏ 215	0.35	1.00	3.00	5.00
❏ 161	0.20	1.00	3.00	5.00	❏ 216	0.35	1.00	3.00	5.00
❏ 162	0.20	1.00	3.00	5.00	❏ 217	0.35	1.00	3.00	5.00
❏ 163	0.20	1.00	3.00	5.00	❏ 218	0.35	1.00	3.00	5.00

	ORIG.	GOOD	FINE	N-MINT
☐ 219	0.35	1.00	3.00	5.00
☐ 220	0.35	1.00	3.00	5.00
☐ 221	0.35	1.00	3.00	5.00
☐ 222	0.35	1.00	3.00	5.00
☐ 223	0.35	1.00	3.00	5.00
☐ 224	0.35	1.00	3.00	5.00
☐ 225	0.35	1.00	3.00	5.00
☐ 226	0.35	1.00	3.00	5.00
☐ 227	0.35	1.00	3.00	5.00
☐ 228	0.35	1.00	3.00	5.00
☐ 229	0.35	1.00	3.00	5.00
☐ 230	0.35	1.00	3.00	5.00
☐ 231	0.35	1.00	3.00	5.00
☐ 232	0.35	1.00	3.00	5.00
☐ 233	0.40	1.00	3.00	5.00
☐ 234 A:Daredevil	0.40	1.00	3.00	5.00
☐ 235 A:Daredevil	0.40	1.00	3.00	5.00
☐ 236	0.40	1.00	3.00	5.00
☐ 237	0.40	1.00	3.00	5.00
☐ 238	0.40	1.00	3.00	5.00
☐ 239	0.40	1.00	3.00	5.00
☐ 240	0.40	1.00	3.00	5.00
☐ 241 Punisher	0.40	13.20	39.60	66.00
☐ 242	0.40	1.00	3.00	5.00
☐ 243	0.40	1.00	3.00	5.00
☐ 244	0.40	1.00	3.00	5.00
☐ 245	0.40	1.00	3.00	5.00
☐ 246	0.40	1.00	3.00	5.00
☐ 247 JBy	0.40	1.20	3.60	6.00
☐ 248 JBy	0.40	1.20	3.60	6.00
☐ 249 JBy	0.50	1.20	3.60	6.00
☐ 250 JBy	0.50	1.20	3.60	6.00
☐ 251 JBy	0.50	1.20	3.60	6.00
☐ 252 JBy	0.50	1.20	3.60	6.00
☐ 253 JBy	0.50	1.20	3.60	6.00
☐ 254 JBy	0.50	0.80	2.40	4.00
☐ 255 JBy, 40th anniv.	0.50	1.20	3.60	6.00
☐ 256	0.50	0.80	2.40	4.00
☐ 257	0.50	0.80	2.40	4.00
☐ 258	0.50	0.80	2.40	4.00
☐ 259	0.50	0.80	2.40	4.00
☐ 260	0.50	0.80	2.40	4.00
☐ 261	0.50	0.80	2.40	4.00
☐ 262	0.50	0.80	2.40	4.00
☐ 263	0.50	1.00	3.00	5.00
☐ 264 MZ, X-Men	0.50	1.00	3.00	5.00
☐ 265 MZ	0.60	0.80	2.40	4.00
☐ 266 MZ	0.60	0.80	2.40	4.00
☐ 267 MZ	0.60	0.80	2.40	4.00
☐ 268 MZ	0.60	0.80	2.40	4.00
☐ 269 I:Team America	0.60	0.80	2.40	4.00
☐ 270	0.60	0.80	2.40	4.00
☐ 271	0.60	0.80	2.40	4.00
☐ 272	0.60	0.80	2.40	4.00
☐ 273	0.60	0.80	2.40	4.00
☐ 274	0.60	0.80	2.40	4.00
☐ 275	0.60	0.80	2.40	4.00
☐ 276	0.60	0.80	2.40	4.00
☐ 277	0.60	0.80	2.40	4.00
☐ 278	0.60	0.80	2.40	4.00
☐ 279	0.60	0.80	2.40	4.00
☐ 280	0.60	0.80	2.40	4.00
☐ 281	0.60	0.80	2.40	4.00
☐ 282 1:new Nomad	0.60	2.40	7.20	12.00
☐ 282 reprint, silver ink	1.75	0.60	1.80	3.00
☐ 283	0.60	0.60	1.80	3.00
☐ 284	0.60	0.60	1.80	3.00
☐ 285	0.60	0.60	1.80	3.00
☐ 286	0.60	0.60	1.80	3.00
☐ 287	0.60	0.60	1.80	3.00
☐ 288	0.60	0.60	1.80	3.00
☐ 289	0.60	0.60	1.80	3.00
☐ 290	0.60	0.60	1.80	3.00
☐ 291	0.60	0.60	1.80	3.00
☐ 292	0.60	0.60	1.80	3.00
☐ 293	0.60	0.60	1.80	3.00
☐ 294	0.60	0.60	1.80	3.00
☐ 295	0.60	0.60	1.80	3.00
☐ 296	0.60	0.60	1.80	3.00
☐ 297	0.60	0.60	1.80	3.00
☐ 298	0.60	0.60	1.80	3.00
☐ 299	0.60	0.60	1.80	3.00
☐ 300 anniversary	0.60	1.40	4.20	7.00
☐ 301	0.60	0.40	1.20	2.00
☐ 302	0.60	0.40	1.20	2.00
☐ 303	0.60	0.40	1.20	2.00
☐ 304	0.65	0.40	1.20	2.00
☐ 305	0.65	0.40	1.20	2.00
☐ 306	0.65	0.40	1.20	2.00
☐ 307	0.65	0.40	1.20	2.00
☐ 308 Secret Wars II	0.65	0.60	1.80	3.00
☐ 309	0.65	0.40	1.20	2.00
☐ 310	0.65	0.40	1.20	2.00
☐ 311	0.65	0.40	1.20	2.00
☐ 312	0.65	0.40	1.20	2.00
☐ 313	0.65	0.40	1.20	2.00
☐ 314	0.75	0.40	1.20	2.00
☐ 315	0.75	0.40	1.20	2.00
☐ 316	0.75	0.40	1.20	2.00
☐ 317	0.75	0.40	1.20	2.00
☐ 318	0.75	0.40	1.20	2.00
☐ 319	0.75	0.40	1.20	2.00
☐ 320	0.75	0.40	1.20	2.00
☐ 321	0.75	0.40	1.20	2.00
☐ 322	0.75	0.40	1.20	2.00
☐ 323	0.75	0.40	1.20	2.00
☐ 324	0.75	0.40	1.20	2.00
☐ 325	0.75	0.40	1.20	2.00
☐ 326	0.75	0.40	1.20	2.00
☐ 327	0.75	0.40	1.20	2.00

	ORIG.	GOOD	FINE	N-MINT
☐ 328	0.75	0.40	1.20	2.00
☐ 329	0.75	0.40	1.20	2.00
☐ 330	0.75	0.40	1.20	2.00
☐ 331	0.75	0.40	1.20	2.00
☐ 332 CA fired	0.75	1.60	4.80	8.00
☐ 333 new CA	0.75	1.20	3.60	6.00
☐ 334 new Bucky	0.75	1.00	3.00	5.00
☐ 335	0.75	1.00	3.00	5.00
☐ 336	0.75	0.40	1.20	2.00
☐ 337 1:The Captain	0.75	0.40	1.20	2.00
☐ 338	0.75	0.40	1.20	2.00
☐ 339 Fall of Mutants	0.75	0.40	1.20	2.00
☐ 340	0.75	0.40	1.20	2.00
☐ 341	0.75	0.40	1.20	2.00
☐ 342	0.75	0.40	1.20	2.00
☐ 343	0.75	0.40	1.20	2.00
☐ 344 giant	1.50	0.80	2.40	4.00
☐ 345	0.75	0.40	1.20	2.00
☐ 346	0.75	0.40	1.20	2.00
☐ 347	0.75	0.40	1.20	2.00
☐ 348	0.75	0.40	1.20	2.00
☐ 349	0.75	0.40	1.20	2.00
☐ 350	1.75	0.80	2.40	4.00
☐ 351 A:Nick Fury	0.75	0.40	1.20	2.00
☐ 352	0.75	0.50	1.50	2.50
☐ 353	0.75	0.50	1.50	2.50
☐ 354	0.75	0.50	1.50	2.50
☐ 355	0.75	0.50	1.50	2.50
☐ 356	0.75	0.50	1.50	2.50
☐ 357	1.00	0.50	1.50	2.50
☐ 358	1.00	0.50	1.50	2.50
☐ 359	1.00	0.50	1.50	2.50
☐ 360	1.00	0.50	1.50	2.50
☐ 361	1.00	0.50	1.50	2.50
☐ 362	1.00	0.50	1.50	2.50
☐ 363	1.00	0.50	1.50	2.50
☐ 364	1.00	0.50	1.50	2.50
☐ 365 vengeance	1.00	0.40	1.20	2.00
☐ 366 vengeance	1.00	0.40	1.20	2.00
☐ 367 vengeance	1.00	0.40	1.20	2.00
☐ 368	1.00	0.40	1.20	2.00
☐ 369	1.00	0.40	1.20	2.00
☐ 370	1.00	0.40	1.20	2.00
☐ 371	1.00	0.40	1.20	2.00
☐ 372 Streets of Poison	1.00	0.30	0.90	1.50
☐ 373 Streets of Poison	1.00	0.30	0.90	1.50
☐ 374 Streets of Poison	1.00	0.30	0.90	1.50
☐ 375 Streets of Poison	1.00	0.30	0.90	1.50
☐ 376 Streets of Poison	1.00	0.30	0.90	1.50
☐ 377 Streets of Poison	1.00	0.30	0.90	1.50
☐ 378 Streets of Poison	1.00	0.30	0.90	1.50
☐ 379	1.00	0.30	0.90	1.50
☐ 380	1.00	0.30	0.90	1.50
☐ 381	1.00	0.30	0.90	1.50
☐ 382	1.00	0.30	0.90	1.50

	ORIG.	GOOD	FINE	N-MINT
☐ 383 50th anniv.	2.00	0.70	2.10	3.50
☐ 384 Jack Frost	1.00	0.30	0.90	1.50
☐ 385	1.00	0.30	0.90	1.50
☐ 386	1.00	0.30	0.90	1.50
☐ 387 Superia Stratagem	1.00	0.30	0.90	1.50
☐ 388 Superia Stratagem	1.00	0.30	0.90	1.50
☐ 389 Superia Stratagem	1.00	0.30	0.90	1.50
☐ 390 Superia Stratagem	1.00	0.30	0.90	1.50
☐ 391 Superia Stratagem	1.00	0.30	0.90	1.50
☐ 392 Superia Stratagem	1.00	0.30	0.90	1.50
☐ 393	1.00	0.30	0.90	1.50
☐ 394	1.00	0.30	0.90	1.50
☐ 395	1.00	0.30	0.90	1.50
☐ 396	1.00	0.30	0.90	1.50
☐ 397	1.25	0.30	0.90	1.50
☐ 398 Galactic Storm	1.25	0.30	0.90	1.50
☐ 399 Galactic Storm	1.25	0.30	0.90	1.50
☐ 400 Galactic Storm, reprint of Avengers #4	2.25	1.00	3.00	5.00
☐ 401	1.25	0.25	0.75	1.25
☐ 402	1.25	0.25	0.75	1.25
☐ 403	1.25	0.25	0.75	1.25
☐ 404	1.25	0.25	0.75	1.25
☐ 405	1.25	0.25	0.75	1.25
☐ 406	1.25	0.25	0.75	1.25
☐ 407	1.25	0.25	0.75	1.25
☐ 408	1.25	0.25	0.75	1.25
☐ 409	1.25	0.25	0.75	1.25
☐ 410	1.25	0.25	0.75	1.25
☐ 411	1.25	0.25	0.75	1.25
☐ 412	1.25	0.25	0.75	1.25
☐ 413	1.25	0.25	0.75	1.25
☐ 414	1.25	0.25	0.75	1.25
☐ 415	1.25	0.25	0.75	1.25
☐ 416	1.25	0.25	0.75	1.25
☐ 417	1.25	0.25	0.75	1.25
☐ 418	1.25	0.25	0.75	1.25
☐ 419	1.25	0.25	0.75	1.25

CAPTAIN AMERICA AND THE CAMPBELL KIDS

	ORIG.	GOOD	FINE	N-MINT
☐ giveaway		0.40	1.20	2.00

CAPTAIN AMERICA ANNUAL

	ORIG.	GOOD	FINE	N-MINT
☐ 1 reprint	0.25	1.40	4.20	7.00
☐ 2 reprint	0.25	1.00	3.00	5.00
☐ 3 JK	0.50	0.60	1.80	3.00
☐ 4 JK	0.50	0.60	1.80	3.00
☐ 5	0.75	0.60	1.80	3.00
☐ 6	1.00	0.60	1.80	3.00
☐ 7	1.00	0.60	1.80	3.00
☐ 8 Wolverine	1.25	3.00	9.00	15.00
☐ 9 Terminus Factor	2.00	0.40	1.20	2.00
☐ 10 Von Strucker	2.00	0.40	1.20	2.00
☐ 11	2.25	0.45	1.35	2.25
☐ 12 trading card	2.95	0.59	1.77	2.95

	ORIG.	GOOD	FINE	N-MINT

CAPTAIN AMERICA GOES TO WAR AGAINST DRUGS
giveaway

CAPTAIN AMERICA SPECIAL EDITION

	ORIG.	GOOD	FINE	N-MINT
1 reprint of Steranko issues	2.00	0.40	1.20	2.00
2 reprint of Steranko issues	2.00	0.40	1.20	2.00

CAPTAIN AMERICA: THE MOVIE SPECIAL

	ORIG.	GOOD	FINE	N-MINT
nn	3.50	0.70	2.10	3.50

CAPTAIN JUSTICE

	ORIG.	GOOD	FINE	N-MINT
1 TV show	1.25	0.25	0.75	1.25
2 TV show	1.25	0.25	0.75	1.25

CAPTAIN MARVEL

	ORIG.	GOOD	FINE	N-MINT
1 GC	0.12	14.00	42.00	70.00
2 GC, V:Skrull	0.12	4.80	14.40	24.00
3 GC	0.12	3.20	9.60	16.00
4 GC	0.12	3.20	9.60	16.00
5 DH	0.12	2.00	6.00	10.00
6 DH	0.12	2.00	6.00	10.00
7 DH	0.12	2.00	6.00	10.00
8 DH	0.12	2.00	6.00	10.00
9 DH	0.12	2.00	6.00	10.00
10 DH	0.12	2.00	6.00	10.00
11 BS(c),	0.12	2.00	6.00	10.00
12	0.12	1.40	4.20	7.00
13	0.12	1.40	4.20	7.00
14	0.12	1.40	4.20	7.00
15	0.15	1.40	4.20	7.00
16	0.15	1.40	4.20	7.00
17 GK/DA, new costume, O:Rick Jones retold	0.15	2.40	7.20	12.00
18	0.15	1.20	3.60	6.00
19	0.15	1.20	3.60	6.00
20	0.15	1.20	3.60	6.00
21	0.15	1.20	3.60	6.00
22	0.20	1.20	3.60	6.00
23	0.20	1.20	3.60	6.00
24	0.20	1.20	3.60	6.00
25 JSn	0.20	7.20	21.60	36.00
26	0.20	6.00	18.00	30.00
27	0.20	5.00	15.00	25.00
28 JSn/AM	0.20	5.00	15.00	25.00
29 JSn/AM	0.20	2.00	6.00	10.00
30 JSn/AM	0.20	5.00	15.00	25.00
31	0.20	3.00	9.00	15.00
32	0.25	3.00	9.00	15.00
33	0.25	3.00	9.00	15.00
34 JSn/JAb, I:Nitro	0.25	1.00	3.00	5.00
35 AA, Ant-Man	0.25	1.00	3.00	5.00
36 JSn, Watcher	0.25	3.60	10.80	18.00
37	0.25	0.40	1.20	2.00
38	0.25	0.40	1.20	2.00
39	0.25	0.40	1.20	2.00

	ORIG.	GOOD	FINE	N-MINT
40	0.25	0.40	1.20	2.00
41	0.25	0.40	1.20	2.00
42	0.25	0.40	1.20	2.00
43	0.25	0.40	1.20	2.00
44	0.25	0.40	1.20	2.00
45	0.25	0.40	1.20	2.00
46	0.30	0.40	1.20	2.00
47	0.30	0.40	1.20	2.00
48	0.30	0.40	1.20	2.00
49	0.30	0.40	1.20	2.00
50	0.30	0.40	1.20	2.00
51	0.30	0.40	1.20	2.00
52	0.30	0.40	1.20	2.00
53	0.35	0.40	1.20	2.00
54	0.35	0.40	1.20	2.00
55	0.35	0.40	1.20	2.00
56	0.35	0.40	1.20	2.00
57	0.35	0.40	1.20	2.00
58	0.35	0.40	1.20	2.00
59	0.35	0.40	1.20	2.00
60	0.35	0.40	1.20	2.00
61	0.35	0.40	1.20	2.00
62	0.40	0.40	1.20	2.00

CAPTAIN MARVEL (Volume 2)

	ORIG.	GOOD	FINE	N-MINT
1 -shot	1.50	0.30	0.90	1.50

CAPTAIN PLANET AND THE PLANETEERS

	ORIG.	GOOD	FINE	N-MINT
1 NA(c) tv	1.00	0.20	0.60	1.00
2	1.00	0.20	0.60	1.00
3	1.00	0.20	0.60	1.00
4	1.00	0.20	0.60	1.00
5	1.25	0.25	0.75	1.25
6	1.25	0.25	0.75	1.25
7	1.25	0.25	0.75	1.25
8	1.25	0.25	0.75	1.25
9	1.25	0.25	0.75	1.25
10	1.25	0.25	0.75	1.25
11	1.25	0.25	0.75	1.25
12	1.25	0.25	0.75	1.25

CAPTAIN SAVAGE AND HIS LEATHERNECK RAIDERS/BATTLEFIELD RAIDERS

	ORIG.	GOOD	FINE	N-MINT
1	0.12	2.00	6.00	10.00
2	0.12	1.20	3.60	6.00
3	0.12	1.00	3.00	5.00
4	0.12	1.00	3.00	5.00
5	0.12	1.00	3.00	5.00
6	0.12	0.80	2.40	4.00
6	0.12	0.80	2.40	4.00
7 Ben Grimm	0.12	1.20	3.60	6.00
8	0.12	0.80	2.40	4.00
9	0.12	0.80	2.40	4.00
10	0.12	0.80	2.40	4.00
11	0.15	0.70	2.10	3.50
12	0.15	0.70	2.10	3.50
13	0.15	0.70	2.10	3.50

	ORIG.	GOOD	FINE	N-MINT
14	0.15	0.70	2.10	3.50
15	0.15	0.70	2.10	3.50
16	0.15	0.70	2.10	3.50
17	0.15	0.70	2.10	3.50
18	0.15	0.70	2.10	3.50
19	0.15	0.70	2.10	3.50

CARE BEARS (Was Star Comic)

	ORIG.	GOOD	FINE	N-MINT
15	1.00	0.20	0.60	1.00
16	1.00	0.20	0.60	1.00
17	1.00	0.20	0.60	1.00
18	1.00	0.20	0.60	1.00
19	1.00	0.20	0.60	1.00
20	1.00	0.20	0.60	1.00

CAT, THE

	ORIG.	GOOD	FINE	N-MINT
1	0.20	3.00	9.00	15.00
2	0.20	2.00	6.00	10.00
3	0.20	2.00	6.00	10.00
4	0.20	2.00	6.00	10.00

CHAMBER OF CHILLS

	ORIG.	GOOD	FINE	N-MINT
1	0.20	1.00	3.00	5.00
2	0.20	0.70	2.10	3.50
3	0.20	0.70	2.10	3.50
4	0.20	0.70	2.10	3.50
5	0.20	0.30	0.90	1.50
6	0.20	0.30	0.90	1.50
7	0.20	0.30	0.90	1.50

CHAMBER OF DARKNESS

	ORIG.	GOOD	FINE	N-MINT
1	0.15	6.40	19.20	32.00
2	0.15	3.00	9.00	15.00
3	0.15	3.00	9.00	15.00
4 B.W. Smith	0.15	9.60	28.80	48.00
5	0.15	1.20	3.60	6.00
6	0.15	1.20	3.60	6.00
7 Wrighton	0.15	4.00	12.00	20.00
8 (becomes Monsters on the Prowl)	0.15	1.20	3.60	6.00

CHAMPIONS

	ORIG.	GOOD	FINE	N-MINT
1 DH, I&O	0.25	2.00	6.00	10.00
2	0.25	0.60	1.80	3.00
3	0.25	0.60	1.80	3.00
4	0.25	0.60	1.80	3.00
5 DH, C:Ghost Rider	0.25	1.20	3.60	6.00
6	0.25	0.30	0.90	1.50
7	0.25	0.30	0.90	1.50
8	0.30	0.30	0.90	1.50
9	0.30	0.30	0.90	1.50
10	0.30	0.30	0.90	1.50
11 JBy	0.30	0.60	1.80	3.00
12 JBy	0.30	0.60	1.80	3.00
13 JBy	0.30	0.60	1.80	3.00
14 JBy	0.30	0.60	1.80	3.00
15 JBy	0.30	0.60	1.80	3.00
16 BH, Dr. Doom	0.35	0.30	0.90	1.50
17 GT/JBy, Sentinels	0.35	0.60	1.80	3.00

CHILDREN OF THE VOYAGER

	ORIG.	GOOD	FINE	N-MINT
1 foil	2.95	0.59	1.77	2.95
2	1.95	0.39	1.17	1.95

CLASSIC PUNISHER

	ORIG.	GOOD	FINE	N-MINT
1 paperback, b&w	4.95	0.99	2.97	4.95

CLASSIC X-MEN

	ORIG.	GOOD	FINE	N-MINT
1 AAd(c)	1.00	1.40	4.20	7.00
2	1.00	0.80	2.40	4.00
3	1.00	0.80	2.40	4.00
4 AAd(c)	1.00	0.60	1.80	3.00
5 AAd(c)	1.00	0.60	1.80	3.00
6 AAd(c)	1.00	0.60	1.80	3.00
7 AAd(c)	1.00	0.60	1.80	3.00
8 AAd(c)	1.00	0.60	1.80	3.00
9 AAd(c)	1.00	0.60	1.80	3.00
10 AAd(c)	1.00	0.60	1.80	3.00
11	1.00	0.60	1.80	3.00
12 AAd(c)	1.00	0.60	1.80	3.00
13 AAd(c)	1.00	0.60	1.80	3.00
14 AAd(c)	1.00	0.60	1.80	3.00
15 AAd(c)	1.00	0.60	1.80	3.00
16 AAd(c)	1.00	0.60	1.80	3.00
17 AAd(c)	1.00	0.60	1.80	3.00
18 AAd(c)	1.00	0.60	1.80	3.00
19 AAd(c)	1.00	0.60	1.80	3.00
20 AAd(c)	1.00	0.60	1.80	3.00
21 AAd(c)	1.00	0.60	1.80	3.00
22 AAd(c)	1.00	0.60	1.80	3.00
23 AAd(c)	1.00	0.60	1.80	3.00
24	1.00	0.60	1.80	3.00
25	1.00	0.60	1.80	3.00
26	1.25	0.50	1.50	2.50
27	1.25	0.50	1.50	2.50
28	1.25	0.50	1.50	2.50
29	1.25	0.50	1.50	2.50
30	1.25	0.50	1.50	2.50
31	1.25	0.50	1.50	2.50
32	1.25	0.50	1.50	2.50
33	1.25	0.50	1.50	2.50
34	1.25	0.50	1.50	2.50
35	1.25	0.50	1.50	2.50
36	1.25	0.50	1.50	2.50
37	1.25	0.50	1.50	2.50
38	1.25	0.50	1.50	2.50
39	1.25	0.50	1.50	2.50
40	1.25	0.50	1.50	2.50
41	1.25	0.50	1.50	2.50
42	1.25	0.50	1.50	2.50
43	1.75	0.40	1.20	2.00
44	1.25	0.25	0.75	1.25
45	1.25	0.25	0.75	1.25

CLOAK & DAGGER (2nd series)

	ORIG.	GOOD	FINE	N-MINT
1 TA	0.65	0.30	0.90	1.50
2 TA	0.65	0.20	0.60	1.00

	ORIG.	GOOD	FINE	N-MINT
☐ 3 TA	0.65	0.20	0.60	1.00
☐ 4 TA Secret Wars II	0.65	0.20	0.60	1.00
☐ 5 TA	0.75	0.20	0.60	1.00
☐ 6 TA	0.75	0.20	0.60	1.00
☐ 7 TA	0.75	0.20	0.60	1.00
☐ 8 TA	0.75	0.20	0.60	1.00
☐ 9 TA	0.75	0.20	0.60	1.00
☐ 10 TA	0.75	0.20	0.60	1.00
☐ 11 TA	1.25	0.25	0.75	1.25

CLOAK & DAGGER (mini-series)

	ORIG.	GOOD	FINE	N-MINT
☐ 1 TA, I: Det. O'Reilly	0.60	0.50	1.50	2.50
☐ 2 TA	0.60	0.30	0.90	1.50
☐ 3 TA	0.60	0.30	0.90	1.50
☐ 4 TA	0.60	0.30	0.90	1.50

CLOAK AND DAGGER
(was Mutant Misadventures of Cloak and Dagger)

	ORIG.	GOOD	FINE	N-MINT
☐ 14	1.50	0.30	0.90	1.50
☐ 15	1.50	0.30	0.90	1.50
☐ 16	1.50	0.30	0.90	1.50
☐ 17 Spider-Man	1.50	0.30	0.90	1.50
☐ 18 Spider-Man, Ghost Rider	1.50	0.30	0.90	1.50
☐ 19 O:retold	2.50	0.50	1.50	2.50

CODENAME: GENETIX

	ORIG.	GOOD	FINE	N-MINT
☐ 1	1.75	0.35	1.05	1.75
☐ 2	1.75	0.35	1.05	1.75
☐ 3	1.75	0.35	1.05	1.75
☐ 4	1.75	0.35	1.05	1.75

CODENAME: SPITFIRE
(was Spitfire and the Troubleshooters)

	ORIG.	GOOD	FINE	N-MINT
☐ 10	0.75	0.20	0.60	1.00
☐ 11	0.75	0.20	0.60	1.00
☐ 12	0.75	0.20	0.60	1.00
☐ 13	0.75	0.20	0.60	1.00

COMBAT KELLY AND HIS DEADLY DOZEN

	ORIG.	GOOD	FINE	N-MINT
☐ 1	0.20	0.40	1.20	2.00
☐ 2	0.20	0.20	0.60	1.00
☐ 3	0.20	0.20	0.60	1.00
☐ 4	0.20	0.20	0.60	1.00
☐ 5	0.20	0.20	0.60	1.00
☐ 6	0.20	0.20	0.60	1.00
☐ 7	0.20	0.20	0.60	1.00
☐ 8	0.20	0.20	0.60	1.00
☐ 9	0.20	0.20	0.60	1.00

COMET MAN, THE

	ORIG.	GOOD	FINE	N-MINT
☐ 1	1.00	0.20	0.60	1.00
☐ 2	1.00	0.20	0.60	1.00
☐ 3	1.00	0.20	0.60	1.00
☐ 4	1.00	0.20	0.60	1.00
☐ 5	1.00	0.20	0.60	1.00
☐ 6	1.00	0.20	0.60	1.00

CONAN SAGA

	ORIG.	GOOD	FINE	N-MINT
☐ 1 BWS b&w, reprints	2.00	0.40	1.20	2.00
☐ 2 BWS b&w, reprints	2.00	0.40	1.20	2.00
☐ 3 BWS b&w, reprints	2.00	0.40	1.20	2.00
☐ 4 BWS b&w, reprints	2.00	0.40	1.20	2.00
☐ 5 BWS b&w, reprints	2.00	0.40	1.20	2.00
☐ 6 BWS b&w, reprints	2.00	0.40	1.20	2.00
☐ 7 BWS b&w, reprints	2.00	0.40	1.20	2.00
☐ 8 BWS b&w, reprints	2.00	0.40	1.20	2.00
☐ 9 BWS b&w, reprints	2.00	0.40	1.20	2.00
☐ 10 b&w, reprints	2.00	0.40	1.20	2.00
☐ 11 b&w, reprints	2.00	0.40	1.20	2.00
☐ 12 b&w, reprints	2.00	0.40	1.20	2.00
☐ 13 b&w, reprints	2.00	0.40	1.20	2.00
☐ 14 b&w, reprints	2.00	0.40	1.20	2.00
☐ 15 b&w, reprints	2.00	0.40	1.20	2.00
☐ 16 b&w, reprints	2.00	0.40	1.20	2.00
☐ 17 b&w, reprints	2.00	0.40	1.20	2.00
☐ 18 b&w, reprints	2.00	0.40	1.20	2.00
☐ 19 b&w, reprints	2.00	0.40	1.20	2.00
☐ 20 b&w, reprints	2.00	0.40	1.20	2.00
☐ 21 b&w, reprints	2.00	0.40	1.20	2.00
☐ 22 b&w, reprints	2.00	0.40	1.20	2.00
☐ 23 b&w, reprints	2.00	0.40	1.20	2.00
☐ 24 b&w, reprints	2.00	0.40	1.20	2.00
☐ 25 b&w, reprints	2.00	0.40	1.20	2.00
☐ 26 b&w, reprints	2.00	0.40	1.20	2.00
☐ 27 b&w, reprints	2.00	0.40	1.20	2.00
☐ 28 b&w, reprints	2.25	0.45	1.35	2.25
☐ 29 b&w, reprints	2.25	0.45	1.35	2.25
☐ 30 b&w, reprints	2.25	0.45	1.35	2.25
☐ 31 b&w, reprints	2.25	0.45	1.35	2.25
☐ 32 b&w, reprints	2.25	0.45	1.35	2.25
☐ 33 b&w, reprints	2.25	0.45	1.35	2.25
☐ 34 b&w, reprints	2.25	0.45	1.35	2.25
☐ 35 b&w, reprints	2.25	0.45	1.35	2.25
☐ 36 b&w, reprints	2.25	0.45	1.35	2.25
☐ 37 b&w, reprints	2.25	0.45	1.35	2.25
☐ 38 b&w, reprints	2.25	0.45	1.35	2.25
☐ 39 b&w, reprints	2.25	0.45	1.35	2.25
☐ 40 b&w, reprints	2.25	0.45	1.35	2.25
☐ 41 b&w, reprints	2.25	0.45	1.35	2.25
☐ 42 b&w, reprints	2.25	0.45	1.35	2.25
☐ 43 b&w, reprints	2.25	0.45	1.35	2.25
☐ 44 b&w, reprints	2.25	0.45	1.35	2.25
☐ 45 b&w, reprints	2.25	0.45	1.35	2.25
☐ 46 b&w, reprints	2.25	0.45	1.35	2.25
☐ 47 b&w, reprints	2.25	0.45	1.35	2.25
☐ 48 b&w, reprints	2.25	0.45	1.35	2.25
☐ 49 b&w, reprints	2.25	0.45	1.35	2.25
☐ 50 b&w, reprints	2.25	0.45	1.35	2.25
☐ 51 b&w, reprints	2.25	0.45	1.35	2.25
☐ 52 b&w, reprints	2.25	0.45	1.35	2.25
☐ 53 b&w, reprints	2.25	0.45	1.35	2.25
☐ 54 b&w, reprints	2.25	0.45	1.35	2.25
☐ 55 b&w, reprints	2.25	0.45	1.35	2.25
☐ 56 b&w, reprints	2.25	0.45	1.35	2.25
☐ 57 b&w, reprints	2.25	0.45	1.35	2.25

	ORIG.	GOOD	FINE	N-MINT
58 b&w, reprints	2.25	0.45	1.35	2.25
59 b&w, reprints	2.25	0.45	1.35	2.25
60 b&w, reprints	2.25	0.45	1.35	2.25
61 b&w, reprints	2.25	0.45	1.35	2.25
62 b&w, reprints	2.25	0.45	1.35	2.25
63 b&w, reprints	2.25	0.45	1.35	2.25
64 b&w, reprints	2.25	0.45	1.35	2.25
65 b&w, reprints	2.25	0.45	1.35	2.25
66 b&w, reprints	2.25	0.45	1.35	2.25
67 b&w, reprints	2.25	0.45	1.35	2.25
68 b&w, reprints	2.25	0.45	1.35	2.25
69 b&w, reprints	2.25	0.45	1.35	2.25
70 b&w, reprints	2.25	0.45	1.35	2.25
71 b&w, reprints	2.25	0.45	1.35	2.25
72 b&w, reprints	2.25	0.45	1.35	2.25
73 b&w, reprints	2.25	0.45	1.35	2.25
74 b&w, reprints	2.25	0.45	1.35	2.25
75 poster, handbook	3.95	0.79	2.37	3.95
76 b&w	2.25	0.45	1.35	2.25
77 b&w	2.25	0.45	1.35	2.25
78 b&w	2.25	0.45	1.35	2.25

CONAN THE BARBARIAN

	ORIG.	GOOD	FINE	N-MINT
1 BS, O:Conan A:Kull	0.15	35.00	105.00	175.00
2 BS, Howard story	0.15	16.00	48.00	80.00
3 BS/TS, low dist.	0.15	20.00	60.00	100.00
4 BS/TS	0.15	10.00	30.00	50.00
5 BS/TS	0.15	10.00	30.00	50.00
6 BS	0.15	6.00	18.00	30.00
7 BS	0.15	6.00	18.00	30.00
8 BS	0.15	6.00	18.00	30.00
9 BS	0.15	6.00	18.00	30.00
10 BS, grant	0.25	8.00	24.00	40.00
11 BS, grant	0.25	8.00	24.00	40.00
12 BS	0.20	7.00	21.00	35.00
13 BS	0.20	7.00	21.00	35.00
14 BS, A:Elric	0.20	8.00	24.00	40.00
15 BS, A:Elric	0.20	8.00	24.00	40.00
16 BS/TS, rep.	0.20	4.00	12.00	20.00
17 GK	0.20	2.40	7.20	12.00
18 GK	0.20	2.40	7.20	12.00
19 BS	0.20	4.00	12.00	20.00
20 BS	0.20	4.00	12.00	20.00
21 BS	0.20	4.00	12.00	20.00
22 BS	0.20	4.00	12.00	20.00
23 GK/BS/TS 1:Red Sonja	0.20	6.80	20.40	34.00
24 BS, Red Sonja	0.20	5.00	15.00	25.00
25 JB/GK/TS, mirrors	0.20	2.40	7.20	12.00
26 JB	0.20	1.00	3.00	5.00
27 JB	0.20	1.00	3.00	5.00
28 JB/GK/TS	0.20	1.10	3.30	5.50
29 JB/GK/TS	0.20	1.10	3.30	5.50
30 JB/GK/TS	0.20	1.10	3.30	5.50
31	0.20	0.70	2.10	3.50
32	0.20	0.70	2.10	3.50

	ORIG.	GOOD	FINE	N-MINT
33	0.20	0.70	2.10	3.50
34	0.20	0.70	2.10	3.50
35	0.20	0.70	2.10	3.50
36	0.20	0.70	2.10	3.50
37 TS/NA	0.20	1.30	3.90	6.50
38	0.25	0.50	1.50	2.50
39	0.25	0.50	1.50	2.50
40	0.25	0.50	1.50	2.50
41 JB/GK	0.25	0.45	1.35	2.25
42 JB/GK	0.25	0.45	1.35	2.25
43 JB/GK	0.25	0.45	1.35	2.25
44	0.25	1.00	3.00	5.00
45	0.25	1.00	3.00	5.00
46	0.20	0.45	1.35	2.25
47	0.20	0.45	1.35	2.25
48	0.20	0.45	1.35	2.25
49	0.20	0.45	1.35	2.25
50	0.20	0.45	1.35	2.25
51	0.20	0.40	1.20	2.00
52	0.20	0.40	1.20	2.00
53	0.20	0.40	1.20	2.00
54	0.20	0.40	1.20	2.00
55	0.20	0.40	1.20	2.00
56	0.20	0.40	1.20	2.00
57	0.20	0.40	1.20	2.00
58	0.25	0.60	1.80	3.00
59	0.25	0.60	1.80	3.00
60	0.25	0.40	1.20	2.00
61	0.25	0.40	1.20	2.00
62	0.25	0.40	1.20	2.00
63	0.25	0.40	1.20	2.00
64	0.25	0.40	1.20	2.00
65 JB/GK	0.25	0.35	1.05	1.75
66 JB/GK	0.30	0.35	1.05	1.75
67 JB/GK, Red Sonja	0.30	0.40	1.20	2.00
68 JB/GK, Red Sonja	0.30	0.40	1.20	2.00
69	0.30	0.35	1.05	1.75
70	0.30	0.35	1.05	1.75
71	0.30	0.30	0.90	1.50
72	0.30	0.30	0.90	1.50
73	0.30	0.30	0.90	1.50
74	0.30	0.30	0.90	1.50
75	0.30	0.30	0.90	1.50
76	0.30	0.30	0.90	1.50
77	0.30	0.30	0.90	1.50
78	0.30	0.30	0.90	1.50
79	0.30	0.30	0.90	1.50
80	0.35	0.30	0.90	1.50
81	0.35	0.30	0.90	1.50
82	0.35	0.30	0.90	1.50
83	0.35	0.25	0.75	1.25
84	0.35	0.25	0.75	1.25
85	0.35	0.25	0.75	1.25
86	0.35	0.25	0.75	1.25
87	0.35	0.25	0.75	1.25

	ORIG.	GOOD	FINE	N-MINT
☐ 88	0.35	0.25	0.75	1.25
☐ 89	0.35	0.25	0.75	1.25
☐ 90	0.35	0.25	0.75	1.25
☐ 91	0.35	0.25	0.75	1.25
☐ 92	0.35	0.25	0.75	1.25
☐ 93	0.35	0.25	0.75	1.25
☐ 94 JB	0.35	0.30	0.90	1.50
☐ 95 JB	0.35	0.30	0.90	1.50
☐ 96 JB	0.35	0.30	0.90	1.50
☐ 97 JB	0.35	0.30	0.90	1.50
☐ 98 JB	0.40	0.30	0.90	1.50
☐ 99 JB	0.40	0.30	0.90	1.50
☐ 100 JB/TS, D:Belit	0.60	0.60	1.80	3.00
☐ 101 JB	0.40	0.30	0.90	1.50
☐ 102 JB	0.40	0.30	0.90	1.50
☐ 103 JB	0.40	0.30	0.90	1.50
☐ 104 JB	0.40	0.30	0.90	1.50
☐ 105 JB	0.40	0.30	0.90	1.50
☐ 106 JB	0.40	0.30	0.90	1.50
☐ 107 JB	0.40	0.30	0.90	1.50
☐ 108 JB	0.40	0.30	0.90	1.50
☐ 109 JB	0.40	0.30	0.90	1.50
☐ 110 JB	0.40	0.30	0.90	1.50
☐ 111 JB	0.40	0.30	0.90	1.50
☐ 112 JB	0.40	0.30	0.90	1.50
☐ 113 JB	0.40	0.30	0.90	1.50
☐ 114 JB	0.40	0.30	0.90	1.50
☐ 115 JB, 10th anniv.	0.75	0.40	1.20	2.00
☐ 116 JB/NA, rep.	0.50	0.30	0.90	1.50
☐ 117	0.50	0.25	0.75	1.25
☐ 118	0.50	0.25	0.75	1.25
☐ 119	0.50	0.25	0.75	1.25
☐ 120	0.50	0.25	0.75	1.25
☐ 121	0.50	0.25	0.75	1.25
☐ 122	0.50	0.25	0.75	1.25
☐ 123	0.50	0.25	0.75	1.25
☐ 124	0.50	0.25	0.75	1.25
☐ 125	0.50	0.25	0.75	1.25
☐ 126	0.50	0.25	0.75	1.25
☐ 127	0.50	0.20	0.60	1.00
☐ 128	0.50	0.20	0.60	1.00
☐ 129	0.50	0.20	0.60	1.00
☐ 130	0.60	0.20	0.60	1.00
☐ 131	0.60	0.20	0.60	1.00
☐ 132	0.60	0.20	0.60	1.00
☐ 133	0.60	0.20	0.60	1.00
☐ 134	0.60	0.20	0.60	1.00
☐ 135	0.60	0.20	0.60	1.00
☐ 136	0.60	0.20	0.60	1.00
☐ 137	0.60	0.20	0.60	1.00
☐ 138	0.60	0.20	0.60	1.00
☐ 139	0.60	0.20	0.60	1.00
☐ 140	0.60	0.20	0.60	1.00
☐ 141	0.60	0.20	0.60	1.00
☐ 142	0.60	0.20	0.60	1.00

	ORIG.	GOOD	FINE	N-MINT
☐ 143	0.60	0.20	0.60	1.00
☐ 144	0.60	0.20	0.60	1.00
☐ 145	0.60	0.20	0.60	1.00
☐ 146	0.60	0.20	0.60	1.00
☐ 147	0.60	0.20	0.60	1.00
☐ 148	0.60	0.20	0.60	1.00
☐ 149	0.60	0.20	0.60	1.00
☐ 150	0.60	0.20	0.60	1.00
☐ 151	0.60	0.20	0.60	1.00
☐ 152	0.60	0.20	0.60	1.00
☐ 153	0.60	0.20	0.60	1.00
☐ 154	0.60	0.20	0.60	1.00
☐ 155	0.60	0.20	0.60	1.00
☐ 156	0.60	0.20	0.60	1.00
☐ 157	0.60	0.20	0.60	1.00
☐ 158	0.60	0.20	0.60	1.00
☐ 159	0.60	0.20	0.60	1.00
☐ 160	0.60	0.20	0.60	1.00
☐ 161	0.60	0.20	0.60	1.00
☐ 162	0.60	0.20	0.60	1.00
☐ 163	0.60	0.20	0.60	1.00
☐ 164	0.60	0.20	0.60	1.00
☐ 165	0.60	0.20	0.60	1.00
☐ 166	0.60	0.20	0.60	1.00
☐ 167	0.60	0.20	0.60	1.00
☐ 168	0.60	0.20	0.60	1.00
☐ 169	0.65	0.20	0.60	1.00
☐ 170	0.65	0.20	0.60	1.00
☐ 171	0.65	0.20	0.60	1.00
☐ 172	0.65	0.20	0.60	1.00
☐ 173	0.65	0.20	0.60	1.00
☐ 174	0.65	0.20	0.60	1.00
☐ 175	0.65	0.20	0.60	1.00
☐ 176	0.65	0.20	0.60	1.00
☐ 177	0.65	0.20	0.60	1.00
☐ 178	0.65	0.20	0.60	1.00
☐ 179	0.75	0.20	0.60	1.00
☐ 180	0.75	0.20	0.60	1.00
☐ 181	0.75	0.20	0.60	1.00
☐ 182	0.75	0.20	0.60	1.00
☐ 183	0.75	0.20	0.60	1.00
☐ 184	0.75	0.20	0.60	1.00
☐ 185	0.75	0.20	0.60	1.00
☐ 186	0.75	0.20	0.60	1.00
☐ 187	0.75	0.20	0.60	1.00
☐ 188	0.75	0.20	0.60	1.00
☐ 189	0.75	0.20	0.60	1.00
☐ 190	0.75	0.20	0.60	1.00
☐ 191	0.75	0.20	0.60	1.00
☐ 192	0.75	0.20	0.60	1.00
☐ 193	0.75	0.20	0.60	1.00
☐ 194	1.00	0.20	0.60	1.00
☐ 195	1.00	0.20	0.60	1.00
☐ 196	1.00	0.20	0.60	1.00
☐ 197	1.00	0.20	0.60	1.00

	ORIG.	GOOD	FINE	N-MINT
❏ 198	1.00	0.20	0.60	1.00
❏ 199	1.00	0.20	0.60	1.00
❏ 200	1.50	0.30	0.90	1.50
❏ 201	1.00	0.20	0.60	1.00
❏ 202	1.00	0.20	0.60	1.00
❏ 203	1.00	0.20	0.60	1.00
❏ 204	1.00	0.20	0.60	1.00
❏ 205	1.00	0.20	0.60	1.00
❏ 206	1.00	0.20	0.60	1.00
❏ 207	1.00	0.20	0.60	1.00
❏ 208	1.00	0.20	0.60	1.00
❏ 209	1.00	0.20	0.60	1.00
❏ 210	1.00	0.20	0.60	1.00
❏ 211	1.00	0.20	0.60	1.00
❏ 212	1.00	0.20	0.60	1.00
❏ 213	1.00	0.20	0.60	1.00
❏ 214	1.00	0.20	0.60	1.00
❏ 215	1.00	0.20	0.60	1.00
❏ 216	1.00	0.20	0.60	1.00
❏ 217	1.00	0.20	0.60	1.00
❏ 218	1.00	0.20	0.60	1.00
❏ 219	1.00	0.20	0.60	1.00
❏ 220	1.00	0.20	0.60	1.00
❏ 221	1.00	0.20	0.60	1.00
❏ 222	1.00	0.20	0.60	1.00
❏ 223	1.00	0.20	0.60	1.00
❏ 224	1.00	0.20	0.60	1.00
❏ 225	1.00	0.20	0.60	1.00
❏ 226	1.00	0.20	0.60	1.00
❏ 227	1.00	0.20	0.60	1.00
❏ 228	1.00	0.20	0.60	1.00
❏ 229	1.00	0.20	0.60	1.00
❏ 230	1.00	0.20	0.60	1.00
❏ 231	1.00	0.20	0.60	1.00
❏ 232 starts over	1.00	0.20	0.60	1.00
❏ 233	1.00	0.20	0.60	1.00
❏ 234	1.00	0.20	0.60	1.00
❏ 235	1.00	0.20	0.60	1.00
❏ 236	1.00	0.20	0.60	1.00
❏ 237	1.00	0.20	0.60	1.00
❏ 238	1.00	0.20	0.60	1.00
❏ 239	1.00	0.20	0.60	1.00
❏ 240	1.00	0.20	0.60	1.00
❏ 241 TMc(c)	1.00	0.60	1.80	3.00
❏ 242 JLee(c)	1.00	0.40	1.20	2.00
❏ 243 Red Sonja	1.00	0.20	0.60	1.00
❏ 244 Red Sonja	1.00	0.20	0.60	1.00
❏ 245 Red Sonja	1.00	0.20	0.60	1.00
❏ 246 Red Sonja	1.00	0.20	0.60	1.00
❏ 247 Red Sonja	1.00	0.20	0.60	1.00
❏ 248 Red Sonja	1.00	0.20	0.60	1.00
❏ 249 Red Sonja	1.00	0.20	0.60	1.00
❏ 250	1.50	0.30	0.90	1.50
❏ 251	1.00	0.20	0.60	1.00
❏ 252	1.00	0.20	0.60	1.00

	ORIG.	GOOD	FINE	N-MINT
❏ 253	1.25	0.25	0.75	1.25
❏ 254	1.25	0.25	0.75	1.25
❏ 255	1.25	0.25	0.75	1.25
❏ 256	1.25	0.25	0.75	1.25
❏ 257	1.25	0.25	0.75	1.25
❏ 258	1.25	0.25	0.75	1.25
❏ 259	1.25	0.25	0.75	1.25
❏ 260	1.25	0.25	0.75	1.25
❏ 261	1.25	0.25	0.75	1.25
❏ 262	1.25	0.25	0.75	1.25
❏ 263	1.25	0.25	0.75	1.25
❏ 264	1.25	0.25	0.75	1.25
❏ 265	1.25	0.25	0.75	1.25
❏ 266	1.25	0.25	0.75	1.25
❏ 267	1.25	0.25	0.75	1.25
❏ 268	1.25	0.25	0.75	1.25
❏ 269	1.25	0.25	0.75	1.25
❏ 270	1.25	0.25	0.75	1.25
❏ 271	1.25	0.25	0.75	1.25
❏ 272	1.25	0.25	0.75	1.25
❏ 273	1.25	0.25	0.75	1.25

CONAN THE BARBARIAN KING-SIZE/ANNUAL

	ORIG.	GOOD	FINE	N-MINT
❏ 1 BS	0.35	2.00	6.00	10.00
❏ 2 BS	0.50	0.60	1.80	3.00
❏ 3 A:Kull	0.60	0.40	1.20	2.00
❏ 4	0.60	0.30	0.90	1.50
❏ 5	0.75	0.30	0.90	1.50
❏ 6	0.75	0.30	0.90	1.50
❏ 7	1.00	0.25	0.75	1.25
❏ 8	1.00	0.25	0.75	1.25
❏ 9	1.00	0.25	0.75	1.25
❏ 10	1.25	0.25	0.75	1.25
❏ 11	1.25	0.25	0.75	1.25

CONAN THE BARBARIAN MOVIE SPECIAL

	ORIG.	GOOD	FINE	N-MINT
❏ 1 JB	0.60	0.20	0.60	1.00
❏ 2 JB	0.60	0.20	0.60	1.00

CONAN THE BARBARIAN SPECIAL

	ORIG.	GOOD	FINE	N-MINT
❏ 1 reprint	2.50	0.50	1.50	2.50

CONAN THE DESTROYER MOVIE SPECIAL

	ORIG.	GOOD	FINE	N-MINT
❏ 1	0.75	0.30	0.90	1.50
❏ 2	0.75	0.30	0.90	1.50

CONAN THE KING (formerly King Conan)

	ORIG.	GOOD	FINE	N-MINT
❏ 21	1.00	0.20	0.60	1.00
❏ 22	1.00	0.20	0.60	1.00
❏ 23	1.00	0.20	0.60	1.00
❏ 24	1.00	0.20	0.60	1.00
❏ 25	1.00	0.20	0.60	1.00
❏ 26	1.00	0.20	0.60	1.00
❏ 27	1.00	0.20	0.60	1.00
❏ 28	1.25	0.25	0.75	1.25
❏ 29	1.25	0.25	0.75	1.25
❏ 30	1.25	0.25	0.75	1.25
❏ 31	1.25	0.25	0.75	1.25
❏ 32	1.25	0.25	0.75	1.25

	ORIG.	GOOD	FINE	N-MINT
33	1.25	0.25	0.75	1.25
34	1.25	0.25	0.75	1.25
35	1.25	0.25	0.75	1.25
36	1.25	0.25	0.75	1.25
37	1.25	0.25	0.75	1.25
38	1.25	0.25	0.75	1.25
39	1.25	0.25	0.75	1.25
40	1.25	0.25	0.75	1.25
41	1.25	0.25	0.75	1.25
42	1.25	0.25	0.75	1.25
43	1.25	0.25	0.75	1.25
44	1.25	0.25	0.75	1.25
45	1.25	0.25	0.75	1.25
46	1.50	0.30	0.90	1.50
47	1.50	0.30	0.90	1.50
48	1.50	0.30	0.90	1.50
49	1.50	0.30	0.90	1.50
50	1.50	0.30	0.90	1.50
51	1.50	0.30	0.90	1.50
52	1.50	0.30	0.90	1.50
53	1.50	0.30	0.90	1.50
54	1.50	0.30	0.90	1.50
55	1.50	0.30	0.90	1.50

COPS: THE JOB

	ORIG.	GOOD	FINE	N-MINT
1	1.25	0.25	0.75	1.25
2	1.25	0.25	0.75	1.25
3	1.25	0.25	0.75	1.25
4	1.25	0.25	0.75	1.25

COUNT DUCKULA

	ORIG.	GOOD	FINE	N-MINT
1 O:Count Duckula	1.00	0.20	0.60	1.00
2	1.00	0.20	0.60	1.00
3 1:Danger Mouse	1.00	0.20	0.60	1.00
4 Danger Mouse	1.00	0.20	0.60	1.00
5 Danger Mouse	1.00	0.20	0.60	1.00
6 Danger Mouse	1.00	0.20	0.60	1.00
7 Danger Mouse	1.00	0.20	0.60	1.00
8 Geraldo Rivera	1.00	0.20	0.60	1.00
9	1.00	0.20	0.60	1.00
10	1.00	0.20	0.60	1.00
11	1.00	0.20	0.60	1.00
12	1.00	0.20	0.60	1.00
13	1.00	0.20	0.60	1.00
14	1.00	0.20	0.60	1.00
15	1.00	0.20	0.60	1.00

CRAZY (black-and-white magazine)

	ORIG.	GOOD	FINE	N-MINT
1	0.40	1.00	3.00	5.00
2	0.40	0.60	1.80	3.00
3	0.40	0.60	1.80	3.00
4	0.40	0.60	1.80	3.00
5	0.40	0.60	1.80	3.00
6	0.40	0.30	0.90	1.50
7	0.40	0.30	0.90	1.50
8	0.50	0.30	0.90	1.50
9	0.50	0.30	0.90	1.50

	ORIG.	GOOD	FINE	N-MINT
10	0.50	0.30	0.90	1.50
11	0.50	0.30	0.90	1.50
12	0.50	0.30	0.90	1.50
13	0.50	0.30	0.90	1.50
14	0.50	0.30	0.90	1.50
15	0.50	0.30	0.90	1.50
16	0.50	0.30	0.90	1.50
17	0.50	0.30	0.90	1.50
18	0.50	0.30	0.90	1.50
19	0.50	0.30	0.90	1.50
20		0.30	0.90	1.50
21		0.30	0.90	1.50
22		0.30	0.90	1.50
23		0.30	0.90	1.50
24		0.30	0.90	1.50
25		0.30	0.90	1.50
26		0.30	0.90	1.50
27		0.30	0.90	1.50
28		0.30	0.90	1.50
29		0.30	0.90	1.50
30		0.30	0.90	1.50
31		0.30	0.90	1.50
32		0.30	0.90	1.50
33		0.30	0.90	1.50
34		0.30	0.90	1.50
35		0.30	0.90	1.50
36		0.30	0.90	1.50
37		0.30	0.90	1.50
38		0.30	0.90	1.50
39		0.30	0.90	1.50
40		0.30	0.90	1.50
41		0.30	0.90	1.50
42		0.30	0.90	1.50
43		0.30	0.90	1.50
44		0.30	0.90	1.50
45		0.30	0.90	1.50
46		0.30	0.90	1.50
47		0.30	0.90	1.50
48		0.30	0.90	1.50
49		0.30	0.90	1.50
50		0.30	0.90	1.50
51		0.30	0.90	1.50
52		0.30	0.90	1.50
53		0.30	0.90	1.50
54		0.30	0.90	1.50
55		0.30	0.90	1.50
56		0.30	0.90	1.50
57		0.30	0.90	1.50
58		0.30	0.90	1.50
59		0.30	0.90	1.50
60		0.30	0.90	1.50
61		0.30	0.90	1.50
62		0.30	0.90	1.50
63		0.30	0.90	1.50
64		0.30	0.90	1.50

	ORIG.	GOOD	FINE	N-MINT
65		0.30	0.90	1.50
66		0.30	0.90	1.50
67		0.30	0.90	1.50
68		0.30	0.90	1.50
69		0.30	0.90	1.50
70		0.30	0.90	1.50
71		0.30	0.90	1.50
72		0.30	0.90	1.50
73		0.30	0.90	1.50
74		0.30	0.90	1.50
75		0.30	0.90	1.50
76		0.30	0.90	1.50
77		0.30	0.90	1.50
78		0.30	0.90	1.50
79		0.30	0.90	1.50
80	0.90	0.30	0.90	1.50
81	0.90	0.30	0.90	1.50
82	1.25	0.30	0.90	1.50
83	0.90	0.30	0.90	1.50
84	0.90	0.30	0.90	1.50
85	1.25	0.30	0.90	1.50
86	0.90	0.30	0.90	1.50
87	0.90	0.30	0.90	1.50
88	0.90	0.30	0.90	1.50
89	0.90	0.30	0.90	1.50
90	0.90	0.30	0.90	1.50
91	1.25	0.30	0.90	1.50
92	1.25	0.30	0.90	1.50
93	1.25	0.30	0.90	1.50
94	1.25	0.30	0.90	1.50

CREATURES ON THE LOOSE
(was Tower of Shadows)

	ORIG.	GOOD	FINE	N-MINT
10 first King Kull story	0.15	3.60	10.80	18.00
11 reprints		0.20	0.60	1.00
12 reprints		0.20	0.60	1.00
13 reprints		0.20	0.60	1.00
14 reprints	0.20	0.20	0.60	1.00
15 reprints	0.20	0.20	0.60	1.00
16 Zullivan of Mars	0.20	0.50	1.50	2.50
17 Zullivan of Mars	0.20	0.50	1.50	2.50
18 Zullivan of Mars	0.20	0.50	1.50	2.50
19 Zullivan of Mars	0.20	0.50	1.50	2.50
20 Zullivan of Mars	0.20	0.50	1.50	2.50
21 Zullivan of Mars	0.20	0.50	1.50	2.50
22 Thongon	0.20	0.80	2.40	4.00
23 Thongon	0.20	0.40	1.20	2.00
24 Thongon	0.20	0.40	1.20	2.00
25 Thongon	0.20	0.40	1.20	2.00
26 Thongon	0.20	0.40	1.20	2.00
27 Thongon	0.20	0.40	1.20	2.00
28 Thongon	0.20	0.40	1.20	2.00
29 Thongon	0.25	0.40	1.20	2.00
30 Man-wolf	0.25	0.80	2.40	4.00
31 Man-wolf	0.25	0.30	0.90	1.50
32 Man-wolf	0.25	0.30	0.90	1.50

	ORIG.	GOOD	FINE	N-MINT
33 Man-wolf	0.25	0.30	0.90	1.50
34 Man-wolf	0.25	0.30	0.90	1.50
35 Man-wolf	0.25	0.30	0.90	1.50
36 Man-wolf	0.25	0.30	0.90	1.50
37 Man-wolf	0.25	0.30	0.90	1.50

CYBERSPACE 3000

	ORIG.	GOOD	FINE	N-MINT
1 glowing cover	2.95	0.59	1.77	2.95
2	1.75	0.35	1.05	1.75
3	1.75	0.35	1.05	1.75
4	1.75	0.35	1.05	1.75

D.P.7

	ORIG.	GOOD	FINE	N-MINT
1	0.75	0.40	1.20	2.00
2	0.75	0.40	1.20	2.00
3	0.75	0.40	1.20	2.00
4	0.75	0.40	1.20	2.00
5	0.75	0.40	1.20	2.00
6	0.75	0.40	1.20	2.00
7	0.75	0.40	1.20	2.00
8	0.75	0.40	1.20	2.00
9	0.75	0.40	1.20	2.00
10	0.75	0.40	1.20	2.00
11	0.75	0.40	1.20	2.00
12	0.75	0.40	1.20	2.00
13	0.75	0.40	1.20	2.00
14	0.75	0.40	1.20	2.00
15	0.75	0.40	1.20	2.00
16	0.75	0.40	1.20	2.00
17	0.75	0.40	1.20	2.00
18	0.75	0.40	1.20	2.00
19	1.25	0.25	0.75	1.25
20	1.25	0.25	0.75	1.25
21	1.25	0.25	0.75	1.25
22	1.25	0.25	0.75	1.25
23 A:Psi-Force	1.25	0.25	0.75	1.25
24	1.25	0.25	0.75	1.25
25 A:Nightmask	1.25	0.25	0.75	1.25
26	1.50	0.30	0.90	1.50
27	1.50	0.30	0.90	1.50
28	1.50	0.30	0.90	1.50
29	1.50	0.30	0.90	1.50
30 I:Capt. Manhattan	1.50	0.40	1.20	2.00
31	1.50	0.40	1.20	2.00
32	1.50	0.40	1.20	2.00

D.P.7 ANNUAL

	ORIG.	GOOD	FINE	N-MINT
1 O:D.P.7	1.25	0.25	0.75	1.25

DAKOTA NORTH

	ORIG.	GOOD	FINE	N-MINT
1	0.75	0.20	0.60	1.00
2	0.75	0.20	0.60	1.00
3	0.75	0.20	0.60	1.00
4	0.75	0.20	0.60	1.00
5	0.75	0.20	0.60	1.00

DAMAGE CONTROL

	ORIG.	GOOD	FINE	N-MINT
1 SpM, Thor	1.00	0.60	1.80	3.00
2 Dr. Doom	1.00	0.40	1.20	2.00

	ORIG.	GOOD	FINE	N-MINT
❏ 3 Iron Man	1.00	0.40	1.20	2.00
❏ 4 Wolverine, Inferno	1.00	0.40	1.20	2.00

DAMAGE CONTROL (Volume 2)

	ORIG.	GOOD	FINE	N-MINT
❏ 1 Capt. America, Thor	1.00	0.40	1.20	2.00
❏ 2 Punisher	1.00	0.40	1.20	2.00
❏ 3 She-Hulk	1.00	0.30	0.90	1.50
❏ 4 Thor, Capt. America, Punisher, SHIELD				
	1.00	0.40	1.20	2.00

DAMAGE CONTROL (Volume 3)

	ORIG.	GOOD	FINE	N-MINT
❏ 1 KBaker, SpM	1.25	0.25	0.75	1.25
❏ 2 Hulk	1.25	0.25	0.75	1.25
❏ 3 Galactus	1.25	0.25	0.75	1.25
❏ 4	1.25	0.25	0.75	1.25

DANCES WITH DEMONS

	ORIG.	GOOD	FINE	N-MINT
❏ 1 foil cover	2.95	0.59	1.77	2.95

DAREDEVIL

	ORIG.	GOOD	FINE	N-MINT
❏ 1 BEv, O:DD	0.12	200.00	600.00	1000.00
❏ 2 JO, V:Electro	0.12	80.00	240.00	400.00
❏ 3 JO, O:Owl	0.12	48.00	144.00	240.00
❏ 4 JO, V:Killgrave	0.12	24.00	72.00	120.00
❏ 5 WW, V:Masked Matador				
	0.12	18.00	54.00	90.00
❏ 6 WW, V:Fellowship of Fear				
	0.12	14.00	42.00	70.00
❏ 7 WW, 1:red costume	0.12	36.00	108.00	180.00
❏ 8 WW	0.12	12.00	36.00	60.00
❏ 9 WW	0.12	12.00	36.00	60.00
❏ 10 WW	0.12	12.00	36.00	60.00
❏ 11	0.12	9.00	27.00	45.00
❏ 12	0.12	9.00	27.00	45.00
❏ 13	0.12	9.00	27.00	45.00
❏ 14	0.12	9.00	27.00	45.00
❏ 15	0.12	9.00	27.00	45.00
❏ 16	0.12	8.00	24.00	40.00
❏ 17 Spider-Man	0.12	15.00	45.00	75.00
❏ 18 JR, Gladiator	0.12	7.00	21.00	35.00
❏ 19 JR, Gladiator	0.12	7.00	21.00	35.00
❏ 20 GC, V:Owl	0.12	6.00	18.00	30.00
❏ 21 GC, V:Owl	0.12	6.00	18.00	30.00
❏ 22 GC	0.12	6.00	18.00	30.00
❏ 23 GC	0.12	6.00	18.00	30.00
❏ 24 GC	0.12	6.00	18.00	30.00
❏ 25 GC	0.12	6.00	18.00	30.00
❏ 26 GC	0.12	6.00	18.00	30.00
❏ 27 GC	0.12	6.00	18.00	30.00
❏ 28 GC	0.12	6.00	18.00	30.00
❏ 29 GC	0.12	6.00	18.00	30.00
❏ 30 GC, A:Thor	0.12	7.20	21.60	36.00
❏ 31 GC, Cobra	0.12	4.00	12.00	20.00
❏ 32 GC, Cobra	0.12	4.00	12.00	20.00
❏ 33 GC, Cobra	0.12	4.00	12.00	20.00
❏ 34 GC, Cobra	0.12	4.00	12.00	20.00
❏ 35 GC, Cobra	0.12	4.00	12.00	20.00
❏ 36 GC, Cobra	0.12	4.00	12.00	20.00

	ORIG.	GOOD	FINE	N-MINT
❏ 37 GC, Cobra	0.12	4.00	12.00	20.00
❏ 38 GC, Cobra	0.12	4.00	12.00	20.00
❏ 39 GC, Cobra	0.12	4.00	12.00	20.00
❏ 40 GC, Cobra	0.12	4.00	12.00	20.00
❏ 41 D:Mike Murdock	0.12	4.00	12.00	20.00
❏ 42 GC	0.12	4.00	12.00	20.00
❏ 43 GC	0.12	4.00	12.00	20.00
❏ 44 GC	0.12	4.00	12.00	20.00
❏ 45 GC	0.12	4.00	12.00	20.00
❏ 46 GC	0.12	4.00	12.00	20.00
❏ 47 GC	0.12	4.00	12.00	20.00
❏ 48 GC	0.12	4.00	12.00	20.00
❏ 49 GC	0.12	4.00	12.00	20.00
❏ 50 BS	0.12	4.00	12.00	20.00
❏ 51 BS	0.12	4.00	12.00	20.00
❏ 52 BS	0.12	4.00	12.00	20.00
❏ 53 GC, O:DD	0.12	4.00	12.00	20.00
❏ 54 GC	0.15	2.00	6.00	10.00
❏ 55 GC	0.15	2.00	6.00	10.00
❏ 56 GC	0.15	2.00	6.00	10.00
❏ 57 GC	0.15	2.00	6.00	10.00
❏ 58 GC	0.15	2.00	6.00	10.00
❏ 59 GC	0.15	2.00	6.00	10.00
❏ 60 GC	0.15	2.00	6.00	10.00
❏ 61 GC	0.15	2.00	6.00	10.00
❏ 62 GC, O:Nighthawk	0.15	2.00	6.00	10.00
❏ 63 GC	0.15	2.00	6.00	10.00
❏ 64 GC	0.15	2.00	6.00	10.00
❏ 65 GC	0.15	2.00	6.00	10.00
❏ 66 GC	0.15	2.00	6.00	10.00
❏ 67 GC	0.15	2.00	6.00	10.00
❏ 68 GC	0.15	2.00	6.00	10.00
❏ 69 GC	0.15	2.00	6.00	10.00
❏ 70 GC	0.15	2.00	6.00	10.00
❏ 71 GC	0.15	2.00	6.00	10.00
❏ 72 GC	0.15	2.00	6.00	10.00
❏ 73 GC	0.15	2.00	6.00	10.00
❏ 74 GC	0.15	2.00	6.00	10.00
❏ 75 GC	0.15	2.00	6.00	10.00
❏ 76 GC	0.15	2.00	6.00	10.00
❏ 77 GC	0.15	2.00	6.00	10.00
❏ 78 GC	0.15	2.00	6.00	10.00
❏ 79 GC	0.15	2.00	6.00	10.00
❏ 80 GC	0.15	2.00	6.00	10.00
❏ 81 GC, giant	0.25	2.00	6.00	10.00
❏ 82 GC	0.20	2.00	6.00	10.00
❏ 83 BS, V:Mr. Hyde	0.20	2.00	6.00	10.00
❏ 84	0.20	2.00	6.00	10.00
❏ 85	0.20	2.00	6.00	10.00
❏ 86	0.20	2.00	6.00	10.00
❏ 87	0.20	2.00	6.00	10.00
❏ 88	0.20	2.00	6.00	10.00
❏ 89	0.20	2.00	6.00	10.00
❏ 90	0.20	2.00	6.00	10.00
❏ 91	0.20	2.00	6.00	10.00

	ORIG.	GOOD	FINE	N-MINT
92	0.20	2.00	6.00	10.00
93	0.20	2.00	6.00	10.00
94	0.20	2.00	6.00	10.00
95	0.20	2.00	6.00	10.00
96	0.20	2.00	6.00	10.00
97	0.20	2.00	6.00	10.00
98	0.20	2.00	6.00	10.00
99	0.20	2.00	6.00	10.00
100 GC, anniversary	0.20	4.80	14.40	24.00
101	0.20	1.00	3.00	5.00
102	0.20	1.00	3.00	5.00
103	0.20	1.00	3.00	5.00
104	0.20	1.00	3.00	5.00
105 O:Moondragon	0.20	1.00	3.00	5.00
106 DH, A:Black Widow	0.20	1.00	3.00	5.00
107 SB, A:Capt. Marvel	0.20	1.00	3.00	5.00
108	0.20	1.00	3.00	5.00
109	0.25	1.00	3.00	5.00
110	0.25	1.00	3.00	5.00
111	0.25	1.00	3.00	5.00
112	0.25	1.00	3.00	5.00
113	0.25	1.00	3.00	5.00
114 1:Death Stalker	0.25	1.00	3.00	5.00
115	0.25	1.00	3.00	5.00
116	0.25	1.00	3.00	5.00
117	0.25	1.00	3.00	5.00
118	0.25	1.00	3.00	5.00
119	0.25	1.00	3.00	5.00
120	0.25	1.00	3.00	5.00
121	0.25	1.00	3.00	5.00
122	0.25	1.00	3.00	5.00
123	0.25	1.00	3.00	5.00
124 GC/KJ, 1:Copperhead	0.25	1.00	3.00	5.00
125 KJ	0.25	1.00	3.00	5.00
126 KJ	0.25	1.00	3.00	5.00
127 KJ	0.25	1.00	3.00	5.00
128 KJ	0.25	1.00	3.00	5.00
129 KJ	0.25	1.00	3.00	5.00
130 KJ	0.25	1.00	3.00	5.00
131 KJ, O:Bullseye	0.25	5.00	15.00	25.00
132	0.25	1.00	3.00	5.00
133	0.25	1.00	3.00	5.00
134	0.25	1.00	3.00	5.00
135	0.25	1.00	3.00	5.00
136	0.25	1.00	3.00	5.00
137	0.30	1.00	3.00	5.00
138 JBy, A:Ghost Rider	0.30	2.00	6.00	10.00
139	0.30	1.00	3.00	5.00
140	0.30	1.00	3.00	5.00
141	0.30	1.00	3.00	5.00
142	0.30	1.00	3.00	5.00
143	0.30	1.00	3.00	5.00
144	0.30	1.00	3.00	5.00
145	0.30	1.00	3.00	5.00
146	0.30	1.00	3.00	5.00
147	0.30	1.00	3.00	5.00
148	0.30	1.00	3.00	5.00
149	0.35	1.00	3.00	5.00
150 KJ, I:Paladin	0.35	1.00	3.00	5.00
151	0.35	1.00	3.00	5.00
152	0.35	1.00	3.00	5.00
153	0.35	1.00	3.00	5.00
154	0.35	1.00	3.00	5.00
155	0.35	1.00	3.00	5.00
156	0.35	1.00	3.00	5.00
157	0.35	1.00	3.00	5.00
158 FM, V:Deathstalker	0.40	8.00	24.00	40.00
159 FM, V:Bullseye	0.40	6.00	18.00	30.00
160 FM, V:Bullseye	0.40	3.20	9.60	16.00
161 FM, V:Bullseye	0.40	3.20	9.60	16.00
162 SD	0.40	0.80	2.40	4.00
163 FM	0.40	2.40	7.20	12.00
164 FM	0.40	2.40	7.20	12.00
165 FM	0.40	2.40	7.20	12.00
166 FM	0.50	2.40	7.20	12.00
167 FM	0.50	2.40	7.20	12.00
168 FM, O&1:Elektra	0.50	7.00	21.00	35.00
169 FM, V:Bullseye	0.50	2.40	7.20	12.00
170 FM, V:Bullseye	0.50	2.40	7.20	12.00
171 FM	0.50	1.60	4.80	8.00
172 FM	0.50	1.60	4.80	8.00
173 FM	0.50	1.60	4.80	8.00
174 FM	0.50	2.40	7.20	12.00
175 FM	0.50	2.40	7.20	12.00
176 FM, A:Elektra	0.50	2.00	6.00	10.00
177 FM	0.50	1.00	3.00	5.00
178 FM	0.60	1.00	3.00	5.00
179 FM	0.60	1.00	3.00	5.00
180 FM	0.60	1.00	3.00	5.00
181 FM, V:Bullseye, D:Elektra	1.00	3.00	9.00	15.00
182 FM, V:Punisher	0.60	2.80	8.40	14.00
183 FM, V:Punisher	0.60	2.80	8.40	14.00
184 FM, V:Punisher	0.60	2.80	8.40	14.00
185 FM	0.60	0.60	1.80	3.00
186 FM	0.60	0.60	1.80	3.00
187 FM	0.60	0.60	1.80	3.00
188 FM	0.60	0.60	1.80	3.00
189 FM	0.60	0.60	1.80	3.00
190 FM	1.00	0.60	1.80	3.00
191 FM	0.60	0.60	1.80	3.00
192 KJ	0.60	0.40	1.20	2.00
193 KJ	0.60	0.40	1.20	2.00
194 KJ	0.60	0.40	1.20	2.00
195 KJ	0.60	0.40	1.20	2.00
196 KJ, A:Wolverine	0.60	2.00	6.00	10.00
197 V:Bullseye	0.60	1.00	3.00	5.00
198	0.60	0.40	1.20	2.00
199	0.60	0.40	1.20	2.00

	ORIG.	GOOD	FINE	N-MINT		ORIG.	GOOD	FINE	N-MINT
☐ 200	0.60	0.40	1.20	2.00	☐ 255 Typhoid Mary	0.75	2.40	7.20	12.00
☐ 201	0.60	0.40	1.20	2.00	☐ 256	0.75	0.80	2.40	4.00
☐ 202	0.60	0.40	1.20	2.00	☐ 257 A:Punisher	0.75	4.80	14.40	24.00
☐ 203	0.60	0.40	1.20	2.00	☐ 258 1:Bengal	0.75	0.30	0.90	1.50
☐ 204	0.60	0.40	1.20	2.00	☐ 259	0.75	0.30	0.90	1.50
☐ 205	0.60	0.40	1.20	2.00	☐ 260 giant	1.50	0.30	0.90	1.50
☐ 206	0.60	0.40	1.20	2.00	☐ 261 A:Human Torch	0.75	0.30	0.90	1.50
☐ 207	0.60	0.40	1.20	2.00	☐ 262 Inferno	0.75	0.30	0.90	1.50
☐ 208	0.60	0.25	0.75	1.25	☐ 263 Inferno	0.75	0.30	0.90	1.50
☐ 209	0.60	0.25	0.75	1.25	☐ 264	0.75	0.30	0.90	1.50
☐ 210	0.60	0.25	0.75	1.25	☐ 265 Inferno	0.75	0.30	0.90	1.50
☐ 211	0.60	0.25	0.75	1.25	☐ 266	0.75	0.30	0.90	1.50
☐ 212	0.60	0.25	0.75	1.25	☐ 267	0.75	0.30	0.90	1.50
☐ 213	0.60	0.25	0.75	1.25	☐ 268	0.75	0.30	0.90	1.50
☐ 214	0.60	0.25	0.75	1.25	☐ 269	0.75	0.30	0.90	1.50
☐ 215	0.60	0.25	0.75	1.25	☐ 270 Spider-Man	1.00	0.80	2.40	4.00
☐ 216	0.60	0.25	0.75	1.25	☐ 271	1.00	0.20	0.60	1.00
☐ 217	0.65	0.25	0.75	1.25	☐ 272 1:Shotgun	1.00	0.20	0.60	1.00
☐ 218	0.65	0.25	0.75	1.25	☐ 273	1.00	0.20	0.60	1.00
☐ 219 FM	0.65	0.80	2.40	4.00	☐ 274	1.00	0.20	0.60	1.00
☐ 220	0.65	0.25	0.75	1.25	☐ 275 Vengeance	1.00	0.30	0.90	1.50
☐ 221	0.65	0.25	0.75	1.25	☐ 276 Vengeance	1.00	0.30	0.90	1.50
☐ 222	0.65	0.25	0.75	1.25	☐ 277	1.00	0.30	0.90	1.50
☐ 223 Secret Wars II	0.65	0.25	0.75	1.25	☐ 278	1.00	0.30	0.90	1.50
☐ 224	0.65	0.25	0.75	1.25	☐ 279	1.00	0.30	0.90	1.50
☐ 225	0.65	0.25	0.75	1.25	☐ 280	1.00	0.30	0.90	1.50
☐ 226 FM	0.65	1.40	4.20	7.00	☐ 281	1.00	0.30	0.90	1.50
☐ 227 FM writer, Kingpin	0.75	1.60	4.80	8.00	☐ 282	1.00	0.30	0.90	1.50
☐ 228 FM writer, layouts	0.75	1.20	3.60	6.00	☐ 283 Capt. America	1.00	0.30	0.90	1.50
☐ 229 FM writer, layouts	0.75	1.20	3.60	6.00	☐ 284	1.00	0.30	0.90	1.50
☐ 230 FM writer, layouts	0.75	1.20	3.60	6.00	☐ 285	1.00	0.30	0.90	1.50
☐ 231 FM writer, layouts	0.75	1.20	3.60	6.00	☐ 286	1.00	0.30	0.90	1.50
☐ 232 FM writer, layouts	0.75	1.20	3.60	6.00	☐ 287	1.00	0.30	0.90	1.50
☐ 233 FM writer, layouts	0.75	1.20	3.60	6.00	☐ 288	1.00	0.30	0.90	1.50
☐ 234	0.75	0.80	2.40	4.00	☐ 289	1.00	0.30	0.90	1.50
☐ 235	0.75	0.80	2.40	4.00	☐ 290	1.00	0.30	0.90	1.50
☐ 236	0.75	0.80	2.40	4.00	☐ 291	1.00	0.30	0.90	1.50
☐ 237	0.75	0.80	2.40	4.00	☐ 292 Punisher	1.00	0.40	1.20	2.00
☐ 238 mutant massacre	0.75	0.80	2.40	4.00	☐ 293 Punisher	1.00	0.40	1.20	2.00
☐ 239 AAd(c)	0.75	0.70	2.10	3.50	☐ 294	1.00	0.20	0.60	1.00
☐ 240	0.75	0.40	1.20	2.00	☐ 295	1.00	0.20	0.60	1.00
☐ 241	0.75	0.40	1.20	2.00	☐ 296	1.00	0.20	0.60	1.00
☐ 242	0.75	0.40	1.20	2.00	☐ 297	1.00	0.20	0.60	1.00
☐ 243	0.75	0.40	1.20	2.00	☐ 298	1.00	0.20	0.60	1.00
☐ 244	0.75	0.40	1.20	2.00	☐ 299	1.00	0.20	0.60	1.00
☐ 245 A:Black Panther	0.75	0.40	1.20	2.00	☐ 300 fall of Kingpin	2.00	0.70	2.10	3.50
☐ 246	0.75	0.40	1.20	2.00	☐ 301 V:Owl	1.25	0.25	0.75	1.25
☐ 247	0.75	0.40	1.20	2.00	☐ 302 V:Owl	1.25	0.25	0.75	1.25
☐ 248 A:Wolverine	0.75	2.40	7.20	12.00	☐ 303 V:Owl	1.25	0.25	0.75	1.25
☐ 249 A:Wolverine	0.75	2.40	7.20	12.00	☐ 304	1.25	0.25	0.75	1.25
☐ 250	0.75	0.20	0.60	1.00	☐ 305	1.25	0.25	0.75	1.25
☐ 251	0.75	0.20	0.60	1.00	☐ 306	1.25	0.25	0.75	1.25
☐ 252 Fall of Mutants	1.25	0.25	0.75	1.25	☐ 307	1.25	0.25	0.75	1.25
☐ 253 Typhoid Mary	0.75	2.40	7.20	12.00	☐ 308	1.25	0.25	0.75	1.25
☐ 254 Typhoid Mary	0.75	2.80	8.40	14.00	☐ 309	1.25	0.25	0.75	1.25

	ORIG.	GOOD	FINE	N-MINT
❑ 310	1.25	0.25	0.75	1.25
❑ 311	1.25	0.25	0.75	1.25
❑ 312	1.25	0.25	0.75	1.25
❑ 313	1.25	0.25	0.75	1.25
❑ 314	1.25	0.25	0.75	1.25
❑ 315	1.25	0.25	0.75	1.25
❑ 316	1.25	0.25	0.75	1.25
❑ 317	1.25	0.25	0.75	1.25
❑ 318	1.25	0.25	0.75	1.25
❑ 319	1.25	0.25	0.75	1.25
❑ 320	1.25	0.25	0.75	1.25

DAREDEVIL ANNUAL

	ORIG.	GOOD	FINE	N-MINT
❑ 1 GC	0.25	4.40	13.20	22.00
❑ 2 reprint	0.25	1.60	4.80	8.00
❑ 3 reprint	0.25	1.60	4.80	8.00
❑ 4 (1976) reprint	0.50	1.00	3.00	5.00
❑ 4 (1989, misnumbered) Atlantis Attacks	2.00	1.00	3.00	5.00
❑ 6 Lifeform	2.00	0.40	1.20	2.00
❑ 7	2.00	0.40	1.20	2.00
❑ 8	2.25	0.45	1.35	2.25
❑ 9 trading card	2.95	0.59	1.77	2.95

DAREDEVIL: MAN WITHOUT FEAR

	ORIG.	GOOD	FINE	N-MINT
❑ 1 FM(w),JRjr,AW	2.95	0.59	1.77	2.95

DARK ANGEL (formerly Hell's Angel)

	ORIG.	GOOD	FINE	N-MINT
❑ 6	1.75	0.35	1.05	1.75
❑ 7	1.75	0.35	1.05	1.75
❑ 8	1.75	0.35	1.05	1.75
❑ 9	1.75	0.35	1.05	1.75
❑ 10	1.75	0.35	1.05	1.75
❑ 11	1.75	0.35	1.05	1.75
❑ 12	1.75	0.35	1.05	1.75
❑ 13	1.75	0.35	1.05	1.75

DARK CRYSTAL

	ORIG.	GOOD	FINE	N-MINT
❑ 1 movie	0.60	0.20	0.60	1.00
❑ 2 movie	0.60	0.20	0.60	1.00

DARK GUARD

	ORIG.	GOOD	FINE	N-MINT
❑ 1 foil cover	2.25	0.45	1.35	2.25

DARKHAWK

	ORIG.	GOOD	FINE	N-MINT
❑ 1	1.00	2.80	8.40	14.00
❑ 2 Spider-Man	1.00	1.60	4.80	8.00
❑ 3 SpM	1.00	1.40	4.20	7.00
❑ 4	1.00	1.00	3.00	5.00
❑ 5	1.00	1.00	3.00	5.00
❑ 6 Daredevil, Capt. America	1.00	0.60	1.80	3.00
❑ 7	1.00	0.60	1.80	3.00
❑ 8	1.00	0.60	1.80	3.00
❑ 9 Punisher	1.00	0.60	1.80	3.00
❑ 10	1.00	0.40	1.20	2.00
❑ 11	1.00	0.40	1.20	2.00
❑ 12	1.25	0.25	0.75	1.25
❑ 13 (Venom)	1.25	2.00	6.00	10.00
❑ 14 (Venom)	1.25	1.60	4.80	8.00

	ORIG.	GOOD	FINE	N-MINT
❑ 15	1.25	0.25	0.75	1.25
❑ 16	1.25	0.25	0.75	1.25
❑ 17	1.25	0.25	0.75	1.25
❑ 18	1.25	0.25	0.75	1.25
❑ 19	1.25	0.25	0.75	1.25
❑ 20	1.25	0.25	0.75	1.25
❑ 21	1.25	0.25	0.75	1.25
❑ 22	1.25	0.25	0.75	1.25
❑ 23	1.25	0.25	0.75	1.25
❑ 24	1.25	0.25	0.75	1.25
❑ 25 foil cover	2.95	0.80	2.40	4.00
❑ 26	1.25	0.25	0.75	1.25
❑ 27	1.25	0.25	0.75	1.25
❑ 28	1.25	0.25	0.75	1.25
❑ 29	1.25	0.25	0.75	1.25
❑ 30	1.25	0.25	0.75	1.25
❑ 31	1.25	0.25	0.75	1.25
❑ 32	1.25	0.25	0.75	1.25

DARKHAWK ANNUAL

	ORIG.	GOOD	FINE	N-MINT
❑ 1	2.25	0.45	1.35	2.25
❑ 2 trading card	2.95	0.59	1.77	2.95

DARKHOLD

	ORIG.	GOOD	FINE	N-MINT
❑ 1 Midnight Sons, polybagged, poster	2.75	0.70	2.10	3.50
❑ 2	1.75	0.35	1.05	1.75
❑ 3	1.75	0.35	1.05	1.75
❑ 4	1.75	0.35	1.05	1.75
❑ 5	1.75	0.35	1.05	1.75
❑ 6	1.75	0.35	1.05	1.75
❑ 7	1.75	0.35	1.05	1.75
❑ 8	1.75	0.35	1.05	1.75
❑ 9	1.75	0.35	1.05	1.75
❑ 10	1.75	0.35	1.05	1.75
❑ 11	1.75	0.35	1.05	1.75
❑ 12	1.75	0.35	1.05	1.75
❑ 13	1.75	0.35	1.05	1.75

DARKMAN

	ORIG.	GOOD	FINE	N-MINT
❑ 1 b&w mag, movie	2.25	0.45	1.35	2.25
❑ 1 comic book	1.50	0.20	0.60	1.00
❑ 2 comic book	1.50	0.20	0.60	1.00
❑ 3 comic book	1.50	0.20	0.60	1.00

DARKMAN (1993 ongoing series)

	ORIG.	GOOD	FINE	N-MINT
❑ 1	3.95	0.79	2.37	3.95
❑ 2	2.95	0.59	1.77	2.95
❑ 3	2.95	0.59	1.77	2.95
❑ 4	2.95	0.59	1.77	2.95
❑ 5	2.95	0.59	1.77	2.95
❑ 6	2.95	0.59	1.77	2.95

DAZZLER

	ORIG.	GOOD	FINE	N-MINT
❑ 1 JR2, direct	0.50	0.50	1.50	2.50
❑ 2 JR2/AA, X-Men	0.50	0.40	1.20	2.00
❑ 3	0.50	0.20	0.60	1.00
❑ 4	0.50	0.20	0.60	1.00
❑ 5	0.50	0.20	0.60	1.00

	ORIG.	GOOD	FINE	N-MINT
6	0.50	0.20	0.60	1.00
7	0.50	0.20	0.60	1.00
8	0.50	0.20	0.60	1.00
9	0.50	0.20	0.60	1.00
10	0.50	0.20	0.60	1.00
11	0.60	0.20	0.60	1.00
12	0.60	0.20	0.60	1.00
13	0.60	0.20	0.60	1.00
14	0.60	0.20	0.60	1.00
15 FS/BSz	0.60	0.30	0.90	1.50
16 FS/BSz	0.60	0.30	0.90	1.50
17 FS, Angel	0.60	0.20	0.60	1.00
18 FS/BSz, FF	0.60	0.30	0.90	1.50
19	0.60	0.20	0.60	1.00
20	0.60	0.20	0.60	1.00
21 giant	1.00	0.20	0.60	1.00
22	0.60	0.20	0.60	1.00
23	0.60	0.20	0.60	1.00
24	0.60	0.20	0.60	1.00
25	0.60	0.20	0.60	1.00
26	0.60	0.20	0.60	1.00
27	0.60	0.20	0.60	1.00
28	0.60	0.20	0.60	1.00
29	0.60	0.20	0.60	1.00
30	0.60	0.20	0.60	1.00
31	0.60	0.20	0.60	1.00
32	0.60	0.20	0.60	1.00
33	0.60	0.20	0.60	1.00
34	0.60	0.20	0.60	1.00
35	0.60	0.20	0.60	1.00
36	0.60	0.20	0.60	1.00
37	0.65	0.20	0.60	1.00
38	0.65	0.20	0.60	1.00
39	0.65	0.20	0.60	1.00
40 Secret Wars II	0.65	0.35	1.05	1.75
41	0.65	0.20	0.60	1.00
42	0.75	0.20	0.60	1.00

DEAD OF NIGHT

	ORIG.	GOOD	FINE	N-MINT
1 reprints	0.20	0.40	1.20	2.00
2 reprints	0.20	0.20	0.60	1.00
3 reprints	0.20	0.20	0.60	1.00
4 reprints	0.20	0.20	0.60	1.00
5 reprints	0.20	0.20	0.60	1.00
6 reprints	0.20	0.20	0.60	1.00
7 reprints	0.20	0.20	0.60	1.00
8 reprints	0.20	0.20	0.60	1.00
9 reprints	0.20	0.20	0.60	1.00
10 reprints	0.20	0.20	0.60	1.00
11 I:Scarecrow	0.25	0.60	1.80	3.00

DEADLIEST HEROES OF KUNG FU, THE

	ORIG.	GOOD	FINE	N-MINT
1 (b&w mag)	1.00	0.20	0.60	1.00

DEADLY FOES OF SPIDER-MAN

	ORIG.	GOOD	FINE	N-MINT
1	1.00	0.60	1.80	3.00
2 SpM	1.00	0.40	1.20	2.00
3 SpM	1.00	0.40	1.20	2.00
4 SpM	1.00	0.40	1.20	2.00

DEADLY HANDS OF KUNG FU (b&w mag)

	ORIG.	GOOD	FINE	N-MINT
1	0.75	0.15	0.45	0.75
2	0.75	0.15	0.45	0.75
3	0.75	0.15	0.45	0.75
4	0.75	0.15	0.45	0.75
5	0.75	0.15	0.45	0.75
6	0.75	0.15	0.45	0.75
7	0.75	0.15	0.45	0.75
8	0.75	0.15	0.45	0.75
9	0.75	0.15	0.45	0.75
10	0.75	0.15	0.45	0.75
11	0.75	0.15	0.45	0.75
12	0.75	0.15	0.45	0.75
13	0.75	0.15	0.45	0.75
14	0.75	0.15	0.45	0.75
15	1.25	0.25	0.75	1.25
16	1.00	0.20	0.60	1.00
17	1.00	0.20	0.60	1.00
18	1.00	0.20	0.60	1.00
19	1.00	0.20	0.60	1.00
20	1.00	0.20	0.60	1.00
21	1.00	0.20	0.60	1.00
22	1.00	0.20	0.60	1.00
23	1.00	0.20	0.60	1.00
24	1.00	0.20	0.60	1.00
25	1.00	0.20	0.60	1.00
26	1.00	0.20	0.60	1.00
27	1.00	0.20	0.60	1.00
28	1.00	0.20	0.60	1.00
29	1.00	0.20	0.60	1.00
30	1.00	0.20	0.60	1.00
31	1.00	0.20	0.60	1.00
32	1.00	0.20	0.60	1.00
33	1.00	0.20	0.60	1.00

DEADLY HANDS OF KUNG FU SPECIAL (b&w mag)

	ORIG.	GOOD	FINE	N-MINT
1	1.00	0.20	0.60	1.00

DEADPOOL

	ORIG.	GOOD	FINE	N-MINT
1 embossed cover	2.50	0.70	2.10	3.50
2	2.00	0.40	1.20	2.00
3	2.00	0.40	1.20	2.00

DEATH'S HEAD

	ORIG.	GOOD	FINE	N-MINT
1	1.75	3.00	9.00	15.00
2	1.75	1.20	3.60	6.00
3	1.75	1.20	3.60	6.00
4	1.75	1.20	3.60	6.00
5	1.75	1.20	3.60	6.00
6	1.75	1.20	3.60	6.00
7	1.75	1.20	3.60	6.00
8 Doctor Who	1.75	1.00	3.00	5.00

	ORIG.	GOOD	FINE	N-MINT
9 Fantastic 4 .... 1.75	1.00	3.00	5.00
10 Iron Man of 2020 .... 1.75	1.00	3.00	5.00

DEATH'S HEAD II

	ORIG.	GOOD	FINE	N-MINT
1 1st printing 1.75	3.00	9.00	15.00
1 2nd printing.................. 1.75	0.35	1.05	1.75
2 1st printing 1.75	2.00	6.00	10.00
2 2nd printing.................. 1.75	0.35	1.05	1.75
3 .... 1.75	1.60	4.80	8.00
4 .... 1.75	1.00	3.00	5.00
5 .... 1.75	0.35	1.05	1.75
6 .... 1.75	0.35	1.05	1.75
9 .... 1.95	0.39	1.17	1.95
10 .... 1.95	0.39	1.17	1.95

DEATH'S HEAD II & THE ORIGIN OF DIE CUT

	ORIG.	GOOD	FINE	N-MINT
1 foil cover 2.95	0.59	1.77	2.95
2 .... 1.75	0.35	1.05	1.75

DEATH'S HEAD II (ongoing series)

	ORIG.	GOOD	FINE	N-MINT
1 .... 1.75	0.35	1.05	1.75
2 .... 1.75	0.35	1.05	1.75
3 .... 1.75	0.35	1.05	1.75
4 .... 1.75	0.35	1.05	1.75
5 .... 1.75	0.35	1.05	1.75
6 .... 1.95	0.39	1.17	1.95
7 .... 1.95	0.39	1.17	1.95
8 .... 1.95	0.39	1.17	1.95
9 .... 1.95	0.39	1.17	1.95
10 .... 1.95	0.39	1.17	1.95

DEATH'S HEAD II (volume 2)

	ORIG.	GOOD	FINE	N-MINT
1	1.00	3.00	5.00

DEATH'S HEAD II/KILLPOWER-BATTLETIDE

	ORIG.	GOOD	FINE	N-MINT
1	0.45	1.35	2.25
2	0.35	1.05	1.75
3	0.35	1.05	1.75
4	0.35	1.05	1.75

DEATH3

	ORIG.	GOOD	FINE	N-MINT
1 foil cover 2.95	0.59	1.77	2.95
2 .... 1.75	0.35	1.05	1.75

DEATHLOK (mini-series)

	ORIG.	GOOD	FINE	N-MINT
1 O:Deathlok.................... 3.95	2.00	6.00	10.00
2 .... 3.95	1.60	4.80	8.00
3 .... 3.95	1.60	4.80	8.00
4 .... 3.95	1.60	4.80	8.00

DEATHLOK (starting July '91)

	ORIG.	GOOD	FINE	N-MINT
1 .... 1.75	1.20	3.60	6.00
2 .... 1.75	0.60	1.80	3.00
3 Dr. Doom 1.75	0.50	1.50	2.50
4 .... 1.75	0.35	1.05	1.75
5 .... 1.75	0.35	1.05	1.75
6 Punisher 1.75	0.35	1.05	1.75
7 Punisher 1.75	0.35	1.05	1.75
8 .... 1.75	0.35	1.05	1.75
9 Ghost Rider 1.75	0.35	1.05	1.75
10 .... 1.75	0.35	1.05	1.75

	ORIG.	GOOD	FINE	N-MINT
11 .... 1.75	0.35	1.05	1.75
12 .... 1.75	0.35	1.05	1.75
13 .... 1.75	0.35	1.05	1.75
14 .... 1.75	0.35	1.05	1.75
15 .... 1.75	0.35	1.05	1.75
16 .... 1.75	0.35	1.05	1.75
17 .... 1.75	0.35	1.05	1.75
18 .... 1.75	0.45	1.35	2.25
19 foil cover..................... 2.25	0.45	1.35	2.25
20 .... 1.75	0.35	1.05	1.75
21 .... 1.75	0.35	1.05	1.75
22 .... 1.75	0.35	1.05	1.75
23 .... 1.75	0.35	1.05	1.75
24 .... 1.75	0.35	1.05	1.75
25 foil cover..................... 2.95	0.59	1.77	2.95
26 .... 1.75	0.35	1.05	1.75
27 .... 1.75	0.35	1.05	1.75

DEATHLOK ANNUAL

	ORIG.	GOOD	FINE	N-MINT
1 .... 2.50	0.50	1.50	2.50

DEATHLOK SPECIAL

	ORIG.	GOOD	FINE	N-MINT
1 reprint.......................... 2.00	0.80	2.40	4.00
2 reprint.......................... 2.00	0.60	1.80	3.00
3 reprint.......................... 2.00	0.60	1.80	3.00
4 reprint.......................... 2.00	0.60	1.80	3.00

DEEP, THE

	ORIG.	GOOD	FINE	N-MINT
1 movie 0.60	0.20	0.60	1.00

DEFENDERS

	ORIG.	GOOD	FINE	N-MINT
1 SB, Hulk 0.20	11.00	33.00	55.00
2 SB, Silver Surfer 0.20	5.00	15.00	25.00
3 SB/JM, Silver Surfer....... 0.20	2.80	8.40	14.00
4 SB/FMc 0.20	2.80	8.40	14.00
5 SB/FMc 0.20	2.80	8.40	14.00
6 SB/FMc 0.20	2.80	8.40	14.00
7 SB, A:Hawkeye 0.20	2.40	7.20	12.00
8 Avengers...................... 0.20	2.40	7.20	12.00
9 Avengers...................... 0.20	2.40	7.20	12.00
10 Avengers.................... 0.20	2.40	7.20	12.00
11 Avengers.................... 0.20	1.60	4.80	8.00
12 .... 0.20	1.60	4.80	8.00
13 .... 0.25	1.60	4.80	8.00
14 .... 0.25	1.60	4.80	8.00
15 .... 0.25	1.60	4.80	8.00
16 .... 0.25	1.60	4.80	8.00
17 .... 0.25	1.60	4.80	8.00
18 .... 0.25	1.60	4.80	8.00
19 .... 0.25	1.60	4.80	8.00
20 SB, Thing 0.25	1.60	4.80	8.00
21 SB 0.25	1.60	4.80	8.00
22 SB 0.25	1.60	4.80	8.00
23 SB 0.25	1.60	4.80	8.00
24 Daredevil.................... 0.25	1.60	4.80	8.00
25 Daredevil.................... 0.25	1.60	4.80	8.00
26 .... 0.25	2.00	6.00	10.00
27 .... 0.25	2.00	6.00	10.00

	ORIG.	GOOD	FINE	N-MINT
☐ 28	0.25	2.00	6.00	10.00
☐ 29	0.25	2.00	6.00	10.00
☐ 30	0.25	1.00	3.00	5.00
☐ 31	0.25	0.80	2.40	4.00
☐ 32 O:Nighthawk	0.25	0.80	2.40	4.00
☐ 33	0.25	0.80	2.40	4.00
☐ 34	0.25	0.80	2.40	4.00
☐ 35	0.25	0.80	2.40	4.00
☐ 36	0.25	0.80	2.40	4.00
☐ 37 SB/KJ	0.25	0.80	2.40	4.00
☐ 38 SB/KJ	0.25	0.80	2.40	4.00
☐ 39 SB/KJ	0.30	0.80	2.40	4.00
☐ 40 SB/KJ	0.30	0.80	2.40	4.00
☐ 41 SB/KJ	0.30	0.80	2.40	4.00
☐ 42 KG/KJ	0.30	0.80	2.40	4.00
☐ 43 KG/KJ	0.30	0.80	2.40	4.00
☐ 44 KG/KJ	0.30	0.80	2.40	4.00
☐ 45 KG/KJ	0.30	0.80	2.40	4.00
☐ 46 KG/KJ	0.30	0.80	2.40	4.00
☐ 47 KG/KJ, Moon Knight	0.30	0.80	2.40	4.00
☐ 48 KG	0.30	0.80	2.40	4.00
☐ 49 KG	0.30	0.80	2.40	4.00
☐ 50 KG	0.30	0.80	2.40	4.00
☐ 51 KG, Moon Knight	0.30	0.60	1.80	3.00
☐ 52 KG, Hulk V:Sub-Mariner	0.30	0.60	1.80	3.00
☐ 53 MG	0.35	0.60	1.80	3.00
☐ 54 MG	0.35	0.60	1.80	3.00
☐ 55	0.35	0.60	1.80	3.00
☐ 56	0.35	0.60	1.80	3.00
☐ 57	0.35	0.60	1.80	3.00
☐ 58	0.35	0.60	1.80	3.00
☐ 59	0.35	0.60	1.80	3.00
☐ 60	0.35	0.60	1.80	3.00
☐ 61	0.35	0.60	1.80	3.00
☐ 62	0.35	0.60	1.80	3.00
☐ 63	0.35	0.60	1.80	3.00
☐ 64	0.35	0.60	1.80	3.00
☐ 65	0.35	0.60	1.80	3.00
☐ 66	0.35	0.60	1.80	3.00
☐ 67	0.35	0.60	1.80	3.00
☐ 68	0.35	0.60	1.80	3.00
☐ 69	0.35	0.60	1.80	3.00
☐ 70	0.35	0.60	1.80	3.00
☐ 71	0.40	0.60	1.80	3.00
☐ 72	0.40	0.60	1.80	3.00
☐ 73 Foolkiller	0.40	1.00	3.00	5.00
☐ 74 Foolkiller	0.40	1.00	3.00	5.00
☐ 75 Foolkiller	0.40	1.00	3.00	5.00
☐ 76	0.40	0.60	1.80	3.00
☐ 77	0.40	0.60	1.80	3.00
☐ 78	0.40	0.60	1.80	3.00
☐ 79	0.40	0.60	1.80	3.00
☐ 80	0.40	0.60	1.80	3.00
☐ 81	0.40	0.60	1.80	3.00

	ORIG.	GOOD	FINE	N-MINT
☐ 82	0.40	0.60	1.80	3.00
☐ 83	0.40	0.60	1.80	3.00
☐ 84	0.40	0.60	1.80	3.00
☐ 85	0.40	0.60	1.80	3.00
☐ 86	0.40	0.60	1.80	3.00
☐ 87	0.50	0.60	1.80	3.00
☐ 88	0.50	0.60	1.80	3.00
☐ 89	0.50	0.60	1.80	3.00
☐ 90 DP/JSt, Daredevil	0.50	0.60	1.80	3.00
☐ 91 DP/JSt, Daredevil	0.50	0.60	1.80	3.00
☐ 92 DP/JSt	0.50	0.60	1.80	3.00
☐ 93 DP/JSt	0.50	0.60	1.80	3.00
☐ 94 DP/JSt	0.50	0.60	1.80	3.00
☐ 95 DP/JSt	0.50	0.60	1.80	3.00
☐ 96 DP/JSt	0.50	0.60	1.80	3.00
☐ 97 DP/JSt	0.50	0.60	1.80	3.00
☐ 98 DP/JSt	0.50	0.60	1.80	3.00
☐ 99 DP/JSt, conflict	0.50	0.60	1.80	3.00
☐ 100 DP/JSt, giant	0.75	1.00	3.00	5.00
☐ 101 DP/JSt, Silver Surfer	0.50	0.40	1.20	2.00
☐ 102 DP/JSt	0.50	0.40	1.20	2.00
☐ 103 DP/JSt	0.60	0.40	1.20	2.00
☐ 104 DP/JSt	0.60	0.40	1.20	2.00
☐ 105 DP/JSt	0.60	0.40	1.20	2.00
☐ 106 DP, Daredevil	0.60	0.40	1.20	2.00
☐ 107 DP/JSt, Enchantress	0.60	0.40	1.20	2.00
☐ 108	0.60	0.40	1.20	2.00
☐ 109	0.60	0.40	1.20	2.00
☐ 110	0.60	0.40	1.20	2.00
☐ 111	0.60	0.40	1.20	2.00
☐ 112	0.60	0.40	1.20	2.00
☐ 113	0.60	0.40	1.20	2.00
☐ 114	0.60	0.40	1.20	2.00
☐ 115	0.60	0.40	1.20	2.00
☐ 116	0.60	0.40	1.20	2.00
☐ 117	0.60	0.40	1.20	2.00
☐ 118	0.60	0.40	1.20	2.00
☐ 119	0.60	0.40	1.20	2.00
☐ 120	0.60	0.40	1.20	2.00
☐ 121	0.60	0.40	1.20	2.00
☐ 122	0.60	0.40	1.20	2.00
☐ 123	0.60	0.40	1.20	2.00
☐ 124	0.60	0.40	1.20	2.00
☐ 125	1.00	0.40	1.20	2.00
☐ 126	1.00	0.40	1.20	2.00
☐ 127	1.00	0.40	1.20	2.00
☐ 128	1.00	0.40	1.20	2.00
☐ 129	1.00	0.40	1.20	2.00
☐ 130	1.00	0.40	1.20	2.00
☐ 131	1.00	0.40	1.20	2.00
☐ 132	1.00	0.40	1.20	2.00
☐ 133	1.00	0.40	1.20	2.00
☐ 134	1.00	0.40	1.20	2.00
☐ 135	1.00	0.40	1.20	2.00

	ORIG.	GOOD	FINE	N-MINT
136	1.00	0.40	1.20	2.00
137	1.00	0.40	1.20	2.00
138	1.00	0.40	1.20	2.00
139 (becomes the New Defenders)	1.00	0.40	1.20	2.00

DEFENDERS ANNUAL

	ORIG.	GOOD	FINE	N-MINT
1 JSn, O:Hulk	0.50	0.60	1.80	3.00
2 GK/KJ, Son of Satan	0.50	0.40	1.20	2.00
3	0.50	0.80	2.40	4.00
4	0.50	0.80	2.40	4.00
5 DH, Guardians	0.50	0.40	1.20	2.00

DEFENDERS OF DYNATRON CITY

	ORIG.	GOOD	FINE	N-MINT
1	1.25	0.25	0.75	1.25
2	1.25	0.25	0.75	1.25
3	1.25	0.25	0.75	1.25
4	1.25	0.25	0.75	1.25
5	1.25	0.25	0.75	1.25
6	1.25	0.25	0.75	1.25

DEFENDERS OF EARTH

	ORIG.	GOOD	FINE	N-MINT
4 (was Star title)	1.00	0.20	0.60	1.00

DENNIS THE MENACE

	ORIG.	GOOD	FINE	N-MINT
1	0.50	0.40	1.20	2.00
2	0.50	0.30	0.90	1.50

DENNIS THE MENACE COMICS DIGEST

	ORIG.	GOOD	FINE	N-MINT
1	1.25	0.25	0.75	1.25
2	1.25	0.25	0.75	1.25
3	1.25	0.25	0.75	1.25

DESTROYER, THE (Volume 1)

	ORIG.	GOOD	FINE	N-MINT
1 (b&w mag)	2.25	0.45	1.35	2.25
2 (b&w mag)	2.25	0.45	1.35	2.25
3 (b&w mag)	2.25	0.45	1.35	2.25
4 (b&w mag)	2.25	0.45	1.35	2.25
5 (b&w mag)	2.25	0.45	1.35	2.25
6 (b&w mag)	2.25	0.45	1.35	2.25

DESTROYER, THE (Volume 2)

	ORIG.	GOOD	FINE	N-MINT
1 color	1.95	0.39	1.17	1.95

DESTROYER, THE (Volume 3)

	ORIG.	GOOD	FINE	N-MINT
1 color	1.95	0.39	1.17	1.95
2 color	1.95	0.39	1.17	1.95
3 color	1.95	0.39	1.17	1.95
4 color	1.95	0.39	1.17	1.95

DEVIL DINOSAUR

	ORIG.	GOOD	FINE	N-MINT
1 JK	0.35	1.00	3.00	5.00
2 JK	0.35	0.70	2.10	3.50
3 JK	0.35	0.50	1.50	2.50
4 JK	0.35	0.50	1.50	2.50
5 JK	0.35	0.50	1.50	2.50
6 JK	0.35	0.30	0.90	1.50
7 JK	0.35	0.30	0.90	1.50
8 JK	0.35	0.30	0.90	1.50
9 JK	0.35	0.30	0.90	1.50

DIGITEK

	ORIG.	GOOD	FINE	N-MINT
1	1.95	0.39	1.17	1.95

	ORIG.	GOOD	FINE	N-MINT
2	1.95	0.39	1.17	1.95
3	2.25	0.45	1.35	2.25
4	2.25	0.45	1.35	2.25

DINO-RIDERS

	ORIG.	GOOD	FINE	N-MINT
1	1.00	0.20	0.60	1.00
2	1.00	0.20	0.60	1.00
3	1.00	0.20	0.60	1.00

DOC SAVAGE

	ORIG.	GOOD	FINE	N-MINT
1	0.20	0.50	1.50	2.50
2	0.20	0.30	0.90	1.50
3	0.20	0.30	0.90	1.50
4	0.20	0.30	0.90	1.50
5	0.20	0.30	0.90	1.50
6	0.20	0.30	0.90	1.50
7	0.20	0.30	0.90	1.50
8	0.20	0.30	0.90	1.50

DOC SAVAGE (b&w mag)

	ORIG.	GOOD	FINE	N-MINT
1	1.00	0.20	0.60	1.00
2	1.00	0.20	0.60	1.00
3	1.00	0.20	0.60	1.00
4	1.00	0.20	0.60	1.00
5	1.00	0.20	0.60	1.00
6	1.00	0.20	0.60	1.00
7	1.00	0.20	0.60	1.00
8	1.00	0.20	0.60	1.00

DOCTOR STRANGE (1974-1987)

	ORIG.	GOOD	FINE	N-MINT
1 DG/FB	0.25	4.00	12.00	20.00
2 DG/FB, A:Defenders	0.25	2.40	7.20	12.00
3 FB/DG, A:Dormammu	0.25	1.20	3.60	6.00
4 DG/FB	0.25	1.20	3.60	6.00
5 DG/FB	0.25	1.20	3.60	6.00
6 GC	0.25	0.40	1.20	2.00
7 GC	0.25	0.40	1.20	2.00
8 GC	0.25	0.40	1.20	2.00
9 GC	0.25	0.40	1.20	2.00
10 GC	0.25	0.40	1.20	2.00
11 GC	0.25	0.40	1.20	2.00
12 GC	0.25	0.40	1.20	2.00
13 GC	0.25	0.40	1.20	2.00
14 GC	0.25	0.30	0.90	1.50
15 GC	0.25	0.30	0.90	1.50
16 GC	0.25	0.30	0.90	1.50
17 GC	0.25	0.30	0.90	1.50
18 GC	0.30	0.30	0.90	1.50
19 GC/AA, I:Xander	0.30	0.40	1.20	2.00
20	0.30	0.30	0.90	1.50
21	0.30	0.30	0.90	1.50
22	0.30	0.30	0.90	1.50
23	0.30	0.30	0.90	1.50
24	0.30	0.30	0.90	1.50
25	0.30	0.40	1.20	2.00
26	0.35	0.40	1.20	2.00
27	0.35	0.20	0.60	1.00
28	0.35	0.20	0.60	1.00

	ORIG.	GOOD	FINE	N-MINT
☐ 29	0.35	0.20	0.60	1.00
☐ 30	0.35	0.20	0.60	1.00
☐ 31	0.35	0.20	0.60	1.00
☐ 32	0.35	0.20	0.60	1.00
☐ 33	0.35	0.20	0.60	1.00
☐ 34	0.35	0.20	0.60	1.00
☐ 35	0.40	0.20	0.60	1.00
☐ 36	0.40	0.20	0.60	1.00
☐ 37	0.40	0.20	0.60	1.00
☐ 38	0.40	0.20	0.60	1.00
☐ 39	0.40	0.20	0.60	1.00
☐ 40	0.40	0.20	0.60	1.00
☐ 41	0.40	0.20	0.60	1.00
☐ 42	0.40	0.20	0.60	1.00
☐ 43	0.50	0.20	0.60	1.00
☐ 44	0.50	0.20	0.60	1.00
☐ 45	0.50	0.20	0.60	1.00
☐ 46	0.50	0.20	0.60	1.00
☐ 47	0.50	0.20	0.60	1.00
☐ 48 A:Brother Voodoo	0.50	0.30	0.90	1.50
☐ 49 A:Baron Mordo	0.50	0.25	0.75	1.25
☐ 50 A:Baron Mordo	0.50	0.25	0.75	1.25
☐ 51	0.60	0.20	0.60	1.00
☐ 52	0.60	0.20	0.60	1.00
☐ 53	0.60	0.20	0.60	1.00
☐ 54 PS	0.60	0.25	0.75	1.25
☐ 55 PS	0.60	0.25	0.75	1.25
☐ 56 PS	0.60	0.25	0.75	1.25
☐ 57	0.60	0.20	0.60	1.00
☐ 58	0.60	0.20	0.60	1.00
☐ 59	0.60	0.20	0.60	1.00
☐ 60	0.60	0.20	0.60	1.00
☐ 61	0.60	0.20	0.60	1.00
☐ 62	0.60	0.20	0.60	1.00
☐ 63	0.60	0.20	0.60	1.00
☐ 64	0.60	0.20	0.60	1.00
☐ 65	0.60	0.20	0.60	1.00
☐ 66	0.60	0.20	0.60	1.00
☐ 67	0.60	0.20	0.60	1.00
☐ 68	0.60	0.20	0.60	1.00
☐ 69	0.60	0.20	0.60	1.00
☐ 70	0.65	0.20	0.60	1.00
☐ 71	0.65	0.20	0.60	1.00
☐ 72	0.65	0.20	0.60	1.00
☐ 73	0.65	0.20	0.60	1.00
☐ 74 Secret Wars II	0.65	0.20	0.60	1.00
☐ 75	0.75	0.20	0.60	1.00
☐ 76	0.75	0.20	0.60	1.00
☐ 77	0.75	0.20	0.60	1.00
☐ 78	0.75	0.20	0.60	1.00
☐ 79	0.75	0.20	0.60	1.00
☐ 80	0.75	0.20	0.60	1.00
☐ 81	0.75	0.20	0.60	1.00

DOCTOR STRANGE (was Strange Tales)

	ORIG.	GOOD	FINE	N-MINT
☐ 169 DA, O:Dr. Strange	0.12	16.00	48.00	80.00

	ORIG.	GOOD	FINE	N-MINT
☐ 170	0.12	10.00	30.00	50.00
☐ 171	0.12	6.00	18.00	30.00
☐ 172	0.12	6.00	18.00	30.00
☐ 173	0.12	6.00	18.00	30.00
☐ 174	0.12	6.00	18.00	30.00
☐ 175	0.12	6.00	18.00	30.00
☐ 176	0.12	6.00	18.00	30.00
☐ 177	0.12	6.00	18.00	30.00
☐ 178	0.12	6.00	18.00	30.00
☐ 179	0.12	6.00	18.00	30.00
☐ 180	0.12	6.00	18.00	30.00
☐ 181	0.12	6.00	18.00	30.00
☐ 182	0.15	6.00	18.00	30.00
☐ 183	0.15	6.00	18.00	30.00

DOCTOR STRANGE ANNUAL

	ORIG.	GOOD	FINE	N-MINT
☐ 1 (1976)	0.50	1.00	3.00	5.00
☐ 2 (1992)	2.25	0.45	1.35	2.25
☐ 3 (1993) with trading card	2.95	0.59	1.77	2.95

DOCTOR STRANGE CLASSICS

	ORIG.	GOOD	FINE	N-MINT
☐ 1 SD rep.	0.30	0.30	0.90	1.50
☐ 2 SD rep.	0.30	0.30	0.90	1.50
☐ 3 AAd (c)	0.30	0.30	0.90	1.50
☐ 4	0.30	0.30	0.90	1.50

DOCTOR STRANGE SPECIAL EDITION

	ORIG.	GOOD	FINE	N-MINT
☐ 1	2.50	0.50	1.50	2.50

DOCTOR STRANGE/ GHOST RIDER SPECIAL

	ORIG.	GOOD	FINE	N-MINT
☐ 1 rep: Dr. Strange #28	1.50	0.30	0.90	1.50

DOCTOR STRANGE: SORCERER SUPREME (beginning 1988)

	ORIG.	GOOD	FINE	N-MINT
☐ 1	1.25	0.80	2.40	4.00
☐ 2 Inferno	1.50	0.60	1.80	3.00
☐ 3	1.50	0.40	1.20	2.00
☐ 4	1.50	0.40	1.20	2.00
☐ 5	1.50	0.40	1.20	2.00
☐ 6	1.50	0.40	1.20	2.00
☐ 7	1.50	0.40	1.20	2.00
☐ 8	1.50	0.40	1.20	2.00
☐ 9	1.50	0.40	1.20	2.00
☐ 10	1.50	0.40	1.20	2.00
☐ 11 Vengeance	1.50	1.00	3.00	5.00
☐ 12 Vengeance	1.50	0.40	1.20	2.00
☐ 13 Vengeance	1.50	0.40	1.20	2.00
☐ 14 vampires	1.50	0.60	1.80	3.00
☐ 15 vampires	1.50	1.60	4.80	8.00
☐ 16 vampires	1.50	0.30	0.90	1.50
☐ 17 vampires	1.50	0.30	0.90	1.50
☐ 18 vampires	1.50	0.30	0.90	1.50
☐ 19 GC	1.50	0.30	0.90	1.50
☐ 20	1.50	0.30	0.90	1.50
☐ 21	1.50	0.30	0.90	1.50
☐ 22	1.50	0.30	0.90	1.50
☐ 23	1.50	0.30	0.90	1.50
☐ 24	1.50	0.30	0.90	1.50

	ORIG.	GOOD	FINE	N-MINT
❏ 25 ....1.50	0.30	0.90	1.50
❏ 26 werewolf 1.50	0.30	0.90	1.50
❏ 27 werewolf 1.50	0.30	0.90	1.50
❏ 28 Ghost Rider 1.50	1.60	4.80	8.00
❏ 29 ....1.75	0.35	1.05	1.75
❏ 30 ....1.75	0.35	1.05	1.75
❏ 31 Infinity Gauntlet............1.75	0.60	1.80	3.00
❏ 32 Infinity Gauntlet............1.75	0.35	1.05	1.75
❏ 33 Infinity Gauntlet............1.75	0.35	1.05	1.75
❏ 34 Infinity Gauntlet............1.75	0.35	1.05	1.75
❏ 35 Infinity Gauntlet............1.75	0.35	1.05	1.75
❏ 36 Infinity Gauntlet............1.75	0.35	1.05	1.75
❏ 37 ....1.75	0.35	1.05	1.75
❏ 38 ....1.75	0.35	1.05	1.75
❏ 39 ....1.75	0.35	1.05	1.75
❏ 40 ....1.75	0.35	1.05	1.75
❏ 41 Wolverine....................1.75	0.35	1.05	1.75
❏ 42 Galactus 1.75	0.35	1.05	1.75
❏ 46 ....1.75	0.35	1.05	1.75
❏ 47 ....1.75	0.35	1.05	1.75
❏ 48 ....1.75	0.35	1.05	1.75
❏ 49 ....1.75	0.35	1.05	1.75
❏ 50 foil cover 2.95	0.59	1.77	2.95
❏ 51 ....1.75	0.35	1.05	1.75
❏ 52 ....1.75	0.35	1.05	1.75
❏ 53 ....1.75	0.35	1.05	1.75
❏ 54 ....1.75	0.35	1.05	1.75
❏ 55 ....1.75	0.35	1.05	1.75
❏ 56 ....1.75	0.35	1.05	1.75
❏ 57 ....1.75	0.35	1.05	1.75

DOCTOR STRANGE: SORCERER SUPREME ANNUAL

	ORIG.	GOOD	FINE	N-MINT
❏ 1 ....2.00	0.45	1.35	2.25
❏ 2 ....2.25	0.45	1.35	2.25
❏ 3 ....2.95	0.59	1.77	2.95

DOCTOR WHO

	ORIG.	GOOD	FINE	N-MINT
❏ 1 BBC TV series...............1.50	0.40	1.20	2.00
❏ 2 ....1.50	0.30	0.90	1.50
❏ 3 ....1.50	0.30	0.90	1.50
❏ 4 ....1.50	0.30	0.90	1.50
❏ 5 ....1.50	0.30	0.90	1.50
❏ 6 ....1.50	0.30	0.90	1.50
❏ 7 ....1.50	0.30	0.90	1.50
❏ 8 ....1.50	0.30	0.90	1.50
❏ 9 ....1.50	0.30	0.90	1.50
❏ 10 ....1.50	0.30	0.90	1.50
❏ 11 ....1.50	0.30	0.90	1.50
❏ 12 ....1.50	0.30	0.90	1.50
❏ 13 ....1.50	0.30	0.90	1.50
❏ 14 ....1.50	0.30	0.90	1.50
❏ 15 ....1.50	0.30	0.90	1.50
❏ 16 ....1.50	0.30	0.90	1.50
❏ 17 ....1.50	0.30	0.90	1.50
❏ 18 ....1.50	0.30	0.90	1.50
❏ 19 ....1.50	0.30	0.90	1.50

	ORIG.	GOOD	FINE	N-MINT
❏ 20 ....1.50	0.30	0.90	1.50
❏ 21 ....1.50	0.30	0.90	1.50
❏ 22 ....1.50	0.30	0.90	1.50
❏ 23 ....1.50	0.30	0.90	1.50

DOOM 2099

	ORIG.	GOOD	FINE	N-MINT
❏ 1 silver cover...................1.75	0.45	1.35	2.25
❏ 2 ....1.25	0.25	0.75	1.25
❏ 3 ....1.25	0.25	0.75	1.25
❏ 4 ....1.25	0.25	0.75	1.25
❏ 5 ....1.25	0.25	0.75	1.25
❏ 6 ....1.25	0.25	0.75	1.25
❏ 7 ....1.25	0.25	0.75	1.25
❏ 8 ....1.25	0.25	0.75	1.25
❏ 9 ....1.25	0.25	0.75	1.25
❏ 10 ....1.25	0.25	0.75	1.25

DOUBLE DRAGON

	ORIG.	GOOD	FINE	N-MINT
❏ 1 ....1.00	0.20	0.60	1.00
❏ 2 ....1.00	0.20	0.60	1.00
❏ 3 ....1.00	0.20	0.60	1.00
❏ 4 ....1.00	0.20	0.60	1.00
❏ 5 ....1.00	0.20	0.60	1.00
❏ 6 ....1.00	0.20	0.60	1.00

DRACULA LIVES! (b&w mag)

	ORIG.	GOOD	FINE	N-MINT
❏ 1 ....0.75	0.15	0.45	0.75
❏ 2 ....0.75	0.15	0.45	0.75
❏ 3 ....0.75	0.15	0.45	0.75
❏ 4 ....0.75	0.15	0.45	0.75
❏ 5 ....0.75	0.15	0.45	0.75
❏ 6 ....0.75	0.15	0.45	0.75
❏ 7 ....0.75	0.15	0.45	0.75
❏ 8 ....0.75	0.15	0.45	0.75
❏ 9 ....0.75	0.15	0.45	0.75
❏ 10 ....0.75	0.15	0.45	0.75
❏ 11 ....0.75	0.15	0.45	0.75
❏ 12 ....0.75	0.15	0.45	0.75
❏ 13 ....0.75	0.15	0.45	0.75

DRACULA LIVES! ANNUAL (b&w mag)

	ORIG.	GOOD	FINE	N-MINT
❏ 1 ....1.25	0.25	0.75	1.25

DRAFT, THE

	ORIG.	GOOD	FINE	N-MINT
❏ 1 D.P.7, Nightmask...........3.50	0.70	2.10	3.50

DRAGON'S CLAWS

	ORIG.	GOOD	FINE	N-MINT
❏ 1 ....1.25	0.40	1.20	2.00
❏ 2 ....1.50	0.30	0.90	1.50
❏ 3	0.30	0.90	1.50
❏ 4	0.30	0.90	1.50
❏ 5 ....1.75	0.35	1.05	1.75
❏ 6 ....1.75	0.35	1.05	1.75
❏ 7 ....1.75	0.35	1.05	1.75
❏ 8 ....1.75	0.35	1.05	1.75
❏ 9 ....1.75	0.35	1.05	1.75
❏ 10 ....1.75	0.35	1.05	1.75

	ORIG.	GOOD	FINE	N-MINT
DRAGONSLAYER				
❑ 1 movie story	0.50	0.20	0.60	1.00
❑ 2 movie story	0.50	0.20	0.60	1.00
DUNE				
❑ 1 movie	0.75	0.30	0.90	1.50
❑ 2 movie	0.75	0.30	0.90	1.50
❑ 3 movie	0.75	0.30	0.90	1.50
ECTOKID				
❑ 1 foil cover	2.50	0.50	1.50	2.50
❑ 2	1.75	0.35	1.05	1.75
ELECTRIC UNDERTOW				
❑ 1 Strikeforce: Morituri	3.95	0.79	2.37	3.95
❑ 2 Strikeforce: Morituri	3.95	0.79	2.37	3.95
❑ 3 Strikeforce: Morituri	3.95	0.79	2.37	3.95
❑ 4 Strikeforce: Morituri	3.95	0.79	2.37	3.95
❑ 5 Strikeforce: Morituri	3.95	0.79	2.37	3.95
ELEKTRA SAGA				
❑ 1 FM rep. Daredevil	2.00	1.60	4.80	8.00
❑ 2 FM rep. Daredevil	2.00	1.60	4.80	8.00
❑ 3 FM rep. Daredevil	2.00	1.60	4.80	8.00
❑ 4 FM rep. Daredevil	2.00	1.60	4.80	8.00
ETERNALS				
❑ 1	0.25	0.20	0.60	1.00
❑ 2	0.25	0.20	0.60	1.00
❑ 3	0.30	0.20	0.60	1.00
❑ 4	0.30	0.20	0.60	1.00
❑ 5	0.30	0.20	0.60	1.00
❑ 6	0.30	0.20	0.60	1.00
❑ 7	0.30	0.20	0.60	1.00
❑ 8	0.30	0.20	0.60	1.00
❑ 9	0.30	0.20	0.60	1.00
❑ 10	0.30	0.20	0.60	1.00
❑ 11	0.30	0.20	0.60	1.00
❑ 12	0.30	0.20	0.60	1.00
❑ 13	0.30	0.20	0.60	1.00
❑ 14	0.30	0.20	0.60	1.00
❑ 15	0.30	0.20	0.60	1.00
❑ 16	0.30	0.20	0.60	1.00
❑ 17	0.35	0.20	0.60	1.00
❑ 18	0.35	0.20	0.60	1.00
❑ 19	0.35	0.20	0.60	1.00
ETERNALS (maxi-series)				
❑ 1	1.25	0.25	0.75	1.25
❑ 2	0.75	0.20	0.60	1.00
❑ 3	0.75	0.20	0.60	1.00
❑ 4	0.75	0.20	0.60	1.00
❑ 5	0.75	0.20	0.60	1.00
❑ 6	0.75	0.20	0.60	1.00
❑ 7	0.75	0.20	0.60	1.00
❑ 8	0.75	0.20	0.60	1.00
❑ 9	0.75	0.20	0.60	1.00
❑ 10	0.75	0.20	0.60	1.00
❑ 11	0.75	0.20	0.60	1.00
❑ 12	1.25	0.25	0.75	1.25

	ORIG.	GOOD	FINE	N-MINT
ETERNALS ANNUAL				
❑	10.50	2.10	6.30	10.50
ETERNALS: THE HEROD FACTOR				
❑ 1	2.50	0.50	1.50	2.50
EVEL KNIEVEL				
❑ giveaway		0.60	1.80	3.00
EXCALIBUR				
❑ 1	1.50	2.40	7.20	12.00
❑ 2	1.50	1.60	4.80	8.00
❑ 3	1.50	1.00	3.00	5.00
❑ 4	1.50	1.00	3.00	5.00
❑ 5	1.50	1.00	3.00	5.00
❑ 6 Inferno	1.50	0.60	1.80	3.00
❑ 7 Inferno	1.50	0.60	1.80	3.00
❑ 8	1.50	0.50	1.50	2.50
❑ 9	1.50	0.50	1.50	2.50
❑ 10	1.50	0.50	1.50	2.50
❑ 11	1.50	0.50	1.50	2.50
❑ 12	1.50	0.50	1.50	2.50
❑ 13	1.50	0.50	1.50	2.50
❑ 14	1.50	0.50	1.50	2.50
❑ 15	1.50	0.50	1.50	2.50
❑ 16	1.50	0.50	1.50	2.50
❑ 17	1.50	0.50	1.50	2.50
❑ 18	1.50	0.50	1.50	2.50
❑ 19	1.50	0.50	1.50	2.50
❑ 20	1.50	0.50	1.50	2.50
❑ 21	1.50	0.50	1.50	2.50
❑ 22	1.50	0.50	1.50	2.50
❑ 23	1.50	0.50	1.50	2.50
❑ 24	1.75	0.50	1.50	2.50
❑ 25	1.75	0.50	1.50	2.50
❑ 26	1.75	0.40	1.20	2.00
❑ 27	1.75	0.40	1.20	2.00
❑ 28	1.75	0.40	1.20	2.00
❑ 29	1.75	0.40	1.20	2.00
❑ 30	1.75	0.40	1.20	2.00
❑ 31	1.75	0.40	1.20	2.00
❑ 32 with $1.50 price	1.50	0.40	1.20	2.00
❑ 32 with $1.75 price	1.75	0.40	1.20	2.00
❑ 33	1.75	0.40	1.20	2.00
❑ 34	1.75	0.40	1.20	2.00
❑ 35	1.75	0.40	1.20	2.00
❑ 36 Outlaws	1.75	0.40	1.20	2.00
❑ 37	1.75	0.40	1.20	2.00
❑ 38	1.75	0.40	1.20	2.00
❑ 39	1.75	0.40	1.20	2.00
❑ 40	1.75	0.40	1.20	2.00
❑ 41	1.75	0.40	1.20	2.00
❑ 42	1.75	0.40	1.20	2.00
❑ 43	1.75	0.40	1.20	2.00
❑ 44	1.75	0.40	1.20	2.00
❑ 45	1.75	0.40	1.20	2.00
❑ 46	1.75	0.40	1.20	2.00

	ORIG.	GOOD	FINE	N-MINT
47	1.75	0.40	1.20	2.00
48	1.75	0.40	1.20	2.00
49	1.75	0.40	1.20	2.00
50		0.40	1.20	2.00
51	1.75	0.40	1.20	2.00
52 A:X-Men	1.75	0.35	1.05	1.75
53	1.75	0.35	1.05	1.75
54	1.75	0.35	1.05	1.75
55	1.75	0.35	1.05	1.75
56	1.75	0.35	1.05	1.75
57	1.75	0.35	1.05	1.75
58	1.75	0.35	1.05	1.75
59	1.75	0.35	1.05	1.75
60	1.75	0.35	1.05	1.75
61	1.75	0.35	1.05	1.75
62	1.75	0.35	1.05	1.75
63	1.75	0.35	1.05	1.75
64	1.75	0.35	1.05	1.75
65	1.75	0.35	1.05	1.75
66	1.75	0.35	1.05	1.75
67	1.75	0.35	1.05	1.75
68	1.75	0.35	1.05	1.75
69	1.75	0.35	1.05	1.75

EXCALIBUR ANNUAL

	ORIG.	GOOD	FINE	N-MINT
1 trading card	2.95	0.59	1.77	2.95

FALCON

	ORIG.	GOOD	FINE	N-MINT
1	0.60	0.25	0.75	1.25
2	0.60	0.20	0.60	1.00
3	0.60	0.20	0.60	1.00
4	0.60	0.20	0.60	1.00

FALLEN ANGELS

	ORIG.	GOOD	FINE	N-MINT
1	0.75	0.20	0.60	1.00
2	0.75	0.20	0.60	1.00
3	0.75	0.20	0.60	1.00
4	0.75	0.20	0.60	1.00
5 D:Don	0.75	0.20	0.60	1.00
6	0.75	0.20	0.60	1.00
7	0.75	0.20	0.60	1.00
8	0.75	0.20	0.60	1.00

FANTASTIC FOUR

	ORIG.	GOOD	FINE	N-MINT
1 JK, 1&O:FF	0.10	1800.00	5400.00	9000.00
2 JK, 1:Skrulls	0.10	480.00	1440.00	2400.00
3 JK, 1:Miracle Man	0.12	250.00	750.00	1250.00
4 JK, R:Sub-Mariner	0.12	320.00	960.00	1600.00
5 JK, 1:Dr. Doom	0.12	280.00	840.00	1400.00
6 JK	0.12	180.00	540.00	900.00
7	0.12	80.00	240.00	400.00
8	0.12	80.00	240.00	400.00
9	0.12	80.00	240.00	400.00
10	0.12	80.00	240.00	400.00
11 JK	0.12	55.00	165.00	275.00
12	0.12	88.00	264.00	440.00
13 JK	0.12	36.00	108.00	180.00
14 JK	0.12	30.00	90.00	150.00

	ORIG.	GOOD	FINE	N-MINT
15 JK	0.12	30.00	90.00	150.00
16 JK	0.12	30.00	90.00	150.00
17 JK	0.12	30.00	90.00	150.00
18 JK	0.12	30.00	90.00	150.00
19 JK	0.12	30.00	90.00	150.00
20 JK	0.12	30.00	90.00	150.00
21 JK	0.12	20.00	60.00	100.00
22 JK	0.12	20.00	60.00	100.00
23 JK	0.12	20.00	60.00	100.00
24 JK	0.12	20.00	60.00	100.00
25 JK Hulk	0.12	56.00	168.00	280.00
26 JK Hulk	0.12	56.00	168.00	280.00
27 JK	0.12	20.00	60.00	100.00
28 JK X-Men	0.12	28.00	84.00	140.00
29 JK	0.12	14.00	42.00	70.00
30 JK	0.12	14.00	42.00	70.00
31 JK	0.12	8.00	24.00	40.00
32 JK	0.12	8.00	24.00	40.00
33 JK	0.12	8.00	24.00	40.00
34 JK	0.12	8.00	24.00	40.00
35 JK	0.12	8.00	24.00	40.00
36 JK	0.12	8.00	24.00	40.00
37 JK	0.12	8.00	24.00	40.00
38 JK	0.12	8.00	24.00	40.00
39 JK	0.12	8.00	24.00	40.00
40 JK	0.12	8.00	24.00	40.00
41 JK, V:Frightful Four	0.12	8.00	24.00	40.00
42 JK, V:Frightful Four	0.12	8.00	24.00	40.00
43 JK, V:Frightful Four	0.12	8.00	24.00	40.00
44 JK, 1:Gorgon	0.12	8.00	24.00	40.00
45 JK	0.12	7.20	21.60	36.00
46 JK	0.12	7.20	21.60	36.00
47 JK, V:Maximus	0.12	7.20	21.60	36.00
48 JK, 1:Silver Surfer	0.12	84.00	252.00	420.00
49 JK, Galactus, Surfer	0.12	28.00	84.00	140.00
50 JK, Galactus, Surfer	0.12	50.00	150.00	250.00
51 JK	0.12	7.20	21.60	36.00
52 1:Black Panther	0.12	10.00	30.00	50.00
53 JK	0.12	7.20	21.60	36.00
54 JK, A:Black Panther	0.12	7.20	21.60	36.00
55 JK, A:Silver Surfer	0.12	11.00	33.00	55.00
56 JK, V:Klaw	0.12	7.20	21.60	36.00
57 JK	0.12	7.20	21.60	36.00
58 JK	0.12	7.20	21.60	36.00
59 JK	0.12	7.20	21.60	36.00
60 JK	0.12	7.20	21.60	36.00
61 JK	0.12	7.20	21.60	36.00
62 JK, 1:Blastaar	0.12	5.00	15.00	25.00
63 JK	0.12	5.00	15.00	25.00
64 JK	0.12	5.00	15.00	25.00
65 JK	0.12	5.00	15.00	25.00
66 JK, 1:Him, A:Crystal	0.12	18.00	54.00	90.00
67 JK, A:Him	0.12	20.00	60.00	100.00
68 JK, V:Mad Thinker	0.12	5.00	15.00	25.00
69 JK, V:Mad Thinker	0.12	5.00	15.00	25.00

	ORIG.	GOOD	FINE	N-MINT
☐ 70 JK, V:Mad Thinker 0.12	5.00	15.00	25.00
☐ 71 JK, V:Mad Thinker 0.12	5.00	15.00	25.00
☐ 72 JK, Surfer.................... 0.12	6.00	18.00	30.00
☐ 73 JK 0.12	3.20	9.60	16.00
☐ 74 JK, Surfer.................... 0.12	4.40	13.20	22.00
☐ 75 JK, Surfer.................... 0.12	4.40	13.20	22.00
☐ 76 JK, Surfer.................... 0.12	4.40	13.20	22.00
☐ 77 JK, Surfer.................... 0.12	4.40	13.20	22.00
☐ 78 .... 0.12	3.20	9.60	16.00
☐ 79 .... 0.12	3.20	9.60	16.00
☐ 80 .... 0.12	3.20	9.60	16.00
☐ 81 .... 0.12	3.20	9.60	16.00
☐ 82 .... 0.12	3.20	9.60	16.00
☐ 83 .... 0.12	3.20	9.60	16.00
☐ 84 JK 0.12	3.20	9.60	16.00
☐ 85 JK 0.12	3.20	9.60	16.00
☐ 86 JK 0.12	3.20	9.60	16.00
☐ 87 JK 0.12	3.20	9.60	16.00
☐ 88 JK 0.12	3.20	9.60	16.00
☐ 89 JK 0.15	3.20	9.60	16.00
☐ 90 JK 0.15	3.20	9.60	16.00
☐ 91 JK, 1:Torgo 0.15	3.20	9.60	16.00
☐ 92 JK, A:Torgo................. 0.15	3.20	9.60	16.00
☐ 93 JK, A:Torgo................. 0.15	3.20	9.60	16.00
☐ 94 JK, 1:Agatha Harkness			
.... 0.15	3.20	9.60	16.00
☐ 95 JK 0.15	3.20	9.60	16.00
☐ 96 JK 0.15	3.20	9.60	16.00
☐ 97 JK 0.15	3.20	9.60	16.00
☐ 98 JK 0.15	3.20	9.60	16.00
☐ 99 JK, A:Inhumans 0.15	3.20	9.60	16.00
☐ 100 JK, anniversary......... 0.15	8.00	24.00	40.00
☐ 101 JK 0.15	2.00	6.00	10.00
☐ 102 JK 0.15	2.00	6.00	10.00
☐ 103 .... 0.15	2.00	6.00	10.00
☐ 104 .... 0.15	2.00	6.00	10.00
☐ 105 .... 0.15	2.00	6.00	10.00
☐ 106 .... 0.15	2.00	6.00	10.00
☐ 107 .... 0.15	2.00	6.00	10.00
☐ 108 .... 0.15	2.00	6.00	10.00
☐ 109 .... 0.15	2.00	6.00	10.00
☐ 110 .... 0.15	2.00	6.00	10.00
☐ 111 .... 0.15	2.00	6.00	10.00
☐ 112 JB, Thing vs. Hulk...... 0.15	3.60	10.80	18.00
☐ 113 JB, 1:Overmind.......... 0.15	1.60	4.80	8.00
☐ 114 JB, V:Overmind 0.15	1.60	4.80	8.00
☐ 115 JB, 1:Eternals 0.15	1.60	4.80	8.00
☐ 116 JB, O:Stranger........... 0.25	1.60	4.80	8.00
☐ 117 JB, V:Diablo............... 0.20	1.60	4.80	8.00
☐ 118 JB, A:Crystal.............. 0.20	1.60	4.80	8.00
☐ 119 JB, V:Klaw 0.20	1.60	4.80	8.00
☐ 120 JB, V:Klaw 0.20	1.60	4.80	8.00
☐ 121 JB 0.20	2.00	6.00	10.00
☐ 122 JB 0.20	1.60	4.80	8.00
☐ 123 JB 0.20	1.60	4.80	8.00

	ORIG.	GOOD	FINE	N-MINT
☐ 124 JB.............................0.20	1.60	4.80	8.00
☐ 125 JB.............................0.20	1.60	4.80	8.00
☐ 126 JB.............................0.20	1.60	4.80	8.00
☐ 127 JB.............................0.20	1.60	4.80	8.00
☐ 128 JB.............................0.20	1.60	4.80	8.00
☐ 129 JB, 1:Thundra 0.20	1.80	5.40	9.00
☐ 130 JB.............................0.20	1.00	3.00	5.00
☐ 131 JB.............................0.20	1.00	3.00	5.00
☐ 132 JB.............................0.20	1.00	3.00	5.00
☐ 133 JB.............................0.20	1.00	3.00	5.00
☐ 134 JB.............................0.20	1.00	3.00	5.00
☐ 135 JB.............................0.20	1.00	3.00	5.00
☐ 136 JB.............................0.20	1.00	3.00	5.00
☐ 137 JB.............................0.20	1.00	3.00	5.00
☐ 138 JB.............................0.20	1.00	3.00	5.00
☐ 139 JB.............................0.20	1.00	3.00	5.00
☐ 140 JB.............................0.20	1.00	3.00	5.00
☐ 141 JB.............................0.20	1.00	3.00	5.00
☐ 142 ....0.20	1.00	3.00	5.00
☐ 143 ....0.20	1.00	3.00	5.00
☐ 144 ....0.20	1.00	3.00	5.00
☐ 145 ....0.20	1.00	3.00	5.00
☐ 146 ....0.25	1.00	3.00	5.00
☐ 147 ....0.25	1.00	3.00	5.00
☐ 148 ....0.25	1.00	3.00	5.00
☐ 149 ....0.25	1.00	3.00	5.00
☐ 150 RB, W:Crystal & Quicksilver			
............................0.25	1.40	4.20	7.00
☐ 151 ....0.25	0.60	1.80	3.00
☐ 152 ....0.25	0.60	1.80	3.00
☐ 153 ....0.25	0.60	1.80	3.00
☐ 154 ....0.25	0.60	1.80	3.00
☐ 155 RB, A:Surfer..............0.25	1.00	3.00	5.00
☐ 156 RB, A:Surfer..............0.25	1.00	3.00	5.00
☐ 157 RB, A:Surfer..............0.25	1.00	3.00	5.00
☐ 158 RB.............................0.25	0.45	1.35	2.25
☐ 159 RB.............................0.25	0.60	1.80	3.00
☐ 160 ....0.25	0.60	1.80	3.00
☐ 161 ....0.25	0.60	1.80	3.00
☐ 162 ....0.25	0.60	1.80	3.00
☐ 163 ....0.25	0.60	1.80	3.00
☐ 164 ....0.25	0.60	1.80	3.00
☐ 165 ....0.25	0.60	1.80	3.00
☐ 166 GP, V:Hulk 0.25	0.60	1.80	3.00
☐ 167 GP, V:Hulk 0.25	0.60	1.80	3.00
☐ 168 ....0.25	0.60	1.80	3.00
☐ 169 ....0.25	0.60	1.80	3.00
☐ 170 ....0.25	0.60	1.80	3.00
☐ 171 ....0.25	0.60	1.80	3.00
☐ 172 ....0.25	0.60	1.80	3.00
☐ 173 ....0.25	0.60	1.80	3.00
☐ 174 ....0.30	0.60	1.80	3.00
☐ 175 ....0.30	0.60	1.80	3.00
☐ 176 ....0.30	0.60	1.80	3.00
☐ 177 ....0.30	0.60	1.80	3.00

	ORIG.	GOOD	FINE	N-MINT
❑ 178	0.30	0.60	1.80	3.00
❑ 179	0.30	0.60	1.80	3.00
❑ 180	0.30	0.60	1.80	3.00
❑ 181	0.30	0.60	1.80	3.00
❑ 182	0.30	0.60	1.80	3.00
❑ 183	0.30	0.60	1.80	3.00
❑ 184	0.30	0.60	1.80	3.00
❑ 185	0.30	0.60	1.80	3.00
❑ 186	0.30	0.60	1.80	3.00
❑ 187	0.30	0.60	1.80	3.00
❑ 188	0.35	0.60	1.80	3.00
❑ 189	0.35	0.60	1.80	3.00
❑ 190	0.35	0.60	1.80	3.00
❑ 191	0.35	0.60	1.80	3.00
❑ 192	0.35	0.60	1.80	3.00
❑ 193	0.35	0.60	1.80	3.00
❑ 194	0.35	0.60	1.80	3.00
❑ 195	0.35	0.60	1.80	3.00
❑ 196	0.35	0.60	1.80	3.00
❑ 197	0.35	0.60	1.80	3.00
❑ 198	0.35	0.60	1.80	3.00
❑ 199	0.35	0.60	1.80	3.00
❑ 200 KP, V:Dr. Doom	0.60	1.00	3.00	5.00
❑ 201 KP	0.35	0.60	1.80	3.00
❑ 202 KP	0.35	0.60	1.80	3.00
❑ 203 KP	0.35	0.60	1.80	3.00
❑ 204	0.35	0.60	1.80	3.00
❑ 205	0.35	0.60	1.80	3.00
❑ 206	0.40	0.60	1.80	3.00
❑ 207	0.40	0.60	1.80	3.00
❑ 208 SB, A:Nova	0.40	1.00	3.00	5.00
❑ 209 JBy, 1:Herbie	0.40	0.70	2.10	3.50
❑ 210 JBy	0.40	0.60	1.80	3.00
❑ 211 JBy	0.40	0.60	1.80	3.00
❑ 212 JBy	0.40	0.60	1.80	3.00
❑ 213 JBy	0.40	0.60	1.80	3.00
❑ 214 JBy	0.40	0.60	1.80	3.00
❑ 215 JBy	0.40	0.60	1.80	3.00
❑ 216 JBy	0.40	0.60	1.80	3.00
❑ 217 JBy, A:Dazzler	0.40	1.00	3.00	5.00
❑ 218	0.40	0.60	1.80	3.00
❑ 219	0.40	0.60	1.80	3.00
❑ 220	0.40	0.60	1.80	3.00
❑ 221	0.40	0.60	1.80	3.00
❑ 222 BS	0.50	0.60	1.80	3.00
❑ 223 BS	0.50	0.60	1.80	3.00
❑ 224 BS	0.50	0.60	1.80	3.00
❑ 225 BS	0.50	0.60	1.80	3.00
❑ 226 BS	0.50	0.60	1.80	3.00
❑ 227 BS	0.50	0.60	1.80	3.00
❑ 228 BS	0.50	0.60	1.80	3.00
❑ 229 BS	0.50	0.60	1.80	3.00
❑ 230 BS	0.50	0.60	1.80	3.00
❑ 231 BS	0.50	0.60	1.80	3.00
❑ 232 JBy	0.50	1.00	3.00	5.00

	ORIG.	GOOD	FINE	N-MINT
❑ 233 JBy	0.50	0.50	1.50	2.50
❑ 234 JBy	0.50	0.50	1.50	2.50
❑ 235 JBy	0.50	0.50	1.50	2.50
❑ 236 JBy, V:Dr. Doom	1.00	0.60	1.80	3.00
❑ 237 JBy	0.50	0.50	1.50	2.50
❑ 238 JBy	0.60	0.45	1.35	2.25
❑ 239 JBy	0.60	0.45	1.35	2.25
❑ 240 JBy, 1:Luna	0.60	0.45	1.35	2.25
❑ 241 JBy, A:Black Panther				
	0.60	0.45	1.35	2.25
❑ 242 JBy, A:Daredevil	0.60	0.50	1.50	2.50
❑ 243 JBy	0.60	0.50	1.50	2.50
❑ 244 JBy	0.60	0.50	1.50	2.50
❑ 245 JBy	0.60	0.50	1.50	2.50
❑ 250 JBy, A:Captain America				
	1.00	0.50	1.50	2.50
❑ 251 JBy, Negative Zone	0.60	0.40	1.20	2.00
❑ 252 JBy, new format	0.60	0.40	1.20	2.00
❑ 253 JBy	0.60	0.40	1.20	2.00
❑ 254 JBy	0.60	0.40	1.20	2.00
❑ 255 JBy	0.60	0.40	1.20	2.00
❑ 256 JBy	0.60	0.40	1.20	2.00
❑ 257 JBy	0.60	0.40	1.20	2.00
❑ 258 JBy	0.60	0.40	1.20	2.00
❑ 259 JBy	0.60	0.40	1.20	2.00
❑ 260 JBy, Silver Surfer, Dr. Doom				
	0.60	0.40	1.20	2.00
❑ 261 JBy	0.60	0.40	1.20	2.00
❑ 262 JBy	0.60	0.40	1.20	2.00
❑ 263 JBy	0.60	0.40	1.20	2.00
❑ 264 JBy	0.60	0.40	1.20	2.00
❑ 265 JBy	0.60	0.40	1.20	2.00
❑ 266 JBy	0.60	0.40	1.20	2.00
❑ 267 JBy	0.60	0.40	1.20	2.00
❑ 268 JBy	0.60	0.40	1.20	2.00
❑ 269 JBy	0.60	0.40	1.20	2.00
❑ 270 JBy	0.60	0.40	1.20	2.00
❑ 271 JBy	0.60	0.40	1.20	2.00
❑ 272 JBy	0.60	0.40	1.20	2.00
❑ 273 JBy	0.60	0.40	1.20	2.00
❑ 274 JBy	0.60	0.40	1.20	2.00
❑ 275 JBy	0.60	0.40	1.20	2.00
❑ 276 JBy	0.60	0.40	1.20	2.00
❑ 277 JBy	0.65	0.40	1.20	2.00
❑ 278 JBy	0.65	0.40	1.20	2.00
❑ 279 JBy	0.65	0.40	1.20	2.00
❑ 280 JBy	0.65	0.40	1.20	2.00
❑ 281 JBy	0.65	0.40	1.20	2.00
❑ 282 JBy Secret Wars II	0.65	0.40	1.20	2.00
❑ 283 JBy	0.65	0.40	1.20	2.00
❑ 284 JBy	0.65	0.40	1.20	2.00
❑ 285 JBy Secret Wars II	0.65	0.40	1.20	2.00
❑ 286 JBy, X-Factor	0.65	0.80	2.40	4.00
❑ 287 JBy	0.75	0.40	1.20	2.00
❑ 288 JBy Secret Wars II	0.75	0.40	1.20	2.00

	ORIG.	GOOD	FINE	N-MINT
❏ 289	0.75	0.30	0.90	1.50
❏ 290	0.75	0.30	0.90	1.50
❏ 291	0.75	0.30	0.90	1.50
❏ 292	0.75	0.30	0.90	1.50
❏ 293	0.75	0.30	0.90	1.50
❏ 294	0.75	0.30	0.90	1.50
❏ 295	0.75	0.30	0.90	1.50
❏ 296	1.50	0.30	0.90	1.50
❏ 297	0.75	0.30	0.90	1.50
❏ 298	0.75	0.30	0.90	1.50
❏ 299	0.75	0.30	0.90	1.50
❏ 300 M:Torch, Alicia	0.75	0.30	0.90	1.50
❏ 301	0.75	0.30	0.90	1.50
❏ 302	0.75	0.30	0.90	1.50
❏ 303	0.75	0.30	0.90	1.50
❏ 304	0.75	0.30	0.90	1.50
❏ 305	0.75	0.30	0.90	1.50
❏ 306	0.75	0.30	0.90	1.50
❏ 307	0.75	0.30	0.90	1.50
❏ 308 I:Fasaud	0.75	0.30	0.90	1.50
❏ 309	0.75	0.30	0.90	1.50
❏ 310	0.75	0.30	0.90	1.50
❏ 311	0.75	0.30	0.90	1.50
❏ 312 Fall of Mutants	0.75	0.30	0.90	1.50
❏ 313	0.75	0.30	0.90	1.50
❏ 314	0.75	0.30	0.90	1.50
❏ 315	0.75	0.30	0.90	1.50
❏ 316	0.75	0.30	0.90	1.50
❏ 317	0.75	0.30	0.90	1.50
❏ 318 Dr. Doom	0.75	0.30	0.90	1.50
❏ 319 Dr. Doom v. Beyonder	1.50	0.30	0.90	1.50
❏ 320 Thing vs. Hulk	0.75	0.30	0.90	1.50
❏ 321 Ms. Marvel vs.She-Hulk	0.75	0.30	0.90	1.50
❏ 322 Inferno	0.75	0.30	0.90	1.50
❏ 323 Inferno	0.75	0.30	0.90	1.50
❏ 324 Inferno	0.75	0.30	0.90	1.50
❏ 325	0.75	0.30	0.90	1.50
❏ 326	0.75	0.30	0.90	1.50
❏ 327	0.75	0.30	0.90	1.50
❏ 328	0.75	0.30	0.90	1.50
❏ 329	0.75	0.30	0.90	1.50
❏ 330	1.00	0.30	0.90	1.50
❏ 331	1.00	0.30	0.90	1.50
❏ 332	1.00	0.30	0.90	1.50
❏ 333	1.00	0.30	0.90	1.50
❏ 334 Vengeance	1.00	0.30	0.90	1.50
❏ 335 Vengeance	1.00	0.30	0.90	1.50
❏ 336 Vengeance	1.00	0.30	0.90	1.50
❏ 337 WS	1.00	0.80	2.40	4.00
❏ 338 WS	1.00	0.40	1.20	2.00
❏ 339 WS	1.00	0.30	0.90	1.50
❏ 340 WS	1.00	0.30	0.90	1.50
❏ 341 WS	1.00	0.30	0.90	1.50
❏ 342	1.00	0.30	0.90	1.50

	ORIG.	GOOD	FINE	N-MINT
❏ 343 WS	1.00	0.30	0.90	1.50
❏ 344 WS	1.00	0.30	0.90	1.50
❏ 345 WS	1.00	0.30	0.90	1.50
❏ 346	1.00	0.30	0.90	1.50
❏ 347 WS,AAd Spider-Man, Hulk, Ghost Rider, Wolverine (1st printing)	1.00	2.00	6.00	10.00
❏ 347 (2nd printing)	1.00	0.80	2.40	4.00
❏ 348 WS,AAd Spider-Man, Hulk, Ghost Rider, Wolverine (1st printing)	1.00	1.40	4.20	7.00
❏ 348 (2nd printing)	1.00	0.80	2.40	4.00
❏ 349 WS,AAd Spider-Man, Hulk, Ghost Rider, Wolverine; Punisher cameo	1.00	1.00	3.00	5.00
❏ 350 WS, Return:Thing	1.50	0.30	0.90	1.50
❏ 351	1.00	0.20	0.60	1.00
❏ 352 WS	1.00	0.20	0.60	1.00
❏ 353 WS	1.00	0.20	0.60	1.00
❏ 354 WS	1.00	0.20	0.60	1.00
❏ 355	1.00	0.20	0.60	1.00
❏ 356 Alicia is Skrull	1.00	0.20	0.60	1.00
❏ 357	1.00	0.20	0.60	1.00
❏ 358 die-cut cover	2.50	1.40	4.20	7.00
❏ 359	1.00	0.20	0.60	1.00
❏ 360	1.00	0.20	0.60	1.00
❏ 361 Dr. Doom	1.25	0.25	0.75	1.25
❏ 362	1.25	0.25	0.75	1.25
❏ 363	1.25	0.25	0.75	1.25
❏ 364	1.25	0.25	0.75	1.25
❏ 365	1.25	0.25	0.75	1.25
❏ 367	1.25	0.25	0.75	1.25
❏ 368	1.25	0.25	0.75	1.25
❏ 369	1.25	0.25	0.75	1.25
❏ 370	1.25	0.25	0.75	1.25
❏ 371 white embossed cover	2.00	2.00	6.00	10.00
❏ 371 second printing, red embossed cover	2.00	0.80	2.40	4.00
❏ 372	1.25	0.25	0.75	1.25
❏ 373	1.25	0.25	0.75	1.25
❏ 374	1.25	0.25	0.75	1.25
❏ 375 foil cover	2.95	0.80	2.40	4.00
❏ 376	1.25	0.25	0.75	1.25
❏ 377	1.25	0.25	0.75	1.25
❏ 378	1.25	0.25	0.75	1.25
❏ 379	1.25	0.25	0.75	1.25
❏ 380	1.25	0.25	0.75	1.25

FANTASTIC FOUR ANNUAL/SPECIAL

	ORIG.	GOOD	FINE	N-MINT
❏ 1 O:FF	0.25	70.00	210.00	350.00
❏ 2 O:Dr. Doom	0.25	48.00	144.00	240.00
❏ 3 W:Sue & Reed	0.25	30.00	90.00	150.00
❏ 4 I:Quasimodo	0.25	7.20	21.60	36.00
❏ 5 Inhumans	0.25	6.00	18.00	30.00
❏ 6	0.25	5.00	15.00	25.00
❏ 7	0.25	2.40	7.20	12.00
❏ 8 reprint	0.25	1.40	4.20	7.00
❏ 9 reprint	0.25	1.40	4.20	7.00

	ORIG.	GOOD	FINE	N-MINT
10 reprint	0.35	1.40	4.20	7.00
11 Invaders	0.50	1.00	3.00	5.00
12 Invaders	0.60	1.00	3.00	5.00
13	0.60	0.60	1.80	3.00
14	0.75	0.60	1.80	3.00
15 GP, Skrulls	0.75	0.40	1.20	2.00
16 JBy	0.75	0.40	1.20	2.00
17 JBy	1.00	0.40	1.20	2.00
18 Kree-Skrull War	1.00	0.40	1.20	2.00
19 JBy	1.25	0.40	1.20	2.00
20	1.25	0.40	1.20	2.00
21 Evolutionary War	1.75	0.40	1.20	2.00
22 Atlantis Attacks	2.00	0.80	2.40	4.00
23 Future Present	2.00	0.40	1.20	2.00
24 Guardians of Galaxy	2.00	0.40	1.20	2.00
25	2.25	0.45	1.35	2.25
26 trading card	2.95	0.59	1.77	2.95

FANTASTIC FOUR ROAST

	ORIG.	GOOD	FINE	N-MINT
1 FH/MG/FM/JB/MA/TA	0.75	0.40	1.20	2.00

FANTASTIC FOUR SPECIAL

	ORIG.	GOOD	FINE	N-MINT
1	2.00	0.40	1.20	2.00

FANTASTIC FOUR UNLIMITED

	ORIG.	GOOD	FINE	N-MINT
1	3.95	0.79	2.37	3.95
2	3.95	0.79	2.37	3.95
3	3.95	0.79	2.37	3.95

FANTASTIC FOUR VS. THE X-MEN

	ORIG.	GOOD	FINE	N-MINT
1	1.50	1.00	3.00	5.00
2	1.50	0.80	2.40	4.00
3	1.50	0.80	2.40	4.00
4	1.50	0.80	2.40	4.00

FANTASY MASTERPIECES

	ORIG.	GOOD	FINE	N-MINT
1 JK/DH/SD	0.12	6.40	19.20	32.00
2 JK/SD/DH	0.12	2.00	6.00	10.00
3	0.25	4.00	12.00	20.00
4	0.25	3.20	9.60	16.00
5	0.25	3.20	9.60	16.00
6	0.25	3.20	9.60	16.00
7	0.25	3.00	9.00	15.00
8	0.25	3.00	9.00	15.00
9	0.25	3.00	9.00	15.00
10	0.25	2.40	7.20	12.00
11 (becomes Marvel Super-Heroes 1967-1982)	0.25	2.40	7.20	12.00

FANTASY MASTERPIECES (Volume 2)

	ORIG.	GOOD	FINE	N-MINT
1 Silver Surfer rep	0.75	0.40	1.20	2.00
2	0.75	0.20	0.60	1.00
3	0.75	0.20	0.60	1.00
4	0.75	0.20	0.60	1.00
5	0.75	0.20	0.60	1.00
6	0.75	0.20	0.60	1.00
7	0.75	0.20	0.60	1.00
8	0.75	0.20	0.60	1.00
9	0.75	0.20	0.60	1.00
10	0.75	0.20	0.60	1.00

	ORIG.	GOOD	FINE	N-MINT
11	0.75	0.20	0.60	1.00
12	0.75	0.20	0.60	1.00
13	0.75	0.20	0.60	1.00
14	0.50	0.20	0.60	1.00

FEAR (ADVENTURE INTO FEAR)

	ORIG.	GOOD	FINE	N-MINT
1 science fiction, giant rep.	0.25	0.30	0.90	1.50
2 science fiction, giant rep.	0.25	0.25	0.75	1.25
3 science fiction, giant rep.	0.25	0.25	0.75	1.25
4 science fiction, giant rep.	0.25	0.25	0.75	1.25
5 science fiction, giant rep.	0.25	0.25	0.75	1.25
6 science fiction, giant rep.	0.25	0.25	0.75	1.25
7 science fiction, reprints	0.20	0.25	0.75	1.25
8 science fiction, reprints	0.20	0.25	0.75	1.25
9 science fiction, reprints	0.20	0.25	0.75	1.25
10 HC, Man-Thing	0.20	1.40	4.20	7.00
11 Man-Thing	0.20	0.60	1.80	3.00
12 Man-Thing	0.20	0.60	1.80	3.00
13 Man-Thing	0.20	0.30	0.90	1.50
14 Man-Thing	0.20	0.30	0.90	1.50
15 Man-Thing	0.20	0.30	0.90	1.50
16 Man-Thing	0.20	0.30	0.90	1.50
17 Man-Thing	0.20	0.30	0.90	1.50
18 Man-Thing	0.20	0.30	0.90	1.50
19 Man-Thing, 1:Howard the Duck	0.20	1.80	5.40	9.00
20 PG, Morbius	0.20	0.40	1.20	2.00
21 Morbius	0.20	0.20	0.60	1.00
22 Morbius	0.25	0.20	0.60	1.00
23 CR, 1st Russell art, Morbius	0.25	0.50	1.50	2.50
24 Morbius	0.25	0.20	0.60	1.00
25 Morbius	0.25	0.20	0.60	1.00
26 Morbius	0.25	0.20	0.60	1.00
27 Morbius	0.25	0.20	0.60	1.00
28 Morbius	0.25	0.20	0.60	1.00
29 Morbius	0.25	0.20	0.60	1.00
30 Morbius	0.25	0.20	0.60	1.00
31 Morbius	0.25	0.20	0.60	1.00

FIGHT MAN

	ORIG.	GOOD	FINE	N-MINT
1	2.00	0.40	1.20	2.00

FIRESTAR

	ORIG.	GOOD	FINE	N-MINT
1	0.75	0.80	2.40	4.00
2 AAd(c)	0.75	1.60	4.80	8.00
3	0.75	0.80	2.40	4.00
4	0.75	0.80	2.40	4.00

FISH POLICE

	ORIG.	GOOD	FINE	N-MINT
1 reprint	1.25	0.25	0.75	1.25
2 reprint	1.25	0.25	0.75	1.25
3 reprint	1.25	0.25	0.75	1.25
4 reprint	1.25	0.25	0.75	1.25
5 reprint	1.25	0.25	0.75	1.25
6 reprint	1.25	0.25	0.75	1.25

FLINTSTONE KIDS (was Star Comic)

	ORIG.	GOOD	FINE	N-MINT
5	1.00	0.20	0.60	1.00

	ORIG.	GOOD	FINE	N-MINT
❏ 6	1.00	0.20	0.60	1.00
❏ 7	1.00	0.20	0.60	1.00
❏ 8	1.00	0.20	0.60	1.00
❏ 9	1.00	0.20	0.60	1.00
❏ 10	1.00	0.20	0.60	1.00
❏ 11	1.00	0.20	0.60	1.00

FLINTSTONES, THE

	ORIG.	GOOD	FINE	N-MINT
❏ 1		0.40	1.20	2.00
❏ 2		0.20	0.60	1.00
❏ 3		0.20	0.60	1.00
❏ 4		0.20	0.60	1.00
❏ 5	0.35	0.20	0.60	1.00
❏ 6	0.35	0.20	0.60	1.00
❏ 7	0.35	0.20	0.60	1.00
❏ 8	0.35	0.20	0.60	1.00
❏ 9	0.35	0.20	0.60	1.00

FOOFUR (was Star Comic)

	ORIG.	GOOD	FINE	N-MINT
❏ 5	1.00	0.20	0.60	1.00
❏ 6	1.00	0.20	0.60	1.00

FOOLKILLER

	ORIG.	GOOD	FINE	N-MINT
❏ 1	1.75	0.35	1.05	1.75
❏ 2	1.75	0.35	1.05	1.75
❏ 3	1.75	0.35	1.05	1.75
❏ 4	1.75	0.35	1.05	1.75
❏ 5	1.75	0.35	1.05	1.75
❏ 6	1.75	0.35	1.05	1.75
❏ 7	1.75	0.35	1.05	1.75
❏ 8 Spider-Man	1.75	0.35	1.05	1.75
❏ 9	1.75	0.35	1.05	1.75
❏ 10	1.75	0.35	1.05	1.75

FOR YOUR EYES ONLY

	ORIG.	GOOD	FINE	N-MINT
❏ 1 movie	0.50	0.20	0.60	1.00
❏ 2 movie	0.50	0.20	0.60	1.00

FRAGGLE ROCK

	ORIG.	GOOD	FINE	N-MINT
❏ 1 rep.	1.00	0.20	0.60	1.00
❏ 2 rep.	1.00	0.20	0.60	1.00
❏ 3 rep.	1.00	0.20	0.60	1.00
❏ 4 rep.	1.00	0.20	0.60	1.00
❏ 5 rep.	1.00	0.20	0.60	1.00

FRANCIS, BROTHER OF THE UNIVERSE

	ORIG.	GOOD	FINE	N-MINT
❏ 1	0.75	0.15	0.45	0.75

FRANKENSTEIN

	ORIG.	GOOD	FINE	N-MINT
❏ 1	0.20	2.40	7.20	12.00
❏ 2	0.20	1.60	4.80	8.00
❏ 3	0.20	1.60	4.80	8.00
❏ 4	0.20	1.60	4.80	8.00
❏ 5	0.20	1.60	4.80	8.00
❏ 6	0.20	1.00	3.00	5.00
❏ 7	0.20	1.00	3.00	5.00
❏ 8	0.20	1.40	4.20	7.00
❏ 9	0.20	1.40	4.20	7.00
❏ 10	0.25	1.00	3.00	5.00
❏ 11	0.25	0.80	2.40	4.00

	ORIG.	GOOD	FINE	N-MINT
❏ 12	0.25	0.80	2.40	4.00
❏ 13	0.25	0.80	2.40	4.00
❏ 14	0.25	0.80	2.40	4.00
❏ 15	0.25	0.80	2.40	4.00
❏ 16	0.25	0.80	2.40	4.00
❏ 17	0.25	0.80	2.40	4.00
❏ 18	0.25	0.80	2.40	4.00

FRED HEMBECK DESTROYS THE MARVEL UNIVERSE

	ORIG.	GOOD	FINE	N-MINT
❏ 1 D:everyone	1.50	0.30	0.90	1.50

FRED HEMBECK SELLS THE MARVEL UNIVERSE

	ORIG.	GOOD	FINE	N-MINT
❏ 1 TA(c,i)	1.25	0.25	0.75	1.25

FREDDY KRUEGER'S NIGHTMARE ON ELM STREET

	ORIG.	GOOD	FINE	N-MINT
❏ 1 O:Freddy Krueger, b&w mag	2.25	0.45	1.35	2.25
❏ 2 b&w mag	2.25	0.45	1.35	2.25

FUN AND GAMES MAGAZINE

	ORIG.	GOOD	FINE	N-MINT
❏ 1	0.50	0.20	0.60	1.00
❏ 2	0.50	0.20	0.60	1.00
❏ 3	0.50	0.20	0.60	1.00
❏ 4	0.50	0.20	0.60	1.00
❏ 5	0.50	0.20	0.60	1.00
❏ 6	0.50	0.20	0.60	1.00
❏ 7	0.50	0.20	0.60	1.00
❏ 8	0.50	0.20	0.60	1.00
❏ 9	0.50	0.20	0.60	1.00
❏ 10	0.50	0.20	0.60	1.00
❏ 11	0.50	0.20	0.60	1.00
❏ 12	0.50	0.20	0.60	1.00
❏ 13	0.50	0.20	0.60	1.00

FURTHER ADVENTURES OF INDIANA JONES, THE

	ORIG.	GOOD	FINE	N-MINT
❏ 1 JBy/TA	0.60	0.30	0.90	1.50
❏ 2 JBy/TA	0.60	0.20	0.60	1.00
❏ 3	0.60	0.20	0.60	1.00
❏ 4	0.60	0.20	0.60	1.00
❏ 5	0.60	0.20	0.60	1.00
❏ 6	0.60	0.20	0.60	1.00
❏ 7	0.60	0.20	0.60	1.00
❏ 8	0.60	0.20	0.60	1.00
❏ 9	0.60	0.20	0.60	1.00
❏ 10	0.60	0.20	0.60	1.00
❏ 11	0.60	0.20	0.60	1.00
❏ 12	0.60	0.20	0.60	1.00
❏ 13	0.60	0.20	0.60	1.00
❏ 14	0.60	0.20	0.60	1.00
❏ 15	0.60	0.20	0.60	1.00
❏ 16	0.60	0.20	0.60	1.00
❏ 17	0.60	0.20	0.60	1.00
❏ 18	0.60	0.20	0.60	1.00
❏ 19	0.60	0.20	0.60	1.00
❏ 20	0.60	0.20	0.60	1.00
❏ 21	0.60	0.20	0.60	1.00
❏ 22	0.60	0.20	0.60	1.00

	ORIG.	GOOD	FINE	N-MINT
❑ 23	0.60	0.20	0.60	1.00
❑ 24	0.60	0.20	0.60	1.00
❑ 25 SD	0.60	0.20	0.60	1.00
❑ 26 SD	0.60	0.20	0.60	1.00
❑ 27 SD	0.60	0.20	0.60	1.00
❑ 28 SD	0.65	0.20	0.60	1.00
❑ 29 SD	0.65	0.20	0.60	1.00
❑ 30 SD	0.65	0.20	0.60	1.00
❑ 31 SD	0.65	0.20	0.60	1.00
❑ 32 SD	0.65	0.20	0.60	1.00
❑ 33	0.65	0.20	0.60	1.00
❑ 34	0.75	0.20	0.60	1.00

G.I. JOE AND THE TRANSFORMERS

	ORIG.	GOOD	FINE	N-MINT
❑ 1	0.75	0.20	0.60	1.00
❑ 2	0.75	0.20	0.60	1.00
❑ 3	0.75	0.20	0.60	1.00
❑ 4	0.75	0.20	0.60	1.00

G.I. JOE COMICS MAGAZINE

	ORIG.	GOOD	FINE	N-MINT
❑ 1 digest	1.50	0.30	0.90	1.50
❑ 2 digest	1.50	0.30	0.90	1.50
❑ 3 digest	1.50	0.30	0.90	1.50
❑ 4 digest	1.50	0.30	0.90	1.50
❑ 5 digest	1.50	0.30	0.90	1.50
❑ 6 digest	1.50	0.30	0.90	1.50
❑ 7 digest	1.50	0.30	0.90	1.50
❑ 8 digest	1.50	0.30	0.90	1.50
❑ 9 digest	1.50	0.30	0.90	1.50
❑ 10 digest	1.50	0.30	0.90	1.50
❑ 11 digest	1.50	0.30	0.90	1.50
❑ 12 digest	1.50	0.30	0.90	1.50
❑ 13 digest	1.50	0.30	0.90	1.50

G.I. JOE EUROPEAN MISSIONS

	ORIG.	GOOD	FINE	N-MINT
❑ 1	1.50	0.30	0.90	1.50
❑ 2	1.50	0.30	0.90	1.50
❑ 3	1.50	0.30	0.90	1.50
❑ 4	1.50	0.30	0.90	1.50
❑ 5	1.50	0.30	0.90	1.50
❑ 6	1.50	0.30	0.90	1.50
❑ 7	1.50	0.30	0.90	1.50
❑ 8	1.50	0.30	0.90	1.50
❑ 9	1.50	0.30	0.90	1.50
❑ 10	1.50	0.30	0.90	1.50
❑ 11	1.50	0.30	0.90	1.50
❑ 12	1.75	0.35	1.05	1.75
❑ 13	1.75	0.35	1.05	1.75
❑ 14	1.75	0.35	1.05	1.75
❑ 15	1.75	0.35	1.05	1.75

G.I. JOE ORDER OF BATTLE

	ORIG.	GOOD	FINE	N-MINT
❑ 1	1.25	0.25	0.75	1.25
❑ 2 Rocky Balboa	1.25	0.60	1.80	3.00
❑ 3	1.25	0.25	0.75	1.25
❑ 4	1.25	0.25	0.75	1.25

G.I. JOE SPECIAL MISSIONS

	ORIG.	GOOD	FINE	N-MINT
❑ 1	0.75	0.20	0.60	1.00

	ORIG.	GOOD	FINE	N-MINT
❑ 2	0.75	0.20	0.60	1.00
❑ 3	0.75	0.20	0.60	1.00
❑ 4	0.75	0.20	0.60	1.00
❑ 5	1.00	0.20	0.60	1.00
❑ 6	1.00	0.20	0.60	1.00
❑ 7	1.00	0.20	0.60	1.00
❑ 8	1.00	0.20	0.60	1.00
❑ 9	1.00	0.20	0.60	1.00
❑ 10	1.00	0.20	0.60	1.00
❑ 11	1.00	0.20	0.60	1.00
❑ 12	1.00	0.20	0.60	1.00
❑ 13	1.00	0.20	0.60	1.00
❑ 14	1.00	0.20	0.60	1.00
❑ 15	1.00	0.20	0.60	1.00
❑ 16	1.00	0.20	0.60	1.00
❑ 17	1.00	0.20	0.60	1.00
❑ 18	1.00	0.20	0.60	1.00
❑ 19	1.00	0.20	0.60	1.00
❑ 20	1.00	0.20	0.60	1.00
❑ 21	1.00	0.20	0.60	1.00
❑ 22	1.00	0.20	0.60	1.00
❑ 23	1.00	0.20	0.60	1.00
❑ 24	1.00	0.20	0.60	1.00
❑ 25	1.00	0.20	0.60	1.00
❑ 26	1.00	0.20	0.60	1.00
❑ 27	1.00	0.20	0.60	1.00
❑ 28	1.00	0.20	0.60	1.00

G.I. JOE YEARBOOK

	ORIG.	GOOD	FINE	N-MINT
❑ 1	1.50	0.80	2.40	4.00
❑ 2	1.50	0.60	1.80	3.00
❑ 3	1.50	0.30	0.90	1.50
❑ 4	1.50	0.30	0.90	1.50

G.I. JOE: A REAL AMERICAN HERO

	ORIG.	GOOD	FINE	N-MINT
❑ 1	1.50	1.60	4.80	8.00
❑ 2	0.60	2.00	6.00	10.00
❑ 3 HT/JAb	0.60	0.80	2.40	4.00
❑ 4 HT/JAb	0.60	0.80	2.40	4.00
❑ 5 HT/JAb	0.60	0.80	2.40	4.00
❑ 6 HT	0.60	0.80	2.40	4.00
❑ 7 HT	0.60	0.80	2.40	4.00
❑ 8 HT	0.60	0.80	2.40	4.00
❑ 9	0.60	0.80	2.40	4.00
❑ 10	0.60	0.80	2.40	4.00
❑ 11	0.60	0.60	1.80	3.00
❑ 12	0.60	0.60	1.80	3.00
❑ 13	0.60	0.60	1.80	3.00
❑ 14	0.60	0.60	1.80	3.00
❑ 15	0.60	0.60	1.80	3.00
❑ 16	0.60	0.60	1.80	3.00
❑ 17	0.60	0.60	1.80	3.00
❑ 18	0.60	0.60	1.80	3.00
❑ 19	0.60	0.60	1.80	3.00
❑ 20	0.60	0.60	1.80	3.00
❑ 21 "silent" issue	0.60	1.20	3.60	6.00

	ORIG.	GOOD	FINE	N-MINT
☐ 22	0.60	0.70	2.10	3.50
☐ 23	0.60	0.70	2.10	3.50
☐ 24	0.60	0.70	2.10	3.50
☐ 25	0.60	0.70	2.10	3.50
☐ 26	0.60	1.00	3.00	5.00
☐ 27	0.60	1.00	3.00	5.00
☐ 28	0.60	0.60	1.80	3.00
☐ 29	0.60	0.60	1.80	3.00
☐ 30	0.60	0.60	1.80	3.00
☐ 31	0.60	0.60	1.80	3.00
☐ 32	0.60	0.60	1.80	3.00
☐ 33	0.60	0.60	1.80	3.00
☐ 34	0.75	0.60	1.80	3.00
☐ 35	0.75	0.60	1.80	3.00
☐ 36	0.75	0.50	1.50	2.50
☐ 37	0.75	0.50	1.50	2.50
☐ 38	0.75	0.50	1.50	2.50
☐ 39	0.75	0.50	1.50	2.50
☐ 40	0.75	0.50	1.50	2.50
☐ 41	0.75	0.50	1.50	2.50
☐ 42	0.75	0.50	1.50	2.50
☐ 43	0.75	0.60	1.80	3.00
☐ 44	0.75	0.25	0.75	1.25
☐ 45	0.75	0.25	0.75	1.25
☐ 46	0.75	0.25	0.75	1.25
☐ 47	0.75	0.25	0.75	1.25
☐ 48	0.75	0.25	0.75	1.25
☐ 49	0.75	0.25	0.75	1.25
☐ 50	1.25	0.60	1.80	3.00
☐ 51	0.75	0.20	0.60	1.00
☐ 52	0.75	0.20	0.60	1.00
☐ 53	0.75	0.20	0.60	1.00
☐ 54	0.75	0.20	0.60	1.00
☐ 55	0.75	0.20	0.60	1.00
☐ 56	0.75	0.20	0.60	1.00
☐ 57	0.75	0.20	0.60	1.00
☐ 58	0.75	0.20	0.60	1.00
☐ 59	1.00	0.20	0.60	1.00
☐ 60 TMc	1.00	1.00	3.00	5.00
☐ 61	1.00	0.20	0.60	1.00
☐ 62	1.00	0.20	0.60	1.00
☐ 63	1.00	0.20	0.60	1.00
☐ 64	1.00	0.20	0.60	1.00
☐ 65	1.00	0.20	0.60	1.00
☐ 66	1.00	0.20	0.60	1.00
☐ 67	1.00	0.20	0.60	1.00
☐ 68	1.00	0.20	0.60	1.00
☐ 69	1.00	0.20	0.60	1.00
☐ 70	1.00	0.20	0.60	1.00
☐ 71	1.00	0.20	0.60	1.00
☐ 72	1.00	0.20	0.60	1.00
☐ 73	1.00	0.20	0.60	1.00
☐ 74	1.00	0.20	0.60	1.00
☐ 75	1.00	0.20	0.60	1.00
☐ 76	1.00	0.20	0.60	1.00

	ORIG.	GOOD	FINE	N-MINT
☐ 77	1.00	0.20	0.60	1.00
☐ 78	1.00	0.20	0.60	1.00
☐ 79	1.00	0.20	0.60	1.00
☐ 80	1.00	0.20	0.60	1.00
☐ 81	1.00	0.20	0.60	1.00
☐ 82	1.00	0.20	0.60	1.00
☐ 83	1.00	0.20	0.60	1.00
☐ 84	1.00	0.20	0.60	1.00
☐ 85	1.00	0.20	0.60	1.00
☐ 86	1.00	0.20	0.60	1.00
☐ 87	1.00	0.20	0.60	1.00
☐ 88	1.00	0.20	0.60	1.00
☐ 89	1.00	0.20	0.60	1.00
☐ 90	1.00	0.20	0.60	1.00
☐ 91	1.00	0.20	0.60	1.00
☐ 92	1.00	0.20	0.60	1.00
☐ 93	1.00	0.20	0.60	1.00
☐ 94	1.00	0.20	0.60	1.00
☐ 95	1.00	0.50	1.50	2.50
☐ 96	1.00	0.20	0.60	1.00
☐ 97	1.00	0.20	0.60	1.00
☐ 98	1.00	0.20	0.60	1.00
☐ 99	1.00	0.20	0.60	1.00
☐ 100	1.50	0.30	0.90	1.50
☐ 101	1.00	0.20	0.60	1.00
☐ 102	1.00	0.20	0.60	1.00
☐ 103	1.00	0.20	0.60	1.00
☐ 104	1.00	0.20	0.60	1.00
☐ 105	1.00	0.20	0.60	1.00
☐ 106	1.00	0.20	0.60	1.00
☐ 107	1.00	0.20	0.60	1.00
☐ 108 Dossiers begin	1.00	0.20	0.60	1.00
☐ 109	1.00	0.20	0.60	1.00
☐ 110	1.00	0.20	0.60	1.00
☐ 111	1.00	0.20	0.60	1.00
☐ 112	1.00	0.20	0.60	1.00
☐ 113	1.00	0.20	0.60	1.00
☐ 114 I:Metal-Head	1.00	0.20	0.60	1.00
☐ 115	1.00	0.20	0.60	1.00
☐ 116	1.00	0.20	0.60	1.00
☐ 117	1.00	0.20	0.60	1.00
☐ 118	1.00	0.20	0.60	1.00
☐ 119	1.00	0.20	0.60	1.00
☐ 120	1.00	0.20	0.60	1.00
☐ 121	1.25	0.25	0.75	1.25
☐ 122	1.25	0.25	0.75	1.25
☐ 123	1.25	0.25	0.75	1.25
☐ 124	1.25	0.25	0.75	1.25
☐ 125	1.25	0.25	0.75	1.25
☐ 126	1.25	0.25	0.75	1.25
☐ 127	1.25	0.25	0.75	1.25
☐ 128	1.25	0.25	0.75	1.25
☐ 129	1.25	0.25	0.75	1.25
☐ 130	1.25	0.25	0.75	1.25
☐ 131	1.25	0.25	0.75	1.25

	ORIG.	GOOD	FINE	N-MINT
☐ 132 .... 1.25	0.25	0.75	1.25
☐ 133 .... 1.25	0.25	0.75	1.25
☐ 134 .... 1.25	0.25	0.75	1.25
☐ 135 trading card.............. 1.75	0.35	1.05	1.75
☐ 136 trading card.............. 1.75	0.35	1.05	1.75
☐ 137 trading card.............. 1.75	0.35	1.05	1.75
☐ 138 trading card.............. 1.75	0.35	1.05	1.75
☐ 139 Transformers 1.25	0.25	0.75	1.25
☐ 140 .... 1.25	0.25	0.75	1.25

GARGOYLE

	ORIG.	GOOD	FINE	N-MINT
☐ 1 .... 0.75	0.25	0.75	1.25
☐ 2 .... 0.75	0.20	0.60	1.00
☐ 3 .... 0.75	0.20	0.60	1.00
☐ 4 .... 0.75	0.20	0.60	1.00

GENE DOGS

	ORIG.	GOOD	FINE	N-MINT
☐ 1 four trading cards.......... 2.75	0.55	1.65	2.75

GENERIC COMIC

	ORIG.	GOOD	FINE	N-MINT
☐ 1 .... 0.60	0.20	0.60	1.00

GHOST RIDER (1973-1983)

	ORIG.	GOOD	FINE	N-MINT
☐ 1 GK, A:Son of Satan 0.20	18.00	54.00	90.00
☐ 2 .... 0.20	8.00	24.00	40.00
☐ 3 .... 0.20	6.00	18.00	30.00
☐ 4 .... 0.20	6.00	18.00	30.00
☐ 5 .... 0.20	6.00	18.00	30.00
☐ 6 .... 0.25	3.60	10.80	18.00
☐ 7 .... 0.25	3.60	10.80	18.00
☐ 8 .... 0.25	3.60	10.80	18.00
☐ 9 .... 0.25	3.60	10.80	18.00
☐ 10 .... 0.25	3.60	10.80	18.00
☐ 11 GK/KJ/SB, A:Hulk........ 0.25	3.60	10.80	18.00
☐ 12 .... 0.25	2.80	8.40	14.00
☐ 13 .... 0.25	2.80	8.40	14.00
☐ 14 .... 0.25	2.80	8.40	14.00
☐ 15 .... 0.25	2.80	8.40	14.00
☐ 16 .... 0.25	2.80	8.40	14.00
☐ 17 .... 0.25	2.80	8.40	14.00
☐ 18 .... 0.25	2.80	8.40	14.00
☐ 19 .... 0.25	2.80	8.40	14.00
☐ 20 GK/KJ/JBy, A:Daredevil			
.... 0.30	3.60	10.80	18.00
☐ 21 .... 0.30	1.60	4.80	8.00
☐ 22 .... 0.30	1.60	4.80	8.00
☐ 23 .... 0.30	1.60	4.80	8.00
☐ 24 .... 0.30	1.60	4.80	8.00
☐ 25 .... 0.30	1.60	4.80	8.00
☐ 26 .... 0.30	1.60	4.80	8.00
☐ 27 .... 0.35	1.60	4.80	8.00
☐ 28 .... 0.35	1.60	4.80	8.00
☐ 29 .... 0.35	1.60	4.80	8.00
☐ 30 .... 0.35	1.60	4.80	8.00
☐ 31 .... 0.35	1.20	3.60	6.00
☐ 32 .... 0.35	1.20	3.60	6.00
☐ 33 .... 0.35	1.20	3.60	6.00
☐ 34 .... 0.35	1.20	3.60	6.00

	ORIG.	GOOD	FINE	N-MINT
☐ 35 .... 0.35	1.20	3.60	6.00
☐ 36 .... 0.40	1.20	3.60	6.00
☐ 37 .... 0.40	1.20	3.60	6.00
☐ 38 .... 0.40	1.20	3.60	6.00
☐ 39 .... 0.40	1.20	3.60	6.00
☐ 40 .... 0.40	1.20	3.60	6.00
☐ 41 .... 0.40	1.00	3.00	5.00
☐ 42 .... 0.40	1.00	3.00	5.00
☐ 43 .... 0.40	1.00	3.00	5.00
☐ 44 .... 0.40	1.00	3.00	5.00
☐ 45 .... 0.40	1.00	3.00	5.00
☐ 46 .... 0.40	1.00	3.00	5.00
☐ 47 .... 0.40	1.00	3.00	5.00
☐ 48 .... 0.50	1.00	3.00	5.00
☐ 49 .... 0.50	1.00	3.00	5.00
☐ 50 DP, A:Night Rider........ 0.75	1.40	4.20	7.00
☐ 51 .... 0.50	0.80	2.40	4.00
☐ 52 .... 0.50	0.80	2.40	4.00
☐ 53 .... 0.50	0.80	2.40	4.00
☐ 54 .... 0.50	0.80	2.40	4.00
☐ 55 .... 0.50	0.80	2.40	4.00
☐ 56 .... 0.50	0.80	2.40	4.00
☐ 57 .... 0.50	0.80	2.40	4.00
☐ 58 .... 0.50	0.80	2.40	4.00
☐ 59 .... 0.50	0.80	2.40	4.00
☐ 60 .... 0.50	0.80	2.40	4.00
☐ 61 .... 0.50	0.80	2.40	4.00
☐ 62 .... 0.50	0.80	2.40	4.00
☐ 63 .... 0.50	0.80	2.40	4.00
☐ 64 .... 0.60	0.80	2.40	4.00
☐ 65 .... 0.60	0.80	2.40	4.00
☐ 66 .... 0.60	0.80	2.40	4.00
☐ 67 .... 0.60	0.80	2.40	4.00
☐ 68 .... 0.60	0.80	2.40	4.00
☐ 69 .... 0.60	0.80	2.40	4.00
☐ 70 .... 0.60	0.80	2.40	4.00
☐ 71 .... 0.60	0.80	2.40	4.00
☐ 72 .... 0.60	0.80	2.40	4.00
☐ 73 .... 0.60	0.80	2.40	4.00
☐ 74 .... 0.60	0.80	2.40	4.00
☐ 75 .... 0.60	0.80	2.40	4.00
☐ 76 .... 0.60	0.80	2.40	4.00
☐ 77 .... 0.60	0.80	2.40	4.00
☐ 78 .... 0.60	0.80	2.40	4.00
☐ 79 .... 0.60	0.80	2.40	4.00
☐ 80 .... 0.60	0.80	2.40	4.00
☐ 81 D:Ghost Rider 0.60	2.40	7.20	12.00

GHOST RIDER (Volume 2, began 1990)

	ORIG.	GOOD	FINE	N-MINT
☐ 1 O, 1st printing.............. 1.95	5.20	15.60	26.00
☐ 1 O, 2nd printing 1.95	2.40	7.20	12.00
☐ 2 .... 1.50	3.60	10.80	18.00
☐ 3 .... 1.50	3.20	9.60	16.00
☐ 4 .... 1.50	4.40	13.20	22.00
☐ 5 Punisher, 1st printing 1.50	4.00	12.00	20.00
☐ 5 2nd printing 1.50	2.00	6.00	10.00

	ORIG.	GOOD	FINE	N-MINT
☐ 6 Punisher	1.50	2.00	6.00	10.00
☐ 7	1.50	1.20	3.60	6.00
☐ 8	1.50	1.20	3.60	6.00
☐ 9 X-Factor	1.50	1.00	3.00	5.00
☐ 10	1.50	0.80	2.40	4.00
☐ 11	1.50	0.80	2.40	4.00
☐ 12 Dr. Strange	1.50	0.30	0.90	1.50
☐ 13	1.50	0.30	0.90	1.50
☐ 14 Johnny Blaze	1.50	0.30	0.90	1.50
☐ 15 glowing cover 1st printing	1.75	3.20	9.60	16.00
☐ 15 2nd printing	1.75	1.40	4.20	7.00
☐ 16 SpM, Hobgoblin	1.75	0.70	2.10	3.50
☐ 17 SpM, Hobgoblin	1.75	0.70	2.10	3.50
☐ 18	1.75	0.60	1.80	3.00
☐ 19	1.75	0.60	1.80	3.00
☐ 20	1.75	0.60	1.80	3.00
☐ 21	1.75	0.60	1.80	3.00
☐ 22	1.75	0.60	1.80	3.00
☐ 23	1.75	0.60	1.80	3.00
☐ 24	1.75	0.60	1.80	3.00
☐ 25 pop-up	2.75	0.55	1.65	2.75
☐ 26 X-Men	1.75	0.35	1.05	1.75
☐ 27 X-Men	1.75	0.50	1.50	2.50
☐ 28 poster	2.50	1.00	3.00	5.00
☐ 29 Wolverine	2.50	0.50	1.50	2.50
☐ 30	2.50	0.50	1.50	2.50
☐ 31 poster	2.50	0.50	1.50	2.50
☐ 32	1.75	0.35	1.05	1.75
☐ 33	1.75	0.35	1.05	1.75
☐ 34	1.75	0.35	1.05	1.75
☐ 35	1.75	0.35	1.05	1.75
☐ 36	1.75	0.35	1.05	1.75
☐ 37	1.75	0.35	1.05	1.75
☐ 38	1.75	0.35	1.05	1.75
☐ 39	1.75	0.35	1.05	1.75
☐ 40 black cover	2.25	0.45	1.35	2.25
☐ 41	1.75	0.35	1.05	1.75
☐ 42	1.75	0.35	1.05	1.75

GHOST RIDER AND CABLE

	ORIG.	GOOD	FINE	N-MINT
☐ 1	3.95	0.79	2.37	3.95

GHOST RIDER ANNUAL

	ORIG.	GOOD	FINE	N-MINT
☐ 1 trading card	2.95	0.59	1.77	2.95

GHOST RIDER POSTER MAGAZINE

	ORIG.	GOOD	FINE	N-MINT
☐ 1	4.95	0.99	2.97	4.95

GHOST RIDER, THE

	ORIG.	GOOD	FINE	N-MINT
☐ 1 1967 Western hero	0.12	4.80	14.40	24.00
☐ 2 1967 Western hero	0.12	2.80	8.40	14.00
☐ 3 1967 Western hero	0.12	2.80	8.40	14.00
☐ 4 1967 Western hero	0.12	2.00	6.00	10.00
☐ 5 1967 Western hero	0.12	2.00	6.00	10.00
☐ 6 1967 Western hero	0.12	2.00	6.00	10.00
☐ 7 1967 Western hero	0.12	2.00	6.00	10.00

GHOST RIDER/ BLAZE: SPIRITS OF VENGEANCE

	ORIG.	GOOD	FINE	N-MINT
☐ 1 poster	2.75	0.70	2.10	3.50
☐ 2	1.75	0.35	1.05	1.75
☐ 3	1.75	0.35	1.05	1.75
☐ 4	1.75	0.35	1.05	1.75
☐ 5 Venom	1.75	0.35	1.05	1.75
☐ 6	1.75	0.35	1.05	1.75
☐ 7	1.75	0.35	1.05	1.75
☐ 8	1.75	0.35	1.05	1.75
☐ 9	1.75	0.35	1.05	1.75
☐ 10	1.75	0.35	1.05	1.75
☐ 11	1.75	0.35	1.05	1.75
☐ 12 glowing cover	2.75	0.55	1.65	2.75
☐ 13 black cover	2.50	0.50	1.50	2.50
☐ 14	1.75	0.35	1.05	1.75

GIANT-SIZE AVENGERS

	ORIG.	GOOD	FINE	N-MINT
☐ 1 RB, rep.	0.50	1.20	3.60	6.00
☐ 2 DC, rep.	0.50	0.80	2.40	4.00
☐ 3 DC, rep.	0.50	0.80	2.40	4.00
☐ 4 DH W:Vision & Scarlet Witch	0.50	0.80	2.40	4.00
☐ 5 rep.	0.50	0.30	0.90	1.50

GIANT-SIZE CAPTAIN AMERICA

	ORIG.	GOOD	FINE	N-MINT
☐ 1 rep:O	0.50	1.20	3.60	6.00

GIANT-SIZE CAPTAIN MARVEL

	ORIG.	GOOD	FINE	N-MINT
☐ 1 rep.	0.50	1.20	3.60	6.00

GIANT-SIZE CHILLERS (1974)

	ORIG.	GOOD	FINE	N-MINT
☐ 1 Dracula, 1-Lilith (becomes Giant-Size Dracula)	0.35	1.20	3.60	6.00

GIANT-SIZE CHILLERS (1975)

	ORIG.	GOOD	FINE	N-MINT
☐ 1	0.50	0.40	1.20	2.00
☐ 2	0.50	0.40	1.20	2.00
☐ 3	0.50	0.40	1.20	2.00

GIANT-SIZE CONAN

	ORIG.	GOOD	FINE	N-MINT
☐ 1 GK/TS/BB	0.50	1.80	5.40	9.00
☐ 2 GK/TS/BS	0.50	1.20	3.60	6.00
☐ 3	0.50	0.40	1.20	2.00
☐ 4	0.50	0.40	1.20	2.00
☐ 5	0.50	0.40	1.20	2.00

GIANT-SIZE CREATURES

	ORIG.	GOOD	FINE	N-MINT
☐ 1 (becomes Giant-Size Werewolf by Night)	0.35	0.80	2.40	4.00

GIANT-SIZE DAREDEVIL

	ORIG.	GOOD	FINE	N-MINT
☐ 1	0.50	1.20	3.60	6.00

GIANT-SIZE DEFENDERS

	ORIG.	GOOD	FINE	N-MINT
☐ 1 Silver Surfer	0.50	2.00	6.00	10.00
☐ 2	0.50	1.20	3.60	6.00
☐ 3	0.50	1.20	3.60	6.00
☐ 4	0.50	1.20	3.60	6.00
☐ 5	0.50	1.20	3.60	6.00

GIANT-SIZE DOC SAVAGE

	ORIG.	GOOD	FINE	N-MINT
☐ 1 movie	0.50	0.60	1.80	3.00

	ORIG.	GOOD	FINE	N-MINT
GIANT-SIZE DOCTOR STRANGE				
❏ 1 .... 0.50		1.20	3.60	6.00
GIANT-SIZE DRACULA (was Giant-Size Chillers)				
❏ 2 .... 0.50		1.00	3.00	5.00
❏ 3 .... 0.50		1.00	3.00	5.00
❏ 4 .... 0.50		1.00	3.00	5.00
❏ 5 JBy................................. 0.50		0.60	1.80	3.00
GIANT-SIZE FANTASTIC FOUR				
(was Giant-Size Super-Stars)				
❏ 2 .... 0.50		1.50	4.50	7.50
❏ 3 .... 0.50		1.50	4.50	7.50
❏ 4 .... 0.50		1.50	4.50	7.50
❏ 5 .... 0.50		1.50	4.50	7.50
❏ 6 .... 0.50		1.50	4.50	7.50
GIANT-SIZE HULK				
❏ 1 reprint 0.50		1.60	4.80	8.00
GIANT-SIZE INVADERS				
❏ 1 O&1:Invaders, rep. O:Sub-Mariner				
.... 0.50		1.20	3.60	6.00
GIANT-SIZE IRON MAN				
❏ 1 reprint 0.50		0.40	1.20	2.00
GIANT-SIZE KID COLT				
❏ 1 .... 0.50		0.60	1.80	3.00
❏ 2 .... 0.50		0.20	0.60	1.00
❏ 3 .... 0.50		0.20	0.60	1.00
GIANT-SIZE MAN-THING				
❏ 1 SD/JK 0.50		1.00	3.00	5.00
❏ 2 .... 0.50		0.60	1.80	3.00
❏ 3 .... 0.50		0.60	1.80	3.00
❏ 4 FB, 1:Howard the Duck . 0.50		1.40	4.20	7.00
❏ 5 FB, Howard the Duck 0.50		1.00	3.00	5.00
GIANT-SIZE MARVEL TRIPLE ACTION				
❏ 1 reprints........................ 0.50		0.60	1.80	3.00
❏ 2 reprints........................ 0.50		0.20	0.60	1.00
GIANT-SIZE MASTER OF KUNG FU				
❏ 1 CR/PG 0.50		1.40	4.20	7.00
❏ 2 .... 0.50		1.00	3.00	5.00
❏ 3 .... 0.50		1.00	3.00	5.00
❏ 4 JK, Yellow Claw............. 0.50		1.20	3.60	6.00
GIANT-SIZE POWER MAN				
❏ 1 .... 0.50		1.20	3.60	6.00
GIANT-SIZE SPIDER-MAN				
❏ 1 DH, reprint 0.50		3.60	10.80	18.00
❏ 2 AM, reprint.................... 0.50		1.20	3.60	6.00
❏ 3 .... 0.50		1.20	3.60	6.00
❏ 4 Punisher 0.50		12.00	36.00	60.00
❏ 5 .... 0.50		1.00	3.00	5.00
❏ 6 .... 0.50		1.00	3.00	5.00
GIANT-SIZE SUPER-HEROES FEATURING				
SPIDER-MAN				
❏ 1 Spider-Man, Man-Wolf... 0.35		9.60	28.80	48.00

	ORIG.	GOOD	FINE	N-MINT
GIANT-SIZE SUPER-STARS				
❏ 1 Fantastic 4, Hulk (becomes Giant-Size				
Fantastic Four)................. 0.35		2.00	6.00	10.00
GIANT-SIZE SUPER-VILLAIN TEAM-UP				
❏ 1 .... 0.50		1.60	4.80	8.00
❏ 2 Dr. Doom, Sub-Mariner.. 0.50		1.00	3.00	5.00
GIANT-SIZE THOR				
❏ 1 GK, rep........................... 0.50		1.00	3.00	5.00
GIANT-SIZE WEREWOLF BY NIGHT				
(was Giant-Size Creatures)				
❏ 2 SD, Frankenstein rep. 0.50		0.60	1.80	3.00
❏ 3 GK................................. 0.50		0.40	1.20	2.00
❏ 4 GK................................. 0.50		0.40	1.20	2.00
❏ 5 GK................................. 0.50		0.40	1.20	2.00
GIANT-SIZE X-MEN				
❏ 1 GK/DC 1&O:New X-Men				
.... 0.50		40.00	120.00	200.00
❏ 2 GK/KJ rep. 0.50		4.00	12.00	20.00
GODZILLA				
❏ 1 .... 0.30		1.20	3.60	6.00
❏ 2 .... 0.30		0.80	2.40	4.00
❏ 3 .... 0.30		0.80	2.40	4.00
❏ 4 .... 0.35		0.80	2.40	4.00
❏ 5 .... 0.35		0.80	2.40	4.00
❏ 6 .... 0.35		0.80	2.40	4.00
❏ 7 .... 0.35		0.80	2.40	4.00
❏ 8 .... 0.35		0.80	2.40	4.00
❏ 9 .... 0.35		0.80	2.40	4.00
❏ 10 .... 0.35		0.80	2.40	4.00
❏ 11 .... 0.35		0.60	1.80	3.00
❏ 12 .... 0.35		0.60	1.80	3.00
❏ 13 .... 0.35		0.60	1.80	3.00
❏ 14 .... 0.35		0.60	1.80	3.00
❏ 15 .... 0.35		0.60	1.80	3.00
❏ 16 .... 0.35		0.60	1.80	3.00
❏ 17 .... 0.35		0.60	1.80	3.00
❏ 18 .... 0.35		0.60	1.80	3.00
❏ 19 .... 0.35		0.60	1.80	3.00
❏ 20 .... 0.35		0.60	1.80	3.00
❏ 21 .... 0.35		0.60	1.80	3.00
❏ 22 .... 0.40		0.60	1.80	3.00
❏ 23 .... 0.40		0.60	1.80	3.00
❏ 24 .... 0.40		0.60	1.80	3.00
GUARDIANS OF THE GALAXY				
❏ 1 .... 1.00		2.40	7.20	12.00
❏ 2 .... 1.00		1.40	4.20	7.00
❏ 3 .... 1.00		0.80	2.40	4.00
❏ 4 .... 1.00		0.80	2.40	4.00
❏ 5 .... 1.00		0.60	1.80	3.00
❏ 6 .... 1.00		0.60	1.80	3.00
❏ 7 .... 1.00		0.60	1.80	3.00
❏ 8 .... 1.00		0.60	1.80	3.00
❏ 9 .... 1.00		0.60	1.80	3.00
❏ 10 .... 1.00		0.60	1.80	3.00

	ORIG.	GOOD	FINE	N-MINT
11	1.00	0.60	1.80	3.00
12	1.00	0.60	1.80	3.00
13 Ghost Rider	1.00	1.60	4.80	8.00
14 Ghost Rider	1.00	1.60	4.80	8.00
15	1.00	0.60	1.80	3.00
16	1.50	0.50	1.50	2.50
17	1.00	0.50	1.50	2.50
18	1.00	0.50	1.50	2.50
19	1.00	0.50	1.50	2.50
20	1.00	0.50	1.50	2.50
21	1.25	0.30	0.90	1.50
22	1.25	0.30	0.90	1.50
23	1.25	0.25	0.75	1.25
24	1.25	0.25	0.75	1.25
25 foil cover	2.50	1.00	3.00	5.00
26	1.25	0.25	0.75	1.25
27	1.25	0.25	0.75	1.25
28	1.25	0.25	0.75	1.25
29	1.25	0.25	0.75	1.25
30	1.25	0.25	0.75	1.25
31	1.25	0.25	0.75	1.25
32	1.25	0.25	0.75	1.25
33	1.25	0.25	0.75	1.25
34	1.25	0.25	0.75	1.25
35 sculpted cover	2.95	0.59	1.77	2.95
36	1.25	0.25	0.75	1.25
37	1.25	0.25	0.75	1.25
38	1.25	0.25	0.75	1.25
39 sculpted foil cover	2.95	0.59	1.77	2.95
40	1.25	0.25	0.75	1.25
41	1.25	0.25	0.75	1.25

GUARDIANS OF THE GALAXY ANNUAL

	ORIG.	GOOD	FINE	N-MINT
1 Korvac Quest	2.00	0.40	1.20	2.00
2	2.25	0.45	1.35	2.25
3 trading card	2.95	0.59	1.77	2.95

GUN RUNNER

	ORIG.	GOOD	FINE	N-MINT
1 four cards	2.75	0.55	1.65	2.75

HAUNT OF HORROR, THE (b&w comics mag)

	ORIG.	GOOD	FINE	N-MINT
1	0.75	0.15	0.45	0.75
2	0.75	0.15	0.45	0.75
3	0.75	0.15	0.45	0.75
4	0.75	0.15	0.45	0.75
5	0.75	0.15	0.45	0.75

HAUNT OF HORROR, THE (digest; not comics)

	ORIG.	GOOD	FINE	N-MINT
June 1973	0.75	0.15	0.45	0.75
August 1973	0.75	0.15	0.45	0.75

HAWKEYE

	ORIG.	GOOD	FINE	N-MINT
tpb	5.95	1.19	3.57	5.95
1	0.60	0.30	0.90	1.50
2	0.60	0.20	0.60	1.00
3	0.60	0.20	0.60	1.00
4	0.60	0.20	0.60	1.00

HEATHCLIFF (was Star Comic)

	ORIG.	GOOD	FINE	N-MINT
23	1.00	0.20	0.60	1.00

	ORIG.	GOOD	FINE	N-MINT
24	1.00	0.20	0.60	1.00
25	1.00	0.20	0.60	1.00
26	1.00	0.20	0.60	1.00
27	1.00	0.20	0.60	1.00
28	1.00	0.20	0.60	1.00
29	1.00	0.20	0.60	1.00
30	1.00	0.20	0.60	1.00
31	1.00	0.20	0.60	1.00
32	1.00	0.20	0.60	1.00
33	1.00	0.20	0.60	1.00
34	1.00	0.20	0.60	1.00
35	1.00	0.20	0.60	1.00
36	1.00	0.20	0.60	1.00
37	1.00	0.20	0.60	1.00
38	1.00	0.20	0.60	1.00
39	1.00	0.20	0.60	1.00
40	1.00	0.20	0.60	1.00
41	1.00	0.20	0.60	1.00
42	1.00	0.20	0.60	1.00
43	1.00	0.20	0.60	1.00
44	1.00	0.20	0.60	1.00
45	1.00	0.20	0.60	1.00
46	1.00	0.20	0.60	1.00
47 Batman parody	1.00	0.20	0.60	1.00
48	1.00	0.20	0.60	1.00
49	1.00	0.20	0.60	1.00
50 giant	1.50	0.30	0.90	1.50
51	1.00	0.20	0.60	1.00
52	1.00	0.20	0.60	1.00
53	1.00	0.20	0.60	1.00
54	1.00	0.20	0.60	1.00
55	1.00	0.20	0.60	1.00
56	1.00	0.20	0.60	1.00

HEATHCLIFF'S FUNHOUSE (was Star Comic)

	ORIG.	GOOD	FINE	N-MINT
6	1.00	0.20	0.60	1.00
7	1.00	0.20	0.60	1.00
8	1.00	0.20	0.60	1.00
9	1.00	0.20	0.60	1.00
10	1.00	0.20	0.60	1.00

HELL'S ANGEL

	ORIG.	GOOD	FINE	N-MINT
1 O:Hell's Angel, A:X-Men	1.75	0.35	1.05	1.75
2	1.75	0.35	1.05	1.75
3	1.75	0.35	1.05	1.75
4	1.75	0.35	1.05	1.75
5 (becomes Dark Angel)	1.75	0.35	1.05	1.75

HELLSTORM: PRINCE OF LIES

	ORIG.	GOOD	FINE	N-MINT
1	2.95	0.60	1.80	3.00
2	2.00	0.40	1.20	2.00
3	2.00	0.40	1.20	2.00
4	2.00	0.40	1.20	2.00
5	2.00	0.40	1.20	2.00

HERCULES PRINCE OF POWER

	ORIG.	GOOD	FINE	N-MINT
1 BL	0.60	0.40	1.20	2.00
2 BL	0.60	0.20	0.60	1.00

	ORIG.	GOOD	FINE	N-MINT
❏ 3 BL 0.60	0.20	0.60	1.00
❏ 4 BL 0.60	0.20	0.60	1.00

HERCULES PRINCE OF POWER (2nd series)

	ORIG.	GOOD	FINE	N-MINT
❏ 1 BL 0.60	0.30	0.90	1.50
❏ 2 .... 0.60	0.20	0.60	1.00
❏ 3 .... 0.60	0.20	0.60	1.00
❏ 4 .... 0.60	0.20	0.60	1.00

HERO

	ORIG.	GOOD	FINE	N-MINT
❏ 1 .... 1.50	0.30	0.90	1.50
❏ 2 .... 1.50	0.30	0.90	1.50
❏ 3 .... 1.50	0.30	0.90	1.50
❏ 4 .... 1.50	0.30	0.90	1.50
❏ 5 .... 1.50	0.30	0.90	1.50
❏ 6 .... 1.50	0.30	0.90	1.50

HERO FOR HIRE

	ORIG.	GOOD	FINE	N-MINT
❏ 1 GT/JR, O:Power Man 1:Luke Cage			
.... 0.20	5.20	15.60	26.00
❏ 2 .... 0.20	2.40	7.20	12.00
❏ 3 .... 0.20	1.60	4.80	8.00
❏ 4 .... 0.20	1.60	4.80	8.00
❏ 5 .... 0.20	1.60	4.80	8.00
❏ 6 .... 0.20	1.00	3.00	5.00
❏ 7 .... 0.20	1.00	3.00	5.00
❏ 8 .... 0.20	1.00	3.00	5.00
❏ 9 .... 0.20	1.00	3.00	5.00
❏ 10 .... 0.20	1.00	3.00	5.00
❏ 11 .... 0.20	1.00	3.00	5.00
❏ 12 .... 0.20	1.00	3.00	5.00
❏ 13 .... 0.20	1.00	3.00	5.00
❏ 14 .... 0.20	1.00	3.00	5.00
❏ 15 .... 0.20	1.00	3.00	5.00
❏ 16 (becomes Power Man) 0.20	1.00	3.00	5.00

HEROES FOR HOPE

	ORIG.	GOOD	FINE	N-MINT
❏ 1 .... 1.50	0.80	2.40	4.00

HOKUM & HEX

	ORIG.	GOOD	FINE	N-MINT
❏ 1 foil cover 2.50	0.50	1.50	2.50

HOOK

	ORIG.	GOOD	FINE	N-MINT
❏ nn bookshelf 5.95	1.19	3.57	5.95
❏ nn magazine 2.95	0.59	1.77	2.95
❏ 1 movie 1.00	0.20	0.60	1.00
❏ 2 movie 1.00	0.20	0.60	1.00
❏ 3 movie 1.00	0.20	0.60	1.00
❏ 4 movie 1.00	0.20	0.60	1.00

HOUSE II: THE SECOND STORY

	ORIG.	GOOD	FINE	N-MINT
❏ 1 movie adapt 2.00	0.40	1.20	2.00

HOWARD THE DUCK

	ORIG.	GOOD	FINE	N-MINT
❏ 1 FB, A:Spider-Man 0.25	1.40	4.20	7.00
❏ 2 FB 0.25	0.80	2.40	4.00
❏ 3 .... 0.25	0.50	1.50	2.50
❏ 4 .... 0.25	0.50	1.50	2.50
❏ 5 .... 0.30	0.50	1.50	2.50
❏ 6 .... 0.30	0.40	1.20	2.00
❏ 7 .... 0.30	0.40	1.20	2.00

	ORIG.	GOOD	FINE	N-MINT
❏ 8 .... 0.30	0.40	1.20	2.00
❏ 9 .... 0.30	0.40	1.20	2.00
❏ 10 .... 0.30	0.40	1.20	2.00
❏ 11 .... 0.30	0.40	1.20	2.00
❏ 12 .... 0.30	1.00	3.00	5.00
❏ 13 .... 0.30	1.00	3.00	5.00
❏ 14 .... 0.30	1.00	3.00	5.00
❏ 15 .... 0.30	0.40	1.20	2.00
❏ 16 .... 0.30	0.40	1.20	2.00
❏ 17 .... 0.30	0.40	1.20	2.00
❏ 18 .... 0.30	0.40	1.20	2.00
❏ 19 .... 0.30	0.40	1.20	2.00
❏ 20 .... 0.30	0.40	1.20	2.00
❏ 21 .... 0.35	0.25	0.75	1.25
❏ 22 .... 0.35	0.25	0.75	1.25
❏ 23 .... 0.35	0.25	0.75	1.25
❏ 24 .... 0.35	0.25	0.75	1.25
❏ 25 .... 0.35	0.25	0.75	1.25
❏ 26 .... 0.35	0.25	0.75	1.25
❏ 27 .... 0.35	0.25	0.75	1.25
❏ 28 .... 0.35	0.25	0.75	1.25
❏ 29 .... 0.35	0.25	0.75	1.25
❏ 30 .... 0.35	0.25	0.75	1.25
❏ 32 .... 0.65	0.20	0.60	1.00
❏ 33 .... 1.50	0.30	0.90	1.50

HOWARD THE DUCK (b&w mag)

	ORIG.	GOOD	FINE	N-MINT
❏ 1 .... 1.00	0.20	0.60	1.00
❏ 2 .... 1.25	0.25	0.75	1.25
❏ 3 .... 1.25	0.25	0.75	1.25
❏ 4 .... 1.25	0.25	0.75	1.25
❏ 5 .... 1.25	0.25	0.75	1.25
❏ 6 .... 1.25	0.25	0.75	1.25
❏ 7 .... 1.25	0.25	0.75	1.25
❏ 8 Batman parody 1.25	0.25	0.75	1.25
❏ 9 .... 1.25	0.25	0.75	1.25

HOWARD THE DUCK (movie adaptation)

	ORIG.	GOOD	FINE	N-MINT
❏ 1 movie 0.75	0.20	0.60	1.00
❏ 2 movie 0.75	0.20	0.60	1.00
❏ 3 movie 0.75	0.20	0.60	1.00

HOWARD THE DUCK ANNUAL

	ORIG.	GOOD	FINE	N-MINT
❏ 1	0.20	0.60	1.00

HULK, THE (color mag)

	ORIG.	GOOD	FINE	N-MINT
❏ 10 (was Rampaging Hulk). 1.50	0.30	0.90	1.50
❏ 11 .... 1.50	0.30	0.90	1.50
❏ 12 .... 1.50	0.30	0.90	1.50
❏ 13 .... 1.50	0.30	0.90	1.50
❏ 14 .... 1.50	0.30	0.90	1.50
❏ 15 .... 1.50	0.30	0.90	1.50
❏ 16 .... 1.50	0.30	0.90	1.50
❏ 17 .... 1.50	0.30	0.90	1.50
❏ 18 .... 1.50	0.30	0.90	1.50
❏ 19 .... 1.50	0.30	0.90	1.50
❏ 20 .... 1.50	0.30	0.90	1.50
❏ 21 .... 1.50	0.30	0.90	1.50

	ORIG.	GOOD	FINE	N-MINT
❏ 22 .... 1.50	0.30	0.90	1.50
❏ 23 .... 1.50	0.30	0.90	1.50
❏ 24 .... 1.50	0.30	0.90	1.50
❏ 25 .... 1.50	0.30	0.90	1.50
❏ 26 .... 1.50	0.30	0.90	1.50
❏ 27 .... 1.50	0.30	0.90	1.50

HUMAN FLY, THE

	ORIG.	GOOD	FINE	N-MINT
❏ 1 .... 0.30	0.40	1.20	2.00
❏ 2 .... 0.30	0.30	0.90	1.50
❏ 3 .... 0.35	0.30	0.90	1.50
❏ 4 .... 0.35	0.30	0.90	1.50
❏ 5 .... 0.35	0.30	0.90	1.50
❏ 6 .... 0.35	0.20	0.60	1.00
❏ 7 .... 0.35	0.20	0.60	1.00
❏ 8 .... 0.35	0.20	0.60	1.00
❏ 9 .... 0.35	0.20	0.60	1.00
❏ 10 .... 0.35	0.20	0.60	1.00
❏ 11 .... 0.35	0.20	0.60	1.00
❏ 12 .... 0.35	0.20	0.60	1.00
❏ 13 .... 0.35	0.20	0.60	1.00
❏ 14 .... 0.35	0.20	0.60	1.00
❏ 15 .... 0.35	0.20	0.60	1.00
❏ 16 .... 0.35	0.20	0.60	1.00
❏ 17 .... 0.35	0.20	0.60	1.00
❏ 18 .... 0.35	0.20	0.60	1.00
❏ 19 .... 0.35	0.20	0.60	1.00

HUMAN TORCH, THE

	ORIG.	GOOD	FINE	N-MINT
❏ 1 reprints........................... 0.25	0.20	0.60	1.00
❏ 2 reprints........................... 0.25	0.20	0.60	1.00
❏ 3 reprints........................... 0.25	0.20	0.60	1.00
❏ 4 reprints........................... 0.25	0.20	0.60	1.00
❏ 5 reprints........................... 0.25	0.20	0.60	1.00
❏ 6 reprints........................... 0.25	0.20	0.60	1.00
❏ 7 reprints........................... 0.25	0.20	0.60	1.00
❏ 8 reprints........................... 0.25	0.20	0.60	1.00

ICEMAN

	ORIG.	GOOD	FINE	N-MINT
❏ 1 .... 0.20	0.15	0.45	0.75
❏ 2 .... 0.20	0.15	0.45	0.75
❏ 3 .... 0.20	0.15	0.45	0.75
❏ 4 .... 0.20	0.15	0.45	0.75

IMPOSSIBLE MAN SUMMER VACATION SPECTACULAR

	ORIG.	GOOD	FINE	N-MINT
❏ 1 .... 0.40	0.40	1.20	2.00
❏ 2 .... 0.40	0.40	1.20	2.00

INCOMPLETE DEATH'S HEAD, THE

	ORIG.	GOOD	FINE	N-MINT
❏ 1 reprints...........................	0.59	1.77	2.95
❏ 2 .... 1.75	0.35	1.05	1.75
❏ 3 .... 1.75	0.35	1.05	1.75
❏ 4 .... 1.75	0.35	1.05	1.75
❏ 5 .... 1.75	0.35	1.05	1.75
❏ 6 .... 1.75	0.35	1.05	1.75
❏ 7 .... 1.75	0.35	1.05	1.75
❏ 8 .... 1.75	0.35	1.05	1.75
❏ 9 .... 1.75	0.35	1.05	1.75

INCREDIBLE HULK

	ORIG.	GOOD	FINE	N-MINT
❏ 1 JK, I:Hulk........................0.12	900.00	2700.00	4500.00
❏ 2 JK/SD, O:retold 0.12	280.00	840.00	1400.00
❏ 3 JK, O:retold 0.12	170.00	510.00	850.00
❏ 4 JK 0.12	120.00	360.00	600.00
❏ 5 ....0.12	120.00	360.00	600.00
❏ 6 ....0.12	170.00	510.00	850.00

INCREDIBLE HULK (was Tales to Astonish)

	ORIG.	GOOD	FINE	N-MINT
❏ 102 O:retold 0.12	36.00	108.00	180.00
❏ 103 I:Space Parasite.........0.12	10.00	30.00	50.00
❏ 104 ....0.12	8.00	24.00	40.00
❏ 105 ....0.12	8.00	24.00	40.00
❏ 106 HT 0.12	6.00	18.00	30.00
❏ 107 HT 0.12	6.00	18.00	30.00
❏ 108 HT 0.12	6.00	18.00	30.00
❏ 109 HT 0.12	6.00	18.00	30.00
❏ 110 HT 0.12	6.00	18.00	30.00
❏ 111 HT/DA 0.12	2.40	7.20	12.00
❏ 112 HT/DA 0.12	2.40	7.20	12.00
❏ 113 HT/DA 0.12	2.40	7.20	12.00
❏ 114 HT/DA 0.12	2.40	7.20	12.00
❏ 115 ....0.12	2.00	6.00	10.00
❏ 116 ....0.12	2.00	6.00	10.00
❏ 117 ....0.12	2.00	6.00	10.00
❏ 118 ....0.15	2.00	6.00	10.00
❏ 119 ....0.15	2.00	6.00	10.00
❏ 120 ....0.15	2.00	6.00	10.00
❏ 121 ....0.15	2.00	6.00	10.00
❏ 122 HT, A:Thing.................0.15	2.00	6.00	10.00
❏ 123 ....0.15	1.00	3.00	5.00
❏ 124 ....0.15	1.00	3.00	5.00
❏ 125 ....0.15	1.00	3.00	5.00
❏ 126 ....0.15	1.00	3.00	5.00
❏ 127 ....0.15	1.00	3.00	5.00
❏ 128 ....0.15	1.00	3.00	5.00
❏ 129 ....0.15	1.00	3.00	5.00
❏ 130 ....0.15	1.00	3.00	5.00
❏ 131 HT, Iron Man 0.15	0.60	1.80	3.00
❏ 132 HT/JSe, V:Hydra........0.15	0.60	1.80	3.00
❏ 133 ....0.15	0.60	1.80	3.00
❏ 134 ....0.15	0.60	1.80	3.00
❏ 135 ....0.15	0.60	1.80	3.00
❏ 136 ....0.15	0.60	1.80	3.00
❏ 137 ....0.15	0.60	1.80	3.00
❏ 138 ....0.15	0.60	1.80	3.00
❏ 139 ....0.15	0.60	1.80	3.00
❏ 140 ....0.15	0.80	2.40	4.00
❏ 141 ....0.15	0.80	2.40	4.00
❏ 142 ....0.15	0.60	1.80	3.00
❏ 143 ....0.15	0.60	1.80	3.00
❏ 144 ....0.15	0.60	1.80	3.00
❏ 145 HT/JSe, O:retold 0.25	0.80	2.40	4.00
❏ 146 HT/JSe 0.20	0.60	1.80	3.00
❏ 147 HT/JSe Parasite.........0.20	0.60	1.80	3.00
❏ 148 HT/JSe 0.20	0.60	1.80	3.00

	ORIG.	GOOD	FINE	N-MINT
☐ 149 HT/JSe	0.20	0.60	1.80	3.00
☐ 150 HT/JSe, I:Viking	0.20	1.00	3.00	5.00
☐ 151	0.20	0.60	1.80	3.00
☐ 152	0.20	0.60	1.80	3.00
☐ 153	0.20	0.60	1.80	3.00
☐ 154	0.20	0.60	1.80	3.00
☐ 155	0.20	0.60	1.80	3.00
☐ 156	0.20	0.60	1.80	3.00
☐ 157	0.20	0.60	1.80	3.00
☐ 158	0.20	0.60	1.80	3.00
☐ 159	0.20	0.60	1.80	3.00
☐ 160	0.20	0.60	1.80	3.00
☐ 161 HT, V:Beast	0.20	0.80	2.40	4.00
☐ 162 HT, T:Wendigo	0.20	0.90	2.70	4.50
☐ 163 HT	0.20	0.60	1.80	3.00
☐ 164 HT	0.20	0.60	1.80	3.00
☐ 165 HT	0.20	0.60	1.80	3.00
☐ 166 HT	0.20	0.60	1.80	3.00
☐ 167 HT	0.20	0.60	1.80	3.00
☐ 168 HT	0.20	0.60	1.80	3.00
☐ 169 HT	0.20	0.60	1.80	3.00
☐ 170 HT	0.20	0.60	1.80	3.00
☐ 171 HT	0.20	0.60	1.80	3.00
☐ 172 HT, X-Men	0.20	4.00	12.00	20.00
☐ 173 HT, V:Cobalt Man	0.20	0.30	0.90	1.50
☐ 174 HT	0.20	0.50	1.50	2.50
☐ 175 HT	0.25	0.50	1.50	2.50
☐ 176 HT	0.25	0.80	2.40	4.00
☐ 177 HT	0.25	0.80	2.40	4.00
☐ 178 HT	0.25	3.60	10.80	18.00
☐ 179 HT, Missing Link	0.25	0.30	0.90	1.50
☐ 180 HT, 1:Wolverine	0.25	20.00	60.00	100.00
☐ 181 HT, A:Wolverine	0.25	60.00	180.00	300.00
☐ 182 I:Crackajack	0.25	15.00	45.00	75.00
☐ 183	0.25	0.40	1.20	2.00
☐ 184	0.25	0.40	1.20	2.00
☐ 185	0.25	0.40	1.20	2.00
☐ 186	0.25	0.40	1.20	2.00
☐ 187	0.25	0.40	1.20	2.00
☐ 188	0.25	0.40	1.20	2.00
☐ 189	0.25	0.40	1.20	2.00
☐ 190	0.25	0.40	1.20	2.00
☐ 191	0.25	0.40	1.20	2.00
☐ 192	0.25	0.40	1.20	2.00
☐ 193	0.25	0.40	1.20	2.00
☐ 194	0.25	0.40	1.20	2.00
☐ 195	0.25	0.40	1.20	2.00
☐ 196	0.25	0.40	1.20	2.00
☐ 197	0.25	0.40	1.20	2.00
☐ 198	0.25	0.40	1.20	2.00
☐ 199	0.25	0.40	1.20	2.00
☐ 200 SB/JSt, Surfer	0.25	4.40	13.20	22.00
☐ 201 SB/JSt	0.25	0.60	1.80	3.00
☐ 202 SB/JSt	0.25	0.60	1.80	3.00
☐ 203 SB/JSt	0.25	0.60	1.80	3.00
☐ 204 HT/JSt, I:Kronus	0.30	0.60	1.80	3.00
☐ 205	0.30	0.60	1.80	3.00
☐ 206	0.30	0.60	1.80	3.00
☐ 207	0.30	0.60	1.80	3.00
☐ 208	0.30	0.60	1.80	3.00
☐ 209	0.30	0.60	1.80	3.00
☐ 210	0.30	0.60	1.80	3.00
☐ 211	0.30	0.60	1.80	3.00
☐ 212	0.30	0.60	1.80	3.00
☐ 213	0.30	0.60	1.80	3.00
☐ 214 SB, Jack of Hearts	0.30	0.60	1.80	3.00
☐ 215	0.30	0.60	1.80	3.00
☐ 216	0.30	0.60	1.80	3.00
☐ 217	0.35	0.60	1.80	3.00
☐ 218	0.35	0.60	1.80	3.00
☐ 219	0.35	0.60	1.80	3.00
☐ 220	0.35	0.60	1.80	3.00
☐ 221	0.35	0.60	1.80	3.00
☐ 222 JSn/AA	0.35	0.60	1.80	3.00
☐ 223	0.35	0.60	1.80	3.00
☐ 224	0.35	0.60	1.80	3.00
☐ 225	0.35	0.60	1.80	3.00
☐ 226	0.35	0.60	1.80	3.00
☐ 227 Doc Samson	0.35	0.60	1.80	3.00
☐ 228	0.35	0.60	1.80	3.00
☐ 229	0.35	0.60	1.80	3.00
☐ 230	0.35	0.60	1.80	3.00
☐ 231	0.35	0.60	1.80	3.00
☐ 232 SB	0.35	0.60	1.80	3.00
☐ 233 SB	0.35	0.60	1.80	3.00
☐ 234 SB	0.35	0.60	1.80	3.00
☐ 235 SB	0.40	0.60	1.80	3.00
☐ 236 SB	0.40	0.60	1.80	3.00
☐ 237 SB	0.40	0.60	1.80	3.00
☐ 238 SB	0.40	0.60	1.80	3.00
☐ 239 SB	0.40	0.60	1.80	3.00
☐ 240 SB	0.40	0.60	1.80	3.00
☐ 241 SB	0.40	0.60	1.80	3.00
☐ 242 SB	0.40	0.60	1.80	3.00
☐ 243 SB	0.40	0.60	1.80	3.00
☐ 244 SB	0.40	0.60	1.80	3.00
☐ 245 SB	0.40	0.60	1.80	3.00
☐ 246 SB	0.40	0.60	1.80	3.00
☐ 247 SB	0.40	0.60	1.80	3.00
☐ 248 SB/JSt, I:Kronus	0.40	0.60	1.80	3.00
☐ 249 SB	0.40	0.60	1.80	3.00
☐ 250 SB, Silver Surfer, giant	0.75	0.80	2.40	4.00
☐ 251	0.50	0.40	1.20	2.00
☐ 252	0.50	0.40	1.20	2.00
☐ 253	0.50	0.40	1.20	2.00
☐ 254	0.50	0.40	1.20	2.00
☐ 255	0.50	0.40	1.20	2.00
☐ 256	0.50	0.40	1.20	2.00
☐ 257	0.50	0.40	1.20	2.00

	ORIG.	GOOD	FINE	N-MINT
☐ 258 .... 0.50	0.40	1.20	2.00
☐ 259 SB 0.50	0.40	1.20	2.00
☐ 260 SB 0.50	0.40	1.20	2.00
☐ 261 SB 0.50	0.40	1.20	2.00
☐ 262 SB 0.50	0.40	1.20	2.00
☐ 263 SB 0.50	0.40	1.20	2.00
☐ 264 SB 0.50	0.40	1.20	2.00
☐ 265 SB 0.50	0.40	1.20	2.00
☐ 266 SB 0.50	0.40	1.20	2.00
☐ 267 SB 0.60	0.40	1.20	2.00
☐ 268 SB 0.60	0.40	1.20	2.00
☐ 269 SB 0.60	0.40	1.20	2.00
☐ 270 SB 0.60	0.40	1.20	2.00
☐ 271 SB 0.60	0.40	1.20	2.00
☐ 272 SB 0.60	0.40	1.20	2.00
☐ 273 SB, Alpha Flight 0.60	0.60	1.80	3.00
☐ 274 SB 0.60	0.40	1.20	2.00
☐ 275 SB 0.60	0.40	1.20	2.00
☐ 276 SB 0.60	0.40	1.20	2.00
☐ 277 SB 0.60	0.40	1.20	2.00
☐ 278 SB 0.60	0.40	1.20	2.00
☐ 279 SB 0.60	0.40	1.20	2.00
☐ 280 SB 0.60	0.40	1.20	2.00
☐ 281 SB 0.60	0.40	1.20	2.00
☐ 282 SB 0.60	0.40	1.20	2.00
☐ 283 SB 0.60	0.40	1.20	2.00
☐ 284 SB 0.60	0.40	1.20	2.00
☐ 285 SB 0.60	0.40	1.20	2.00
☐ 286 SB 0.60	0.40	1.20	2.00
☐ 287 SB 0.60	0.40	1.20	2.00
☐ 288 SB 0.60	0.40	1.20	2.00
☐ 289 SB 0.60	0.40	1.20	2.00
☐ 290 SB 0.60	0.40	1.20	2.00
☐ 291 SB 0.60	0.40	1.20	2.00
☐ 292 SB 0.60	0.40	1.20	2.00
☐ 293 SB 0.60	0.40	1.20	2.00
☐ 294 SB 0.60	0.40	1.20	2.00
☐ 295 SB 0.60	0.40	1.20	2.00
☐ 296 SB 0.60	0.40	1.20	2.00
☐ 297 SB 0.60	0.40	1.20	2.00
☐ 298 SB 0.60	0.40	1.20	2.00
☐ 299 SB 0.60	0.40	1.20	2.00
☐ 300 SB A:Spider-Man, giant			
.... 1.00	1.20	3.60	6.00
☐ 301 SB 0.60	0.30	0.90	1.50
☐ 302 SB 0.60	0.30	0.90	1.50
☐ 303 SB 0.60	0.30	0.90	1.50
☐ 304 SB 0.60	0.30	0.90	1.50
☐ 305 SB 0.60	0.30	0.90	1.50
☐ 306 SB 0.65	0.30	0.90	1.50
☐ 307 SB 0.65	0.30	0.90	1.50
☐ 308 SB 0.65	0.30	0.90	1.50
☐ 309 SB 0.65	0.30	0.90	1.50
☐ 310 SB 0.65	0.30	0.90	1.50
☐ 311 SB 0.65	0.30	0.90	1.50

	ORIG.	GOOD	FINE	N-MINT
☐ 312 Secret Wars II 0.65	0.30	0.90	1.50
☐ 313 Alpha Flight 0.65	0.20	0.60	1.00
☐ 314 JBy 0.65	1.00	3.00	5.00
☐ 315 JBy 0.65	0.60	1.80	3.00
☐ 316 JBy 0.75	0.60	1.80	3.00
☐ 317 JBy 0.75	0.60	1.80	3.00
☐ 318 JBy 0.75	0.60	1.80	3.00
☐ 319 JBy 0.75	0.60	1.80	3.00
☐ 320 .... 0.75	0.60	1.80	3.00
☐ 321 .... 0.75	0.65	1.95	3.25
☐ 322 .... 0.75	0.65	1.95	3.25
☐ 323 .... 0.75	0.65	1.95	3.25
☐ 324 Hulk seen as gray 0.75	2.40	7.20	12.00
☐ 326 .... 0.75	0.65	1.95	3.25
☐ 327 .... 0.75	0.65	1.95	3.25
☐ 328 .... 0.75	0.65	1.95	3.25
☐ 329 .... 0.75	0.65	1.95	3.25
☐ 330 TMc 0.75	5.60	16.80	28.00
☐ 331 TMc Hulk turns gray ... 0.75	3.60	10.80	18.00
☐ 332 TMc 0.75	2.40	7.20	12.00
☐ 333 TMc 0.75	2.40	7.20	12.00
☐ 334 TMc 0.75	2.40	7.20	12.00
☐ 335 TMc 0.75	2.40	7.20	12.00
☐ 336 TMc A:X-Factor 0.75	2.00	6.00	10.00
☐ 337 TMc A:X-Factor 0.75	2.00	6.00	10.00
☐ 338 TMc 0.75	2.00	6.00	10.00
☐ 339 TMc 0.75	2.00	6.00	10.00
☐ 340 TMc A:Wolverine 0.75	10.00	30.00	50.00
☐ 341 TMc V:Man-Bull 0.75	2.00	6.00	10.00
☐ 342 TMc 0.75	2.00	6.00	10.00
☐ 343 TMc 0.75	2.00	6.00	10.00
☐ 344 TMc 0.75	2.00	6.00	10.00
☐ 345 TMc 1.50	2.00	6.00	10.00
☐ 346 TMc 0.75	2.00	6.00	10.00
☐ 347 .... 0.75	0.40	1.20	2.00
☐ 348 .... 0.75	0.40	1.20	2.00
☐ 350 Hulk vs. Thing 0.75	0.80	2.40	4.00
☐ 351 .... 0.75	0.60	1.80	3.00
☐ 352 .... 0.75	0.60	1.80	3.00
☐ 353 .... 0.75	0.60	1.80	3.00
☐ 354 .... 0.75	0.60	1.80	3.00
☐ 355 .... 0.75	0.60	1.80	3.00
☐ 356 .... 0.75	0.60	1.80	3.00
☐ 357 .... 0.75	0.60	1.80	3.00
☐ 358 .... 0.75	0.60	1.80	3.00
☐ 359 .... 1.00	0.60	1.80	3.00
☐ 360 .... 1.00	0.60	1.80	3.00
☐ 361 Iron Man 1.00	0.40	1.20	2.00
☐ 362 .... 1.00	0.40	1.20	2.00
☐ 363 Acts of Vengeance 1.00	0.40	1.20	2.00
☐ 364 WS(c) Countdown 1.00	0.60	1.80	3.00
☐ 365 WS(c) Countdown 1.00	0.60	1.80	3.00
☐ 366 WS(c) Countdown 1.00	0.60	1.80	3.00
☐ 367 WS(c) Countdown 1.00	4.40	13.20	22.00
☐ 368 .... 1.00	2.40	7.20	12.00

	ORIG.	GOOD	FINE	N-MINT
❑ 369 .... 1.00		2.40	7.20	12.00
❑ 370 Dr. Strange, Sub-Mariner				
.... 1.00		1.60	4.80	8.00
❑ 371 Dr. Strange, Sub-Mariner				
.... 1.00		1.60	4.80	8.00
❑ 372 Green Hulk returns 1.00		4.00	12.00	20.00
❑ 373 .... 1.00		1.20	3.60	6.00
❑ 374 .... 1.00		1.20	3.60	6.00
❑ 375 .... 1.00		1.20	3.60	6.00
❑ 376 .... 1.00		1.20	3.60	6.00
❑ 377 1:new Hulk, 1st printing				
.... 1.00		4.40	13.20	22.00
❑ 377 2nd printing............... 1.00		0.60	1.80	3.00
❑ 378 Rhino as Santa 1.00		0.60	1.80	3.00
❑ 379 .... 1.00		1.20	3.60	6.00
❑ 380 .... 1.00		1.20	3.60	6.00
❑ 381 .... 1.00		1.20	3.60	6.00
❑ 382 .... 1.00		1.20	3.60	6.00
❑ 383 Infinity Gauntlet.......... 1.00		1.00	3.00	5.00
❑ 384 Infinity Gauntlet.......... 1.00		1.00	3.00	5.00
❑ 385 Infinity Gauntlet.......... 1.00		1.00	3.00	5.00
❑ 386 Infinity Gauntlet.......... 1.00		1.00	3.00	5.00
❑ 387 Infinity Gauntlet.......... 1.00		1.00	3.00	5.00
❑ 388 1:Speedfreek 1.00		0.60	1.80	3.00
❑ 389 .... 1.00		0.50	1.50	2.50
❑ 390 .... 1.25		0.50	1.50	2.50
❑ 391 X-Factor.................... 1.25		0.50	1.50	2.50
❑ 392 .... 1.25		0.50	1.50	2.50
❑ 393 green foil cover 2.50		2.00	6.00	10.00
❑ 395 .... 1.25		0.60	1.80	3.00
❑ 396 .... 1.25		0.60	1.80	3.00
❑ 397 .... 1.25		0.60	1.80	3.00
❑ 398 .... 1.25		0.60	1.80	3.00
❑ 399 .... 1.25		0.60	1.80	3.00
❑ 400 shiny cover 2.50		1.20	3.60	6.00
❑ 401 .... 1.25		0.25	0.75	1.25
❑ 402 .... 1.25		0.25	0.75	1.25
❑ 403 .... 1.25		0.25	0.75	1.25
❑ 404 .... 1.25		0.25	0.75	1.25
❑ 405 .... 1.25		0.25	0.75	1.25
❑ 406 .... 1.25		0.25	0.75	1.25
❑ 407 .... 1.25		0.25	0.75	1.25
❑ 408 .... 1.25		0.25	0.75	1.25
❑ 409 .... 1.25		0.25	0.75	1.25
❑ 410 .... 1.25		0.25	0.75	1.25

INCREDIBLE HULK AND WOLVERINE

	ORIG.	GOOD	FINE	N-MINT
❑ 1 reprint 2.00		0.40	1.20	2.00

INCREDIBLE HULK ANNUAL/SPECIAL

	ORIG.	GOOD	FINE	N-MINT
❑ 1 Steranko cover 0.25		8.40	25.20	42.00
❑ 2 reprint 0.25		4.80	14.40	24.00
❑ 3 reprint 0.25		2.00	6.00	10.00
❑ 4 .... 0.50		1.20	3.60	6.00
❑ 5 .... 0.50		1.20	3.60	6.00
❑ 6 HT, Dr. Strange 0.60		1.00	3.00	5.00

	ORIG.	GOOD	FINE	N-MINT
❑ 7 JBy/BL, Spider-Man 0.60		1.40	4.20	7.00
❑ 8 Alpha Flight................... 0.75		0.40	1.20	2.00
❑ 9 .... 0.75		0.40	1.20	2.00
❑ 10 .... 0.75		0.40	1.20	2.00
❑ 11 .... 1.00		0.40	1.20	2.00
❑ 12 .... 1.00		0.20	0.60	1.00
❑ 13 .... 1.00		0.20	0.60	1.00
❑ 14 .... 1.25		0.25	0.75	1.25
❑ 15 .... 1.25		0.25	0.75	1.25
❑ 16 Lifeform 2.00		0.40	1.20	2.00
❑ 17 Subterranean 2.00		0.40	1.20	2.00
❑ 18 .... 2.25		0.45	1.35	2.25
❑ 19 1:Lazarus, trading card				
.... 2.95		0.59	1.77	2.95

INCREDIBLE HULK POSTER MAGAZINE

	ORIG.	GOOD	FINE	N-MINT
❑ 1 tv show......................... 1.50		0.79	2.37	3.95
❑ 1 comics.......................... 3.95		0.79	2.37	3.95

INCREDIBLE HULK VS. QUASIMODO

	ORIG.	GOOD	FINE	N-MINT
❑ 1 .... 0.60		0.60	1.80	3.00

INCREDIBLE HULK: FUTURE IMPERFECT

	ORIG.	GOOD	FINE	N-MINT
❑ 1 GP............................... 5.95		1.19	3.57	5.95
❑ 2 GP............................... 5.95		1.19	3.57	5.95

INDIANA JONES AND THE LAST CRUSADE

	ORIG.	GOOD	FINE	N-MINT
❑ 1 b&w mag.......................		0.59	1.77	2.95
❑ 1 comic book.................... 1.00		0.20	0.60	1.00
❑ 2 comic book.................... 1.00		0.20	0.60	1.00
❑ 3 comic book.................... 1.00		0.20	0.60	1.00
❑ 4 comic book.................... 1.00		0.20	0.60	1.00

INDIANA JONES AND THE TEMPLE OF DOOM

	ORIG.	GOOD	FINE	N-MINT
❑ 1 movie 0.75		0.20	0.60	1.00
❑ 2 movie 0.75		0.20	0.60	1.00
❑ 3 movie 0.75		0.20	0.60	1.00

INFINITY CRUSADE, THE

	ORIG.	GOOD	FINE	N-MINT
❑ 1 foil cover....................... 3.50		0.70	2.10	3.50
❑ 2 .... 2.50		0.50	1.50	2.50
❑ 3 .... 2.50		0.50	1.50	2.50
❑ 4 .... 2.50		0.50	1.50	2.50

INFINITY GAUNTLET

	ORIG.	GOOD	FINE	N-MINT
❑ 1 GP, Thanos, Surfer, SpM, Avengers				
.... 2.50		2.00	6.00	10.00
❑ 2 GP, Thanos, Surfer, SpM, Avengers				
.... 2.50		1.20	3.60	6.00
❑ 3 GP, Thanos, Surfer, SpM, Avengers				
.... 2.50		1.20	3.60	6.00
❑ 4 GP, Thanos, Surfer, SpM, Avengers				
.... 2.50		1.20	3.60	6.00
❑ 5 GP(c) Ron Lim 2.50		1.20	3.60	6.00
❑ 6 GP(c) Ron Lim 2.50		1.20	3.60	6.00

INFINITY WAR

	ORIG.	GOOD	FINE	N-MINT
❑ 1 .... 2.50		1.00	3.00	5.00
❑ 2 .... 2.50		0.60	1.80	3.00
❑ 3 .... 2.50		0.60	1.80	3.00
❑ 4 .... 2.50		0.60	1.80	3.00

	ORIG.	GOOD	FINE	N-MINT
5	2.50	0.60	1.80	3.00
6	2.50	0.60	1.80	3.00

INHUMANS

	ORIG.	GOOD	FINE	N-MINT
1 GP, V:Blastaar	0.12	0.60	1.80	3.00
2	0.12	0.30	0.90	1.50
3	0.12	0.30	0.90	1.50
4	0.12	0.30	0.90	1.50
5	0.30	0.30	0.90	1.50
6	0.30	0.30	0.90	1.50
7	0.30	0.20	0.60	1.00
8	0.30	0.20	0.60	1.00
9	0.30	0.20	0.60	1.00
10	0.30	0.20	0.60	1.00
11	0.30	0.20	0.60	1.00
12	0.30	0.20	0.60	1.00

INHUMANS SPECIAL

	ORIG.	GOOD	FINE	N-MINT
1	1.50	0.30	0.90	1.50

INVADERS ANNUAL, THE (1977)

	ORIG.	GOOD	FINE	N-MINT
1	0.50	1.00	3.00	5.00

INVADERS, THE (first series)

	ORIG.	GOOD	FINE	N-MINT
1	0.25	2.00	6.00	10.00
2	0.25	1.40	4.20	7.00
3	0.25	1.20	3.60	6.00
4	0.25	1.20	3.60	6.00
5	0.25	1.20	3.60	6.00
6	0.25	0.80	2.40	4.00
7	0.25	0.80	2.40	4.00
8	0.30	0.80	2.40	4.00
9	0.30	0.80	2.40	4.00
10	0.30	0.80	2.40	4.00
11	0.30	0.80	2.40	4.00
12	0.30	0.80	2.40	4.00
13	0.30	0.80	2.40	4.00
14	0.30	0.80	2.40	4.00
15	0.30	0.80	2.40	4.00
16	0.30	0.80	2.40	4.00
17	0.30	0.80	2.40	4.00
18	0.30	0.80	2.40	4.00
19	0.30	0.80	2.40	4.00
20	0.30	1.20	3.60	6.00
21	0.30	0.60	1.80	3.00
22	0.35	0.60	1.80	3.00
23	0.35	0.60	1.80	3.00
24	0.35	0.60	1.80	3.00
25	0.35	0.60	1.80	3.00
26	0.35	0.60	1.80	3.00
27	0.35	0.60	1.80	3.00
28	0.35	0.60	1.80	3.00
29	0.35	0.60	1.80	3.00
30	0.35	0.60	1.80	3.00
31	0.35	0.60	1.80	3.00
32	0.35	0.60	1.80	3.00
33	0.35	0.60	1.80	3.00
34	0.35	0.60	1.80	3.00
35	0.35	0.60	1.80	3.00
36	0.35	0.60	1.80	3.00
37	0.35	0.60	1.80	3.00
38	0.35	0.60	1.80	3.00
39	0.35	0.60	1.80	3.00
40	0.40	0.60	1.80	3.00
41 giant	0.60	0.60	1.80	3.00

INVADERS, THE (second series, 1993)

	ORIG.	GOOD	FINE	N-MINT
1	1.75	0.35	1.05	1.75
2	1.75	0.35	1.05	1.75
3	1.75	0.35	1.05	1.75
4	1.75	0.35	1.05	1.75

IRON FIST

	ORIG.	GOOD	FINE	N-MINT
1 JBy	0.25	9.60	28.80	48.00
2 JBy	0.25	4.00	12.00	20.00
3 JBy	0.25	4.00	12.00	20.00
4 JBy	0.25	4.00	12.00	20.00
5 JBy	0.25	4.00	12.00	20.00
6 JBy	0.25	4.00	12.00	20.00
7 JBy	0.30	4.00	12.00	20.00
8 JBy	0.30	4.00	12.00	20.00
9 JBy	0.30	4.00	12.00	20.00
10 JBy	0.30	4.00	12.00	20.00
11 JBy	0.30	4.00	12.00	20.00
12 JBy	0.30	4.00	12.00	20.00
13 JBy	0.30	4.00	12.00	20.00
14 JBy 1:Sabretooth	0.30	50.00	150.00	250.00
15 JBy, A:Wolverine	0.30	13.00	39.00	65.00

IRON MAN

	ORIG.	GOOD	FINE	N-MINT
1 JCr/GC	0.12	80.00	240.00	400.00
2 JCr, I:Demolisher	0.12	20.00	60.00	100.00
3 JCr	0.12	12.00	36.00	60.00
4 JCr	0.12	10.00	30.00	50.00
5 JCr	0.12	10.00	30.00	50.00
6 JCr/GT	0.12	7.00	21.00	35.00
7 JCr/GT	0.12	7.00	21.00	35.00
8 JCr/GT	0.12	7.00	21.00	35.00
9 JCr/GT	0.12	7.00	21.00	35.00
10 JCr/GT	0.12	7.00	21.00	35.00
11	0.12	5.00	15.00	25.00
12	0.12	5.00	15.00	25.00
13	0.12	5.00	15.00	25.00
14	0.12	5.00	15.00	25.00
15	0.12	5.00	15.00	25.00
16	0.15	4.00	12.00	20.00
17	0.15	4.00	12.00	20.00
18	0.15	4.00	12.00	20.00
19	0.15	4.00	12.00	20.00
20	0.15	4.00	12.00	20.00
21	0.15	2.40	7.20	12.00
22	0.15	2.40	7.20	12.00
23	0.15	2.40	7.20	12.00
24	0.15	2.40	7.20	12.00
25	0.15	2.40	7.20	12.00

	ORIG.	GOOD	FINE	N-MINT
❏ 26	0.15	2.40	7.20	12.00
❏ 27	0.15	2.40	7.20	12.00
❏ 28	0.15	2.40	7.20	12.00
❏ 29	0.15	2.40	7.20	12.00
❏ 30	0.15	2.40	7.20	12.00
❏ 31	0.15	2.00	6.00	10.00
❏ 32	0.15	2.00	6.00	10.00
❏ 33	0.15	2.00	6.00	10.00
❏ 34	0.15	2.00	6.00	10.00
❏ 35	0.15	2.00	6.00	10.00
❏ 36	0.15	2.00	6.00	10.00
❏ 37	0.15	2.00	6.00	10.00
❏ 38	0.15	2.00	6.00	10.00
❏ 39	0.15	2.00	6.00	10.00
❏ 40	0.15	2.00	6.00	10.00
❏ 41	0.15	2.00	6.00	10.00
❏ 42	0.15	2.00	6.00	10.00
❏ 43 GT/JM, A:Midas	0.25	2.00	6.00	10.00
❏ 44 GT	0.20	1.60	4.80	8.00
❏ 45 GT	0.20	1.60	4.80	8.00
❏ 46 GT	0.20	1.60	4.80	8.00
❏ 47 BS/JM, O:retold	0.20	3.00	9.00	15.00
❏ 48	0.20	1.60	4.80	8.00
❏ 49	0.20	1.60	4.80	8.00
❏ 50	0.20	1.60	4.80	8.00
❏ 51	0.20	1.60	4.80	8.00
❏ 52	0.20	1.60	4.80	8.00
❏ 53	0.20	1.60	4.80	8.00
❏ 54	0.20	1.60	4.80	8.00
❏ 55 JSn, I:Destroyer, Thanos	0.20	22.00	66.00	110.00
❏ 56 JSn, I:Fangor	0.20	2.40	7.20	12.00
❏ 57	0.20	1.20	3.60	6.00
❏ 58	0.20	1.20	3.60	6.00
❏ 59	0.20	1.20	3.60	6.00
❏ 60	0.20	1.20	3.60	6.00
❏ 61	0.20	1.20	3.60	6.00
❏ 62	0.20	1.20	3.60	6.00
❏ 63	0.20	1.20	3.60	6.00
❏ 64	0.20	1.20	3.60	6.00
❏ 65	0.20	1.20	3.60	6.00
❏ 66	0.20	1.20	3.60	6.00
❏ 67	0.20	1.20	3.60	6.00
❏ 68 GT, O:retold	0.25	2.00	6.00	10.00
❏ 69 GT	0.25	1.20	3.60	6.00
❏ 70 GT	0.25	1.20	3.60	6.00
❏ 71 GT	0.25	1.20	3.60	6.00
❏ 72 GT/NA, comic con	0.25	1.20	3.60	6.00
❏ 73	0.25	1.20	3.60	6.00
❏ 74	0.25	1.20	3.60	6.00
❏ 75	0.25	1.20	3.60	6.00
❏ 76	0.25	1.20	3.60	6.00
❏ 77	0.25	1.20	3.60	6.00
❏ 78	0.25	1.20	3.60	6.00
❏ 79	0.25	1.20	3.60	6.00
❏ 80	0.25	1.20	3.60	6.00
❏ 81	0.25	1.20	3.60	6.00
❏ 82	0.25	1.20	3.60	6.00
❏ 83	0.25	1.20	3.60	6.00
❏ 84	0.25	1.20	3.60	6.00
❏ 85	0.25	1.20	3.60	6.00
❏ 86	0.25	1.20	3.60	6.00
❏ 87	0.25	1.20	3.60	6.00
❏ 88	0.25	1.20	3.60	6.00
❏ 89	0.25	1.20	3.60	6.00
❏ 90	0.30	1.20	3.60	6.00
❏ 91	0.30	1.20	3.60	6.00
❏ 92	0.30	1.20	3.60	6.00
❏ 93	0.30	1.20	3.60	6.00
❏ 94	0.30	1.20	3.60	6.00
❏ 95	0.30	1.20	3.60	6.00
❏ 96	0.30	1.20	3.60	6.00
❏ 97	0.30	1.20	3.60	6.00
❏ 98	0.30	1.20	3.60	6.00
❏ 99	0.30	1.20	3.60	6.00
❏ 100 GT/JSn(c), Mandarin	0.30	3.00	9.00	15.00
❏ 101	0.30	0.80	2.40	4.00
❏ 102	0.30	0.80	2.40	4.00
❏ 103	0.30	0.80	2.40	4.00
❏ 104	0.35	0.80	2.40	4.00
❏ 105	0.35	0.80	2.40	4.00
❏ 106	0.35	0.80	2.40	4.00
❏ 107	0.35	0.80	2.40	4.00
❏ 108	0.35	0.80	2.40	4.00
❏ 109	0.35	0.80	2.40	4.00
❏ 110	0.35	0.80	2.40	4.00
❏ 111	0.35	0.80	2.40	4.00
❏ 112	0.35	0.80	2.40	4.00
❏ 113	0.35	0.80	2.40	4.00
❏ 114	0.35	0.80	2.40	4.00
❏ 115	0.35	0.80	2.40	4.00
❏ 116	0.35	0.80	2.40	4.00
❏ 117 BL/JR2	0.35	1.40	4.20	7.00
❏ 118 JBy/BL	0.35	1.00	3.00	5.00
❏ 119 BL/JR2, alcoholism	0.35	1.20	3.60	6.00
❏ 120	0.35	1.20	3.60	6.00
❏ 121	0.35	1.20	3.60	6.00
❏ 122	0.40	1.20	3.60	6.00
❏ 123	0.40	1.20	3.60	6.00
❏ 124	0.40	1.20	3.60	6.00
❏ 125	0.40	1.20	3.60	6.00
❏ 126	0.40	1.20	3.60	6.00
❏ 127	0.40	1.20	3.60	6.00
❏ 128 BL/JR2, alcoholism	0.40	1.00	3.00	5.00
❏ 129	0.40	0.60	1.80	3.00
❏ 130	0.40	0.60	1.80	3.00
❏ 131	0.40	0.60	1.80	3.00
❏ 132	0.40	0.60	1.80	3.00
❏ 133	0.40	0.60	1.80	3.00

	ORIG.	GOOD	FINE	N-MINT		ORIG.	GOOD	FINE	N-MINT
134	0.40	0.60	1.80	3.00	189	0.60	0.40	1.20	2.00
135	0.40	0.60	1.80	3.00	190	0.60	0.40	1.20	2.00
136	0.40	0.60	1.80	3.00	191 LMc old Iron Man	0.60	0.40	1.20	2.00
137	0.40	0.60	1.80	3.00	192	0.60	0.40	1.20	2.00
138	0.50	0.60	1.80	3.00	193	0.65	0.40	1.20	2.00
139	0.50	0.60	1.80	3.00	194	0.65	0.40	1.20	2.00
140	0.50	0.60	1.80	3.00	195	0.65	0.40	1.20	2.00
141	0.50	0.60	1.80	3.00	196	0.65	0.40	1.20	2.00
142	0.50	0.60	1.80	3.00	197 Secret Wars II	0.65	0.40	1.20	2.00
143	0.50	0.60	1.80	3.00	198	0.65	0.40	1.20	2.00
144	0.50	0.60	1.80	3.00	199	0.65	0.40	1.20	2.00
145	0.50	0.60	1.80	3.00	200	1.25	1.20	3.60	6.00
146	0.50	0.60	1.80	3.00	201	0.60	0.20	0.60	1.00
147	0.50	0.60	1.80	3.00	202	0.60	0.20	0.60	1.00
148	0.50	0.60	1.80	3.00	203	0.75	0.20	0.60	1.00
149	0.50	0.60	1.80	3.00	204	0.75	0.20	0.60	1.00
150	0.75	0.60	1.80	3.00	205	0.75	0.20	0.60	1.00
151	0.50	0.40	1.20	2.00	206	0.75	0.20	0.60	1.00
152	0.50	0.40	1.20	2.00	207	0.75	0.20	0.60	1.00
153	0.50	0.40	1.20	2.00	208	0.75	0.20	0.60	1.00
154	0.60	0.40	1.20	2.00	209	0.75	0.20	0.60	1.00
155	0.60	0.40	1.20	2.00	210	0.75	0.20	0.60	1.00
156	0.60	0.40	1.20	2.00	211	0.75	0.20	0.60	1.00
157	0.60	0.40	1.20	2.00	212	0.75	0.20	0.60	1.00
158	0.60	0.40	1.20	2.00	213	0.75	0.20	0.60	1.00
159 PS, Diablo	0.60	0.40	1.20	2.00	214	0.75	0.20	0.60	1.00
160 Serpent Squad	0.60	0.40	1.20	2.00	215	0.75	0.20	0.60	1.00
161 Moon Knight	0.60	0.40	1.20	2.00	216	0.75	0.20	0.60	1.00
162	0.60	0.40	1.20	2.00	217	0.75	0.20	0.60	1.00
163	0.60	0.40	1.20	2.00	218	0.75	0.20	0.60	1.00
164	0.60	0.40	1.20	2.00	219	0.75	0.20	0.60	1.00
165	0.60	0.40	1.20	2.00	220 D:Spymaster	0.75	0.20	0.60	1.00
166	0.60	0.40	1.20	2.00	221	0.75	0.20	0.60	1.00
167 LMc, alcoholism	0.60	0.40	1.20	2.00	222	0.75	0.20	0.60	1.00
168 LMc, Machine Man	0.60	0.40	1.20	2.00	223	0.75	0.20	0.60	1.00
169 new Iron Man	0.60	2.40	7.20	12.00	224	0.75	0.20	0.60	1.00
170	0.60	0.80	2.40	4.00	225 Armor Wars	1.25	1.20	3.60	6.00
171	0.60	0.40	1.20	2.00	226 Armor Wars	0.75	0.80	2.40	4.00
172	0.60	0.40	1.20	2.00	227 Armor Wars	0.75	0.80	2.40	4.00
173 LMc	0.60	0.40	1.20	2.00	228 Armor Wars	0.75	0.80	2.40	4.00
174 LMc	0.60	0.40	1.20	2.00	229 Armor Wars	0.75	0.80	2.40	4.00
175 LMc	0.60	0.40	1.20	2.00	230 Armor Wars	0.75	0.80	2.40	4.00
176 LMc	0.60	0.40	1.20	2.00	231 Armor Wars	0.75	0.80	2.40	4.00
177 LMc	0.60	0.40	1.20	2.00	232 BWS, Flexographic	0.75	0.60	1.80	3.00
178 LMc	0.60	0.40	1.20	2.00	232 BWS, offset	0.75	0.60	1.80	3.00
179 LMc	0.60	0.40	1.20	2.00	233 A:Ant-Man	0.75	0.20	0.60	1.00
180 LMc	0.60	0.40	1.20	2.00	234 A:Spider-Man	0.75	0.20	0.60	1.00
181 LMc	0.60	0.40	1.20	2.00	235	0.75	0.20	0.60	1.00
182 LMc	0.60	0.40	1.20	2.00	236	0.75	0.20	0.60	1.00
183 LMc	0.60	0.40	1.20	2.00	237	0.75	0.20	0.60	1.00
184 LMc	0.60	0.40	1.20	2.00	238	0.75	0.20	0.60	1.00
185 LMc	0.60	0.40	1.20	2.00	239	0.75	0.20	0.60	1.00
186	0.60	0.40	1.20	2.00	240	0.75	0.20	0.60	1.00
187	0.60	0.40	1.20	2.00	241	0.75	0.20	0.60	1.00
188	0.60	0.40	1.20	2.00	242 Stark shot	0.75	0.50	1.50	2.50

	ORIG.	GOOD	FINE	N-MINT
☐ 243 Stark crippled............ 0.75	0.50	1.50	2.50
☐ 244 .... 1.50	0.30	0.90	1.50
☐ 245 .... 0.75	0.30	0.90	1.50
☐ 246 .... 1.00	0.20	0.60	1.00
☐ 247 .... 1.00	0.20	0.60	1.00
☐ 248 Stark cured 1.00	0.20	0.60	1.00
☐ 249 Dr. Doom 1.00	0.20	0.60	1.00
☐ 250 Dr. Doom, Acts 1.50	0.30	0.90	1.50
☐ 251 Acts of Vengeance 1.00	0.20	0.60	1.00
☐ 252 Acts of Vengeance 1.00	0.20	0.60	1.00
☐ 253 JBy(c) 1.00	0.20	0.60	1.00
☐ 254 .... 1.00	0.20	0.60	1.00
☐ 255 .... 1.00	0.20	0.60	1.00
☐ 256 .... 1.00	0.20	0.60	1.00
☐ 257 .... 1.00	0.20	0.60	1.00
☐ 258 .... 1.00	0.60	1.80	3.00
☐ 259 Armor Wars II 1.00	0.40	1.20	2.00
☐ 260 Armor Wars II 1.00	0.40	1.20	2.00
☐ 261 Armor Wars II 1.00	0.40	1.20	2.00
☐ 262 Armor Wars II 1.00	0.40	1.20	2.00
☐ 263 Armor Wars II 1.00	0.40	1.20	2.00
☐ 264 Armor Wars II 1.00	0.40	1.20	2.00
☐ 265 Armor Wars II 1.00	0.40	1.20	2.00
☐ 266 Armor Wars II 1.00	0.40	1.20	2.00
☐ 267 .... 1.00	0.20	0.60	1.00
☐ 268 O:retold.................... 1.00	0.20	0.60	1.00
☐ 269 .... 1.00	0.20	0.60	1.00
☐ 270 .... 1.00	0.20	0.60	1.00
☐ 271 .... 1.00	0.20	0.60	1.00
☐ 272 .... 1.00	0.20	0.60	1.00
☐ 273 .... 1.00	0.20	0.60	1.00
☐ 274 .... 1.00	0.20	0.60	1.00
☐ 275 .... 1.50	0.30	0.90	1.50
☐ 276 .... 1.00	0.20	0.60	1.00
☐ 277 .... 1.25	0.25	0.75	1.25
☐ 278 Galactic Storm 1.25	0.25	0.75	1.25
☐ 279 Galactic Storm 1.25	0.25	0.75	1.25
☐ 280 .... 1.25	0.25	0.75	1.25
☐ 281 .... 1.25	0.25	0.75	1.25
☐ 282 .... 1.25	0.25	0.75	1.25
☐ 283 .... 1.25	0.25	0.75	1.25
☐ 284 .... 1.25	1.60	4.80	8.00
☐ 285 .... 1.25	0.25	0.75	1.25
☐ 286 .... 1.25	0.25	0.75	1.25
☐ 287 .... 1.25	0.25	0.75	1.25
☐ 288 silver foil cover 2.50	0.80	2.40	4.00
☐ 289 .... 1.25	0.25	0.75	1.25
☐ 290 foil cover 2.95	0.59	1.77	2.95
☐ 291 .... 1.25	0.25	0.75	1.25
☐ 292 .... 1.25	0.25	0.75	1.25
☐ 293 .... 1.25	0.25	0.75	1.25
☐ 294 .... 1.25	0.25	0.75	1.25
☐ 295 .... 1.25	0.25	0.75	1.25
☐ 296 .... 1.25	0.25	0.75	1.25

	ORIG.	GOOD	FINE	N-MINT
IRON MAN AND SUB-MARINER			
☐ 1 GC,JCr.........................0.12	35.00	105.00	175.00
IRON MAN ANNUAL			
☐ 1 reprint.............................0.25	3.00	9.00	15.00
☐ 2 reprint.............................0.25	1.60	4.80	8.00
☐ 3 ....0.50	0.80	2.40	4.00
☐ 4 ....0.50	0.80	2.40	4.00
☐ 5 ....1.00	0.80	2.40	4.00
☐ 6 ....1.00	0.60	1.80	3.00
☐ 7 West Coast Avengers 1.00	0.40	1.20	2.00
☐ 8 ....1.25	0.40	1.20	2.00
☐ 9 ....1.25	0.40	1.20	2.00
☐ 10 Atlantis Attacks 2.00	0.40	1.20	2.00
☐ 11 Terminus Factor...........2.00	0.40	1.20	2.00
☐ 12 Subterranean Wars......2.00	0.40	1.20	2.00
☐ 13 ....2.25	0.45	1.35	2.25
☐ 14 trading card 2.95	0.59	1.77	2.95
IRON MANUAL, THE			
☐ 1 ....1.75	0.35	1.05	1.75
ISLAND OF DR. MOREAU, THE			
☐ 1 movie 0.50	0.20	0.60	1.00
JACK OF HEARTS			
☐ 1 ....0.60	0.30	0.90	1.50
☐ 2 ....0.60	0.20	0.60	1.00
☐ 3 ....0.60	0.20	0.60	1.00
☐ 4 ....0.60	0.20	0.60	1.00
JAMES BOND JR.			
☐ 1 TV cartoon 1.00	0.25	0.75	1.25
☐ 2 TV cartoon 1.25	0.25	0.75	1.25
☐ 3 TV cartoon 1.25	0.25	0.75	1.25
☐ 4 TV cartoon 1.25	0.25	0.75	1.25
☐ 5 TV cartoon 1.25	0.25	0.75	1.25
☐ 6 TV cartoon 1.25	0.25	0.75	1.25
☐ 8 ....1.25	0.25	0.75	1.25
☐ 9 ....1.25	0.25	0.75	1.25
☐ 10 ....1.25	0.25	0.75	1.25
☐ 11 ....1.25	0.25	0.75	1.25
☐ 12 ....1.25	0.25	0.75	1.25
JOHN CARTER OF MARS			
☐ 1 ....0.30	0.80	2.40	4.00
☐ 2 ....0.30	0.60	1.80	3.00
☐ 3 ....0.30	0.60	1.80	3.00
☐ 4 ....0.30	0.60	1.80	3.00
☐ 5 ....0.30	0.40	1.20	2.00
☐ 6 ....0.35	0.40	1.20	2.00
☐ 7 ....0.35	0.40	1.20	2.00
☐ 8 ....0.35	0.40	1.20	2.00
☐ 9 ....0.35	0.40	1.20	2.00
☐ 10 ....0.35	0.40	1.20	2.00
☐ 11 ....0.35	0.30	0.90	1.50
☐ 12 ....0.35	0.30	0.90	1.50
☐ 13 ....0.35	0.30	0.90	1.50
☐ 14 ....0.35	0.30	0.90	1.50
☐ 15 ....0.35	0.30	0.90	1.50

	ORIG.	GOOD	FINE	N-MINT
☐ 16	0.35	0.30	0.90	1.50
☐ 17	0.35	0.30	0.90	1.50
☐ 18 F. Miller	0.35	0.60	1.80	3.00
☐ 19	0.35	0.30	0.90	1.50
☐ 20	0.35	0.30	0.90	1.50
☐ 21	0.35	0.30	0.90	1.50
☐ 22	0.35	0.30	0.90	1.50
☐ 23	0.35	0.30	0.90	1.50
☐ 24	0.40	0.30	0.90	1.50
☐ 25	0.40	0.30	0.90	1.50
☐ 26	0.40	0.30	0.90	1.50
☐ 27	0.40	0.30	0.90	1.50
☐ 28	0.40	0.30	0.90	1.50

JOHN CARTER OF MARS ANNUAL

	ORIG.	GOOD	FINE	N-MINT
☐ 1	0.50	0.60	1.80	3.00
☐ 2	0.60	0.40	1.20	2.00
☐ 3	0.60	0.40	1.20	2.00

JOURNEY INTO MYSTERY

	ORIG.	GOOD	FINE	N-MINT
☐ 1	0.10	150.00	450.00	750.00
☐ 2	0.10	60.00	180.00	300.00
☐ 3	0.10	55.00	165.00	275.00
☐ 4	0.10	45.00	135.00	225.00
☐ 5	0.10	45.00	135.00	225.00
☐ 6	0.10	36.00	108.00	180.00
☐ 7	0.10	36.00	108.00	180.00
☐ 8	0.10	36.00	108.00	180.00
☐ 9	0.10	36.00	108.00	180.00
☐ 10	0.10	36.00	108.00	180.00
☐ 11	0.10	30.00	90.00	150.00
☐ 12	0.10	30.00	90.00	150.00
☐ 13	0.10	30.00	90.00	150.00
☐ 14	0.10	30.00	90.00	150.00
☐ 15	0.10	30.00	90.00	150.00
☐ 16	0.10	30.00	90.00	150.00
☐ 17	0.10	30.00	90.00	150.00
☐ 18	0.10	30.00	90.00	150.00
☐ 19	0.10	30.00	90.00	150.00
☐ 20	0.10	30.00	90.00	150.00
☐ 21	0.10	45.00	135.00	225.00
☐ 22	0.10	30.00	90.00	150.00
☐ 23	0.10	18.00	54.00	90.00
☐ 24	0.10	18.00	54.00	90.00
☐ 25	0.10	18.00	54.00	90.00
☐ 26	0.10	18.00	54.00	90.00
☐ 27	0.10	18.00	54.00	90.00
☐ 28	0.10	18.00	54.00	90.00
☐ 29	0.10	18.00	54.00	90.00
☐ 30	0.10	18.00	54.00	90.00
☐ 31	0.10	18.00	54.00	90.00
☐ 32	0.10	18.00	54.00	90.00
☐ 33	0.10	20.00	60.00	100.00
☐ 34	0.10	20.00	60.00	100.00
☐ 35	0.10	18.00	54.00	90.00
☐ 36	0.10	18.00	54.00	90.00

	ORIG.	GOOD	FINE	N-MINT
☐ 37	0.10	18.00	54.00	90.00
☐ 38	0.10	18.00	54.00	90.00
☐ 39	0.10	20.00	60.00	100.00
☐ 40	0.10	18.00	54.00	90.00
☐ 41	0.10	15.00	45.00	75.00
☐ 42	0.10	15.00	45.00	75.00
☐ 43	0.10	15.00	45.00	75.00
☐ 44	0.10	15.00	45.00	75.00
☐ 45	0.10	15.00	45.00	75.00
☐ 46	0.10	15.00	45.00	75.00
☐ 47	0.10	15.00	45.00	75.00
☐ 48	0.10	15.00	45.00	75.00
☐ 49	0.10	15.00	45.00	75.00
☐ 50	0.10	15.00	45.00	75.00
☐ 51	0.10	12.00	36.00	60.00
☐ 52	0.10	12.00	36.00	60.00
☐ 53	0.10	12.00	36.00	60.00
☐ 54	0.10	12.00	36.00	60.00
☐ 55	0.10	12.00	36.00	60.00
☐ 56	0.10	12.00	36.00	60.00
☐ 57	0.10	12.00	36.00	60.00
☐ 58	0.10	12.00	36.00	60.00
☐ 59	0.10	12.00	36.00	60.00
☐ 60	0.10	12.00	36.00	60.00
☐ 61	0.10	12.00	36.00	60.00
☐ 62	0.10	18.00	54.00	90.00
☐ 63	0.10	12.00	36.00	60.00
☐ 64	0.10	12.00	36.00	60.00
☐ 65	0.10	12.00	36.00	60.00
☐ 66	0.10	12.00	36.00	60.00
☐ 67	0.10	12.00	36.00	60.00
☐ 68	0.10	12.00	36.00	60.00
☐ 69	0.10	12.00	36.00	60.00
☐ 70	0.10	12.00	36.00	60.00
☐ 71	0.10	12.00	36.00	60.00
☐ 72	0.10	12.00	36.00	60.00
☐ 73	0.10	12.00	36.00	60.00
☐ 74	0.10	12.00	36.00	60.00
☐ 75	0.10	12.00	36.00	60.00
☐ 76	0.12	10.00	30.00	50.00
☐ 77	0.12	10.00	30.00	50.00
☐ 78	0.12	10.00	30.00	50.00
☐ 79	0.12	10.00	30.00	50.00
☐ 80	0.12	10.00	30.00	50.00
☐ 81	0.12	10.00	30.00	50.00
☐ 82	0.12	10.00	30.00	50.00
☐ 83 JK/SD, O:I:Thor	0.12	480.00	1440.00	2400.00
☐ 84 JK/SD/DH, I:Executioner	0.12	100.00	300.00	500.00
☐ 85 JK/SD, 1:Loki	0.12	60.00	180.00	300.00
☐ 86 JK/SD/DH, 1:Odin	0.12	40.00	120.00	200.00
☐ 87 JK/SD	0.12	28.00	84.00	140.00
☐ 88 JK/SD	0.12	28.00	84.00	140.00
☐ 89 JK/SD	0.12	28.00	84.00	140.00
☐ 90 SD, 1:Carbon-Copy	0.12	16.00	48.00	80.00

	ORIG.	GOOD	FINE	N-MINT
☐ 91 JSt/SD, 1:Sandu 0.12	14.00	42.00	70.00
☐ 92 JSt/SD, Loki 0.12	18.00	54.00	90.00
☐ 93 JK/SD, 1:Radioactive Man			
.... 0.12	18.00	54.00	90.00
☐ 94 JSt/SD, Loki 0.12	14.00	42.00	70.00
☐ 95 JSt/SD 0.12	12.00	36.00	60.00
☐ 96 JSt/SD, Merlin.............. 0.12	12.00	36.00	60.00
☐ 97 JK 0.12	16.00	48.00	80.00
☐ 98 JK 0.12	16.00	48.00	80.00
☐ 99 JK 0.12	16.00	48.00	80.00
☐ 100 JK 0.12	16.00	48.00	80.00
☐ 101 JK, Iron Man, Giant Man			
.... 0.12	9.00	27.00	45.00
☐ 102 JK 0.12	9.00	27.00	45.00
☐ 103 JK 0.12	9.00	27.00	45.00
☐ 104 JK, giants................... 0.12	9.00	27.00	45.00
☐ 105 JK, Hyde, Cobra 0.12	9.00	27.00	45.00
☐ 106 JK, O:Balder 0.12	9.00	27.00	45.00
☐ 107 JK, I:Grey Gargoyle ... 0.12	9.00	27.00	45.00
☐ 108 JK, Dr. Strange 0.12	9.00	27.00	45.00
☐ 109 JK, Magneto 0.12	12.00	36.00	60.00
☐ 110 JK, Hyde-Cobra-Loki . 0.12	9.00	27.00	45.00
☐ 111 JK, Hyde-Cobra-Loki . 0.12	8.00	24.00	40.00
☐ 112 JK, Hulk 0.12	20.00	60.00	100.00
☐ 113 JK, Grey Gargoyle 0.12	8.00	24.00	40.00
☐ 114 JK, 1:Absorbing Man . 0.12	8.00	24.00	40.00
☐ 115 JK, O:Loki 0.12	8.00	24.00	40.00
☐ 116 JK, Loki, Daredevil..... 0.12	8.00	24.00	40.00
☐ 117 JK, Loki...................... 0.12	8.00	24.00	40.00
☐ 118 JK, 1st Destroyer 0.12	8.00	24.00	40.00
☐ 119 JK 0.12	8.00	24.00	40.00
☐ 120 JK 0.12	8.00	24.00	40.00
☐ 121 JK 0.12	8.00	24.00	40.00
☐ 122 JK 0.12	8.00	24.00	40.00
☐ 123 JK 0.12	8.00	24.00	40.00
☐ 124 JK 0.12	8.00	24.00	40.00
☐ 125 JK (becomes Thor) 0.12	8.00	24.00	40.00

JOURNEY INTO MYSTERY
(second series, beginning 1972)

	ORIG.	GOOD	FINE	N-MINT
☐ 1 .... 0.20	0.20	0.60	1.00
☐ 2 .... 0.20	0.20	0.60	1.00
☐ 3 .... 0.20	0.20	0.60	1.00
☐ 4 .... 0.20	0.20	0.60	1.00
☐ 5 .... 0.20	0.20	0.60	1.00
☐ 6 .... 0.20	0.20	0.60	1.00
☐ 7 .... 0.20	0.20	0.60	1.00
☐ 8 .... 0.20	0.20	0.60	1.00
☐ 9 .... 0.20	0.20	0.60	1.00
☐ 10 .... 0.20	0.20	0.60	1.00
☐ 11 .... 0.25	0.20	0.60	1.00
☐ 12 .... 0.25	0.20	0.60	1.00
☐ 13 .... 0.25	0.20	0.60	1.00
☐ 14 .... 0.25	0.20	0.60	1.00
☐ 15 .... 0.25	0.20	0.60	1.00
☐ 16 .... 0.25	0.20	0.60	1.00

	ORIG.	GOOD	FINE	N-MINT
☐ 17 .... 0.25	0.20	0.60	1.00
☐ 18 .... 0.25	0.20	0.60	1.00
☐ 19 .... 0.25	0.20	0.60	1.00

JOURNEY INTO MYSTERY KING-SIZE ANNUAL
(1965)

	ORIG.	GOOD	FINE	N-MINT
☐ 1 JK, I:Hercules (becomes Thor Annual)			
.... 0.25	20.00	60.00	100.00

JUNGLE ACTION

	ORIG.	GOOD	FINE	N-MINT
☐ 1 reprints 0.20	0.30	0.90	1.50
☐ 2 reprints 0.20	0.20	0.60	1.00
☐ 3 reprints 0.20	0.20	0.60	1.00
☐ 4 reprints 0.20	0.20	0.60	1.00
☐ 5 Black Panther................. 0.20	0.20	0.60	1.00
☐ 6 Black Panther................. 0.20	0.20	0.60	1.00
☐ 7 Black Panther................. 0.20	0.20	0.60	1.00
☐ 8 Black Panther................. 0.20	0.20	0.60	1.00
☐ 9 Black Panther................. 0.25	0.20	0.60	1.00
☐ 10 Black Panther............... 0.25	0.20	0.60	1.00
☐ 11 Black Panther............... 0.25	0.20	0.60	1.00
☐ 12 Black Panther............... 0.25	0.20	0.60	1.00
☐ 13 Black Panther............... 0.25	0.20	0.60	1.00
☐ 14 Black Panther............... 0.25	0.20	0.60	1.00
☐ 15 Black Panther............... 0.25	0.20	0.60	1.00
☐ 16 Black Panther............... 0.25	0.20	0.60	1.00
☐ 17 Black Panther............... 0.25	0.20	0.60	1.00
☐ 18 Black Panther............... 0.25	0.20	0.60	1.00
☐ 19 Black Panther............... 0.25	0.20	0.60	1.00
☐ 20 Black Panther............... 0.25	0.20	0.60	1.00
☐ 21 Black Panther............... 0.25	0.20	0.60	1.00
☐ 22 Black Panther............... 0.25	0.20	0.60	1.00
☐ 23 Black Panther............... 0.30	0.20	0.60	1.00
☐ 24 Black Panther............... 0.30	0.20	0.60	1.00

JUSTICE

	ORIG.	GOOD	FINE	N-MINT
☐ 1 .... 0.75	0.20	0.60	1.00
☐ 2 .... 0.75	0.20	0.60	1.00
☐ 3 .... 0.75	0.20	0.60	1.00
☐ 4 .... 0.75	0.20	0.60	1.00
☐ 5 .... 0.75	0.20	0.60	1.00
☐ 6 .... 0.75	0.20	0.60	1.00
☐ 7 .... 0.75	0.20	0.60	1.00
☐ 8 .... 0.75	0.20	0.60	1.00
☐ 9 .... 0.75	0.20	0.60	1.00
☐ 10 .... 0.75	0.20	0.60	1.00
☐ 11 .... 0.75	0.20	0.60	1.00
☐ 12 .... 0.75	0.20	0.60	1.00
☐ 13 .... 0.75	0.20	0.60	1.00
☐ 14 .... 0.75	0.20	0.60	1.00
☐ 15 .... 0.75	0.20	0.60	1.00
☐ 16 .... 0.75	0.20	0.60	1.00
☐ 17 .... 0.75	0.20	0.60	1.00
☐ 18 .... 0.75	0.20	0.60	1.00
☐ 19 .... 1.25	0.25	0.75	1.25
☐ 20 .... 1.25	0.25	0.75	1.25
☐ 21 .... 1.25	0.25	0.75	1.25

	ORIG.	GOOD	FINE	N-MINT
22	1.25	0.25	0.75	1.25
23	1.25	0.25	0.75	1.25
24	1.25	0.25	0.75	1.25
25	1.25	0.25	0.75	1.25
26	1.50	0.30	0.90	1.50
27	1.50	0.30	0.90	1.50
28	1.50	0.30	0.90	1.50
29	1.50	0.30	0.90	1.50
30	1.50	0.30	0.90	1.50
31	1.50	0.30	0.90	1.50
32	1.50	0.30	0.90	1.50

KA-ZAR (1970)

	ORIG.	GOOD	FINE	N-MINT
1 giant	0.25	1.20	3.60	6.00
2 giant	0.25	1.00	3.00	5.00
3 giant	0.25	1.00	3.00	5.00

KA-ZAR (1972)

	ORIG.	GOOD	FINE	N-MINT
1 O:Savage Land	0.20	0.60	1.80	3.00
2 DH	0.20	0.40	1.20	2.00
3 DH	0.25	0.40	1.20	2.00
4 DH	0.25	0.40	1.20	2.00
5 DH	0.25	0.40	1.20	2.00
6 JB	0.25	0.30	0.90	1.50
7 JB	0.25	0.30	0.90	1.50
8 JB	0.25	0.30	0.90	1.50
9 JB	0.25	0.30	0.90	1.50
10 JB	0.25	0.30	0.90	1.50
11	0.25	0.20	0.60	1.00
12	0.25	0.20	0.60	1.00
13	0.25	0.20	0.60	1.00
14	0.25	0.20	0.60	1.00
15	0.25	0.20	0.60	1.00
16	0.30	0.20	0.60	1.00
17	0.30	0.20	0.60	1.00
18	0.30	0.20	0.60	1.00
19	0.30	0.20	0.60	1.00
20	0.30	0.20	0.60	1.00

KA-ZAR THE SAVAGE (1981)

	ORIG.	GOOD	FINE	N-MINT
1 BA, O	0.50	0.30	0.90	1.50
2 BA	0.50	0.20	0.60	1.00
3 BA	0.50	0.20	0.60	1.00
4 BA	0.50	0.20	0.60	1.00
5 BA	0.50	0.20	0.60	1.00
6 BA	0.50	0.20	0.60	1.00
7 BA	0.50	0.20	0.60	1.00
8 BA	0.50	0.20	0.60	1.00
9 BA	0.50	0.20	0.60	1.00
10 BA, direct distribution	0.75	0.50	1.50	2.50
11 BA/GK, Zabu	0.75	0.30	0.90	1.50
12 BA, panel missing	0.75	0.30	0.90	1.50
12 rep.	0.75	0.40	1.20	2.00
13 BA	0.75	0.30	0.90	1.50
14	0.75	0.20	0.60	1.00
15	0.75	0.20	0.60	1.00
16	0.75	0.20	0.60	1.00

	ORIG.	GOOD	FINE	N-MINT
17	0.75	0.20	0.60	1.00
18	0.75	0.20	0.60	1.00
19	0.75	0.20	0.60	1.00
20	0.75	0.20	0.60	1.00
21	0.75	0.20	0.60	1.00
22	0.75	0.20	0.60	1.00
23	0.75	0.20	0.60	1.00
24	0.75	0.20	0.60	1.00
25	0.75	0.20	0.60	1.00
26	0.75	0.20	0.60	1.00
27	0.75	0.20	0.60	1.00
28	0.75	0.20	0.60	1.00
29	1.00	0.20	0.60	1.00
30	1.00	0.20	0.60	1.00
31	1.00	0.20	0.60	1.00
32	1.00	0.20	0.60	1.00
33	1.00	0.20	0.60	1.00
34	1.00	0.20	0.60	1.00

KICKERS, INC.

	ORIG.	GOOD	FINE	N-MINT
1	0.75	0.20	0.60	1.00
2	0.75	0.20	0.60	1.00
3	0.75	0.20	0.60	1.00
4	0.75	0.20	0.60	1.00
5	0.75	0.20	0.60	1.00
6	0.75	0.20	0.60	1.00
7	0.75	0.20	0.60	1.00
8	0.75	0.20	0.60	1.00
9	0.75	0.20	0.60	1.00
10	0.75	0.20	0.60	1.00
11	0.75	0.20	0.60	1.00
12	0.75	0.20	0.60	1.00

KID 'N PLAY

	ORIG.	GOOD	FINE	N-MINT
1	1.25	0.25	0.75	1.25
2	1.25	0.25	0.75	1.25
3	1.25	0.25	0.75	1.25
4	1.25	0.25	0.75	1.25
5	1.25	0.25	0.75	1.25
6	1.25	0.25	0.75	1.25
7	1.25	0.25	0.75	1.25
8	1.25	0.25	0.75	1.25
9	1.25	0.25	0.75	1.25

KILLPOWER: THE EARLY YEARS

	ORIG.	GOOD	FINE	N-MINT
1 foil cover	2.95	0.59	1.77	2.95

KING CONAN

	ORIG.	GOOD	FINE	N-MINT
1 JB, wife & son	0.75	0.50	1.50	2.50
2 JB	0.75	0.30	0.90	1.50
3 JB	0.75	0.30	0.90	1.50
4	0.75	0.20	0.60	1.00
5	0.75	0.20	0.60	1.00
6	0.75	0.20	0.60	1.00
7 BS	0.75	0.40	1.20	2.00
8 BS	0.75	0.40	1.20	2.00
9	1.00	0.20	0.60	1.00
10	1.00	0.20	0.60	1.00

	ORIG.	GOOD	FINE	N-MINT
11	1.00	0.20	0.60	1.00
12	1.00	0.20	0.60	1.00
13	1.00	0.20	0.60	1.00
14	1.00	0.20	0.60	1.00
15	1.00	0.20	0.60	1.00
16	1.00	0.20	0.60	1.00
17	1.00	0.20	0.60	1.00
18	1.00	0.20	0.60	1.00
19 (becomes Conan the King) 1.00		0.20	0.60	1.00

KITTY PRYDE & WOLVERINE

	ORIG.	GOOD	FINE	N-MINT
1 AM	0.75	1.60	4.80	8.00
2 AM	0.75	1.20	3.60	6.00
3 AM	0.75	1.00	3.00	5.00
4 AM	0.75	1.00	3.00	5.00
5 AM	0.75	1.00	3.00	5.00
6 AM	0.75	1.00	3.00	5.00

KNIGHTS OF PENDRAGON, THE (1990-1991)

	ORIG.	GOOD	FINE	N-MINT
1	1.95	0.39	1.17	1.95
2	1.95	0.39	1.17	1.95
3	1.95	0.39	1.17	1.95
4	1.95	0.39	1.17	1.95
5	1.95	0.39	1.17	1.95
6	1.95	0.39	1.17	1.95
7	1.95	0.39	1.17	1.95
8	1.95	0.39	1.17	1.95
9	1.95	0.39	1.17	1.95
10	1.95	0.39	1.17	1.95
11	1.95	0.39	1.17	1.95
12	1.95	0.39	1.17	1.95
13	1.95	0.39	1.17	1.95
14	1.95	0.39	1.17	1.95
15	1.95	0.39	1.17	1.95
16	1.95	0.39	1.17	1.95
17	1.95	0.39	1.17	1.95

KNIGHTS OF PENDRAGON, THE (1992) (was Pendragon)

	ORIG.	GOOD	FINE	N-MINT
5	1.75	0.35	1.05	1.75
6	1.75	0.35	1.05	1.75
7	1.75	0.35	1.05	1.75
8	1.75	0.35	1.05	1.75
9	1.75	0.35	1.05	1.75
10	1.75	0.35	1.05	1.75
11	1.75	0.35	1.05	1.75
12	1.75	0.35	1.05	1.75
13	1.75	0.35	1.05	1.75
14	1.75	0.35	1.05	1.75
15	1.75	0.35	1.05	1.75

KREE/SKRULL WAR STARRING THE AVENGERS, THE

	ORIG.	GOOD	FINE	N-MINT
1 reprint	2.50	0.50	1.50	2.50
2 reprint	2.50	0.50	1.50	2.50

KRULL

	ORIG.	GOOD	FINE	N-MINT
1 movie	0.60	0.20	0.60	1.00
2 movie	0.60	0.20	0.60	1.00

KULL AND THE BARBARIANS

	ORIG.	GOOD	FINE	N-MINT
1 b&w mag	1.00	0.20	0.60	1.00
2 b&w mag	1.00	0.20	0.60	1.00
3 b&w mag	1.00	0.20	0.60	1.00

KULL THE CONQUEROR (1971)

	ORIG.	GOOD	FINE	N-MINT
1 WW/RA, O:Kull	0.15	1.00	3.00	5.00
2 JSe	0.15	0.80	2.40	4.00
3 JSe	0.20	0.80	2.40	4.00
4 JSe	0.20	0.60	1.80	3.00
5 JSe	0.20	0.60	1.80	3.00
6	0.20	0.40	1.20	2.00
7	0.20	0.40	1.20	2.00
8	0.20	0.40	1.20	2.00
9	0.20	0.40	1.20	2.00
10	0.20	0.40	1.20	2.00
11	0.20	0.30	0.90	1.50
12	0.20	0.30	0.90	1.50
13	0.20	0.30	0.90	1.50
14 JSn/MP	0.25	0.35	1.05	1.75
15 SD/MP, rep.	0.25	0.30	0.90	1.50
16	0.25	0.20	0.60	1.00
17 AA	0.25	0.20	0.60	1.00
18 AA	0.30	0.20	0.60	1.00
19 AA	0.30	0.20	0.60	1.00
20 AA	0.30	0.20	0.60	1.00
21	0.30	0.20	0.60	1.00
22	0.30	0.20	0.60	1.00
23	0.30	0.20	0.60	1.00
24	0.35	0.20	0.60	1.00
25	0.35	0.20	0.60	1.00
26	0.35	0.20	0.60	1.00
27	0.35	0.20	0.60	1.00
28	0.35	0.20	0.60	1.00
29	0.35	0.20	0.60	1.00

KULL THE CONQUEROR (1982)

	ORIG.	GOOD	FINE	N-MINT
1 JB, Brule	2.00	0.50	1.50	2.50
2 Misareena	2.00	0.40	1.20	2.00

KULL THE CONQUEROR (1983)

	ORIG.	GOOD	FINE	N-MINT
1 JB, Iraina	1.25	0.30	0.90	1.50
2 JB	1.25	0.25	0.75	1.25
3 JB	1.00	0.20	0.60	1.00
4 JB	1.00	0.20	0.60	1.00
5	0.60	0.20	0.60	1.00
6	0.60	0.20	0.60	1.00
7	0.60	0.20	0.60	1.00
8	0.60	0.20	0.60	1.00
9	0.65	0.20	0.60	1.00
10	0.65	0.20	0.60	1.00

LABYRINTH

	ORIG.	GOOD	FINE	N-MINT
1 movie	0.75	0.20	0.60	1.00

	ORIG.	GOOD	FINE	N-MINT
❏ 2 movie	0.75	0.20	0.60	1.00
❏ 3 movie	0.75	0.20	0.60	1.00

LAFF-A-LYMPICS

	ORIG.	GOOD	FINE	N-MINT
❏ 1 Hanna-Barbera	0.35	0.30	0.90	1.50
❏ 2 Hanna-Barbera	0.35	0.20	0.60	1.00
❏ 3 Hanna-Barbera	0.35	0.20	0.60	1.00
❏ 4 Hanna-Barbera	0.35	0.20	0.60	1.00
❏ 5 Hanna-Barbera	0.35	0.20	0.60	1.00
❏ 6 Hanna-Barbera	0.35	0.20	0.60	1.00
❏ 7 Hanna-Barbera	0.35	0.20	0.60	1.00
❏ 8 Hanna-Barbera	0.35	0.20	0.60	1.00
❏ 9 Hanna-Barbera	0.35	0.20	0.60	1.00
❏ 10 Hanna-Barbera	0.35	0.20	0.60	1.00
❏ 11 Hanna-Barbera	0.35	0.20	0.60	1.00
❏ 12 Hanna-Barbera	0.35	0.20	0.60	1.00
❏ 13 Hanna-Barbera	0.35	0.20	0.60	1.00

LAST STARFIGHTER

	ORIG.	GOOD	FINE	N-MINT
❏ 1 movie	0.75	0.20	0.60	1.00
❏ 2 movie	0.75	0.20	0.60	1.00
❏ 3 movie	0.75	0.20	0.60	1.00

LEGION OF MONSTERS, THE

	ORIG.	GOOD	FINE	N-MINT
❏ 1 b&w, magazine	1.00	0.20	0.60	1.00

LEGION OF NIGHT

	ORIG.	GOOD	FINE	N-MINT
❏ 1	4.95	0.99	2.97	4.95
❏ 2	4.95	0.99	2.97	4.95

LETHAL FOES OF SPIDER-MAN

	ORIG.	GOOD	FINE	N-MINT
❏ 1	1.75	0.35	1.05	1.75
❏ 2	1.75	0.35	1.05	1.75

LIFE OF CAPTAIN MARVEL

	ORIG.	GOOD	FINE	N-MINT
❏ 1 Baxter rep.	2.00	0.40	1.20	2.00
❏ 2 Baxter rep.	2.00	0.40	1.20	2.00
❏ 3 Baxter rep.	2.00	0.40	1.20	2.00
❏ 4 Baxter rep.	2.00	0.40	1.20	2.00
❏ 5 Baxter rep.	2.00	0.40	1.20	2.00

LIFE OF POPE JOHN-PAUL II

	ORIG.	GOOD	FINE	N-MINT
❏ 1 JSt	1.50	0.30	0.90	1.50

LOGAN'S RUN

	ORIG.	GOOD	FINE	N-MINT
❏ 1 GP, movie	0.30	0.30	0.90	1.50
❏ 2 GP, movie	0.30	0.20	0.60	1.00
❏ 3 GP, movie	0.30	0.20	0.60	1.00
❏ 4 GP, movie	0.30	0.20	0.60	1.00
❏ 5 GP, movie	0.30	0.20	0.60	1.00
❏ 6 GP, movie	0.30	0.20	0.60	1.00
❏ 7 GP, movie	0.30	0.20	0.60	1.00

LONGSHOT

	ORIG.	GOOD	FINE	N-MINT
❏ 1 AAd	0.75	4.80	14.40	24.00
❏ 2 AAd	0.75	4.00	12.00	20.00
❏ 3 AAd	0.75	3.20	9.60	16.00
❏ 4 AAd	0.75	3.20	9.60	16.00
❏ 5 AAd	0.75	3.20	9.60	16.00
❏ 6 AAd double-size	1.25	3.60	10.80	18.00

MACHINE MAN (1978-1981)

	ORIG.	GOOD	FINE	N-MINT
❏ 1	0.35	0.40	1.20	2.00

	ORIG.	GOOD	FINE	N-MINT
❏ 2	0.35	0.30	0.90	1.50
❏ 3	0.35	0.25	0.75	1.25
❏ 4	0.35	0.25	0.75	1.25
❏ 5	0.35	0.25	0.75	1.25
❏ 6	0.35	0.20	0.60	1.00
❏ 7	0.35	0.20	0.60	1.00
❏ 8	0.35	0.20	0.60	1.00
❏ 9	0.35	0.20	0.60	1.00
❏ 10	0.40	0.20	0.60	1.00
❏ 11	0.40	0.20	0.60	1.00
❏ 12	0.40	0.20	0.60	1.00
❏ 13	0.40	0.20	0.60	1.00
❏ 14	0.40	0.20	0.60	1.00
❏ 15	0.40	0.20	0.60	1.00
❏ 16	0.40	0.20	0.60	1.00
❏ 17	0.50	0.20	0.60	1.00
❏ 18 A:Alpha Flight	0.50	1.00	3.00	5.00

MACHINE MAN (1984-1985)

	ORIG.	GOOD	FINE	N-MINT
❏ 1 HT/BS	0.75	0.60	1.80	3.00
❏ 2 HT/BS	0.75	0.40	1.20	2.00
❏ 3 HT/BS	0.75	0.40	1.20	2.00
❏ 4 HT/BS	0.75	0.40	1.20	2.00

MAD DOG

	ORIG.	GOOD	FINE	N-MINT
❏ 1 TV show tie-in	1.25	0.25	0.75	1.25
❏ 2	1.25	0.25	0.75	1.25
❏ 3	1.25	0.25	0.75	1.25
❏ 4	1.25	0.25	0.75	1.25
❏ 5	1.25	0.25	0.75	1.25

MADBALLS (was Star Comic)

	ORIG.	GOOD	FINE	N-MINT
❏ 9	1.00	0.20	0.60	1.00
❏ 10	1.00	0.20	0.60	1.00

MAGIK

	ORIG.	GOOD	FINE	N-MINT
❏ 1 Illyana & Storm	0.60	0.50	1.50	2.50
❏ 2 Illyana & Storm	0.60	0.50	1.50	2.50
❏ 3	0.60	0.40	1.20	2.00
❏ 4	0.60	0.40	1.20	2.00

MAN FROM ATLANTIS

	ORIG.	GOOD	FINE	N-MINT
❏ 1 TV series, giant	1.00	0.30	0.90	1.50
❏ 2	0.35	0.20	0.60	1.00
❏ 3	0.35	0.20	0.60	1.00
❏ 4	0.35	0.20	0.60	1.00
❏ 5	0.35	0.20	0.60	1.00
❏ 6	0.35	0.20	0.60	1.00
❏ 7	0.35	0.20	0.60	1.00

MAN-THING (1974-1975)

	ORIG.	GOOD	FINE	N-MINT
❏ 1 FB/JM, A:Howard the Duck	0.20	3.00	9.00	15.00
❏ 2	0.20	0.80	2.40	4.00
❏ 3 Foolkiller	0.20	2.00	6.00	10.00
❏ 4 Foolkiller	0.20	1.20	3.60	6.00
❏ 5	0.25	0.60	1.80	3.00
❏ 6 MP	0.25	0.60	1.80	3.00
❏ 7 MP	0.25	0.40	1.20	2.00
❏ 8 MP	0.25	0.40	1.20	2.00

	ORIG.	GOOD	FINE	N-MINT
❏ 9 MP	0.25	0.40	1.20	2.00
❏ 10 MP	0.25	0.40	1.20	2.00
❏ 11 MP	0.25	0.40	1.20	2.00
❏ 12	0.25	0.20	0.60	1.00
❏ 13	0.25	0.20	0.60	1.00
❏ 14	0.25	0.20	0.60	1.00
❏ 15	0.25	0.20	0.60	1.00
❏ 22 JM, C:Howard the Duck	0.25	0.30	0.90	1.50

MAN-THING (1979-1981)

	ORIG.	GOOD	FINE	N-MINT
❏ 1	0.40	0.40	1.20	2.00
❏ 2	0.40	0.40	1.20	2.00
❏ 3	0.40	0.20	0.60	1.00
❏ 4	0.40	0.20	0.60	1.00
❏ 5	0.40	0.20	0.60	1.00
❏ 6	0.50	0.20	0.60	1.00
❏ 7	0.50	0.20	0.60	1.00
❏ 8	0.50	0.20	0.60	1.00
❏ 9	0.50	0.20	0.60	1.00
❏ 10	0.50	0.20	0.60	1.00
❏ 11	0.50	0.20	0.60	1.00

MARC SPECTOR: MOON KNIGHT

	ORIG.	GOOD	FINE	N-MINT
❏ 1	1.50	1.00	3.00	5.00
❏ 2	1.50	0.80	2.40	4.00
❏ 3	1.50	0.60	1.80	3.00
❏ 4	1.50	0.60	1.80	3.00
❏ 5	1.50	0.60	1.80	3.00
❏ 6 Brother Voodoo	1.50	0.30	0.90	1.50
❏ 7 Brother Voodoo	1.50	0.30	0.90	1.50
❏ 8 Punisher, Acts of Vengeance	1.50	1.60	4.80	8.00
❏ 9 Punisher, Acts of Vengeance	1.50	1.60	4.80	8.00
❏ 10 Acts	1.50	0.30	0.90	1.50
❏ 11	1.50	0.30	0.90	1.50
❏ 12	1.50	0.30	0.90	1.50
❏ 13	1.50	0.30	0.90	1.50
❏ 14	1.50	0.30	0.90	1.50
❏ 15 Trial	1.50	0.30	0.90	1.50
❏ 16 Trial	1.50	0.30	0.90	1.50
❏ 17 Trial	1.50	0.30	0.90	1.50
❏ 18 Trial	1.50	0.30	0.90	1.50
❏ 19 SpM, Punisher	1.50	1.60	4.80	8.00
❏ 20 SpM, Punisher	1.50	1.40	4.20	7.00
❏ 21 SpM, Punisher	1.50	1.00	3.00	5.00
❏ 22	1.50	0.30	0.90	1.50
❏ 23	1.50	0.30	0.90	1.50
❏ 24	1.50	0.30	0.90	1.50
❏ 25 Ghost Rider	2.50	0.30	0.90	1.50
❏ 26	1.50	0.30	0.90	1.50
❏ 27	1.50	0.30	0.90	1.50
❏ 28	1.50	0.30	0.90	1.50
❏ 29	1.50	0.30	0.90	1.50
❏ 30	1.50	0.30	0.90	1.50

	ORIG.	GOOD	FINE	N-MINT
❏ 31	1.50	0.30	0.90	1.50
❏ 32	1.50	0.30	0.90	1.50
❏ 33	1.50	0.30	0.90	1.50
❏ 34	1.50	0.30	0.90	1.50
❏ 35	1.75	0.35	1.05	1.75
❏ 36 Punisher	1.75	0.35	1.05	1.75
❏ 37 Punisher	1.75	0.35	1.05	1.75
❏ 38 Punisher	1.75	0.35	1.05	1.75
❏ 39 Dr. Doom	1.75	0.35	1.05	1.75
❏ 40	1.75	0.35	1.05	1.75
❏ 41	1.75	0.35	1.05	1.75
❏ 42	1.75	0.35	1.05	1.75
❏ 43	1.75	0.35	1.05	1.75
❏ 44	1.75	0.35	1.05	1.75
❏ 45	1.75	0.35	1.05	1.75
❏ 46	1.75	0.35	1.05	1.75
❏ 47	1.75	0.35	1.05	1.75
❏ 48	1.75	0.35	1.05	1.75
❏ 49	1.75	0.35	1.05	1.75
❏ 50 die-cut cover	2.95	0.59	1.77	2.95
❏ 51	1.75	0.35	1.05	1.75
❏ 52	1.75	0.35	1.05	1.75
❏ 53	1.75	0.35	1.05	1.75
❏ 54	1.75	0.35	1.05	1.75

MARK HAZZARD: MERC

	ORIG.	GOOD	FINE	N-MINT
❏ 1	0.75	0.20	0.60	1.00
❏ 2	0.75	0.20	0.60	1.00
❏ 3	0.75	0.20	0.60	1.00
❏ 4	0.75	0.20	0.60	1.00
❏ 5	0.75	0.20	0.60	1.00
❏ 6	0.75	0.20	0.60	1.00
❏ 7	0.75	0.20	0.60	1.00
❏ 8	0.75	0.20	0.60	1.00
❏ 9	0.75	0.20	0.60	1.00
❏ 10	0.75	0.20	0.60	1.00
❏ 11	0.75	0.20	0.60	1.00
❏ 12	0.75	0.20	0.60	1.00

MARK HAZZARD: MERC ANNUAL

	ORIG.	GOOD	FINE	N-MINT
❏ 1 D:Hazzard	1.25	0.25	0.75	1.25

MARVEL ACTION UNIVERSE

	ORIG.	GOOD	FINE	N-MINT
❏ 1 SM rep.	1.00	0.20	0.60	1.00

MARVEL AGE

	ORIG.	GOOD	FINE	N-MINT
❏ 1	0.25	0.40	1.20	2.00
❏ 2	0.25	0.20	0.60	1.00
❏ 3	0.25	0.20	0.60	1.00
❏ 4	0.25	0.20	0.60	1.00
❏ 5	0.25	0.20	0.60	1.00
❏ 6	0.25	0.20	0.60	1.00
❏ 7	0.25	0.20	0.60	1.00
❏ 8	0.25	0.20	0.60	1.00
❏ 9	0.25	0.20	0.60	1.00
❏ 10	0.25	0.20	0.60	1.00
❏ 11	0.25	0.20	0.60	1.00
❏ 12	0.25	0.20	0.60	1.00

	ORIG.	GOOD	FINE	N-MINT		ORIG.	GOOD	FINE	N-MINT
❏ 13	0.25	0.20	0.60	1.00	❏ 68	0.50	0.20	0.60	1.00
❏ 14	0.25	0.20	0.60	1.00	❏ 69	0.50	0.20	0.60	1.00
❏ 15	0.35	0.20	0.60	1.00	❏ 70	0.50	0.20	0.60	1.00
❏ 16	0.35	0.20	0.60	1.00	❏ 71	0.50	0.20	0.60	1.00
❏ 17	0.35	0.20	0.60	1.00	❏ 72	0.50	0.20	0.60	1.00
❏ 18	0.35	0.20	0.60	1.00	❏ 73	0.50	0.20	0.60	1.00
❏ 19	0.35	0.20	0.60	1.00	❏ 74	0.50	0.20	0.60	1.00
❏ 20	0.35	0.20	0.60	1.00	❏ 75	0.50	0.20	0.60	1.00
❏ 21	0.35	0.20	0.60	1.00	❏ 76	0.50	0.20	0.60	1.00
❏ 22	0.35	0.20	0.60	1.00	❏ 77	0.50	0.20	0.60	1.00
❏ 23	0.35	0.20	0.60	1.00	❏ 78	0.50	0.20	0.60	1.00
❏ 24	0.35	0.20	0.60	1.00	❏ 79	0.75	0.20	0.60	1.00
❏ 25	0.35	0.20	0.60	1.00	❏ 80	0.75	0.20	0.60	1.00
❏ 26	0.35	0.20	0.60	1.00	❏ 81	0.75	0.20	0.60	1.00
❏ 27	0.35	0.20	0.60	1.00	❏ 82	0.75	0.20	0.60	1.00
❏ 28	0.35	0.20	0.60	1.00	❏ 83	0.75	0.20	0.60	1.00
❏ 29	0.35	0.20	0.60	1.00	❏ 84	0.75	0.20	0.60	1.00
❏ 30	0.35	0.20	0.60	1.00	❏ 85	0.75	0.20	0.60	1.00
❏ 31	0.35	0.20	0.60	1.00	❏ 86	1.00	0.20	0.60	1.00
❏ 32 AAd	0.35	0.20	0.60	1.00	❏ 87	1.00	0.20	0.60	1.00
❏ 33	0.35	0.20	0.60	1.00	❏ 88	1.00	0.20	0.60	1.00
❏ 34	0.35	0.20	0.60	1.00	❏ 89	1.00	0.20	0.60	1.00
❏ 35	0.35	0.20	0.60	1.00	❏ 90	1.00	0.20	0.60	1.00
❏ 36	0.35	0.20	0.60	1.00	❏ 91	1.00	0.20	0.60	1.00
❏ 37	0.35	0.20	0.60	1.00	❏ 92	1.00	0.20	0.60	1.00
❏ 38	0.35	0.20	0.60	1.00	❏ 93	1.00	0.20	0.60	1.00
❏ 39	0.35	0.20	0.60	1.00	❏ 94	1.00	0.20	0.60	1.00
❏ 40	0.35	0.20	0.60	1.00	❏ 95 Capt. America issue	1.00	0.20	0.60	1.00
❏ 41	0.50	0.20	0.60	1.00	❏ 96	1.00	0.20	0.60	1.00
❏ 42	0.50	0.20	0.60	1.00	❏ 97	1.00	0.20	0.60	1.00
❏ 43	0.50	0.20	0.60	1.00	❏ 98	1.00	0.20	0.60	1.00
❏ 44	0.50	0.20	0.60	1.00	❏ 99	1.00	0.20	0.60	1.00
❏ 45	0.50	0.20	0.60	1.00	❏ 100	1.00	0.20	0.60	1.00
❏ 46	0.50	0.20	0.60	1.00	❏ 101	1.00	0.20	0.60	1.00
❏ 47	0.50	0.20	0.60	1.00	❏ 102	1.00	0.20	0.60	1.00
❏ 48	0.50	0.20	0.60	1.00	❏ 103	1.00	0.20	0.60	1.00
❏ 49	0.50	0.20	0.60	1.00	❏ 104	1.00	0.20	0.60	1.00
❏ 50	0.50	0.20	0.60	1.00	❏ 105	1.00	0.20	0.60	1.00
❏ 51	0.50	0.20	0.60	1.00	❏ 106	1.00	0.20	0.60	1.00
❏ 52	0.50	0.20	0.60	1.00	❏ 107	1.00	0.20	0.60	1.00
❏ 53	0.50	0.20	0.60	1.00	❏ 108	1.00	0.20	0.60	1.00
❏ 54 SM wedding	0.50	0.20	0.60	1.00	❏ 109	1.00	0.20	0.60	1.00
❏ 55	0.50	0.20	0.60	1.00	❏ 110	1.00	0.20	0.60	1.00
❏ 56	0.50	0.20	0.60	1.00	❏ 111	1.00	0.20	0.60	1.00
❏ 57	0.50	0.20	0.60	1.00	❏ 112	1.00	0.20	0.60	1.00
❏ 58	0.50	0.20	0.60	1.00	❏ 113	1.00	0.20	0.60	1.00
❏ 59	0.50	0.20	0.60	1.00	❏ 114	1.00	0.20	0.60	1.00
❏ 60	0.50	0.20	0.60	1.00	❏ 115	1.00	0.20	0.60	1.00
❏ 61	0.50	0.20	0.60	1.00	❏ 116	1.00	0.20	0.60	1.00
❏ 62	0.50	0.20	0.60	1.00	❏ 117	1.00	0.20	0.60	1.00
❏ 63	0.50	0.20	0.60	1.00	❏ 118 with card	1.50	0.30	0.90	1.50
❏ 64	0.50	0.20	0.60	1.00	❏ 119	1.00	0.20	0.60	1.00
❏ 65	0.50	0.20	0.60	1.00	❏ 120	1.00	0.20	0.60	1.00
❏ 66	0.50	0.20	0.60	1.00	❏ 121	1.00	0.20	0.60	1.00
❏ 67	0.50	0.20	0.60	1.00	❏ 122	1.00	0.20	0.60	1.00

	ORIG.	GOOD	FINE	N-MINT
❏ 123	1.00	0.20	0.60	1.00
❏ 124	1.00	0.20	0.60	1.00
❏ 125	1.00	0.20	0.60	1.00
❏ 126	1.00	0.20	0.60	1.00
❏ 127	1.00	0.20	0.60	1.00
❏ 128	1.00	0.20	0.60	1.00

MARVEL AGE ANNUAL

	ORIG.	GOOD	FINE	N-MINT
❏ 1	0.50	0.30	0.90	1.50
❏ 2	0.50	0.30	0.90	1.50
❏ 3 FH,TA,JBu,MR	0.75	0.20	0.60	1.00
❏ 4 Wolverine	0.75	0.20	0.60	1.00

MARVEL AGE PREVIEW

	ORIG.	GOOD	FINE	N-MINT
❏ 1 1990	1.50	0.30	0.90	1.50
❏ 2 1992	2.25	0.45	1.35	2.25

MARVEL AND DC PRESENT

	ORIG.	GOOD	FINE	N-MINT
❏ 1 WS/TA, X-Men & Titans	2.00	3.00	9.00	15.00

MARVEL CHILLERS

	ORIG.	GOOD	FINE	N-MINT
❏ 1 Modred	0.25	0.40	1.20	2.00
❏ 2 Modred	0.25	0.20	0.60	1.00
❏ 3 Tigra	0.25	0.20	0.60	1.00
❏ 4 Tigra	0.25	0.20	0.60	1.00
❏ 5 Tigra	0.25	0.20	0.60	1.00
❏ 6 Tigra	0.25	0.40	1.20	2.00
❏ 7 Tigra	0.30	0.20	0.60	1.00

MARVEL CLASSIC COMICS

	ORIG.	GOOD	FINE	N-MINT
❏ 1	0.50	0.60	1.80	3.00
❏ 2	0.50	0.60	1.80	3.00
❏ 3	0.50	0.60	1.80	3.00
❏ 4	0.50	0.60	1.80	3.00
❏ 5	0.50	0.60	1.80	3.00
❏ 6	0.50	0.60	1.80	3.00
❏ 7	0.50	0.60	1.80	3.00
❏ 8	0.50	0.60	1.80	3.00
❏ 9	0.50	0.60	1.80	3.00
❏ 10	0.50	0.60	1.80	3.00
❏ 11	0.50	0.60	1.80	3.00
❏ 12	0.50	0.60	1.80	3.00
❏ 13	0.50	0.60	1.80	3.00
❏ 14	0.50	0.60	1.80	3.00
❏ 15	0.50	0.60	1.80	3.00
❏ 16	0.50	0.60	1.80	3.00
❏ 17	0.50	0.60	1.80	3.00
❏ 18	0.50	0.60	1.80	3.00
❏ 19	0.50	0.60	1.80	3.00
❏ 20	0.50	0.60	1.80	3.00
❏ 21	0.50	0.60	1.80	3.00
❏ 22	0.50	0.60	1.80	3.00
❏ 23	0.50	0.60	1.80	3.00
❏ 24	0.50	0.60	1.80	3.00
❏ 25	0.50	0.60	1.80	3.00
❏ 26	0.50	0.60	1.80	3.00
❏ 27	0.60	0.60	1.80	3.00
❏ 28	0.60	0.80	2.40	4.00
❏ 29	0.60	0.60	1.80	3.00

	ORIG.	GOOD	FINE	N-MINT
❏ 30	0.60	0.60	1.80	3.00
❏ 31	0.60	0.60	1.80	3.00
❏ 32	0.60	0.60	1.80	3.00
❏ 33	0.60	0.60	1.80	3.00
❏ 34	0.60	0.60	1.80	3.00
❏ 35	0.60	0.60	1.80	3.00
❏ 36	0.60	0.60	1.80	3.00

MARVEL COLLECTOR'S EDITION

	ORIG.	GOOD	FINE	N-MINT
❏ 1 SpM, Wolverine, Ghost Rider, Charleston Chew promotion, $.50 and a candy bar wrapper	1.50	0.30	0.90	1.50

MARVEL COLLECTORS' ITEM CLASSICS

	ORIG.	GOOD	FINE	N-MINT
❏ 1 reprints	0.25	8.00	24.00	40.00
❏ 2 reprints	0.25	4.40	13.20	22.00
❏ 3 reprints	0.25	2.40	7.20	12.00
❏ 4 reprints	0.25	2.40	7.20	12.00
❏ 5 reprints	0.25	2.40	7.20	12.00
❏ 6	0.25	1.60	4.80	8.00
❏ 7	0.25	1.60	4.80	8.00
❏ 8	0.25	1.60	4.80	8.00
❏ 9	0.25	1.60	4.80	8.00
❏ 10	0.25	1.60	4.80	8.00
❏ 11	0.25	1.60	4.80	8.00
❏ 12	0.25	1.60	4.80	8.00
❏ 13	0.25	1.60	4.80	8.00
❏ 14	0.25	1.60	4.80	8.00
❏ 15	0.25	1.60	4.80	8.00
❏ 16	0.25	1.60	4.80	8.00
❏ 17	0.25	1.60	4.80	8.00
❏ 18	0.25	1.60	4.80	8.00
❏ 19	0.25	1.60	4.80	8.00
❏ 20	0.25	1.60	4.80	8.00
❏ 21	0.25	1.60	4.80	8.00
❏ 22 reprints (becomes Marvel's Greatest Comics)	0.25	1.60	4.80	8.00

MARVEL COMICS PRESENTS

	ORIG.	GOOD	FINE	N-MINT
❏ 1 Wolverine	1.25	2.40	7.20	12.00
❏ 2 Wolverine	1.25	1.20	3.60	6.00
❏ 3 Wolverine	1.25	0.80	2.40	4.00
❏ 4 Wolverine	1.25	0.80	2.40	4.00
❏ 5 Wolverine	1.25	0.80	2.40	4.00
❏ 6 Wolverine	1.25	0.80	2.40	4.00
❏ 7 Wolverine	1.25	0.80	2.40	4.00
❏ 8 Wolverine	1.25	0.80	2.40	4.00
❏ 9 Wolverine	1.25	0.80	2.40	4.00
❏ 10 Wolverine	1.25	0.80	2.40	4.00
❏ 11 Colossus	1.25	0.50	1.50	2.50
❏ 12 Colossus	1.25	0.50	1.50	2.50
❏ 13 Colossus	1.25	0.50	1.50	2.50
❏ 14 Colossus	1.25	0.50	1.50	2.50
❏ 15 Colossus	1.25	0.50	1.50	2.50
❏ 16 Colossus	1.25	0.50	1.50	2.50
❏ 17 Cyclops	1.25	0.80	2.40	4.00

	ORIG.	GOOD	FINE	N-MINT
☐ 18 JBy, She-Hulk, Cyclops				
.... 1.25	0.60	1.80	3.00
☐ 19 Cyclops...................... 1.25	0.60	1.80	3.00
☐ 20 Cyclops...................... 1.25	0.60	1.80	3.00
☐ 21 Cyclops...................... 1.25	0.60	1.80	3.00
☐ 22 Cyclops...................... 1.25	0.60	1.80	3.00
☐ 23 Cyclops...................... 1.25	0.60	1.80	3.00
☐ 24 Cyclops, Havok............ 1.25	0.60	1.80	3.00
☐ 25 Havok 1.25	0.50	1.50	2.50
☐ 26 Havok 1.25	0.50	1.50	2.50
☐ 27 Havok 1.25	0.50	1.50	2.50
☐ 28 Havok 1.25	0.50	1.50	2.50
☐ 29 Havok 1.25	0.50	1.50	2.50
☐ 30 Havok 1.25	0.50	1.50	2.50
☐ 31 Havok, Excalibur.......... 1.25	0.80	2.40	4.00
☐ 32 TMc(c) Excalibur.......... 1.25	0.80	2.40	4.00
☐ 33 Excalibur..................... 1.25	0.80	2.40	4.00
☐ 34 Excalibur..................... 1.25	0.80	2.40	4.00
☐ 35 Excalibur..................... 1.25	0.60	1.80	3.00
☐ 36 Excalibur..................... 1.25	0.60	1.80	3.00
☐ 37 Excalibur..................... 1.25	0.60	1.80	3.00
☐ 38 Excalibur..................... 1.25	0.60	1.80	3.00
☐ 39 Wolverine.................... 1.25	0.60	1.80	3.00
☐ 40 Wolverine.................... 1.25	0.60	1.80	3.00
☐ 41 Wolverine.................... 1.25	0.60	1.80	3.00
☐ 42 Wolverine.................... 1.25	0.60	1.80	3.00
☐ 43 Wolverine.................... 1.25	0.60	1.80	3.00
☐ 44 Wolverine.................... 1.25	0.60	1.80	3.00
☐ 45 Wolverine.................... 1.25	0.60	1.80	3.00
☐ 46 Wolverine.................... 1.25	0.60	1.80	3.00
☐ 47 Wolverine.................... 1.25	0.60	1.80	3.00
☐ 48 Wolverine, SPM........... 1.25	2.00	6.00	10.00
☐ 49 Wolverine, SpM 1.25	1.20	3.60	6.00
☐ 50 Wolverine, SpM 1.25	1.20	3.60	6.00
☐ 51 Wolverine.................... 1.25	0.50	1.50	2.50
☐ 52 Wolverine.................... 1.25	0.50	1.50	2.50
☐ 53 Wolverine.................... 1.25	0.50	1.50	2.50
☐ 54 Wolverine & Hulk 1.25	0.40	1.20	2.00
☐ 55 Wolverine & Hulk 1.25	0.40	1.20	2.00
☐ 56 Wolverine & Hulk 1.25	0.40	1.20	2.00
☐ 57 Wolverine & Hulk 1.25	0.40	1.20	2.00
☐ 58 Wolverine & Hulk 1.25	0.40	1.20	2.00
☐ 59 Wolverine & Hulk 1.25	0.40	1.20	2.00
☐ 60 Wolverine & Hulk 1.25	0.40	1.20	2.00
☐ 61 Wolverine & Hulk 1.25	0.40	1.20	2.00
☐ 62 Wolverine.................... 1.25	0.80	2.40	4.00
☐ 63 Wolverine.................... 1.25	0.80	2.40	4.00
☐ 64 Wolverine, Ghost Rider 1.25	1.40	4.20	7.00
☐ 65 Wolverine, Ghost Rider 1.25	1.00	3.00	5.00
☐ 66 Wolverine, Ghost Rider 1.25	0.60	1.80	3.00
☐ 67 Wolverine, Ghost Rider 1.25	0.60	1.80	3.00
☐ 68 Wolverine, Ghost Rider 1.25	0.60	1.80	3.00
☐ 69 Wolverine, Ghost Rider 1.25	0.60	1.80	3.00
☐ 70 Wolverine, Ghost Rider 1.25	0.60	1.80	3.00
☐ 71 Wolverine, Ghost Rider 1.25	0.60	1.80	3.00

	ORIG.	GOOD	FINE	N-MINT
☐ 72 BWS, Weapon X..........1.25	2.80	8.40	14.00
☐ 73 BWS, Weapon X..........1.25	2.00	6.00	10.00
☐ 74 BWS, Weapon X..........1.25	1.60	4.80	8.00
☐ 75 BWS, Weapon X..........1.25	1.60	4.80	8.00
☐ 76 BWS, Weapon X..........1.25	1.60	4.80	8.00
☐ 77 BWS, Weapon X.........1.25	0.80	2.40	4.00
☐ 78 BWS, Weapon X.........1.25	0.80	2.40	4.00
☐ 79 BWS, Weapon X.........1.25	0.80	2.40	4.00
☐ 80 BWS, Weapon X.........1.25	0.80	2.40	4.00
☐ 81 BWS, Weapon X.........1.25	0.80	2.40	4.00
☐ 82 BWS, Weapon X.........1.25	0.80	2.40	4.00
☐ 83 BWS, Weapon X.........1.25	0.80	2.40	4.00
☐ 84 BWS, Weapon X.........1.25	0.80	2.40	4.00
☐ 85 Wolverine 1.25	0.60	1.80	3.00
☐ 86 Wolverine 1.25	0.60	1.80	3.00
☐ 87 Wolverine 1.25	0.60	1.80	3.00
☐ 88 Wolverine 1.25	0.60	1.80	3.00
☐ 89 Wolverine 1.25	0.60	1.80	3.00
☐ 90 Wolverine 1.25	0.60	1.80	3.00
☐ 91 Wolverine 1.25	0.60	1.80	3.00
☐ 92 Wolverine 1.25	0.60	1.80	3.00
☐ 93 Wolverine 1.25	0.60	1.80	3.00
☐ 94 Wolverine 1.25	0.60	1.80	3.00
☐ 95 Wolverine 1.50	0.60	1.80	3.00
☐ 96 Wolverine 1.50	0.60	1.80	3.00
☐ 97 Wolverine 1.50	0.60	1.80	3.00
☐ 98 Wolverine 1.50	0.60	1.80	3.00
☐ 99 Wolverine 1.50	0.60	1.80	3.00
☐ 100 Wolverine 1.50	1.20	3.60	6.00
☐ 101 Wolverine 1.50	0.40	1.20	2.00
☐ 102 Wolverine 1.50	0.40	1.20	2.00
☐ 103 Wolverine 1.50	0.40	1.20	2.00
☐ 104 Wolverine 1.50	0.40	1.20	2.00
☐ 105 Wolverine 1.50	0.40	1.20	2.00
☐ 108 Wolverine, Ghost Rider1.50	0.40	1.20	2.00
☐ 109 Wolverine, Ghost Rider1.50	0.40	1.20	2.00
☐ 110 Wolverine, Ghost Rider1.50	0.40	1.20	2.00
☐ 111 Infinity War, Wolverine, Ghost Rider			
....1.50	0.40	1.20	2.00
☐ 112 Wolverine, Ghost Rider1.50	0.30	0.90	1.50
☐ 113 Wolverine, Ghost Rider1.50	0.30	0.90	1.50
☐ 114 Wolverine, Ghost Rider1.50	0.30	0.90	1.50
☐ 115 Wolverine, Ghost Rider1.50	0.30	0.90	1.50
☐ 116 Wolverine, Ghost Rider1.50	0.30	0.90	1.50
☐ 117 Wolverine, Ghost Rider, Venom			
....1.50	0.80	2.40	4.00
☐ 118 Wolverine 1.50	0.40	1.20	2.00
☐ 119 Wolverine 1.50	0.40	1.20	2.00
☐ 120 Wolverine 1.50	0.30	0.90	1.50
☐ 121 Wolverine 1.50	0.30	0.90	1.50
☐ 122 Wolverine 1.50	0.30	0.90	1.50
☐ 123 Wolverine 1.50	0.30	0.90	1.50
☐ 124 Wolverine 1.50	0.30	0.90	1.50
☐ 125 Wolverine 1.50	0.30	0.90	1.50
☐ 126 Wolverine 1.50	0.30	0.90	1.50

	ORIG.	GOOD	FINE	N-MINT
❑ 127 Wolverine	1.50	0.30	0.90	1.50
❑ 128 Wolverine	1.50	0.30	0.90	1.50
❑ 129 Wolverine	1.50	0.30	0.90	1.50
❑ 130 Wolverine	1.50	0.30	0.90	1.50
❑ 131 Wolverine	1.50	0.30	0.90	1.50
❑ 132 Wolverine	1.50	0.30	0.90	1.50
❑ 133 Wolverine	1.50	0.30	0.90	1.50
❑ 134 Wolverine	1.50	0.30	0.90	1.50
❑ 135 Wolverine	1.50	0.30	0.90	1.50
❑ 136 Wolverine	1.50	0.30	0.90	1.50
❑ 137 Wolverine	1.50	0.30	0.90	1.50
❑ 138 Wolverine	1.50	0.30	0.90	1.50

MARVEL COMICS SUPER SPECIAL
(magazine size)

	ORIG.	GOOD	FINE	N-MINT
❑ 1 Kiss	1.50	0.30	0.90	1.50
❑ 2 Conan	1.50	0.30	0.90	1.50
❑ 3 Close Encounters	1.50	0.30	0.90	1.50
❑ 4 Beatles (becomes Marvel Super Special)				
	1.50	0.30	0.90	1.50

MARVEL DOUBLE FEATURE

	ORIG.	GOOD	FINE	N-MINT
❑ 1	0.20	0.20	0.60	1.00
❑ 2	0.20	0.20	0.60	1.00
❑ 3	0.20	0.20	0.60	1.00
❑ 4	0.25	0.20	0.60	1.00
❑ 5	0.25	0.20	0.60	1.00
❑ 6	0.25	0.20	0.60	1.00
❑ 7	0.25	0.20	0.60	1.00
❑ 8	0.25	0.20	0.60	1.00
❑ 9	0.25	0.20	0.60	1.00
❑ 10	0.25	0.20	0.60	1.00
❑ 11	0.25	0.20	0.60	1.00
❑ 12	0.25	0.20	0.60	1.00
❑ 13	0.25	0.20	0.60	1.00
❑ 14	0.25	0.20	0.60	1.00
❑ 15	0.25	0.20	0.60	1.00
❑ 16	0.25	0.20	0.60	1.00
❑ 17	0.25	0.20	0.60	1.00
❑ 18	0.30	0.20	0.60	1.00
❑ 19	0.30	0.20	0.60	1.00
❑ 20	0.30	0.20	0.60	1.00
❑ 21	0.30	0.20	0.60	1.00

MARVEL FANFARE

	ORIG.	GOOD	FINE	N-MINT
❑ 1 MG/TA, SpM/DD	1.25	2.40	7.20	12.00
❑ 2 MG, SpM/FF	1.25	2.00	6.00	10.00
❑ 3 DC, X-Men	1.25	1.60	4.80	8.00
❑ 4 PS/TA/MG, X-Men; MG, Deathlok				
	1.25	1.60	4.80	8.00
❑ 5 MR, Dr. Strange/CA	1.25	0.80	2.40	4.00
❑ 6 SpM/Dr. Strange	1.25	0.60	1.80	3.00
❑ 7 Hulk/DD	1.25	0.50	1.50	2.50
❑ 8	1.50	0.40	1.20	2.00
❑ 9	1.50	0.40	1.20	2.00
❑ 10	1.50	0.40	1.20	2.00
❑ 11	1.50	0.40	1.20	2.00

	ORIG.	GOOD	FINE	N-MINT
❑ 12	1.50	0.40	1.20	2.00
❑ 13 AAd (c)	1.50	0.40	1.20	2.00
❑ 14	1.50	0.40	1.20	2.00
❑ 15 BS, Thing	1.50	0.50	1.50	2.50
❑ 16	1.50	0.40	1.20	2.00
❑ 17	1.50	0.40	1.20	2.00
❑ 18 FM, Capt. America	1.50	0.80	2.40	4.00
❑ 19 JSn, Thing & Hulk	1.50	0.30	0.90	1.50
❑ 20 JSn, Thing & Hulk	1.50	0.30	0.90	1.50
❑ 21 JSn, Thing & Hulk	1.50	0.30	0.90	1.50
❑ 22 JSn, Thing & Hulk	1.50	0.30	0.90	1.50
❑ 23 JSn, Thing & Hulk	1.50	0.30	0.90	1.50
❑ 24	1.50	0.30	0.90	1.50
❑ 25	1.50	0.30	0.90	1.50
❑ 26	1.50	0.30	0.90	1.50
❑ 27	1.50	0.30	0.90	1.50
❑ 28	1.50	0.30	0.90	1.50
❑ 29	1.50	0.30	0.90	1.50
❑ 30	1.50	0.30	0.90	1.50
❑ 31	1.50	0.30	0.90	1.50
❑ 32	1.50	0.30	0.90	1.50
❑ 33 Wolverine, X-Men	1.50	0.60	1.80	3.00
❑ 34 Warriors 3	1.50	0.30	0.90	1.50
❑ 35 Warriors 3	1.50	0.30	0.90	1.50
❑ 36 Warriors 3	1.50	0.30	0.90	1.50
❑ 37 Warriors 3	1.50	0.30	0.90	1.50
❑ 38 Moon Knight	1.50	0.30	0.90	1.50
❑ 39 Hawkeye, Moon Knight	1.95	0.39	1.17	1.95
❑ 40 Angel, Storm	1.95	0.39	1.17	1.95
❑ 41 DG, Dr. Strange	1.95	0.39	1.17	1.95
❑ 42 Spider-Man	1.95	0.80	2.40	4.00
❑ 43 Sub-Mariner, Torch	1.95	0.39	1.17	1.95
❑ 44 Iron Man	1.95	0.39	1.17	1.95
❑ 45 JBy(c) all pin-ups	1.95	0.39	1.17	1.95
❑ 46 Fantastic Four	1.95	0.39	1.17	1.95
❑ 47 Hulk, Spider-Man	1.95	0.60	1.80	3.00
❑ 48 She-Hulk	1.95	0.39	1.17	1.95
❑ 49 Dr. Strange	1.95	0.39	1.17	1.95
❑ 50 X-Factor	2.25	0.45	1.35	2.25
❑ 51 Silver Surfer	2.95	0.59	1.77	2.95
❑ 52 Black Knight	2.25	0.45	1.35	2.25
❑ 53 Black Knight	2.25	0.45	1.35	2.25
❑ 54 Black Knight	2.25	0.45	1.35	2.25
❑ 55 Power Pack, Wolverine				
	2.25	0.45	1.35	2.25
❑ 56 Shanna	2.25	0.45	1.35	2.25
❑ 57 Shanna	2.25	0.45	1.35	2.25
❑ 58 Shanna	2.25	0.45	1.35	2.25
❑ 59 Shanna	2.25	0.45	1.35	2.25
❑ 60 WS(i), Denys Cowan, Black Panther, Rogue, Daredevil				
	2.25	0.45	1.35	2.25

MARVEL FEATURE (1971-1973)

	ORIG.	GOOD	FINE	N-MINT
❑ 1 NA(c), O:Defenders	0.25	11.00	33.00	55.00
❑ 2 BEv, Sub-Mariner rep.	0.25	4.40	13.20	22.00
❑ 3 BEv, Defenders	0.20	4.40	13.20	22.00

	ORIG.	GOOD	FINE	N-MINT
☐ 4 Ant-Man	0.20	2.00	6.00	10.00
☐ 5 Ant-Man	0.20	1.00	3.00	5.00
☐ 6 Ant-Man	0.20	1.00	3.00	5.00
☐ 7 CR, Ant-Man	0.20	1.00	3.00	5.00
☐ 8 CR, Ant-Man	0.20	1.00	3.00	5.00
☐ 9 CR, Ant-Man	0.20	1.00	3.00	5.00
☐ 10 CR, Ant-Man	0.20	1.00	3.00	5.00
☐ 11 Thing	0.20	1.60	4.80	8.00
☐ 12 Thing	0.20	1.60	4.80	8.00

MARVEL FEATURE (1975-1976)

	ORIG.	GOOD	FINE	N-MINT
☐ 1 NA, Red Sonja	0.25	0.50	1.50	2.50
☐ 2 Red Sonja	0.25	0.40	1.20	2.00
☐ 3 Red Sonja	0.25	0.40	1.20	2.00
☐ 4 Red Sonja	0.25	0.40	1.20	2.00
☐ 5 Red Sonja	0.25	0.40	1.20	2.00
☐ 6 Red Sonja	0.30	0.40	1.20	2.00
☐ 7 Red Sonja	0.30	0.40	1.20	2.00

MARVEL FUMETTI BOOK, THE

	ORIG.	GOOD	FINE	N-MINT
☐ 1 photos	1.00	0.20	0.60	1.00

MARVEL GUIDE TO COLLECTING COMICS, THE

	ORIG.	GOOD	FINE	N-MINT
☐ 1 1982, no cover price				

MARVEL HOLIDAY SPECIAL

	ORIG.	GOOD	FINE	N-MINT
☐ 1993	2.95	0.59	1.77	2.95
☐ 1 AAd	2.25	0.45	1.35	2.25

MARVEL ILLUSTRATED: SWIMSUIT ISSUE

	ORIG.	GOOD	FINE	N-MINT
☐ 1	3.95	0.79	2.37	3.95

MARVEL MASTERPIECES COLLECTION

	ORIG.	GOOD	FINE	N-MINT
☐ 1 Joe Jusko	2.95	0.59	1.77	2.95
☐ 2 Joe Jusko	2.95	0.59	1.77	2.95
☐ 3 Joe Jusko	2.95	0.59	1.77	2.95
☐ 4 Joe Jusko	2.95	0.59	1.77	2.95

MARVEL MILESTONE EDITION: AMAZING FANTASY #15

	ORIG.	GOOD	FINE	N-MINT
☐ reprint	2.95	0.59	1.77	2.95

MARVEL MILESTONE EDITION: AMAZING SPIDER-MAN #1

	ORIG.	GOOD	FINE	N-MINT
☐	2.95	0.59	1.77	2.95

MARVEL MILESTONE EDITION: AMAZING SPIDER-MAN #129

	ORIG.	GOOD	FINE	N-MINT
☐ reprint, O:Punisher	2.95	0.59	1.77	2.95

MARVEL MILESTONE EDITION: AVENGERS #1

	ORIG.	GOOD	FINE	N-MINT
☐ reprint, O:Avengers	2.95	0.59	1.77	2.95

MARVEL MILESTONE EDITION: FANTASTIC FOUR #1

	ORIG.	GOOD	FINE	N-MINT
☐ reprint	2.95	0.59	1.77	2.95

MARVEL MILESTONE EDITION: FANTASTIC FOUR #5

	ORIG.	GOOD	FINE	N-MINT
☐	2.95	0.59	1.77	2.95

MARVEL MILESTONE EDITION: GIANT-SIZE X-MEN #1

	ORIG.	GOOD	FINE	N-MINT
☐ reprint	3.95	0.79	2.37	3.95

MARVEL MILESTONE EDITION: INCREDIBLE HULK #1

	ORIG.	GOOD	FINE	N-MINT
☐ reprint	2.95	0.59	1.77	2.95

	ORIG.	GOOD	FINE	N-MINT
MARVEL MILESTONE EDITION: IRON FIST #14				
☐	2.95	0.59	1.77	2.95
MARVEL MILESTONE EDITION: IRON MAN #55				
☐	2.95	0.59	1.77	2.95
MARVEL MILESTONE EDITION: TALES OF SUSPENSE #39				
☐ O:Iron Man	2.95	0.59	1.77	2.95
MARVEL MILESTONE EDITION: X-MEN #1				
☐	2.95	0.59	1.77	2.95
MARVEL MILESTONE EDITION: X-MEN #9				
☐	2.95	0.59	1.77	2.95
MARVEL MOVIE PREMIERE				
☐ 1 b&w mag	1.00	0.20	0.60	1.00
MARVEL NO-PRIZE BOOK, THE				
☐ 1 mistakes	1.00	0.20	0.60	1.00
MARVEL POSTER BOOK				
☐ 1 TMc		0.50	1.50	2.50

MARVEL PREMIERE

	ORIG.	GOOD	FINE	N-MINT
☐ 1 GK, O:Warlock	0.20	10.00	30.00	50.00
☐ 2 JK, Yellow Claw	0.20	5.00	15.00	25.00
☐ 3 BS, Dr. Strange	0.20	5.00	15.00	25.00
☐ 4 FB/BS, Dr. Strange	0.20	2.40	7.20	12.00
☐ 5 MP/CR, Dr. Strange	0.20	1.40	4.20	7.00
☐ 6 MP/FB, Dr. Strange	0.20	1.40	4.20	7.00
☐ 7 MP/CR, Dr. Strange	0.20	1.40	4.20	7.00
☐ 8 JSn, Dr. Strange	0.20	1.40	4.20	7.00
☐ 9 FB, Dr. Strange	0.20	1.40	4.20	7.00
☐ 10 NA/FB, Dr. Strange	0.20	1.40	4.20	7.00
☐ 11 NA/FB, Dr. Strange	0.20	1.40	4.20	7.00
☐ 12 NA/FB, Dr. Strange	0.20	1.40	4.20	7.00
☐ 13 NA/FB, Dr. Strange	0.20	1.40	4.20	7.00
☐ 14 NA/FB, Dr. Strange	0.20	1.40	4.20	7.00
☐ 15 GK O:Iron Fist	0.25	16.00	48.00	80.00
☐ 16 Iron Fist	0.25	2.40	7.20	12.00
☐ 17 Iron Fist	0.25	2.40	7.20	12.00
☐ 18 Iron Fist	0.25	2.40	7.20	12.00
☐ 19 Iron Fist	0.25	2.40	7.20	12.00
☐ 20 Iron Fist	0.25	2.40	7.20	12.00
☐ 21 Iron Fist	0.25	2.40	7.20	12.00
☐ 22 Iron Fist	0.25	2.40	7.20	12.00
☐ 23 PB, Iron Fist	0.25	2.00	6.00	10.00
☐ 24 PB, Iron Fist	0.25	2.00	6.00	10.00
☐ 25 JBy, Iron Fist ends	0.25	4.80	14.40	24.00
☐ 26 JK, Hercules	0.25	1.00	3.00	5.00
☐ 27 Satana	0.25	1.00	3.00	5.00
☐ 28 Legion of Monsters	0.25	2.80	8.40	14.00
☐ 29 JK, O:Red Raven	0.25	0.40	1.20	2.00
☐ 30 JK, Liberty Legion	0.25	0.40	1.20	2.00
☐ 31 JK, 1:Wood-God	0.25	0.40	1.20	2.00
☐ 32 HC, Monark	0.30	0.40	1.20	2.00
☐ 33 HC, Monark	0.30	0.40	1.20	2.00
☐ 34 HC, Solomon Kane	0.30	0.40	1.20	2.00
☐ 35 3-D Man	0.30	0.40	1.20	2.00
☐ 36 3-D Man	0.30	0.40	1.20	2.00

	ORIG.	GOOD	FINE	N-MINT
❏ 37 3-D Man	0.30	0.40	1.20	2.00
❏ 38 Weirdworld	0.30	0.60	1.80	3.00
❏ 39 Torpedo	0.35	0.30	0.90	1.50
❏ 40 Torpedo	0.35	0.30	0.90	1.50
❏ 41 Seeker 3000	0.35	0.30	0.90	1.50
❏ 42 Tigra	0.35	0.30	0.90	1.50
❏ 43 1:Paladin	0.35	0.30	0.90	1.50
❏ 44 KG, Jack of Hearts	0.35	0.40	1.20	2.00
❏ 45 Man-Wolf	0.35	0.30	0.90	1.50
❏ 46 GP, War God	0.35	0.30	0.90	1.50
❏ 47 JBy, O:new Ant-Man	0.35	0.50	1.50	2.50
❏ 48 JBy, Ant-Man	0.40	0.40	1.20	2.00
❏ 49 Falcon	0.40	0.20	0.60	1.00
❏ 50 Alice Cooper	0.40	1.00	3.00	5.00
❏ 51 Black Panther	0.40	0.30	0.90	1.50
❏ 52 Black Panther	0.40	0.30	0.90	1.50
❏ 53 Black Panther	0.40	0.30	0.90	1.50
❏ 54 GD, Caleb Hammer	0.40	0.20	0.60	1.00
❏ 55 Wonder Man	0.40	0.60	1.80	3.00
❏ 56 TA/HC, Dominic Fortune	0.50	0.30	0.90	1.50
❏ 57 WS, Doctor Who	0.50	0.50	1.50	2.50
❏ 58 TA/FM, Doctor Who	0.50	0.50	1.50	2.50
❏ 59 Doctor Who	0.50	0.40	1.20	2.00
❏ 60 WS, Doctor Who	0.50	0.40	1.20	2.00
❏ 61 TS, Star Lord	0.50	0.30	0.90	1.50

MARVEL PRESENTS

	ORIG.	GOOD	FINE	N-MINT
❏ 1 Bloodstone	0.25	0.40	1.20	2.00
❏ 2 Bloodstone	0.25	0.20	0.60	1.00
❏ 3 Guardians of the Galaxy	0.25	1.00	3.00	5.00
❏ 4 Guardians of the Galaxy	0.25	0.80	2.40	4.00
❏ 5 Guardians of the Galaxy	0.25	0.80	2.40	4.00
❏ 6 Guardians of the Galaxy	0.25	0.80	2.40	4.00
❏ 7 Guardians of the Galaxy	0.30	0.80	2.40	4.00
❏ 8 Guardians of the Galaxy	0.30	0.20	0.60	1.00
❏ 9 Guardians of the Galaxy	0.30	0.80	2.40	4.00
❏ 10 Guardians of the Galaxy	0.30	0.20	0.60	1.00
❏ 11 Guardians of the Galaxy	0.30	0.80	2.40	4.00
❏ 12 Guardians of the Galaxy	0.30	0.80	2.40	4.00

MARVEL PREVIEW '93

	ORIG.	GOOD	FINE	N-MINT
❏	3.95	0.79	2.37	3.95

MARVEL PREVIEW (b&w mag)

	ORIG.	GOOD	FINE	N-MINT
❏ 1 Man-Gods	1.00	0.20	0.60	1.00
❏ 2 Punisher	1.00	0.20	0.60	1.00
❏ 3 Blade	1.00	0.20	0.60	1.00
❏ 4 Star-Lord	1.00	0.20	0.60	1.00
❏ 5 Sherlock Holmes	1.00	0.20	0.60	1.00
❏ 6 Sherlock Holmes	1.00	0.20	0.60	1.00
❏ 7 Satanna	1.00	0.20	0.60	1.00
❏ 8 Morbius	1.00	0.20	0.60	1.00
❏ 9 Man-God	1.00	0.20	0.60	1.00

	ORIG.	GOOD	FINE	N-MINT
❏ 10 Thor	1.00	0.20	0.60	1.00
❏ 11 Star-Lord	1.00	0.20	0.60	1.00
❏ 12 horror	1.00	0.20	0.60	1.00
❏ 13 UFO	1.00	0.20	0.60	1.00
❏ 14 Star-Lord	1.00	0.20	0.60	1.00
❏ 15 Star-Lord	1.00	0.20	0.60	1.00
❏ 16 terror	1.00	0.20	0.60	1.00
❏ 17 Blackmark	1.00	0.20	0.60	1.00
❏ 18 Star-Lord	1.25	0.25	0.75	1.25
❏ 19 Kull	1.25	0.25	0.75	1.25
❏ 20 Bizarre Adventures	1.25	0.25	0.75	1.25
❏ 21 Moon Knight	1.25	0.25	0.75	1.25
❏ 22 Merlin	1.25	0.25	0.75	1.25
❏ 23 Bizarre Adventures	1.25	0.25	0.75	1.25
❏ 24 (becomes Bizarre Adventures) Paradox	1.25	0.25	0.75	1.25

MARVEL SAGA

	ORIG.	GOOD	FINE	N-MINT
❏ 1	1.00	0.30	0.90	1.50
❏ 2	1.00	0.30	0.90	1.50
❏ 3	1.00	0.30	0.90	1.50
❏ 4	1.00	0.30	0.90	1.50
❏ 5	1.00	0.30	0.90	1.50
❏ 6	1.00	0.30	0.90	1.50
❏ 7	1.00	0.30	0.90	1.50
❏ 8	1.00	0.30	0.90	1.50
❏ 9	1.00	0.30	0.90	1.50
❏ 10	1.00	0.30	0.90	1.50
❏ 11	1.00	0.20	0.60	1.00
❏ 12	1.00	0.20	0.60	1.00
❏ 13	1.00	0.20	0.60	1.00
❏ 14	1.00	0.20	0.60	1.00
❏ 15	1.00	0.20	0.60	1.00
❏ 16	1.00	0.20	0.60	1.00
❏ 17	1.00	0.20	0.60	1.00
❏ 18	1.00	0.20	0.60	1.00
❏ 19	1.00	0.20	0.60	1.00
❏ 20	1.00	0.20	0.60	1.00
❏ 21	1.00	0.20	0.60	1.00
❏ 22 O:Mary Jane	1.00	0.20	0.60	1.00
❏ 23	1.00	0.20	0.60	1.00
❏ 24	1.00	0.20	0.60	1.00
❏ 25 O:Silver Surfer	1.00	0.20	0.60	1.00

MARVEL SPECIAL EDITION (tabloid)

	ORIG.	GOOD	FINE	N-MINT
❏ 1 Star Wars	1.00	0.20	0.60	1.00
❏ 2 Star Wars	1.00	0.20	0.60	1.00
❏ 1 Spectacular Spider-Man	1.50	0.30	0.90	1.50
❏ 1 Close Encounters of the Third Kind	1.50	0.30	0.90	1.50
❏ 3 Star Wars	2.50	0.50	1.50	2.50

MARVEL SPECTACULAR

	ORIG.	GOOD	FINE	N-MINT
❏ 1 reprints	0.20	0.20	0.60	1.00
❏ 2 reprints	0.20	0.20	0.60	1.00
❏ 3 reprints	0.20	0.20	0.60	1.00
❏ 4 reprints	0.20	0.20	0.60	1.00

	ORIG.	GOOD	FINE	N-MINT
5 reprints	0.20	0.20	0.60	1.00
6	0.20	0.20	0.60	1.00
7	0.25	0.20	0.60	1.00
8	0.25	0.20	0.60	1.00
9	0.25	0.20	0.60	1.00
10	0.25	0.20	0.60	1.00
11	0.25	0.20	0.60	1.00
12	0.25	0.20	0.60	1.00
13	0.25	0.20	0.60	1.00
14	0.25	0.20	0.60	1.00
15	0.25	0.20	0.60	1.00
16	0.25	0.20	0.60	1.00
17	0.25	0.20	0.60	1.00
18	0.25	0.20	0.60	1.00
19	0.25	0.20	0.60	1.00

MARVEL SPOTLIGHT (1971-1977)

	ORIG.	GOOD	FINE	N-MINT
1 WW/NA, O:Red Wolf	0.15	4.00	12.00	20.00
2 1:Werewolf	0.25	6.00	18.00	30.00
3 Werewolf	0.20	2.40	7.20	12.00
4 Werewolf	0.20	2.40	7.20	12.00
5 SD/MP, 1&O:Ghost Rider	0.20	25.00	75.00	125.00
6 Ghost Rider	0.20	11.00	33.00	55.00
7 Ghost Rider	0.20	8.40	25.20	42.00
8 Ghost Rider	0.20	8.40	25.20	42.00
9 Ghost Rider	0.20	8.40	25.20	42.00
10 Ghost Rider	0.20	8.40	25.20	42.00
11 Ghost Rider	0.20	8.40	25.20	42.00
12 SD, 1&O:Son of Satan	0.20	3.60	10.80	18.00
13 Son of Satan	0.20	2.00	6.00	10.00
14 Son of Satan	0.20	2.00	6.00	10.00
15 Son of Satan	0.25	2.00	6.00	10.00
16 Son of Satan	0.25	2.00	6.00	10.00
17 Son of Satan	0.25	2.00	6.00	10.00
18 Son of Satan	0.25	2.00	6.00	10.00
19 Son of Satan	0.25	2.00	6.00	10.00
20 Son of Satan	0.25	2.00	6.00	10.00
21 Son of Satan	0.25	2.00	6.00	10.00
22 Son of Satan	0.25	3.00	9.00	15.00
23 Son of Satan	0.25	1.20	3.60	6.00
24 Son of Satan	0.25	1.20	3.60	6.00
25 Sinbad	0.25	0.40	1.20	2.00
26 Scarecrow	0.25	0.40	1.20	2.00
27 Sub-Mariner	0.25	0.60	1.80	3.00
28 Moon Knight	0.25	2.40	7.20	12.00
29 JK, Moon Knight	0.25	2.00	6.00	10.00
30 JB, Warriors 3	0.30	0.20	0.60	1.00
31 HC/JSn, A:Nick Fury	0.30	1.40	4.20	7.00
32 1:Spider-Woman	0.30	1.60	4.80	8.00
33 Deathlok	0.30	1.60	4.80	8.00

MARVEL SPOTLIGHT (1979-1981)

	ORIG.	GOOD	FINE	N-MINT
1 PB, Capt. Marvel	0.40	0.20	0.60	1.00
2 TA/FM(c), Capt. Marvel	0.40	0.30	0.90	1.50

	ORIG.	GOOD	FINE	N-MINT
3 PB, Capt. Marvel	0.40	0.30	0.90	1.50
4 PB, Capt. Marvel	0.40	0.30	0.90	1.50
5 FM(c), SD, Dragon Lord	0.40	0.25	0.75	1.25
6 Star Lord	0.40	0.30	0.90	1.50
7 Star Lord	0.40	0.30	0.90	1.50
8 TA/FM, Capt. Marvel	0.50	0.40	1.20	2.00
9 SD Capt. Universe	0.50	0.30	0.90	1.50
10 SD Capt. Universe	0.50	0.30	0.90	1.50
11 SD Capt. Universe	0.50	0.30	0.90	1.50

MARVEL SPRING SPECIAL

	ORIG.	GOOD	FINE	N-MINT
1 Elvira		0.40	1.20	2.00

MARVEL SUPER ACTION (1977-1981)

	ORIG.	GOOD	FINE	N-MINT
1 reprints	0.30	0.40	1.20	2.00
2 reprints	0.30	0.20	0.60	1.00
3 reprints	0.30	0.20	0.60	1.00
4 reprint	0.35	0.20	0.60	1.00
5 reprint	0.35	0.20	0.60	1.00
6 reprint	0.35	0.20	0.60	1.00
7 reprint	0.35	0.20	0.60	1.00
8 reprint	0.35	0.20	0.60	1.00
9 reprint	0.35	0.20	0.60	1.00
10 reprint	0.35	0.20	0.60	1.00
11 reprint	0.35	0.20	0.60	1.00
12 reprint	0.35	0.20	0.60	1.00
13 reprint	0.35	0.20	0.60	1.00
14 reprints	0.40	0.20	0.60	1.00
15 reprints	0.40	0.20	0.60	1.00
16 reprints	0.40	0.20	0.60	1.00
17 reprints	0.40	0.20	0.60	1.00
18 reprints	0.40	0.20	0.60	1.00
19 reprints	0.40	0.20	0.60	1.00
20 reprints	0.40	0.20	0.60	1.00
21 reprints	0.40	0.20	0.60	1.00
22 reprints	0.40	0.20	0.60	1.00
23 reprints	0.50	0.20	0.60	1.00
24 reprints	0.50	0.20	0.60	1.00
25 reprints	0.50	0.20	0.60	1.00
26 reprints	0.50	0.20	0.60	1.00
27 reprints	0.50	0.20	0.60	1.00
28 reprints	0.50	0.20	0.60	1.00
29 reprints	0.50	0.20	0.60	1.00
30 reprints	0.50	0.20	0.60	1.00
31 reprints	0.50	0.20	0.60	1.00
32 reprints	0.50	0.20	0.60	1.00
33 reprints	0.50	0.20	0.60	1.00
34 reprints	0.50	0.20	0.60	1.00
35 reprints	0.50	0.20	0.60	1.00
36 reprints	0.50	0.20	0.60	1.00
37 reprints	0.50	0.20	0.60	1.00

MARVEL SUPER SPECIAL (was Marvel Comics Super Special) (magazine size)

	ORIG.	GOOD	FINE	N-MINT
5 Jaws 2	1.50	0.30	0.90	1.50
6 Kiss	1.50	0.30	0.90	1.50

	ORIG.	GOOD	FINE	N-MINT
❏ 8 Battlestar Galactica,				
tabloid 1.50	0.30	0.90	1.50
❏ 8 Battlestar Galactica 1.50	0.30	0.90	1.50
❏ 9 Conan 1.50	0.30	0.90	1.50
❏ 10 Starlord 1.50	0.30	0.90	1.50
❏ 11 Warriors of Shadow				
Realm 1.50	0.30	0.90	1.50
❏ 12 Warriors of Shadow				
Realm 1.50	0.30	0.90	1.50
❏ 13 Warriors of Shadow				
Realm 1.50	0.30	0.90	1.50
❏ 14 Meteor 1.50	0.30	0.90	1.50
❏ 15 Star Trek: Motion				
Picture 1.50	0.30	0.90	1.50
❏ 16 Empire Strikes Back 2.00	0.40	1.20	2.00
❏ 17 Xanadu 2.00	0.40	1.20	2.00
❏ 18 Raiders of the Lost Ark				
...... 2.50	0.50	1.50	2.50
❏ 19 For Your Eyes Only 2.50	0.50	1.50	2.50
❏ 20 Dragonslayer 2.50	0.50	1.50	2.50
❏ 21 Conan movie 2.50	0.50	1.50	2.50
❏ 22 Bladerunner, comic size				
...... 2.50	0.50	1.50	2.50
❏ 23 Annie 2.50	0.50	1.50	2.50
❏ 24 Dark Crystal 2.50	0.50	1.50	2.50
❏ 25 Rock & Rule, comic size				
...... 2.50	0.50	1.50	2.50
❏ 26 Octopussy 2.50	0.50	1.50	2.50
❏ 27 Return of the Jedi 2.50	0.50	1.50	2.50
❏ 28 Krull 2.50	0.50	1.50	2.50
❏ 29 Tarzan of the Apes 2.00	0.40	1.20	2.00
❏ 30 Indiana Jones Temple of Doom				
...... 2.50	0.50	1.50	2.50
❏ 31 The Last Starfighter 2.50	0.50	1.50	2.50
❏ 32 Muppets Take Manhattan				
...... 2.50	0.50	1.50	2.50
❏ 33 Buckaroo Banzai 2.50	0.50	1.50	2.50
❏ 34 Sheena 2.50	0.50	1.50	2.50
❏ 35 Conan the Destroyer ... 2.50	0.50	1.50	2.50
❏ 36 Dune 2.50	0.50	1.50	2.50
❏ 37 2010 ...... 2.00	0.40	1.20	2.00
❏ 38 Red Sonja 2.00	0.40	1.20	2.00
❏ 39 Santa Claus: the Movie				
...... 2.50	0.50	1.50	2.50
❏ 40 Labyrinth 2.50	0.50	1.50	2.50
❏ 41 Howard the Duck 2.50	0.50	1.50	2.50

MARVEL SUPER-HEROES (1966)

	ORIG.	GOOD	FINE	N-MINT
❏ 1 reprints 0.25			

MARVEL SUPER-HEROES (1967-1982)
(was Fantasy Masterpiece)

	ORIG.	GOOD	FINE	N-MINT
❏ 12 1:Captain Marvel 0.25	13.00	39.00	65.00
❏ 13 ...... 0.25	8.00	24.00	40.00
❏ 14 ...... 0.25	3.60	10.80	18.00
❏ 15 ...... 0.25	2.40	7.20	12.00
❏ 16 ...... 0.25	2.00	6.00	10.00

	ORIG.	GOOD	FINE	N-MINT
❏ 17 ...... 0.25	2.00	6.00	10.00
❏ 18 ...... 0.25	4.40	13.20	22.00
❏ 19 ...... 0.25	2.00	6.00	10.00
❏ 20 ...... 0.25	2.00	6.00	10.00
❏ 21 ...... 0.25	0.60	1.80	3.00
❏ 22 ...... 0.25	0.60	1.80	3.00
❏ 23 ...... 0.25	0.60	1.80	3.00
❏ 24 ...... 0.25	0.60	1.80	3.00
❏ 25 ...... 0.25	0.60	1.80	3.00
❏ 26 ...... 0.25	0.60	1.80	3.00
❏ 27 ...... 0.25	0.60	1.80	3.00
❏ 28 ...... 0.25	0.60	1.80	3.00
❏ 29 ...... 0.25	0.60	1.80	3.00
❏ 30 ...... 0.25	0.60	1.80	3.00
❏ 31 ...... 0.25	0.40	1.20	2.00
❏ 32 reprints 0.20	0.40	1.20	2.00
❏ 33 reprints 0.20	0.40	1.20	2.00
❏ 34 reprints 0.20	0.40	1.20	2.00
❏ 35 reprints 0.20	0.40	1.20	2.00
❏ 36 reprints 0.20	0.40	1.20	2.00
❏ 37 reprints 0.20	0.40	1.20	2.00
❏ 38 reprints 0.20	0.40	1.20	2.00
❏ 39 reprints 0.20	0.40	1.20	2.00
❏ 40 reprints 0.20	0.40	1.20	2.00
❏ 41 reprints 0.20	0.40	1.20	2.00
❏ 42 reprints 0.20	0.40	1.20	2.00
❏ 43 reprint 0.25	0.20	0.60	1.00
❏ 44 reprint 0.25	0.20	0.60	1.00
❏ 45 reprint 0.25	0.20	0.60	1.00
❏ 46 reprint 0.25	0.20	0.60	1.00
❏ 47 reprint 0.25	0.20	0.60	1.00
❏ 48 reprint 0.25	0.20	0.60	1.00
❏ 49 reprint 0.25	0.20	0.60	1.00
❏ 50 reprint 0.25	0.20	0.60	1.00
❏ 51 reprints 0.25	0.20	0.60	1.00
❏ 52 reprints 0.25	0.20	0.60	1.00
❏ 53 reprints 0.25	0.20	0.60	1.00
❏ 54 reprints 0.25	0.20	0.60	1.00
❏ 55 reprints 0.25	0.20	0.60	1.00
❏ 56 reprints 0.25	0.20	0.60	1.00
❏ 57 reprints 0.25	0.20	0.60	1.00
❏ 58 reprints 0.25	0.20	0.60	1.00
❏ 59 reprints 0.30	0.20	0.60	1.00
❏ 60 reprints 0.30	0.20	0.60	1.00
❏ 61 reprints 0.30	0.20	0.60	1.00
❏ 62 reprints 0.30	0.20	0.60	1.00
❏ 63 reprints 0.30	0.20	0.60	1.00
❏ 64 reprints 0.30	0.20	0.60	1.00
❏ 65 reprints 0.30	0.20	0.60	1.00
❏ 66 reprints 0.30	0.20	0.60	1.00
❏ 67 reprints 0.30	0.20	0.60	1.00
❏ 68 reprints 0.30	0.20	0.60	1.00
❏ 69 reprints 0.30	0.20	0.60	1.00
❏ 70 reprints 0.30	0.20	0.60	1.00
❏ 71 reprints 0.30	0.20	0.60	1.00

	ORIG.	GOOD	FINE	N-MINT
❏ 72 reprints	0.35	0.20	0.60	1.00
❏ 73 reprints	0.35	0.20	0.60	1.00
❏ 74 reprints	0.35	0.20	0.60	1.00
❏ 75 reprints	0.35	0.20	0.60	1.00
❏ 76 reprints	0.35	0.20	0.60	1.00
❏ 77 reprints	0.35	0.20	0.60	1.00
❏ 78 reprints	0.35	0.20	0.60	1.00
❏ 79 reprints	0.35	0.20	0.60	1.00
❏ 80 reprints	0.35	0.20	0.60	1.00
❏ 81 reprints	0.35	0.20	0.60	1.00
❏ 82 reprints	0.35	0.20	0.60	1.00
❏ 83 reprints	0.35	0.20	0.60	1.00
❏ 84 reprints	0.35	0.20	0.60	1.00
❏ 85 reprints	0.35	0.20	0.60	1.00
❏ 86 reprints	0.35	0.20	0.60	1.00
❏ 87 reprints	0.35	0.20	0.60	1.00
❏ 88 reprints	0.35	0.20	0.60	1.00
❏ 89 reprints	0.35	0.20	0.60	1.00
❏ 90 reprints	0.35	0.20	0.60	1.00
❏ 91 reprints	0.40	0.20	0.60	1.00
❏ 92 reprints	0.40	0.20	0.60	1.00
❏ 93 reprints	0.40	0.20	0.60	1.00
❏ 94 reprints	0.40	0.20	0.60	1.00
❏ 95 reprints	0.40	0.20	0.60	1.00
❏ 96 reprints	0.40	0.20	0.60	1.00
❏ 97 reprints	0.40	0.20	0.60	1.00
❏ 98 reprints	0.40	0.20	0.60	1.00
❏ 99 reprints	0.40	0.20	0.60	1.00
❏ 100 reprints	0.40	0.20	0.60	1.00
❏ 101 reprints	0.40	0.20	0.60	1.00
❏ 102 reprints	0.40	0.20	0.60	1.00
❏ 103 reprints	0.40	0.20	0.60	1.00
❏ 104 reprints	0.40	0.20	0.60	1.00
❏ 105 reprints	0.40	0.20	0.60	1.00

MARVEL SUPER-HEROES (1990-)

	ORIG.	GOOD	FINE	N-MINT
❏ 1 80 pages	2.95	0.59	1.77	2.95
❏ 2 80 pages	2.95	0.59	1.77	2.95
❏ 3 80 pages	2.95	0.59	1.77	2.95
❏ 4 80 pages	2.95	0.59	1.77	2.95
❏ 5 80 pages	2.95	0.59	1.77	2.95
❏ 6 AAd(c)	2.25	0.45	1.35	2.25
❏ 7	2.25	0.45	1.35	2.25
❏ 8	2.25	0.45	1.35	2.25
❏ 9	2.50	0.50	1.50	2.50
❏ 10	2.50	0.50	1.50	2.50
❏ 11 Ghost Rider	2.50	0.50	1.50	2.50
❏ 12	2.50	0.50	1.50	2.50
❏ 13 Iron Man	2.75	0.55	1.65	2.75
❏ 14	2.75	0.55	1.65	2.75

MARVEL SUPER-HEROES CONTEST OF CHAMPIONS

	ORIG.	GOOD	FINE	N-MINT
❏ 1 Alpha Flight	0.25	2.00	6.00	10.00
❏ 2 JR2 X-Men	0.25	1.60	4.80	8.00
❏ 3 JR2 X-Men	0.25	2.00	6.00	10.00

MARVEL SUPER-HEROES SECRET WARS

	ORIG.	GOOD	FINE	N-MINT
❏ 1 MZ, X-Men, Avengers, FF in all	0.75	0.80	2.40	4.00
❏ 2 MZ	0.75	0.60	1.80	3.00
❏ 3 MZ	0.75	0.60	1.80	3.00
❏ 4 MZ	0.75	0.60	1.80	3.00
❏ 5 MZ	0.75	0.60	1.80	3.00
❏ 6 MZ	0.75	0.50	1.50	2.50
❏ 7 MZ	0.75	0.50	1.50	2.50
❏ 8 MZ	0.75	0.50	1.50	2.50
❏ 9 MZ	0.75	0.50	1.50	2.50
❏ 10 MZ	0.75	0.50	1.50	2.50
❏ 11 MZ	0.75	0.50	1.50	2.50
❏ 12 MZ	1.00	0.50	1.50	2.50

MARVEL SWIMSUIT SPECIAL

	ORIG.	GOOD	FINE	N-MINT
❏ 1	3.95	0.79	2.37	3.95
❏ 2	4.50	0.90	2.70	4.50

MARVEL TAILS

	ORIG.	GOOD	FINE	N-MINT
❏ 1 1:Peter Porker	0.60	0.30	0.90	1.50

MARVEL TALES (reprints)

	ORIG.	GOOD	FINE	N-MINT
❏ 1 O:Spider-Man	0.25	40.00	120.00	200.00
❏ 2 O:X-Men	0.25	12.00	36.00	60.00
❏ 3 1:Torch	0.25	6.00	18.00	30.00
❏ 4	0.25	2.40	7.20	12.00
❏ 5	0.25	2.40	7.20	12.00
❏ 6	0.25	2.40	7.20	12.00
❏ 7	0.25	2.40	7.20	12.00
❏ 8	0.25	2.40	7.20	12.00
❏ 9	0.25	2.40	7.20	12.00
❏ 10	0.25	2.40	7.20	12.00
❏ 11	0.25	2.40	7.20	12.00
❏ 12	0.25	2.40	7.20	12.00
❏ 13 Marvel Boy	0.25	1.80	5.40	9.00
❏ 14	0.25	1.00	3.00	5.00
❏ 15	0.25	1.00	3.00	5.00
❏ 16	0.25	0.80	2.40	4.00
❏ 17	0.25	0.80	2.40	4.00
❏ 18	0.25	0.80	2.40	4.00
❏ 19	0.25	0.80	2.40	4.00
❏ 20	0.25	0.80	2.40	4.00
❏ 21	0.25	0.80	2.40	4.00
❏ 22	0.25	0.80	2.40	4.00
❏ 23	0.25	0.80	2.40	4.00
❏ 24	0.25	0.80	2.40	4.00
❏ 25	0.25	0.80	2.40	4.00
❏ 26	0.25	0.80	2.40	4.00
❏ 27	0.25	0.80	2.40	4.00
❏ 28	0.25	0.80	2.40	4.00
❏ 29	0.25	0.80	2.40	4.00

	ORIG.	GOOD	FINE	N-MINT			ORIG.	GOOD	FINE	N-MINT
☐ 30	0.25	0.80	2.40	4.00	☐ 85		0.30	0.80	2.40	4.00
☐ 31	0.25	0.80	2.40	4.00	☐ 86		0.35	0.80	2.40	4.00
☐ 32	0.25	0.80	2.40	4.00	☐ 87		0.35	0.80	2.40	4.00
☐ 33	0.25	0.80	2.40	4.00	☐ 88		0.35	0.80	2.40	4.00
☐ 34	0.20	0.80	2.40	4.00	☐ 89		0.35	0.80	2.40	4.00
☐ 35	0.20	0.80	2.40	4.00	☐ 90		0.35	0.80	2.40	4.00
☐ 36	0.20	0.80	2.40	4.00	☐ 91		0.35	0.80	2.40	4.00
☐ 37	0.20	0.80	2.40	4.00	☐ 92		0.35	0.80	2.40	4.00
☐ 38	0.20	0.80	2.40	4.00	☐ 93		0.35	0.80	2.40	4.00
☐ 39	0.20	0.80	2.40	4.00	☐ 94		0.35	0.80	2.40	4.00
☐ 40	0.20	0.80	2.40	4.00	☐ 95		0.35	0.80	2.40	4.00
☐ 41	0.20	0.80	2.40	4.00	☐ 96		0.35	0.80	2.40	4.00
☐ 42	0.20	0.80	2.40	4.00	☐ 97		0.35	0.80	2.40	4.00
☐ 43	0.20	0.80	2.40	4.00	☐ 98 D:Gwen Stacy	0.35	0.80	2.40	4.00
☐ 44	0.20	0.80	2.40	4.00	☐ 99 D:Green Goblin	0.35	0.80	2.40	4.00
☐ 45	0.20	0.80	2.40	4.00	☐ 100 TA/SD/GK/MN	0.60	0.80	2.40	4.00
☐ 46	0.20	0.80	2.40	4.00	☐ 101		0.35	0.40	1.20	2.00
☐ 47	0.20	0.80	2.40	4.00	☐ 102		0.35	0.40	1.20	2.00
☐ 48	0.20	0.80	2.40	4.00	☐ 103		0.35	0.40	1.20	2.00
☐ 49	0.20	0.80	2.40	4.00	☐ 104		0.35	0.40	1.20	2.00
☐ 50	0.20	0.80	2.40	4.00	☐ 105		0.35	0.40	1.20	2.00
☐ 51	0.25	0.80	2.40	4.00	☐ 106 rep. 1:Punisher	0.40	1.00	3.00	5.00
☐ 52	0.25	0.80	2.40	4.00	☐ 107		0.40	0.40	1.20	2.00
☐ 53	0.25	0.80	2.40	4.00	☐ 108		0.40	0.40	1.20	2.00
☐ 54	0.25	0.80	2.40	4.00	☐ 109		0.40	0.40	1.20	2.00
☐ 55	0.25	0.80	2.40	4.00	☐ 110		0.40	0.40	1.20	2.00
☐ 56	0.25	0.80	2.40	4.00	☐ 111 Punisher	0.40	1.00	3.00	5.00
☐ 57	0.25	0.80	2.40	4.00	☐ 112 Punisher	0.40	1.00	3.00	5.00
☐ 58	0.25	0.80	2.40	4.00	☐ 113		0.40	0.40	1.20	2.00
☐ 59	0.25	0.80	2.40	4.00	☐ 114		0.40	0.40	1.20	2.00
☐ 60	0.25	0.80	2.40	4.00	☐ 115		0.40	0.40	1.20	2.00
☐ 61	0.25	0.80	2.40	4.00	☐ 116		0.40	0.40	1.20	2.00
☐ 62	0.25	0.80	2.40	4.00	☐ 117		0.40	0.40	1.20	2.00
☐ 63	0.25	0.80	2.40	4.00	☐ 118		0.40	0.40	1.20	2.00
☐ 64	0.25	0.80	2.40	4.00	☐ 119		0.40	0.40	1.20	2.00
☐ 65	0.25	0.80	2.40	4.00	☐ 120		0.40	0.40	1.20	2.00
☐ 66	0.25	0.80	2.40	4.00	☐ 121		0.50	0.40	1.20	2.00
☐ 67	0.25	0.80	2.40	4.00	☐ 122		0.50	0.40	1.20	2.00
☐ 68	0.25	0.80	2.40	4.00	☐ 123		0.50	0.40	1.20	2.00
☐ 69	0.25	0.80	2.40	4.00	☐ 124		0.50	0.40	1.20	2.00
☐ 70	0.25	0.80	2.40	4.00	☐ 125		0.50	0.40	1.20	2.00
☐ 71	0.30	0.80	2.40	4.00	☐ 126		0.50	0.40	1.20	2.00
☐ 72	0.30	0.80	2.40	4.00	☐ 127		0.50	0.40	1.20	2.00
☐ 73	0.30	0.80	2.40	4.00	☐ 128		0.50	0.40	1.20	2.00
☐ 74	0.30	0.80	2.40	4.00	☐ 129		0.50	0.40	1.20	2.00
☐ 75	0.30	0.80	2.40	4.00	☐ 130		0.50	0.40	1.20	2.00
☐ 76	0.30	0.80	2.40	4.00	☐ 131		0.50	0.40	1.20	2.00
☐ 77	0.30	0.80	2.40	4.00	☐ 132		0.50	0.40	1.20	2.00
☐ 78	0.30	0.80	2.40	4.00	☐ 133		0.50	0.40	1.20	2.00
☐ 79	0.30	0.80	2.40	4.00	☐ 134		0.50	0.40	1.20	2.00
☐ 80	0.30	0.80	2.40	4.00	☐ 135		0.50	0.40	1.20	2.00
☐ 81	0.30	0.80	2.40	4.00	☐ 136		0.50	0.40	1.20	2.00
☐ 82	0.30	0.80	2.40	4.00	☐ 137 1&O:Spider-Man	0.60	0.80	2.40	4.00
☐ 83	0.30	0.80	2.40	4.00	☐ 138 Amazing Spider-Man #1				
☐ 84	0.30	0.80	2.40	4.00		0.60	0.80	2.40	4.00

	ORIG.	GOOD	FINE	N-MINT		ORIG.	GOOD	FINE	N-MINT
❑ 141	0.60	0.40	1.20	2.00	❑ 196	0.75	0.40	1.20	2.00
❑ 142	0.60	0.40	1.20	2.00	❑ 197	0.75	0.40	1.20	2.00
❑ 143	0.60	0.40	1.20	2.00	❑ 198	0.75	0.40	1.20	2.00
❑ 144	0.60	0.40	1.20	2.00	❑ 199	0.75	0.40	1.20	2.00
❑ 145	0.60	0.40	1.20	2.00	❑ 200 TMc(c)	1.25	0.60	1.80	3.00
❑ 146	0.60	0.40	1.20	2.00	❑ 201 TMc(c)	0.75	0.40	1.20	2.00
❑ 147	0.60	0.40	1.20	2.00	❑ 202 TMc(c)	0.75	0.40	1.20	2.00
❑ 148	0.60	0.40	1.20	2.00	❑ 203 TMc(c)	0.75	0.40	1.20	2.00
❑ 149	0.60	0.40	1.20	2.00	❑ 204 TMc(c)	0.75	0.40	1.20	2.00
❑ 150	0.60	0.40	1.20	2.00	❑ 205 TMc(c)	0.75	0.40	1.20	2.00
❑ 151	0.60	0.40	1.20	2.00	❑ 206 TMc(c)	0.75	0.40	1.20	2.00
❑ 152	0.60	0.40	1.20	2.00	❑ 207 TMc(c)	0.75	0.40	1.20	2.00
❑ 153	0.60	0.40	1.20	2.00	❑ 208 TMc(c)	0.75	0.40	1.20	2.00
❑ 154	0.60	0.40	1.20	2.00	❑ 209 TMc(c) 1:Punisher	0.75	0.40	1.20	2.00
❑ 155	0.60	0.40	1.20	2.00	❑ 210 TMc(c) A:Punisher	0.75	0.40	1.20	2.00
❑ 156	0.60	0.40	1.20	2.00	❑ 211 TMc(c) A:Punisher	0.75	0.40	1.20	2.00
❑ 157	0.60	0.40	1.20	2.00	❑ 212 TMc(c) A:Punisher	0.75	0.40	1.20	2.00
❑ 158	0.60	0.40	1.20	2.00	❑ 213 TMc(c) A:Punisher	0.75	0.40	1.20	2.00
❑ 159	0.60	0.40	1.20	2.00	❑ 214 TMc(c) A:Punisher	0.75	0.40	1.20	2.00
❑ 160	0.60	0.40	1.20	2.00	❑ 215 TMc(c) A:Punisher	0.75	0.40	1.20	2.00
❑ 161	0.60	0.40	1.20	2.00	❑ 216 TMc(c) A:Punisher	0.75	0.40	1.20	2.00
❑ 162	0.60	0.40	1.20	2.00	❑ 217 TMc(c) A:Punisher	0.75	0.40	1.20	2.00
❑ 163	0.60	0.40	1.20	2.00	❑ 218 TMc(c) A:Punisher	0.75	0.40	1.20	2.00
❑ 164	0.60	0.40	1.20	2.00	❑ 219 TMc(c) A:Punisher	0.75	0.40	1.20	2.00
❑ 165	0.60	0.40	1.20	2.00	❑ 220 TMc(c) A:Punisher	0.75	0.40	1.20	2.00
❑ 166	0.60	0.40	1.20	2.00	❑ 221 TMc(c) A:Punisher	0.75	0.40	1.20	2.00
❑ 167	0.60	0.40	1.20	2.00	❑ 222 TMc(c) A:Punisher	0.75	0.40	1.20	2.00
❑ 168	0.60	0.40	1.20	2.00	❑ 223 TMc(c)	0.75	0.40	1.20	2.00
❑ 169	0.60	0.40	1.20	2.00	❑ 224 TMc(c)	0.75	0.40	1.20	2.00
❑ 170	0.60	0.40	1.20	2.00	❑ 225 TMc(c)	0.75	0.40	1.20	2.00
❑ 171	0.60	0.40	1.20	2.00	❑ 226 TMc(c)	0.75	0.40	1.20	2.00
❑ 172	0.60	0.40	1.20	2.00	❑ 227 TMc(c)	1.00	0.40	1.20	2.00
❑ 173	0.60	0.40	1.20	2.00	❑ 228 TMc(c)	1.00	0.40	1.20	2.00
❑ 174	0.65	0.40	1.20	2.00	❑ 229 TMc(c)	1.00	0.40	1.20	2.00
❑ 175	0.65	0.40	1.20	2.00	❑ 230 TMc(c)	1.00	0.40	1.20	2.00
❑ 176	0.65	0.40	1.20	2.00	❑ 231 TMc(c)	1.00	0.40	1.20	2.00
❑ 177	0.65	0.40	1.20	2.00	❑ 232 TMc(c)	1.00	0.40	1.20	2.00
❑ 178	0.65	0.40	1.20	2.00	❑ 233 TMc(c)	1.00	0.40	1.20	2.00
❑ 179	0.65	0.40	1.20	2.00	❑ 234 TMc(c)	1.00	0.40	1.20	2.00
❑ 180	0.65	0.40	1.20	2.00	❑ 235 TMc(c)	1.00	0.40	1.20	2.00
❑ 181	0.65	0.40	1.20	2.00	❑ 236 TMc(c)	1.00	0.40	1.20	2.00
❑ 182	0.65	0.40	1.20	2.00	❑ 237 TMc(c)	1.00	0.40	1.20	2.00
❑ 183	0.65	0.40	1.20	2.00	❑ 238 TMc(c)	1.00	0.40	1.20	2.00
❑ 184	0.75	0.40	1.20	2.00	❑ 239 TMc(c)	1.00	0.40	1.20	2.00
❑ 185	0.75	0.40	1.20	2.00	❑ 240	1.00	0.20	0.60	1.00
❑ 186	0.75	0.40	1.20	2.00	❑ 241	1.00	0.20	0.60	1.00
❑ 187	0.75	0.40	1.20	2.00	❑ 242	1.00	0.20	0.60	1.00
❑ 188	0.75	0.40	1.20	2.00	❑ 243	1.00	0.20	0.60	1.00
❑ 189	0.75	0.40	1.20	2.00	❑ 244	1.00	0.20	0.60	1.00
❑ 190	0.75	0.40	1.20	2.00	❑ 245	1.00	0.20	0.60	1.00
❑ 191	0.75	0.40	1.20	2.00	❑ 246	1.00	0.20	0.60	1.00
❑ 192	0.75	0.40	1.20	2.00	❑ 247	1.00	0.20	0.60	1.00
❑ 193	0.75	0.40	1.20	2.00	❑ 248	1.00	0.20	0.60	1.00
❑ 194	0.75	0.40	1.20	2.00	❑ 249	1.00	0.20	0.60	1.00
❑ 195	0.75	0.40	1.20	2.00	❑ 250	1.50	0.30	0.90	1.50

	ORIG.	GOOD	FINE	N-MINT
251	1.00	0.20	0.60	1.00
252	1.00	0.20	0.60	1.00
253 Moebius(c)	1.50	0.30	0.90	1.50
254	1.00	0.20	0.60	1.00
255	1.00	0.20	0.60	1.00
256	1.00	0.20	0.60	1.00
257	1.00	0.20	0.60	1.00
258	1.25	0.25	0.75	1.25
259	1.25	0.25	0.75	1.25
260	1.25	0.25	0.75	1.25
261	1.25	0.25	0.75	1.25
262 X-Men	1.25	0.25	0.75	1.25
263	1.25	0.25	0.75	1.25
264	1.25	0.25	0.75	1.25
265	1.25	0.25	0.75	1.25
266	1.25	0.25	0.75	1.25
267	1.25	0.25	0.75	1.25
268	1.25	0.25	0.75	1.25
269	1.25	0.25	0.75	1.25
270	1.25	0.25	0.75	1.25
271	1.25	0.25	0.75	1.25
272	1.25	0.25	0.75	1.25
273	1.25	0.25	0.75	1.25
274	1.25	0.25	0.75	1.25
275	1.25	0.25	0.75	1.25
276	1.25	0.25	0.75	1.25
277	1.25	0.25	0.75	1.25
278	1.25	0.25	0.75	1.25

MARVEL TEAM-UP

	ORIG.	GOOD	FINE	N-MINT
1 SpM/Torch	0.20	10.00	30.00	50.00
2 SpM/Torch	0.20	6.00	18.00	30.00
3 SpM/Torch	0.20	6.00	18.00	30.00
4 GK, SpM/X-Men	0.20	8.00	24.00	40.00
5 GK, SpM/Vision	0.20	1.80	5.40	9.00
6 GK, SpM/Thing	0.20	1.80	5.40	9.00
7 RA, SpM/Thor	0.20	1.80	5.40	9.00
8 SpM/Cat	0.20	1.80	5.40	9.00
9 RA, SpM/Iron Man	0.20	1.80	5.40	9.00
10 SpM/Torch	0.20	1.80	5.40	9.00
11 SpM/Inhumans	0.20	1.20	3.60	6.00
12 SpM/Werewolf	0.20	1.20	3.60	6.00
13 GK, SpM/Capt. America	0.20	1.20	3.60	6.00
14 GK, SpM/Sub-Mariner	0.20	1.20	3.60	6.00
15 SpM/Ghost Rider	0.20	2.40	7.20	12.00
16 GK, SpM/Capt. Marvel	0.20	2.00	6.00	10.00
17 GK, SpM/Mr. Fantastic	0.20	2.00	6.00	10.00
18 GK, Torch/Hulk	0.20	2.00	6.00	10.00
19 GK, SpM/Ka-Zar	0.20	2.00	6.00	10.00
20 SpM/Black Panther	0.20	2.00	6.00	10.00
21 SpM/Dr. Strange	0.25	1.00	3.00	5.00
22 SpM/Hawkeye	0.25	1.00	3.00	5.00

	ORIG.	GOOD	FINE	N-MINT
23 Torch/Iceman, A:X-Men	0.25	1.00	3.00	5.00
24 SpM/Brother Voodoo	0.25	1.00	3.00	5.00
25 SpM/Daredevil	0.25	1.00	3.00	5.00
26 Torch/Thor	0.25	1.00	3.00	5.00
27 SpM/Hulk	0.25	1.00	3.00	5.00
28 SpM/Hercules	0.25	1.00	3.00	5.00
29 Torch/Iron Man	0.25	1.00	3.00	5.00
30 SpM/Falcon	0.25	1.00	3.00	5.00
31 SpM/Iron Fist	0.25	1.00	3.00	5.00
32 Torch/Son of Satan	0.25	1.00	3.00	5.00
33 SpM/Nighthawk	0.25	1.00	3.00	5.00
34 SpM/Valkyrie	0.25	1.00	3.00	5.00
35 Torch/Dr. Strange	0.25	1.00	3.00	5.00
36 SpM/Frankenstein	0.25	1.00	3.00	5.00
37 SpM/Man-Wolf	0.25	1.00	3.00	5.00
38 SpM/Beast	0.25	1.00	3.00	5.00
39 SpM/Torch	0.25	1.00	3.00	5.00
40 SpM/Sons of Tiger	0.25	1.00	3.00	5.00
41 SpM/Scarlet Witch	0.25	1.00	3.00	5.00
42 SpM/Scarlet Witch, Vision	0.25	1.00	3.00	5.00
43 SpM/Dr. Doom	0.25	1.00	3.00	5.00
44 SpM/Moondragon	0.25	1.00	3.00	5.00
45 SpM/Killraven	0.25	1.00	3.00	5.00
46 SpM/Deathlok	0.25	2.00	6.00	10.00
47 SpM/Thing	0.25	1.00	3.00	5.00
48 SpM/Iron Man	0.25	1.00	3.00	5.00
49 SpM/Iron Man	0.30	1.00	3.00	5.00
50 SpM/Dr. Strange	0.30	1.00	3.00	5.00
51 SpM/Iron Man	0.30	0.60	1.80	3.00
52 SpM/Capt. America	0.30	0.60	1.80	3.00
53 JBy, SpM/Hulk, A:X-Men	0.30	2.40	7.20	12.00
54 JBy, SpM/Hulk, A:Woodgod	0.30	1.20	3.60	6.00
55 JBy, SpM/Warlock	0.30	1.20	3.60	6.00
56 SpM/Daredevil	0.30	0.60	1.80	3.00
57 SpM/Black Widow	0.30	0.60	1.80	3.00
58 SpM/Ghost Rider	0.30	1.20	3.60	6.00
59 JBy, SpM/Yellowjacket & Wasp	0.30	0.70	2.10	3.50
60 JBy, SpM/Wasp, A:Yellowjacket	0.30	0.70	2.10	3.50
61 JBy, SpM/Torch	0.30	0.70	2.10	3.50
62 JBy, SpM/Ms. Marvel	0.30	0.70	2.10	3.50
63 JBy, SpM/Iron Fist	0.35	1.00	3.00	5.00
64 JBy, SpM/Daughters of Dragon	0.35	0.70	2.10	3.50

	ORIG.	GOOD	FINE	N-MINT
☐ 65 JBy, SpM/Capt. Britain				
.... 0.35	0.80	2.40	4.00
☐ 66 JBy, SpM/Capt. Britain				
.... 0.35	0.80	2.40	4.00
☐ 67 JBy, SpM/Tigra 0.35	0.70	2.10	3.50
☐ 68 JBy, SpM/Man-Thing ... 0.35	0.70	2.10	3.50
☐ 69 JBy, SpM/Havok 0.35	0.80	2.40	4.00
☐ 70 JBy, SpM/Thor 0.35	0.70	2.10	3.50
☐ 71 SpM/Falcon 0.35	0.40	1.20	2.00
☐ 72 SpM/Iron Man 0.35	0.40	1.20	2.00
☐ 73 SpM/Daredevil 0.35	0.25	0.75	1.25
☐ 74 SpM/Not Ready for Prime Time Players				
.... 0.35	0.60	1.80	3.00
☐ 75 JBy, SpM/Power Man .. 0.35	0.60	1.80	3.00
☐ 76 SpM/Dr. Strange 0.35	0.40	1.20	2.00
☐ 77 HC, SpM/Ms. Marvel ... 0.35	0.40	1.20	2.00
☐ 78 SpM/Wonder Man 0.35	0.60	1.80	3.00
☐ 79 JBy/TA, SpM/Red Sonja				
.... 0.35	0.40	1.20	2.00
☐ 80 SpM/Dr. Strange & Clea				
.... 0.35	0.40	1.20	2.00
☐ 81 SpM/Satana 0.40	0.40	1.20	2.00
☐ 82 SpM/Black Widow 0.40	0.40	1.20	2.00
☐ 83 SpM/Nick Fury 0.40	0.40	1.20	2.00
☐ 84 SpM/Shang-Chi 0.40	0.60	1.80	3.00
☐ 85 SpM/Shang-Chi 0.40	0.60	1.80	3.00
☐ 86 SpM/Guardians of Galaxy				
.... 0.40	0.60	1.80	3.00
☐ 87 GC, SpM/Black Panther				
.... 0.40	0.40	1.20	2.00
☐ 88 SpM/Invisible Girl 0.40	0.40	1.20	2.00
☐ 89 SpM/Nightcrawler 0.40	0.60	1.80	3.00
☐ 90 SpM/Beast 0.40	0.40	1.20	2.00
☐ 91 SpM/Ghost Rider 0.40	0.80	2.40	4.00
☐ 92 CI, SpM/Hawkeye 0.40	0.40	1.20	2.00
☐ 93 CI, SpM/Werewolf 0.40	0.40	1.20	2.00
☐ 94 MZ, SpM/Shroud 0.40	0.40	1.20	2.00
☐ 95 SpM/Mockingbird 0.40	0.40	1.20	2.00
☐ 96 SpM/Howard the Duck . 0.40	0.40	1.20	2.00
☐ 97 Hulk/Spider-Woman 0.50	0.40	1.20	2.00
☐ 98 SpM/Black Widow 0.50	0.40	1.20	2.00
☐ 99 SpM/Machine Man 0.50	0.40	1.20	2.00
☐ 100 FM/JBy, SpM/FF, 1:Karma				
.... 0.50	2.00	6.00	10.00
☐ 101 SpM/Nighthawk 0.50	0.40	1.20	2.00
☐ 102 SpM/Doc Samson 0.50	0.40	1.20	2.00
☐ 103 SpM/Ant-Man 0.50	0.40	1.20	2.00
☐ 104 Hulk/Ka-Zar 0.50	0.40	1.20	2.00
☐ 105 Power Man & Iron Fist & Hulk				
.... 0.50	0.40	1.20	2.00
☐ 106 SpM/Capt. America ... 0.50	0.40	1.20	2.00
☐ 107 SpM/She-Hulk 0.50	0.40	1.20	2.00
☐ 108 SpM/Paladin 0.50	0.40	1.20	2.00
☐ 109 SpM/Dazzler 0.50	0.40	1.20	2.00
☐ 110 SpM/Iron Man 0.50	0.40	1.20	2.00

	ORIG.	GOOD	FINE	N-MINT
☐ 111 SpM/Devil-Slayer 0.50	0.40	1.20	2.00
☐ 112 SpM/King Kull 0.50	0.40	1.20	2.00
☐ 113 SpM/Quasar 0.60	0.40	1.20	2.00
☐ 114 SpM/Falcon 0.60	0.40	1.20	2.00
☐ 115 SpM/Thor 0.60	0.40	1.20	2.00
☐ 116 SpM/Valkyrie 0.60	0.40	1.20	2.00
☐ 117 SpM/Wolverine 0.60	0.80	2.40	4.00
☐ 118 SpM/Prof. X 0.60	0.40	1.20	2.00
☐ 119 KGa, SpM/Gargoyle ... 0.60	0.40	1.20	2.00
☐ 120 KGa, SpM/Dominic Fortune				
.... 0.60	0.40	1.20	2.00
☐ 121 KGa, SpM/Torch 0.60	0.40	1.20	2.00
☐ 122 Man-Thing/DD 0.60	0.40	1.20	2.00
☐ 123 Man-Thing/DD 0.60	0.40	1.20	2.00
☐ 124 KGa, SpM/Beast 0.60	0.40	1.20	2.00
☐ 125 KGa, SpM/Tigra 0.60	0.40	1.20	2.00
☐ 126 BH, SpM/Hulk 0.60	0.40	1.20	2.00
☐ 127 KGa, SpM/Watcher 0.60	0.40	1.20	2.00
☐ 128 .... 0.60	0.40	1.20	2.00
☐ 129 .... 0.60	0.40	1.20	2.00
☐ 130 .... 0.60	0.40	1.20	2.00
☐ 131 .... 0.60	0.40	1.20	2.00
☐ 132 .... 0.60	0.40	1.20	2.00
☐ 133 .... 0.60	0.40	1.20	2.00
☐ 134 Jack of Hearts 0.60	0.40	1.20	2.00
☐ 135 Kitty Pryde 0.60	0.40	1.20	2.00
☐ 136 Wonder Man 0.60	0.40	1.20	2.00
☐ 137 Aunt May & Franklin Richards				
.... 0.60	0.40	1.20	2.00
☐ 138 Sandman/Nick Fury ... 0.60	0.40	1.20	2.00
☐ 139 Sandman/Nick Fury ... 0.60	0.40	1.20	2.00
☐ 140 Sandman/Nick Fury ... 0.60	0.40	1.20	2.00
☐ 141 SpM new costume 0.60	0.40	1.20	2.00
☐ 142 SpM/Capt. Marvel 0.60	0.40	1.20	2.00
☐ 143 SpM/Starfox 0.60	0.40	1.20	2.00
☐ 144 SpM/Moon Knight 0.60	0.40	1.20	2.00
☐ 145 SpM/Iron Man 0.60	0.40	1.20	2.00
☐ 146 SpM 0.60	0.40	1.20	2.00
☐ 147 SpM/Torch 0.60	0.40	1.20	2.00
☐ 148 .... 0.60	0.40	1.20	2.00
☐ 149 .... 0.60	0.40	1.20	2.00
☐ 150 SpM/X-Men 1.00	0.80	2.40	4.00

MARVEL TEAM-UP ANNUAL

	ORIG.	GOOD	FINE	N-MINT
☐ 1 A: X-Men 0.50	2.40	7.20	12.00
☐ 2 A:SpM/Hulk 0.75	0.40	1.20	2.00
☐ 3 A:Hulk/Power Man 0.75	0.30	0.90	1.50
☐ 4 A:Daredevil/Moon Knight				
.... 0.75	0.50	1.50	2.50
☐ 5 A:SpM/Thing/Scarlet Witch				
.... 1.00	0.40	1.20	2.00
☐ 6 A:New Mutants/Cloak & Dagger				
.... 1.00	0.60	1.80	3.00
☐ 7 A: Alpha Flight 1.00	0.60	1.80	3.00

	ORIG.	GOOD	FINE	N-MINT
MARVEL TREASURY EDITION				
☐ 1 SD, SpM	1.50	1.20	3.60	6.00
☐ 2 JK/FF, Silver Surfer	1.50	0.70	2.10	3.50
☐ 3 Thor	1.50	0.70	2.10	3.50
☐ 4 BS, Conan	1.50	0.90	2.70	4.50
☐ 5 O:Hulk	1.50	0.70	2.10	3.50
☐ 6 SD, Dr. Strange	1.50	0.70	2.10	3.50
☐ 7 JK, Avengers	1.50	0.90	2.70	4.50
☐ 8 Xmas	1.50	0.90	2.70	4.50
☐ 9 Super-Hero Team-up	1.50	0.70	2.10	3.50
☐ 10 Thor	1.50	0.70	2.10	3.50
☐ 11 FF	1.50	0.70	2.10	3.50
☐ 12 Howard the Duck, new stories				
	1.50	0.70	2.10	3.50
☐ 13 Xmas	1.50	0.70	2.10	3.50
☐ 14 SpM	1.50	0.70	2.10	3.50
☐ 15 BS, Conan/Red Sonja	1.50	0.90	2.70	4.50
☐ 16 Defenders	1.50	0.60	1.80	3.00
☐ 17 Hulk	1.50	0.60	1.80	3.00
☐ 18 SpM, X-Men	2.00	0.70	2.10	3.50
☐ 19 Conan	2.00	0.90	2.70	4.50
☐ 20 Hulk	2.00	0.50	1.50	2.50
☐ 21 FF	2.00	0.50	1.50	2.50
☐ 22 SpM	2.00	0.50	1.50	2.50
☐ 23 Conan	2.00	0.60	1.80	3.00
☐ 24 Hulk	2.00	0.50	1.50	2.50
☐ 25 SpM/Hulk	2.00	0.50	1.50	2.50
☐ 26 Hulk, Wolverine & Hercules				
	2.00	1.00	3.00	5.00
☐ 27 Hulk/SpM	2.00	0.60	1.80	3.00
☐ 28 SpM/Superman	2.50	1.60	4.80	8.00
MARVEL TREASURY OF OZ				
☐ 1 Land of Oz	1.50	1.20	3.60	6.00
MARVEL TREASURY SPECIAL				
☐ 1 Giant Super-Hero Holiday Grab Bag				
	1.50	1.00	3.00	5.00
☐ 2 Captain America's Bicentennial Battles (1976)				
	1.50	1.00	3.00	5.00
MARVEL TRIPLE ACTION				
☐ 1 reprints	0.25	0.40	1.20	2.00
☐ 2	0.20	0.20	0.60	1.00
☐ 3	0.20	0.20	0.60	1.00
☐ 4	0.20	0.20	0.60	1.00
☐ 5	0.20	0.20	0.60	1.00
☐ 6	0.20	0.20	0.60	1.00
☐ 7	0.20	0.20	0.60	1.00
☐ 8	0.20	0.20	0.60	1.00
☐ 9	0.20	0.20	0.60	1.00
☐ 10	0.20	0.20	0.60	1.00
☐ 11	0.20	0.20	0.60	1.00
☐ 12	0.20	0.20	0.60	1.00
☐ 13	0.20	0.20	0.60	1.00
☐ 14	0.20	0.20	0.60	1.00
☐ 15	0.20	0.20	0.60	1.00

	ORIG.	GOOD	FINE	N-MINT
☐ 16	0.20	0.20	0.60	1.00
☐ 17	0.20	0.20	0.60	1.00
☐ 18	0.25	0.20	0.60	1.00
☐ 19	0.25	0.20	0.60	1.00
☐ 20	0.25	0.20	0.60	1.00
☐ 21	0.25	0.20	0.60	1.00
☐ 22	0.25	0.20	0.60	1.00
☐ 23	0.25	0.20	0.60	1.00
☐ 24	0.25	0.20	0.60	1.00
☐ 25	0.25	0.20	0.60	1.00
☐ 26	0.25	0.20	0.60	1.00
☐ 27	0.25	0.20	0.60	1.00
☐ 28	0.25	0.20	0.60	1.00
☐ 29	0.25	0.20	0.60	1.00
☐ 30	0.25	0.20	0.60	1.00
☐ 31	0.30	0.20	0.60	1.00
☐ 32	0.30	0.20	0.60	1.00
☐ 33	0.30	0.20	0.60	1.00
☐ 34	0.30	0.20	0.60	1.00
☐ 35	0.30	0.20	0.60	1.00
☐ 36	0.30	0.20	0.60	1.00
☐ 37	0.30	0.20	0.60	1.00
☐ 38	0.30	0.20	0.60	1.00
☐ 39	0.30	0.20	0.60	1.00
☐ 40	0.30	0.20	0.60	1.00
☐ 41	0.30	0.20	0.60	1.00
☐ 42	0.30	0.20	0.60	1.00
☐ 43	0.30	0.20	0.60	1.00
☐ 44	0.30	0.20	0.60	1.00
☐ 45	0.30	0.20	0.60	1.00
☐ 46	0.30	0.20	0.60	1.00
☐ 47	0.30	0.20	0.60	1.00
MARVEL TWO-IN-ONE (all have Thing)				
☐ 1 Man-Thing	0.20	3.60	10.80	18.00
☐ 2 Sub-Mariner	0.20	0.80	2.40	4.00
☐ 3 Daredevil, A:Black Widow				
	0.25	0.80	2.40	4.00
☐ 4 Capt. America	0.25	0.80	2.40	4.00
☐ 5 Guardians of Galaxy	0.25	3.00	9.00	15.00
☐ 6 Dr. Strange	0.25	2.00	6.00	10.00
☐ 7 Valkyrie, A:Dr. Strange	0.25	0.60	1.80	3.00
☐ 8 Ghost Rider	0.25	2.00	6.00	10.00
☐ 9 Thor	0.25	0.60	1.80	3.00
☐ 10 Black Widow	0.25	0.60	1.80	3.00
☐ 11 Golem	0.25	0.50	1.50	2.50
☐ 12 Iron Man	0.25	0.50	1.50	2.50
☐ 13 Power Man	0.25	0.50	1.50	2.50
☐ 14 Son of Satan	0.25	0.50	1.50	2.50
☐ 15 Morbius	0.25	0.50	1.50	2.50
☐ 16 Ka-Zar	0.25	0.50	1.50	2.50
☐ 17 SpM	0.25	0.50	1.50	2.50
☐ 18 SpM	0.25	0.50	1.50	2.50
☐ 19 Tigra	0.30	0.50	1.50	2.50
☐ 20 Liberty Legion	0.30	0.50	1.50	2.50
☐ 21 Doc Savage, A:Torch	0.30	0.30	0.90	1.50

	ORIG.	GOOD	FINE	N-MINT
☐ 22 Thor & Torch	0.30	0.30	0.90	1.50
☐ 23 Thor, Torch	0.30	0.30	0.90	1.50
☐ 24 SB, Black Goliath	0.30	0.30	0.90	1.50
☐ 25 Iron Fist	0.30	0.30	0.90	1.50
☐ 26 Nick Fury	0.30	0.30	0.90	1.50
☐ 27 Deathlok	0.30	0.80	2.40	4.00
☐ 28 Sub-Mariner	0.30	0.30	0.90	1.50
☐ 29 Shang-Chi	0.30	0.30	0.90	1.50
☐ 30 JB, Spider-Woman	0.30	0.30	0.90	1.50
☐ 31 Spider-Woman	0.30	0.30	0.90	1.50
☐ 32 Invisible Girl	0.30	0.30	0.90	1.50
☐ 33 Mordred	0.35	0.30	0.90	1.50
☐ 34 Nighthawk	0.35	0.25	0.75	1.25
☐ 35 Skull the Slayer	0.35	0.25	0.75	1.25
☐ 36 Mr. Fantastic	0.35	0.25	0.75	1.25
☐ 37 Matt Murdock	0.35	0.25	0.75	1.25
☐ 38 Daredevil	0.35	0.25	0.75	1.25
☐ 39 Vision, A:Daredevil	0.35	0.25	0.75	1.25
☐ 40 Black Panther	0.35	0.25	0.75	1.25
☐ 41 Brother Voodoo	0.35	0.25	0.75	1.25
☐ 42 Capt. America	0.35	0.25	0.75	1.25
☐ 43 JBy, Man-Thing	0.35	0.70	2.10	3.50
☐ 44 GD, Hercules	0.35	0.20	0.60	1.00
☐ 45 GD, Capt. Marvel	0.35	0.20	0.60	1.00
☐ 46 Hulk	0.35	0.20	0.60	1.00
☐ 47 GD, Yancy Street Gang	0.35	0.20	0.60	1.00
☐ 48 Jack of Hearts	0.35	0.25	0.75	1.25
☐ 49 GD, Dr. Strange	0.35	0.20	0.60	1.00
☐ 50 JBy/JS, 2 Things	0.35	0.80	2.40	4.00
☐ 51 FM/BMc, Beast	0.40	1.00	3.00	5.00
☐ 52 Moon Knight	0.40	0.50	1.50	2.50
☐ 53 JBy/JS, Quasar	0.40	0.60	1.80	3.00
☐ 54 JBy/JS, Deathlok	0.40	2.80	8.40	14.00
☐ 55 JBy/JS, Giant Man	0.40	0.60	1.80	3.00
☐ 56 GP/GD, Thundar	0.40	0.20	0.60	1.00
☐ 57 GP/GD, Wundarr	0.40	0.20	0.60	1.00
☐ 58 GP/GD, Aquarian	0.40	0.20	0.60	1.00
☐ 59 Torch	0.40	0.20	0.60	1.00
☐ 60 GP/GD, Impossible Man	0.40	0.20	0.60	1.00
☐ 61 GD, Starhawk	0.40	0.25	0.75	1.25
☐ 62 GD, Moondragon	0.40	0.25	0.75	1.25
☐ 63 GD, Warlock	0.40	0.25	0.75	1.25
☐ 64 GP/GD, Stingray	0.40	0.20	0.60	1.00
☐ 65 GP/GD, Triton	0.40	0.20	0.60	1.00
☐ 66 GD, Scarlet Witch	0.40	0.20	0.60	1.00
☐ 67 Hyperion	0.50	0.20	0.60	1.00
☐ 68 Angel	0.50	0.20	0.60	1.00
☐ 69 Guardians of Galaxy	0.50	0.60	1.80	3.00
☐ 70 Inhumans	0.50	0.20	0.60	1.00
☐ 71 Mr. Fantastic	0.50	0.20	0.60	1.00
☐ 72 Stingray	0.50	0.20	0.60	1.00
☐ 73 Quasar	0.50	0.20	0.60	1.00
☐ 74 Puppet Master	0.50	0.20	0.60	1.00

	ORIG.	GOOD	FINE	N-MINT
☐ 75 Avengers	0.50	0.20	0.60	1.00
☐ 76 Iceman	0.50	0.20	0.60	1.00
☐ 77 Man-Thing	0.50	0.20	0.60	1.00
☐ 78 Wonder Man	0.50	0.20	0.60	1.00
☐ 79 Blue Diamond	0.50	0.20	0.60	1.00
☐ 80 Ghost Rider	0.50	1.00	3.00	5.00
☐ 81 Sub-Mariner	0.50	0.20	0.60	1.00
☐ 82 Capt. America	0.50	0.20	0.60	1.00
☐ 83 Sasquatch	0.60	0.60	1.80	3.00
☐ 84 Alpha Flight	0.60	0.60	1.80	3.00
☐ 85 Giant-Man	0.60	0.20	0.60	1.00
☐ 86 Sandman	0.60	0.20	0.60	1.00
☐ 87 Ant-Man	0.60	0.20	0.60	1.00
☐ 88 She-Hulk	0.60	0.20	0.60	1.00
☐ 89 Torch	0.60	0.20	0.60	1.00
☐ 90 Spider-Man	0.60	0.20	0.60	1.00
☐ 91 Ghost Rider	0.60	0.80	2.40	4.00
☐ 92 Jocasta	0.60	0.20	0.60	1.00
☐ 93 D:Jocasta	0.60	0.20	0.60	1.00
☐ 94 Power Man	0.60	0.20	0.60	1.00
☐ 95 Living Mummy	0.60	0.20	0.60	1.00
☐ 96	0.60	0.20	0.60	1.00
☐ 97 Iron Man	0.60	0.20	0.60	1.00
☐ 98	0.60	0.20	0.60	1.00
☐ 99	0.60	0.20	0.60	1.00
☐ 100 Ben Grimm, JBy script	1.00	0.30	0.90	1.50

MARVEL TWO-IN-ONE ANNUAL

	ORIG.	GOOD	FINE	N-MINT
☐ 1	0.50	0.40	1.20	2.00
☐ 2 JSn D:Thanos	0.60	1.00	3.00	5.00
☐ 3	0.60	0.30	0.90	1.50
☐ 4	0.60	0.30	0.90	1.50
☐ 5	0.75	0.30	0.90	1.50
☐ 6	0.75	0.30	0.90	1.50
☐ 7	1.00	0.30	0.90	1.50

MARVEL YEAR IN REVIEW

	ORIG.	GOOD	FINE	N-MINT
☐ 1 TMc(c) (1989)	3.95	0.79	2.37	3.95
☐ 2 1990	3.95	0.79	2.37	3.95
☐ 3 1991	3.95	0.79	2.37	3.95
☐ 4 1992		0.79	2.37	3.95

MARVEL'S GREATEST COMICS

	ORIG.	GOOD	FINE	N-MINT
☐ 23 reprints	0.25	0.20	0.60	1.00
☐ 24 reprints	0.25	0.20	0.60	1.00
☐ 25 reprints	0.25	0.20	0.60	1.00
☐ 26 reprints	0.25	0.20	0.60	1.00
☐ 27 reprints	0.25	0.20	0.60	1.00
☐ 28 reprints	0.25	0.20	0.60	1.00
☐ 29 reprints	0.25	0.20	0.60	1.00
☐ 30 reprints	0.25	0.20	0.60	1.00
☐ 31 reprints	0.25	0.20	0.60	1.00
☐ 32 reprints	0.25	0.20	0.60	1.00
☐ 33 reprints	0.25	0.20	0.60	1.00
☐ 34 reprints	0.25	0.20	0.60	1.00
☐ 35 reprints	0.20	0.20	0.60	1.00

	ORIG.	GOOD	FINE	N-MINT
❏ 36 reprints	0.20	0.20	0.60	1.00
❏ 37 reprints	0.20	0.20	0.60	1.00
❏ 38 reprints	0.20	0.20	0.60	1.00
❏ 39 reprints	0.20	0.20	0.60	1.00
❏ 40 reprints	0.20	0.20	0.60	1.00
❏ 41 reprints	0.20	0.20	0.60	1.00
❏ 42 reprints	0.20	0.20	0.60	1.00
❏ 43 reprints	0.20	0.20	0.60	1.00
❏ 44 reprints	0.20	0.20	0.60	1.00
❏ 45 reprints	0.20	0.20	0.60	1.00
❏ 46 reprints	0.20	0.20	0.60	1.00
❏ 47 reprints	0.20	0.20	0.60	1.00
❏ 48 reprints	0.20	0.20	0.60	1.00
❏ 49 reprints	0.25	0.20	0.60	1.00
❏ 50 reprints	0.25	0.20	0.60	1.00
❏ 51 reprints	0.25	0.20	0.60	1.00
❏ 52 reprints	0.25	0.20	0.60	1.00
❏ 53 reprints	0.25	0.20	0.60	1.00
❏ 54 reprints	0.25	0.20	0.60	1.00
❏ 55 reprints	0.25	0.20	0.60	1.00
❏ 56 reprints	0.25	0.20	0.60	1.00
❏ 57 reprints	0.25	0.20	0.60	1.00
❏ 58 reprints	0.25	0.20	0.60	1.00
❏ 59 reprints	0.25	0.20	0.60	1.00
❏ 60 reprints	0.25	0.20	0.60	1.00
❏ 61 reprints	0.25	0.20	0.60	1.00
❏ 62 reprints	0.25	0.20	0.60	1.00
❏ 63 reprints	0.25	0.20	0.60	1.00
❏ 64 reprints	0.25	0.20	0.60	1.00
❏ 65 reprints	0.30	0.20	0.60	1.00
❏ 66 reprints	0.30	0.20	0.60	1.00
❏ 67 reprints	0.30	0.20	0.60	1.00
❏ 68 reprints	0.30	0.20	0.60	1.00
❏ 69 reprints	0.30	0.20	0.60	1.00
❏ 70 reprints	0.30	0.20	0.60	1.00
❏ 71 reprints	0.30	0.20	0.60	1.00
❏ 72 reprints	0.30	0.20	0.60	1.00
❏ 73 reprints	0.30	0.20	0.60	1.00
❏ 74 reprints	0.35	0.20	0.60	1.00
❏ 75 reprints	0.35	0.20	0.60	1.00
❏ 76 reprints	0.35	0.20	0.60	1.00
❏ 77 reprints	0.35	0.20	0.60	1.00
❏ 78 reprints	0.35	0.20	0.60	1.00
❏ 79 reprints	0.35	0.20	0.60	1.00
❏ 80	0.35	0.20	0.60	1.00
❏ 81	0.35	0.20	0.60	1.00
❏ 82	0.35	0.20	0.60	1.00
❏ 83	0.35	0.20	0.60	1.00
❏ 84	0.35	0.20	0.60	1.00
❏ 85	0.35	0.20	0.60	1.00
❏ 86	0.35	0.20	0.60	1.00
❏ 87	0.35	0.20	0.60	1.00
❏ 88	0.40	0.20	0.60	1.00
❏ 89	0.40	0.20	0.60	1.00
❏ 90	0.40	0.20	0.60	1.00

	ORIG.	GOOD	FINE	N-MINT
❏ 91	0.40	0.20	0.60	1.00
❏ 92	0.40	0.20	0.60	1.00
❏ 93	0.40	0.20	0.60	1.00
❏ 94	0.40	0.20	0.60	1.00
❏ 95	0.40	0.20	0.60	1.00
❏ 96	0.40	0.20	0.60	1.00

MASTER OF KUNG FU
(was Special Marvel Edition)

	ORIG.	GOOD	FINE	N-MINT
❏ 17 JSn, I:Black Jack Tarr	0.20	3.00	9.00	15.00
❏ 18 PG	0.25	2.00	6.00	10.00
❏ 19 PG	0.25	2.00	6.00	10.00
❏ 20 PG	0.25	2.00	6.00	10.00
❏ 21	0.25	1.00	3.00	5.00
❏ 22 PG	0.25	1.00	3.00	5.00
❏ 23	0.25	1.00	3.00	5.00
❏ 24 JSn/WS	0.25	1.00	3.00	5.00
❏ 25 PG	0.25	1.00	3.00	5.00
❏ 26	0.25	1.00	3.00	5.00
❏ 27	0.25	1.00	3.00	5.00
❏ 28	0.25	1.00	3.00	5.00
❏ 29 PG	0.25	1.00	3.00	5.00
❏ 30 PG	0.25	1.00	3.00	5.00
❏ 31 PG	0.25	1.00	3.00	5.00
❏ 32	0.25	0.60	1.80	3.00
❏ 33 PG	0.25	0.60	1.80	3.00
❏ 34 PG	0.25	0.60	1.80	3.00
❏ 35 PG	0.25	0.60	1.80	3.00
❏ 36	0.25	0.40	1.20	2.00
❏ 37	0.25	0.40	1.20	2.00
❏ 38 PG	0.25	0.40	1.20	2.00
❏ 39 PG	0.25	0.40	1.20	2.00
❏ 40 PG	0.25	0.40	1.20	2.00
❏ 41	0.25	0.40	1.20	2.00
❏ 42 PG	0.25	0.40	1.20	2.00
❏ 43 PG	0.25	0.40	1.20	2.00
❏ 44 PG	0.30	0.40	1.20	2.00
❏ 45 PG	0.30	0.40	1.20	2.00
❏ 46 PG	0.30	0.40	1.20	2.00
❏ 47 PG	0.30	0.40	1.20	2.00
❏ 48 PG	0.30	0.40	1.20	2.00
❏ 49 PG	0.30	0.40	1.20	2.00
❏ 50 PG	0.30	0.40	1.20	2.00
❏ 51 PG	0.30	0.40	1.20	2.00
❏ 52	0.30	0.20	0.60	1.00
❏ 53	0.30	0.20	0.60	1.00
❏ 54	0.30	0.20	0.60	1.00
❏ 55	0.30	0.20	0.60	1.00
❏ 56	0.30	0.20	0.60	1.00
❏ 57	0.30	0.20	0.60	1.00
❏ 58	0.35	0.20	0.60	1.00
❏ 59	0.35	0.20	0.60	1.00
❏ 60	0.35	0.20	0.60	1.00
❏ 61	0.35	0.20	0.60	1.00
❏ 62	0.35	0.20	0.60	1.00

	ORIG.	GOOD	FINE	N-MINT
63	0.35	0.20	0.60	1.00
64	0.35	0.20	0.60	1.00
65	0.35	0.20	0.60	1.00
66	0.35	0.20	0.60	1.00
67	0.35	0.20	0.60	1.00
68	0.35	0.20	0.60	1.00
69	0.35	0.20	0.60	1.00
70	0.35	0.20	0.60	1.00
71	0.35	0.20	0.60	1.00
72	0.35	0.20	0.60	1.00
73	0.35	0.20	0.60	1.00
74	0.35	0.20	0.60	1.00
75	0.35	0.20	0.60	1.00
76	0.40	0.20	0.60	1.00
77	0.40	0.20	0.60	1.00
78	0.40	0.20	0.60	1.00
79	0.40	0.20	0.60	1.00
80	0.40	0.20	0.60	1.00
81	0.40	0.20	0.60	1.00
82	0.40	0.20	0.60	1.00
83	0.40	0.20	0.60	1.00
84	0.40	0.20	0.60	1.00
85	0.40	0.20	0.60	1.00
86	0.40	0.20	0.60	1.00
87	0.40	0.20	0.60	1.00
88	0.40	0.20	0.60	1.00
89	0.40	0.20	0.60	1.00
90	0.40	0.20	0.60	1.00
91 GD	0.40	0.40	1.20	2.00
92 GD	0.50	0.40	1.20	2.00
93 GD	0.50	0.40	1.20	2.00
94 GD	0.50	0.40	1.20	2.00
95 GD	0.50	0.40	1.20	2.00
96 GD	0.50	0.40	1.20	2.00
97 GD	0.50	0.40	1.20	2.00
98 GD	0.50	0.40	1.20	2.00
99 GD	0.50	0.40	1.20	2.00
100 GD	0.75	0.40	1.20	2.00
101 GD	0.50	0.40	1.20	2.00
102 GD, 1:Day pencils	0.50	0.40	1.20	2.00
103 GD	0.50	0.40	1.20	2.00
104	0.50	0.40	1.20	2.00
105	0.50	0.40	1.20	2.00
106 GD, C:Velcro	0.50	0.40	1.20	2.00
107 GD, A:Sata	0.50	0.40	1.20	2.00
108 GD	0.60	0.40	1.20	2.00
109 GD	0.60	0.40	1.20	2.00
110 GD	0.60	0.40	1.20	2.00
111 GD	0.60	0.40	1.20	2.00
112 GD	0.60	0.40	1.20	2.00
113 GD	0.60	0.40	1.20	2.00
114	0.60	0.40	1.20	2.00
115 GD	0.60	0.40	1.20	2.00
116 GD	0.60	0.40	1.20	2.00
117 GD	0.60	0.40	1.20	2.00

	ORIG.	GOOD	FINE	N-MINT
118 GD, double size	1.00	0.40	1.20	2.00
119 GD	0.60	0.40	1.20	2.00
120 GD	0.60	0.40	1.20	2.00
121	0.60	0.40	1.20	2.00
122	0.60	0.40	1.20	2.00
123	0.60	0.40	1.20	2.00
124	0.60	0.40	1.20	2.00
125	1.00	0.40	1.20	2.00

MASTER OF KUNG FU ANNUAL

	ORIG.	GOOD	FINE	N-MINT
1 (1976)	0.50	0.80	2.40	4.00

MASTER OF KUNG FU: BLEEDING BLACK

	ORIG.	GOOD	FINE	N-MINT
1	2.95	0.59	1.77	2.95

MEPHISTO VS. ...

	ORIG.	GOOD	FINE	N-MINT
1 JB, Fantastic Four	1.50	0.30	0.90	1.50
2 JB, X-Factor	1.50	0.30	0.90	1.50
3 JB, X-Men	1.50	0.30	0.90	1.50
4 JB, Avengers	1.50	0.30	0.90	1.50

METEOR MAN

	ORIG.	GOOD	FINE	N-MINT
1 movie adaptation	2.25	0.45	1.35	2.25

METEOR MAN (series)

	ORIG.	GOOD	FINE	N-MINT
1	1.25	0.25	0.75	1.25
2	1.25	0.25	0.75	1.25

MICRONAUTS

	ORIG.	GOOD	FINE	N-MINT
1 MG, O:	0.35	0.40	1.20	2.00
2 MG	0.35	0.30	0.90	1.50
3 MG	0.35	0.30	0.90	1.50
4 MG	0.35	0.30	0.90	1.50
5 MG	0.40	0.30	0.90	1.50
6 MG	0.40	0.30	0.90	1.50
7 MG	0.40	0.30	0.90	1.50
8 MG	0.40	0.30	0.90	1.50
9 MG	0.40	0.30	0.90	1.50
10 MG	0.40	0.30	0.90	1.50
11 MG	0.40	0.30	0.90	1.50
12 MG	0.40	0.30	0.90	1.50
13	0.40	0.25	0.75	1.25
14	0.40	0.25	0.75	1.25
15	0.40	0.25	0.75	1.25
16	0.40	0.25	0.75	1.25
17	0.40	0.25	0.75	1.25
18	0.40	0.25	0.75	1.25
19	0.40	0.25	0.75	1.25
20	0.40	0.25	0.75	1.25
21	0.50	0.25	0.75	1.25
22	0.50	0.25	0.75	1.25
23	0.50	0.25	0.75	1.25
24	0.50	0.25	0.75	1.25
25	0.50	0.25	0.75	1.25
26 PB	0.50	0.25	0.75	1.25
27 PB	0.50	0.25	0.75	1.25
28 PB	0.50	0.25	0.75	1.25
29 PB	0.50	0.25	0.75	1.25
30 PB	0.50	0.25	0.75	1.25
31 PB Dr. Strange	0.50	0.20	0.60	1.00

	ORIG.	GOOD	FINE	N-MINT
❏ 32 PB Dr. Strange	0.50	0.20	0.60	1.00
❏ 33 PB Dr. Strange	0.50	0.20	0.60	1.00
❏ 34 PB Dr. Strange	0.50	0.20	0.60	1.00
❏ 35	0.75	0.40	1.20	2.00
❏ 36	0.50	0.40	1.20	2.00
❏ 37 X-Men	0.60	0.60	1.80	3.00
❏ 38 direct sale	0.75	0.60	1.80	3.00
❏ 39	0.75	0.35	1.05	1.75
❏ 40	0.75	0.35	1.05	1.75
❏ 41	0.75	0.20	0.60	1.00
❏ 42	0.75	0.20	0.60	1.00
❏ 43	0.75	0.20	0.60	1.00
❏ 44	0.75	0.20	0.60	1.00
❏ 45	0.75	0.20	0.60	1.00
❏ 46	0.75	0.20	0.60	1.00
❏ 47	0.75	0.20	0.60	1.00
❏ 48 BG, 1st Guice	0.75	0.40	1.20	2.00
❏ 49	0.75	0.20	0.60	1.00
❏ 50	0.75	0.20	0.60	1.00
❏ 51	0.75	0.20	0.60	1.00
❏ 52	0.75	0.20	0.60	1.00
❏ 53	0.75	0.20	0.60	1.00
❏ 54	0.75	0.20	0.60	1.00
❏ 55	0.75	0.20	0.60	1.00
❏ 56	0.75	0.20	0.60	1.00
❏ 57	1.00	0.20	0.60	1.00
❏ 58	0.75	0.20	0.60	1.00
❏ 59	0.75	0.20	0.60	1.00

MICRONAUTS (2nd Series)

	ORIG.	GOOD	FINE	N-MINT
❏ 1 Makers	0.60	0.30	0.90	1.50
❏ 2	0.60	0.20	0.60	1.00
❏ 3	0.60	0.20	0.60	1.00
❏ 4	0.60	0.20	0.60	1.00
❏ 5	0.60	0.20	0.60	1.00
❏ 6	0.60	0.20	0.60	1.00
❏ 7	0.65	0.20	0.60	1.00
❏ 8	0.65	0.20	0.60	1.00
❏ 9	0.65	0.20	0.60	1.00
❏ 10	0.65	0.20	0.60	1.00
❏ 11	0.65	0.20	0.60	1.00
❏ 12	0.65	0.20	0.60	1.00
❏ 13	0.65	0.20	0.60	1.00
❏ 14	0.65	0.20	0.60	1.00
❏ 15	0.65	0.20	0.60	1.00
❏ 16 Secret Wars II	0.65	0.20	0.60	1.00
❏ 17	0.75	0.20	0.60	1.00
❏ 18	0.75	0.20	0.60	1.00
❏ 19	0.75	0.20	0.60	1.00
❏ 20	0.75	0.20	0.60	1.00

MICRONAUTS ANNUAL

	ORIG.	GOOD	FINE	N-MINT
❏ 1 SD	0.75	0.40	1.20	2.00
❏ 2 SD	0.75	0.30	0.90	1.50

MICRONAUTS SPECIAL EDITION

	ORIG.	GOOD	FINE	N-MINT
❏ 1	2.00	0.40	1.20	2.00

	ORIG.	GOOD	FINE	N-MINT
❏ 2	2.00	0.40	1.20	2.00
❏ 3	2.00	0.40	1.20	2.00
❏ 4	2.00	0.40	1.20	2.00
❏ 5	2.00	0.40	1.20	2.00

MIDNIGHT SONS UNLIMITED

	ORIG.	GOOD	FINE	N-MINT
❏ 1	3.95	0.79	2.37	3.95
❏ 2	3.95	0.79	2.37	3.95

MIGHTY MARVEL WESTERN, THE

	ORIG.	GOOD	FINE	N-MINT
❏ 1	0.25	0.60	1.80	3.00
❏ 2	0.25	0.40	1.20	2.00
❏ 3	0.25	0.40	1.20	2.00
❏ 4	0.25	0.40	1.20	2.00
❏ 5	0.25	0.40	1.20	2.00
❏ 6	0.25	0.30	0.90	1.50
❏ 7	0.25	0.30	0.90	1.50
❏ 8	0.25	0.30	0.90	1.50
❏ 9	0.25	0.30	0.90	1.50
❏ 10	0.25	0.30	0.90	1.50
❏ 11	0.25	0.30	0.90	1.50
❏ 12	0.25	0.30	0.90	1.50
❏ 13	0.25	0.30	0.90	1.50
❏ 14	0.25	0.30	0.90	1.50
❏ 15	0.25	0.30	0.90	1.50
❏ 16	0.25	0.30	0.90	1.50
❏ 17	0.20	0.30	0.90	1.50
❏ 18	0.20	0.30	0.90	1.50
❏ 19	0.20	0.30	0.90	1.50
❏ 20	0.20	0.30	0.90	1.50
❏ 21	0.20	0.20	0.60	1.00
❏ 22	0.20	0.20	0.60	1.00
❏ 23	0.20	0.20	0.60	1.00
❏ 24	0.20	0.20	0.60	1.00
❏ 25	0.20	0.20	0.60	1.00
❏ 26	0.20	0.20	0.60	1.00
❏ 27	0.20	0.20	0.60	1.00
❏ 28	0.20	0.20	0.60	1.00
❏ 29	0.20	0.20	0.60	1.00
❏ 30	0.20	0.20	0.60	1.00
❏ 31	0.20	0.20	0.60	1.00
❏ 32	0.20	0.20	0.60	1.00
❏ 33	0.20	0.20	0.60	1.00
❏ 34	0.25	0.20	0.60	1.00
❏ 35	0.25	0.20	0.60	1.00
❏ 36	0.25	0.20	0.60	1.00
❏ 37	0.25	0.20	0.60	1.00
❏ 38	0.25	0.20	0.60	1.00
❏ 39	0.25	0.20	0.60	1.00
❏ 40	0.25	0.20	0.60	1.00
❏ 41	0.25	0.20	0.60	1.00
❏ 42	0.25	0.20	0.60	1.00
❏ 43	0.25	0.20	0.60	1.00
❏ 44	0.25	0.20	0.60	1.00
❏ 45	0.25	0.20	0.60	1.00
❏ 46	0.25	0.20	0.60	1.00

	ORIG.	GOOD	FINE	N-MINT
MIGHTY MOUSE				
1 Batman parody	1.00	0.20	0.60	1.00
2	1.00	0.20	0.60	1.00
3 Bat-Bat, Sub-Mariner parody				
	1.00	0.20	0.60	1.00
4 GP(c), Crisis parody	1.00	0.20	0.60	1.00
5 Crisis parody	1.00	0.20	0.60	1.00
6 McFarlane parody	1.00	0.20	0.60	1.00
7 computer art	1.00	0.20	0.60	1.00
8	1.00	0.20	0.60	1.00
9	1.00	0.20	0.60	1.00
10 Letterman parody	1.00	0.20	0.60	1.00
MIGHTY THOR ANNUAL, THE (was Thor Annual)				
14 (1989)	2.00	0.60	1.80	3.00
15 (1990)	2.00	0.50	1.50	2.50
16 (1991)		0.50	1.50	2.50
17 (1992)	2.25	0.50	1.50	2.50
18 (1993) card	2.95	0.59	1.77	2.95
MIGHTY THOR, THE (formerly Thor)				
411	1.00	0.20	0.60	1.00
412	1.00	0.20	0.60	1.00
413	1.00	0.20	0.60	1.00
414	1.00	0.20	0.60	1.00
412 Vengeance, New Warriors				
	1.00	4.40	13.20	22.00
413	1.00	0.20	0.60	1.00
414	1.00	0.20	0.60	1.00
415 O:Thor revised	1.00	0.20	0.60	1.00
416	1.00	0.20	0.60	1.00
417	1.00	0.20	0.60	1.00
418	1.00	0.20	0.60	1.00
419 Black Galaxy	1.00	0.20	0.60	1.00
420 Black Galaxy	1.00	0.20	0.60	1.00
421 Black Galaxy	1.00	0.20	0.60	1.00
422 Black Galaxy	1.00	0.20	0.60	1.00
423 Black Galaxy	1.00	0.20	0.60	1.00
424 Black Galaxy	1.00	0.20	0.60	1.00
425	1.00	0.20	0.60	1.00
426	1.00	0.20	0.60	1.00
427 Excalibur	1.00	0.20	0.60	1.00
428 Excalibur	1.00	0.20	0.60	1.00
429 Ghost Rider	1.00	0.80	2.40	4.00
430 Ghost Rider	1.00	0.60	1.80	3.00
431	1.00	0.20	0.60	1.00
432 JK, D:Loki, 1:new Thor, reprint O:Thor				
	1.00	0.30	0.90	1.50
433	1.00	0.20	0.60	1.00
434	1.00	0.20	0.60	1.00
435	1.00	0.20	0.60	1.00
436	1.00	0.20	0.60	1.00
437	1.00	0.20	0.60	1.00
438	1.00	0.20	0.60	1.00
439	1.00	0.20	0.60	1.00
440	1.00	0.20	0.60	1.00

	ORIG.	GOOD	FINE	N-MINT
441	1.00	0.20	0.60	1.00
442	1.00	0.20	0.60	1.00
443	1.00	0.20	0.60	1.00
444	1.25	0.25	0.75	1.25
445 Galactic Storm	1.25	0.25	0.75	1.25
446 Galactic Storm	1.25	0.25	0.75	1.25
447	1.25	0.25	0.75	1.25
448 Spider-Man	1.25	0.25	0.75	1.25
449	1.25	0.25	0.75	1.25
450 reprints origin of Loki				
	2.50	0.50	1.50	2.50
451	1.25	0.25	0.75	1.25
452	1.25	0.25	0.75	1.25
453	1.25	0.25	0.75	1.25
454	1.25	0.25	0.75	1.25
455	1.25	0.25	0.75	1.25
456	1.25	0.25	0.75	1.25
457	1.25	0.25	0.75	1.25
458	1.25	0.25	0.75	1.25
459	1.25	0.25	0.75	1.25
460	1.25	0.25	0.75	1.25
461	1.25	0.25	0.75	1.25
462	1.25	0.25	0.75	1.25
463	1.25	0.25	0.75	1.25
464	1.25	0.25	0.75	1.25
465	1.25	0.25	0.75	1.25
466	1.25	0.25	0.75	1.25
MONSTER MADNESS (b&w mag; not comics)				
1	0.60	0.12	0.36	0.60
2	0.60	0.12	0.36	0.60
3	0.60	0.12	0.36	0.60
MONSTERS OF THE MOVIES **(b&w mag; not comics)**				
1	1.00	0.20	0.60	1.00
2	1.00	0.20	0.60	1.00
3	1.00	0.20	0.60	1.00
4	1.00	0.20	0.60	1.00
5	1.00	0.20	0.60	1.00
6	1.00	0.20	0.60	1.00
7	1.00	0.20	0.60	1.00
8	1.00	0.20	0.60	1.00
MONSTERS OF THE MOVIES ANNUAL				
1	1.25	0.25	0.75	1.25
MONSTERS ON THE PROWL **(was Chamber of Darkness)**				
9 reprint	0.15	0.25	0.75	1.25
10 reprint	0.15	0.25	0.75	1.25
11 reprint	0.15	0.25	0.75	1.25
12 reprint	0.15	0.25	0.75	1.25
13 reprint	0.25	0.25	0.75	1.25
14 reprint	0.25	0.25	0.75	1.25
15 reprint	0.20	0.25	0.75	1.25
16 King Kull	0.20	0.25	0.75	1.25
17 reprints	0.20	0.25	0.75	1.25
18 reprints	0.20	0.25	0.75	1.25

	ORIG.	GOOD	FINE	N-MINT
19 reprints	0.20	0.25	0.75	1.25
20 reprints	0.20	0.25	0.75	1.25
21 reprints	0.20	0.25	0.75	1.25
22 reprints	0.20	0.25	0.75	1.25
23 reprints	0.20	0.25	0.75	1.25
24 reprints	0.20	0.25	0.75	1.25
25 reprints	0.20	0.25	0.75	1.25
26 reprints	0.20	0.25	0.75	1.25
27 reprints	0.20	0.25	0.75	1.25
28 reprints	0.25	0.25	0.75	1.25
29 reprints	0.25	0.25	0.75	1.25
30 reprints	0.25	0.25	0.75	1.25

MONSTERS TO LAUGH WITH
(b&w mag; not comics)

	ORIG.	GOOD	FINE	N-MINT
1	0.25	4.00	12.00	20.00
2	0.25	2.40	7.20	12.00
3 (becomes Monsters Unlimited)	0.25	2.40	7.20	12.00

MONSTERS UNLEASHED (b&w mag)

	ORIG.	GOOD	FINE	N-MINT
1	0.75	0.15	0.45	0.75
2 Frankenstein	0.75	0.15	0.45	0.75
3 Frankenstein, Man-Thing, Son of Satan	0.75	0.15	0.45	0.75
4 Frankenstein	0.75	0.15	0.45	0.75
5 Frankenstein, Man-Thing	0.75	0.15	0.45	0.75
6 Frankenstein, Werewolf	0.75	0.15	0.45	0.75
7 Frankenstein, Werewolf	0.75	0.15	0.45	0.75
8 Frankenstein, Man-Thing	0.75	0.15	0.45	0.75
9 Frankenstein, Man-Thing, Wendigo	0.75	0.15	0.45	0.75
10 Frankenstein, Tigra	0.75	0.15	0.45	0.75
11 Gabriel	0.75	0.15	0.45	0.75

MONSTERS UNLEASHED ANNUAL

	ORIG.	GOOD	FINE	N-MINT
1 reprints	1.25	0.25	0.75	1.25

MONSTERS UNLIMITED (b&w mag; not comics)

	ORIG.	GOOD	FINE	N-MINT
4 (was Monsters to Laugh with)	0.25	1.60	4.80	8.00
5	0.25	1.60	4.80	8.00
6	0.25	1.60	4.80	8.00
7	0.25	1.60	4.80	8.00

MOON KNIGHT
(also see Marc Spector, Moon Knight)

	ORIG.	GOOD	FINE	N-MINT
1 BSz, O:Moon Knight	0.50	0.90	2.70	4.50
2 BSz	0.50	0.40	1.20	2.00
3 BSz	0.50	0.40	1.20	2.00
4 BSz	0.50	0.40	1.20	2.00
5 BSz	0.50	0.40	1.20	2.00
6 BSz	0.50	0.40	1.20	2.00
7 BSz	0.50	0.40	1.20	2.00
8 BSz, V:Moon Kings	0.50	0.45	1.35	2.25
9 BSz, V:Midnight Man	0.50	0.30	0.90	1.50
10 BSz, V:Midnight Man	0.50	0.30	0.90	1.50

	ORIG.	GOOD	FINE	N-MINT
11 BSz, V:Creed	0.50	0.45	1.35	2.25
12 BSz	0.50	0.25	0.75	1.25
13 BSz	0.50	0.25	0.75	1.25
14 BSz	0.75	0.25	0.75	1.25
15 FM (c)/BSz, direct	0.75	0.70	2.10	3.50
16 V:Blacksmith	0.75	0.40	1.20	2.00
17 BSz	0.75	0.30	0.90	1.50
18 BSz, V:Slayers Elite	0.75	0.40	1.20	2.00
19 BSz, V:Arsenal	0.75	0.30	0.90	1.50
20 BSz, V:Arsenal	0.75	0.30	0.90	1.50
21	0.75	0.25	0.75	1.25
22	0.75	0.25	0.75	1.25
23	0.75	0.25	0.75	1.25
24	0.75	0.25	0.75	1.25
25 BSz	1.00	0.40	1.20	2.00
26	0.75	0.20	0.60	1.00
27	0.75	0.20	0.60	1.00
28	0.75	0.20	0.60	1.00
29	0.75	0.20	0.60	1.00
30	0.75	0.20	0.60	1.00
31	0.75	0.20	0.60	1.00
32	0.75	0.20	0.60	1.00
33	0.75	0.20	0.60	1.00
34	0.75	0.20	0.60	1.00
35 KN, X-Men	1.00	0.35	1.05	1.75
36	0.75	0.20	0.60	1.00
37	0.75	0.20	0.60	1.00
38	0.75	0.20	0.60	1.00

MOON KNIGHT (Second Series, 1985)

	ORIG.	GOOD	FINE	N-MINT
1	1.25	0.35	1.05	1.75
2	0.65	0.20	0.60	1.00
3	0.65	0.20	0.60	1.00
4	0.65	0.20	0.60	1.00
5	0.65	0.20	0.60	1.00
6	0.65	0.20	0.60	1.00

MOON KNIGHT SPECIAL

	ORIG.	GOOD	FINE	N-MINT
1 Shang-Chi	2.50	0.50	1.50	2.50

MOON KNIGHT SPECIAL EDITION

	ORIG.	GOOD	FINE	N-MINT
1 BSz, reprints	2.00	0.40	1.20	2.00
2 BSz, reprints	2.00	0.40	1.20	2.00
3 BSz, reprints	2.00	0.40	1.20	2.00

MORBIUS REVISITED

	ORIG.	GOOD	FINE	N-MINT
1 reprint	1.95	0.39	1.17	1.95
2 reprint	1.95	0.39	1.17	1.95
3 reprint	1.95	0.39	1.17	1.95

MORBIUS: THE LIVING VAMPIRE

	ORIG.	GOOD	FINE	N-MINT
1 poster	2.75	0.80	2.40	4.00
2	1.75	0.40	1.20	2.00
3	1.75	0.35	1.05	1.75
4 Spider-Man	1.75	0.35	1.05	1.75
5	1.75	0.35	1.05	1.75
6	1.75	0.35	1.05	1.75
7	1.75	0.35	1.05	1.75
8	1.75	0.35	1.05	1.75

	ORIG.	GOOD	FINE	N-MINT
9	1.75	0.35	1.05	1.75
10	1.75	0.35	1.05	1.75
11	1.75	0.35	1.05	1.75
12	2.95	0.59	1.77	2.95
12 black cover	2.25	0.45	1.35	2.25
13	1.75	0.35	1.05	1.75
14	1.75	0.35	1.05	1.75

MORTIGAN GOTH: IMMORTALIS

	ORIG.	GOOD	FINE	N-MINT
1 foil cover	2.95	0.59	1.77	2.95

MOTHER TERESA OF CALCUTTA

	ORIG.	GOOD	FINE	N-MINT
1	1.25	0.25	0.75	1.25

MOTORMOUTH

	ORIG.	GOOD	FINE	N-MINT
1	1.75	0.60	1.80	3.00
2	1.75	0.40	1.20	2.00
3 Punisher	1.75	0.35	1.05	1.75
4	1.75	0.35	1.05	1.75
5 (becomes Motormouth & Killpower)	1.75	0.35	1.05	1.75

MOTORMOUTH & KILLPOWER
(was Motormouth)

	ORIG.	GOOD	FINE	N-MINT
6	1.75	0.35	1.05	1.75
7	1.75	0.35	1.05	1.75
8	1.75	0.35	1.05	1.75
9	1.75	0.35	1.05	1.75
10	1.75	0.35	1.05	1.75
11	1.75	0.35	1.05	1.75
12	1.75	0.35	1.05	1.75

MS. MARVEL

	ORIG.	GOOD	FINE	N-MINT
1	0.30	1.00	3.00	5.00
2	0.30	0.70	2.10	3.50
3	0.30	0.50	1.50	2.50
4	0.30	0.50	1.50	2.50
5	0.30	0.60	1.80	3.00
6	0.30	0.30	0.90	1.50
7	0.30	0.30	0.90	1.50
8	0.30	0.30	0.90	1.50
9	0.30	0.30	0.90	1.50
10	0.30	0.30	0.90	1.50
11	0.35	0.30	0.90	1.50
12	0.35	0.30	0.90	1.50
13	0.35	0.30	0.90	1.50
14	0.35	0.30	0.90	1.50
15	0.35	0.30	0.90	1.50
16	0.35	0.30	0.90	1.50
17	0.35	0.30	0.90	1.50
18	0.35	0.30	0.90	1.50
19	0.35	0.30	0.90	1.50
20	0.35	0.40	1.20	2.00
21	0.35	0.30	0.90	1.50
22	0.35	0.30	0.90	1.50
23	0.35	0.30	0.90	1.50

MUPPET BABIES (Was Star Comic)

	ORIG.	GOOD	FINE	N-MINT
18	1.00	0.20	0.60	1.00
19	1.00	0.20	0.60	1.00

	ORIG.	GOOD	FINE	N-MINT
20	1.00	0.20	0.60	1.00
21	1.00	0.20	0.60	1.00
22	1.00	0.20	0.60	1.00
23	1.00	0.20	0.60	1.00
24	1.00	0.20	0.60	1.00
25	1.00	0.20	0.60	1.00
26	1.00	0.20	0.60	1.00

MUTANT MISADVENTURES OF CLOAK & DAGGER

	ORIG.	GOOD	FINE	N-MINT
1	1.25	0.25	0.75	1.25
2	1.50	0.30	0.90	1.50
3	1.50	0.30	0.90	1.50
4 Inferno	1.50	0.30	0.90	1.50
5	1.50	0.30	0.90	1.50
6	1.50	0.30	0.90	1.50
7	1.50	0.30	0.90	1.50
8	1.50	0.30	0.90	1.50
9 Avengers, Acts of Vengeance	2.50	0.50	1.50	2.50
10	1.50	0.30	0.90	1.50
11	1.50	0.30	0.90	1.50
12	1.50	0.30	0.90	1.50
13 (becomes Cloak & Dagger)	1.50	0.30	0.90	1.50

MY LOVE (1969-1976)

	ORIG.	GOOD	FINE	N-MINT
1	0.15	0.20	0.60	1.00
2	0.15	0.20	0.60	1.00
3	0.15	0.20	0.60	1.00
4	0.15	0.20	0.60	1.00
5	0.15	0.20	0.60	1.00
6	0.15	0.20	0.60	1.00
7	0.15	0.20	0.60	1.00
8	0.15	0.20	0.60	1.00
9	0.15	0.20	0.60	1.00
10	0.15	0.20	0.60	1.00
11	0.15	0.20	0.60	1.00
12	0.15	0.20	0.60	1.00
13	0.15	0.20	0.60	1.00
14	0.15	0.20	0.60	1.00
15	0.15	0.20	0.60	1.00
16	0.15	0.20	0.60	1.00
17	0.15	0.20	0.60	1.00
18	0.15	0.20	0.60	1.00
19	0.20	0.20	0.60	1.00
20	0.20	0.20	0.60	1.00
21	0.20	0.20	0.60	1.00
22	0.20	0.20	0.60	1.00
23	0.20	0.20	0.60	1.00
24	0.20	0.20	0.60	1.00
25	0.20	0.20	0.60	1.00
26	0.20	0.20	0.60	1.00
27	0.20	0.20	0.60	1.00
28	0.20	0.20	0.60	1.00
29	0.20	0.20	0.60	1.00
30	0.20	0.20	0.60	1.00

	ORIG.	GOOD	FINE	N-MINT
❏ 31	0.20	0.20	0.60	1.00
❏ 32	0.20	0.20	0.60	1.00
❏ 33	0.20	0.20	0.60	1.00
❏ 34	0.20	0.20	0.60	1.00
❏ 35	0.20	0.20	0.60	1.00
❏ 36	0.20	0.20	0.60	1.00
❏ 37	0.20	0.20	0.60	1.00
❏ 38	0.20	0.20	0.60	1.00
❏ 39	0.20	0.20	0.60	1.00

MYS-TECH WARS

	ORIG.	GOOD	FINE	N-MINT
❏ 1	1.75	0.35	1.05	1.75
❏ 2	1.75	0.35	1.05	1.75
❏ 3	1.75	0.35	1.05	1.75
❏ 4	1.75	0.35	1.05	1.75

NAM MAGAZINE, THE
(really The 'Nam Magazine)

	ORIG.	GOOD	FINE	N-MINT
❏ 1 b&w rep.	2.00	0.40	1.20	2.00
❏ 2 b&w rep.	2.00	0.40	1.20	2.00
❏ 3 b&w rep.	2.00	0.40	1.20	2.00
❏ 4 b&w rep.	2.00	0.40	1.20	2.00
❏ 5 b&w rep.	2.00	0.40	1.20	2.00
❏ 6 b&w rep.	2.00	0.40	1.20	2.00
❏ 7 b&w rep.	2.00	0.40	1.20	2.00
❏ 8 b&w rep.	2.00	0.40	1.20	2.00
❏ 9 b&w rep.	2.00	0.40	1.20	2.00
❏ 10 b&w rep.	2.00	0.40	1.20	2.00

NAM, THE (really The 'Nam)

	ORIG.	GOOD	FINE	N-MINT
❏ 1 MG,1st printing	0.75	1.40	4.20	7.00
❏ 1 MG reprint	0.75	0.80	2.40	4.00
❏ 2 MG	0.75	1.00	3.00	5.00
❏ 3	0.75	0.80	2.40	4.00
❏ 4	0.75	0.80	2.40	4.00
❏ 5	0.75	0.80	2.40	4.00
❏ 6 MG	0.75	0.40	1.20	2.00
❏ 7 MG	0.75	0.40	1.20	2.00
❏ 8 MG	0.75	0.40	1.20	2.00
❏ 9 D:Mike	0.75	0.40	1.20	2.00
❏ 10	0.75	0.40	1.20	2.00
❏ 11	0.75	0.40	1.20	2.00
❏ 12	0.75	0.40	1.20	2.00
❏ 13	0.75	0.40	1.20	2.00
❏ 14	0.75	0.40	1.20	2.00
❏ 15	0.75	0.40	1.20	2.00
❏ 16	0.75	0.40	1.20	2.00
❏ 17	0.75	0.40	1.20	2.00
❏ 18	1.25	0.30	0.90	1.50
❏ 19	1.25	0.30	0.90	1.50
❏ 20	1.25	0.30	0.90	1.50
❏ 21	1.25	0.30	0.90	1.50
❏ 22	1.25	0.30	0.90	1.50
❏ 23	1.25	0.30	0.90	1.50
❏ 24	1.25	0.30	0.90	1.50
❏ 25	1.25	0.30	0.90	1.50
❏ 26	1.50	0.30	0.90	1.50

	ORIG.	GOOD	FINE	N-MINT
❏ 27	1.50	0.30	0.90	1.50
❏ 28	1.50	0.30	0.90	1.50
❏ 29	1.50	0.30	0.90	1.50
❏ 30	1.50	0.30	0.90	1.50
❏ 31	1.50	0.30	0.90	1.50
❏ 32	1.50	0.30	0.90	1.50
❏ 33	1.50	0.30	0.90	1.50
❏ 34	1.50	0.30	0.90	1.50
❏ 35	1.50	0.30	0.90	1.50
❏ 36	1.50	0.30	0.90	1.50
❏ 37	1.50	0.30	0.90	1.50
❏ 38	1.50	0.30	0.90	1.50
❏ 39	1.50	0.30	0.90	1.50
❏ 40	1.50	0.30	0.90	1.50
❏ 41 Capt. America, Thor, Iron Man	1.50	0.40	1.20	2.00
❏ 42	1.50	0.30	0.90	1.50
❏ 43	1.50	0.30	0.90	1.50
❏ 44	1.50	0.30	0.90	1.50
❏ 45	1.50	0.30	0.90	1.50
❏ 46	1.50	0.30	0.90	1.50
❏ 47	1.50	0.30	0.90	1.50
❏ 48	1.50	0.30	0.90	1.50
❏ 49	1.50	0.30	0.90	1.50
❏ 50	1.50	0.30	0.90	1.50
❏ 51	1.50	0.30	0.90	1.50
❏ 52 Punisher (1st printing)	1.50	1.60	4.80	8.00
❏ 52 (2nd printing)	1.50	0.30	0.90	1.50
❏ 53 Punisher (1st printing)	1.50	0.80	2.40	4.00
❏ 53 (2nd printing)	1.50	0.30	0.90	1.50
❏ 54	1.50	0.30	0.90	1.50
❏ 55	1.50	0.30	0.90	1.50
❏ 56	1.50	0.30	0.90	1.50
❏ 57	1.50	0.30	0.90	1.50
❏ 58	1.50	0.30	0.90	1.50
❏ 59	1.50	0.30	0.90	1.50
❏ 60	1.50	0.30	0.90	1.50
❏ 61	1.50	0.30	0.90	1.50
❏ 62	1.50	0.30	0.90	1.50
❏ 63	1.50	0.30	0.90	1.50
❏ 64	1.50	0.30	0.90	1.50
❏ 65	1.75	0.35	1.05	1.75
❏ 66	1.75	0.35	1.05	1.75
❏ 67 Punisher	1.75	0.35	1.05	1.75
❏ 68 Punisher	1.75	0.35	1.05	1.75
❏ 69 Punisher	1.75	0.35	1.05	1.75
❏ 70	1.75	0.35	1.05	1.75
❏ 71	1.75	0.35	1.05	1.75
❏ 72	1.75	0.35	1.05	1.75
❏ 73	1.75	0.35	1.05	1.75
❏ 74	1.75	0.35	1.05	1.75
❏ 75	2.25	0.45	1.35	2.25
❏ 76	1.75	0.35	1.05	1.75
❏ 77	1.75	0.35	1.05	1.75
❏ 78	1.75	0.35	1.05	1.75

	ORIG.	GOOD	FINE	N-MINT
79 .... 1.75	0.35	1.05	1.75
80 .... 1.75	0.35	1.05	1.75
81 .... 1.75	0.35	1.05	1.75
82 .... 1.75	0.35	1.05	1.75
83 .... 1.75	0.35	1.05	1.75
84 last issue..................... 1.75	0.35	1.05	1.75

NAMOR THE SUB-MARINER

	ORIG.	GOOD	FINE	N-MINT
1 JBy, O:Sub-Mariner 1.00	1.00	3.00	5.00
2 JBy.................................. 1.00	0.80	2.40	4.00
3 JBy.................................. 1.00	0.60	1.80	3.00
4 JBy.................................. 1.00	0.60	1.80	3.00
5 JBy.................................. 1.00	0.60	1.80	3.00
6 JBy.................................. 1.00	0.30	0.90	1.50
7 JBy.................................. 1.00	0.30	0.90	1.50
8 JBy.................................. 1.00	0.30	0.90	1.50
9 JBy.................................. 1.00	0.30	0.90	1.50
10 JBy................................ 1.00	0.30	0.90	1.50
11 JBy................................ 1.00	0.30	0.90	1.50
12 JBy, Torch, Capt. America 1.00	0.30	0.90	1.50
13 JBy................................ 1.00	0.20	0.60	1.00
14 JBy................................ 1.00	0.20	0.60	1.00
15 JBy................................ 1.00	0.20	0.60	1.00
16 JBy................................ 1.00	0.20	0.60	1.00
17 JBy................................ 1.00	0.20	0.60	1.00
18 JBy................................ 1.00	0.20	0.60	1.00
19 JBy................................ 1.00	0.20	0.60	1.00
20 JBy................................ 1.00	0.20	0.60	1.00
21 JBy................................ 1.00	0.20	0.60	1.00
22 JBy................................ 1.00	0.20	0.60	1.00
23 JBy................................ 1.25	0.25	0.75	1.25
24 JBy Wolverine.............. 1.25	0.25	0.75	1.25
25 JBy................................ 1.25	0.25	0.75	1.25
26 .... 1.25	4.80	14.40	24.00
27 .... 1.25	3.60	10.80	18.00
28 .... 1.25	2.40	7.20	12.00
29 .... 1.25	2.40	7.20	12.00
30 .... 1.25	2.40	7.20	12.00
31 .... 1.25	2.40	7.20	12.00
32 .... 1.25	1.60	4.80	8.00
33 .... 1.25	1.00	3.00	5.00
34 .... 1.25	1.00	3.00	5.00
35 .... 1.25	1.00	3.00	5.00
36 .... 1.25	0.60	1.80	3.00
37 .... 2.00	1.00	3.00	5.00
38 .... 1.25	0.25	0.75	1.25
39 .... 1.25	0.25	0.75	1.25
40 .... 1.25	0.25	0.75	1.25
41 .... 1.25	0.25	0.75	1.25
42 .... 1.25	0.25	0.75	1.25
43 .... 1.25	0.25	0.75	1.25

NAMOR THE SUB-MARINER ANNUAL

	ORIG.	GOOD	FINE	N-MINT
1 Subterranean Wars 2.00	0.40	1.20	2.00

	ORIG.	GOOD	FINE	N-MINT
2 .... 2.25	0.45	1.35	2.25
3 card 2.95	0.59	1.77	2.95

NEW DEFENDERS (formerly The Defenders)

	ORIG.	GOOD	FINE	N-MINT
140 .... 0.60	0.20	0.60	1.00
141 .... 0.60	0.20	0.60	1.00
142 AAd(c) 0.65	0.20	0.60	1.00
143 .... 0.65	0.20	0.60	1.00
144 .... 0.65	0.20	0.60	1.00
145 .... 0.65	0.20	0.60	1.00
146 .... 0.65	0.20	0.60	1.00
147 .... 0.65	0.20	0.60	1.00
148 .... 0.65	0.20	0.60	1.00
149 .... 0.65	0.20	0.60	1.00
150 .... 1.25	0.25	0.75	1.25
151 .... 0.65	0.20	0.60	1.00
152 Secret Wars II 1.25	0.25	0.75	1.25

NEW MUTANTS

	ORIG.	GOOD	FINE	N-MINT
1 BMc................................ 0.60	2.40	7.20	12.00
2 BMc, V:Sentinels........... 0.60	1.60	4.80	8.00
3 BMc, V:Brood................ 0.60	1.00	3.00	5.00
4 .... 0.60	0.80	2.40	4.00
5 .... 0.60	0.80	2.40	4.00
6 .... 0.60	0.80	2.40	4.00
7 .... 0.60	0.80	2.40	4.00
8 .... 0.60	0.80	2.40	4.00
9 .... 0.60	0.80	2.40	4.00
10 .... 0.60	0.80	2.40	4.00
11 .... 0.60	0.80	2.40	4.00
12 .... 0.60	0.80	2.40	4.00
13 .... 0.60	0.80	2.40	4.00
14 .... 0.60	0.80	2.40	4.00
15 SB, X-Men.................... 0.60	0.80	2.40	4.00
16 .... 0.60	0.80	2.40	4.00
17 .... 0.60	0.80	2.40	4.00
18 BSz, Moonstar I 0.60	1.60	4.80	8.00
19 BSz 0.60	0.60	1.80	3.00
20 BSz 0.60	0.60	1.80	3.00
21 BSz 1.00	0.60	1.80	3.00
22 BSz 0.60	0.50	1.50	2.50
23 BSz 0.60	0.50	1.50	2.50
24 BSz 0.60	0.50	1.50	2.50
25 .... 0.60	0.50	1.50	2.50
26 .... 0.65	0.50	1.50	2.50
27 .... 0.65	0.50	1.50	2.50
28 .... 0.65	0.50	1.50	2.50
29 .... 0.65	0.50	1.50	2.50
30 Secret Wars II 0.65	0.50	1.50	2.50
31 .... 0.65	0.50	1.50	2.50
32 .... 0.65	0.50	1.50	2.50
33 .... 0.65	0.50	1.50	2.50
34 .... 0.65	0.50	1.50	2.50
35 .... 0.75	0.50	1.50	2.50
36 AAd(c), Secret Wars II 0.75	0.60	1.80	3.00

	ORIG.	GOOD	FINE	N-MINT
❏ 37 Secret Wars II	0.75	0.60	1.80	3.00
❏ 38 AAd(c)	0.75	0.60	1.80	3.00
❏ 39 AAd(c)	0.75	0.60	1.80	3.00
❏ 40	0.75	0.60	1.80	3.00
❏ 41	0.75	0.60	1.80	3.00
❏ 42	0.75	0.60	1.80	3.00
❏ 43	0.75	0.60	1.80	3.00
❏ 44	0.75	0.60	1.80	3.00
❏ 45	0.75	0.60	1.80	3.00
❏ 46 mutant massacre	0.75	0.60	1.80	3.00
❏ 47	0.75	0.60	1.80	3.00
❏ 48	0.75	0.60	1.80	3.00
❏ 49	0.75	0.60	1.80	3.00
❏ 50	1.25	0.60	1.80	3.00
❏ 51	0.75	0.60	1.80	3.00
❏ 52	0.75	0.60	1.80	3.00
❏ 53	0.75	0.60	1.80	3.00
❏ 54	0.75	0.60	1.80	3.00
❏ 55	0.75	0.60	1.80	3.00
❏ 56	0.75	0.60	1.80	3.00
❏ 57	0.75	0.60	1.80	3.00
❏ 58 registration card	0.75	1.00	3.00	5.00
❏ 59 Fall of Mutants	0.75	1.00	3.00	5.00
❏ 60 Fall, D:Cipher	1.25	1.00	3.00	5.00
❏ 61 Fall, new costumes	0.75	1.20	3.60	6.00
❏ 62	0.75	0.60	1.80	3.00
❏ 63	1.00	0.60	1.80	3.00
❏ 64	1.00	0.60	1.80	3.00
❏ 65	1.00	0.60	1.80	3.00
❏ 66	1.00	0.60	1.80	3.00
❏ 67	1.00	0.60	1.80	3.00
❏ 68	1.00	0.60	1.80	3.00
❏ 69	1.00	0.60	1.80	3.00
❏ 70 Inferno	1.00	0.60	1.80	3.00
❏ 71 Inferno	1.00	0.60	1.80	3.00
❏ 72 Inferno	1.00	0.60	1.80	3.00
❏ 73 Inferno	1.50	0.60	1.80	3.00
❏ 74	1.00	0.60	1.80	3.00
❏ 75	1.00	0.60	1.80	3.00
❏ 76 Sub-Mariner	1.00	0.60	1.80	3.00
❏ 77	1.00	0.60	1.80	3.00
❏ 78	1.00	0.60	1.80	3.00
❏ 79	1.00	0.60	1.80	3.00
❏ 80	1.00	0.60	1.80	3.00
❏ 81	1.00	0.60	1.80	3.00
❏ 82	1.00	0.60	1.80	3.00
❏ 83	1.00	0.60	1.80	3.00
❏ 84 Vengeance	1.00	0.60	1.80	3.00
❏ 85 TMc(c) Vengeance	1.00	0.60	1.80	3.00
❏ 86 TMc(c) Vengeance	1.00	4.40	13.20	22.00
❏ 87 TMc(c) 1:Cable	1.00	13.00	39.00	65.00
❏ 88 TMc(c)	1.00	5.00	15.00	25.00
❏ 89 TMc(c)	1.00	2.40	7.20	12.00
❏ 90	1.00	2.40	7.20	12.00
❏ 91	1.00	2.40	7.20	12.00

	ORIG.	GOOD	FINE	N-MINT
❏ 92	1.00	2.40	7.20	12.00
❏ 93 TMc(c)	1.00	5.20	15.60	26.00
❏ 94	1.00	2.00	6.00	10.00
❏ 95 X-Tinction	1.00	2.00	6.00	10.00
❏ 96 X-Tinction	1.00	2.80	8.40	14.00
❏ 97 X-Tinction	1.00	2.80	8.40	14.00
❏ 98 I:Deadpool, Gideon, Domino	1.00	2.00	6.00	10.00
❏ 99 L:Sunspot	1.00	1.60	4.80	8.00
❏ 100 1st printing I:X-Force	1.50	2.00	6.00	10.00
❏ 100 2nd printing	1.50	0.80	2.40	4.00

NEW MUTANTS ANNUAL/SPECIAL

	ORIG.	GOOD	FINE	N-MINT
❏ 1 AAd, 1985	1.00	1.20	3.60	6.00
❏ 2 1986	1.25	0.80	2.40	4.00
❏ 3 1987	1.25	0.80	2.40	4.00
❏ 4 Evolutionary War, 1988	1.75	0.80	2.40	4.00
❏ 5 Atlantis Attacks, 1989	2.00	0.60	1.80	3.00
❏ 6 Future Present, 1990	2.00	0.60	1.80	3.00
❏ 7 Kings of Pain, 1991	2.00	0.40	1.20	2.00

NEW MUTANTS SPECIAL EDITION

	ORIG.	GOOD	FINE	N-MINT
❏ 1 (1985)	1.50	0.30	0.90	1.50

NEW MUTANTS SUMMER SPECIAL, THE

	ORIG.	GOOD	FINE	N-MINT
❏ 1	2.95	0.59	1.77	2.95

NEW WARRIORS

	ORIG.	GOOD	FINE	N-MINT
❏ 1	1.00	4.00	12.00	20.00
❏ 2	1.00	3.00	9.00	15.00
❏ 3	1.00	2.00	6.00	10.00
❏ 4	1.00	1.40	4.20	7.00
❏ 5	1.00	1.20	3.60	6.00
❏ 6	1.00	1.20	3.60	6.00
❏ 7 A:Punisher	1.00	1.60	4.80	8.00
❏ 8 A:Punisher	1.00	1.60	4.80	8.00
❏ 9 Punisher	1.00	1.20	3.60	6.00
❏ 10	1.00	1.00	3.00	5.00
❏ 11 Wolverine	1.00	1.00	3.00	5.00
❏ 12	1.00	0.80	2.40	4.00
❏ 13	1.00	0.80	2.40	4.00
❏ 14 Darkhawk, Namor	1.00	0.40	1.20	2.00
❏ 15	1.00	0.40	1.20	2.00
❏ 16	1.00	0.40	1.20	2.00
❏ 17 F4	1.00	0.40	1.20	2.00
❏ 18	1.00	0.40	1.20	2.00
❏ 19	1.00	0.40	1.20	2.00
❏ 20	1.25	0.40	1.20	2.00
❏ 21	1.25	0.40	1.20	2.00
❏ 22	1.25	0.40	1.20	2.00
❏ 23	1.25	0.40	1.20	2.00
❏ 24	1.25	0.40	1.20	2.00
❏ 25	2.50	1.20	3.60	6.00
❏ 26	1.25	0.25	0.75	1.25
❏ 27	1.25	0.25	0.75	1.25
❏ 28	1.25	0.25	0.75	1.25
❏ 29	1.25	0.25	0.75	1.25
❏ 30	1.25	0.25	0.75	1.25

	ORIG.	GOOD	FINE	N-MINT
31	1.25	0.25	0.75	1.25
32	1.25	0.25	0.75	1.25
33	1.25	0.25	0.75	1.25
34	1.25	0.25	0.75	1.25
35	1.25	0.25	0.75	1.25
36	1.25	0.25	0.75	1.25
37	1.25	0.25	0.75	1.25
38	1.25	0.25	0.75	1.25
39	1.25	0.25	0.75	1.25

NEW WARRIORS ANNUAL

	ORIG.	GOOD	FINE	N-MINT
1 Kings of Pain (1991)	2.00	1.00	3.00	5.00
2 (1992)	2.25	0.60	1.80	3.00
3 trading card (1993)	2.95	0.59	1.77	2.95

NFL SUPERPRO (one-shot, 1990)

	ORIG.	GOOD	FINE	N-MINT
1 O:SuperPro	3.95	1.00	3.00	5.00

NFL SUPERPRO (series, begins 1991)

	ORIG.	GOOD	FINE	N-MINT
1 A:SpM	1.00	0.20	0.60	1.00
2	1.00	0.20	0.60	1.00
3	1.00	0.20	0.60	1.00
4	1.00	0.20	0.60	1.00
5	1.25	0.25	0.75	1.25
6	1.25	0.25	0.75	1.25
7	1.25	0.25	0.75	1.25
8 Capt. America	1.25	0.25	0.75	1.25
9	1.25	0.25	0.75	1.25
10	1.25	0.25	0.75	1.25
11	1.25	0.25	0.75	1.25
12	1.25	0.25	0.75	1.25

NICK FURY VS. S.H.I.E.L.D.

	ORIG.	GOOD	FINE	N-MINT
1	3.50	4.00	12.00	20.00
2 BSz(c)	3.50	4.00	12.00	20.00
3	3.50	2.00	6.00	10.00
4	3.50	2.00	6.00	10.00
5	3.50	2.00	6.00	10.00
6	3.50	2.00	6.00	10.00

NICK FURY, AGENT OF S.H.I.E.L.D. (1968-1971)

	ORIG.	GOOD	FINE	N-MINT
1	0.12	8.00	24.00	40.00
2	0.12	4.80	14.40	24.00
3	0.12	3.00	9.00	15.00
4	0.12	3.00	9.00	15.00
5	0.12	3.00	9.00	15.00
6	0.12	1.60	4.80	8.00
7	0.12	1.60	4.80	8.00
8	0.12	0.80	2.40	4.00
9	0.12	0.80	2.40	4.00
10	0.12	0.80	2.40	4.00
11	0.12	0.80	2.40	4.00
12	0.12	0.80	2.40	4.00
13	0.12	0.80	2.40	4.00
14	0.15	0.80	2.40	4.00
15	0.15	0.80	2.40	4.00
16	0.25	0.80	2.40	4.00
17	0.25	0.80	2.40	4.00
18	0.25	0.80	2.40	4.00

NICK FURY, AGENT OF S.H.I.E.L.D. (1983)

	ORIG.	GOOD	FINE	N-MINT
1 reprints	2.00	0.40	1.20	2.00
2 reprints	2.00	0.40	1.20	2.00

NICK FURY, AGENT OF S.H.I.E.L.D. (1989-1993)

	ORIG.	GOOD	FINE	N-MINT
1	1.50	0.40	1.20	2.00
2	1.50	0.30	0.90	1.50
3	1.50	0.30	0.90	1.50
4	1.50	0.30	0.90	1.50
5	1.50	0.30	0.90	1.50
6	1.50	0.30	0.90	1.50
7	1.50	0.30	0.90	1.50
8	1.50	0.30	0.90	1.50
9	1.50	0.30	0.90	1.50
10	1.50	0.30	0.90	1.50
11	1.50	0.30	0.90	1.50
12	1.50	0.30	0.90	1.50
13	1.50	0.30	0.90	1.50
14	1.50	0.30	0.90	1.50
15	1.50	0.30	0.90	1.50
16	1.50	0.30	0.90	1.50
17	1.50	0.30	0.90	1.50
18	1.50	0.30	0.90	1.50
19	1.50	0.30	0.90	1.50
20	1.50	0.30	0.90	1.50
21	1.50	0.30	0.90	1.50
22	1.50	0.30	0.90	1.50
23	1.50	0.30	0.90	1.50
24	1.50	0.30	0.90	1.50
25	1.50	0.30	0.90	1.50
26	1.50	0.30	0.90	1.50
27	1.50	0.30	0.90	1.50
28	1.50	0.30	0.90	1.50
29	1.50	0.30	0.90	1.50
30	1.50	0.30	0.90	1.50
31	1.50	0.30	0.90	1.50
32	1.75	0.35	1.05	1.75
33	1.75	0.35	1.05	1.75
34	1.75	0.35	1.05	1.75
35	1.75	0.35	1.05	1.75
36	1.75	0.35	1.05	1.75
37	1.75	0.35	1.05	1.75
38	1.75	0.35	1.05	1.75
39	1.75	0.35	1.05	1.75
40	1.75	0.35	1.05	1.75
41	1.75	0.35	1.05	1.75
42	1.75	0.35	1.05	1.75
43	1.75	0.35	1.05	1.75
44	1.75	0.35	1.05	1.75
45	1.75	0.35	1.05	1.75
46	1.75	0.35	1.05	1.75
47	1.75	0.35	1.05	1.75

NIGHT NURSE

	ORIG.	GOOD	FINE	N-MINT
1	0.20	0.30	0.90	1.50
2	0.20	0.30	0.90	1.50

	ORIG.	GOOD	FINE	N-MINT
3	0.20	0.30	0.90	1.50
4	0.20	0.30	0.90	1.50

NIGHT THRASHER

	ORIG.	GOOD	FINE	N-MINT
1 foil cover	2.95	0.59	1.77	2.95
2	1.75	0.35	1.05	1.75

NIGHT THRASHER: FOUR CONTROL

	ORIG.	GOOD	FINE	N-MINT
1	2.00	0.40	1.20	2.00
2	2.00	0.40	1.20	2.00
3	2.00	0.40	1.20	2.00
4	2.00	0.40	1.20	2.00

NIGHTCAT

	ORIG.	GOOD	FINE	N-MINT
1 O:Nightcat	3.95	0.79	2.37	3.95

NIGHTCRAWLER

	ORIG.	GOOD	FINE	N-MINT
1 DC	0.75	1.00	3.00	5.00
2	0.75	0.70	2.10	3.50
3	0.75	0.70	2.10	3.50
4	0.75	0.70	2.10	3.50

NIGHTMASK

	ORIG.	GOOD	FINE	N-MINT
1	0.75	0.20	0.60	1.00
2	0.75	0.20	0.60	1.00
3	0.75	0.20	0.60	1.00
4	0.75	0.20	0.60	1.00
5	0.75	0.20	0.60	1.00
6	0.75	0.20	0.60	1.00
7	0.75	0.20	0.60	1.00
8	0.75	0.20	0.60	1.00
9	0.75	0.20	0.60	1.00
10	0.75	0.20	0.60	1.00
11	0.75	0.20	0.60	1.00
12	0.75	0.20	0.60	1.00

NIGHTSTALKERS

	ORIG.	GOOD	FINE	N-MINT
1 poster	2.75	0.55	1.65	2.75
2	1.75	0.35	1.05	1.75
3	1.75	0.35	1.05	1.75
4	1.75	0.35	1.05	1.75
5	1.75	0.35	1.05	1.75
6	1.75	0.35	1.05	1.75
7	1.75	0.35	1.05	1.75
8	1.75	0.35	1.05	1.75
9	1.75	0.35	1.05	1.75
10	1.75	0.35	1.05	1.75
11	1.75	0.35	1.05	1.75
12	1.75	0.35	1.05	1.75

NOMAD (1992-)

	ORIG.	GOOD	FINE	N-MINT
1 gatefold cover	2.00	0.80	2.40	4.00
2	1.75	0.50	1.50	2.50
3	1.75	0.35	1.05	1.75
4	1.75	0.35	1.05	1.75
5	1.75	0.35	1.05	1.75
6	1.75	0.35	1.05	1.75
7 Infinity War	1.75	0.35	1.05	1.75
8	1.75	0.35	1.05	1.75
9	1.75	0.35	1.05	1.75

	ORIG.	GOOD	FINE	N-MINT
10	1.75	0.35	1.05	1.75
11	1.75	0.35	1.05	1.75
12	1.75	0.35	1.05	1.75
13	1.75	0.35	1.05	1.75
14	1.75	0.35	1.05	1.75
15	1.75	0.35	1.05	1.75
16	1.75	0.35	1.05	1.75
17	1.75	0.35	1.05	1.75
18	1.75	0.35	1.05	1.75

NOMAD (mini-series)

	ORIG.	GOOD	FINE	N-MINT
1	1.50	0.80	2.40	4.00
2	1.50	0.60	1.80	3.00
3	1.50	0.40	1.20	2.00
4	1.50	0.40	1.20	2.00

NOT BRAND ECHH

	ORIG.	GOOD	FINE	N-MINT
1	0.12	7.20	21.60	36.00
2	0.12	3.60	10.80	18.00
3	0.12	3.60	10.80	18.00
4	0.12	3.60	10.80	18.00
5	0.12	3.60	10.80	18.00
6	0.12	3.00	9.00	15.00
7	0.12	3.00	9.00	15.00
8	0.12	3.00	9.00	15.00
9	0.25	3.00	9.00	15.00
10	0.25	3.00	9.00	15.00
11	0.25	2.40	7.20	12.00
12	0.25	2.40	7.20	12.00
13	0.25	2.40	7.20	12.00

NOVA

	ORIG.	GOOD	FINE	N-MINT
1 O:Nova	0.30	2.40	7.20	12.00
2	0.30	1.60	4.80	8.00
3	0.30	1.20	3.60	6.00
4	0.30	1.20	3.60	6.00
5	0.30	1.20	3.60	6.00
6	0.30	1.00	3.00	5.00
7	0.30	1.00	3.00	5.00
8	0.30	1.00	3.00	5.00
9	0.30	1.00	3.00	5.00
10	0.30	1.00	3.00	5.00
11	0.30	0.80	2.40	4.00
12	0.30	0.80	2.40	4.00
13	0.30	0.80	2.40	4.00
14	0.30	0.80	2.40	4.00
15	0.35	0.80	2.40	4.00
16	0.35	0.80	2.40	4.00
17	0.35	0.80	2.40	4.00
18	0.35	0.80	2.40	4.00
19	0.35	0.80	2.40	4.00
20	0.35	0.80	2.40	4.00
21	0.35	0.80	2.40	4.00
22	0.35	0.80	2.40	4.00
23	0.35	0.80	2.40	4.00
24	0.30			
25	0.40			

	ORIG.	GOOD	FINE	N-MINT
Nth MAN				
1	1.00	0.20	0.60	1.00
2	1.00	0.20	0.60	1.00
3	1.00	0.20	0.60	1.00
4	1.00	0.20	0.60	1.00
5	1.00	0.20	0.60	1.00
6	1.00	0.20	0.60	1.00
7	1.00	0.20	0.60	1.00
8	1.00	0.20	0.60	1.00
9	1.00	0.20	0.60	1.00
10	1.00	0.20	0.60	1.00
11	1.00	0.20	0.60	1.00
12	1.00	0.20	0.60	1.00
13	1.00	0.20	0.60	1.00
14	1.00	0.20	0.60	1.00
15	1.00	0.20	0.60	1.00
16	1.00	0.20	0.60	1.00
OBNOXIO THE CLOWN				
1 X-Men	0.60	0.20	0.60	1.00
OFFICIAL HANDBOOK OF THE CONAN UNIVERSE				
1	1.25	0.25	0.75	1.25
OFFICIAL HANDBOOK OF THE CONAN UNIVERSE (1993)				
no number or price, sold with Conan Saga #75				
OFFICIAL HANDBOOK OF THE MARVEL UNIVERSE				
1	1.00	1.20	3.60	6.00
2	1.00	0.90	2.70	4.50
3	1.00	0.80	2.40	4.00
4	1.00	0.70	2.10	3.50
5	1.00	0.70	2.10	3.50
6	1.00	0.60	1.80	3.00
7	1.00	0.60	1.80	3.00
8	1.00	0.60	1.80	3.00
9	1.00	0.60	1.80	3.00
10	1.00	0.60	1.80	3.00
11	1.00	0.60	1.80	3.00
12	1.00	0.60	1.80	3.00
13	1.00	0.50	1.50	2.50
14	1.00	0.80	2.40	4.00
15	1.00	0.80	2.40	4.00
20	1.00	0.90	2.70	4.50
21	1.00	0.90	2.70	4.50
22	1.00	0.90	2.70	4.50
23	1.00	0.90	2.70	4.50
24	1.00	0.90	2.70	4.50
25	1.00	0.90	2.70	4.50
OFFICIAL HANDBOOK OF THE MARVEL UNIVERSE (2nd series)				
1	1.50	0.80	2.40	4.00
2	1.50	0.60	1.80	3.00
3	1.50	0.60	1.80	3.00
4	1.50	0.60	1.80	3.00
5	1.50	0.60	1.80	3.00
6	1.50	0.60	1.80	3.00
7	1.50	0.60	1.80	3.00
8	1.50	0.60	1.80	3.00
9	1.50	0.60	1.80	3.00
10	1.50	0.60	1.80	3.00
11	1.50	0.50	1.50	2.50
12	1.50	0.50	1.50	2.50
13	1.50	0.50	1.50	2.50
14	1.50	0.50	1.50	2.50
15	1.50	0.50	1.50	2.50
16	1.50	0.50	1.50	2.50
17	1.50	0.50	1.50	2.50
18	1.50	0.50	1.50	2.50
19	1.50	0.50	1.50	2.50
20	1.50	0.50	1.50	2.50
OFFICIAL HANDBOOK OF THE MARVEL UNIVERSE MASTER EDITION (looseleaf)				
1	3.95	0.79	2.37	3.95
2	3.95	0.79	2.37	3.95
3	3.95	0.79	2.37	3.95
4	3.95	0.79	2.37	3.95
5	3.95	0.79	2.37	3.95
6	3.95	0.79	2.37	3.95
7	3.95	0.79	2.37	3.95
8	3.95	0.79	2.37	3.95
9	3.95	0.79	2.37	3.95
10	3.95	0.79	2.37	3.95
11	3.95	0.79	2.37	3.95
12	4.50	0.90	2.70	4.50
13	4.50	0.90	2.70	4.50
14	4.50	0.90	2.70	4.50
15	4.50	0.90	2.70	4.50
16	4.50	0.90	2.70	4.50
17	4.50	0.90	2.70	4.50
18	4.50	0.90	2.70	4.50
19	4.50	0.90	2.70	4.50
20	4.50	0.90	2.70	4.50
21	4.50	0.90	2.70	4.50
22	4.50	0.90	2.70	4.50
23	4.50	0.90	2.70	4.50
24	4.50	0.90	2.70	4.50
25	4.50	0.90	2.70	4.50
26	4.50	0.90	2.70	4.50
27	4.50	0.90	2.70	4.50
28	4.95	0.99	2.97	4.95
29	4.95	0.99	2.97	4.95
30	4.95	0.99	2.97	4.95
31	4.95	0.99	2.97	4.95
32	4.95	0.99	2.97	4.95
33	4.95	0.99	2.97	4.95
OFFICIAL HANDBOOK OF THE MARVEL UNIVERSE UPDATE '89				
1	1.50	0.30	0.90	1.50
2	1.50	0.30	0.90	1.50
3	1.50	0.30	0.90	1.50

	ORIG.	GOOD	FINE	N-MINT
❏ 4	1.50	0.30	0.90	1.50
❏ 5	1.50	0.30	0.90	1.50
❏ 6	1.50	0.30	0.90	1.50
❏ 7	1.50	0.30	0.90	1.50
❏ 8	1.50	0.30	0.90	1.50

OFFICIAL MARVEL INDEX TO MARVEL TEAM-UP

	ORIG.	GOOD	FINE	N-MINT
❏ 1	1.25	0.25	0.75	1.25
❏ 2	1.25	0.25	0.75	1.25
❏ 3	1.25	0.25	0.75	1.25
❏ 4	1.25	0.25	0.75	1.25
❏ 5	1.25	0.25	0.75	1.25
❏ 6	1.25	0.25	0.75	1.25

OFFICIAL MARVEL INDEX TO THE AMAZING SPIDER-MAN

	ORIG.	GOOD	FINE	N-MINT
❏ 1	1.25	0.30	0.90	1.50
❏ 2	1.25	0.25	0.75	1.25
❏ 3	1.25	0.25	0.75	1.25
❏ 4	1.25	0.25	0.75	1.25
❏ 5	1.25	0.25	0.75	1.25
❏ 6	1.25	0.25	0.75	1.25
❏ 7	1.25	0.25	0.75	1.25
❏ 8	1.25	0.25	0.75	1.25
❏ 9	1.25	0.25	0.75	1.25

OFFICIAL MARVEL INDEX TO THE AVENGERS

	ORIG.	GOOD	FINE	N-MINT
❏ 1	2.95	0.59	1.77	2.95
❏ 2	2.95	0.59	1.77	2.95
❏ 3	2.95	0.59	1.77	2.95
❏ 4	2.95	0.59	1.77	2.95
❏ 5	2.95	0.59	1.77	2.95
❏ 6	2.95	0.59	1.77	2.95
❏ 7	2.95	0.59	1.77	2.95

OFFICIAL MARVEL INDEX TO THE FANTASTIC FOUR

	ORIG.	GOOD	FINE	N-MINT
❏ 1	1.25	0.25	0.75	1.25
❏ 2	1.25	0.25	0.75	1.25
❏ 3	1.25	0.25	0.75	1.25
❏ 4	1.25	0.25	0.75	1.25
❏ 5	1.25	0.25	0.75	1.25
❏ 6	1.25	0.25	0.75	1.25
❏ 7	1.25	0.25	0.75	1.25
❏ 8	1.25	0.25	0.75	1.25
❏ 9	1.25	0.25	0.75	1.25
❏ 10	1.25	0.25	0.75	1.25
❏ 11	1.25	0.25	0.75	1.25
❏ 12	1.25	0.25	0.75	1.25

OFFICIAL MARVEL INDEX TO THE X-MEN

	ORIG.	GOOD	FINE	N-MINT
❏ 1	2.95	0.59	1.77	2.95
❏ 2	2.95	0.59	1.77	2.95
❏ 3	2.95	0.59	1.77	2.95
❏ 4	2.95	0.59	1.77	2.95
❏ 5	2.95	0.59	1.77	2.95
❏ 6	2.95	0.59	1.77	2.95
❏ 7	2.95	0.59	1.77	2.95

OMEGA THE UNKNOWN

	ORIG.	GOOD	FINE	N-MINT
❏ 1	0.25	1.20	3.60	6.00
❏ 2	0.25	0.60	1.80	3.00
❏ 3	0.25	0.60	1.80	3.00
❏ 4	0.30	0.60	1.80	3.00
❏ 5	0.30	0.60	1.80	3.00
❏ 6	0.30	0.60	1.80	3.00
❏ 7	0.30	0.60	1.80	3.00
❏ 8	0.30	1.00	3.00	5.00
❏ 9	0.30	1.00	3.00	5.00
❏ 10	0.30	1.00	3.00	5.00
❏ 11	0.30	1.00	3.00	5.00

OPEN SPACE

	ORIG.	GOOD	FINE	N-MINT
❏ 1	4.95	1.20	3.60	6.00
❏ 2	4.95	0.99	2.97	4.95
❏ 3	4.95	0.99	2.97	4.95
❏ 4	4.95	0.99	2.97	4.95

ORIGINAL GHOST RIDER RIDES AGAIN, THE

	ORIG.	GOOD	FINE	N-MINT
❏ 1 reprint	1.50	0.30	0.90	1.50
❏ 2 reprint	1.50	0.30	0.90	1.50
❏ 3 reprint	1.50	0.30	0.90	1.50
❏ 4 reprint	1.50	0.30	0.90	1.50
❏ 5 reprint	1.50	0.30	0.90	1.50
❏ 6 reprint	1.50	0.30	0.90	1.50
❏ 7 reprint	1.50	0.30	0.90	1.50

ORIGINAL GHOST RIDER, THE

	ORIG.	GOOD	FINE	N-MINT
❏ 1 O:reprinted	1.75	0.35	1.05	1.75
❏ 2 reprints	1.75	0.35	1.05	1.75
❏ 3 reprints	1.75	0.35	1.05	1.75
❏ 4 reprints	1.75	0.35	1.05	1.75
❏ 5 reprints	1.75	0.35	1.05	1.75
❏ 6 reprints	1.75	0.35	1.05	1.75
❏ 7 reprints	1.75	0.35	1.05	1.75
❏ 8 reprints	1.75	0.35	1.05	1.75
❏ 9 reprints	1.75	0.35	1.05	1.75
❏ 10 reprints	1.75	0.35	1.05	1.75
❏ 11 reprints	1.75	0.35	1.05	1.75
❏ 12 reprints	1.75	0.35	1.05	1.75
❏ 13 reprints	1.75	0.35	1.05	1.75
❏ 14 reprints	1.75	0.35	1.05	1.75
❏ 15 reprints	1.75	0.35	1.05	1.75
❏ 16 reprints	1.75	0.35	1.05	1.75

OUR LOVE STORY

	ORIG.	GOOD	FINE	N-MINT
❏ 1	0.15	2.00	6.00	10.00
❏ 2	0.15	1.00	3.00	5.00
❏ 3	0.15	1.00	3.00	5.00
❏ 4	0.15	1.00	3.00	5.00
❏ 5 Steranko	0.15	4.00	12.00	20.00
❏ 6	0.15	1.00	3.00	5.00
❏ 7	0.15	1.00	3.00	5.00
❏ 8	0.15	1.00	3.00	5.00
❏ 9	0.15	1.00	3.00	5.00
❏ 10	0.15	1.00	3.00	5.00
❏ 11	0.15	0.60	1.80	3.00

	ORIG.	GOOD	FINE	N-MINT
12	0.15	0.60	1.80	3.00
13	0.15	0.60	1.80	3.00
14	0.15	0.60	1.80	3.00
15	0.15	0.20	0.60	1.00
16	0.15	0.20	0.60	1.00
17	0.15	0.20	0.60	1.00
18	0.20	0.20	0.60	1.00
19	0.20	0.20	0.60	1.00
20	0.20	0.20	0.60	1.00
21	0.20	0.20	0.60	1.00
22	0.20	0.20	0.60	1.00
23	0.20	0.20	0.60	1.00
24	0.20	0.20	0.60	1.00
25	0.20	0.20	0.60	1.00
26	0.20	0.20	0.60	1.00
27	0.20	0.20	0.60	1.00
28	0.20	0.20	0.60	1.00
29	0.20	0.20	0.60	1.00
30	0.20	0.20	0.60	1.00
31	0.20	0.20	0.60	1.00
32	0.20	0.20	0.60	1.00
33	0.20	0.20	0.60	1.00
34	0.20	0.20	0.60	1.00
35	0.20	0.20	0.60	1.00
36	0.20	0.20	0.60	1.00
37	0.20	0.20	0.60	1.00
38	0.20	0.20	0.60	1.00

PENDRAGON

	ORIG.	GOOD	FINE	N-MINT
1 Iron Man	1.75	0.35	1.05	1.75
2	1.75	0.35	1.05	1.75
3	1.75	0.35	1.05	1.75
4 (becomes Knights of Pendragon)				
	1.75	0.35	1.05	1.75

PETER PARKER THE SPECTACULAR SPIDER-MAN (was Spectacular Spider-Man)

	ORIG.	GOOD	FINE	N-MINT
48 Prowler	0.50	0.80	2.40	4.00
49 Prowler	0.50	0.80	2.40	4.00
50 JR2/JM, Smuggler	0.50	0.80	2.40	4.00
51 FM(c)	0.50	0.80	2.40	4.00
52 FM(c)	0.50	0.80	2.40	4.00
53 JM/FS, Tinker	0.50	0.80	2.40	4.00
54	0.50	0.80	2.40	4.00
55	0.50	0.80	2.40	4.00
56	0.50	0.80	2.40	4.00
57	0.50	0.80	2.40	4.00
58 JBy	0.50	1.20	3.60	6.00
59 JM	0.50	0.80	2.40	4.00
60 JM/FM(c) O:retold	0.75	1.20	3.60	6.00
61	0.50	0.60	1.80	3.00
62	0.60	0.60	1.80	3.00
63	0.60	0.60	1.80	3.00
64 I: Cloak & Dagger	0.60	2.80	8.40	14.00
65	0.60	0.60	1.80	3.00
66	0.60	0.60	1.80	3.00
67	0.60	0.60	1.80	3.00

	ORIG.	GOOD	FINE	N-MINT
68	0.60	0.60	1.80	3.00
69 Cloak & Dagger	0.60	1.40	4.20	7.00
70 Cloak & Dagger	0.60	1.40	4.20	7.00
71	0.60	0.50	1.50	2.50
72	0.60	0.50	1.50	2.50
73	0.60	0.50	1.50	2.50
74	0.60	0.50	1.50	2.50
75	1.00	0.50	1.50	2.50
76	0.60	0.50	1.50	2.50
77	0.60	0.50	1.50	2.50
78	0.60	0.50	1.50	2.50
79	0.60	0.50	1.50	2.50
80	0.60	0.50	1.50	2.50
81 Punisher	0.60	3.00	9.00	15.00
82 Punisher	0.60	3.00	9.00	15.00
83 Punisher	0.60	3.00	9.00	15.00
84	0.60	0.60	1.80	3.00
85	0.60	0.60	1.80	3.00
86	0.60	0.60	1.80	3.00
87	0.60	0.60	1.80	3.00
88	0.60	0.60	1.80	3.00
89	0.60	0.60	1.80	3.00
90 AM, new costume	0.60	0.50	1.50	2.50
91	0.60	0.50	1.50	2.50
92	0.60	0.50	1.50	2.50
93	0.60	0.50	1.50	2.50
94	0.60	0.50	1.50	2.50
95	0.60	0.50	1.50	2.50
96	0.60	0.50	1.50	2.50
97	0.60	0.50	1.50	2.50
98	0.60	0.50	1.50	2.50
99	0.60	0.50	1.50	2.50
100	1.00	1.00	3.00	5.00
101	0.65	0.50	1.50	2.50
102	0.65	0.50	1.50	2.50
103	0.65	0.50	1.50	2.50
104	0.65	0.50	1.50	2.50
105	0.65	0.50	1.50	2.50
106	0.65	0.50	1.50	2.50
107 D:Jean DeWolff	0.65	0.80	2.40	4.00
108	0.65	0.50	1.50	2.50
109	0.65	0.50	1.50	2.50
110	0.65	0.50	1.50	2.50
111 Secret Wars II	0.75	0.50	1.50	2.50
112	0.75	0.50	1.50	2.50
113	0.75	0.50	1.50	2.50
114	0.75	0.50	1.50	2.50
115	0.75	0.50	1.50	2.50
116 Sabretooth	0.75	1.60	4.80	8.00
117	0.75	0.50	1.50	2.50
118	0.75	0.50	1.50	2.50
119 Sabretooth	0.75	1.20	3.60	6.00
120	0.75	0.50	1.50	2.50
121	0.75	0.50	1.50	2.50
122	0.75	0.50	1.50	2.50

	ORIG.	GOOD	FINE	N-MINT
☐ 123	0.75	0.50	1.50	2.50
☐ 124	0.75	0.50	1.50	2.50
☐ 125	0.75	0.50	1.50	2.50
☐ 126	0.75	0.50	1.50	2.50
☐ 127	0.75	0.50	1.50	2.50
☐ 128	0.75	0.50	1.50	2.50
☐ 129	0.75	0.50	1.50	2.50
☐ 130	0.75	0.50	1.50	2.50
☐ 131 Kraven	0.75	1.80	5.40	9.00
☐ 132 Kraven (becomes The Spectacular Spider-Man)0.75				
1.805.40				9.00

PETER PARKER, THE SPECTACULAR SPIDER-MAN ANNUAL

	ORIG.	GOOD	FINE	N-MINT
☐ 4	1.00	0.40	1.20	2.00
☐ 5	1.25	0.30	0.90	1.50
☐ 6 (becomes The Spectacular Spider-Man Annual)				
	1.25	0.30	0.90	1.50

PHOENIX: THE UNTOLD STORY

	ORIG.	GOOD	FINE	N-MINT
☐ 1 X-Men	2.00	1.20	3.60	6.00

PINOCCHIO AND THE EMPEROR OF THE NIGHT

	ORIG.	GOOD	FINE	N-MINT
☐ 1 movie	1.25	0.25	0.75	1.25

PIRATES OF DARK WATER

	ORIG.	GOOD	FINE	N-MINT
☐ 1	1.00	0.20	0.60	1.00
☐ 2	1.00	0.20	0.60	1.00
☐ 3	1.00	0.20	0.60	1.00
☐ 4	1.25	0.25	0.75	1.25
☐ 5	1.25	0.25	0.75	1.25
☐ 6	1.25	0.25	0.75	1.25
☐ 7	1.25	0.25	0.75	1.25
☐ 8	1.25	0.25	0.75	1.25
☐ 9	1.25	0.25	0.75	1.25

PITT, THE

	ORIG.	GOOD	FINE	N-MINT
☐ 1	3.25	0.65	1.95	3.25

POLICE ACADEMY

	ORIG.	GOOD	FINE	N-MINT
☐ 1	1.00	0.20	0.60	1.00
☐ 2	1.00	0.20	0.60	1.00
☐ 3	1.00	0.20	0.60	1.00
☐ 4	1.00	0.20	0.60	1.00
☐ 5	1.00	0.20	0.60	1.00
☐ 6	1.00	0.20	0.60	1.00

POWER MAN & IRON FIST (formerly Power Man)

	ORIG.	GOOD	FINE	N-MINT
☐ 50 JBy	0.35	1.60	4.80	8.00
☐ 51	0.35	0.40	1.20	2.00
☐ 52	0.35	0.40	1.20	2.00
☐ 53	0.35	0.40	1.20	2.00
☐ 54 O:Iron Fist	0.35	1.60	4.80	8.00
☐ 55	0.35	0.40	1.20	2.00
☐ 56	0.35	0.40	1.20	2.00
☐ 57 X-Men	0.40	1.60	4.80	8.00
☐ 58 1:El Aquila	0.40	0.40	1.20	2.00
☐ 59 BL	0.40	0.40	1.20	2.00
☐ 60 BL	0.40	0.40	1.20	2.00
☐ 61 BL	0.40	0.40	1.20	2.00
☐ 62 BL	0.40	0.40	1.20	2.00

	ORIG.	GOOD	FINE	N-MINT
☐ 63 BL	0.40	0.40	1.20	2.00
☐ 64 BL	0.40	0.40	1.20	2.00
☐ 65 BL	0.50	0.40	1.20	2.00
☐ 66 FM(c), Sabretooth	0.50	10.00	30.00	50.00
☐ 67	0.50	0.40	1.20	2.00
☐ 68 FM(c)	0.50	0.40	1.20	2.00
☐ 69	0.50	0.40	1.20	2.00
☐ 70 FM(c)	0.50	0.40	1.20	2.00
☐ 71 FM(c)	0.50	0.40	1.20	2.00
☐ 72 FM(c)	0.50	0.40	1.20	2.00
☐ 73 FM(c)	0.50	0.40	1.20	2.00
☐ 74 FM(c)	0.50	0.40	1.20	2.00
☐ 75 origins	0.75	0.60	1.80	3.00
☐ 76	0.50	0.40	1.20	2.00
☐ 77	0.60	0.40	1.20	2.00
☐ 78	0.60	5.00	15.00	25.00
☐ 79	0.60	0.30	0.90	1.50
☐ 80	0.60	0.30	0.90	1.50
☐ 81	0.60	0.30	0.90	1.50
☐ 82	0.60	0.30	0.90	1.50
☐ 83	0.60	0.30	0.90	1.50
☐ 84 Sabretooth	0.60	6.00	18.00	30.00
☐ 85	0.60	0.20	0.60	1.00
☐ 86 Moon Knight	0.60	0.60	1.80	3.00
☐ 87 Moon Knight	0.60	0.60	1.80	3.00
☐ 88	0.60	0.20	0.60	1.00
☐ 89	0.60	0.20	0.60	1.00
☐ 90	0.60	0.20	0.60	1.00
☐ 91	0.60	0.20	0.60	1.00
☐ 92	0.60	0.20	0.60	1.00
☐ 93	0.60	0.20	0.60	1.00
☐ 94	0.60	0.20	0.60	1.00
☐ 95	0.60	0.20	0.60	1.00
☐ 96	0.60	0.20	0.60	1.00
☐ 97	0.60	0.20	0.60	1.00
☐ 98	0.60	0.20	0.60	1.00
☐ 99	0.60	0.20	0.60	1.00
☐ 100	1.00	0.20	0.60	1.00
☐ 101	0.60	0.20	0.60	1.00
☐ 102	0.60	0.20	0.60	1.00
☐ 103	0.60	0.20	0.60	1.00
☐ 104	0.60	0.20	0.60	1.00
☐ 105	0.60	0.20	0.60	1.00
☐ 106	0.60	0.20	0.60	1.00
☐ 107	0.60	0.20	0.60	1.00
☐ 108	0.60	0.20	0.60	1.00
☐ 109	0.60	0.20	0.60	1.00
☐ 110	0.60	0.20	0.60	1.00
☐ 111	0.60	0.20	0.60	1.00
☐ 112	0.60	0.20	0.60	1.00
☐ 113	0.60	0.20	0.60	1.00
☐ 114	0.60	0.20	0.60	1.00
☐ 115	0.60	0.20	0.60	1.00
☐ 116	0.65	0.20	0.60	1.00
☐ 117	0.65	0.20	0.60	1.00

	ORIG.	GOOD	FINE	N-MINT
118	0.65	0.20	0.60	1.00
119	0.65	0.20	0.60	1.00
120	0.65	0.20	0.60	1.00
121 Secret Wars II	0.65	0.20	0.60	1.00
122	0.75	0.20	0.60	1.00
123	0.75	0.20	0.60	1.00
124	0.75	0.20	0.60	1.00
125 D:Iron Fist	1.25	1.20	3.60	6.00

POWER MAN (formerly Hero for Hire)

	ORIG.	GOOD	FINE	N-MINT
17 GT, A:Iron Man	0.20	1.60	4.80	8.00
18	0.20	0.80	2.40	4.00
19	0.25	0.80	2.40	4.00
20	0.25	0.80	2.40	4.00
21	0.25	0.60	1.80	3.00
22	0.25	0.60	1.80	3.00
23	0.25	0.60	1.80	3.00
24	0.25	0.60	1.80	3.00
25	0.25	0.60	1.80	3.00
26	0.25	0.60	1.80	3.00
27 GP	0.25	0.60	1.80	3.00
28	0.25	0.60	1.80	3.00
29	0.25	0.60	1.80	3.00
30	0.25	0.60	1.80	3.00
31 NA	0.25	0.60	1.80	3.00
32	0.25	0.60	1.80	3.00
33	0.25	0.60	1.80	3.00
34	0.25	0.60	1.80	3.00
35	0.30	0.60	1.80	3.00
36	0.30	0.60	1.80	3.00
37	0.30	0.60	1.80	3.00
38	0.30	0.60	1.80	3.00
39	0.30	0.60	1.80	3.00
40	0.30	0.60	1.80	3.00
41	0.30	0.60	1.80	3.00
42	0.30	0.60	1.80	3.00
43	0.30	0.60	1.80	3.00
44	0.30	0.60	1.80	3.00
45 JSn, A:Mace	0.30	0.60	1.80	3.00
46 GT, 1:Zzax	0.30	0.60	1.80	3.00
47 BS, A:Iron Fist	0.30	1.00	3.00	5.00
48 JBy, 1:Power Man/Iron Fist	0.35	1.00	3.00	5.00
49 JBy, A:Iron Fist (becomes Power Man & Iron Fist)	0.35	1.00	3.00	5.00

POWER MAN ANNUAL

	ORIG.	GOOD	FINE	N-MINT
1 (1976)	0.50	0.60	1.80	3.00

POWER PACHYDERMS

	ORIG.	GOOD	FINE	N-MINT
1 one-shop parody	1.25	0.25	0.75	1.25

POWER PACK

	ORIG.	GOOD	FINE	N-MINT
1 V: Snarks	1.00	0.60	1.80	3.00
1 paperback	0.60	1.59	4.77	7.95
2	0.60	0.40	1.20	2.00
3	0.60	0.40	1.20	2.00
4	0.60	0.40	1.20	2.00

	ORIG.	GOOD	FINE	N-MINT
5	0.60	0.40	1.20	2.00
6	0.60	0.40	1.20	2.00
7	0.60	0.40	1.20	2.00
8	0.60	0.40	1.20	2.00
9	0.65	0.40	1.20	2.00
10	0.65	0.40	1.20	2.00
11	0.65	0.25	0.75	1.25
12 A:X-Men	0.65	0.80	2.40	4.00
13	0.65	0.30	0.90	1.50
14	0.65	0.30	0.90	1.50
15	0.65	0.30	0.90	1.50
16	0.65	0.30	0.90	1.50
17	0.65	0.30	0.90	1.50
18 Secret Wars II	0.65	0.30	0.90	1.50
19 Wolverine	1.25	1.40	4.20	7.00
20	0.75	0.30	0.90	1.50
21	0.75	0.30	0.90	1.50
22	0.75	0.30	0.90	1.50
23	0.75	0.30	0.90	1.50
24	0.75	0.30	0.90	1.50
25	1.25	0.30	0.90	1.50
26	1.00	0.30	0.90	1.50
27 mutant massacre	1.00	0.80	2.40	4.00
28 A:FF,Avengers	1.00	0.30	0.90	1.50
29	1.00	0.30	0.90	1.50
30	1.00	0.30	0.90	1.50
31 I:Trash	1.00	0.30	0.90	1.50
32	1.00	0.30	0.90	1.50
33	1.00	0.30	0.90	1.50
34	1.00	0.30	0.90	1.50
35 Fall of Mutants	1.00	0.30	0.90	1.50
36	1.00	0.30	0.90	1.50
37	1.00	0.30	0.90	1.50
38	1.00	0.30	0.90	1.50
39	1.25	0.30	0.90	1.50
40	1.25	0.30	0.90	1.50
41	1.25	0.30	0.90	1.50
42 Inferno	1.25	0.30	0.90	1.50
43 Inferno	1.50	0.30	0.90	1.50
44 Inferno	1.50	0.30	0.90	1.50
45	1.50	0.30	0.90	1.50
46 A:Punisher	1.50	0.80	2.40	4.00
47	1.50	0.30	0.90	1.50
48	1.50	0.30	0.90	1.50
49	1.50	0.30	0.90	1.50
50	1.95	0.39	1.17	1.95
51 1:Numinus	1.50	0.30	0.90	1.50
52	1.50	0.30	0.90	1.50
53 Acts of Vengeance	1.50	0.30	0.90	1.50
54	1.50	0.30	0.90	1.50
55	1.50	0.30	0.90	1.50
56	1.50	0.30	0.90	1.50
57	1.50	0.30	0.90	1.50
58 Galactus	1.50	0.30	0.90	1.50
59	1.50	0.30	0.90	1.50

	ORIG.	GOOD	FINE	N-MINT
☐ 60	1.50	0.30	0.90	1.50
☐ 61	1.50	0.30	0.90	1.50
☐ 62	1.50	0.30	0.90	1.50

POWER PACK HOLIDAY SPECIAL

	ORIG.	GOOD	FINE	N-MINT
☐ 1	2.25	0.45	1.35	2.25

PRINCE NAMOR, THE SUB-MARINER

	ORIG.	GOOD	FINE	N-MINT
☐ 1	0.75	0.40	1.20	2.00
☐ 2	0.75	0.20	0.60	1.00
☐ 3	0.75	0.20	0.60	1.00
☐ 4	0.75	0.20	0.60	1.00

PSI-FORCE

	ORIG.	GOOD	FINE	N-MINT
☐ 1	0.75	0.35	1.05	1.75
☐ 2	0.75	0.35	1.05	1.75
☐ 3	0.75	0.35	1.05	1.75
☐ 4	0.75	0.35	1.05	1.75
☐ 5	0.75	0.35	1.05	1.75
☐ 6	0.75	0.35	1.05	1.75
☐ 7	0.75	0.35	1.05	1.75
☐ 8	0.75	0.35	1.05	1.75
☐ 9	0.75	0.35	1.05	1.75
☐ 10	0.75	0.35	1.05	1.75
☐ 11	0.75	0.35	1.05	1.75
☐ 12	0.75	0.35	1.05	1.75
☐ 13	0.75	0.35	1.05	1.75
☐ 14	0.75	0.35	1.05	1.75
☐ 15	0.75	0.35	1.05	1.75
☐ 16	0.75	0.35	1.05	1.75
☐ 17	0.75	0.35	1.05	1.75
☐ 18	0.75	0.35	1.05	1.75
☐ 19	1.25	0.35	1.05	1.75
☐ 20	1.25	0.25	0.75	1.25
☐ 21	1.25	0.25	0.75	1.25
☐ 22	1.25	0.25	0.75	1.25
☐ 23	1.25	0.25	0.75	1.25
☐ 24	1.25	0.25	0.75	1.25
☐ 25	1.25	0.25	0.75	1.25
☐ 26	1.50	0.30	0.90	1.50
☐ 27	1.50	0.30	0.90	1.50
☐ 28	1.50	0.30	0.90	1.50
☐ 29	1.50	0.30	0.90	1.50
☐ 30	1.50	0.30	0.90	1.50
☐ 31	1.50	0.30	0.90	1.50
☐ 32	1.50	0.30	0.90	1.50

PSI-FORCE ANNUAL

	ORIG.	GOOD	FINE	N-MINT
☐ 1 (1987)	1.25	0.25	0.75	1.25

PUNISHER (mini-series)

	ORIG.	GOOD	FINE	N-MINT
☐ 1	1.25	10.00	30.00	50.00
☐ 2	0.75	6.00	18.00	30.00
☐ 3	0.75	3.20	9.60	16.00
☐ 4	0.75	3.20	9.60	16.00
☐ 5	0.75	3.20	9.60	16.00

PUNISHER 2099

	ORIG.	GOOD	FINE	N-MINT
☐ 1 foil cover	1.75	0.35	1.05	1.75
☐ 2	1.25	0.25	0.75	1.25

	ORIG.	GOOD	FINE	N-MINT
☐ 3	1.25	0.25	0.75	1.25
☐ 4	1.25	0.25	0.75	1.25
☐ 5	1.25	0.25	0.75	1.25
☐ 6	1.25	0.25	0.75	1.25
☐ 7	1.25	0.25	0.75	1.25
☐ 8	1.25	0.25	0.75	1.25
☐ 9	1.25	0.25	0.75	1.25

PUNISHER ANNUAL, THE

	ORIG.	GOOD	FINE	N-MINT
☐ 1 Evolutionary War	1.75	2.00	6.00	10.00
☐ 2 Atlantis Attacks	2.00	1.60	4.80	8.00
☐ 3 Lifeform	2.00	0.40	1.20	2.00
☐ 4 Von Strucker	2.00	0.40	1.20	2.00
☐ 5	2.25	0.45	1.35	2.25

PUNISHER ARMORY, THE

	ORIG.	GOOD	FINE	N-MINT
☐ 1 weapons	1.50	1.60	4.80	8.00
☐ 2	1.75	0.60	1.80	3.00
☐ 3		0.60	1.80	3.00
☐ 4	2.00	0.40	1.20	2.00
☐ 5	2.00	0.40	1.20	2.00
☐ 6	2.00	0.40	1.20	2.00
☐ 7	2.00	0.40	1.20	2.00

PUNISHER BACK TO SCHOOL SPECIAL, THE

	ORIG.	GOOD	FINE	N-MINT
☐ 1	2.95	0.59	1.77	2.95

PUNISHER HOLIDAY SPECIAL

	ORIG.	GOOD	FINE	N-MINT
☐ 1 foil cover	2.95	0.59	1.77	2.95

PUNISHER MAGAZINE

	ORIG.	GOOD	FINE	N-MINT
☐ 1 b&w, reprints	2.25	0.45	1.35	2.25
☐ 2 b&w, reprints	2.25	0.45	1.35	2.25
☐ 3 b&w, reprints	2.25	0.45	1.35	2.25
☐ 4 b&w, reprints	2.25	0.45	1.35	2.25
☐ 5 b&w, reprints	2.25	0.45	1.35	2.25
☐ 6 b&w, reprints	2.25	0.45	1.35	2.25
☐ 7 b&w, reprints	2.25	0.45	1.35	2.25
☐ 8 b&w, reprints	2.25	0.45	1.35	2.25
☐ 9 b&w, reprints	2.25	0.45	1.35	2.25
☐ 10 b&w, reprints	2.25	0.45	1.35	2.25
☐ 11 b&w, reprints	2.25	0.45	1.35	2.25
☐ 12 b&w, reprints	2.25	0.45	1.35	2.25
☐ 13 b&w, reprints	2.25	0.45	1.35	2.25
☐ 14 b&w, reprints	2.25	0.45	1.35	2.25
☐ 15 b&w, reprints	2.25	0.45	1.35	2.25
☐ 16 b&w, reprints	2.25	0.45	1.35	2.25

PUNISHER MOVIE SPECIAL

	ORIG.	GOOD	FINE	N-MINT
☐ nn	5.95	1.19	3.57	5.95

PUNISHER P.O.V.

	ORIG.	GOOD	FINE	N-MINT
☐ 1 BW	4.95	1.20	3.60	6.00
☐ 2 BW	4.95	1.20	3.60	6.00
☐ 3 BW	4.95	1.20	3.60	6.00
☐ 4 BW	4.95	1.20	3.60	6.00

PUNISHER SUMMER SPECIAL

	ORIG.	GOOD	FINE	N-MINT
☐ 1	2.95	0.59	1.77	2.95
☐ 3	2.50	0.50	1.50	2.50

	ORIG.	GOOD	FINE	N-MINT
PUNISHER WAR JOURNAL				
1	1.50	3.60	10.80	18.00
2 Daredevil	1.50	3.00	9.00	15.00
3 Daredevil	1.50	3.00	9.00	15.00
4	1.50	2.00	6.00	10.00
5	1.50	2.00	6.00	10.00
6 Wolverine	1.50	4.00	12.00	20.00
7 Wolverine	1.50	2.40	7.20	12.00
8	1.50	1.40	4.20	7.00
9	1.50	1.40	4.20	7.00
10	1.50	1.40	4.20	7.00
11	1.50	1.40	4.20	7.00
12 Vengeance	1.50	1.00	3.00	5.00
13 Vengeance	1.50	1.00	3.00	5.00
14 Spider-Man	1.50	1.60	4.80	8.00
15	1.50	1.00	3.00	5.00
16	1.50	0.60	1.80	3.00
17	1.50	0.60	1.80	3.00
18	1.50	0.60	1.80	3.00
19	1.50	0.40	1.20	2.00
20	1.50	0.40	1.20	2.00
21	1.50	0.40	1.20	2.00
22	1.50	0.40	1.20	2.00
23	1.75	0.40	1.20	2.00
24	1.75	0.35	1.05	1.75
25	1.75	0.35	1.05	1.75
26	1.75	0.35	1.05	1.75
27	1.75	0.35	1.05	1.75
28	1.75	0.35	1.05	1.75
29	1.75	0.35	1.05	1.75
30 Ghost Rider	1.75	0.60	1.80	3.00
31	1.75	0.35	1.05	1.75
32	1.75	0.35	1.05	1.75
33	1.75	0.35	1.05	1.75
34	1.75	0.35	1.05	1.75
35	1.75	0.35	1.05	1.75
36	1.75	0.35	1.05	1.75
37	1.75	0.35	1.05	1.75
38	1.75	0.35	1.05	1.75
39	1.75	0.35	1.05	1.75
40	1.75	0.35	1.05	1.75
41	1.75	0.35	1.05	1.75
42	1.75	0.35	1.05	1.75
43	1.75	0.35	1.05	1.75
44	1.75	0.35	1.05	1.75
45	1.75	0.35	1.05	1.75
46	1.75	0.35	1.05	1.75
47	1.75	0.35	1.05	1.75
48	1.75	0.35	1.05	1.75
49	1.75	0.35	1.05	1.75
50 Wolverine	2.95	0.59	1.77	2.95
51	1.75	0.35	1.05	1.75
52	1.75	0.35	1.05	1.75
53	1.75	0.35	1.05	1.75
54	1.75	0.35	1.05	1.75
55	1.75	0.35	1.05	1.75
56	1.75	0.35	1.05	1.75
57	1.75	0.35	1.05	1.75
58	1.75	0.35	1.05	1.75
PUNISHER WAR ZONE				
1 diecut cover	2.25	0.80	2.40	4.00
2	1.75	0.35	1.05	1.75
3	1.75	0.35	1.05	1.75
4	1.75	0.35	1.05	1.75
5	1.75	0.35	1.05	1.75
6	1.75	0.35	1.05	1.75
7	1.75	0.35	1.05	1.75
8	1.75	0.35	1.05	1.75
9	1.75	0.35	1.05	1.75
10	1.75	0.35	1.05	1.75
11	1.75	0.35	1.05	1.75
12	1.75	0.35	1.05	1.75
13	1.75	0.35	1.05	1.75
14	1.75	0.35	1.05	1.75
15	1.75	0.35	1.05	1.75
16	1.75	0.35	1.05	1.75
17	1.75	0.35	1.05	1.75
18	1.75	0.35	1.05	1.75
19	1.75	0.35	1.05	1.75
PUNISHER WAR ZONE ANNUAL				
1 card	2.95	0.59	1.77	2.95
PUNISHER, THE (ongoing series)				
1	0.75	5.00	15.00	25.00
2	0.75	2.80	8.40	14.00
3	0.75	2.00	6.00	10.00
4	0.75	2.00	6.00	10.00
5	0.75	2.00	6.00	10.00
6	0.75	2.00	6.00	10.00
7	0.75	2.00	6.00	10.00
8	1.00	2.00	6.00	10.00
9	1.00	2.00	6.00	10.00
10 Daredevil	1.00	4.80	14.40	24.00
11	1.00	1.20	3.60	6.00
12	1.00	1.00	3.00	5.00
13	1.00	1.00	3.00	5.00
14	1.00	1.00	3.00	5.00
15	1.00	1.00	3.00	5.00
16	1.00	1.00	3.00	5.00
17	1.00	1.00	3.00	5.00
18 V:Kingpin	1.00	1.00	3.00	5.00
19	1.00	0.80	2.40	4.00
20	1.00	0.80	2.40	4.00
21	1.00	0.80	2.40	4.00
22	1.00	0.80	2.40	4.00
23	1.00	0.80	2.40	4.00
24	1.00	0.80	2.40	4.00
25	1.75	0.50	1.50	2.50
26	1.00	0.40	1.20	2.00
27	1.00	0.40	1.20	2.00

	ORIG.	GOOD	FINE	N-MINT
❑ 28 Vengeance	1.00	0.40	1.20	2.00
❑ 29 Vengeance	1.00	0.40	1.20	2.00
❑ 30	1.00	0.40	1.20	2.00
❑ 31	1.00	0.40	1.20	2.00
❑ 32	1.00	0.40	1.20	2.00
❑ 33	1.00	0.40	1.20	2.00
❑ 34	1.00	0.40	1.20	2.00
❑ 35 Jigsaw Puzzle	1.00	0.20	0.60	1.00
❑ 36 Jigsaw Puzzle	1.00	0.20	0.60	1.00
❑ 37 Jigsaw Puzzle	1.00	0.20	0.60	1.00
❑ 38 Jigsaw Puzzle	1.00	0.20	0.60	1.00
❑ 39 Jigsaw Puzzle	1.00	0.20	0.60	1.00
❑ 40 Jigsaw Puzzle	1.00	0.20	0.60	1.00
❑ 41	1.00	0.20	0.60	1.00
❑ 42	1.00	0.20	0.60	1.00
❑ 43	1.00	0.20	0.60	1.00
❑ 44	1.00	0.20	0.60	1.00
❑ 45	1.00	0.20	0.60	1.00
❑ 46	1.00	0.20	0.60	1.00
❑ 47	1.00	0.20	0.60	1.00
❑ 48	1.00	0.20	0.60	1.00
❑ 49	1.00	0.20	0.60	1.00
❑ 50	1.50	0.30	0.90	1.50
❑ 51	1.00	0.20	0.60	1.00
❑ 52	1.00	0.20	0.60	1.00
❑ 53	1.00	0.20	0.60	1.00
❑ 54	1.00	0.20	0.60	1.00
❑ 55	1.00	0.20	0.60	1.00
❑ 56	1.00	0.20	0.60	1.00
❑ 57 photo cover	1.00	0.20	0.60	1.00
❑ 58	1.00	0.20	0.60	1.00
❑ 59	1.00	0.20	0.60	1.00
❑ 60 Cage	1.25	0.25	0.75	1.25
❑ 61 Cage	1.25	0.25	0.75	1.25
❑ 62	1.25	0.25	0.75	1.25
❑ 63	1.25	0.25	0.75	1.25
❑ 64	1.25	0.25	0.75	1.25
❑ 65	1.25	0.25	0.75	1.25
❑ 66	1.25	0.25	0.75	1.25
❑ 67	1.25	0.25	0.75	1.25
❑ 68	1.25	0.25	0.75	1.25
❑ 69	1.25	0.25	0.75	1.25
❑ 70	1.25	0.25	0.75	1.25
❑ 71	1.25	0.25	0.75	1.25
❑ 72	1.25	0.25	0.75	1.25
❑ 73	1.25	0.25	0.75	1.25
❑ 74	1.25	0.25	0.75	1.25
❑ 75 foil cover	2.75	0.55	1.65	2.75
❑ 76	1.25	0.25	0.75	1.25
❑ 77	1.25	0.25	0.75	1.25
❑ 78	1.25	0.25	0.75	1.25
❑ 79	1.25	0.25	0.75	1.25
❑ 80	1.25	0.25	0.75	1.25
❑ 81	1.25	0.25	0.75	1.25

	ORIG.	GOOD	FINE	N-MINT
❑ 82	1.25	0.25	0.75	1.25
❑ 83	1.25	0.25	0.75	1.25

PUNISHER/CAPTAIN AMERICA: BLOOD & GLORY

	ORIG.	GOOD	FINE	N-MINT
❑ 1	5.95	1.19	3.57	5.95
❑ 2	5.95	1.19	3.57	5.95
❑ 3	5.95	1.19	3.57	5.95

PUNISHER: ORIGIN MICRO CHIP

	ORIG.	GOOD	FINE	N-MINT
❑ 1	1.75	0.35	1.05	1.75
❑ 2	1.75	0.35	1.05	1.75

PUNISHER: THE GHOSTS OF INNOCENTS

	ORIG.	GOOD	FINE	N-MINT
❑ 1	5.95	1.19	3.57	5.95
❑ 2	5.95	1.19	3.57	5.95

PUSSYCAT

	ORIG.	GOOD	FINE	N-MINT
❑ 1 (b&w mag) Wally Wood, Bill Ward	0.35	5.00	15.00	25.00

QUASAR

	ORIG.	GOOD	FINE	N-MINT
❑ 1	1.00	0.80	2.40	4.00
❑ 2	1.00	0.60	1.80	3.00
❑ 3	1.00	0.40	1.20	2.00
❑ 4	1.00	0.40	1.20	2.00
❑ 5 Vengeance	1.00	0.40	1.20	2.00
❑ 6 Vengeance	1.00	0.40	1.20	2.00
❑ 7 Spider-Man	1.00	0.80	2.40	4.00
❑ 8	1.00	0.30	0.90	1.50
❑ 9	1.00	0.30	0.90	1.50
❑ 10	1.00	0.30	0.90	1.50
❑ 11 Phoenix	1.00	0.30	0.90	1.50
❑ 12	1.00	0.30	0.90	1.50
❑ 13	1.00	0.30	0.90	1.50
❑ 14 TMc(c)	1.00	0.30	0.90	1.50
❑ 15	1.00	0.30	0.90	1.50
❑ 16 48 pages	1.50	0.30	0.90	1.50
❑ 17	1.00	0.30	0.90	1.50
❑ 18	1.50	0.30	0.90	1.50
❑ 19	1.00	0.30	0.90	1.50
❑ 20 F4	1.00	0.30	0.90	1.50
❑ 21	1.00	0.20	0.60	1.00
❑ 22	1.00	0.20	0.60	1.00
❑ 23	1.00	0.20	0.60	1.00
❑ 24	1.00	0.20	0.60	1.00
❑ 25 new costume	1.00	0.20	0.60	1.00
❑ 26 Infinity Gauntlet	1.00	0.20	0.60	1.00
❑ 27 Infinity Gauntlet	1.00	0.20	0.60	1.00
❑ 28	1.00	0.20	0.60	1.00
❑ 29	1.00	0.20	0.60	1.00
❑ 30	1.00	0.20	0.60	1.00
❑ 31 New Universe	1.25	0.25	0.75	1.25
❑ 32 Galactic Storm	1.25	0.25	0.75	1.25
❑ 33 Galactic Storm	1.25	0.25	0.75	1.25
❑ 34 Galactic Storm	1.25	0.25	0.75	1.25
❑ 35 Galactic Storm	1.25	0.25	0.75	1.25
❑ 38 Infinity War	1.25	0.25	0.75	1.25
❑ 39 Infinity War	1.25	0.25	0.75	1.25

	ORIG.	GOOD	FINE	N-MINT
❏ 40 Infinity War	1.25	0.25	0.75	1.25
❏ 41	1.25	0.25	0.75	1.25
❏ 42	1.25	0.25	0.75	1.25
❏ 43	1.25	0.25	0.75	1.25
❏ 44	1.25	0.25	0.75	1.25
❏ 45	1.25	0.25	0.75	1.25
❏ 46	1.25	0.25	0.75	1.25
❏ 47	1.25	0.25	0.75	1.25
❏ 48	1.25	0.25	0.75	1.25
❏ 49	1.25	0.25	0.75	1.25
❏ 50 foil cover	2.95	0.59	1.77	2.95
❏ 51	1.25	0.25	0.75	1.25

QUASAR SPECIAL EDITION

	ORIG.	GOOD	FINE	N-MINT
❏ 1 reprints Quasar #32	1.25	0.25	0.75	1.25
❏ 2 reprints Quasar #33	1.25	0.25	0.75	1.25
❏ 3 reprints Quasar #34	1.25	0.25	0.75	1.25

QUESTPROBE

	ORIG.	GOOD	FINE	N-MINT
❏ 1 JR Hulk	0.75	0.20	0.60	1.00
❏ 2 AM/JM Spider-Man	0.75	0.20	0.60	1.00
❏ 3 Thing	0.75	0.20	0.60	1.00

RAIDERS OF THE LOST ARK

	ORIG.	GOOD	FINE	N-MINT
❏ 1 JB/KJ movie	0.50	0.30	0.90	1.50
❏ 2 JB/KJ	0.50	0.20	0.60	1.00
❏ 3 JB/KJ	0.50	0.20	0.60	1.00

RAMPAGING HULK, THE (b&w mag)

	ORIG.	GOOD	FINE	N-MINT
❏ 1	1.00	0.20	0.60	1.00
❏ 2	1.00	0.20	0.60	1.00
❏ 3	1.00	0.20	0.60	1.00
❏ 4	1.00	0.20	0.60	1.00
❏ 5	1.00	0.20	0.60	1.00
❏ 6	1.00	0.20	0.60	1.00
❏ 7	1.00	0.20	0.60	1.00
❏ 8	1.00	0.20	0.60	1.00
❏ 9 (becomes the Hulk)	1.00	0.20	0.60	1.00

RAVAGE 2099

	ORIG.	GOOD	FINE	N-MINT
❏ 1 foil cover	1.75	0.35	1.05	1.75
❏ 2	1.25	0.25	0.75	1.25
❏ 3	1.25	0.25	0.75	1.25
❏ 4	1.25	0.25	0.75	1.25
❏ 5	1.25	0.25	0.75	1.25
❏ 6	1.25	0.25	0.75	1.25
❏ 7	1.25	0.25	0.75	1.25
❏ 8	1.25	0.25	0.75	1.25
❏ 9	1.25	0.25	0.75	1.25
❏ 10	1.25	0.25	0.75	1.25
❏ 11	1.25	0.25	0.75	1.25

RAWHIDE KID (1955-1979)

	ORIG.	GOOD	FINE	N-MINT
❏ 1	0.10	60.00	180.00	300.00
❏ 2	0.10	40.00	120.00	200.00
❏ 3	0.10	28.00	84.00	140.00
❏ 4	0.10	28.00	84.00	140.00
❏ 5	0.10	28.00	84.00	140.00
❏ 6	0.10	16.00	48.00	80.00
❏ 7	0.10	16.00	48.00	80.00

	ORIG.	GOOD	FINE	N-MINT
❏ 8	0.10	16.00	48.00	80.00
❏ 9	0.10	16.00	48.00	80.00
❏ 10	0.10	16.00	48.00	80.00
❏ 11	0.10	7.20	21.60	36.00
❏ 12	0.10	7.20	21.60	36.00
❏ 13	0.10	7.20	21.60	36.00
❏ 14	0.10	7.20	21.60	36.00
❏ 15	0.10	7.20	21.60	36.00
❏ 16	0.10	7.20	21.60	36.00
❏ 17	0.10	7.20	21.60	36.00
❏ 18	0.10	7.20	21.60	36.00
❏ 19	0.10	7.20	21.60	36.00
❏ 20	0.10	7.20	21.60	36.00
❏ 21	0.10	7.20	21.60	36.00
❏ 22	0.10	7.20	21.60	36.00
❏ 23	0.10	13.00	39.00	65.00
❏ 24	0.10	6.00	18.00	30.00
❏ 25	0.10	6.00	18.00	30.00
❏ 26	0.10	6.00	18.00	30.00
❏ 27	0.12	6.00	18.00	30.00
❏ 28	0.12	6.00	18.00	30.00
❏ 29	0.12	6.00	18.00	30.00
❏ 30	0.12	6.00	18.00	30.00
❏ 31	0.12	5.20	15.60	26.00
❏ 32	0.12	5.20	15.60	26.00
❏ 33	0.12	5.20	15.60	26.00
❏ 34	0.12	5.20	15.60	26.00
❏ 35	0.12	5.20	15.60	26.00
❏ 36	0.12	5.20	15.60	26.00
❏ 37	0.12	5.20	15.60	26.00
❏ 38	0.12	5.20	15.60	26.00
❏ 39	0.12	5.20	15.60	26.00
❏ 40	0.12	5.20	15.60	26.00
❏ 41	0.12	5.20	15.60	26.00
❏ 42	0.12	5.20	15.60	26.00
❏ 43	0.12	5.20	15.60	26.00
❏ 44	0.12	5.20	15.60	26.00
❏ 45	0.12	5.20	15.60	26.00
❏ 46	0.12	5.20	15.60	26.00
❏ 47	0.12	2.40	7.20	12.00
❏ 48	0.12	2.40	7.20	12.00
❏ 49	0.12	2.40	7.20	12.00
❏ 50	0.12	2.40	7.20	12.00
❏ 51	0.12	2.40	7.20	12.00
❏ 52	0.12	2.40	7.20	12.00
❏ 53	0.12	2.40	7.20	12.00
❏ 54	0.12	2.40	7.20	12.00
❏ 55	0.12	2.40	7.20	12.00
❏ 56	0.12	2.40	7.20	12.00
❏ 57	0.12	2.40	7.20	12.00
❏ 58	0.12	2.40	7.20	12.00
❏ 59	0.12	2.40	7.20	12.00
❏ 60	0.12	2.40	7.20	12.00
❏ 61	0.12	2.40	7.20	12.00
❏ 62	0.12	2.40	7.20	12.00

	ORIG.	GOOD	FINE	N-MINT
❏ 63	0.12	2.40	7.20	12.00
❏ 64	0.12	2.40	7.20	12.00
❏ 65	0.12	2.40	7.20	12.00
❏ 66	0.12	2.40	7.20	12.00
❏ 67	0.12	2.40	7.20	12.00
❏ 68	0.12	2.40	7.20	12.00
❏ 69	0.12	2.40	7.20	12.00
❏ 70	0.12	2.40	7.20	12.00
❏ 71	0.15	1.00	3.00	5.00
❏ 72	0.15	1.00	3.00	5.00
❏ 73	0.15	1.00	3.00	5.00
❏ 74	0.15	1.00	3.00	5.00
❏ 75	0.15	1.00	3.00	5.00
❏ 76	0.15	1.00	3.00	5.00
❏ 77	0.15	1.00	3.00	5.00
❏ 78	0.15	1.00	3.00	5.00
❏ 79	0.15	1.00	3.00	5.00
❏ 80	0.15	1.00	3.00	5.00
❏ 81	0.15	1.00	3.00	5.00
❏ 82	0.15	1.00	3.00	5.00
❏ 83	0.15	1.00	3.00	5.00
❏ 84	0.20	1.00	3.00	5.00
❏ 85	0.20	1.00	3.00	5.00
❏ 86	0.20	1.00	3.00	5.00
❏ 87	0.20	1.00	3.00	5.00
❏ 88	0.20	1.00	3.00	5.00
❏ 89	0.20	1.00	3.00	5.00
❏ 90	0.20	1.00	3.00	5.00
❏ 91	0.20	1.00	3.00	5.00
❏ 92	0.20	1.00	3.00	5.00
❏ 93	0.20	1.00	3.00	5.00
❏ 94	0.20	1.00	3.00	5.00
❏ 95	0.20	1.00	3.00	5.00
❏ 96	0.20	1.00	3.00	5.00
❏ 97	0.25	1.00	3.00	5.00
❏ 98	0.25	1.00	3.00	5.00
❏ 99	0.25	1.00	3.00	5.00
❏ 100	0.25	2.40	7.20	12.00
❏ 101	0.25	1.00	3.00	5.00
❏ 102	0.25	1.00	3.00	5.00
❏ 103	0.25	1.00	3.00	5.00
❏ 104	0.25	1.00	3.00	5.00
❏ 105	0.25	1.00	3.00	5.00
❏ 106	0.25	1.00	3.00	5.00
❏ 107	0.25	1.00	3.00	5.00
❏ 108	0.25	1.00	3.00	5.00
❏ 109	0.25	1.00	3.00	5.00
❏ 110	0.25	1.00	3.00	5.00
❏ 111	0.25	1.00	3.00	5.00
❏ 112	0.25	1.00	3.00	5.00
❏ 113	0.25	1.00	3.00	5.00
❏ 114	0.25	1.00	3.00	5.00
❏ 115	0.25	1.00	3.00	5.00
❏ 116		0.60	1.80	3.00
❏ 117		0.60	1.80	3.00

	ORIG.	GOOD	FINE	N-MINT
❏ 118		0.60	1.80	3.00
❏ 119		0.60	1.80	3.00
❏ 120		0.60	1.80	3.00
❏ 121		0.60	1.80	3.00
❏ 122		0.60	1.80	3.00
❏ 123		0.60	1.80	3.00
❏ 124		0.60	1.80	3.00
❏ 125		0.60	1.80	3.00
❏ 126		0.60	1.80	3.00
❏ 127		0.60	1.80	3.00
❏ 128		0.60	1.80	3.00
❏ 129		0.60	1.80	3.00
❏ 130		0.60	1.80	3.00
❏ 131		0.60	1.80	3.00
❏ 132		0.60	1.80	3.00
❏ 133		0.60	1.80	3.00
❏ 134		0.60	1.80	3.00
❏ 135		0.60	1.80	3.00
❏ 136		0.60	1.80	3.00
❏ 137		0.60	1.80	3.00
❏ 138		0.60	1.80	3.00
❏ 139		0.60	1.80	3.00
❏ 140		0.60	1.80	3.00
❏ 141	0.30	0.60	1.80	3.00
❏ 142		0.60	1.80	3.00
❏ 143		0.60	1.80	3.00
❏ 144		0.60	1.80	3.00
❏ 145		0.60	1.80	3.00
❏ 146		0.60	1.80	3.00
❏ 147		0.60	1.80	3.00
❏ 148		0.60	1.80	3.00
❏ 149		0.60	1.80	3.00
❏ 150		0.60	1.80	3.00
❏ 151		0.60	1.80	3.00

RAWHIDE KID (mini-series)

	ORIG.	GOOD	FINE	N-MINT
❏ 1	0.75	0.20	0.60	1.00
❏ 2	0.75	0.20	0.60	1.00
❏ 3	0.75	0.20	0.60	1.00
❏ 4	0.75	0.20	0.60	1.00

RAWHIDE KID SPECIAL

	ORIG.	GOOD	FINE	N-MINT
❏ 1 reprints, 1971	0.25	1.00	3.00	5.00

RAZORLINE: THE FIRST CUT

	ORIG.	GOOD	FINE	N-MINT
❏ 1 sampler	0.75	0.15	0.45	0.75

RED SONJA (1976-1979)

	ORIG.	GOOD	FINE	N-MINT
❏ 1 FT	0.30	0.50	1.50	2.50
❏ 2 FT	0.30	0.35	1.05	1.75
❏ 3 FT	0.30	0.35	1.05	1.75
❏ 4 FT	0.30	0.35	1.05	1.75
❏ 5 FT	0.30	0.35	1.05	1.75
❏ 6	0.35	0.20	0.60	1.00
❏ 7	0.35	0.20	0.60	1.00
❏ 8	0.35	0.20	0.60	1.00
❏ 9	0.35	0.20	0.60	1.00
❏ 10	0.35	0.20	0.60	1.00

	ORIG.	GOOD	FINE	N-MINT
11 .... 0.35	0.20	0.60	1.00
12 .... 0.35	0.20	0.60	1.00
13 .... 0.35	0.20	0.60	1.00
14 .... 0.35	0.20	0.60	1.00
15 .... 0.40	0.20	0.60	1.00

RED SONJA (1983)

	ORIG.	GOOD	FINE	N-MINT
1 .... 0.60	0.40	1.20	2.00
2 .... 0.60	0.30	0.90	1.50

RED SONJA (1983-1986)

	ORIG.	GOOD	FINE	N-MINT
1 .... 1.00	0.40	1.20	2.00
2 .... 1.00	0.30	0.90	1.50
3 .... 1.00	0.30	0.90	1.50
4 .... 1.00	0.30	0.90	1.50
5 .... 0.60	0.30	0.90	1.50
6 .... 0.60	0.30	0.90	1.50
7 .... 0.60	0.30	0.90	1.50
8 .... 0.65	0.30	0.90	1.50
9 .... 0.65	0.30	0.90	1.50
10 .... 0.65	0.30	0.90	1.50
11 .... 0.65	0.30	0.90	1.50
12 .... 0.75	0.30	0.90	1.50
13 .... 0.75	0.30	0.90	1.50

RED SONJA: THE MOVIE

	ORIG.	GOOD	FINE	N-MINT
1 movie 0.75	0.20	0.60	1.00
2 movie 0.75	0.20	0.60	1.00

RED WOLF

	ORIG.	GOOD	FINE	N-MINT
1 .... 0.20	0.20	0.60	1.00
2 .... 0.20	0.20	0.60	1.00
3 .... 0.20	0.20	0.60	1.00
4 .... 0.20	0.20	0.60	1.00
5 .... 0.20	0.20	0.60	1.00
6 .... 0.20	0.20	0.60	1.00
7 .... 0.20	0.20	0.60	1.00
8 .... 0.20	0.20	0.60	1.00
9 .... 0.20	0.20	0.60	1.00

REN & STIMPY SHOW, THE

	ORIG.	GOOD	FINE	N-MINT
1 Ren scratch&sniff card .. 2.25	7.00	21.00	35.00
1 Stimpy scratch&sniff card			
.... 2.25	7.00	21.00	35.00
1 second printing 2.25	2.00	6.00	10.00
1 third printing.................. 2.25	1.00	3.00	5.00
2 .... 1.75	4.80	14.40	24.00
2 second printing 1.75	0.80	2.40	4.00
3 .... 1.75	3.00	9.00	15.00
3 second printing 1.75	0.80	2.40	4.00
4 .... 1.75	2.00	6.00	10.00
5 .... 1.75	2.00	6.00	10.00
6 Spider-Man 1.75	1.40	4.20	7.00
7 Spider-Man 1.75	1.00	3.00	5.00
8 .... 1.75	0.60	1.80	3.00
9 .... 1.75	0.60	1.80	3.00
10 .... 1.75	0.35	1.05	1.75
11 .... 1.75	0.35	1.05	1.75

	ORIG.	GOOD	FINE	N-MINT

REQUIEM FOR DRACULA

	ORIG.	GOOD	FINE	N-MINT
1 reprints 2.00	0.40	1.20	2.00

RETURN OF THE JEDI

	ORIG.	GOOD	FINE	N-MINT
1 AW, movie...................... 0.60	0.30	0.90	1.50
2 AW, movie...................... 0.60	0.30	0.90	1.50
3 AW 0.60	0.20	0.60	1.00
4 AW 0.60	0.20	0.60	1.00

RINGO KID (1970-1976)

	ORIG.	GOOD	FINE	N-MINT
1 .... 0.15	0.40	1.20	2.00
2 .... 0.15	0.20	0.60	1.00
3 .... 0.15	0.20	0.60	1.00
4 .... 0.15	0.20	0.60	1.00
5 .... 0.15	0.20	0.60	1.00
6 .... 0.15	0.20	0.60	1.00
7 .... 0.15	0.20	0.60	1.00
8 .... 0.15	0.20	0.60	1.00
9 .... 0.15	0.20	0.60	1.00
10 .... 0.15	0.20	0.60	1.00
11 .... 0.15	0.20	0.60	1.00
12 .... 0.25	0.20	0.60	1.00
12 .... 0.25	0.20	0.60	1.00
13 .... 0.20	0.20	0.60	1.00
14 .... 0.20	0.20	0.60	1.00
15 .... 0.20	0.20	0.60	1.00
16 .... 0.20	0.20	0.60	1.00
17 .... 0.20	0.20	0.60	1.00
18 .... 0.20	0.20	0.60	1.00
19 .... 0.20	0.20	0.60	1.00
20 .... 0.20	0.20	0.60	1.00
21 .... 0.20	0.20	0.60	1.00
22 .... 0.20	0.20	0.60	1.00
23 .... 0.20	0.20	0.60	1.00
24 .... 0.20	0.20	0.60	1.00
25 .... 0.20	0.20	0.60	1.00
26 .... 0.20	0.20	0.60	1.00
27 .... 0.20	0.20	0.60	1.00
28 .... 0.20	0.20	0.60	1.00
29 .... 0.20	0.20	0.60	1.00
30 .... 0.20	0.20	0.60	1.00

ROBOCOP

	ORIG.	GOOD	FINE	N-MINT
1 movie adaptation, mag... 2.00	0.60	1.80	3.00
1 movie, bookshelf 4.95	0.99	2.97	4.95

ROBOCOP (ongoing series)

	ORIG.	GOOD	FINE	N-MINT
1 .... 1.50	1.60	4.80	8.00
2 .... 1.50	1.00	3.00	5.00
3 .... 1.50	0.60	1.80	3.00
4 .... 1.50	0.60	1.80	3.00
5 .... 1.50	0.30	0.90	1.50
6 .... 1.50	0.30	0.90	1.50
7 .... 1.50	0.30	0.90	1.50
8 .... 1.50	0.30	0.90	1.50
9 .... 1.50	0.30	0.90	1.50
10 .... 1.50	0.30	0.90	1.50
11 .... 1.50	0.30	0.90	1.50

	ORIG.	GOOD	FINE	N-MINT
❏ 12	1.50	0.30	0.90	1.50
❏ 13	1.50	0.30	0.90	1.50
❏ 14	1.50	0.30	0.90	1.50
❏ 15	1.50	0.30	0.90	1.50
❏ 16	1.50	0.30	0.90	1.50
❏ 17	1.50	0.30	0.90	1.50
❏ 18	1.50	0.30	0.90	1.50
❏ 19	1.50	0.30	0.90	1.50
❏ 20	1.50	0.30	0.90	1.50
❏ 21	1.50	0.30	0.90	1.50
❏ 22	1.50	0.30	0.90	1.50
❏ 23	1.50	0.30	0.90	1.50

ROBOCOP 2

	ORIG.	GOOD	FINE	N-MINT
❏ 1 bookshelf, movie	4.95	0.99	2.97	4.95
❏ 1 b&w mag, movie	2.25	0.45	1.35	2.25
❏ 1 comic book, movie	1.00	0.20	0.60	1.00
❏ 2 comic book, movie	1.00	0.20	0.60	1.00
❏ 3 comic book, movie	1.00	0.20	0.60	1.00

ROBOTIX

	ORIG.	GOOD	FINE	N-MINT
❏ 1	0.75	0.40	1.20	2.00

ROCKET RACCOON

	ORIG.	GOOD	FINE	N-MINT
❏ 1	0.75	0.25	0.75	1.25
❏ 2	0.75	0.20	0.60	1.00
❏ 3	0.75	0.20	0.60	1.00
❏ 4	0.75	0.20	0.60	1.00

ROM

	ORIG.	GOOD	FINE	N-MINT
❏ 1 SB, O:	0.40	0.80	2.40	4.00
❏ 2 SB,FM(c)	0.40	0.50	1.50	2.50
❏ 3 SB,FM(c)	0.40	0.50	1.50	2.50
❏ 4 SB	0.40	0.40	1.20	2.00
❏ 5 SB	0.40	0.40	1.20	2.00
❏ 6 SB	0.40	0.30	0.90	1.50
❏ 7 SB	0.40	0.30	0.90	1.50
❏ 8 SB	0.40	0.30	0.90	1.50
❏ 9 SB	0.40	0.30	0.90	1.50
❏ 10 SB	0.50	0.30	0.90	1.50
❏ 11 SB	0.50	0.30	0.90	1.50
❏ 12 SB	0.50	0.30	0.90	1.50
❏ 13 SB	0.50	0.25	0.75	1.25
❏ 14 SB	0.50	0.25	0.75	1.25
❏ 15 SB	0.50	0.25	0.75	1.25
❏ 16 SB	0.50	0.25	0.75	1.25
❏ 17 SB, X-Men	0.50	0.80	2.40	4.00
❏ 18 SB, X-Men	0.50	0.80	2.40	4.00
❏ 19 SB/JSt, C:X-Men	0.50	0.30	0.90	1.50
❏ 20 SB/JSt	0.50	0.25	0.75	1.25
❏ 21 SB/JSt	0.50	0.25	0.75	1.25
❏ 22 SB/JSt	0.50	0.25	0.75	1.25
❏ 23 SB/JSt	0.50	0.25	0.75	1.25
❏ 24 SB/JSt	0.50	0.25	0.75	1.25
❏ 25 SB/JSt, double size	0.75	0.30	0.90	1.50
❏ 26	0.60	0.25	0.75	1.25
❏ 27	0.60	0.25	0.75	1.25
❏ 28	0.60	0.25	0.75	1.25

	ORIG.	GOOD	FINE	N-MINT
❏ 29	0.60	0.25	0.75	1.25
❏ 30	0.60	0.25	0.75	1.25
❏ 31	0.60	0.25	0.75	1.25
❏ 32	0.60	0.25	0.75	1.25
❏ 33	0.60	0.25	0.75	1.25
❏ 34	0.60	0.25	0.75	1.25
❏ 35	0.60	0.25	0.75	1.25
❏ 36	0.60	0.20	0.60	1.00
❏ 37	0.60	0.20	0.60	1.00
❏ 38	0.60	0.20	0.60	1.00
❏ 39	0.60	0.20	0.60	1.00
❏ 40	0.60	0.20	0.60	1.00
❏ 41	0.60	0.20	0.60	1.00
❏ 42	0.60	0.20	0.60	1.00
❏ 43	0.60	0.20	0.60	1.00
❏ 44	0.60	0.20	0.60	1.00
❏ 45	0.60	0.20	0.60	1.00
❏ 46	0.60	0.20	0.60	1.00
❏ 47	0.60	0.20	0.60	1.00
❏ 48	0.60	0.20	0.60	1.00
❏ 49	0.60	0.20	0.60	1.00
❏ 50	1.00	0.20	0.60	1.00
❏ 51	0.60	0.20	0.60	1.00
❏ 52	0.60	0.20	0.60	1.00
❏ 53	0.60	0.20	0.60	1.00
❏ 54	0.60	0.20	0.60	1.00
❏ 55	0.60	0.20	0.60	1.00
❏ 56 Alpha Flight	0.60	0.25	0.75	1.25
❏ 57 Alpha Flight	0.60	0.25	0.75	1.25
❏ 58 Dire Wraiths	0.60	0.20	0.60	1.00
❏ 59 SD	0.60	0.20	0.60	1.00
❏ 60 SD	0.60	0.20	0.60	1.00
❏ 61 SD	0.60	0.20	0.60	1.00
❏ 62 SD	0.60	0.20	0.60	1.00
❏ 63 SD	0.60	0.20	0.60	1.00
❏ 64	0.60	0.20	0.60	1.00
❏ 65	0.65	0.20	0.60	1.00
❏ 66	0.65	0.20	0.60	1.00
❏ 67	0.65	0.20	0.60	1.00
❏ 68	0.65	0.20	0.60	1.00
❏ 69	0.65	0.20	0.60	1.00
❏ 70	0.65	0.20	0.60	1.00
❏ 71	0.65	0.20	0.60	1.00
❏ 72 Secret Wars II	0.65	0.20	0.60	1.00
❏ 73	0.75	0.20	0.60	1.00

	ORIG.	GOOD	FINE	N-MINT
74 .... 0.75	0.20	0.60	1.00
75 .... 0.75	0.20	0.60	1.00

ROM ANNUAL

	ORIG.	GOOD	FINE	N-MINT
1 Stardust (1982) 1.00	0.30	0.90	1.50
2 (1983) 1.00	0.25	0.75	1.25
3 (1984) 1.00	0.25	0.75	1.25
4 (1985) 1.25	0.25	0.75	1.25

S.H.I.E.L.D. (1973)

	ORIG.	GOOD	FINE	N-MINT
1 .... 0.20	0.40	1.20	2.00
2 .... 0.20	0.40	1.20	2.00
3 .... 0.20	0.40	1.20	2.00
4 .... 0.20	0.40	1.20	2.00
5 .... 0.20	0.40	1.20	2.00

SABRETOOTH

	ORIG.	GOOD	FINE	N-MINT
1 diecut cover 2.95	0.80	2.40	4.00
2 .... 2.95	0.59	1.77	2.95

SAGA OF CRYSTAR, CRYSTAL WARRIOR, THE

	ORIG.	GOOD	FINE	N-MINT
1 Origin 2.00	0.40	1.20	2.00
2 .... 0.60	0.20	0.60	1.00
3 .... 0.60	0.20	0.60	1.00
4 .... 0.60	0.20	0.60	1.00
5 .... 0.60	0.20	0.60	1.00
6 .... 0.60	0.20	0.60	1.00
7 .... 0.60	0.20	0.60	1.00
8 .... 0.60	0.20	0.60	1.00
9 .... 0.60	0.20	0.60	1.00
10 .... 0.60	0.20	0.60	1.00
11 Alpha Flight 1.00	0.20	0.60	1.00

SAGA OF THE ORIGINAL HUMAN TORCH, THE

	ORIG.	GOOD	FINE	N-MINT
1 RB O:Human Torch 1.50	0.30	0.90	1.50
2 O:Toro 1.50	0.30	0.90	1.50
3 D:Hitler 1.50	0.30	0.90	1.50
4 .... 1.50	0.30	0.90	1.50

SAGA OF THE SUB-MARINER, THE

	ORIG.	GOOD	FINE	N-MINT
1 O:Sub-Mariner 1.25	0.60	1.80	3.00
2 .... 1.50	0.40	1.20	2.00
3 .... 1.50	0.40	1.20	2.00
4 Human Torch 1.50	0.40	1.20	2.00
5 Torch, Capt. America, Invaders			
.... 1.50	0.40	1.20	2.00
6 Torch, Capt. America, Invaders			
1.50 .... 0.40	1.20	2.00	
7 Fantastic Four 1.50	0.40	1.20	2.00
8 F4, Avengers 1.50	0.40	1.20	2.00
9 F4, Avengers 1.50	0.40	1.20	2.00
10 .... 1.50	0.40	1.20	2.00
11 .... 1.50	0.40	1.20	2.00
12 .... 1.50	0.40	1.20	2.00

SAINT SINNER

	ORIG.	GOOD	FINE	N-MINT
1 foil cover 2.50	0.50	1.50	2.50

SAVAGE RETURN OF DRACULA

	ORIG.	GOOD	FINE	N-MINT
1 reprints 2.00	0.40	1.20	2.00

SAVAGE SHE-HULK, THE

	ORIG.	GOOD	FINE	N-MINT
1 O: 0.40	0.40	1.20	2.00
2 .... 0.40	0.20	0.60	1.00
3 .... 0.40	0.20	0.60	1.00
4 .... 0.40	0.20	0.60	1.00
5 .... 0.40	0.20	0.60	1.00
6 .... 0.40	0.20	0.60	1.00
7 .... 0.40	0.20	0.60	1.00
8 .... 0.50	0.20	0.60	1.00
9 .... 0.50	0.20	0.60	1.00
10 .... 0.50	0.20	0.60	1.00
11 .... 0.50	0.20	0.60	1.00
12 .... 0.50	0.20	0.60	1.00
13 .... 0.50	0.20	0.60	1.00
14 .... 0.50	0.20	0.60	1.00
15 .... 0.50	0.20	0.60	1.00
16 .... 0.50	0.20	0.60	1.00
17 .... 0.50	0.20	0.60	1.00
18 .... 0.50	0.20	0.60	1.00
19 .... 0.50	0.20	0.60	1.00
20 .... 0.50	0.20	0.60	1.00
21 .... 0.50	0.20	0.60	1.00
22 .... 0.50	0.20	0.60	1.00
23 .... 0.50	0.20	0.60	1.00
24 .... 0.60	0.20	0.60	1.00
25 double size 1.00	0.25	0.75	1.25

SAVAGE SWORD OF CONAN

	ORIG.	GOOD	FINE	N-MINT
1 O:Blackmark, b&w 1.00	12.00	36.00	60.00
2 .... 1.00	6.00	18.00	30.00
3 .... 1.00	3.00	9.00	15.00
4 .... 1.00	3.00	9.00	15.00
5 .... 1.00	3.00	9.00	15.00
6 .... 1.00	1.60	4.80	8.00
7 .... 1.00	1.60	4.80	8.00
8 .... 1.00	1.60	4.80	8.00
9 .... 1.00	1.60	4.80	8.00
10 .... 1.00	1.60	4.80	8.00
11 .... 1.00	1.60	4.80	8.00
12 .... 1.00	1.60	4.80	8.00
13 .... 1.00	1.60	4.80	8.00
14 .... 1.00	1.60	4.80	8.00
15 .... 1.00	1.60	4.80	8.00
16 .... 1.00	1.60	4.80	8.00
17 .... 1.00	1.60	4.80	8.00
18 .... 1.00	1.60	4.80	8.00
19 .... 1.00	1.60	4.80	8.00
20 .... 1.00	1.60	4.80	8.00
21 .... 1.00	1.20	3.60	6.00
22 .... 1.00	1.20	3.60	6.00
23 .... 1.00	1.20	3.60	6.00
24 .... 1.00	1.20	3.60	6.00
25 .... 1.00	1.20	3.60	6.00
26 .... 1.00	1.20	3.60	6.00
27 .... 1.00	1.20	3.60	6.00
28 .... 1.00	1.20	3.60	6.00

	ORIG.	GOOD	FINE	N-MINT		ORIG.	GOOD	FINE	N-MINT
❏ 29	1.00	1.20	3.60	6.00	❏ 84	1.50	1.20	3.60	6.00
❏ 30	1.00	1.20	3.60	6.00	❏ 85	1.50	1.20	3.60	6.00
❏ 31	1.00	1.20	3.60	6.00	❏ 86	1.50	1.20	3.60	6.00
❏ 32	1.00	1.20	3.60	6.00	❏ 87	1.50	1.20	3.60	6.00
❏ 33	1.00	1.20	3.60	6.00	❏ 88	1.50	1.20	3.60	6.00
❏ 34	1.00	1.20	3.60	6.00	❏ 89	1.50	1.20	3.60	6.00
❏ 35	1.00	1.20	3.60	6.00	❏ 90	1.50	1.20	3.60	6.00
❏ 36	1.00	1.20	3.60	6.00	❏ 91	1.50	1.20	3.60	6.00
❏ 37	1.00	1.20	3.60	6.00	❏ 92	1.50	1.20	3.60	6.00
❏ 38	1.00	1.20	3.60	6.00	❏ 93	1.50	1.20	3.60	6.00
❏ 39	1.00	1.20	3.60	6.00	❏ 94	1.50	1.20	3.60	6.00
❏ 40	1.00	1.20	3.60	6.00	❏ 95	1.50	1.20	3.60	6.00
❏ 41	1.00	1.20	3.60	6.00	❏ 96	1.50	1.20	3.60	6.00
❏ 42	1.00	1.20	3.60	6.00	❏ 97	1.50	1.20	3.60	6.00
❏ 43	1.00	1.20	3.60	6.00	❏ 98	1.50	1.20	3.60	6.00
❏ 44	1.00	1.20	3.60	6.00	❏ 99	1.50	1.20	3.60	6.00
❏ 45	1.25	1.20	3.60	6.00	❏ 100	1.50	1.20	3.60	6.00
❏ 46	1.25	1.20	3.60	6.00	❏ 101	1.50	1.00	3.00	5.00
❏ 47	1.25	1.20	3.60	6.00	❏ 102	1.50	1.00	3.00	5.00
❏ 48	1.25	1.20	3.60	6.00	❏ 103	1.50	1.00	3.00	5.00
❏ 49	1.25	1.20	3.60	6.00	❏ 104	1.50	1.00	3.00	5.00
❏ 50	1.25	1.20	3.60	6.00	❏ 105	1.50	1.00	3.00	5.00
❏ 51	1.25	1.20	3.60	6.00	❏ 106	1.50	1.00	3.00	5.00
❏ 52	1.25	1.20	3.60	6.00	❏ 107	1.50	1.00	3.00	5.00
❏ 53	1.25	1.20	3.60	6.00	❏ 108	1.50	1.00	3.00	5.00
❏ 54	1.25	1.20	3.60	6.00	❏ 109	1.50	1.00	3.00	5.00
❏ 55	1.25	1.20	3.60	6.00	❏ 110	1.50	1.00	3.00	5.00
❏ 56	1.25	1.20	3.60	6.00	❏ 111	1.50	1.00	3.00	5.00
❏ 57	1.25	1.20	3.60	6.00	❏ 112	1.50	1.00	3.00	5.00
❏ 58	1.25	1.20	3.60	6.00	❏ 113	1.50	1.00	3.00	5.00
❏ 59	1.25	1.20	3.60	6.00	❏ 114	1.50	1.00	3.00	5.00
❏ 60	1.25	1.20	3.60	6.00	❏ 115	1.50	1.00	3.00	5.00
❏ 61	1.25	1.20	3.60	6.00	❏ 116	1.50	1.00	3.00	5.00
❏ 62	1.25	1.20	3.60	6.00	❏ 117	1.50	1.00	3.00	5.00
❏ 63	1.25	1.20	3.60	6.00	❏ 118	1.50	1.00	3.00	5.00
❏ 64	1.25	1.20	3.60	6.00	❏ 119	1.50	1.00	3.00	5.00
❏ 65	1.25	1.20	3.60	6.00	❏ 120	1.50	1.00	3.00	5.00
❏ 66	1.25	1.20	3.60	6.00	❏ 121	1.50	1.00	3.00	5.00
❏ 67	1.25	1.20	3.60	6.00	❏ 122	1.50	1.00	3.00	5.00
❏ 68	1.25	1.20	3.60	6.00	❏ 123	1.50	1.00	3.00	5.00
❏ 69	1.25	1.20	3.60	6.00	❏ 124	1.50	1.00	3.00	5.00
❏ 70	1.25	1.20	3.60	6.00	❏ 125	1.50	1.00	3.00	5.00
❏ 71	1.50	1.20	3.60	6.00	❏ 126	1.50	1.00	3.00	5.00
❏ 72	1.50	1.20	3.60	6.00	❏ 127	1.50	1.00	3.00	5.00
❏ 73	1.50	1.20	3.60	6.00	❏ 128	1.50	1.00	3.00	5.00
❏ 74	1.50	1.20	3.60	6.00	❏ 129	1.50	1.00	3.00	5.00
❏ 75	1.50	1.20	3.60	6.00	❏ 130	1.50	1.00	3.00	5.00
❏ 76	1.50	1.20	3.60	6.00	❏ 131	1.50	1.00	3.00	5.00
❏ 77	1.50	1.20	3.60	6.00	❏ 132	1.50	1.00	3.00	5.00
❏ 78	1.50	1.20	3.60	6.00	❏ 133	1.50	1.00	3.00	5.00
❏ 79	1.50	1.20	3.60	6.00	❏ 134	1.50	1.00	3.00	5.00
❏ 80	1.50	1.20	3.60	6.00	❏ 135	2.00	1.00	3.00	5.00
❏ 81	1.50	1.20	3.60	6.00	❏ 136	2.00	1.00	3.00	5.00
❏ 82	1.50	1.20	3.60	6.00	❏ 137	2.00	1.00	3.00	5.00
❏ 83	1.50	1.20	3.60	6.00	❏ 138	2.00	1.00	3.00	5.00

	ORIG.	GOOD	FINE	N-MINT
139	2.00	1.00	3.00	5.00
140	2.00	1.00	3.00	5.00
141	2.00	1.00	3.00	5.00
142	2.00	1.00	3.00	5.00
143	2.00	1.00	3.00	5.00
144	2.00	1.00	3.00	5.00
145	2.00	1.00	3.00	5.00
146	2.00	1.00	3.00	5.00
147	2.00	1.00	3.00	5.00
148	2.00	1.00	3.00	5.00
149	2.00	1.00	3.00	5.00
150	2.00	1.00	3.00	5.00
151	2.00	0.80	2.40	4.00
152	2.00	0.80	2.40	4.00
153	2.00	0.80	2.40	4.00
154	2.00	0.80	2.40	4.00
155	2.00	0.80	2.40	4.00
156	2.00	0.80	2.40	4.00
157	2.00	0.80	2.40	4.00
158	2.00	0.80	2.40	4.00
159	2.00	0.80	2.40	4.00
160	2.00	0.80	2.40	4.00
161	2.00	0.80	2.40	4.00
162	2.00	0.80	2.40	4.00
163	2.00	0.80	2.40	4.00
164	2.25	0.80	2.40	4.00
165	2.25	0.80	2.40	4.00
166	2.25	0.80	2.40	4.00
167	2.25	0.80	2.40	4.00
168	2.25	0.80	2.40	4.00
169	2.25	0.80	2.40	4.00
170	2.25	0.80	2.40	4.00
171	2.25	0.80	2.40	4.00
172	2.25	0.80	2.40	4.00
173	2.25	0.80	2.40	4.00
174	2.25	0.80	2.40	4.00
175	2.25	0.80	2.40	4.00
176	2.25	0.60	1.80	3.00
177	2.25	0.60	1.80	3.00
178	2.25	0.60	1.80	3.00
179	2.25	0.60	1.80	3.00
180	2.25	0.60	1.80	3.00
181	2.25	0.60	1.80	3.00
182	2.25	0.60	1.80	3.00
183	2.25	0.60	1.80	3.00
184	2.25	0.60	1.80	3.00
185	2.25	0.60	1.80	3.00
186	2.25	0.60	1.80	3.00
187	2.25	0.60	1.80	3.00
188	2.25	0.60	1.80	3.00
189	2.25	0.60	1.80	3.00
190	2.25	0.60	1.80	3.00
191	2.25	0.45	1.35	2.25
192	2.25	0.45	1.35	2.25
193	2.25	0.45	1.35	2.25

	ORIG.	GOOD	FINE	N-MINT
194	2.25	0.45	1.35	2.25
195	2.25	0.45	1.35	2.25
196	2.25	0.45	1.35	2.25
197	2.25	0.45	1.35	2.25
198	2.25	0.45	1.35	2.25
199	2.25	0.45	1.35	2.25
200	2.25	0.45	1.35	2.25
201	2.25	0.45	1.35	2.25
202	2.25	0.45	1.35	2.25
203	2.25	0.45	1.35	2.25
204	2.25	0.45	1.35	2.25
205	2.25	0.45	1.35	2.25
206	2.25	0.45	1.35	2.25
207	2.25	0.45	1.35	2.25
208	2.25	0.45	1.35	2.25
209	2.25	0.45	1.35	2.25
210	2.25	0.45	1.35	2.25
211	2.25	0.45	1.35	2.25
212	2.25	0.45	1.35	2.25
213	2.25	0.45	1.35	2.25
214	2.25	0.45	1.35	2.25

SAVAGE SWORD OF CONAN ANNUAL

	ORIG.	GOOD	FINE	N-MINT
1 b&w	1.25	0.50	1.50	2.50

SAVAGE TALES (1971-1974)

	ORIG.	GOOD	FINE	N-MINT
1 BWS, JR, GM b&w mag; Conan, 1&O:Man-Thing	1.00	18.00	54.00	90.00
2 BWS, AW, FB, GM, BWr	1.00	7.20	21.60	36.00
3 AW, BWS, JSt, FB	1.00	4.00	12.00	20.00
4 NA, GK	1.00	1.60	4.80	8.00
5 NA, GK	1.00	1.60	4.80	8.00
6	1.00	0.60	1.80	3.00
7	1.00	0.60	1.80	3.00
8	1.00	0.60	1.80	3.00
9	1.00	0.60	1.80	3.00
10	1.00	0.60	1.80	3.00

SAVAGE TALES (2nd series)

	ORIG.	GOOD	FINE	N-MINT
1 b&w mag MG, 1:'Nam	1.50	1.50	4.50	7.50
2	1.50	0.30	0.90	1.50
3	1.50	0.30	0.90	1.50
4 'Nam	1.50	0.60	1.80	3.00
5	1.50	0.30	0.90	1.50
6	1.50	0.30	0.90	1.50
7	1.50	0.30	0.90	1.50
8	1.50	0.30	0.90	1.50

SAVAGE TALES ANNUAL (1975)

	ORIG.	GOOD	FINE	N-MINT
1 b&w GK O:Ka-Zar	1.25	0.60	1.80	3.00

SECRET DEFENDERS, THE

	ORIG.	GOOD	FINE	N-MINT
1 foil cover	2.50	0.50	1.50	2.50
2	1.75	0.35	1.05	1.75
3	1.75	0.35	1.05	1.75
4	1.75	0.35	1.05	1.75
5	1.75	0.35	1.05	1.75
6	1.75	0.35	1.05	1.75
7	1.75	0.35	1.05	1.75

	ORIG.	GOOD	FINE	N-MINT
SECRET WARS II				
❏ 1 A:X-Men, New Mutants..	0.75	0.40	1.20	2.00
❏ 2	0.75	0.30	0.90	1.50
❏ 3	0.75	0.30	0.90	1.50
❏ 4	0.75	0.30	0.90	1.50
❏ 5	0.75	0.30	0.90	1.50
❏ 6	0.75	0.30	0.90	1.50
❏ 7	0.75	0.30	0.90	1.50
❏ 8	0.75	0.30	0.90	1.50
❏ 9 double size	1.25	0.40	1.20	2.00
SECTAURS				
❏ 1	0.75	0.30	0.90	1.50
❏ 2	0.75	0.25	0.75	1.25
❏ 3	0.75	0.20	0.60	1.00
❏ 4	0.75	0.20	0.60	1.00
❏ 5	0.75	0.20	0.60	1.00
❏ 6	0.75	0.20	0.60	1.00
❏ 7	0.75	0.20	0.60	1.00
❏ 8	0.75	0.20	0.60	1.00
SEMPER FI'				
❏ 1 JSe	0.75	0.20	0.60	1.00
❏ 2 JSe	0.75	0.20	0.60	1.00
❏ 3 JSe	0.75	0.20	0.60	1.00
❏ 4 JSe	0.75	0.20	0.60	1.00
❏ 5 JSe	0.75	0.20	0.60	1.00
❏ 6 JSe	0.75	0.20	0.60	1.00
❏ 7 JSe	0.75	0.20	0.60	1.00
❏ 8 JSe	0.75	0.20	0.60	1.00
❏ 9 JSe	0.75	0.20	0.60	1.00
SENSATIONAL SHE-HULK				
❏ 1 JBy	1.50	0.60	1.80	3.00
❏ 2 JBy	1.50	0.50	1.50	2.50
❏ 3 JBy	1.50	0.50	1.50	2.50
❏ 4 JBy A:Blonde Phantom..	1.50	0.40	1.20	2.00
❏ 5 JBy	1.50	0.40	1.20	2.00
❏ 6 JBy	1.50	0.40	1.20	2.00
❏ 7 JBy	1.50	0.40	1.20	2.00
❏ 8 JBy	1.50	0.40	1.20	2.00
❏ 9	1.50	0.30	0.90	1.50
❏ 10	1.50	0.30	0.90	1.50
❏ 11	1.50	0.30	0.90	1.50
❏ 12	1.50	0.30	0.90	1.50
❏ 13	1.50	0.30	0.90	1.50
❏ 14	1.50	0.30	0.90	1.50
❏ 15	1.50	0.30	0.90	1.50
❏ 16	1.50	0.30	0.90	1.50
❏ 17	1.50	0.30	0.90	1.50
❏ 18	1.50	0.30	0.90	1.50
❏ 19	1.50	0.30	0.90	1.50
❏ 20	1.50	0.30	0.90	1.50
❏ 21 Blonde Phantom	1.50	0.30	0.90	1.50
❏ 22 Blonde Phantom	1.50	0.30	0.90	1.50
❏ 23 Blonde Phantom	1.50	0.30	0.90	1.50
❏ 24 Death's Head	1.50	0.30	0.90	1.50

	ORIG.	GOOD	FINE	N-MINT
❏ 25 Hercules	1.50	0.30	0.90	1.50
❏ 26	1.50	0.30	0.90	1.50
❏ 27 white inside covers	1.50	0.30	0.90	1.50
❏ 28	1.50	0.30	0.90	1.50
❏ 29	1.50	0.30	0.90	1.50
❏ 30	1.50	0.30	0.90	1.50
❏ 31 JBy	1.50	0.30	0.90	1.50
❏ 32 JBy	1.50	0.30	0.90	1.50
❏ 33 JBy	1.50	0.30	0.90	1.50
❏ 34 JBy	1.50	0.30	0.90	1.50
❏ 35 JBy	1.50	0.30	0.90	1.50
❏ 36 JBy	1.75	0.35	1.05	1.75
❏ 37 JBy	1.75	0.35	1.05	1.75
❏ 38 JBy	1.75	0.35	1.05	1.75
❏ 39 JBy	1.75	0.35	1.05	1.75
❏ 40 JBy	1.75	0.35	1.05	1.75
❏ 41 JBy	1.75	0.35	1.05	1.75
❏ 43	1.75	0.35	1.05	1.75
❏ 44 JBy	1.75	0.35	1.05	1.75
❏ 45	1.75	0.35	1.05	1.75
❏ 46	1.75	0.35	1.05	1.75
❏ 47	1.75	0.35	1.05	1.75
❏ 48 JBy	1.75	0.35	1.05	1.75
❏ 49	1.75	0.35	1.05	1.75
❏ 50 JBy,DG,FM,WS,TA,WP,HC, foil cover	2.95	0.59	1.77	2.95
❏ 51	1.75	0.35	1.05	1.75
❏ 52	1.75	0.35	1.05	1.75
❏ 53	1.75	0.35	1.05	1.75
❏ 54	1.75	0.35	1.05	1.75
❏ 55	1.75	0.35	1.05	1.75
❏ 56	1.75	0.35	1.05	1.75
SGT. FURY AND HIS HOWLING COMMANDOS				
❏ 1	0.12	90.00	270.00	450.00
❏ 2	0.12	40.00	120.00	200.00
❏ 3	0.12	25.00	75.00	125.00
❏ 4	0.12	25.00	75.00	125.00
❏ 5	0.12	25.00	75.00	125.00
❏ 6	0.12	12.00	36.00	60.00
❏ 7	0.12	12.00	36.00	60.00
❏ 8	0.12	12.00	36.00	60.00
❏ 9	0.12	12.00	36.00	60.00
❏ 10	0.12	12.00	36.00	60.00
❏ 11	0.12	7.20	21.60	36.00
❏ 12	0.12	7.20	21.60	36.00
❏ 13 A:Captain America	0.12	25.00	75.00	125.00
❏ 14	0.12	7.20	21.60	36.00
❏ 15	0.12	7.20	21.60	36.00
❏ 16	0.12	7.20	21.60	36.00
❏ 17	0.12	7.20	21.60	36.00
❏ 18	0.12	7.20	21.60	36.00
❏ 19	0.12	7.20	21.60	36.00
❏ 20	0.12	7.20	21.60	36.00
❏ 21	0.12	4.00	12.00	20.00
❏ 22	0.12	4.00	12.00	20.00

	ORIG.	GOOD	FINE	N-MINT		ORIG.	GOOD	FINE	N-MINT
❏ 23	0.12	4.00	12.00	20.00	❏ 78	0.15	2.40	7.20	12.00
❏ 24	0.12	4.00	12.00	20.00	❏ 79	0.15	2.40	7.20	12.00
❏ 25	0.12	4.00	12.00	20.00	❏ 80	0.15	2.40	7.20	12.00
❏ 26	0.12	4.00	12.00	20.00	❏ 81	0.15	2.40	7.20	12.00
❏ 27	0.12	4.00	12.00	20.00	❏ 82	0.15	2.40	7.20	12.00
❏ 28	0.12	4.00	12.00	20.00	❏ 83	0.15	2.40	7.20	12.00
❏ 29	0.12	4.00	12.00	20.00	❏ 84	0.15	2.40	7.20	12.00
❏ 30	0.12	4.00	12.00	20.00	❏ 85	0.15	2.40	7.20	12.00
❏ 31	0.12	4.00	12.00	20.00	❏ 86	0.15	2.40	7.20	12.00
❏ 32	0.12	4.00	12.00	20.00	❏ 87	0.15	2.40	7.20	12.00
❏ 33	0.12	4.00	12.00	20.00	❏ 88	0.15	2.40	7.20	12.00
❏ 34	0.12	4.00	12.00	20.00	❏ 89	0.15	2.40	7.20	12.00
❏ 35	0.12	4.00	12.00	20.00	❏ 90	0.15	2.40	7.20	12.00
❏ 36	0.12	4.00	12.00	20.00	❏ 91	0.15	2.40	7.20	12.00
❏ 37	0.12	4.00	12.00	20.00	❏ 92	0.25	2.40	7.20	12.00
❏ 38	0.12	4.00	12.00	20.00	❏ 93	0.20	2.40	7.20	12.00
❏ 39	0.12	4.00	12.00	20.00	❏ 94	0.20	2.40	7.20	12.00
❏ 40	0.12	4.00	12.00	20.00	❏ 95	0.20	2.40	7.20	12.00
❏ 41	0.12	4.00	12.00	20.00	❏ 96	0.20	2.40	7.20	12.00
❏ 42	0.12	4.00	12.00	20.00	❏ 97	0.20	2.40	7.20	12.00
❏ 43	0.12	4.00	12.00	20.00	❏ 98	0.20	2.40	7.20	12.00
❏ 44	0.12	4.00	12.00	20.00	❏ 99	0.20	2.40	7.20	12.00
❏ 45	0.12	4.00	12.00	20.00	❏ 100	0.20	3.60	10.80	18.00
❏ 46	0.12	4.00	12.00	20.00	❏ 101	0.20	0.80	2.40	4.00
❏ 47	0.12	4.00	12.00	20.00	❏ 102	0.20	0.80	2.40	4.00
❏ 48	0.12	4.00	12.00	20.00	❏ 103	0.20	0.80	2.40	4.00
❏ 49	0.12	4.00	12.00	20.00	❏ 104	0.20	0.80	2.40	4.00
❏ 50	0.12	4.00	12.00	20.00	❏ 105	0.20	0.80	2.40	4.00
❏ 51	0.12	2.80	8.40	14.00	❏ 106	0.20	0.80	2.40	4.00
❏ 52	0.12	2.80	8.40	14.00	❏ 107	0.20	0.80	2.40	4.00
❏ 53	0.12	2.80	8.40	14.00	❏ 108	0.20	0.80	2.40	4.00
❏ 54	0.12	2.80	8.40	14.00	❏ 109	0.20	0.80	2.40	4.00
❏ 55	0.12	2.80	8.40	14.00	❏ 110	0.20	0.80	2.40	4.00
❏ 56	0.12	2.80	8.40	14.00	❏ 111	0.20	0.80	2.40	4.00
❏ 57	0.12	2.80	8.40	14.00	❏ 112	0.20	0.80	2.40	4.00
❏ 58	0.12	2.80	8.40	14.00	❏ 113	0.20	0.80	2.40	4.00
❏ 59	0.12	2.80	8.40	14.00	❏ 114	0.20	0.80	2.40	4.00
❏ 60	0.12	2.80	8.40	14.00	❏ 115	0.20	0.80	2.40	4.00
❏ 61	0.12	2.80	8.40	14.00	❏ 116	0.20	0.80	2.40	4.00
❏ 62	0.12	2.80	8.40	14.00	❏ 117	0.20	0.80	2.40	4.00
❏ 63	0.12	2.80	8.40	14.00	❏ 118	0.20	0.80	2.40	4.00
❏ 64	0.12	2.80	8.40	14.00	❏ 119	0.25	0.80	2.40	4.00
❏ 65	0.12	2.80	8.40	14.00	❏ 120	0.25	0.80	2.40	4.00
❏ 66	0.12	2.80	8.40	14.00	❏ 121	0.25	0.80	2.40	4.00
❏ 67	0.12	2.80	8.40	14.00	❏ 122	0.25	0.80	2.40	4.00
❏ 68	0.15	2.80	8.40	14.00	❏ 123	0.25	0.80	2.40	4.00
❏ 69	0.15	2.80	8.40	14.00	❏ 124	0.25	0.80	2.40	4.00
❏ 70	0.15	2.80	8.40	14.00	❏ 125	0.25	0.80	2.40	4.00
❏ 71	0.15	2.40	7.20	12.00	❏ 126	0.25	0.80	2.40	4.00
❏ 72	0.15	2.40	7.20	12.00	❏ 127	0.25	0.80	2.40	4.00
❏ 73	0.15	2.40	7.20	12.00	❏ 128	0.25	0.80	2.40	4.00
❏ 74	0.15	2.40	7.20	12.00	❏ 129	0.25	0.80	2.40	4.00
❏ 75	0.15	2.40	7.20	12.00	❏ 130	0.25	0.80	2.40	4.00
❏ 76	0.15	2.40	7.20	12.00	❏ 131	0.25	0.80	2.40	4.00
❏ 77	0.15	2.40	7.20	12.00	❏ 132	0.25	0.80	2.40	4.00

	ORIG.	GOOD	FINE	N-MINT
133	0.25	0.80	2.40	4.00
134	0.25	0.80	2.40	4.00
135	0.30	0.80	2.40	4.00
136	0.30	0.80	2.40	4.00
137	0.30	0.80	2.40	4.00
138	0.30	0.80	2.40	4.00
139	0.30	0.80	2.40	4.00
140	0.30	0.80	2.40	4.00
141	0.30	0.60	1.80	3.00
142	0.30	0.60	1.80	3.00
143	0.30	0.60	1.80	3.00
144	0.30	0.60	1.80	3.00
145	0.30	0.60	1.80	3.00
146	0.30	0.60	1.80	3.00
147	0.30	0.60	1.80	3.00
148	0.30	0.60	1.80	3.00
149	0.30	0.60	1.80	3.00
150	0.30	0.60	1.80	3.00
151	0.30	0.60	1.80	3.00
152	0.30	0.60	1.80	3.00
153	0.30	0.60	1.80	3.00
154	0.30	0.60	1.80	3.00
155	0.30	0.60	1.80	3.00
156	0.30	0.60	1.80	3.00
157	0.30	0.60	1.80	3.00
158	0.30	0.60	1.80	3.00
159	0.30	0.60	1.80	3.00
160	0.30	0.60	1.80	3.00
161	0.30	0.60	1.80	3.00
162	0.30	0.60	1.80	3.00
163	0.30	0.60	1.80	3.00
164	0.30	0.60	1.80	3.00
165	0.30	0.60	1.80	3.00
166	0.30	0.60	1.80	3.00
167	0.30	0.60	1.80	3.00

SGT. FURY AND HIS HOWLING COMMANDOS ANNUAL

	ORIG.	GOOD	FINE	N-MINT
1 (1965-1971)	0.25	5.00	15.00	25.00
2 (1965-1971)	0.25	1.00	3.00	5.00
3 (1965-1971)	0.25	1.00	3.00	5.00
4 (1965-1971)	0.25	1.00	3.00	5.00
5 (1965-1971)	0.25	1.00	3.00	5.00
6 (1965-1971)	0.25	1.00	3.00	5.00
7 (1965-1971)	0.25	1.00	3.00	5.00

SHADOW RIDERS

	ORIG.	GOOD	FINE	N-MINT
1 embossed cover	2.50	0.50	1.50	2.50
2	1.75	0.35	1.05	1.75
3	1.75	0.35	1.05	1.75
4	1.75	0.35	1.05	1.75

SHADOWMASTERS

	ORIG.	GOOD	FINE	N-MINT
1 O:Shadowmasters	3.95	1.40	4.20	7.00
2	3.95	1.00	3.00	5.00
3	3.95	1.00	3.00	5.00
4	3.95	1.00	3.00	5.00

SHANNA THE SHE-DEVIL

	ORIG.	GOOD	FINE	N-MINT
1	0.20	0.20	0.60	1.00
2	0.20	0.20	0.60	1.00
3	0.20	0.20	0.60	1.00
4	0.20	0.20	0.60	1.00
5	0.20	0.20	0.60	1.00

SHE-HULK: CEREMONY

	ORIG.	GOOD	FINE	N-MINT
1 leg shaving	3.95	0.79	2.37	3.95
2	3.95	0.79	2.37	3.95

SHEENA

	ORIG.	GOOD	FINE	N-MINT
1 GM, movie	0.75	0.20	0.60	1.00
2 GM, movie	0.75	0.20	0.60	1.00

SHOGUN WARRIORS (1978-)

	ORIG.	GOOD	FINE	N-MINT
1	0.35	0.40	1.20	2.00
2	0.35	0.30	0.90	1.50
3	0.35	0.30	0.90	1.50
4	0.40	0.30	0.90	1.50
5	0.40	0.30	0.90	1.50
6	0.40	0.30	0.90	1.50
7	0.40	0.30	0.90	1.50
8	0.40	0.30	0.90	1.50
9	0.40	0.30	0.90	1.50
10	0.40	0.30	0.90	1.50
11	0.40	0.30	0.90	1.50
12	0.40	0.30	0.90	1.50
13	0.40	0.30	0.90	1.50
14	0.40	0.30	0.90	1.50
15	0.40	0.30	0.90	1.50
16	0.40	0.30	0.90	1.50
17	0.40	0.30	0.90	1.50
18	0.40	0.30	0.90	1.50
19	0.40	0.30	0.90	1.50
20	0.50	0.30	0.90	1.50

SILVER HAWKS (was Star Comic)

	ORIG.	GOOD	FINE	N-MINT
6	1.00	0.20	0.60	1.00
7	1.00	0.20	0.60	1.00

SILVER SABLE AND THE WILD PACK

	ORIG.	GOOD	FINE	N-MINT
1 foil cover	2.00	0.80	2.40	4.00
2	1.25	0.25	0.75	1.25
3	1.25	0.25	0.75	1.25
4	1.25	0.25	0.75	1.25
5	1.25	0.25	0.75	1.25
6	1.25	0.25	0.75	1.25
7	1.25	0.25	0.75	1.25
8	1.25	0.25	0.75	1.25
9	1.25	0.25	0.75	1.25
10	1.25	0.25	0.75	1.25
11	1.25	0.25	0.75	1.25
12	1.25	0.25	0.75	1.25
13	1.25	0.25	0.75	1.25
14	1.25	0.25	0.75	1.25
15	1.25	0.25	0.75	1.25
16	1.25	0.25	0.75	1.25

	ORIG.	GOOD	FINE	N-MINT
SILVER SURFER (1968-1970)				
☐ 1	0.25	60.00	180.00	300.00
☐ 2	0.25	20.00	60.00	100.00
☐ 3	0.25	18.00	54.00	90.00
☐ 4	0.25	56.00	168.00	280.00
☐ 5	0.25	13.00	39.00	65.00
☐ 6	0.25	13.00	39.00	65.00
☐ 7	0.25	13.00	39.00	65.00
☐ 8	0.15	13.00	39.00	65.00
☐ 9	0.15	13.00	39.00	65.00
☐ 10	0.15	13.00	39.00	65.00
☐ 11	0.15	7.20	21.60	36.00
☐ 12	0.15	7.20	21.60	36.00
☐ 13	0.15	7.20	21.60	36.00
☐ 14	0.15	7.20	21.60	36.00
☐ 15	0.15	7.20	21.60	36.00
☐ 16	0.15	7.20	21.60	36.00
☐ 17	0.15	7.20	21.60	36.00
☐ 18	0.15	7.20	21.60	36.00
SILVER SURFER (1982 one-shot)				
☐ 1 JBy	1.00	2.00	6.00	10.00
SILVER SURFER (1987, Volume 3)				
☐ 1 MR	1.25	2.40	7.20	12.00
☐ 2	0.75	1.60	4.80	8.00
☐ 3	0.75	1.00	3.00	5.00
☐ 4	0.75	1.00	3.00	5.00
☐ 5	0.75	1.00	3.00	5.00
☐ 6	0.75	0.80	2.40	4.00
☐ 7	0.75	0.80	2.40	4.00
☐ 8	0.75	0.80	2.40	4.00
☐ 9	0.75	0.80	2.40	4.00
☐ 10	0.75	0.80	2.40	4.00
☐ 11	1.00	0.80	2.40	4.00
☐ 12	1.00	0.80	2.40	4.00
☐ 13	1.00	0.80	2.40	4.00
☐ 14	1.00	0.80	2.40	4.00
☐ 15	1.00	1.60	4.80	8.00
☐ 16	1.00	0.80	2.40	4.00
☐ 17	1.00	0.80	2.40	4.00
☐ 18	1.00	0.80	2.40	4.00
☐ 19	1.00	0.80	2.40	4.00
☐ 20	1.00	0.80	2.40	4.00
☐ 21	1.00	0.80	2.40	4.00
☐ 22	1.00	0.80	2.40	4.00
☐ 23	1.00	0.80	2.40	4.00
☐ 24	1.00	0.80	2.40	4.00
☐ 25	1.50	0.80	2.40	4.00
☐ 26	1.00	0.80	2.40	4.00
☐ 27	1.00	0.80	2.40	4.00
☐ 28	1.00	0.80	2.40	4.00
☐ 29	1.00	0.80	2.40	4.00
☐ 30	1.00	0.80	2.40	4.00
☐ 31	1.50	0.80	2.40	4.00
☐ 32	1.00	0.80	2.40	4.00

	ORIG.	GOOD	FINE	N-MINT
☐ 33	1.00	0.80	2.40	4.00
☐ 34 Thanos	1.00	3.60	10.80	18.00
☐ 35 Thanos	1.00	2.40	7.20	12.00
☐ 36 Thanos	1.00	1.20	3.60	6.00
☐ 37 Thanos	1.00	1.20	3.60	6.00
☐ 38 Thanos	1.00	1.20	3.60	6.00
☐ 39 Thanos	1.00	1.20	3.60	6.00
☐ 40	1.00	0.50	1.50	2.50
☐ 41	1.00	0.50	1.50	2.50
☐ 42	1.00	0.50	1.50	2.50
☐ 43	1.00	0.50	1.50	2.50
☐ 44	1.00	0.80	2.40	4.00
☐ 45	1.00	1.40	4.20	7.00
☐ 46 R: Adam Warlock	1.00	1.60	4.80	8.00
☐ 47	1.00	1.20	3.60	6.00
☐ 48	1.00	0.40	1.20	2.00
☐ 49	1.00	0.40	1.20	2.00
☐ 50 silver cover, 1st printing				
	1.50	3.60	10.80	18.00
☐ 50 2nd printing	1.50	1.20	3.60	6.00
☐ 51 Infinity Gauntlet	1.00	0.60	1.80	3.00
☐ 52 Infinity Gauntlet	1.00	0.60	1.80	3.00
☐ 53 Infinity Gauntlet	1.00	0.60	1.80	3.00
☐ 54 Infinity Gauntlet	1.00	0.60	1.80	3.00
☐ 55 Infinity Gauntlet	1.00	0.60	1.80	3.00
☐ 56 Infinity Gauntlet	1.00	0.60	1.80	3.00
☐ 57 Infinity Gauntlet	1.00	0.60	1.80	3.00
☐ 58 Infinity Gauntlet	1.00	0.60	1.80	3.00
☐ 59 Infinity Gauntlet	1.00	0.60	1.80	3.00
☐ 60	1.00	0.40	1.20	2.00
☐ 61	1.00	0.40	1.20	2.00
☐ 62	1.25	0.25	0.75	1.25
☐ 63	1.25	0.25	0.75	1.25
☐ 64	1.25	0.25	0.75	1.25
☐ 65	1.25	0.25	0.75	1.25
☐ 66	1.25	0.25	0.75	1.25
☐ 69	1.25	0.25	0.75	1.25
☐ 70	1.25	0.25	0.75	1.25
☐ 71	1.25	0.25	0.75	1.25
☐ 72	1.25	0.25	0.75	1.25
☐ 73	1.25	0.25	0.75	1.25
☐ 74	1.25	0.25	0.75	1.25
☐ 75 silver foil cover	2.50	0.50	1.50	2.50
☐ 76	1.25	0.25	0.75	1.25
☐ 77	1.25	0.25	0.75	1.25
☐ 78	1.25	0.25	0.75	1.25
☐ 79	1.25	0.25	0.75	1.25
☐ 80	1.25	0.25	0.75	1.25
☐ 81	1.25	0.25	0.75	1.25
☐ 82	1.75	0.35	1.05	1.75
☐ 83	1.75	0.35	1.05	1.75
☐ 84	1.75	0.35	1.05	1.75
SILVER SURFER ANNUAL				
☐ 1 Evolutionary War (1988)				
	1.75	1.60	4.80	8.00

	ORIG.	GOOD	FINE	N-MINT
❑ 2 Atlantis Attacks (1989)				
..................................2.00	1.00	3.00	5.00
❑ 3 Lifeform (1990) 2.00	0.40	1.20	2.00
❑ 4 (1991) 2.00	0.40	1.20	2.00
❑ 5 (1992) 2.25	0.45	1.35	2.25
❑ 6 trading card....................2.95	0.59	1.77	2.95

SILVER SURFER/WARLOCK: RESURRECTION

	ORIG.	GOOD	FINE	N-MINT
❑ 1 ....2.50	0.50	1.50	2.50
❑ 2 ....2.50	0.50	1.50	2.50
❑ 3 ....2.50	0.50	1.50	2.50
❑ 4 ....2.50	0.50	1.50	2.50

SKULL THE SLAYER

	ORIG.	GOOD	FINE	N-MINT
❑ 1 ....0.25	0.40	1.20	2.00
❑ 2 ....0.25	0.30	0.90	1.50
❑ 3 ....0.25	0.30	0.90	1.50
❑ 4 ....0.25	0.30	0.90	1.50
❑ 5 ....0.25	0.30	0.90	1.50
❑ 6 ....0.25	0.30	0.90	1.50
❑ 7 ....0.30	0.30	0.90	1.50
❑ 8 ....0.30	0.30	0.90	1.50

SLAPSTICK

	ORIG.	GOOD	FINE	N-MINT
❑ 1 ....1.25	0.25	0.75	1.25
❑ 2 ....1.25	0.25	0.75	1.25
❑ 3 ....1.25	0.25	0.75	1.25
❑ 4 ....1.25	0.25	0.75	1.25

SLEDGE HAMMER

	ORIG.	GOOD	FINE	N-MINT
❑ 1 TV tie-in 1.00	0.20	0.60	1.00
❑ 2 TV tie-in 1.00	0.20	0.60	1.00

SLEEPWALKER

	ORIG.	GOOD	FINE	N-MINT
❑ 1 1:Sleepwalker................1.00	1.00	3.00	5.00
❑ 2 1:8-Ball 1.00	0.40	1.20	2.00
❑ 3 ....1.00	0.40	1.20	2.00
❑ 4 ....1.00	0.40	1.20	2.00
❑ 5 Spider-Man 1.00	0.20	0.60	1.00
❑ 6 ....1.00	0.20	0.60	1.00
❑ 7 Infinity Gauntlet.............1.00	0.20	0.60	1.00
❑ 8 Deathlok 1.25	0.25	0.75	1.25
❑ 9 ....1.25	0.25	0.75	1.25
❑ 10 ....1.25	0.25	0.75	1.25
❑ 11 ....1.25	0.25	0.75	1.25
❑ 12 ....1.25	0.25	0.75	1.25
❑ 13 ....1.25	0.25	0.75	1.25
❑ 14 ....1.25	0.25	0.75	1.25
❑ 15 ....1.25	0.25	0.75	1.25
❑ 16 ....1.25	0.25	0.75	1.25
❑ 17 ....1.25	0.25	0.75	1.25
❑ 18 ....1.25	0.25	0.75	1.25
❑ 19 ....2.00	0.40	1.20	2.00
❑ 20 ....1.25	0.25	0.75	1.25
❑ 21 ....1.25	0.25	0.75	1.25
❑ 22 ....1.25	0.25	0.75	1.25
❑ 23 ....1.25	0.25	0.75	1.25
❑ 24 ....1.25	0.25	0.75	1.25
❑ 25 foil cover 2.95	0.59	1.77	2.95

	ORIG.	GOOD	FINE	N-MINT
❑ 26 ....1.25	0.25	0.75	1.25
❑ 27 ....1.25	0.25	0.75	1.25
❑ 28 ....1.25	0.25	0.75	1.25

SLEEPWALKER HOLIDAY SPECIAL

	ORIG.	GOOD	FINE	N-MINT
❑ 1 ....2.00	0.40	1.20	2.00

SMURFS TREASURY EDITION, THE

	ORIG.	GOOD	FINE	N-MINT
❑ 1 ....2.50	0.50	1.50	2.50

SMURFS, THE

	ORIG.	GOOD	FINE	N-MINT
❑ 1 ....0.60	0.12	0.36	0.60
❑ 2 ....0.60	0.12	0.36	0.60
❑ 3 ....0.60	0.12	0.36	0.60

SOLARMAN

	ORIG.	GOOD	FINE	N-MINT
❑ 1 O:Solarman...................1.00	0.20	0.60	1.00
❑ 2 ....1.00	0.20	0.60	1.00

SOLO AVENGERS

	ORIG.	GOOD	FINE	N-MINT
❑ 1 ....0.75	0.60	1.80	3.00
❑ 2 ....0.75	0.40	1.20	2.00
❑ 3 ....0.75	0.20	0.60	1.00
❑ 4 ....0.75	0.20	0.60	1.00
❑ 5 ....0.75	0.20	0.60	1.00
❑ 6 ....0.75	0.20	0.60	1.00
❑ 7 ....0.75	0.20	0.60	1.00
❑ 8 ....0.75	0.20	0.60	1.00
❑ 9 ....0.75	0.20	0.60	1.00
❑ 10 ....0.75	0.20	0.60	1.00
❑ 11 ....0.75	0.20	0.60	1.00
❑ 12 ....0.75	0.20	0.60	1.00
❑ 13 ....0.75	0.20	0.60	1.00
❑ 14 ....0.75	0.20	0.60	1.00
❑ 15 ....0.75	0.20	0.60	1.00
❑ 16 ....0.75	0.20	0.60	1.00
❑ 17 ....0.75	0.20	0.60	1.00
❑ 18 ....0.75	0.20	0.60	1.00
❑ 19 ....0.75	0.20	0.60	1.00
❑ 20 (becomes Avengers Spotlight)				
..................................0.75	0.20	0.60	1.00

SOLOMON KANE

	ORIG.	GOOD	FINE	N-MINT
❑ 1 ....1.25	0.25	0.75	1.25
❑ 2 ....0.65	0.20	0.60	1.00
❑ 3 ....0.65	0.20	0.60	1.00
❑ 4 ....0.75	0.20	0.60	1.00
❑ 5 ....0.75	0.20	0.60	1.00
❑ 6 ....0.75	0.20	0.60	1.00

SON OF SATAN

	ORIG.	GOOD	FINE	N-MINT
❑ 1 ....0.25	1.20	3.60	6.00
❑ 2 ....0.25	0.60	1.80	3.00
❑ 3 ....0.25	0.40	1.20	2.00
❑ 4 ....0.25	0.40	1.20	2.00
❑ 5 ....0.25	0.40	1.20	2.00
❑ 6 ....0.30	0.40	1.20	2.00
❑ 7 ....0.30	0.40	1.20	2.00
❑ 8 ....0.30	0.40	1.20	2.00

	ORIG.	GOOD	FINE	N-MINT
SOVIET SUPER SOLDIERS				
❏ 1 .... 2.00	0.40	1.20	2.00
SPECIAL COLLECTORS' EDITION				
❏ 1 Kung Fu tabloid 1.00	0.20	0.60	1.00
SPECIAL MARVEL EDITION				
❏ 1 .... 0.25	0.60	1.80	3.00
❏ 2 .... 0.25	0.30	0.90	1.50
❏ 3 .... 0.25	0.30	0.90	1.50
❏ 4 .... 0.25	0.30	0.90	1.50
❏ 5 .... 0.20	0.40	1.20	2.00
❏ 6 .... 0.20	0.40	1.20	2.00
❏ 7 .... 0.20	0.40	1.20	2.00
❏ 8 .... 0.20	0.40	1.20	2.00
❏ 9 .... 0.20	0.40	1.20	2.00
❏ 10 .... 0.20	0.40	1.20	2.00
❏ 11 .... 0.20	0.40	1.20	2.00
❏ 12 .... 0.20	0.40	1.20	2.00
❏ 13 .... 0.20	0.40	1.20	2.00
❏ 14 .... 0.20	0.40	1.20	2.00
❏ 15 1:Master of Kung Fu 0.20	4.00	12.00	20.00
❏ 16 (becomes Master of Kung Fu)				
.... 0.20	2.00	6.00	10.00
SPECTACULAR SPIDER-MAN				
❏ 1 b&w mag 0.35			
❏ 2 color mag 0.35			
SPECTACULAR SPIDER-MAN ANNUAL				
❏ 1 RB/JM, Dr. Octopus (1979)				
.... 0.75	0.80	2.40	4.00
❏ 2 JM, 1, O:Rapier (1980) .. 0.75	0.60	1.80	3.00
❏ 3 (1981) (becomes Peter Paker, The Spectacular Spider-Man Annual) 0.75	0.40	1.20	2.00
SPECTACULAR SPIDER-MAN ANNUAL				
(was Peter Parker, the Spectacular Spider-Man Annual)				
❏ 7 .... 1.25	0.30	0.90	1.50
❏ 8 Evolutionary War (1988) 1.75	0.60	1.80	3.00
❏ 9 Atlantis Attacks (1989)... 2.00	0.60	1.80	3.00
❏ 10 tiny Spider-Man (1990) 2.00	0.40	1.20	2.00
❏ 11 Vibranium Vendetta (1991)				
.... 2.00	0.40	1.20	2.00
❏ 12 (1992) 2.25	0.45	1.35	2.25
❏ 13 trading card 2.95	0.59	1.77	2.95
SPECTACULAR SPIDER-MAN, THE				
❏ 1 SB, Tarantula 0.30	8.80	26.40	44.00
❏ 2 SB, Kraven 0.30	4.00	12.00	20.00
❏ 3 SB 0.30	2.80	8.40	14.00
❏ 4 SB 0.30	2.80	8.40	14.00
❏ 5 SB 0.30	2.80	8.40	14.00
❏ 6 .... 0.30	3.00	9.00	15.00
❏ 7 .... 0.30	3.00	9.00	15.00
❏ 8 .... 0.30	3.00	9.00	15.00
❏ 9 .... 0.30	1.40	4.20	7.00
❏ 10 .... 0.30	1.40	4.20	7.00
❏ 11 SB 0.35	1.20	3.60	6.00

	ORIG.	GOOD	FINE	N-MINT
❏ 12 SB 0.35	1.20	3.60	6.00
❏ 13 SB 0.35	1.20	3.60	6.00
❏ 14 SB 0.35	1.20	3.60	6.00
❏ 15 SB 0.35	1.20	3.60	6.00
❏ 16 SB 0.35	1.20	3.60	6.00
❏ 17 Angel/Iceman 0.35	1.20	3.60	6.00
❏ 18 Angel/Iceman 0.35	1.20	3.60	6.00
❏ 19 .... 0.35	1.00	3.00	5.00
❏ 20 .... 0.35	1.00	3.00	5.00
❏ 21 .... 0.35	1.00	3.00	5.00
❏ 22 .... 0.35	1.00	3.00	5.00
❏ 23 .... 0.35	1.00	3.00	5.00
❏ 24 .... 0.35	1.00	3.00	5.00
❏ 25 .... 0.35	1.00	3.00	5.00
❏ 26 .... 0.35	1.00	3.00	5.00
❏ 27 DC/FM, ... 0.35	3.00	9.00	15.00
❏ 28 FM, DD 0.35	2.00	6.00	10.00
❏ 29 .... 0.35	0.80	2.40	4.00
❏ 30 .... 0.40	0.80	2.40	4.00
❏ 31 .... 0.40	0.80	2.40	4.00
❏ 32 .... 0.40	0.80	2.40	4.00
❏ 33 .... 0.40	0.80	2.40	4.00
❏ 34 .... 0.40	0.80	2.40	4.00
❏ 35 .... 0.40	0.80	2.40	4.00
❏ 36 .... 0.40	0.80	2.40	4.00
❏ 37 .... 0.40	0.80	2.40	4.00
❏ 38 .... 0.40	2.00	6.00	10.00
❏ 39 .... 0.40	0.80	2.40	4.00
❏ 40 .... 0.40	0.80	2.40	4.00
❏ 41 .... 0.40	0.80	2.40	4.00
❏ 42 .... 0.40	0.80	2.40	4.00
❏ 43 .... 0.40	0.80	2.40	4.00
❏ 44 .... 0.40	0.80	2.40	4.00
❏ 45 Vulture 0.40	0.80	2.40	4.00
❏ 46 FM(c), Cobra 0.50	0.80	2.40	4.00
❏ 47 .... 0.50	0.60	1.80	3.00
❏ 48 (becomes Peter Parker, The Spectacular Spider-Man)				
.... 0.50	0.60	1.80	3.00
SPECTACULAR SPIDER-MAN, THE (was Peter Parker, The Spectacular Spider-Man)				
❏ 133 .... 0.75	0.40	1.20	2.00
❏ 134 .... 0.75	0.40	1.20	2.00
❏ 135 .... 0.75	0.40	1.20	2.00
❏ 136 .... 0.75	0.40	1.20	2.00
❏ 137 .... 0.75	0.40	1.20	2.00
❏ 138 .... 1.00	0.40	1.20	2.00
❏ 139 O:Tombstone 1.00	0.40	1.20	2.00
❏ 140 C:Punisher 1.00	1.00	3.00	5.00
❏ 141 A:Punisher 1.00	1.60	4.80	8.00
❏ 142 A:Punisher 1.00	2.00	6.00	10.00
❏ 143 A:Punisher 1.00	1.60	4.80	8.00
❏ 144 .... 1.00	0.40	1.20	2.00
❏ 145 .... 1.00	0.40	1.20	2.00
❏ 146 Inferno 1.00	0.40	1.20	2.00
❏ 147 Inferno 1.00	0.40	1.20	2.00

	ORIG.	GOOD	FINE	N-MINT
❑ 148 Inferno	1.00	0.40	1.20	2.00
❑ 149	1.00	0.40	1.20	2.00
❑ 150	1.00	0.40	1.20	2.00
❑ 151	1.00	0.40	1.20	2.00
❑ 152	1.00	0.40	1.20	2.00
❑ 153	1.00	0.40	1.20	2.00
❑ 154	1.00	0.40	1.20	2.00
❑ 155	1.00	0.40	1.20	2.00
❑ 156	1.00	0.40	1.20	2.00
❑ 157	1.00	0.40	1.20	2.00
❑ 158 Acts of Vengeance, cosmic power	1.00	2.00	6.00	10.00
❑ 159 Vengeance, power	1.00	1.20	3.60	6.00
❑ 160 Vengeance, power	1.00	1.20	3.60	6.00
❑ 161	1.00	0.40	1.20	2.00
❑ 162	1.00	0.40	1.20	2.00
❑ 163 Hobgoblin	1.00	0.40	1.20	2.00
❑ 164	1.00	0.30	0.90	1.50
❑ 165 D:Arranger	1.00	0.30	0.90	1.50
❑ 166	1.00	0.30	0.90	1.50
❑ 167	1.00	0.30	0.90	1.50
❑ 168 Avengers	1.00	0.30	0.90	1.50
❑ 169 Avengers	1.00	0.30	0.90	1.50
❑ 170	1.00	0.30	0.90	1.50
❑ 171	1.00	0.30	0.90	1.50
❑ 172	1.00	0.30	0.90	1.50
❑ 173 Dr. Octopus	1.00	0.30	0.90	1.50
❑ 174 Dr. Octopus	1.00	0.30	0.90	1.50
❑ 175 Dr. Octopus	1.00	0.30	0.90	1.50
❑ 176 O&1:Corona	1.00	0.30	0.90	1.50
❑ 177	1.00	0.30	0.90	1.50
❑ 178	1.00	0.30	0.90	1.50
❑ 179	1.00	0.30	0.90	1.50
❑ 180 Green Goblin	1.00	0.40	1.20	2.00
❑ 181 Green Goblin	1.00	0.40	1.20	2.00
❑ 182 Green Goblin	1.00	0.40	1.20	2.00
❑ 183 Green Goblin	1.00	0.40	1.20	2.00
❑ 184	1.00	0.20	0.60	1.00
❑ 185	1.25	0.25	0.75	1.25
❑ 186 Vulture	1.25	0.25	0.75	1.25
❑ 187 Vulture	1.25	0.25	0.75	1.25
❑ 188 Vulture	1.25	0.25	0.75	1.25
❑ 189 hologram cover	2.95	0.59	1.77	2.95
❑ 189 hologram cover, 2nd printing	2.95	0.59	1.77	2.95
❑ 190	1.25	0.25	0.75	1.25
❑ 191	1.25	0.25	0.75	1.25
❑ 192	1.25	0.25	0.75	1.25
❑ 193	1.25	0.25	0.75	1.25
❑ 194	1.25	0.25	0.75	1.25
❑ 195	1.25	0.25	0.75	1.25
❑ 196	1.25	0.25	0.75	1.25
❑ 197	1.25	0.25	0.75	1.25
❑ 198 X-Men	1.25	0.25	0.75	1.25
❑ 199	1.25	0.25	0.75	1.25

	ORIG.	GOOD	FINE	N-MINT
❑ 200 foil cover	2.95	0.59	1.77	2.95
❑ 201 maximum carnage	1.25	0.50	1.50	2.50
❑ 202	1.25	0.25	0.75	1.25
❑ 203	1.25	0.25	0.75	1.25
❑ 204	1.25	0.25	0.75	1.25
❑ 205	1.25	0.25	0.75	1.25

SPEEDBALL

	ORIG.	GOOD	FINE	N-MINT
❑ 1 SD,O:Speedball	0.75	0.60	1.80	3.00
❑ 2 SD	0.75	0.40	1.20	2.00
❑ 3 SD	0.75	0.40	1.20	2.00
❑ 4 SD	0.75	0.40	1.20	2.00
❑ 5 SD	0.75	0.40	1.20	2.00
❑ 6 SD	0.75	0.40	1.20	2.00
❑ 7 SD	0.75	0.40	1.20	2.00
❑ 8 SD	0.75	0.40	1.20	2.00
❑ 9 SD	0.75	0.40	1.20	2.00
❑ 10 SD	0.75	0.40	1.20	2.00

SPELLBOUND

	ORIG.	GOOD	FINE	N-MINT
❑ 1	1.50	0.30	0.90	1.50
❑ 2	1.50	0.30	0.90	1.50
❑ 3	1.50	0.30	0.90	1.50
❑ 4	1.50	0.30	0.90	1.50
❑ 5	1.50	0.30	0.90	1.50
❑ 6	2.25	0.45	1.35	2.25

SPIDER-MAN

	ORIG.	GOOD	FINE	N-MINT
❑ 7-Eleven giveaway, child abuse, verbal				
❑ 1 TMc silver cover	1.75	1.60	4.80	8.00
❑ 1 TMc bagged silver cover	2.00	5.00	15.00	25.00
❑ 1 TMc newsstand cover	1.75	1.60	4.80	8.00
❑ 1 TMc bagged newsstand	1.75	4.00	12.00	20.00
❑ 1 TMc gold cover, 2nd printing, direct sale	1.75	1.20	3.60	6.00
❑ 1 TMc gold cover, 2nd printing, UPC box	1.75	2.00	6.00	10.00
❑ 1 TMc platinum cover, giveaway		75.00	225.00	375.00
❑ 2 TMc, Lizard	1.75	1.20	3.60	6.00
❑ 3 TMc, Lizard	1.75	0.60	1.80	3.00
❑ 4 TMc, Lizard	1.75	0.60	1.80	3.00
❑ 5 TMc, Lizard	1.75	0.60	1.80	3.00
❑ 6 TMc, Ghost Rider	1.75	1.20	3.60	6.00
❑ 7 TMc, Ghost Rider	1.75	1.40	4.20	7.00
❑ 8 TMc, Wolverine, Wendigo	1.75	0.60	1.80	3.00
❑ 9 TMc, Wolverine, Wendigo	1.75	0.60	1.80	3.00
❑ 10 TMc, Wolverine, Wendigo	1.75	0.60	1.80	3.00
❑ 11 TMc, Wolverine, Wendigo	1.75	0.60	1.80	3.00
❑ 12 TMc, Wolverine, Wendigo	1.75	0.60	1.80	3.00
❑ 13 TMc	1.75	0.60	1.80	3.00
❑ 14	1.75	0.60	1.80	3.00
❑ 15 Erik Larsen	1.75	0.60	1.80	3.00
❑ 16 TMc, X-Force	1.75	0.80	2.40	4.00

	ORIG.	GOOD	FINE	N-MINT
☐ 17 AW........................1.75	0.60	1.80	3.00
☐ 18 Ghost Rider 1.75	1.00	3.00	5.00
☐ 19 ....1.75	0.70	2.10	3.50
☐ 20 ....1.75	0.70	2.10	3.50
☐ 21 Deathlok 1.75	0.50	1.50	2.50
☐ 22 ....1.75	0.50	1.50	2.50
☐ 23 Deathlok, Torch, Ghost Rider			
.................................1.75	0.35	1.05	1.75
☐ 24 ....1.75	0.35	1.05	1.75
☐ 25 ....1.75	0.35	1.05	1.75
☐ 26 hologram cover...........3.50	0.70	2.10	3.50
☐ 27 ....1.75	0.35	1.05	1.75
☐ 28 ....1.75	0.35	1.05	1.75
☐ 29 ....1.75	0.35	1.05	1.75
☐ 30 ....1.75	0.35	1.05	1.75
☐ 31 ....1.75	0.35	1.05	1.75
☐ 32 ....1.75	0.35	1.05	1.75
☐ 33 Punisher 1.75	0.35	1.05	1.75
☐ 34 Punisher 1.75	0.35	1.05	1.75
☐ 35 maximum carnage 1.75	0.60	1.80	3.00
☐ 36 maximum carnage 1.75	0.35	1.05	1.75
☐ 37 maximum carnage 1.75	0.35	1.05	1.75
☐ 38 ....1.75	0.35	1.05	1.75
☐ 39 ....1.75	0.35	1.05	1.75

SPIDER-MAN & HIS AMAZING FRIENDS

	ORIG.	GOOD	FINE	N-MINT
☐ 1 A:Iceman I:Firestar 0.50	0.20	0.60	1.00

SPIDER-MAN & THE NEW MUTANTS

	ORIG.	GOOD	FINE	N-MINT
☐ nn giveaway, child abuse ...	1.00	3.00	5.00

SPIDER-MAN 2099

	ORIG.	GOOD	FINE	N-MINT
☐ 1 O:Spider-Man 2099 ....1.75	1.20	3.60	6.00
☐ 1 autographed by Rick Leonardi & Al Williamson, with			
certificate of authenticity 1.75	2.00	6.00	10.00
☐ 2 ....1.25	0.80	2.40	4.00
☐ 3 ....1.25	0.60	1.80	3.00
☐ 4 ....1.25	0.60	1.80	3.00
☐ 5 ....1.25	0.25	0.75	1.25
☐ 6 ....1.25	0.25	0.75	1.25
☐ 7 ....1.25	0.25	0.75	1.25
☐ 8 ....1.25	0.25	0.75	1.25
☐ 9 ....1.25	0.25	0.75	1.25
☐ 10 ....1.25	0.25	0.75	1.25
☐ 11 ....1.25	0.25	0.75	1.25
☐ 12 ....1.25	0.25	0.75	1.25

SPIDER-MAN AND DAREDEVIL SPECIAL EDITION

	ORIG.	GOOD	FINE	N-MINT
☐ 1 (1983) 2.00	0.40	1.20	2.00

SPIDER-MAN AND THE DALLAS COWBOYS

	ORIG.	GOOD	FINE	N-MINT
☐ nn, 'Danger in Dallas' giveaway	3.00	9.00	15.00

SPIDER-MAN AND THE INCREDIBLE HULK

	ORIG.	GOOD	FINE	N-MINT
☐ nn, 'Chaos in Kansas City' giveaway			
....	3.00	9.00	15.00

SPIDER-MAN CLASSICS

	ORIG.	GOOD	FINE	N-MINT
☐ 1 reprints.........................1.25	0.25	0.75	1.25
☐ 2 reprints.........................1.25	0.25	0.75	1.25

	ORIG.	GOOD	FINE	N-MINT
☐ 3 reprints 1.25	0.25	0.75	1.25
☐ 4 reprints 1.25	0.25	0.75	1.25
☐ 5 reprints 1.25	0.25	0.75	1.25
☐ 6 reprints 1.25	0.25	0.75	1.25
☐ 7 reprints 1.25	0.25	0.75	1.25

SPIDER-MAN COMICS MAGAZINE

	ORIG.	GOOD	FINE	N-MINT
☐ 1 digest 1.50	0.30	0.90	1.50
☐ 2 digest 1.50	0.30	0.90	1.50
☐ 3 digest 1.50	0.30	0.90	1.50
☐ 4 digest 1.50	0.30	0.90	1.50
☐ 5 digest 1.50	0.30	0.90	1.50
☐ 6 digest 1.50	0.30	0.90	1.50
☐ 7 digest 1.50	0.30	0.90	1.50
☐ 8 digest 1.50	0.30	0.90	1.50
☐ 9 digest 1.50	0.30	0.90	1.50
☐ 10 digest 1.50	0.30	0.90	1.50
☐ 11 digest 1.50	0.30	0.90	1.50
☐ 12 digest 1.50	0.30	0.90	1.50
☐ 13 digest 1.50	0.30	0.90	1.50

SPIDER-MAN SAGA

	ORIG.	GOOD	FINE	N-MINT
☐ 1 retelling 2.95	0.59	1.77	2.95
☐ 2 retelling 2.95	0.59	1.77	2.95
☐ 3 retelling 2.95	0.59	1.77	2.95
☐ 4 retelling 2.95	0.59	1.77	2.95

SPIDER-MAN SPECIAL EDITION

	ORIG.	GOOD	FINE	N-MINT
☐ 1 Venom, UNICEF tie-in, poster, donation1.003.00			5.00

SPIDER-MAN UNLIMITED

	ORIG.	GOOD	FINE	N-MINT
☐ 1 Carnage 3.95	0.79	2.37	3.95
☐ 2 Carnage 3.95	0.79	2.37	3.95

SPIDER-MAN VS. THE HULK

	ORIG.	GOOD	FINE	N-MINT
☐ nn, giveaway	3.00	9.00	15.00

SPIDER-MAN VS. WOLVERINE

	ORIG.	GOOD	FINE	N-MINT
☐ bookshelf...........................4.95	0.99	2.97	4.95
☐ 1 ....2.50	5.60	16.80	28.00

SPIDER-MAN, FIRE-STAR AND ICEMAN

	ORIG.	GOOD	FINE	N-MINT
☐ nn, 'Danger in Denver' giveaway	3.60	10.80	18.00

SPIDER-MAN, POWER PACK

	ORIG.	GOOD	FINE	N-MINT
☐ 1 giveaway, no cover price, 1984			

SPIDER-MAN, STORM AND POWER MAN

	ORIG.	GOOD	FINE	N-MINT
☐ nn, 'Smokescreen' giveaway	4.00	12.00	20.00

SPIDER-MAN: 'CHRISTMAS IN DALLAS'

	ORIG.	GOOD	FINE	N-MINT
☐ nn, giveaway			

SPIDER-WOMAN

	ORIG.	GOOD	FINE	N-MINT
☐ 1 CI, O:.............................0.35	0.25	0.75	1.25
☐ 2 ....0.35	0.20	0.60	1.00
☐ 3 ....0.35	0.20	0.60	1.00
☐ 4 ....0.35	0.20	0.60	1.00
☐ 5 ....0.35	0.20	0.60	1.00
☐ 6 ....0.35	0.20	0.60	1.00
☐ 7 ....0.35	0.20	0.60	1.00
☐ 8 ....0.35	0.20	0.60	1.00
☐ 9 ....0.35	0.20	0.60	1.00
☐ 10 ....0.35	0.20	0.60	1.00

	ORIG.	GOOD	FINE	N-MINT
❑ 11	0.35	0.20	0.60	1.00
❑ 12	0.35	0.20	0.60	1.00
❑ 13	0.35	0.20	0.60	1.00
❑ 14	0.40	0.20	0.60	1.00
❑ 15	0.40	0.20	0.60	1.00
❑ 16	0.40	0.20	0.60	1.00
❑ 17	0.40	0.20	0.60	1.00
❑ 18	0.40	0.20	0.60	1.00
❑ 19	0.40	0.20	0.60	1.00
❑ 20	0.40	0.20	0.60	1.00
❑ 21	0.40	0.20	0.60	1.00
❑ 22	0.40	0.20	0.60	1.00
❑ 23	0.40	0.20	0.60	1.00
❑ 24	0.40	0.20	0.60	1.00
❑ 25	0.40	0.20	0.60	1.00
❑ 26 JBy(c)	0.40	0.20	0.60	1.00
❑ 27	0.40	0.20	0.60	1.00
❑ 28	0.40	0.20	0.60	1.00
❑ 29	0.40	0.20	0.60	1.00
❑ 30	0.50	0.20	0.60	1.00
❑ 31	0.50	0.20	0.60	1.00
❑ 32	0.50	0.20	0.60	1.00
❑ 33	0.50	0.20	0.60	1.00
❑ 34	0.50	0.20	0.60	1.00
❑ 35	0.50	0.20	0.60	1.00
❑ 36	0.50	0.20	0.60	1.00
❑ 37 TA, A: X-Men	0.50	0.50	1.50	2.50
❑ 38 A:X-Men	0.50	0.40	1.20	2.00
❑ 39	0.50	0.20	0.60	1.00
❑ 40	0.50	0.20	0.60	1.00
❑ 41	0.50	0.20	0.60	1.00
❑ 42	0.60	0.20	0.60	1.00
❑ 43	0.60	0.20	0.60	1.00
❑ 44	0.60	0.20	0.60	1.00
❑ 45	0.60	0.20	0.60	1.00
❑ 46	0.60	0.20	0.60	1.00
❑ 47	0.60	0.20	0.60	1.00
❑ 48	0.60	0.20	0.60	1.00
❑ 49	0.60	0.20	0.60	1.00
❑ 50 D:Spider-Woman	1.00	0.30	0.90	1.50

SPIDEY SUPER STORIES

	ORIG.	GOOD	FINE	N-MINT
❑ 1	0.35	0.40	1.20	2.00
❑ 2	0.35	0.30	0.90	1.50
❑ 3	0.35	0.30	0.90	1.50
❑ 4	0.35	0.30	0.90	1.50
❑ 5	0.35	0.30	0.90	1.50
❑ 6	0.35	0.20	0.60	1.00
❑ 7	0.35	0.20	0.60	1.00
❑ 8	0.35	0.20	0.60	1.00
❑ 9	0.35	0.20	0.60	1.00
❑ 10	0.35	0.20	0.60	1.00
❑ 11	0.35	0.20	0.60	1.00
❑ 12	0.35	0.20	0.60	1.00
❑ 13	0.35	0.20	0.60	1.00
❑ 14	0.35	0.20	0.60	1.00

	ORIG.	GOOD	FINE	N-MINT
❑ 15	0.35	0.20	0.60	1.00
❑ 16	0.35	0.20	0.60	1.00
❑ 17	0.35	0.20	0.60	1.00
❑ 18	0.35	0.20	0.60	1.00
❑ 19	0.35	0.20	0.60	1.00
❑ 20	0.35	0.20	0.60	1.00
❑ 21	0.35	0.20	0.60	1.00
❑ 22	0.35	0.20	0.60	1.00
❑ 23	0.35	0.20	0.60	1.00
❑ 24	0.35	0.20	0.60	1.00
❑ 25	0.35	0.20	0.60	1.00
❑ 26	0.35	0.20	0.60	1.00
❑ 27	0.35	0.20	0.60	1.00
❑ 28	0.35	0.20	0.60	1.00
❑ 29	0.35	0.20	0.60	1.00
❑ 30	0.35	0.20	0.60	1.00
❑ 31	0.35	0.20	0.60	1.00
❑ 32	0.35	0.20	0.60	1.00
❑ 33	0.35	0.20	0.60	1.00
❑ 34	0.35	0.20	0.60	1.00
❑ 35	0.35	0.20	0.60	1.00
❑ 36	0.35	0.20	0.60	1.00
❑ 37	0.35	0.20	0.60	1.00
❑ 38	0.35	0.20	0.60	1.00
❑ 39	0.35	0.20	0.60	1.00
❑ 40	0.40	0.20	0.60	1.00
❑ 41	0.40	0.20	0.60	1.00
❑ 42	0.40	0.20	0.60	1.00
❑ 43	0.40	0.20	0.60	1.00
❑ 44	0.40	0.20	0.60	1.00
❑ 45	0.40	0.20	0.60	1.00
❑ 46	0.50	0.20	0.60	1.00
❑ 47	0.50	0.20	0.60	1.00
❑ 48	0.50	0.20	0.60	1.00
❑ 49	0.50	0.20	0.60	1.00
❑ 50	0.50	0.20	0.60	1.00
❑ 51	0.50	0.20	0.60	1.00
❑ 52	0.50	0.20	0.60	1.00
❑ 53	0.50	0.20	0.60	1.00
❑ 54	0.50	0.20	0.60	1.00
❑ 55	0.50	0.20	0.60	1.00
❑ 56	0.60	0.20	0.60	1.00
❑ 57	0.60	0.20	0.60	1.00

SPITFIRE & THE TROUBLESHOOTERS

	ORIG.	GOOD	FINE	N-MINT
❑ 1	0.75	0.20	0.60	1.00
❑ 2	0.75	0.20	0.60	1.00
❑ 3	0.75	0.20	0.60	1.00
❑ 4	0.75	0.20	0.60	1.00
❑ 5	0.75	0.20	0.60	1.00
❑ 6	0.75	0.20	0.60	1.00
❑ 7	0.75	0.20	0.60	1.00
❑ 8	0.75	0.20	0.60	1.00
❑ 9 (becomes Codename: Spitfire)	0.75	0.20	0.60	1.00

	ORIG.	GOOD	FINE	N-MINT
SPOOF				
❏ 1	0.15	0.20	0.60	1.00
❏ 2	0.20	0.20	0.60	1.00
❏ 3	0.20	0.20	0.60	1.00
❏ 4	0.20	0.20	0.60	1.00
❏ 5	0.20	0.20	0.60	1.00
SQUADRON SUPREME				
❏ 1	1.25	0.25	0.75	1.25
❏ 2	0.75	0.20	0.60	1.00
❏ 3	0.75	0.20	0.60	1.00
❏ 4	0.75	0.20	0.60	1.00
❏ 5	0.75	0.20	0.60	1.00
❏ 6	0.75	0.20	0.60	1.00
❏ 7	0.75	0.20	0.60	1.00
❏ 8	0.75	0.20	0.60	1.00
❏ 9	0.75	0.20	0.60	1.00
❏ 10	0.75	0.20	0.60	1.00
❏ 11	0.75	0.20	0.60	1.00
❏ 12	1.25	0.25	0.75	1.25
STAR BRAND				
❏ 1	0.75	0.20	0.60	1.00
❏ 2	0.75	0.20	0.60	1.00
❏ 3	0.75	0.20	0.60	1.00
❏ 4	0.75	0.20	0.60	1.00
❏ 5	0.75	0.20	0.60	1.00
❏ 6	0.75	0.20	0.60	1.00
❏ 7	0.75	0.20	0.60	1.00
❏ 8	0.75	0.20	0.60	1.00
❏ 9	0.75	0.20	0.60	1.00
❏ 10 (becomes The Star Brand)	0.75	0.25	0.75	1.25
STAR BRAND ANNUAL				
❏ 1 (1987)	1.25	0.25	0.75	1.25
STAR BRAND, THE (was Star Brand)				
❏ 11 JBy	0.75	0.20	0.60	1.00
❏ 12 JBy	0.75	0.20	0.60	1.00
❏ 13 JBy	1.25	0.25	0.75	1.25
❏ 14 JBy	1.25	0.25	0.75	1.25
❏ 15 JBy	1.25	0.25	0.75	1.25
❏ 16 JBy	1.25	0.25	0.75	1.25
❏ 17 JBy	1.50	0.30	0.90	1.50
❏ 18 JBy	1.50	0.30	0.90	1.50
❏ 19 JBy	1.50	0.30	0.90	1.50
STAR TREK				
❏ 1	0.40	1.20	3.60	6.00
❏ 2	0.40	0.60	1.80	3.00
❏ 3	0.40	0.60	1.80	3.00
❏ 4	0.40	0.60	1.80	3.00
❏ 5	0.40	0.60	1.80	3.00
❏ 6	0.50	0.40	1.20	2.00
❏ 7	0.50	0.40	1.20	2.00
❏ 8	0.50	0.40	1.20	2.00
❏ 9	0.50	0.40	1.20	2.00
❏ 10	0.50	0.40	1.20	2.00

	ORIG.	GOOD	FINE	N-MINT
❏ 11	0.50	0.40	1.20	2.00
❏ 12	0.50	0.40	1.20	2.00
❏ 13	0.50	0.40	1.20	2.00
❏ 14	0.50	0.40	1.20	2.00
❏ 15	0.50	0.40	1.20	2.00
❏ 16	0.50	0.40	1.20	2.00
❏ 17	0.50	0.40	1.20	2.00
❏ 18	0.60	0.40	1.20	2.00
STAR WARS				
❏ 1 HC 30 movie	0.30	5.00	15.00	25.00
❏ 1 HC 35 movie	0.35	50.00	150.00	250.00
❏ 2 HC movie	0.30	2.00	6.00	10.00
❏ 3 HC movie	0.30	2.00	6.00	10.00
❏ 4 HC low distribution	0.30	2.00	6.00	10.00
❏ 5 HC	0.35	1.40	4.20	7.00
❏ 6 HC	0.35	1.40	4.20	7.00
❏ 7 HC	0.35	1.40	4.20	7.00
❏ 8 HC	0.35	1.40	4.20	7.00
❏ 9 HC	0.35	1.40	4.20	7.00
❏ 10 HC	0.35	1.40	4.20	7.00
❏ 11	0.35	1.20	3.60	6.00
❏ 12	0.35	1.20	3.60	6.00
❏ 13	0.35	1.20	3.60	6.00
❏ 14	0.35	1.20	3.60	6.00
❏ 15	0.35	1.20	3.60	6.00
❏ 16	0.35	1.20	3.60	6.00
❏ 17 low distribution	0.35	1.20	3.60	6.00
❏ 18 low distribution	0.35	1.20	3.60	6.00
❏ 19 low distribution	0.35	1.20	3.60	6.00
❏ 20	0.35	1.20	3.60	6.00
❏ 21	0.35	1.00	3.00	5.00
❏ 22	0.35	1.00	3.00	5.00
❏ 23	0.40	1.00	3.00	5.00
❏ 24	0.40	1.00	3.00	5.00
❏ 25	0.40	1.00	3.00	5.00
❏ 26	0.40	1.00	3.00	5.00
❏ 27	0.40	1.00	3.00	5.00
❏ 28	0.40	1.00	3.00	5.00
❏ 29	0.40	1.00	3.00	5.00
❏ 30	0.40	1.00	3.00	5.00
❏ 31	0.40	1.00	3.00	5.00
❏ 32	0.40	1.00	3.00	5.00
❏ 33	0.40	1.00	3.00	5.00
❏ 34	0.40	1.00	3.00	5.00
❏ 35	0.40	1.00	3.00	5.00
❏ 36	0.40	1.00	3.00	5.00
❏ 37	0.40	1.00	3.00	5.00
❏ 38 TA/MG	0.40	1.00	3.00	5.00
❏ 39 AW Empire	0.50	1.00	3.00	5.00
❏ 40 AW Empire	0.50	1.00	3.00	5.00
❏ 41 AW Empire	0.50	1.00	3.00	5.00
❏ 42 AW Empire	0.50	1.00	3.00	5.00
❏ 43 AW Empire	0.50	1.00	3.00	5.00
❏ 44 AW Empire	0.50	1.00	3.00	5.00
❏ 45	0.50	1.00	3.00	5.00

	ORIG.	GOOD	FINE	N-MINT
❑ 46	0.50	1.00	3.00	5.00
❑ 47	0.50	1.00	3.00	5.00
❑ 48	0.50	1.00	3.00	5.00
❑ 49	0.50	1.00	3.00	5.00
❑ 50 WS/AW, TP giant	0.75	1.40	4.20	7.00
❑ 51	0.50	0.80	2.40	4.00
❑ 52	0.50	0.80	2.40	4.00
❑ 53	0.50	0.80	2.40	4.00
❑ 54	0.50	0.80	2.40	4.00
❑ 55	0.60	0.80	2.40	4.00
❑ 56	0.60	0.80	2.40	4.00
❑ 57	0.60	0.80	2.40	4.00
❑ 58	0.60	0.80	2.40	4.00
❑ 59	0.60	0.80	2.40	4.00
❑ 60	0.60	0.80	2.40	4.00
❑ 61	0.60	0.80	2.40	4.00
❑ 62	0.60	0.80	2.40	4.00
❑ 63	0.60	0.80	2.40	4.00
❑ 64	0.60	0.80	2.40	4.00
❑ 65	0.60	0.80	2.40	4.00
❑ 66	0.60	0.80	2.40	4.00
❑ 67	0.60	0.80	2.40	4.00
❑ 68	0.60	0.80	2.40	4.00
❑ 69	0.60	0.80	2.40	4.00
❑ 70	0.60	0.80	2.40	4.00
❑ 71	0.60	0.60	1.80	3.00
❑ 72	0.60	0.60	1.80	3.00
❑ 73	0.60	0.60	1.80	3.00
❑ 74	0.60	0.60	1.80	3.00
❑ 75	0.60	0.60	1.80	3.00
❑ 76	0.60	0.60	1.80	3.00
❑ 77	0.60	0.60	1.80	3.00
❑ 78	0.60	0.60	1.80	3.00
❑ 79	0.60	0.60	1.80	3.00
❑ 80	0.60	0.60	1.80	3.00
❑ 81	0.60	0.60	1.80	3.00
❑ 82	0.60	0.60	1.80	3.00
❑ 83	0.60	0.60	1.80	3.00
❑ 84	0.60	0.60	1.80	3.00
❑ 85	0.60	0.60	1.80	3.00
❑ 86	0.60	0.60	1.80	3.00
❑ 87	0.60	0.60	1.80	3.00
❑ 88	0.60	0.60	1.80	3.00
❑ 89	0.60	0.60	1.80	3.00
❑ 90	0.60	0.60	1.80	3.00
❑ 91	0.60	0.60	1.80	3.00
❑ 92	1.00	0.60	1.80	3.00
❑ 93	0.60	0.60	1.80	3.00
❑ 94	0.65	0.60	1.80	3.00
❑ 95	0.65	0.60	1.80	3.00
❑ 96	0.65	0.60	1.80	3.00
❑ 97	0.65	0.60	1.80	3.00
❑ 98	0.65	0.60	1.80	3.00
❑ 99	0.65	0.60	1.80	3.00
❑ 100	1.25	1.00	3.00	5.00
❑ 101	0.65	0.60	1.80	3.00
❑ 102	0.65	0.60	1.80	3.00
❑ 103	0.65	0.60	1.80	3.00
❑ 104	0.75	0.60	1.80	3.00
❑ 105	0.75	0.60	1.80	3.00
❑ 106	0.75	0.60	1.80	3.00
❑ 107	0.75	0.60	1.80	3.00

STAR WARS ANNUAL

	ORIG.	GOOD	FINE	N-MINT
❑ 1 (1979)	0.75	2.00	6.00	10.00
❑ 2 (1982)	1.00	1.20	3.60	6.00
❑ 3 (1983)	1.00	1.20	3.60	6.00

STAR-LORD

	ORIG.	GOOD	FINE	N-MINT
❑ 1 JBy	1.50	0.30	0.90	1.50

STARRIORS

	ORIG.	GOOD	FINE	N-MINT
❑ 1	0.75	0.30	0.90	1.50
❑ 2	0.75	0.20	0.60	1.00
❑ 3	0.75	0.20	0.60	1.00
❑ 4	0.75	0.20	0.60	1.00

STEELTOWN ROCKERS

	ORIG.	GOOD	FINE	N-MINT
❑ 1	1.00	0.20	0.60	1.00
❑ 2	1.00	0.20	0.60	1.00
❑ 3	1.00	0.20	0.60	1.00
❑ 4	1.00	0.20	0.60	1.00
❑ 5	1.00	0.20	0.60	1.00
❑ 6	1.00	0.20	0.60	1.00

STRANGE TALES

	ORIG.	GOOD	FINE	N-MINT
❑ 1	0.10	200.00	600.00	1000.00
❑ 2	0.10	90.00	270.00	450.00
❑ 3	0.10	70.00	210.00	350.00
❑ 4	0.10	70.00	210.00	350.00
❑ 5	0.10	70.00	210.00	350.00
❑ 6	0.10	45.00	135.00	225.00
❑ 7	0.10	45.00	135.00	225.00
❑ 8	0.10	45.00	135.00	225.00
❑ 9	0.10	45.00	135.00	225.00
❑ 10	0.10	45.00	135.00	225.00
❑ 11	0.10	35.00	105.00	175.00
❑ 12	0.10	35.00	105.00	175.00
❑ 13	0.10	35.00	105.00	175.00
❑ 14	0.10	35.00	105.00	175.00
❑ 15	0.10	35.00	105.00	175.00
❑ 16	0.10	35.00	105.00	175.00
❑ 17	0.10	35.00	105.00	175.00
❑ 18	0.10	35.00	105.00	175.00
❑ 19	0.10	35.00	105.00	175.00
❑ 20	0.10	35.00	105.00	175.00
❑ 21	0.10	24.00	72.00	120.00
❑ 22	0.10	24.00	72.00	120.00
❑ 23	0.10	24.00	72.00	120.00
❑ 24	0.10	24.00	72.00	120.00
❑ 25	0.10	24.00	72.00	120.00
❑ 26	0.10	24.00	72.00	120.00
❑ 27	0.10	24.00	72.00	120.00
❑ 28	0.10	24.00	72.00	120.00

	ORIG.	GOOD	FINE	N-MINT
29	0.10	24.00	72.00	120.00
30	0.10	24.00	72.00	120.00
31	0.10	24.00	72.00	120.00
32	0.10	24.00	72.00	120.00
33	0.10	24.00	72.00	120.00
34	0.10	24.00	72.00	120.00
35	0.10	20.00	60.00	100.00
36	0.10	20.00	60.00	100.00
37	0.10	20.00	60.00	100.00
38	0.10	20.00	60.00	100.00
39	0.10	20.00	60.00	100.00
40	0.10	20.00	60.00	100.00
41	0.10	20.00	60.00	100.00
42	0.10	20.00	60.00	100.00
43	0.10	20.00	60.00	100.00
44	0.10	20.00	60.00	100.00
45	0.10	20.00	60.00	100.00
46	0.10	20.00	60.00	100.00
47	0.10	20.00	60.00	100.00
48	0.10	20.00	60.00	100.00
49	0.10	20.00	60.00	100.00
50	0.10	20.00	60.00	100.00
51	0.10	20.00	60.00	100.00
52	0.10	20.00	60.00	100.00
53	0.10	20.00	60.00	100.00
54	0.10	20.00	60.00	100.00
55	0.10	20.00	60.00	100.00
56	0.10	20.00	60.00	100.00
57	0.10	20.00	60.00	100.00
58	0.10	20.00	60.00	100.00
59	0.10	20.00	60.00	100.00
60	0.10	20.00	60.00	100.00
61	0.10	14.00	42.00	70.00
62	0.10	14.00	42.00	70.00
63	0.10	14.00	42.00	70.00
64	0.10	14.00	42.00	70.00
65	0.10	14.00	42.00	70.00
66	0.10	14.00	42.00	70.00
67	0.10	14.00	42.00	70.00
68	0.10	14.00	42.00	70.00
69	0.10	14.00	42.00	70.00
70	0.10	14.00	42.00	70.00
71	0.10	12.00	36.00	60.00
72	0.10	12.00	36.00	60.00
73	0.10	12.00	36.00	60.00
74	0.10	12.00	36.00	60.00
75	0.10	12.00	36.00	60.00
76	0.10	12.00	36.00	60.00
77	0.10	12.00	36.00	60.00
78	0.10	12.00	36.00	60.00
79	0.10	16.00	48.00	80.00
80	0.10	10.00	30.00	50.00
81	0.10	10.00	30.00	50.00
82	0.10	10.00	30.00	50.00
83	0.10	10.00	30.00	50.00

	ORIG.	GOOD	FINE	N-MINT
84	0.10	10.00	30.00	50.00
85	0.10	10.00	30.00	50.00
86	0.10	10.00	30.00	50.00
87	0.10	10.00	30.00	50.00
88	0.10	10.00	30.00	50.00
89	0.10	10.00	30.00	50.00
90	0.10	10.00	30.00	50.00
91	0.10	10.00	30.00	50.00
92	0.10	10.00	30.00	50.00
93	0.10	10.00	30.00	50.00
94	0.10	10.00	30.00	50.00
95	0.10	10.00	30.00	50.00
96	0.10	10.00	30.00	50.00
97	0.10	10.00	30.00	50.00
98	0.10	10.00	30.00	50.00
99	0.10	10.00	30.00	50.00
100	0.12	16.00	48.00	80.00
101 SD/JK, Human Torch	0.12	100.00	300.00	500.00
102 SD/JK	0.12	64.00	192.00	320.00
103 SD/JK	0.12	24.00	72.00	120.00
104 SD/JK	0.12	24.00	72.00	120.00
105 SD/JK	0.12	24.00	72.00	120.00
106 SD, A:FF	0.12	20.00	60.00	100.00
107 SD, Torch V:Sub-Mariner	0.12	30.00	90.00	150.00
108 SD/JK	0.12	20.00	60.00	100.00
109 SD/JK	0.12	20.00	60.00	100.00
110 SD, 1:Dr. Strange	0.12	120.00	360.00	600.00
111 SD, 1:Asbestos	0.12	52.00	156.00	260.00
112 SD	0.12	18.00	54.00	90.00
113 SD	0.12	18.00	54.00	90.00
114 SD/JK, Capt. America	0.12	40.00	120.00	200.00
115 SD, O:Dr. Strange	0.12	60.00	180.00	300.00
116	0.12	12.00	36.00	60.00
117	0.12	12.00	36.00	60.00
118	0.12	12.00	36.00	60.00
119	0.12	12.00	36.00	60.00
120	0.12	12.00	36.00	60.00
121 SP	0.12	8.00	24.00	40.00
122 SP	0.12	8.00	24.00	40.00
123 SP	0.12	8.00	24.00	40.00
124 SP	0.12	8.00	24.00	40.00
125 SP	0.12	8.00	24.00	40.00
126 SP	0.12	8.00	24.00	40.00
127 SP	0.12	8.00	24.00	40.00
128 SP	0.12	8.00	24.00	40.00
129 SP	0.12	8.00	24.00	40.00
130 SD, C:Beatles	0.12	9.60	28.80	48.00
131 SD, Thing/Torch	0.12	6.40	19.20	32.00
132 SD, Thing/Torch	0.12	6.40	19.20	32.00
133 SD, Thing/Torch	0.12	6.40	19.20	32.00
134 SD, L:Torch, A:Watcher	0.12	6.40	19.20	32.00
135 SD/JK, 1:SHIELD	0.12	16.00	48.00	80.00

	ORIG.	GOOD	FINE	N-MINT
❏ 136 SD/JK, Dr. Strange 0.12	6.00	18.00	30.00
❏ 137 .... 0.12	3.00	9.00	15.00
❏ 138 .... 0.12	3.00	9.00	15.00
❏ 139 .... 0.12	3.00	9.00	15.00
❏ 140 .... 0.12	3.00	9.00	15.00
❏ 141 .... 0.12	3.00	9.00	15.00
❏ 142 .... 0.12	3.00	9.00	15.00
❏ 143 .... 0.12	3.00	9.00	15.00
❏ 144 .... 0.12	3.00	9.00	15.00
❏ 145 .... 0.12	3.00	9.00	15.00
❏ 146 .... 0.12	3.00	9.00	15.00
❏ 147 .... 0.12	3.00	9.00	15.00
❏ 148 BEv/JK, O:Ancient One			
.... 0.12	3.20	9.60	16.00
❏ 149 BEv/JK...................... 0.12	2.40	7.20	12.00
❏ 150 BEv/JK/JB, 1:Buscema			
.... 0.12	2.40	7.20	12.00
❏ 151 BEv/JK/JSo, 1:Steranko			
.... 0.12	4.00	12.00	20.00
❏ 152 .... 0.12	2.40	7.20	12.00
❏ 153 .... 0.12	2.40	7.20	12.00
❏ 154 .... 0.12	2.40	7.20	12.00
❏ 155 .... 0.12	2.40	7.20	12.00
❏ 156 .... 0.12	2.40	7.20	12.00
❏ 157 .... 0.12	2.40	7.20	12.00
❏ 158 .... 0.12	2.40	7.20	12.00
❏ 159 JSo, O:Fury 0.12	3.00	9.00	15.00
❏ 160 .... 0.12	2.40	7.20	12.00
❏ 161 .... 0.12	2.40	7.20	12.00
❏ 162 .... 0.12	2.40	7.20	12.00
❏ 163 .... 0.12	2.40	7.20	12.00
❏ 164 .... 0.12	2.40	7.20	12.00
❏ 165 .... 0.12	2.40	7.20	12.00
❏ 166 .... 0.12	2.40	7.20	12.00
❏ 167 JSo/DA 0.12	3.00	9.00	15.00
❏ 168 JSo/DA, O:Br. Voodoo (ends 1967 series)			
.... 0.12	2.40	7.20	12.00
❏ 169 Br. Voodoo (begins 1973 series)			
.... 0.20	0.40	1.20	2.00
❏ 170 Br. Voodoo................. 0.20	0.40	1.20	2.00
❏ 171 Br. Voodoo................. 0.20	0.40	1.20	2.00
❏ 172 Br. Voodoo................. 0.20	0.40	1.20	2.00
❏ 173 Br. Voodoo................. 0.20	0.40	1.20	2.00
❏ 174 JB/JM, O:Golem 0.25	0.20	0.60	1.00
❏ 175 SD, Rep-Torr 0.25	0.20	0.60	1.00
❏ 176 Golem 0.25	0.20	0.60	1.00
❏ 177 Golem 0.25	0.20	0.60	1.00
❏ 178 JSn, O:Warlock........... 0.25	1.20	3.60	6.00
❏ 179 JSn, Warlock 0.25	0.80	2.40	4.00
❏ 180 JSn, Warlock 0.25	0.80	2.40	4.00
❏ 181 JSn, Warlock 0.25	0.80	2.40	4.00
❏ 182 rep. 0.25	0.20	0.60	1.00
❏ 183 rep. 0.25	0.20	0.60	1.00
❏ 184 rep. 0.25	0.20	0.60	1.00
❏ 185 rep. 0.25	0.20	0.60	1.00

	ORIG.	GOOD	FINE	N-MINT
❏ 186 rep.............................0.25	0.20	0.60	1.00
❏ 187 rep.............................0.30	0.20	0.60	1.00
❏ 188 rep.............................0.30	0.20	0.60	1.00

STRANGE TALES (Volume 2)

	ORIG.	GOOD	FINE	N-MINT
❏ 1 Dr. Strange, Cloak & Dagger			
.....................................0.75	0.40	1.20	2.00
❏ 2 ....0.75	0.40	1.20	2.00
❏ 3 ....0.75	0.40	1.20	2.00
❏ 4 ....0.75	0.40	1.20	2.00
❏ 5 ....0.75	0.40	1.20	2.00
❏ 6 ....0.75	0.40	1.20	2.00
❏ 7 ....0.75	0.40	1.20	2.00
❏ 8 ....0.75	0.40	1.20	2.00
❏ 9 ....0.75	0.40	1.20	2.00
❏ 10 ....0.75	0.40	1.20	2.00
❏ 11 ....0.75	0.40	1.20	2.00
❏ 12 ....0.75	0.40	1.20	2.00
❏ 13 ....0.75	0.40	1.20	2.00
❏ 14 ....0.75	0.40	1.20	2.00
❏ 15 ....0.75	0.40	1.20	2.00
❏ 16 ....0.75	0.40	1.20	2.00
❏ 17 ....0.75	0.40	1.20	2.00
❏ 18 X-Factor 0.75	0.20	0.60	1.00
❏ 19 last 0.75	0.20	0.60	1.00

STRANGE TALES ANNUAL

	ORIG.	GOOD	FINE	N-MINT
❏ 1 reprint (1962) 0.25	30.00	90.00	150.00
❏ 2 SpM/Torch (1963)..........0.25	36.00	108.00	180.00

STREET POET RAY

	ORIG.	GOOD	FINE	N-MINT
❏ 1 b&w 2.95	0.59	1.77	2.95
❏ 2 b&w 2.95	0.59	1.77	2.95
❏ 3 b&w 2.95	0.59	1.77	2.95
❏ 4 b&w 2.95	0.59	1.77	2.95

STRIKEFORCE: MORITURI

	ORIG.	GOOD	FINE	N-MINT
❏ 1 ....0.75	0.40	1.20	2.00
❏ 2 ....0.75	0.40	1.20	2.00
❏ 3 ....0.75	0.40	1.20	2.00
❏ 4 ....0.75	0.40	1.20	2.00
❏ 5 ....0.75	0.40	1.20	2.00
❏ 6 ....0.75	0.40	1.20	2.00
❏ 7 ....0.75	0.40	1.20	2.00
❏ 8 ....0.75	0.40	1.20	2.00
❏ 9 ....0.75	0.40	1.20	2.00
❏ 10 ....0.75	0.40	1.20	2.00
❏ 11 ....0.75	0.40	1.20	2.00
❏ 12 ....0.75	0.40	1.20	2.00
❏ 13 ....1.25	0.40	1.20	2.00
❏ 14 ....0.75	0.25	0.75	1.25
❏ 15 ....1.00	0.25	0.75	1.25
❏ 16 ....1.00	0.25	0.75	1.25
❏ 17 ....1.00	0.25	0.75	1.25
❏ 18 ....1.00	0.25	0.75	1.25
❏ 19 ....1.00	0.25	0.75	1.25
❏ 20 ....1.00	0.25	0.75	1.25
❏ 21 ....1.25	0.25	0.75	1.25

	ORIG.	GOOD	FINE	N-MINT
❑ 22	1.25	0.25	0.75	1.25
❑ 23	1.25	0.25	0.75	1.25
❑ 24	1.50	0.30	0.90	1.50
❑ 25	1.25	0.30	0.90	1.50
❑ 26	1.50	0.30	0.90	1.50
❑ 27	1.50	0.30	0.90	1.50
❑ 28	1.50	0.30	0.90	1.50
❑ 29	1.50	0.30	0.90	1.50
❑ 30	1.50	0.30	0.90	1.50
❑ 31	1.50	0.30	0.90	1.50

STRYFE'S STRIKE FILE

	ORIG.	GOOD	FINE	N-MINT
❑ 1	1.75	0.35	1.05	1.75

SUB-MARINER

	ORIG.	GOOD	FINE	N-MINT
❑ 1 JB, O:Sub-Mariner	0.12	28.00	84.00	140.00
❑ 2 JB, A:Triton	0.12	8.00	24.00	40.00
❑ 3 JB, A:Triton	0.12	4.00	12.00	20.00
❑ 4 JB	0.12	2.40	7.20	12.00
❑ 5 JB	0.12	2.40	7.20	12.00
❑ 6 JB	0.12	2.40	7.20	12.00
❑ 7 JB	0.12	2.40	7.20	12.00
❑ 8	0.12	2.40	7.20	12.00
❑ 9	0.12	1.60	4.80	8.00
❑ 10	0.12	1.60	4.80	8.00
❑ 11	0.12	1.40	4.20	7.00
❑ 12	0.12	1.40	4.20	7.00
❑ 13	0.12	1.40	4.20	7.00
❑ 14 Human Torch	0.12	1.40	4.20	7.00
❑ 15	0.12	1.00	3.00	5.00
❑ 16	0.15	1.00	3.00	5.00
❑ 17	0.15	1.00	3.00	5.00
❑ 18	0.15	1.00	3.00	5.00
❑ 19	0.15	1.00	3.00	5.00
❑ 20	0.15	1.00	3.00	5.00
❑ 21	0.15	1.00	3.00	5.00
❑ 22 Dr. Strange	0.15	1.00	3.00	5.00
❑ 23	0.15	0.40	1.20	2.00
❑ 24	0.15	0.40	1.20	2.00
❑ 25	0.15	0.50	1.50	2.50
❑ 26	0.15	0.50	1.50	2.50
❑ 27 SB	0.15	1.00	3.00	5.00
❑ 28	0.15	0.50	1.50	2.50
❑ 29 SB, V:Hercules	0.15	0.30	0.90	1.50
❑ 30 SB, A:Capt. Marvel	0.15	0.40	1.20	2.00
❑ 31	0.15	0.30	0.90	1.50
❑ 32	0.15	0.30	0.90	1.50
❑ 33 SB/JM, I:Namora	0.15	0.40	1.20	2.00
❑ 34 SB/JM, A:Surfer & Hulk	0.15	0.80	2.40	4.00
❑ 35 SB/JM, A:Surfer & Hulk	0.15	0.80	2.40	4.00
❑ 36 BWr/SB, M:Lady Dorma	0.15	0.50	1.50	2.50
❑ 37 RA, D:Lady Dorma	0.15	0.40	1.20	2.00
❑ 38	0.15	0.30	0.90	1.50

	ORIG.	GOOD	FINE	N-MINT
❑ 39	0.15	0.30	0.90	1.50
❑ 40	0.15	0.30	0.90	1.50
❑ 41 GT	0.15	0.25	0.75	1.25
❑ 42 GT	0.15	0.25	0.75	1.25
❑ 43	0.25	0.40	1.20	2.00
❑ 44	0.20	0.40	1.20	2.00
❑ 45	0.20	0.40	1.20	2.00
❑ 46 GC	0.20	0.25	0.75	1.25
❑ 47 GC	0.20	0.25	0.75	1.25
❑ 48 GC	0.20	0.25	0.75	1.25
❑ 49 GC	0.20	0.25	0.75	1.25
❑ 50 BEv, 1:Nita	0.20	0.35	1.05	1.75
❑ 51 BEv	0.20	0.30	0.90	1.50
❑ 52 BEv	0.20	0.30	0.90	1.50
❑ 53 BEv	0.20	0.30	0.90	1.50
❑ 54 BEv	0.20	0.30	0.90	1.50
❑ 55 BEv	0.20	0.30	0.90	1.50
❑ 56	0.20	0.25	0.75	1.25
❑ 57	0.20	0.25	0.75	1.25
❑ 58 BEv	0.20	0.30	0.90	1.50
❑ 59 BEv	0.20	0.30	0.90	1.50
❑ 60 BEv	0.20	0.30	0.90	1.50
❑ 61	0.20	0.25	0.75	1.25
❑ 62	0.20	0.25	0.75	1.25
❑ 63	0.20	0.25	0.75	1.25
❑ 64	0.20	0.25	0.75	1.25
❑ 65	0.20	0.25	0.75	1.25
❑ 66	0.20	0.25	0.75	1.25
❑ 67	0.20	0.25	0.75	1.25
❑ 68	0.20	0.25	0.75	1.25
❑ 69	0.20	0.25	0.75	1.25
❑ 70	0.25	0.25	0.75	1.25
❑ 71	0.25	0.25	0.75	1.25
❑ 72	0.25	0.25	0.75	1.25

SUB-MARINER ANNUAL

	ORIG.	GOOD	FINE	N-MINT
❑ 1 SB, rep.	0.25	0.40	1.20	2.00
❑ 2 BEv, rep.	0.25	0.35	1.05	1.75

SUBURBAN JERSEY NINJA SHE-DEVILS

	ORIG.	GOOD	FINE	N-MINT
❑ 1	1.50	0.30	0.90	1.50

SUPER HEROES PUZZLES AND GAMES

❑ giveaway, SpM,Hulk,Capt. America,Spider-Woman

SUPER SOLDIERS

	ORIG.	GOOD	FINE	N-MINT
❑ 1 foil cover	2.50	0.50	1.50	2.50
❑ 2	1.75	0.35	1.05	1.75
❑ 3	1.75	0.35	1.05	1.75
❑ 4	1.75	0.35	1.05	1.75
❑ 5	1.75	0.35	1.05	1.75
❑ 6	1.75	0.35	1.05	1.75
❑ 7	1.75	0.35	1.05	1.75

SUPER-VILLAIN CLASSICS

	ORIG.	GOOD	FINE	N-MINT
❑ 1 O:Galactus, reprint	0.60			

SUPER-VILLAIN TEAM-UP

	ORIG.	GOOD	FINE	N-MINT
❑ 1	0.25	0.80	2.40	4.00
❑ 2	0.25	0.50	1.50	2.50

	ORIG.	GOOD	FINE	N-MINT
3	0.25	0.50	1.50	2.50
4	0.25	0.50	1.50	2.50
5	0.25	0.50	1.50	2.50
6	0.25	0.30	0.90	1.50
7	0.25	0.30	0.90	1.50
8	0.30	0.30	0.90	1.50
9	0.30	0.30	0.90	1.50
10	0.30	0.30	0.90	1.50
11	0.30	0.30	0.90	1.50
12	0.30	0.30	0.90	1.50
13	0.30	0.30	0.90	1.50
14	0.30	0.30	0.90	1.50
15	0.30	0.30	0.90	1.50
16	0.40	0.30	0.90	1.50
17	0.40	0.30	0.90	1.50

SUPERNATURAL THRILLERS

	ORIG.	GOOD	FINE	N-MINT
1	0.20	0.20	0.60	1.00
2	0.20	0.20	0.60	1.00
3 REHoward story	0.20	0.20	0.60	1.00
4	0.20	0.20	0.60	1.00
5 I:Living Mummy	0.20	0.20	0.60	1.00
6	0.20	0.20	0.60	1.00
7 Living Mummy	0.25	0.20	0.60	1.00
8 Living Mummy	0.25	0.20	0.60	1.00
9 Living Mummy	0.25	0.20	0.60	1.00
10 Living Mummy	0.25	0.20	0.60	1.00
11 Living Mummy	0.25	0.20	0.60	1.00
12 Living Mummy	0.25	0.20	0.60	1.00
13 Living Mummy	0.25	0.20	0.60	1.00
14 Living Mummy	0.25	0.20	0.60	1.00
15 Living Mummy	0.25	0.20	0.60	1.00

SWEET XVI

	ORIG.	GOOD	FINE	N-MINT
1	1.00	0.20	0.60	1.00
2	1.00	0.20	0.60	1.00
3	1.00	0.20	0.60	1.00
4	1.00	0.20	0.60	1.00
5	1.00	0.20	0.60	1.00
6	1.00	0.20	0.60	1.00

SWEET XVI BACK TO SCHOOL SPECIAL

	ORIG.	GOOD	FINE	N-MINT
1	2.25	0.45	1.35	2.25

TALES OF ASGARD (1968)

	ORIG.	GOOD	FINE	N-MINT
1	0.25	6.00	18.00	30.00

TALES OF ASGARD (1984)

	ORIG.	GOOD	FINE	N-MINT
1	1.25	0.40	1.20	2.00

TALES OF G.I. JOE

	ORIG.	GOOD	FINE	N-MINT
1 rep.	2.25	0.45	1.35	2.25
2 rep.	1.50	0.45	1.35	2.25
3 rep.	1.50	0.45	1.35	2.25
4 rep.	1.50	0.45	1.35	2.25
5 rep.	1.50	0.45	1.35	2.25
6 rep.	1.50	0.30	0.90	1.50
7 rep.	1.50	0.30	0.90	1.50
8 rep.	1.50	0.30	0.90	1.50
9 rep.	1.50	0.30	0.90	1.50

	ORIG.	GOOD	FINE	N-MINT
10 rep.	1.50	0.30	0.90	1.50
11 rep.	1.50	0.30	0.90	1.50
12 rep.	1.50	0.30	0.90	1.50
13 rep.	1.50	0.30	0.90	1.50
14 rep.	1.50	0.30	0.90	1.50
15 rep.	1.50	0.30	0.90	1.50

TALES OF SUSPENSE

	ORIG.	GOOD	FINE	N-MINT
1	0.10	140.00	420.00	700.00
2	0.10	60.00	180.00	300.00
3	0.10	50.00	150.00	250.00
4	0.10	60.00	180.00	300.00
5	0.10	36.00	108.00	180.00
6	0.10	36.00	108.00	180.00
7	0.10	36.00	108.00	180.00
8	0.10	36.00	108.00	180.00
9	0.10	36.00	108.00	180.00
10	0.10	36.00	108.00	180.00
11	0.10	25.00	75.00	125.00
12	0.10	25.00	75.00	125.00
13	0.10	25.00	75.00	125.00
14	0.10	25.00	75.00	125.00
15	0.10	25.00	75.00	125.00
16	0.10	25.00	75.00	125.00
17	0.10	25.00	75.00	125.00
18	0.10	25.00	75.00	125.00
19	0.10	25.00	75.00	125.00
20	0.10	25.00	75.00	125.00
21	0.10	20.00	60.00	100.00
22	0.10	20.00	60.00	100.00
23	0.10	20.00	60.00	100.00
24	0.10	20.00	60.00	100.00
25	0.10	20.00	60.00	100.00
26	0.12	18.00	54.00	90.00
27	0.12	18.00	54.00	90.00
28	0.12	18.00	54.00	90.00
29	0.12	18.00	54.00	90.00
30	0.12	18.00	54.00	90.00
31	0.12	18.00	54.00	90.00
32	0.12	18.00	54.00	90.00
33	0.12	18.00	54.00	90.00
34	0.12	18.00	54.00	90.00
35	0.12	18.00	54.00	90.00
36	0.12	18.00	54.00	90.00
37	0.12	18.00	54.00	90.00
38	0.12	18.00	54.00	90.00
39 JK, O:1:Iron Man	0.12	440.00	1320.00	2200.00
40 JK	0.12	170.00	510.00	850.00
41 JK	0.12	120.00	360.00	600.00
42 DH/SD, I:Mad Pharoah	0.12	40.00	120.00	200.00
43	0.12	40.00	120.00	200.00
44	0.12	40.00	120.00	200.00
45	0.12	40.00	120.00	200.00
46	0.12	36.00	108.00	180.00
47	0.12	36.00	108.00	180.00
48 SD, new costume	0.12	45.00	135.00	225.00

	ORIG.	GOOD	FINE	N-MINT
49 SD, A:Angel 0.12	20.00	60.00	100.00
50 DH, 1:Mandarin 0.12	14.00	42.00	70.00
51 DH, Scarecrow 0.12	12.00	36.00	60.00
52 DH, 1:Black Widow 0.12	20.00	60.00	100.00
53 DH, O:Watcher 0.12	14.00	42.00	70.00
54 DH 0.12	12.00	36.00	60.00
55 DH 0.12	12.00	36.00	60.00
56 DH 0.12	12.00	36.00	60.00
57 DH, 1:Hawkeye............ 0.12	32.00	96.00	160.00
58 DH, Capt. America starts			
.... 0.12	45.00	135.00	225.00
59 DH/JK, I:Jarvis 0.12	40.00	120.00	200.00
60 DJ/JK, Assassins 0.12	13.00	39.00	65.00
61 DH/JK, Assassins 0.12	8.00	24.00	40.00
62 DH/JK, Assassins 0.12	8.00	24.00	40.00
63 O:Capt. America 0.12	28.00	84.00	140.00
64 .... 0.12	13.00	39.00	65.00
65 .... 0.12	13.00	39.00	65.00
66 .... 0.12	13.00	39.00	65.00
67 .... 0.12	6.00	18.00	30.00
68 .... 0.12	6.00	18.00	30.00
69 .... 0.12	6.00	18.00	30.00
70 .... 0.12	6.00	18.00	30.00
71 .... 0.12	6.00	18.00	30.00
72 .... 0.12	6.00	18.00	30.00
73 .... 0.12	6.00	18.00	30.00
74 .... 0.12	6.00	18.00	30.00
75 .... 0.12	6.00	18.00	30.00
76 .... 0.12	6.00	18.00	30.00
77 .... 0.12	6.00	18.00	30.00
78 .... 0.12	6.00	18.00	30.00
79 .... 0.12	6.00	18.00	30.00
80 .... 0.12	6.00	18.00	30.00
81 .... 0.12	6.00	18.00	30.00
82 .... 0.12	6.00	18.00	30.00
83 .... 0.12	6.00	18.00	30.00
84 .... 0.12	6.00	18.00	30.00
85 .... 0.12	6.00	18.00	30.00
86 .... 0.12	6.00	18.00	30.00
87 .... 0.12	6.00	18.00	30.00
88 GK/GC, Red Skull 0.12	6.00	18.00	30.00
89 GK/GC, Red Skull 0.12	6.00	18.00	30.00
90 GK/GC, Red Skull 0.12	6.00	18.00	30.00
91 GK/GC, Red Skull 0.12	6.00	18.00	30.00
92 GK/GC, Red Skull 0.12	6.00	18.00	30.00
93 GK/GC, Red Skull 0.12	6.00	18.00	30.00
94 GK/GC, Red Skull 0.12	6.00	18.00	30.00
95 GK/GC, Red Skull........ 0.12	6.00	18.00	30.00
96 GK/GC, Red Skull........ 0.12	6.00	18.00	30.00
97 GK/GC, Red Skull........ 0.12	6.00	18.00	30.00
98 GK/GC, Red Skull........ 0.12	6.00	18.00	30.00
99 GK/GC, Red Skull (becomes Captain America)			
.... 0.12	6.00	18.00	30.00

TALES OF THE ZOMBIE (b&w mag)

	ORIG.	GOOD	FINE	N-MINT
1 O:Zombie 0.75	0.15	0.45	0.75

	ORIG.	GOOD	FINE	N-MINT
2 .... 0.75	0.15	0.45	0.75
3 .... 0.75	0.15	0.45	0.75
4 .... 0.75	0.15	0.45	0.75
5 .... 0.75	0.15	0.45	0.75
6 .... 0.75	0.15	0.45	0.75
7 .... 0.75	0.15	0.45	0.75
8 .... 0.75	0.15	0.45	0.75
9 .... 0.75	0.15	0.45	0.75
10 .... 0.75	0.15	0.45	0.75

TALES OF THE ZOMBIE ANNUAL

	ORIG.	GOOD	FINE	N-MINT
1 reprints 1.25	0.25	0.75	1.25

TALES TO ASTONISH

	ORIG.	GOOD	FINE	N-MINT
1 .... 0.10	140.00	420.00	700.00
2 .... 0.10	60.00	180.00	300.00
3 .... 0.10	45.00	135.00	225.00
4 .... 0.10	45.00	135.00	225.00
5 .... 0.10	45.00	135.00	225.00
6 .... 0.10	25.00	75.00	125.00
7 .... 0.10	25.00	75.00	125.00
8 .... 0.10	25.00	75.00	125.00
9 .... 0.10	25.00	75.00	125.00
10 .... 0.10	25.00	75.00	125.00
11 .... 0.10	20.00	60.00	100.00
12 .... 0.10	20.00	60.00	100.00
13 .... 0.10	20.00	60.00	100.00
14 .... 0.10	20.00	60.00	100.00
15 .... 0.10	20.00	60.00	100.00
16 .... 0.10	20.00	60.00	100.00
17 .... 0.10	20.00	60.00	100.00
18 .... 0.10	20.00	60.00	100.00
19 .... 0.10	20.00	60.00	100.00
20 .... 0.10	20.00	60.00	100.00
21 .... 0.10	18.00	54.00	90.00
22 .... 0.10	18.00	54.00	90.00
23 .... 0.10	18.00	54.00	90.00
24 .... 0.10	18.00	54.00	90.00
25 .... 0.10	18.00	54.00	90.00
26 .... 0.10	18.00	54.00	90.00
27 SD/JK, 1:Ant-Man 0.10	360.00	1080.00	1800.00
28 SD/JK............................ 0.12	16.00	48.00	80.00
29 SD/JK............................ 0.12	16.00	48.00	80.00
30 SD/JK............................ 0.12	16.00	48.00	80.00
31 SD/JK............................ 0.12	16.00	48.00	80.00
32 SD/JK............................ 0.12	16.00	48.00	80.00
33 SD/JK............................ 0.12	16.00	48.00	80.00
34 SD/JK............................ 0.12	16.00	48.00	80.00
35 SD/JK, 2:Ant-Man 0.12	200.00	600.00	1000.00
36 SD/JK............................ 0.12	80.00	240.00	400.00
37 SD/JK............................ 0.12	40.00	120.00	200.00
38 .... 0.12	30.00	90.00	150.00
39 .... 0.12	30.00	90.00	150.00
40 .... 0.12	30.00	90.00	150.00
41 DH/SD........................... 0.12	30.00	90.00	150.00
42 DH/SD........................... 0.12	30.00	90.00	150.00

	ORIG.	GOOD	FINE	N-MINT
❏ 43 DH/SD 0.12	30.00	90.00	150.00
❏ 44 JK/SD, O:Wasp 0.12	40.00	120.00	200.00
❏ 45 DH/SD 0.12	18.00	54.00	90.00
❏ 46 DH/SD 0.12	18.00	54.00	90.00
❏ 47 DH/SD 0.12	18.00	54.00	90.00
❏ 48 DH/SD 0.12	18.00	54.00	90.00
❏ 49 JK/DH/AM, Giant Man			
.... 0.12	24.00	72.00	120.00
❏ 50 JK/SD, Human Top I.... 0.12	12.00	36.00	60.00
❏ 51 JK, Human Top II......... 0.12	12.00	36.00	60.00
❏ 52 1:Black Knight.............. 0.12	12.00	36.00	60.00
❏ 53 .... 0.12	12.00	36.00	60.00
❏ 54 .... 0.12	12.00	36.00	60.00
❏ 55 .... 0.12	12.00	36.00	60.00
❏ 56 .... 0.12	12.00	36.00	60.00
❏ 57 .... 0.12	20.00	60.00	100.00
❏ 58 .... 0.12	12.00	36.00	60.00
❏ 59 Giant-Man vs. Hulk 0.12	28.00	84.00	140.00
❏ 60 Hulk begins.................. 0.12	36.00	108.00	180.00
❏ 61 .... 0.12	11.00	33.00	55.00
❏ 62 .... 0.12	11.00	33.00	55.00
❏ 63 .... 0.12	11.00	33.00	55.00
❏ 64 .... 0.12	11.00	33.00	55.00
❏ 65 .... 0.12	11.00	33.00	55.00
❏ 66 .... 0.12	11.00	33.00	55.00
❏ 67 .... 0.12	11.00	33.00	55.00
❏ 68 .... 0.12	11.00	33.00	55.00
❏ 69 .... 0.12	11.00	33.00	55.00
❏ 70 Sub-Mariner begins 0.12	16.00	48.00	80.00
❏ 71 .... 0.12	6.00	18.00	30.00
❏ 72 .... 0.12	6.00	18.00	30.00
❏ 73 .... 0.12	6.00	18.00	30.00
❏ 74 .... 0.12	6.00	18.00	30.00
❏ 75 .... 0.12	6.00	18.00	30.00
❏ 76 .... 0.12	6.00	18.00	30.00
❏ 77 .... 0.12	6.00	18.00	30.00
❏ 78 .... 0.12	6.00	18.00	30.00
❏ 79 .... 0.12	6.00	18.00	30.00
❏ 80 GC/JK 0.12	6.00	18.00	30.00
❏ 81 GC/JK 0.12	6.00	18.00	30.00
❏ 82 GC/JK 0.12	6.00	18.00	30.00
❏ 83 .... 0.12	6.00	18.00	30.00
❏ 84 .... 0.12	6.00	18.00	30.00
❏ 85 .... 0.12	6.00	18.00	30.00
❏ 86 .... 0.12	6.00	18.00	30.00
❏ 87 .... 0.12	6.00	18.00	30.00
❏ 88 .... 0.12	6.00	18.00	30.00
❏ 89 .... 0.12	6.00	18.00	30.00
❏ 90 .... 0.12	6.00	18.00	30.00
❏ 91 .... 0.12	6.00	18.00	30.00
❏ 92 Silver Surfer................ 0.12	9.60	28.80	48.00
❏ 93 Silver Surfer................ 0.12	9.60	28.80	48.00
❏ 94 .... 0.12	3.20	9.60	16.00
❏ 95 .... 0.12	6.00	18.00	30.00
❏ 96 .... 0.12	6.00	18.00	30.00

	ORIG.	GOOD	FINE	N-MINT
❏ 97 ....0.12	6.00	18.00	30.00
❏ 98 ....0.12	6.00	18.00	30.00
❏ 99 ....0.12	6.00	18.00	30.00
❏ 100 Hulk vs. Sub-Mariner .0.12	7.20	21.60	36.00
❏ 101 (becomes The Incredible Hulk)			
....0.12	6.00	18.00	30.00

TALES TO ASTONISH (2nd series)

	ORIG.	GOOD	FINE	N-MINT
❏ 1 JB, Sub-Mariner rep.........	0.40	1.20	2.00
❏ 2 JB, Sub-Mariner rep.........	0.30	0.90	1.50
❏ 3 JB, Sub-Mariner rep.........	0.30	0.90	1.50
❏ 4 JB, Sub-Mariner rep.........	0.30	0.90	1.50
❏ 5 JB, Sub-Mariner rep.........	0.30	0.90	1.50
❏ 6 JB, Sub-Mariner rep.........	0.30	0.90	1.50
❏ 7 JB, Sub-Mariner rep.........	0.30	0.90	1.50
❏ 8 JB, Sub-Mariner rep.........	0.30	0.90	1.50
❏ 9 JB, Sub-Mariner rep.........	0.30	0.90	1.50
❏ 10 JB, Sub-Mariner rep.......	0.30	0.90	1.50
❏ 11 JB, Sub-Mariner rep.......	0.30	0.90	1.50
❏ 12 JB, Sub-Mariner rep.......	0.30	0.90	1.50
❏ 13 JB, Sub-Mariner rep.......	0.30	0.90	1.50
❏ 14 JB, Sub-Mariner rep.......	0.30	0.90	1.50

TARZAN OF THE APES

	ORIG.	GOOD	FINE	N-MINT
❏ 1 O:Tarzan 0.60	0.20	0.60	1.00
❏ 2 O:Tarzan 0.60	0.20	0.60	1.00

TARZAN, LORD OF THE JUNGLE

	ORIG.	GOOD	FINE	N-MINT
❏ 1 ....0.30	0.50	1.50	2.50
❏ 2 ....0.30	0.30	0.90	1.50
❏ 3 ....0.30	0.30	0.90	1.50
❏ 4 ....0.30	0.30	0.90	1.50
❏ 5 ....0.30	0.30	0.90	1.50
❏ 6 ....0.35	0.20	0.60	1.00
❏ 7 ....0.35	0.20	0.60	1.00
❏ 8 ....0.35	0.20	0.60	1.00
❏ 9 ....0.35	0.20	0.60	1.00
❏ 10 ....0.35	0.20	0.60	1.00
❏ 11 ....0.35	0.20	0.60	1.00
❏ 12 ....0.35	0.20	0.60	1.00
❏ 13 ....0.35	0.20	0.60	1.00
❏ 14 ....0.35	0.20	0.60	1.00
❏ 15 ....0.35	0.20	0.60	1.00
❏ 16 ....0.35	0.20	0.60	1.00
❏ 17 ....0.35	0.20	0.60	1.00
❏ 18 ....0.35	0.20	0.60	1.00
❏ 19 ....0.35	0.20	0.60	1.00
❏ 20 ....0.35	0.20	0.60	1.00
❏ 21 ....0.35	0.20	0.60	1.00
❏ 22 ....0.35	0.20	0.60	1.00
❏ 23 ....0.35	0.20	0.60	1.00
❏ 24 ....0.40	0.20	0.60	1.00
❏ 25 ....0.40	0.20	0.60	1.00
❏ 26 ....0.40	0.20	0.60	1.00
❏ 27 ....0.40	0.20	0.60	1.00
❏ 28 ....0.40	0.20	0.60	1.00
❏ 29 ....0.40	0.20	0.60	1.00

	ORIG.	GOOD	FINE	N-MINT
TARZAN, LORD OF THE JUNGLE ANNUAL				
1 (1977)	0.50	0.40	1.20	2.00
2 (1978)	0.60	0.40	1.20	2.00
3 (1979)	0.60	0.40	1.20	2.00
TEAM AMERICA				
1 O:Team America	0.60	0.30	0.90	1.50
2 LMc	0.60	0.20	0.60	1.00
3 LMc	0.60	0.20	0.60	1.00
4 LMc	0.60	0.20	0.60	1.00
5	0.60	0.20	0.60	1.00
6	0.60	0.20	0.60	1.00
7	0.60	0.20	0.60	1.00
8	0.60	0.20	0.60	1.00
9	0.60	0.20	0.60	1.00
10	0.60	0.20	0.60	1.00
11 Ghost Rider	0.60	0.60	1.80	3.00
12 DP, Marauder unmasked	1.00	0.20	0.60	1.00
TERMINATOR 2: JUDGMENT DAY				
nn b&w reprint	2.25	0.45	1.35	2.25
1 movie	1.00	0.20	0.60	1.00
2 movie	1.00	0.20	0.60	1.00
3 movie	1.00	0.20	0.60	1.00
TERROR, INC.				
1	1.75	0.35	1.05	1.75
2	1.75	0.35	1.05	1.75
3	1.75	0.35	1.05	1.75
4	1.75	0.35	1.05	1.75
5	1.75	0.35	1.05	1.75
6	1.75	0.35	1.05	1.75
7	1.75	0.35	1.05	1.75
8	1.75	0.35	1.05	1.75
9	1.75	0.35	1.05	1.75
10 Wolverine	1.75	0.35	1.05	1.75
11	1.75	0.35	1.05	1.75
12	1.75	0.35	1.05	1.75
13	1.75	0.35	1.05	1.75
THANOS QUEST, THE				
1	4.95	3.00	9.00	15.00
2	4.95	2.00	6.00	10.00
THING, THE				
1 JBy, Origin	0.60	0.50	1.50	2.50
2 JBy	0.60	0.30	0.90	1.50
3	0.60	0.20	0.60	1.00
4	0.60	0.20	0.60	1.00
5	0.60	0.20	0.60	1.00
6	0.60	0.20	0.60	1.00
7	0.60	0.20	0.60	1.00
8	0.60	0.20	0.60	1.00
9	0.60	0.20	0.60	1.00
10	0.60	0.20	0.60	1.00
11	0.60	0.20	0.60	1.00
12	0.60	0.20	0.60	1.00
13	0.60	0.20	0.60	1.00

	ORIG.	GOOD	FINE	N-MINT
14	0.60	0.20	0.60	1.00
15	0.60	0.20	0.60	1.00
16	0.60	0.20	0.60	1.00
17	0.60	0.20	0.60	1.00
18	0.60	0.20	0.60	1.00
19	0.60	0.20	0.60	1.00
20	0.60	0.20	0.60	1.00
21	0.60	0.20	0.60	1.00
22	0.65	0.20	0.60	1.00
23	0.65	0.20	0.60	1.00
24	0.65	0.20	0.60	1.00
25	0.65	0.20	0.60	1.00
26	0.65	0.20	0.60	1.00
27	0.65	0.20	0.60	1.00
28	0.65	0.20	0.60	1.00
29	0.65	0.20	0.60	1.00
30 Secret Wars II	0.65	0.20	0.60	1.00
31	0.75	0.20	0.60	1.00
32	0.75	0.20	0.60	1.00
33	0.75	0.20	0.60	1.00
34	0.75	0.20	0.60	1.00
35	0.75	0.20	0.60	1.00
36	0.75	0.20	0.60	1.00
THOR (formerly Journey into Mystery)				
126 JK, Hercules	0.12	16.00	48.00	80.00
127 JK	0.12	6.00	18.00	30.00
128 JK	0.12	6.00	18.00	30.00
129 JK	0.12	6.00	18.00	30.00
130 JK	0.12	6.00	18.00	30.00
131 JK	0.12	6.00	18.00	30.00
132 JK	0.12	6.00	18.00	30.00
133 JK	0.12	6.00	18.00	30.00
134 JK, I:High Evolutionary	0.12	9.60	28.80	48.00
135 JK	0.12	6.00	18.00	30.00
136 JK	0.12	6.00	18.00	30.00
137 JK	0.12	6.00	18.00	30.00
138 JK	0.12	6.00	18.00	30.00
139 JK	0.12	6.00	18.00	30.00
140 JK	0.12	6.00	18.00	30.00
141 JK	0.12	4.40	13.20	22.00
142 JK	0.12	4.40	13.20	22.00
143 JK	0.12	4.40	13.20	22.00
144 JK	0.12	4.40	13.20	22.00
145 JK	0.12	4.40	13.20	22.00
146 JK, O:Inhumans	0.12	4.40	13.20	22.00
147 JK	0.12	4.40	13.20	22.00
148 JK	0.12	4.40	13.20	22.00
149 JK	0.12	4.40	13.20	22.00
150 JK	0.12	4.40	13.20	22.00
151 JK	0.12	4.40	13.20	22.00
152 JK	0.12	4.40	13.20	22.00
153 JK	0.12	4.40	13.20	22.00
154 JK	0.12	4.40	13.20	22.00
155 JK	0.12	4.40	13.20	22.00

	ORIG.	GOOD	FINE	N-MINT
❏ 156 JK	0.12	4.40	13.20	22.00
❏ 157 JK	0.12	4.40	13.20	22.00
❏ 158 JK, O:Don Blake	0.12	10.00	30.00	50.00
❏ 159 JK	0.12	4.40	13.20	22.00
❏ 160 JK	0.12	4.40	13.20	22.00
❏ 161 JK	0.12	4.40	13.20	22.00
❏ 162 JK, O:Galactus	0.12	4.40	13.20	22.00
❏ 163 JK	0.12	4.40	13.20	22.00
❏ 164 JK	0.12	4.40	13.20	22.00
❏ 165 JK, Him/Warlock	0.15	8.00	24.00	40.00
❏ 166 JK, Him/Warlock	0.15	8.00	24.00	40.00
❏ 167 JK, Sif	0.15	4.40	13.20	22.00
❏ 168 JK, O:Galactus	0.15	6.00	18.00	30.00
❏ 169 JK, O:Galactus	0.15	6.00	18.00	30.00
❏ 170	0.15	3.60	10.80	18.00
❏ 171	0.15	3.60	10.80	18.00
❏ 172	0.15	3.60	10.80	18.00
❏ 173	0.15	3.60	10.80	18.00
❏ 174	0.15	3.60	10.80	18.00
❏ 175	0.15	3.60	10.80	18.00
❏ 176	0.15	3.60	10.80	18.00
❏ 177	0.15	3.60	10.80	18.00
❏ 178	0.15	3.60	10.80	18.00
❏ 179	0.15	3.60	10.80	18.00
❏ 180 NA	0.15	2.00	6.00	10.00
❏ 181 NA	0.15	2.00	6.00	10.00
❏ 182	0.15	1.00	3.00	5.00
❏ 183	0.15	1.00	3.00	5.00
❏ 184	0.15	1.00	3.00	5.00
❏ 185	0.15	1.00	3.00	5.00
❏ 186	0.15	1.00	3.00	5.00
❏ 187	0.15	1.00	3.00	5.00
❏ 188	0.15	1.00	3.00	5.00
❏ 189	0.15	1.00	3.00	5.00
❏ 190	0.15	1.00	3.00	5.00
❏ 191	0.15	1.00	3.00	5.00
❏ 192	0.15	1.00	3.00	5.00
❏ 193 JB/SB, Silver Surfer	0.25	2.40	7.20	12.00
❏ 194	0.20	1.00	3.00	5.00
❏ 195	0.20	1.00	3.00	5.00
❏ 196	0.20	1.00	3.00	5.00
❏ 197	0.20	1.00	3.00	5.00
❏ 198	0.20	1.00	3.00	5.00
❏ 199	0.20	1.00	3.00	5.00
❏ 200 JB, Ragnarok	0.20	1.20	3.60	6.00
❏ 201 JB	0.20	0.50	1.50	2.50
❏ 202 JB	0.20	0.50	1.50	2.50
❏ 203 JB	0.20	0.50	1.50	2.50
❏ 204 JB	0.20	0.50	1.50	2.50
❏ 205 JB	0.20	0.50	1.50	2.50
❏ 206 JB	0.20	0.50	1.50	2.50
❏ 207 JB	0.20	0.50	1.50	2.50
❏ 208 JB	0.20	0.50	1.50	2.50
❏ 209 JB	0.20	0.50	1.50	2.50
❏ 210 JB	0.20	0.50	1.50	2.50
❏ 211 JB	0.20	0.50	1.50	2.50
❏ 212 JB	0.20	0.50	1.50	2.50
❏ 213 JB	0.20	0.50	1.50	2.50
❏ 214	0.20	0.25	0.75	1.25
❏ 215	0.20	0.25	0.75	1.25
❏ 216	0.20	0.25	0.75	1.25
❏ 217	0.20	0.25	0.75	1.25
❏ 218	0.20	0.25	0.75	1.25
❏ 219	0.20	0.25	0.75	1.25
❏ 220	0.20	0.25	0.75	1.25
❏ 221	0.20	0.30	0.90	1.50
❏ 222	0.20	0.30	0.90	1.50
❏ 223	0.25	0.30	0.90	1.50
❏ 224	0.25	0.30	0.90	1.50
❏ 225	0.25	0.30	0.90	1.50
❏ 226	0.25	0.30	0.90	1.50
❏ 227	0.25	0.30	0.90	1.50
❏ 228	0.25	0.30	0.90	1.50
❏ 229	0.25	0.30	0.90	1.50
❏ 230	0.25	0.30	0.90	1.50
❏ 231	0.25	0.30	0.90	1.50
❏ 232	0.25	0.30	0.90	1.50
❏ 233	0.25	0.30	0.90	1.50
❏ 234	0.25	0.30	0.90	1.50
❏ 235	0.25	0.30	0.90	1.50
❏ 236	0.25	0.30	0.90	1.50
❏ 237	0.25	0.30	0.90	1.50
❏ 238	0.25	0.30	0.90	1.50
❏ 239	0.25	0.30	0.90	1.50
❏ 240	0.25	0.30	0.90	1.50
❏ 241 JB	0.25	0.30	0.90	1.50
❏ 242 JB	0.25	0.30	0.90	1.50
❏ 243 JB	0.25	0.30	0.90	1.50
❏ 244 JB	0.25	0.30	0.90	1.50
❏ 245 JB	0.25	0.30	0.90	1.50
❏ 246 JB	0.25	0.30	0.90	1.50
❏ 247 JB	0.25	0.30	0.90	1.50
❏ 248 JB	0.25	0.30	0.90	1.50
❏ 249 JB	0.25	0.30	0.90	1.50
❏ 250 JB	0.25	0.30	0.90	1.50
❏ 251	0.30	0.30	0.90	1.50
❏ 252	0.30	0.30	0.90	1.50
❏ 253	0.30	0.30	0.90	1.50
❏ 254	0.30	0.30	0.90	1.50
❏ 255	0.30	0.30	0.90	1.50
❏ 256	0.30	0.30	0.90	1.50
❏ 257	0.30	0.30	0.90	1.50
❏ 258	0.30	0.30	0.90	1.50
❏ 259	0.30	0.30	0.90	1.50
❏ 260 WS	0.30	0.80	2.40	4.00
❏ 261 WS	0.30	0.30	0.90	1.50
❏ 262 WS	0.30	0.30	0.90	1.50
❏ 263 WS	0.30	0.30	0.90	1.50
❏ 264 WS	0.30	0.30	0.90	1.50
❏ 265 WS	0.35	0.30	0.90	1.50

	ORIG.	GOOD	FINE	N-MINT
266 WS	0.35	0.30	0.90	1.50
267 WS	0.35	0.30	0.90	1.50
268 WS	0.35	0.20	0.60	1.00
269 WS	0.35	0.20	0.60	1.00
270 WS	0.35	0.20	0.60	1.00
271 WS	0.35	0.20	0.60	1.00
272	0.35	0.21	0.63	1.05
273	0.35	0.21	0.63	1.05
274	0.35	0.21	0.63	1.05
275	0.35	0.21	0.63	1.05
276	0.35	0.21	0.63	1.05
277	0.35	0.21	0.63	1.05
278	0.35	0.21	0.63	1.05
279	0.35	0.21	0.63	1.05
280	0.35	0.21	0.63	1.05
281	0.35	0.21	0.63	1.05
282	0.35	0.21	0.63	1.05
283	0.40	0.21	0.63	1.05
284	0.40	0.21	0.63	1.05
285	0.40	0.21	0.63	1.05
286	0.40	0.21	0.63	1.05
287	0.40	0.21	0.63	1.05
288	0.40	0.21	0.63	1.05
289	0.40	0.21	0.63	1.05
290	0.40	0.21	0.63	1.05
291	0.40	0.21	0.63	1.05
292	0.40	0.21	0.63	1.05
293	0.40	0.21	0.63	1.05
294 KP, O:Odin	0.40	0.20	0.60	1.00
295 KP	0.40	0.20	0.60	1.00
296 KP	0.40	0.20	0.60	1.00
297 KP	0.40	0.20	0.60	1.00
298 KP	0.40	0.20	0.60	1.00
299 KP	0.50	0.20	0.60	1.00
300 KP, giant	0.75	0.30	0.90	1.50
301	0.50	0.20	0.60	1.00
302	0.50	0.20	0.60	1.00
303	0.50	0.20	0.60	1.00
304	0.50	0.20	0.60	1.00
305	0.50	0.20	0.60	1.00
306	0.50	0.20	0.60	1.00
307	0.50	0.20	0.60	1.00
308	0.50	0.20	0.60	1.00
309	0.50	0.20	0.60	1.00
310	0.50	0.20	0.60	1.00
311	0.50	0.20	0.60	1.00
312	0.50	0.20	0.60	1.00
313	0.50	0.20	0.60	1.00
314	0.50	0.20	0.60	1.00
315	0.60	0.20	0.60	1.00
316	0.60	0.20	0.60	1.00
317	0.60	0.20	0.60	1.00
318	0.60	0.20	0.60	1.00
319	0.60	0.20	0.60	1.00
320	0.60	0.20	0.60	1.00

	ORIG.	GOOD	FINE	N-MINT
321	0.60	0.20	0.60	1.00
322	0.60	0.20	0.60	1.00
323	0.60	0.20	0.60	1.00
324	0.60	0.20	0.60	1.00
325	0.60	0.20	0.60	1.00
326	0.60	0.20	0.60	1.00
327	0.60	0.20	0.60	1.00
328	0.60	0.20	0.60	1.00
329	0.60	0.20	0.60	1.00
330	0.60	0.20	0.60	1.00
331	0.60	0.20	0.60	1.00
332	0.60	0.20	0.60	1.00
333	0.60	0.20	0.60	1.00
334	0.60	0.20	0.60	1.00
335	0.60	0.20	0.60	1.00
336	0.60	0.20	0.60	1.00
337 1:Simonson Thor	0.60	1.20	3.60	6.00
338 WS Beta Ray Bill	0.60	0.80	2.40	4.00
339 WS, Beta Ray Bill	0.60	0.50	1.50	2.50
340 WS Beta Ray Bill	0.60	0.40	1.20	2.00
341 WS	0.60	0.30	0.90	1.50
342 WS	0.60	0.30	0.90	1.50
343 WS	0.60	0.30	0.90	1.50
344 WS	0.60	0.30	0.90	1.50
345 WS	0.60	0.30	0.90	1.50
346 WS	0.60	0.30	0.90	1.50
347 WS	0.60	0.30	0.90	1.50
348 WS	0.60	0.30	0.90	1.50
349 WS	0.60	0.30	0.90	1.50
350 WS	0.60	0.30	0.90	1.50
351 WS	0.60	0.30	0.90	1.50
352 WS	0.60	0.30	0.90	1.50
353 WS	0.60	0.30	0.90	1.50
354 WS	0.65	0.30	0.90	1.50
355 WS	0.65	0.30	0.90	1.50
356 WS	0.65	0.30	0.90	1.50
357 WS	0.65	0.30	0.90	1.50
358 WS	0.65	0.30	0.90	1.50
359 WS	0.65	0.30	0.90	1.50
360 WS	0.65	0.30	0.90	1.50
361 WS	0.65	0.30	0.90	1.50
362 WS	0.65	0.30	0.90	1.50
363 WS Secret Wars II	0.65	0.30	0.90	1.50
364	0.75	0.30	0.90	1.50
365	0.75	0.30	0.90	1.50
366	0.75	0.30	0.90	1.50
367	0.75	0.30	0.90	1.50
368	0.75	0.30	0.90	1.50
369	0.75	0.30	0.90	1.50
370	0.75	0.30	0.90	1.50
371	0.75	0.30	0.90	1.50
372	0.75	0.30	0.90	1.50
373 mutant massacre	0.75	0.60	1.80	3.00
374 mutant massacre	0.75	0.60	1.80	3.00
375	0.75	0.30	0.90	1.50

	ORIG.	GOOD	FINE	N-MINT
376	0.75	0.30	0.90	1.50
377	0.75	0.30	0.90	1.50
378	0.75	0.30	0.90	1.50
379	0.75	0.30	0.90	1.50
380	0.75	0.30	0.90	1.50
381	0.75	0.30	0.90	1.50
382	1.25	0.30	0.90	1.50
383 Secret Wars II	0.75	0.30	0.90	1.50
384 Thor of 2537	0.75	0.30	0.90	1.50
385 A:Hulk	0.75	0.40	1.20	2.00
386	0.75	0.30	0.90	1.50
387	0.75	0.30	0.90	1.50
388	0.75	0.30	0.90	1.50
389	0.75	0.30	0.90	1.50
390	0.75	0.20	0.60	1.00
391	0.75	0.20	0.60	1.00
392	0.75	0.20	0.60	1.00
393	0.75	0.20	0.60	1.00
394	0.75	0.20	0.60	1.00
395	0.75	0.20	0.60	1.00
396	0.75	0.20	0.60	1.00
397	0.75	0.20	0.60	1.00
398	0.75	0.20	0.60	1.00
399	0.75	0.20	0.60	1.00
400 anniversary	1.75	0.60	1.80	3.00
401	0.75	0.20	0.60	1.00
402	0.75	0.20	0.60	1.00
403	0.75	0.20	0.60	1.00
404	0.75	0.20	0.60	1.00
405	0.75	0.20	0.60	1.00
406	0.75	0.20	0.60	1.00
407	1.00	0.20	0.60	1.00
408	1.00	0.20	0.60	1.00
409	1.00	0.20	0.60	1.00
410	1.00	0.20	0.60	1.00
411 Acts of Vengeance, 1:New Warriors (becomes The Mighty Thor)	1.00	2.80	8.40	14.00

THOR ANNUAL
(was Journey into Mystery Annual)

	ORIG.	GOOD	FINE	N-MINT
2 JK (1966)	0.25	8.00	24.00	40.00
3 JK, reprint (1971)	0.25	2.00	6.00	10.00
4 JK, reprint (1971)	0.25	2.00	6.00	10.00
5 JK/JB (1976)	0.50	1.00	3.00	5.00
6 JK/JB (1977)	0.50	1.00	3.00	5.00
7 (1978)	0.60	0.60	1.80	3.00
8 (1979)	0.75	0.60	1.80	3.00
9 (1981)	0.75	0.60	1.80	3.00
10 (1982)	1.00	0.60	1.80	3.00
11 (1983)	1.00	0.60	1.80	3.00
12 (1984)	1.00	0.60	1.80	3.00
13 (1985) (becomes Mighty Thor Annual)	1.25	0.60	1.80	3.00

THOR CORPS

	ORIG.	GOOD	FINE	N-MINT
1	1.75	0.35	1.05	1.75

THUNDERCATS (Former Star Comic)

	ORIG.	GOOD	FINE	N-MINT
22	1.00	0.20	0.60	1.00
23	1.00	0.20	0.60	1.00
24	1.00	0.20	0.60	1.00

THUNDERSTRIKE

	ORIG.	GOOD	FINE	N-MINT
1 foil cover	2.95	0.59	1.77	2.95

TIME BANDITS

	ORIG.	GOOD	FINE	N-MINT
1 movie	1.00	0.20	0.60	1.00

TOMB OF DARKNESS (was Beware)

	ORIG.	GOOD	FINE	N-MINT
9	0.25	0.20	0.60	1.00
10	0.25	0.20	0.60	1.00
11	0.25	0.20	0.60	1.00
12	0.25	0.20	0.60	1.00
13	0.25	0.20	0.60	1.00
14	0.25	0.20	0.60	1.00
15	0.25	0.20	0.60	1.00
16	0.25	0.20	0.60	1.00
17	0.25	0.20	0.60	1.00
18	0.25	0.20	0.60	1.00
19	0.25	0.20	0.60	1.00
20	0.25	0.20	0.60	1.00
21	0.25	0.20	0.60	1.00
22	0.25	0.20	0.60	1.00
23	0.25	0.20	0.60	1.00

TOMB OF DRACULA

	ORIG.	GOOD	FINE	N-MINT
1 GC	0.20	9.00	27.00	45.00
2 GC	0.20	6.00	18.00	30.00
3 GC	0.20	4.80	14.40	24.00
4 GC	0.20	4.80	14.40	24.00
5 GC	0.20	4.80	14.40	24.00
6 GC	0.20	2.40	7.20	12.00
7 GC	0.20	2.40	7.20	12.00
8 GC	0.20	2.40	7.20	12.00
9 GC	0.20	2.40	7.20	12.00
10 GC	0.20	3.60	10.80	18.00
11 GC	0.20	2.00	6.00	10.00
12 GC	0.20	2.00	6.00	10.00
13 GC	0.20	2.80	8.40	14.00
14 GC	0.20	2.00	6.00	10.00
15 GC	0.20	2.00	6.00	10.00
16 GC	0.20	2.00	6.00	10.00
17 GC	0.20	2.00	6.00	10.00
18 GC	0.20	2.00	6.00	10.00
19 GC	0.20	2.00	6.00	10.00
20 GC	0.25	2.00	6.00	10.00
21 GC	0.25	1.60	4.80	8.00
22 GC	0.25	1.60	4.80	8.00
23 GC	0.25	1.60	4.80	8.00
24 GC	0.25	1.60	4.80	8.00
25 GC	0.25	1.60	4.80	8.00
26 GC	0.25	1.60	4.80	8.00
27 GC	0.25	1.60	4.80	8.00
28 GC	0.25	1.60	4.80	8.00
29 GC	0.25	1.60	4.80	8.00

	ORIG.	GOOD	FINE	N-MINT
❏ 30 GC	0.25	1.60	4.80	8.00
❏ 31 GC	0.25	1.60	4.80	8.00
❏ 32 GC	0.25	1.60	4.80	8.00
❏ 33 GC	0.25	1.60	4.80	8.00
❏ 34 GC	0.25	1.60	4.80	8.00
❏ 35 GC	0.25	1.60	4.80	8.00
❏ 36 GC	0.25	1.60	4.80	8.00
❏ 37 GC	0.25	1.60	4.80	8.00
❏ 38 GC	0.25	1.60	4.80	8.00
❏ 39 GC	0.25	1.60	4.80	8.00
❏ 40 GC	0.25	1.60	4.80	8.00
❏ 41 GC	0.25	1.20	3.60	6.00
❏ 42 GC	0.25	1.20	3.60	6.00
❏ 43 GC	0.25	1.20	3.60	6.00
❏ 44 GC	0.25	1.20	3.60	6.00
❏ 45 GC	0.25	1.20	3.60	6.00
❏ 46 GC	0.25	1.20	3.60	6.00
❏ 47 GC	0.25	1.20	3.60	6.00
❏ 48 GC	0.30	1.20	3.60	6.00
❏ 49 GC	0.30	1.20	3.60	6.00
❏ 50 GC	0.30	1.20	3.60	6.00
❏ 51 GC	0.30	1.20	3.60	6.00
❏ 52 GC	0.30	1.20	3.60	6.00
❏ 53 GC	0.30	1.20	3.60	6.00
❏ 54 GC	0.30	1.20	3.60	6.00
❏ 55 GC	0.30	1.20	3.60	6.00
❏ 56 GC	0.30	1.20	3.60	6.00
❏ 57 GC	0.30	1.20	3.60	6.00
❏ 58 GC	0.30	1.20	3.60	6.00
❏ 59 GC	0.30	1.20	3.60	6.00
❏ 60 GC	0.30	1.20	3.60	6.00
❏ 61 GC	0.35	1.20	3.60	6.00
❏ 62 GC	0.35	1.20	3.60	6.00
❏ 63 GC	0.35	1.20	3.60	6.00
❏ 64 GC	0.35	1.20	3.60	6.00
❏ 65 GC	0.35	1.20	3.60	6.00
❏ 66 GC	0.35	1.20	3.60	6.00
❏ 67 GC	0.35	1.20	3.60	6.00
❏ 68 GC	0.35	1.20	3.60	6.00
❏ 69 GC	0.35	1.20	3.60	6.00
❏ 70 D:Dracula	0.60	1.20	3.60	6.00

TOMB OF DRACULA (b&w mag)

	ORIG.	GOOD	FINE	N-MINT
❏ 1	1.25	0.25	0.75	1.25
❏ 2	1.25	0.25	0.75	1.25
❏ 3	1.25	0.25	0.75	1.25
❏ 4	1.25	0.25	0.75	1.25
❏ 5	1.25	0.25	0.75	1.25
❏ 6	1.25	0.25	0.75	1.25

TOMMY

	ORIG.	GOOD	FINE	N-MINT
❏ (b&w mag; not comics) nn, filmbook	1.00	0.20	0.60	1.00

TOWER OF SHADOWS

	ORIG.	GOOD	FINE	N-MINT
❏ 1	0.15	0.80	2.40	4.00
❏ 2	0.15	0.60	1.80	3.00

	ORIG.	GOOD	FINE	N-MINT
❏ 3	0.15	0.60	1.80	3.00
❏ 4	0.15	0.60	1.80	3.00
❏ 5	0.15	0.40	1.20	2.00
❏ 6	0.15	0.40	1.20	2.00
❏ 7	0.15	0.40	1.20	2.00
❏ 8	0.15	0.40	1.20	2.00
❏ 9	0.15	0.40	1.20	2.00

TOXIC AVENGER

	ORIG.	GOOD	FINE	N-MINT
❏ 1 O:Toxic Avenger	1.50	0.30	0.90	1.50
❏ 2	1.50	0.30	0.90	1.50
❏ 3	1.50	0.30	0.90	1.50
❏ 4	1.50	0.30	0.90	1.50
❏ 5	1.50	0.30	0.90	1.50
❏ 6	1.50	0.30	0.90	1.50
❏ 7	1.50	0.30	0.90	1.50
❏ 8	1.50	0.30	0.90	1.50
❏ 9	1.50	0.30	0.90	1.50
❏ 10	1.50	0.30	0.90	1.50
❏ 11	1.50	0.30	0.90	1.50

TOXIC CRUSADERS

	ORIG.	GOOD	FINE	N-MINT
❏ 1	1.25	0.25	0.75	1.25
❏ 2	1.25	0.25	0.75	1.25
❏ 3	1.25	0.25	0.75	1.25
❏ 4	1.25	0.25	0.75	1.25
❏ 5	1.25	0.25	0.75	1.25
❏ 6	1.25	0.25	0.75	1.25
❏ 7	1.25	0.25	0.75	1.25
❏ 8	1.25	0.25	0.75	1.25

TRANSFORMERS

	ORIG.	GOOD	FINE	N-MINT
❏ 1	0.75	0.80	2.40	4.00
❏ 2	0.75	0.60	1.80	3.00
❏ 3 SpM	0.75	0.40	1.20	2.00
❏ 4	0.75	0.40	1.20	2.00
❏ 5	0.75	0.40	1.20	2.00
❏ 6	0.75	0.40	1.20	2.00
❏ 7	0.75	0.40	1.20	2.00
❏ 8	0.75	0.40	1.20	2.00
❏ 9	0.75	0.40	1.20	2.00
❏ 10	0.75	0.40	1.20	2.00
❏ 11	0.75	0.30	0.90	1.50
❏ 12	0.75	0.30	0.90	1.50
❏ 13	0.75	0.30	0.90	1.50
❏ 14	0.75	0.30	0.90	1.50
❏ 15	0.75	0.20	0.60	1.00
❏ 16	0.75	0.20	0.60	1.00
❏ 17	0.75	0.20	0.60	1.00
❏ 18	0.75	0.20	0.60	1.00
❏ 19	0.75	0.20	0.60	1.00
❏ 20	0.75	0.20	0.60	1.00
❏ 21	0.75	0.20	0.60	1.00
❏ 22	0.75	0.20	0.60	1.00
❏ 23	0.75	0.20	0.60	1.00
❏ 24	0.75	0.20	0.60	1.00
❏ 25	0.75	0.20	0.60	1.00

	ORIG.	GOOD	FINE	N-MINT
❏ 26	0.75	0.20	0.60	1.00
❏ 27	0.75	0.20	0.60	1.00
❏ 28	1.00	0.20	0.60	1.00
❏ 29	1.00	0.20	0.60	1.00
❏ 30	1.00	0.20	0.60	1.00
❏ 31	1.00	0.20	0.60	1.00
❏ 32	1.00	0.20	0.60	1.00
❏ 33	1.00	0.20	0.60	1.00
❏ 34	1.00	0.20	0.60	1.00
❏ 35	1.00	0.20	0.60	1.00
❏ 36	1.00	0.20	0.60	1.00
❏ 37	1.00	0.20	0.60	1.00
❏ 38	1.00	0.20	0.60	1.00
❏ 39	1.00	0.20	0.60	1.00
❏ 40	1.00	0.20	0.60	1.00
❏ 41	1.00	0.20	0.60	1.00
❏ 42	1.00	0.20	0.60	1.00
❏ 43	1.00	0.20	0.60	1.00
❏ 44	1.00	0.20	0.60	1.00
❏ 45	1.00	0.20	0.60	1.00
❏ 46	1.00	0.20	0.60	1.00
❏ 47	1.00	0.20	0.60	1.00
❏ 48	1.00	0.20	0.60	1.00
❏ 49	1.00	0.20	0.60	1.00
❏ 50	1.50	0.30	0.90	1.50
❏ 51	1.00	0.20	0.60	1.00
❏ 52	1.00	0.20	0.60	1.00
❏ 53	1.00	0.20	0.60	1.00
❏ 54	1.00	0.20	0.60	1.00
❏ 55	1.00	0.20	0.60	1.00
❏ 56	1.00	0.20	0.60	1.00
❏ 57	1.00	0.20	0.60	1.00
❏ 58	1.00	0.20	0.60	1.00
❏ 59	1.00	0.20	0.60	1.00
❏ 60	1.00	0.20	0.60	1.00
❏ 61	1.00	0.20	0.60	1.00
❏ 62	1.00	0.20	0.60	1.00
❏ 63	1.00	0.20	0.60	1.00
❏ 64	1.00	0.20	0.60	1.00
❏ 65	1.00	0.20	0.60	1.00
❏ 66	1.00	0.20	0.60	1.00
❏ 67	1.00	0.20	0.60	1.00
❏ 68	1.00	0.20	0.60	1.00
❏ 69	1.00	0.20	0.60	1.00
❏ 70	1.00	0.20	0.60	1.00
❏ 71	1.00	0.20	0.60	1.00
❏ 72	1.00	0.20	0.60	1.00
❏ 73	1.00	0.20	0.60	1.00
❏ 74	1.00	0.20	0.60	1.00
❏ 75	1.50	0.30	0.90	1.50
❏ 76	1.00	0.20	0.60	1.00
❏ 77	1.00	0.20	0.60	1.00
❏ 78	1.00	0.20	0.60	1.00
❏ 79	1.00	0.20	0.60	1.00
❏ 80	1.00	0.20	0.60	1.00

	ORIG.	GOOD	FINE	N-MINT
TRANSFORMERS COMICS MAGAZINE				
❏ 1 digest	1.50	0.30	0.90	1.50
❏ 2	1.50	0.30	0.90	1.50
❏ 3	1.50	0.30	0.90	1.50
❏ 4	1.50	0.30	0.90	1.50
❏ 5	1.50	0.30	0.90	1.50
❏ 6	1.50	0.30	0.90	1.50
❏ 7	1.50	0.30	0.90	1.50
❏ 8	1.50	0.30	0.90	1.50
❏ 9	1.50	0.30	0.90	1.50
❏ 10	1.50	0.30	0.90	1.50
TRANSFORMERS MOVIE				
❏ 1	0.75	0.20	0.60	1.00
❏ 2	0.75	0.20	0.60	1.00
❏ 3	0.75	0.20	0.60	1.00
TRANSFORMERS UNIVERSE				
❏ 1	1.25	0.25	0.75	1.25
❏ 2	1.25	0.25	0.75	1.25
❏ 3	1.25	0.25	0.75	1.25
❏ 4	1.25	0.25	0.75	1.25
TRANSFORMERS: HEADMASTERS, THE				
❏ 1	1.00	0.20	0.60	1.00
❏ 2	1.00	0.20	0.60	1.00
❏ 3	1.00	0.20	0.60	1.00
❏ 4	0.75	0.15	0.45	0.75
U.S. 1				
❏ 1 HT, origin	0.60	0.40	1.20	2.00
❏ 2	0.60	0.20	0.60	1.00
❏ 3	0.60	0.20	0.60	1.00
❏ 4	0.60	0.20	0.60	1.00
❏ 5	0.60	0.20	0.60	1.00
❏ 6	0.60	0.20	0.60	1.00
❏ 7	0.60	0.20	0.60	1.00
❏ 8	0.60	0.20	0.60	1.00
❏ 9	0.60	0.20	0.60	1.00
❏ 10	0.60	0.20	0.60	1.00
❏ 11	0.60	0.20	0.60	1.00
❏ 12	0.60	0.20	0.60	1.00
U.S.AGENT				
❏ 1	1.75	0.35	1.05	1.75
❏ 2	1.75	0.35	1.05	1.75
❏ 3	1.75	0.35	1.05	1.75
❏ 4	1.75	0.35	1.05	1.75
UNCANNY X-MEN (formerly X-Men)				
❏ 142 JBy/TA	0.50	3.00	9.00	15.00
❏ 143 JBy/TA	0.50	3.00	9.00	15.00
❏ 144	0.50	1.60	4.80	8.00
❏ 145	0.50	1.60	4.80	8.00
❏ 146	0.50	1.60	4.80	8.00
❏ 147	0.50	1.60	4.80	8.00
❏ 148	0.50	1.60	4.80	8.00
❏ 149	0.50	1.60	4.80	8.00
❏ 150	0.75	1.60	4.80	8.00
❏ 151	0.75	1.20	3.60	6.00

	ORIG.	GOOD	FINE	N-MINT
❏ 152	0.75	1.20	3.60	6.00
❏ 153	0.60	1.20	3.60	6.00
❏ 154	0.60	1.20	3.60	6.00
❏ 155	0.60	1.20	3.60	6.00
❏ 156	0.60	1.20	3.60	6.00
❏ 157	0.60	1.20	3.60	6.00
❏ 158	0.60	1.20	3.60	6.00
❏ 159 BSz, A:Dracula	0.60	1.20	3.60	6.00
❏ 160	0.60	1.20	3.60	6.00
❏ 161	0.60	1.20	3.60	6.00
❏ 162	0.60	1.20	3.60	6.00
❏ 163	0.60	1.20	3.60	6.00
❏ 164 DC, I:Binary	0.60	1.20	3.60	6.00
❏ 165	0.60	1.60	4.80	8.00
❏ 166 PS	1.00	1.20	3.60	6.00
❏ 167 PS	0.60	1.20	3.60	6.00
❏ 168	0.60	1.20	3.60	6.00
❏ 169	0.60	1.20	3.60	6.00
❏ 170	0.60	1.20	3.60	6.00
❏ 171 Rogue joins	0.60	1.40	4.20	7.00
❏ 172	0.60	1.40	4.20	7.00
❏ 173	0.60	1.00	3.00	5.00
❏ 174	0.60	1.00	3.00	5.00
❏ 175	1.00	1.00	3.00	5.00
❏ 176	0.60	1.00	3.00	5.00
❏ 177	0.60	1.00	3.00	5.00
❏ 178	0.60	1.00	3.00	5.00
❏ 179	0.60	1.00	3.00	5.00
❏ 180	0.60	1.00	3.00	5.00
❏ 181	0.60	1.00	3.00	5.00
❏ 182	0.60	1.00	3.00	5.00
❏ 183	0.60	1.00	3.00	5.00
❏ 184	0.60	1.00	3.00	5.00
❏ 185	0.60	1.00	3.00	5.00
❏ 186 BS/TA, Storm	1.00	1.00	3.00	5.00
❏ 187 JR2	0.60	1.00	3.00	5.00
❏ 188 JR2	0.60	1.00	3.00	5.00
❏ 189 JR2	0.60	1.00	3.00	5.00
❏ 190 JR2	0.60	1.00	3.00	5.00
❏ 191 JR2	0.60	1.00	3.00	5.00
❏ 192 JR2	0.60	1.00	3.00	5.00
❏ 193 JR2, 20th anniv	1.25	1.00	3.00	5.00
❏ 194 JR2	0.65	1.00	3.00	5.00
❏ 195 JR2	0.65	1.00	3.00	5.00
❏ 196 JR2 Secret Wars II	0.65	1.00	3.00	5.00
❏ 197 JR2	0.65	1.00	3.00	5.00
❏ 198	0.65	1.00	3.00	5.00
❏ 199	0.65	1.00	3.00	5.00
❏ 200	1.25	2.40	7.20	12.00
❏ 201	0.65	6.40	19.20	32.00
❏ 202 Secret Wars II	0.75	1.00	3.00	5.00
❏ 203 Secret Wars II	0.75	1.00	3.00	5.00
❏ 204	0.75	1.00	3.00	5.00
❏ 205	0.75	3.60	10.80	18.00
❏ 206	0.75	1.00	3.00	5.00
❏ 207	0.75	1.00	3.00	5.00
❏ 208	0.75	1.00	3.00	5.00
❏ 209	0.75	1.00	3.00	5.00
❏ 210 massacre	0.75	3.20	9.60	16.00
❏ 211 massacre	0.75	3.20	9.60	16.00
❏ 212 massacre	0.75	6.40	19.20	32.00
❏ 213 massacre	0.75	6.40	19.20	32.00
❏ 214	0.75	1.20	3.60	6.00
❏ 215	0.75	1.20	3.60	6.00
❏ 216	0.75	1.20	3.60	6.00
❏ 217	0.75	1.20	3.60	6.00
❏ 218	0.75	1.20	3.60	6.00
❏ 219	0.75	1.20	3.60	6.00
❏ 220	0.75	1.20	3.60	6.00
❏ 221	0.75	1.20	3.60	6.00
❏ 222	0.75	2.80	8.40	14.00
❏ 223	0.75	1.20	3.60	6.00
❏ 224 registration card	0.75	0.80	2.40	4.00
❏ 225 Fall of Mutants	0.75	1.60	4.80	8.00
❏ 226 Fall of Mutants	1.25	1.20	3.60	6.00
❏ 227 Fall of Mutants	0.75	1.20	3.60	6.00
❏ 228	0.75	0.70	2.10	3.50
❏ 229	1.00	0.70	2.10	3.50
❏ 230	1.00	0.70	2.10	3.50
❏ 231	1.00	0.70	2.10	3.50
❏ 232	1.00	0.70	2.10	3.50
❏ 233	1.00	0.70	2.10	3.50
❏ 234	1.00	0.70	2.10	3.50
❏ 235	1.00	0.70	2.10	3.50
❏ 236	1.00	0.70	2.10	3.50
❏ 237	1.00	0.70	2.10	3.50
❏ 238	1.00	0.70	2.10	3.50
❏ 239 Inferno	1.00	0.70	2.10	3.50
❏ 240 Inferno	1.00	0.70	2.10	3.50
❏ 241 Inferno	1.00	0.70	2.10	3.50
❏ 242 Inferno	1.50	0.70	2.10	3.50
❏ 243 Inferno	1.00	0.70	2.10	3.50
❏ 244	1.00	1.60	4.80	8.00
❏ 245	1.00	0.70	2.10	3.50
❏ 246	1.00	0.70	2.10	3.50
❏ 247	1.00	0.70	2.10	3.50
❏ 248 Jim Lee art	1.00	6.40	19.20	32.00
❏ 248 reprint	1.25	0.25	0.75	1.25
❏ 249	1.00	1.00	3.00	5.00
❏ 250	1.00	1.00	3.00	5.00
❏ 251	1.00	1.00	3.00	5.00
❏ 252	1.00	1.00	3.00	5.00
❏ 253	1.00	1.00	3.00	5.00
❏ 254	1.00	1.00	3.00	5.00
❏ 255	1.00	1.00	3.00	5.00
❏ 256 Vengeance	1.00	2.40	7.20	12.00
❏ 257 Vengeance	1.00	2.40	7.20	12.00
❏ 258 Vengeance	1.00	2.40	7.20	12.00
❏ 259	1.00	0.80	2.40	4.00
❏ 260	1.00	0.80	2.40	4.00

	ORIG.	GOOD	FINE	N-MINT
261	1.00	0.80	2.40	4.00
262	1.00	0.80	2.40	4.00
263	1.00	0.80	2.40	4.00
264	1.00	0.80	2.40	4.00
265	1.00	0.80	2.40	4.00
266	1.00	8.00	24.00	40.00
267	1.00	4.00	12.00	20.00
268	1.00	5.60	16.80	28.00
269	1.00	2.00	6.00	10.00
270 X-Tinction	1.00	2.40	7.20	12.00
271 X-Tinction	1.00	1.40	4.20	7.00
272 X-Tinction	1.00	1.40	4.20	7.00
273 JBy, MG	1.00	1.40	4.20	7.00
274 Magneto, Nick Fury, Ka-Zar				
	1.00	1.20	3.60	6.00
275	1.50	2.00	6.00	10.00
276	1.00	0.80	2.40	4.00
277	1.00	0.80	2.40	4.00
278	1.00	0.80	2.40	4.00
279	1.00	0.80	2.40	4.00
280	1.00	0.80	2.40	4.00
281 1st printing, new team				
	1.00	1.50	4.50	7.50
281 2nd printing	1.00	0.20	0.60	1.00
282	1.00	1.20	3.60	6.00
283	1.00	2.00	6.00	10.00
284	1.00	0.50	1.50	2.50
285	1.25	0.80	2.40	4.00
286	1.25	0.80	2.40	4.00
287	1.25	0.80	2.40	4.00
288	1.25	0.80	2.40	4.00
289	1.25	0.50	1.50	2.50
290	1.25	0.50	1.50	2.50
291	1.25	0.25	0.75	1.25
292	1.25	0.25	0.75	1.25
293	1.25	0.25	0.75	1.25
294 X-cutioner's song; with card				
	1.50	0.30	0.90	1.50
295 with card	1.50	0.30	0.90	1.50
296 with card	1.50	0.30	0.90	1.50
297	1.25	0.25	0.75	1.25
298	1.25	0.25	0.75	1.25
299	1.25	0.25	0.75	1.25
300 shiny cover	3.95	1.20	3.60	6.00
301	1.25	0.25	0.75	1.25
302	1.25	0.25	0.75	1.25
303	1.25	0.25	0.75	1.25

UNCANNY X-MEN ANNUAL (was X-Men Annual)

	ORIG.	GOOD	FINE	N-MINT
5 BA/BMc, A:FF (1981)	0.75	2.00	6.00	10.00
6 BSz, A:Dracula (1982)	1.00	2.00	6.00	10.00
7 MG (1983)	1.00	1.60	4.80	8.00
8 Kitty (1984)	1.00	1.60	4.80	8.00
9 AAd (1985)	1.25	2.40	7.20	12.00
10 AAd (1986)	1.25	2.40	7.20	12.00
11 (1987)	1.25	1.20	3.60	6.00

	ORIG.	GOOD	FINE	N-MINT
12 AAd Evolutionary War (1988)				
	1.75	0.80	2.40	4.00
13 Atlantis Attacks (1989)				
	2.00	0.80	2.40	4.00
14 Future Present (1990)	2.00	1.20	3.60	6.00
15 Kings of Pain (1991)	2.00	0.80	2.40	4.00
16 Shattershot (1992)	2.25	0.60	1.80	3.00
17 trading card (1993)	2.95	0.59	1.77	2.95

UNKNOWN WORLDS OF SCIENCE FICTION (b&w mag)

	ORIG.	GOOD	FINE	N-MINT
1	1.25	0.25	0.75	1.25
2	0.75	0.15	0.45	0.75
3	0.75	0.15	0.45	0.75
4	0.75	0.15	0.45	0.75
5	0.75	0.15	0.45	0.75
6	0.75	0.15	0.45	0.75

UNKNOWN WORLDS OF SCIENCE FICTION SPECIAL

	ORIG.	GOOD	FINE	N-MINT
1 reprints	1.25	0.25	0.75	1.25

VAMPIRE TALES (b&w mag)

	ORIG.	GOOD	FINE	N-MINT
1	0.75	0.15	0.45	0.75
2	0.75	0.15	0.45	0.75
3	0.75	0.15	0.45	0.75
4	0.75	0.15	0.45	0.75
5	0.75	0.15	0.45	0.75
6	0.75	0.15	0.45	0.75
7	0.75	0.15	0.45	0.75
8	0.75	0.15	0.45	0.75
9	0.75	0.15	0.45	0.75
10	0.75	0.15	0.45	0.75
11	0.75	0.15	0.45	0.75

VAMPIRE TALES ANNUAL

	ORIG.	GOOD	FINE	N-MINT
1 reprints	1.25	0.25	0.75	1.25

VENOM: FUNERAL PYRE

	ORIG.	GOOD	FINE	N-MINT
1 foil cover, Punisher	2.95	0.59	1.77	2.95

VENOM: LETHAL PROTECTOR

	ORIG.	GOOD	FINE	N-MINT
1 foil cover	2.95	1.60	4.80	8.00
1 gold edition		15.00	45.00	75.00
1 black cover	2.95	60.00	180.00	300.00
2	2.95	0.80	2.40	4.00
3	2.95	0.70	2.10	3.50
4	2.95	0.59	1.77	2.95
5	2.95	0.59	1.77	2.95
6	2.95	0.59	1.77	2.95

VINTAGE PACK

	ORIG.	GOOD	FINE	N-MINT
20 Marvel comic-book reprints				
	19.95	3.99	11.97	19.95

VISION & SCARLET WITCH

	ORIG.	GOOD	FINE	N-MINT
1	0.60	0.35	1.05	1.75
2	0.60	0.25	0.75	1.25
3	0.60	0.25	0.75	1.25
4	0.60	0.25	0.75	1.25

VISION & SCARLET WITCH (2nd series)

	ORIG.	GOOD	FINE	N-MINT
1	1.25	0.25	0.75	1.25

	ORIG.	GOOD	FINE	N-MINT
2	0.75	0.20	0.60	1.00
3	0.75	0.20	0.60	1.00
4	0.75	0.20	0.60	1.00
5	0.75	0.20	0.60	1.00
6	0.75	0.20	0.60	1.00
7	0.75	0.20	0.60	1.00
8	0.75	0.20	0.60	1.00
9	0.75	0.20	0.60	1.00
10	0.75	0.20	0.60	1.00
12	1.25	0.25	0.75	1.25

VISIONARIES (was Star Comic)

	ORIG.	GOOD	FINE	N-MINT
3	1.00	0.20	0.60	1.00
4	1.00	0.20	0.60	1.00
5	1.00	0.20	0.60	1.00
6	1.00	0.20	0.60	1.00

WAR IS HELL

	ORIG.	GOOD	FINE	N-MINT
1 reprints	0.20	0.30	0.90	1.50
2 reprints	0.20	0.20	0.60	1.00
3 reprints	0.20	0.20	0.60	1.00
4 reprints	0.20	0.20	0.60	1.00
5 reprints	0.20	0.20	0.60	1.00
6 reprints	0.20	0.20	0.60	1.00
7 reprints	0.25	0.20	0.60	1.00
8 reprints	0.25	0.20	0.60	1.00
9	0.25	0.40	1.20	2.00
10	0.25	0.40	1.20	2.00
11	0.25	0.40	1.20	2.00
12	0.25	0.40	1.20	2.00
13	0.25	0.40	1.20	2.00
14	0.25	0.40	1.20	2.00
15	0.25	0.40	1.20	2.00

WAR, THE

	ORIG.	GOOD	FINE	N-MINT
1	3.50	0.70	2.10	3.50
2	3.50	0.70	2.10	3.50
3	3.50	0.70	2.10	3.50
4	3.50	0.70	2.10	3.50

WARHEADS

	ORIG.	GOOD	FINE	N-MINT
1 Wolverine	1.75	0.35	1.05	1.75
2	1.75	0.35	1.05	1.75
3	1.75	0.35	1.05	1.75
4	1.75	0.35	1.05	1.75
5	1.75	0.35	1.05	1.75
6	1.75	0.35	1.05	1.75
7	1.75	0.35	1.05	1.75
8	1.75	0.35	1.05	1.75
9	1.75	0.35	1.05	1.75
10	1.75	0.35	1.05	1.75
11	1.75	0.35	1.05	1.75
12	1.75	0.35	1.05	1.75
13	1.75	0.35	1.05	1.75
14	1.75	0.35	1.05	1.75

WARHEADS: BLACK DAWN

	ORIG.	GOOD	FINE	N-MINT
1 foil cover	2.95	0.59	1.77	2.95
2	1.75	0.35	1.05	1.75

WARLOCK (1972-)

	ORIG.	GOOD	FINE	N-MINT
1 GK Origin	0.20	8.00	24.00	40.00
2	0.20	3.20	9.60	16.00
3	0.20	3.20	9.60	16.00
4 GK	0.20	2.00	6.00	10.00
5	0.20	2.00	6.00	10.00
6	0.20	2.00	6.00	10.00
7	0.20	2.00	6.00	10.00
8 (1973)	0.20	2.00	6.00	10.00
9 JSn (1975)	0.25	2.80	8.40	14.00
10 JSn	0.25	6.40	19.20	32.00
11 JSn	0.25	3.20	9.60	16.00
12 JSn	0.25	2.40	7.20	12.00
13 JSn	0.25	2.40	7.20	12.00
14 JSn	0.25	2.40	7.20	12.00
15 JSn	0.30	5.20	15.60	26.00

WARLOCK (1982-1983)

	ORIG.	GOOD	FINE	N-MINT
1 JSn, rep	2.00	0.80	2.40	4.00
2 JSn, rep	2.00	0.60	1.80	3.00
3 JSn, rep	2.00	0.60	1.80	3.00
4 JSn, rep	2.00	0.60	1.80	3.00
5 JSn, rep	2.00	0.60	1.80	3.00
6 JSn, rep	2.00	0.60	1.80	3.00

WARLOCK (1992)

	ORIG.	GOOD	FINE	N-MINT
1 reprints	2.50	0.50	1.50	2.50
2 reprints	2.50	0.50	1.50	2.50
3 reprints	2.50	0.50	1.50	2.50
4 reprints	2.50	0.50	1.50	2.50
5 reprints	2.50	0.50	1.50	2.50
6 reprints	2.50	0.50	1.50	2.50

WARLOCK AND THE INFINITY WATCH

	ORIG.	GOOD	FINE	N-MINT
1	1.75	1.20	3.60	6.00
2	1.75	0.80	2.40	4.00
3	1.75	0.60	1.80	3.00
4	1.75	0.60	1.80	3.00
5	1.75	0.60	1.80	3.00
6	1.75	0.60	1.80	3.00
7	1.75	0.60	1.80	3.00
8	1.75	0.60	1.80	3.00
9 Infinity war	1.75	0.35	1.05	1.75
10	1.75	0.35	1.05	1.75
11	1.75	0.35	1.05	1.75
12	1.75	0.35	1.05	1.75
13	1.75	0.35	1.05	1.75
14	1.75	0.35	1.05	1.75
15	1.75	0.35	1.05	1.75
16	1.75	0.35	1.05	1.75
17	1.75	0.35	1.05	1.75
18	1.75	0.35	1.05	1.75
19	1.75	0.35	1.05	1.75
20	1.75	0.35	1.05	1.75
21	1.75	0.35	1.05	1.75

WARLOCK CHRONICLES, THE

	ORIG.	GOOD	FINE	N-MINT
1 foil embossed cover	2.95	0.59	1.77	2.95

	ORIG.	GOOD	FINE	N-MINT
❏ 2	2.00	0.40	1.20	2.00
❏ 3	2.00	0.40	1.20	2.00
❏ 4	2.00	0.40	1.20	2.00

WCW: WORLD CHAMPIONSHIP WRESTLING

	ORIG.	GOOD	FINE	N-MINT
❏ 1	1.25	0.25	0.75	1.25
❏ 2	1.25	0.25	0.75	1.25
❏ 3	1.25	0.25	0.75	1.25
❏ 4	1.25	0.25	0.75	1.25
❏ 5	1.25	0.25	0.75	1.25
❏ 6	1.25	0.25	0.75	1.25
❏ 7	1.25	0.25	0.75	1.25
❏ 8	1.25	0.25	0.75	1.25
❏ 9	1.25	0.25	0.75	1.25
❏ 10	1.25	0.25	0.75	1.25
❏ 11	1.25	0.25	0.75	1.25
❏ 12	1.25	0.25	0.75	1.25

WEB OF SPIDER-MAN

	ORIG.	GOOD	FINE	N-MINT
❏ 1	0.65	6.00	18.00	30.00
❏ 2	0.65	3.00	9.00	15.00
❏ 3	0.65	2.00	6.00	10.00
❏ 4	0.65	2.00	6.00	10.00
❏ 5	0.65	2.00	6.00	10.00
❏ 6 Secret Wars II	0.65	1.40	4.20	7.00
❏ 7	0.65	1.60	4.80	8.00
❏ 8	0.65	1.20	3.60	6.00
❏ 9	0.65	1.20	3.60	6.00
❏ 10	0.65	1.20	3.60	6.00
❏ 11	0.75	0.80	2.40	4.00
❏ 12	0.75	0.80	2.40	4.00
❏ 13	0.75	0.80	2.40	4.00
❏ 14	0.75	0.80	2.40	4.00
❏ 15	0.75	0.80	2.40	4.00
❏ 16	0.75	0.70	2.10	3.50
❏ 17	0.75	0.70	2.10	3.50
❏ 18	0.75	0.70	2.10	3.50
❏ 19	0.75	0.70	2.10	3.50
❏ 20	0.75	0.70	2.10	3.50
❏ 21	0.75	0.70	2.10	3.50
❏ 22	0.75	0.70	2.10	3.50
❏ 23	0.75	0.70	2.10	3.50
❏ 24	0.75	0.70	2.10	3.50
❏ 25	0.75	0.70	2.10	3.50
❏ 26	0.75	0.70	2.10	3.50
❏ 27	0.75	0.70	2.10	3.50
❏ 28	0.75	0.70	2.10	3.50
❏ 29 A:Wolverine	0.75	4.80	14.40	24.00
❏ 30	0.75	2.40	7.20	12.00
❏ 31 V:Kraven	0.75	2.00	6.00	10.00
❏ 32 V:Kraven	0.75	2.00	6.00	10.00
❏ 33 BSz(c)	0.75	0.40	1.20	2.00
❏ 34	0.75	0.35	1.05	1.75
❏ 35	0.75	0.35	1.05	1.75
❏ 36	0.75	0.35	1.05	1.75
❏ 37	0.75	0.35	1.05	1.75

	ORIG.	GOOD	FINE	N-MINT
❏ 38 V:Hobgoblin	1.00	0.80	2.40	4.00
❏ 39 Cult of Love	1.00	0.40	1.20	2.00
❏ 40 Cult of Love	1.00	0.40	1.20	2.00
❏ 41 Cult of Love	1.00	0.40	1.20	2.00
❏ 42 Cult of Love	1.00	0.40	1.20	2.00
❏ 43 Cult of Love	1.00	0.40	1.20	2.00
❏ 44 A:Hulk	1.00	0.40	1.20	2.00
❏ 45 V:Vulture	1.00	0.40	1.20	2.00
❏ 46	1.00	0.40	1.20	2.00
❏ 47 Hobgoblin, Inferno	1.00	1.20	3.60	6.00
❏ 48 Hobgoblin, Inferno	1.00	2.40	7.20	12.00
❏ 49	1.00	0.40	1.20	2.00
❏ 50	1.50	0.40	1.20	2.00
❏ 51	1.00	0.40	1.20	2.00
❏ 52	1.00	0.40	1.20	2.00
❏ 53	1.00	0.40	1.20	2.00
❏ 54	1.00	0.40	1.20	2.00
❏ 55	1.00	0.40	1.20	2.00
❏ 56	1.00	0.40	1.20	2.00
❏ 57	1.00	0.40	1.20	2.00
❏ 58 Vengeance	1.00	0.40	1.20	2.00
❏ 59 Vengeance	1.00	0.40	1.20	2.00
❏ 60 Vengeance	1.00	0.40	1.20	2.00
❏ 61 Vengeance	1.00	0.40	1.20	2.00
❏ 62	1.00	0.40	1.20	2.00
❏ 63	1.00	0.40	1.20	2.00
❏ 64 Vengeance	1.00	0.20	0.60	1.00
❏ 65 Vengeance	1.00	0.20	0.60	1.00
❏ 66	1.00	0.20	0.60	1.00
❏ 67	1.00	0.20	0.60	1.00
❏ 68	1.00	0.20	0.60	1.00
❏ 69	1.00	0.20	0.60	1.00
❏ 70	1.00	0.20	0.60	1.00
❏ 71	1.00	0.20	0.60	1.00
❏ 72	1.00	0.20	0.60	1.00
❏ 73	1.00	0.20	0.60	1.00
❏ 74	1.00	0.20	0.60	1.00
❏ 75	1.00	0.20	0.60	1.00
❏ 76 Fantastic Four	1.00	0.20	0.60	1.00
❏ 77	1.00	0.20	0.60	1.00
❏ 78 Cloak & Dagger	1.00	0.20	0.60	1.00
❏ 79	1.00	0.20	0.60	1.00
❏ 80	1.00	0.20	0.60	1.00
❏ 81	1.00	0.20	0.60	1.00
❏ 82	1.00	0.20	0.60	1.00
❏ 83	1.00	0.20	0.60	1.00
❏ 84	1.00	0.20	0.60	1.00
❏ 85	1.25	0.25	0.75	1.25
❏ 86	1.25	0.25	0.75	1.25
❏ 87	1.25	0.25	0.75	1.25
❏ 88	1.25	0.25	0.75	1.25
❏ 89	1.25	0.25	0.75	1.25
❏ 90 hologram	2.95	0.59	1.77	2.95
❏ 90 hologram, 2nd printing	1.25	0.25	0.75	1.25
❏ 91	1.25	0.25	0.75	1.25

	ORIG.	GOOD	FINE	N-MINT
92	1.25	0.25	0.75	1.25
93	1.25	0.25	0.75	1.25
94	1.25	0.25	0.75	1.25
95	1.25	0.25	0.75	1.25
96	1.25	0.25	0.75	1.25
97	1.25	0.25	0.75	1.25
98	1.25	0.25	0.75	1.25
99	1.25	0.25	0.75	1.25
100 foil cover	2.95	0.59	1.77	2.95
101	1.25	0.50	1.50	2.50
102 maximum carnage	1.25	0.25	0.75	1.25
103	1.25	0.25	0.75	1.25
104	1.25	0.25	0.75	1.25
105	1.25	0.25	0.75	1.25

WEB OF SPIDER-MAN ANNUAL

	ORIG.	GOOD	FINE	N-MINT
1 (1985)	1.25	1.00	3.00	5.00
2 (1986)	1.25	0.80	2.40	4.00
3 pin-ups (1987)	1.25	0.45	1.35	2.25
4 Evolutionary War, 1:Poison, (1988)	1.75	0.40	1.20	2.00
5 Atlantis Attacks (1989)	2.00	0.40	1.20	2.00
6 Tiny Spidey (1990)	2.00	0.40	1.20	2.00
7 Vivranium Vendetta (1991)	2.00	0.40	1.20	2.00
8 (1992)	2.25	0.45	1.35	2.25
9 trading card (1993)	2.95	0.59	1.77	2.95

WEDDING OF DRACULA

	ORIG.	GOOD	FINE	N-MINT
1 reprints	2.00	0.40	1.20	2.00

WEIRD WONDER TALES (1973-1977)

	ORIG.	GOOD	FINE	N-MINT
1 reprints	0.20	0.30	0.90	1.50

WEIRD WONDER TALES (1973-1977)

	ORIG.	GOOD	FINE	N-MINT
2 reprints	0.20	0.20	0.60	1.00
3 reprints	0.20	0.20	0.60	1.00
4	0.25	0.20	0.60	1.00
5	0.25	0.20	0.60	1.00
6	0.25	0.20	0.60	1.00
7	0.25	0.20	0.60	1.00
8	0.25	0.20	0.60	1.00
9	0.25	0.20	0.60	1.00
10	0.25	0.20	0.60	1.00
11	0.25	0.20	0.60	1.00
12	0.25	0.20	0.60	1.00
13	0.25	0.20	0.60	1.00
14	0.25	0.20	0.60	1.00
15	0.25	0.20	0.60	1.00
16	0.25	0.20	0.60	1.00
17	0.25	0.20	0.60	1.00
18	0.30	0.20	0.60	1.00
19 Dr. Druid	0.30	0.20	0.60	1.00
20 Dr. Druid	0.30	0.20	0.60	1.00
21 Dr. Druid	0.30	0.20	0.60	1.00
22 Dr. Druid	0.30	0.20	0.60	1.00

WEREWOLF BY NIGHT

	ORIG.	GOOD	FINE	N-MINT
1 MP	0.20	2.00	6.00	10.00
2 MP	0.20	0.80	2.40	4.00
3 MP	0.20	0.60	1.80	3.00
4 MP	0.20	0.60	1.80	3.00
5 MP	0.20	0.60	1.80	3.00
6 MP	0.20	0.60	1.80	3.00
7 MP	0.20	0.60	1.80	3.00
8	0.20	0.40	1.20	2.00
9	0.20	0.40	1.20	2.00
10	0.20	0.40	1.20	2.00
11	0.20	0.40	1.20	2.00
12	0.20	0.40	1.20	2.00
13	0.20	0.40	1.20	2.00
14	0.20	0.40	1.20	2.00
15	0.20	0.40	1.20	2.00
16	0.20	0.40	1.20	2.00
17	0.25	0.40	1.20	2.00
18	0.25	0.40	1.20	2.00
19	0.25	0.40	1.20	2.00
20	0.25	0.40	1.20	2.00
21	0.25	0.40	1.20	2.00
22	0.25	0.40	1.20	2.00
23	0.25	0.40	1.20	2.00
24	0.25	0.40	1.20	2.00
25	0.25	0.40	1.20	2.00
26	0.25	0.40	1.20	2.00
27	0.25	0.40	1.20	2.00
28	0.25	0.40	1.20	2.00
29	0.25	0.40	1.20	2.00
30	0.25	0.40	1.20	2.00
31	0.25	0.40	1.20	2.00
32 O&1:Moon Knight	0.25	5.00	15.00	25.00
33 Moon Knight	0.25	2.40	7.20	12.00
34	0.25	0.40	1.20	2.00
35	0.25	0.40	1.20	2.00
36	0.25	0.40	1.20	2.00
37 BWr, A:Moon Knight	0.25	1.40	4.20	7.00
38	0.25	0.40	1.20	2.00
39	0.25	0.40	1.20	2.00
40	0.30	0.40	1.20	2.00
41	0.30	0.40	1.20	2.00
42	0.30	0.40	1.20	2.00
43	0.30	0.40	1.20	2.00

WEST COAST AVENGERS

	ORIG.	GOOD	FINE	N-MINT
1 BH	0.75	1.00	3.00	5.00
2 BH	0.75	0.40	1.20	2.00
3 BH	0.75	0.40	1.20	2.00
4 BH	0.75	0.40	1.20	2.00

WEST COAST AVENGERS (2nd series)

	ORIG.	GOOD	FINE	N-MINT
1	1.25	1.20	3.60	6.00
2	0.65	0.80	2.40	4.00
3	0.65	0.60	1.80	3.00
4	0.65	0.60	1.80	3.00

	ORIG.	GOOD	FINE	N-MINT
❑ 5	0.75	0.60	1.80	3.00
❑ 6	0.75	0.60	1.80	3.00
❑ 7	0.75	0.60	1.80	3.00
❑ 8	0.75	0.60	1.80	3.00
❑ 9	0.75	0.60	1.80	3.00
❑ 10	0.75	0.60	1.80	3.00
❑ 11	0.75	0.40	1.20	2.00
❑ 12	0.75	0.40	1.20	2.00
❑ 13	0.75	0.40	1.20	2.00
❑ 14	0.75	0.40	1.20	2.00
❑ 15	0.75	0.40	1.20	2.00
❑ 16	0.75	0.40	1.20	2.00
❑ 17	0.75	0.40	1.20	2.00
❑ 18	0.75	0.40	1.20	2.00
❑ 19	0.75	0.40	1.20	2.00
❑ 20	0.75	0.40	1.20	2.00
❑ 21	0.75	0.35	1.05	1.75
❑ 22	0.75	0.35	1.05	1.75
❑ 23	0.75	0.35	1.05	1.75
❑ 24	0.75	0.35	1.05	1.75
❑ 25	0.75	0.35	1.05	1.75
❑ 26	0.75	0.35	1.05	1.75
❑ 27	0.75	0.35	1.05	1.75
❑ 28	0.75	0.35	1.05	1.75
❑ 29	0.75	0.35	1.05	1.75
❑ 30	0.75	0.35	1.05	1.75
❑ 31	0.75	0.35	1.05	1.75
❑ 32	0.75	0.35	1.05	1.75
❑ 33	0.75	0.35	1.05	1.75
❑ 34	0.75	0.35	1.05	1.75
❑ 35	0.75	0.35	1.05	1.75
❑ 36	0.75	0.35	1.05	1.75
❑ 37	0.75	0.35	1.05	1.75
❑ 38	0.75	0.35	1.05	1.75
❑ 39	0.75	0.35	1.05	1.75
❑ 40	0.75	0.35	1.05	1.75
❑ 41	0.75	0.35	1.05	1.75
❑ 42 JBy	0.75	0.20	0.60	1.00
❑ 43 JBy	0.75	0.20	0.60	1.00
❑ 44 JBy	0.75	0.20	0.60	1.00
❑ 45 JBy	0.75	0.20	0.60	1.00
❑ 46 1:Great Lakes Avengers	0.75	0.20	0.60	1.00
❑ 47 (becomes Avengers West Coast)	0.75	0.20	0.60	1.00

WEST COAST AVENGERS ANNUAL

	ORIG.	GOOD	FINE	N-MINT
❑ 1 (1986)	1.25	0.40	1.20	2.00
❑ 2 (1987)	1.25	0.40	1.20	2.00
❑ 3 Evolutionary War (1988) (becomes Avengers West Coast Annual)	1.75	0.60	1.80	3.00

WESTERN GUNFIGHTERS (1970-1972)

	ORIG.	GOOD	FINE	N-MINT
❑ 1	0.25	0.60	1.80	3.00
❑ 2	0.25	0.40	1.20	2.00
❑ 3	0.25	0.40	1.20	2.00

	ORIG.	GOOD	FINE	N-MINT
❑ 4	0.25	0.40	1.20	2.00
❑ 5	0.25	0.40	1.20	2.00
❑ 6	0.25	0.40	1.20	2.00
❑ 7	0.25	0.20	0.60	1.00
❑ 8	0.25	0.20	0.60	1.00
❑ 9	0.25	0.20	0.60	1.00
❑ 10	0.25	0.20	0.60	1.00
❑ 11	0.25	0.20	0.60	1.00
❑ 12	0.25	0.20	0.60	1.00
❑ 13	0.25	0.20	0.60	1.00
❑ 14	0.25	0.20	0.60	1.00
❑ 15	0.25	0.20	0.60	1.00
❑ 16	0.25	0.20	0.60	1.00
❑ 17	0.25	0.20	0.60	1.00
❑ 18	0.25	0.20	0.60	1.00
❑ 19	0.25	0.20	0.60	1.00
❑ 20	0.25	0.20	0.60	1.00
❑ 21	0.25	0.20	0.60	1.00
❑ 22	0.25	0.20	0.60	1.00
❑ 23	0.25	0.20	0.60	1.00
❑ 24	0.25	0.20	0.60	1.00
❑ 25	0.25	0.20	0.60	1.00
❑ 26	0.25	0.20	0.60	1.00
❑ 27	0.25	0.20	0.60	1.00
❑ 28	0.25	0.20	0.60	1.00
❑ 29	0.25	0.20	0.60	1.00
❑ 30	0.25	0.20	0.60	1.00
❑ 31	0.25	0.20	0.60	1.00
❑ 32	0.25	0.20	0.60	1.00
❑ 33	0.25	0.20	0.60	1.00

WESTERN TEAM-UP

	ORIG.	GOOD	FINE	N-MINT
❑ 1 (1933)	0.20	0.20	0.60	1.00

WHAT IF? (Volume 1, 1977-1988)

	ORIG.	GOOD	FINE	N-MINT
❑ 1 Spider-Man	0.50	3.00	9.00	15.00
❑ 2 GK(c), Hulk	0.50	1.60	4.80	8.00
❑ 3 GK/KJ, Avengers	0.50	0.80	2.40	4.00
❑ 4 GK(c)	0.50	0.80	2.40	4.00
❑ 5 Capt. America	0.50	0.80	2.40	4.00
❑ 6 Fantastic Four	0.60	0.70	2.10	3.50
❑ 7 GK(c), Spider-Man	0.60	1.00	3.00	5.00
❑ 8 GK(c), Daredevil	0.60	0.80	2.40	4.00
❑ 9 JK(c), O:Marvel Boy	0.60	0.60	1.80	3.00
❑ 10 JB, Thor	0.60	0.50	1.50	2.50
❑ 11 JK, Fantastic Four	0.60	0.40	1.20	2.00
❑ 12 Hulk	0.60	0.40	1.20	2.00
❑ 13 JB, Conan	0.60	0.80	2.40	4.00
❑ 14 Sgt. Fury	0.60	0.40	1.20	2.00
❑ 15 CI, Nova	0.60	0.40	1.20	2.00
❑ 16 Fu Manchu	0.60	0.40	1.20	2.00
❑ 17 CI, Ghost Rider	0.60	1.00	3.00	5.00
❑ 18 TS, Dr. Strange	0.60	0.40	1.20	2.00
❑ 19 PB, Spider-Man	0.75	0.60	1.80	3.00
❑ 20 Avengers	0.75	0.40	1.20	2.00
❑ 21 GC, Sub-Mariner	0.75	0.40	1.20	2.00

	ORIG.	GOOD	FINE	N-MINT
22 Dr. Doom	0.75	0.40	1.20	2.00
23 JB, Hulk	0.75	0.40	1.20	2.00
24 GK/RB, Spider-Man	0.75	0.60	1.80	3.00
25 Thor, Avengers	0.75	0.40	1.20	2.00
26 JBy(c), Capt. America				
	0.75	0.40	1.20	2.00
27 FM(c), X-Men	0.75	1.80	5.40	9.00
28 FM, Daredevil	0.75	1.80	5.40	9.00
29 MG(c), Avengers	0.75	0.30	0.90	1.50
30 RB, Spider-Man	0.75	0.60	1.80	3.00
31 Wolverine	1.00	3.20	9.60	16.00
32 Avengers	1.00	0.40	1.20	2.00
33 BL, Dazzler	1.00	0.40	1.20	2.00
34 FH/FM/JBy/BSz	1.00	0.40	1.20	2.00
35 FM, Elektra	1.00	0.50	1.50	2.50
36 JBy, Fantastic Four	1.00	0.40	1.20	2.00
37 Beast	1.00	0.40	1.20	2.00
38 Daredevil	1.00	0.40	1.20	2.00
39 Thor, Conan	1.00	0.40	1.20	2.00
40 Dr. Strange	1.00	0.40	1.20	2.00
41 Sub-Mariner	1.00	0.40	1.20	2.00
42 Fantastic Four	1.00	0.40	1.20	2.00
43 Hulk	1.00	0.40	1.20	2.00
44 Hulk	1.00	0.40	1.20	2.00
45 Hulk	1.00	0.40	1.20	2.00
46 Spider-Man	1.00	0.40	1.20	2.00
47 Thor, Loki	1.00	0.40	1.20	2.00

WHAT IF? (Volume 2, 1989)

	ORIG.	GOOD	FINE	N-MINT
1 Avengers	1.25	1.00	3.00	5.00
2 Daredevil	1.25	0.80	2.40	4.00
3 Capt. America	1.25	0.80	2.40	4.00
4 Spider-Man	1.25	0.80	2.40	4.00
5 Avengers	1.25	0.40	1.20	2.00
6 X-Men	1.25	1.60	4.80	8.00
7 Wolverine	1.25	1.60	4.80	8.00
8 Iron Man	1.25	0.60	1.80	3.00
9 X-Men	1.25	0.60	1.80	3.00
10 Punisher	1.25	0.60	1.80	3.00
11 Fantastic Four	1.25	0.25	0.75	1.25
12 X-Men	1.25	0.40	1.20	2.00
13 X-Men	1.25	0.40	1.20	2.00
14 Capt. Marvel	1.25	0.25	0.75	1.25
15 F4, Galactus	1.25	0.25	0.75	1.25
16 Wolverine, Conan	1.25	0.80	2.40	4.00
17 D:Spider-Man	1.25	0.25	0.75	1.25
18 FF, Dr. Doom	1.25	0.25	0.75	1.25
19	1.25	0.25	0.75	1.25
20 SpM	1.25	0.25	0.75	1.25
21 SpM, D:Black Cat	1.25	0.25	0.75	1.25
22 Silver Surfer	1.25	0.60	1.80	3.00
23 X-Men	1.25	0.60	1.80	3.00
24 vampire Wolverine	1.25	0.25	0.75	1.25
25 Atlantis Attacks	1.25	0.60	1.80	3.00
26 Punisher	1.25	0.60	1.80	3.00
27 Namor, F4	1.25	0.25	0.75	1.25

	ORIG.	GOOD	FINE	N-MINT
28 Captain America	1.25	0.25	0.75	1.25
29 Captain America, Avengers				
	1.25	0.25	0.75	1.25
30	1.25	0.25	0.75	1.25
31	1.25	0.25	0.75	1.25
32 Phoenix	1.25	0.25	0.75	1.25
33 Phoenix	1.25	0.25	0.75	1.25
34 humor	1.25	0.25	0.75	1.25
35 F4, SpM, Dr. Doom	1.25	0.25	0.75	1.25
36	1.25	0.25	0.75	1.25
37 Wolverine	1.25	0.40	1.20	2.00
38 Thor	1.25	0.25	0.75	1.25
41 Avengers vs. Galactus	1.75	0.35	1.05	1.75
42 Spider-Man	1.25	0.25	0.75	1.25
43 Wolverine	1.25	0.25	0.75	1.25
44 Venom, Punisher	1.25	0.25	0.75	1.25
45 Ghost Rider	1.25	0.25	0.75	1.25
46 Cable	1.25	0.25	0.75	1.25
47 Magneto	1.25	0.25	0.75	1.25
48 Daredevil	1.25	0.25	0.75	1.25
49 Silver Surfer	1.25	0.25	0.75	1.25
50 Hulk/Wolverine, silver sculpted cover				
	2.95	0.59	1.77	2.95
51 Punisher/Capt. America				
	1.25	0.25	0.75	1.25
52 Dr. Doom	1.25	0.25	0.75	1.25
53 SpM,Hulk,Iron Man 2020				
	1.25	0.25	0.75	1.25
54 Death's Head	1.25	0.25	0.75	1.25

WHAT IF? SPECIAL (1988)

	ORIG.	GOOD	FINE	N-MINT
1 Iron Man	1.50	0.30	0.90	1.50

WHAT THE--?!

	ORIG.	GOOD	FINE	N-MINT
1	1.25	0.25	0.75	1.25
2	1.25	0.25	0.75	1.25
3 TMc	1.25	0.25	0.75	1.25
4	1.25	0.25	0.75	1.25
5	1.50	0.30	0.90	1.50
6 JBy/TA	1.00	0.30	0.90	1.50
7 JBy(c)	1.25	0.25	0.75	1.25
8 JBy(c)	1.25	0.25	0.75	1.25
9 JBy(c)	1.25	0.25	0.75	1.25
10 JBy(c)	1.25	0.25	0.75	1.25
11 JBy(c)	1.25	0.25	0.75	1.25
12 JBy(c)	1.25	0.25	0.75	1.25
13 JBy(c)	1.25	0.25	0.75	1.25
14 JBy(c)	1.25	0.25	0.75	1.25
15	1.25	0.25	0.75	1.25
16 EC parody	1.25	0.25	0.75	1.25
17	1.25	0.25	0.75	1.25
18	1.25	0.25	0.75	1.25
19	1.25	0.25	0.75	1.25
20	1.25	0.25	0.75	1.25
21	1.25	0.25	0.75	1.25
22	1.25	0.25	0.75	1.25

	ORIG.	GOOD	FINE	N-MINT
❏ 23 ......1.25		0.25	0.75	1.25
❏ 24 ......1.25		0.25	0.75	1.25
❏ 25 ......2.50		0.50	1.50	2.50
❏ 26 ......2.50		0.50	1.50	2.50
❏ 27 ......2.50		0.50	1.50	2.50

WILD THING

	ORIG.	GOOD	FINE	N-MINT
❏ 1 embossed cover 2.50		0.50	1.50	2.50
❏ 2 ......1.75		0.35	1.05	1.75
❏ 3 ......1.75		0.35	1.05	1.75
❏ 4 ......1.75		0.35	1.05	1.75
❏ 5 ......1.75		0.35	1.05	1.75
❏ 6 ......1.75		0.35	1.05	1.75

WILLOW

	ORIG.	GOOD	FINE	N-MINT
❏ 1 movie 1.00		0.20	0.60	1.00
❏ 2 movie 1.00		0.20	0.60	1.00
❏ 3 movie 1.00		0.20	0.60	1.00

WOLFPACK

	ORIG.	GOOD	FINE	N-MINT
❏ 1 ......0.75		0.20	0.60	1.00
❏ 2 ......0.75		0.20	0.60	1.00
❏ 3 ......0.75		0.20	0.60	1.00
❏ 4 ......0.75		0.20	0.60	1.00
❏ 5 ......0.75		0.20	0.60	1.00
❏ 6 ......0.75		0.20	0.60	1.00
❏ 7 ......0.75		0.20	0.60	1.00
❏ 8 ......0.75		0.20	0.60	1.00
❏ 9 ......0.75		0.20	0.60	1.00
❏ 10 ......0.75		0.20	0.60	1.00
❏ 11 ......0.75		0.20	0.60	1.00
❏ 12 ......0.75		0.20	0.60	1.00

WOLVERINE (mini-series)

	ORIG.	GOOD	FINE	N-MINT
❏ 1 FM, I:Mariko 0.60		6.00	18.00	30.00
❏ 2 FM 0.60		4.00	12.00	20.00
❏ 3 FM 0.60		4.00	12.00	20.00
❏ 4 FM 0.60		4.00	12.00	20.00

WOLVERINE (ongoing series)

	ORIG.	GOOD	FINE	N-MINT
❏ 1 ......1.50		6.40	19.20	32.00
❏ 2 ......1.50		3.60	10.80	18.00
❏ 3 ......1.50		1.60	4.80	8.00
❏ 4 ......1.50		1.60	4.80	8.00
❏ 5 ......1.50		1.60	4.80	8.00
❏ 6 ......1.50		1.20	3.60	6.00
❏ 7 ......1.50		1.20	3.60	6.00
❏ 8 Hulk 1.50		1.60	4.80	8.00
❏ 9 ......1.50		1.20	3.60	6.00
❏ 10 BSz 1.50		6.00	18.00	30.00
❏ 11 ......1.50		1.00	3.00	5.00
❏ 12 ......1.50		1.00	3.00	5.00
❏ 13 ......1.50		1.00	3.00	5.00
❏ 14 ......1.50		1.00	3.00	5.00
❏ 15 ......1.50		1.00	3.00	5.00
❏ 16 ......1.50		1.00	3.00	5.00
❏ 17 ......1.50		1.00	3.00	5.00
❏ 18 ......1.50		1.00	3.00	5.00
❏ 19 JBy, Vengeance 1.50		1.00	3.00	5.00

	ORIG.	GOOD	FINE	N-MINT
❏ 20 JBy, Vengeance 1.50		1.00	3.00	5.00
❏ 21 JBy/KJ 1.50		0.80	2.40	4.00
❏ 22 JBy 1.50		0.80	2.40	4.00
❏ 23 JBy 1.50		0.80	2.40	4.00
❏ 24 ......1.50		0.80	2.40	4.00
❏ 25 ......1.50		0.80	2.40	4.00
❏ 26 ......1.75		0.80	2.40	4.00
❏ 27 Lazarus Project 1.75		1.20	3.60	6.00
❏ 28 Lazarus Project 1.75		1.20	3.60	6.00
❏ 29 Lazarus Project 1.75		1.20	3.60	6.00
❏ 30 Lazarus Project 1.75		1.20	3.60	6.00
❏ 31 ......1.75		1.00	3.00	5.00
❏ 32 ......1.75		1.00	3.00	5.00
❏ 33 ......1.75		1.00	3.00	5.00
❏ 34 ......1.75		1.00	3.00	5.00
❏ 35 ......1.75		1.00	3.00	5.00
❏ 36 ......1.75		1.00	3.00	5.00
❏ 37 ......1.75		1.00	3.00	5.00
❏ 38 ......1.75		1.00	3.00	5.00
❏ 39 ......1.75		1.00	3.00	5.00
❏ 40 ......1.75		1.00	3.00	5.00
❏ 41 ......1.75		2.00	6.00	10.00
❏ 42 ......1.75		1.20	3.60	6.00
❏ 43 ......1.75		1.00	3.00	5.00
❏ 44 ......1.75		0.50	1.50	2.50
❏ 45 ......1.75		0.80	2.40	4.00
❏ 46 ......1.75		0.80	2.40	4.00
❏ 47 ......1.75		0.50	1.50	2.50
❏ 48 Logan's past 1.75		0.50	1.50	2.50
❏ 49 Logan's past 1.75		0.50	1.50	2.50
❏ 50 diecut cover 2.50		1.60	4.80	8.00
❏ 51 ......1.75		0.40	1.20	2.00
❏ 52 ......1.75		0.40	1.20	2.00
❏ 53 ......1.75		0.35	1.05	1.75
❏ 54 ......1.75		0.35	1.05	1.75
❏ 55 ......1.75		0.35	1.05	1.75
❏ 56 ......1.75		0.35	1.05	1.75
❏ 57 ......1.75		0.35	1.05	1.75
❏ 58 ......1.75		0.35	1.05	1.75
❏ 59 ......1.75		0.35	1.05	1.75
❏ 60 ......1.75		0.80	2.40	4.00
❏ 61 ......1.75		0.80	2.40	4.00
❏ 62 ......1.75		0.80	2.40	4.00
❏ 63 ......1.75		0.80	2.40	4.00
❏ 64 ......1.75		0.80	2.40	4.00
❏ 65 ......1.75		0.35	1.05	1.75
❏ 66 ......1.75		0.35	1.05	1.75
❏ 67 ......1.75		0.35	1.05	1.75
❏ 68 ......1.75		0.35	1.05	1.75
❏ 69 ......1.75		0.35	1.05	1.75
❏ 70 ......1.75		0.35	1.05	1.75
❏ 71 ......1.75		0.35	1.05	1.75
❏ 72 ......1.75		0.35	1.05	1.75
❏ 73 ......1.75		0.35	1.05	1.75

	ORIG.	GOOD	FINE	N-MINT
WOLVERINE AND THE PUNISHER: DAMAGING EVIDENCE				
❑ 1 ....2.00	0.40	1.20	2.00
WOLVERINE SAGA, THE				
❑ 1 O:Wolverine.................3.95	1.20	3.60	6.00
❑ 2 ....3.95	1.00	3.00	5.00
❑ 3 ....3.95	1.00	3.00	5.00
❑ 4 ....3.95	1.00	3.00	5.00
WONDER MAN (1986 one-shot)				
❑ 1 ....1.25	0.80	2.40	4.00
WONDER MAN (beginning 1991)				
❑ 1 poster.......................1.00	0.50	1.50	2.50
❑ 2 ....1.00	0.40	1.20	2.00
❑ 3 1:Splice.................1.00	0.40	1.20	2.00
❑ 4 ....1.00	0.28	0.84	1.40
❑ 5 ....1.00	0.28	0.84	1.40
❑ 6 ....1.25	0.28	0.84	1.40
❑ 7 ....1.25	0.30	0.90	1.50
❑ 8 Galactic Storm.............1.25	0.25	0.75	1.25
❑ 9 Galactic Storm.............1.25	0.25	0.75	1.25
❑ 10 ....1.25	0.25	0.75	1.25
❑ 11 ....1.25	0.25	0.75	1.25
❑ 12 ....1.25	0.25	0.75	1.25
❑ 13 ....1.25	0.25	0.75	1.25
❑ 14 ....1.25	0.25	0.75	1.25
❑ 15 ....1.25	0.25	0.75	1.25
❑ 16 ....1.25	0.25	0.75	1.25
❑ 17 ....1.25	0.25	0.75	1.25
❑ 18 ....1.25	0.25	0.75	1.25
❑ 19 ....1.25	0.25	0.75	1.25
❑ 20 ....1.25	0.25	0.75	1.25
❑ 21 ....1.25	0.25	0.75	1.25
❑ 22 ....1.25	0.25	0.75	1.25
❑ 23 ....1.25	0.25	0.75	1.25
❑ 24 ....1.25	0.25	0.75	1.25
WONDER MAN ANNUAL				
❑ 1 (1992).......................2.25	0.45	1.35	2.25
❑ 2 trading card (1993)........2.95	0.59	1.77	2.95
WORLDS UNKNOWN				
❑ 1 ....0.20	0.20	0.60	1.00
❑ 2 ....0.20	0.20	0.60	1.00
❑ 3 ....0.20	0.20	0.60	1.00
❑ 4 ....0.20	0.20	0.60	1.00
❑ 5 ....0.20	0.20	0.60	1.00
❑ 6 ....0.20	0.20	0.60	1.00
❑ 7 ....0.25	0.20	0.60	1.00
❑ 8 ....0.25	0.20	0.60	1.00
WYATT EARP (1960-1961, revival of old title)				
❑ 30 ....0.20	0.20	0.60	1.00
❑ 31 ....0.20	0.20	0.60	1.00
❑ 32 ....0.20	0.20	0.60	1.00
❑ 33 ....0.20	0.20	0.60	1.00
❑ 34 ....0.20	0.20	0.60	1.00

	ORIG.	GOOD	FINE	N-MINT
X-FACTOR				
❑ 1 ....1.25	2.40	7.20	12.00
❑ 2 ....0.75	1.00	3.00	5.00
❑ 3 ....0.75	1.00	3.00	5.00
❑ 4 ....0.75	1.00	3.00	5.00
❑ 5 ....0.75	1.00	3.00	5.00
❑ 6 ....0.75	0.80	2.40	4.00
❑ 7 ....0.75	0.80	2.40	4.00
❑ 8 ....0.75	0.80	2.40	4.00
❑ 9 massacre 0.75	0.80	2.40	4.00
❑ 10 massacre 0.75	0.80	2.40	4.00
❑ 11 massacre 0.75	0.80	2.40	4.00
❑ 12 ....0.75	0.60	1.80	3.00
❑ 13 ....0.75	0.60	1.80	3.00
❑ 14 ....0.75	0.60	1.80	3.00
❑ 15 ....0.75	0.60	1.80	3.00
❑ 16 ....0.75	0.60	1.80	3.00
❑ 17 ....0.75	0.60	1.80	3.00
❑ 18 ....0.75	0.60	1.80	3.00
❑ 19 ....0.75	0.60	1.80	3.00
❑ 20 ....0.75	0.60	1.80	3.00
❑ 21 ....0.75	0.60	1.80	3.00
❑ 22 ....0.75	0.60	1.80	3.00
❑ 23 registration card 0.75	2.00	6.00	10.00
❑ 24 Fall of Mutants 0.75	2.00	6.00	10.00
❑ 25 Fall of Mutants 0.75	2.00	6.00	10.00
❑ 26 Fall of Mutants 0.75	2.00	6.00	10.00
❑ 27 ....0.75	0.40	1.20	2.00
❑ 28 ....1.00	0.40	1.20	2.00
❑ 29 ....1.00	0.40	1.20	2.00
❑ 30 ....1.00	0.40	1.20	2.00
❑ 31 ....1.00	0.40	1.20	2.00
❑ 32 A:Avengers 1.00	0.40	1.20	2.00
❑ 33 ....1.00	0.40	1.20	2.00
❑ 34 ....1.00	0.40	1.20	2.00
❑ 35 Inferno........................1.00	0.40	1.20	2.00
❑ 36 Inferno........................1.00	0.40	1.20	2.00
❑ 37 Inferno........................1.00	0.40	1.20	2.00
❑ 38 Inferno........................1.50	0.50	1.50	2.50
❑ 39 Inferno........................1.00	0.50	1.50	2.50
❑ 40 RL 1.00	1.60	4.80	8.00
❑ 41 ....1.00	0.40	1.20	2.00
❑ 42 ....1.00	0.40	1.20	2.00
❑ 43 ....1.00	0.40	1.20	2.00
❑ 44 ....1.00	0.40	1.20	2.00
❑ 45 ....1.00	0.40	1.20	2.00
❑ 46 ....1.00	0.40	1.20	2.00
❑ 47 ....1.00	0.40	1.20	2.00
❑ 48 ....1.00	0.40	1.20	2.00
❑ 49 ....1.00	0.40	1.20	2.00
❑ 50 TMc(c) Acts of Vengeance				
........................1.50	0.40	1.20	2.00
❑ 51 ....1.00	1.20	3.60	6.00
❑ 52 ....1.00	1.20	3.60	6.00
❑ 53 ....1.00	1.20	3.60	6.00

	ORIG.	GOOD	FINE	N-MINT
54	1.00	0.20	0.60	1.00
55	1.00	0.20	0.60	1.00
56	1.00	0.20	0.60	1.00
57	1.00	0.20	0.60	1.00
58	1.00	0.20	0.60	1.00
59	1.00	0.20	0.60	1.00
60 X-Tinction	1.00	1.60	4.80	8.00
61 X-Tinction	1.00	1.20	3.60	6.00
62 X-Tinction	1.00	1.20	3.60	6.00
63	1.00	1.60	4.80	8.00
64	1.00	1.20	3.60	6.00
65	1.00	1.20	3.60	6.00
66	1.00	0.35	1.05	1.75
67	1.00	0.35	1.05	1.75
68	1.00	0.35	1.05	1.75
69	1.00	0.35	1.05	1.75
70	1.00	0.40	1.20	2.00
71 new team	1.00	1.40	4.20	7.00
71 2nd printing	1.00	0.20	0.60	1.00
72	1.00	0.60	1.80	3.00
73	1.00	0.60	1.80	3.00
74	1.00	0.60	1.80	3.00
75	1.75	0.50	1.50	2.50
76	1.25	0.25	0.75	1.25
77	1.25	0.25	0.75	1.25
78	1.25	0.25	0.75	1.25
79	1.25	0.25	0.75	1.25
80	1.25	0.25	0.75	1.25
81	1.25	0.25	0.75	1.25
82	1.25	0.25	0.75	1.25
83	1.25	0.25	0.75	1.25
84 bagged, with card, X-Cutioner's Song				
	1.50	0.30	0.90	1.50
85 bagged, with card	1.50	0.30	0.90	1.50
86 bagged, with card	1.50	0.30	0.90	1.50
87	1.25	0.25	0.75	1.25
88	1.25	0.25	0.75	1.25
89	1.25	0.25	0.75	1.25
90	1.25	0.25	0.75	1.25
91	1.25	0.25	0.75	1.25
92 hologram cover	3.50	0.70	2.10	3.50
93	1.25	0.25	0.75	1.25
94	1.25	0.25	0.75	1.25

X-FACTOR ANNUAL

	ORIG.	GOOD	FINE	N-MINT
1 (1986)	1.25	1.00	3.00	5.00
2 (1987)	1.25	0.60	1.80	3.00
3 Evolutionary War (1988)				
	1.75	0.40	1.20	2.00
4 Atlantis Attacks (1989)				
	2.00	0.40	1.20	2.00
5 Future Present (1990)	2.00	0.40	1.20	2.00
6 Kings of Pain (1991)	2.00	0.40	1.20	2.00
7 Shattershot (1992)	2.25	0.45	1.35	2.25
8 trading card (1993)	2.95	0.59	1.77	2.95

X-FORCE

	ORIG.	GOOD	FINE	N-MINT
1 with Cable card	1.50	2.00	6.00	10.00
1 with Deadpool card	1.50	1.20	3.60	6.00
1 with Shatterstar card	1.50	1.20	3.60	6.00
1 with Sunspot & Gideon card				
	1.50	1.20	3.60	6.00
1 with X-Force group card.	1.50	1.50	4.50	7.50
1 2nd printing	1.50	0.30	0.90	1.50
2	1.00	0.60	1.80	3.00
3	1.00	0.60	1.80	3.00
4 SpM	1.00	0.80	2.40	4.00
5 R:Brotherhood of Evil Mutants				
	1.00	0.40	1.20	2.00
6	1.00	0.40	1.20	2.00
7	1.25	0.25	0.75	1.25
8	1.25	0.25	0.75	1.25
9	1.25	0.25	0.75	1.25
10	1.25	0.25	0.75	1.25
11	1.25	0.25	0.75	1.25
12	1.25	0.25	0.75	1.25
13	1.25	0.25	0.75	1.25
14	1.25	0.25	0.75	1.25
15	1.25	0.25	0.75	1.25
16 w/card, X-Cutioner's Song				
	1.50	0.30	0.90	1.50
17 with card	1.50	0.30	0.90	1.50
18 with card	1.50	0.30	0.90	1.50
19	1.25	0.25	0.75	1.25
20	1.25	0.25	0.75	1.25
21	1.25	0.25	0.75	1.25
22	1.25	0.25	0.75	1.25
23	1.25	0.25	0.75	1.25
24	1.25	0.25	0.75	1.25
25 hologram cover	3.50	0.70	2.10	3.50

X-FORCE ANNUAL

	ORIG.	GOOD	FINE	N-MINT
1 Shattershot (1992)	2.25	0.45	1.35	2.25

X-MEN (1963-)

	ORIG.	GOOD	FINE	N-MINT
1 JK, O:X-Men 1:Magneto	0.12	560.00	1680.00	2800.00
2 JK, 1:Vanisher	0.12	160.00	480.00	800.00
3 JK, 1:Blob	0.12	60.00	180.00	300.00
4 JK, 1:Evil Mutants	0.12	80.00	240.00	400.00
5 JK, A:Evil Mutants	0.12	60.00	180.00	300.00
6	0.12	30.00	90.00	150.00
7	0.12	30.00	90.00	150.00
8 JK	0.12	30.00	90.00	150.00
9 JK	0.12	30.00	90.00	150.00
10 JK	0.12	30.00	90.00	150.00
11	0.12	20.00	60.00	100.00
12	0.12	20.00	60.00	100.00
13	0.12	20.00	60.00	100.00
14	0.12	20.00	60.00	100.00
15	0.12	20.00	60.00	100.00
16	0.12	20.00	60.00	100.00
17	0.12	15.00	45.00	75.00

	ORIG.	GOOD	FINE	N-MINT
☐ 18	0.12	15.00	45.00	75.00
☐ 19	0.12	15.00	45.00	75.00
☐ 20	0.12	15.00	45.00	75.00
☐ 21	0.12	11.00	33.00	55.00
☐ 22	0.12	11.00	33.00	55.00
☐ 23	0.12	11.00	33.00	55.00
☐ 24	0.12	11.00	33.00	55.00
☐ 25	0.12	11.00	33.00	55.00
☐ 26	0.12	11.00	33.00	55.00
☐ 27	0.12	11.00	33.00	55.00
☐ 28 1:Banshee	0.12	13.00	39.00	65.00
☐ 29	0.12	10.00	30.00	50.00
☐ 30	0.12	10.00	30.00	50.00
☐ 31	0.12	8.00	24.00	40.00
☐ 32	0.12	8.00	24.00	40.00
☐ 33	0.12	8.00	24.00	40.00
☐ 34	0.12	8.00	24.00	40.00
☐ 35 JK(c), A:Spider-Man, Banshee				
	0.12	10.00	30.00	50.00
☐ 36	0.12	8.00	24.00	40.00
☐ 37	0.12	8.00	24.00	40.00
☐ 38	0.12	10.00	30.00	50.00
☐ 39	0.12	8.00	24.00	40.00
☐ 40	0.12	8.00	24.00	40.00
☐ 41	0.12	8.00	24.00	40.00
☐ 42	0.12	8.00	24.00	40.00
☐ 43	0.12	8.00	24.00	40.00
☐ 44 DH, A:Magneto	0.12	8.00	24.00	40.00
☐ 45	0.12	8.00	24.00	40.00
☐ 46	0.12	8.00	24.00	40.00
☐ 47	0.12	8.00	24.00	40.00
☐ 48	0.12	8.00	24.00	40.00
☐ 49 JSo/DH, C:Magneto	0.12	8.00	24.00	40.00
☐ 50 JSo, Magneto	0.12	7.00	21.00	35.00
☐ 51 JSo, Magneto	0.12	7.00	21.00	35.00
☐ 52 DH/MSe/JSt, O:Lorna Dane				
	0.12	4.80	14.40	24.00
☐ 53 BS, Smith's 1st	0.12	7.00	21.00	35.00
☐ 54 BS/DH, O:Havok	0.12	5.00	15.00	25.00
☐ 55 BS/DH, O:Havok	0.12	5.00	15.00	25.00
☐ 56 NA	0.12	7.00	21.00	35.00
☐ 57 NA	0.12	7.00	21.00	35.00
☐ 58 NA	0.15	7.00	21.00	35.00
☐ 59 NA	0.15	7.00	21.00	35.00
☐ 60 NA	0.15	7.00	21.00	35.00
☐ 61 NA	0.15	7.00	21.00	35.00
☐ 62 NA	0.15	7.00	21.00	35.00
☐ 63 NA	0.15	7.00	21.00	35.00
☐ 64 DH, O:Sunfire	0.15	4.00	12.00	20.00
☐ 65 NA, A:Havok, SHIELD	0.15	6.40	19.20	32.00
☐ 66 SB, A:Hulk, Havok	0.15	2.00	6.00	10.00
☐ 67 reprint	0.25	2.00	6.00	10.00
☐ 68 reprint	0.25	2.00	6.00	10.00
☐ 69 reprint	0.25	2.00	6.00	10.00
☐ 70 reprint	0.25	2.00	6.00	10.00

	ORIG.	GOOD	FINE	N-MINT
☐ 71 reprint	0.25	2.00	6.00	10.00
☐ 72 reprint	0.25	2.00	6.00	10.00
☐ 73 reprint	0.25	2.00	6.00	10.00
☐ 74 reprint	0.25	2.00	6.00	10.00
☐ 75 reprint	0.25	2.00	6.00	10.00
☐ 76 reprint	0.25	2.00	6.00	10.00
☐ 77 reprint	0.25	2.00	6.00	10.00
☐ 78 reprint	0.25	2.00	6.00	10.00
☐ 79 reprint	0.25	2.00	6.00	10.00
☐ 80 reprint	0.25	2.00	6.00	10.00
☐ 81 reprint	0.25	2.00	6.00	10.00
☐ 82 reprint	0.25	2.00	6.00	10.00
☐ 83 reprint	0.25	2.00	6.00	10.00
☐ 84 reprint	0.25	2.00	6.00	10.00
☐ 85 reprint	0.25	2.00	6.00	10.00
☐ 86 reprint	0.25	2.00	6.00	10.00
☐ 87 reprint	0.25	2.00	6.00	10.00
☐ 88 reprint	0.25	2.00	6.00	10.00
☐ 89 reprint	0.25	2.00	6.00	10.00
☐ 90 reprint	0.25	2.00	6.00	10.00
☐ 91 reprint	0.25	2.00	6.00	10.00
☐ 92 reprint	0.25	2.00	6.00	10.00
☐ 93 reprint	0.25	2.00	6.00	10.00
☐ 94 GK/DC/BMc, I:New X-Men				
	0.25	25.00	75.00	125.00
☐ 95 GK/DC, D:Thunderbird				
	0.25	10.00	30.00	50.00
☐ 96	0.25	6.00	18.00	30.00
☐ 97	0.25	6.00	18.00	30.00
☐ 98	0.25	6.00	18.00	30.00
☐ 99	0.25	6.00	18.00	30.00
☐ 100 DC	0.25	8.00	24.00	40.00
☐ 101 DC, I:Phoenix, A:Juggernaut				
	0.30	6.00	18.00	30.00
☐ 102 DC, O:Storm	0.30	4.00	12.00	20.00
☐ 103	0.30	3.20	9.60	16.00
☐ 104	0.30	3.20	9.60	16.00
☐ 105	0.30	3.20	9.60	16.00
☐ 106	0.30	3.20	9.60	16.00
☐ 107	0.30	3.20	9.60	16.00
☐ 108 DC/JBy/TA, A:FF	0.35	7.20	21.60	36.00
☐ 109 DC/JBy/TA, I:Weapon Alpha				
	0.35	7.20	21.60	36.00
☐ 110 DC/TA, A:Warhawk	0.35	3.40	10.20	17.00
☐ 111 DC/JBy/TA, A:Beast, Magneto				
	0.35	3.20	9.60	16.00
☐ 112	0.35	2.80	8.40	14.00
☐ 113	0.35	2.80	8.40	14.00
☐ 114	0.35	2.80	8.40	14.00
☐ 115	0.35	2.80	8.40	14.00
☐ 116	0.35	2.80	8.40	14.00
☐ 117	0.35	2.80	8.40	14.00
☐ 118	0.35	2.80	8.40	14.00
☐ 119	0.35	2.80	8.40	14.00

	ORIG.	GOOD	FINE	N-MINT
☐ 120 JBy/TA, I:Alpha Flight				
............0.35		6.00	18.00	30.00
☐ 121 DC/JBy/TA, A:Alpha Flight				
............0.40		7.00	21.00	35.00
☐ 122 DC/JBy/TA, I:Hellfire Club				
............0.40		2.20	6.60	11.00
☐ 123 ....0.40		2.00	6.00	10.00
☐ 124 ....0.40		2.00	6.00	10.00
☐ 125 ....0.40		2.00	6.00	10.00
☐ 126 ....0.40		2.00	6.00	10.00
☐ 127 ....0.40		2.00	6.00	10.00
☐ 128 ....0.40		2.00	6.00	10.00
☐ 129 JBy/TA, I:Kitty Pryde				
............0.40		2.40	7.20	12.00
☐ 130 JR2/JBy/TA, I:Dazzler				
............0.40		2.70	8.10	13.50
☐ 131 JBy/TA, A:Angel 0.40		1.80	5.40	9.00
☐ 132 JBy/TA, A:Angel 0.40		1.80	5.40	9.00
☐ 133 JBy/TA, A:Angel 0.40		1.80	5.40	9.00
☐ 134 JBy/TA, A:Angel 0.40		1.80	5.40	9.00
☐ 135 JBy/TA, A:Angel 0.40		1.80	5.40	9.00
☐ 136 JBy/TA, A:Angel 0.40		1.80	5.40	9.00
☐ 137 JBy/TA, A:Angel 0.75		1.80	5.40	9.00
☐ 138 JBy/TA, A:Angel 0.50		1.80	5.40	9.00
☐ 139 JBy/TA 0.50		2.40	7.20	12.00
☐ 140 JBy/TA 0.50		2.40	7.20	12.00
☐ 141 JBy/TA (becomes Uncanny X-Men)				
............0.50		1.00	3.00	5.00

X-MEN (1991-)

	ORIG.	GOOD	FINE	N-MINT
☐ 1 cover A: Storm 1.50		0.40	1.20	2.00
☐ 1 cover B: Colossus 1.50		0.40	1.20	2.00
☐ 1 cover C: Wolverine 1.50		0.40	1.20	2.00
☐ 1 cover D: Magneto 1.50		0.40	1.20	2.00
☐ 1 cover E: double gatefold 3.95		1.00	3.00	5.00
☐ 2 ....1.00		0.40	1.20	2.00
☐ 3 ....1.00		0.40	1.20	2.00
☐ 4 ....1.00		1.00	3.00	5.00
☐ 5 ....1.25		0.40	1.20	2.00
☐ 6 ....1.25		1.00	3.00	5.00
☐ 7 ....1.25		0.80	2.40	4.00
☐ 8 ....1.25		0.40	1.20	2.00
☐ 9 ....1.25		0.25	0.75	1.25
☐ 10 ....1.25		0.25	0.75	1.25
☐ 11 ....1.25		0.25	0.75	1.25
☐ 12 ....1.25		0.25	0.75	1.25
☐ 13 ....1.25		0.25	0.75	1.25
☐ 14 X-Cutioner's Song, trading card				
............1.50		0.30	0.90	1.50
☐ 15 bagged, with card 1.50		0.30	0.90	1.50
☐ 16 bagged, with card 1.50		0.30	0.90	1.50
☐ 17 ....1.25		0.25	0.75	1.25
☐ 18 ....1.25		0.25	0.75	1.25
☐ 19 ....1.25		0.25	0.75	1.25
☐ 20 ....1.25		0.25	0.75	1.25
☐ 21 ....1.25		0.25	0.75	1.25

	ORIG.	GOOD	FINE	N-MINT
☐ 22 ....1.25		0.25	0.75	1.25
☐ 23 ....1.25		0.25	0.75	1.25
☐ 24 ....1.25		0.25	0.75	1.25

X-MEN ADVENTURES

	ORIG.	GOOD	FINE	N-MINT
☐ 1 TV cartoon version 1.25		0.50	1.50	2.50
☐ 2 ....1.25		0.25	0.75	1.25
☐ 3 ....1.25		0.25	0.75	1.25
☐ 4 ....1.25		0.25	0.75	1.25
☐ 5 ....1.25		0.25	0.75	1.25
☐ 6 ....1.25		0.25	0.75	1.25
☐ 7 ....1.25		0.25	0.75	1.25
☐ 8 ....1.25		0.25	0.75	1.25
☐ 9 ....1.25		0.25	0.75	1.25
☐ 10 ....1.25		0.25	0.75	1.25
☐ 11 ....1.25		0.25	0.75	1.25

X-MEN ANNIVERSARY MAGAZINE

	ORIG.	GOOD	FINE	N-MINT
☐ 1 ....3.95		0.79	2.37	3.95

X-MEN ANNUAL

	ORIG.	GOOD	FINE	N-MINT
☐ 1 reprint 0.25		6.00	18.00	30.00
☐ 2 reprint 0.12		4.00	12.00	20.00
☐ 3 FM/GP/TA, I:Arkon (1979)				
............0.75		1.60	4.80	8.00
☐ 4 JR2, A:Dr. Strange (1980) (becomes Uncanny X-Men				
Annual) 0.75		1.60	4.80	8.00

X-MEN ANNUAL (second series, '92-on)

	ORIG.	GOOD	FINE	N-MINT
☐ 1 (1992) 2.25		0.45	1.35	2.25

X-MEN AT THE STATE FAIR

	ORIG.	GOOD	FINE	N-MINT
☐ 1 Dallas Times-Herald		6.00	18.00	30.00

X-MEN CLASSIC (was Classic X-Men)

	ORIG.	GOOD	FINE	N-MINT
☐ 46 reprints 1.25		0.25	0.75	1.25
☐ 47 reprints 1.25		0.25	0.75	1.25
☐ 48 reprints 1.25		0.25	0.75	1.25
☐ 49 reprints 1.25		0.25	0.75	1.25
☐ 50 reprints 1.25		0.25	0.75	1.25
☐ 51 reprints 1.25		0.25	0.75	1.25
☐ 52 reprints 1.25		0.25	0.75	1.25
☐ 53 reprints 1.25		0.25	0.75	1.25
☐ 54 reprints 1.25		0.25	0.75	1.25
☐ 55 reprints 1.25		0.25	0.75	1.25
☐ 56 reprints 1.25		0.25	0.75	1.25
☐ 57 reprints 1.25		0.25	0.75	1.25
☐ 58 reprints 1.25		0.25	0.75	1.25
☐ 59 reprints 1.25		0.25	0.75	1.25
☐ 60 reprints 1.25		0.25	0.75	1.25
☐ 61 reprints 1.25		0.25	0.75	1.25
☐ 62 reprints 1.25		0.25	0.75	1.25
☐ 63 reprints 1.25		0.25	0.75	1.25
☐ 64 reprints 1.25		0.25	0.75	1.25
☐ 65 reprints 1.25		0.25	0.75	1.25
☐ 66 reprints 1.25		0.25	0.75	1.25
☐ 67 reprints 1.25		0.25	0.75	1.25
☐ 68 reprints 1.25		0.25	0.75	1.25
☐ 69 reprints 1.25		0.25	0.75	1.25
☐ 70 reprints 1.25		0.25	0.75	1.25

	ORIG.	GOOD	FINE	N-MINT
❏ 71 reprints	1.25	0.25	0.75	1.25
❏ 72 reprints	1.25	0.25	0.75	1.25
❏ 73 reprints	1.25	0.25	0.75	1.25
❏ 74 reprints	1.25	0.25	0.75	1.25
❏ 75 reprints	1.25	0.25	0.75	1.25
❏ 76 reprints	1.25	0.25	0.75	1.25
❏ 77 reprints	1.25	0.25	0.75	1.25
❏ 78 reprints	1.25	0.25	0.75	1.25
❏ 79 reprints	1.75	0.35	1.05	1.75
❏ 80 reprints	1.25	0.25	0.75	1.25
❏ 81 reprints	1.25	0.25	0.75	1.25
❏ 82 reprints	1.25	0.25	0.75	1.25
❏ 83 reprints	1.25	0.25	0.75	1.25
❏ 84 reprints	1.25	0.25	0.75	1.25
❏ 85 reprints	1.25	0.25	0.75	1.25
❏ 86 reprints	1.25	0.25	0.75	1.25
❏ 87 reprints	1.25	0.25	0.75	1.25

X-MEN CLASSICS

	ORIG.	GOOD	FINE	N-MINT
❏ 1 reprint	2.00	0.50	1.50	2.50
❏ 2 reprint	2.00	0.50	1.50	2.50
❏ 3 reprint	2.00	0.50	1.50	2.50

X-MEN POSTER MAGAZINE

	ORIG.	GOOD	FINE	N-MINT
❏ 1 (1992)	4.95	0.99	2.97	4.95
❏ 2	4.95	0.99	2.97	4.95

X-MEN SPECIAL EDITION (1982)

	ORIG.	GOOD	FINE	N-MINT
❏ 1 reprint	2.00	0.40	1.20	2.00

X-MEN SPOTLIGHT ON THE STARJAMMERS

	ORIG.	GOOD	FINE	N-MINT
❏ 1 DC	2.50	0.90	2.70	4.50
❏ 2 DC	2.50	0.90	2.70	4.50

X-MEN UNLIMITED

	ORIG.	GOOD	FINE	N-MINT
❏ 1	3.95	0.79	2.37	3.95
❏ 2	3.95	0.79	2.37	3.95

X-MEN VS. THE AVENGERS

	ORIG.	GOOD	FINE	N-MINT
❏ 1	1.50	0.30	0.90	1.50
❏ 2	1.50	0.30	0.90	1.50
❏ 3	1.50	0.30	0.90	1.50
❏ 4	1.50	0.30	0.90	1.50

X-MEN/ALPHA FLIGHT

	ORIG.	GOOD	FINE	N-MINT
❏ 1	1.50	0.80	2.40	4.00
❏ 2	1.50	0.80	2.40	4.00

X-MEN/MICRONAUTS

	ORIG.	GOOD	FINE	N-MINT
❏ 1 BG, Limited Series	0.60	0.60	1.80	3.00
❏ 2	0.60	0.40	1.20	2.00
❏ 3	0.60	0.40	1.20	2.00
❏ 4	0.60	0.40	1.20	2.00

X-TERMINATORS

	ORIG.	GOOD	FINE	N-MINT
❏ 1 Inferno	1.00	0.20	0.60	1.00
❏ 2 Inferno	1.00	0.20	0.60	1.00
❏ 3 Inferno	1.00	0.20	0.60	1.00
❏ 4 Inferno	1.00	0.20	0.60	1.00

YUPPIES FROM HELL

	ORIG.	GOOD	FINE	N-MINT
❏ 1 b&w	2.95	0.59	1.77	2.95
❏ 2 b&w, Son of...	2.95	0.59	1.77	2.95

	ORIG.	GOOD	FINE	N-MINT
❏ 3 b&w, Sex, Lies	2.95	0.59	1.77	2.95

ZORRO

	ORIG.	GOOD	FINE	N-MINT
❏ 1	1.00	0.20	0.60	1.00
❏ 2	1.00	0.20	0.60	1.00
❏ 3	1.00	0.20	0.60	1.00
❏ 4	1.00	0.20	0.60	1.00
❏ 5	1.00	0.20	0.60	1.00
❏ 6	1.00	0.20	0.60	1.00
❏ 7	1.00	0.20	0.60	1.00
❏ 8	1.00	0.20	0.60	1.00
❏ 9	1.00	0.20	0.60	1.00
❏ 10 ATh(c)	1.00	0.20	0.60	1.00
❏ 11 ATh(c)	1.00	0.20	0.60	1.00
❏ 12 ATh(c)	1.00	0.20	0.60	1.00

MARVEL UK

ACTION FORCE

	ORIG.	GOOD	FINE	N-MINT
❏ 1 (reprinted in U.S. as G.I. Joe European Missions)	1.00	0.20	0.60	1.00
❏ 2	1.00	0.20	0.60	1.00
❏ 3	1.00	0.20	0.60	1.00
❏ 4	1.00	0.20	0.60	1.00
❏ 5	1.00	0.20	0.60	1.00
❏ 6	1.00	0.20	0.60	1.00
❏ 7	1.00	0.20	0.60	1.00
❏ 8	1.00	0.20	0.60	1.00
❏ 9	1.00	0.20	0.60	1.00
❏ 10	1.00	0.20	0.60	1.00
❏ 11	1.00	0.20	0.60	1.00
❏ 12	1.00	0.20	0.60	1.00
❏ 13	1.00	0.20	0.60	1.00
❏ 14	1.00	0.20	0.60	1.00
❏ 15	1.00	0.20	0.60	1.00
❏ 16	1.00	0.20	0.60	1.00
❏ 17	1.00	0.20	0.60	1.00
❏ 18	1.00	0.20	0.60	1.00
❏ 19	1.00	0.20	0.60	1.00
❏ 20	1.00	0.20	0.60	1.00
❏ 21	1.00	0.20	0.60	1.00
❏ 22	1.00	0.20	0.60	1.00
❏ 23	1.00	0.20	0.60	1.00

ACTION FORCE HOLIDAY SPECIAL (1987)

	ORIG.	GOOD	FINE	N-MINT
❏	1.50	0.30	0.90	1.50

AVENGERS, THE

❏ reprints

BLAKE'S 7 (based on TV series)

❏ 1 no U.S. price
❏ 2 no U.S. price
❏ 3 no U.S. price
❏ 4 no U.S. price
❏ 5 no U.S. price
❏ 6 no U.S. price
❏ 7 no U.S. price

	ORIG.	GOOD	FINE	N-MINT
❏ 8 no U.S. price				
❏ 9 no U.S. price				
❏ 10 no U.S. price				
❏ 11 no U.S. price				
❏ 12 no U.S. price				
❏ 13 no U.S. price				
❏ 14 no U.S. price				
❏ 15 no U.S. price				
❏ 16 no U.S. price				
❏ 17 no U.S. price				
❏ 18 no U.S. price				
❏ 19 no U.S. price				
❏ 20 no U.S. price				
❏ 21 no U.S. price				
❏ 22 no U.S. price				
❏ 23 no U.S. price				

BLAKE'S 7 SUMMER SPECIAL
❏ no U.S. price ....

CAPTAIN BRITAIN (Oct. '76-July '77) (combined with Spider-Man comic as Spider-Man and Captain Britan)

	ORIG.	GOOD	FINE	N-MINT
❏ 1 No U.S. price				
❏ 2 No U.S. price				
❏ 3 No U.S. price				
❏ 4 No U.S. price				
❏ 5 No U.S. price				
❏ 6 No U.S. price				
❏ 7 No U.S. price				
❏ 8 No U.S. price				
❏ 9 No U.S. price				
❏ 10 No U.S. price				
❏ 11 No U.S. price				
❏ 12 No U.S. price				
❏ 13 No U.S. price				
❏ 14 No U.S. price				
❏ 15 No U.S. price				
❏ 16 No U.S. price				
❏ 17 No U.S. price				
❏ 18 No U.S. price				
❏ 19 No U.S. price				
❏ 20 No U.S. price				
❏ 21 No U.S. price				
❏ 22 No U.S. price				
❏ 23 No U.S. price				
❏ 24 No U.S. price				
❏ 25 No U.S. price				
❏ 26 No U.S. price				
❏ 27 No U.S. price				
❏ 28 No U.S. price				
❏ 29 No U.S. price				
❏ 30 No U.S. price				
❏ 31 No U.S. price				
❏ 32 No U.S. price				
❏ 33 No U.S. price				
❏ 34 No U.S. price				

	ORIG.	GOOD	FINE	N-MINT
❏ 35 No U.S. price				
❏ 36 No U.S. price				
❏ 37 No U.S. price				
❏ 38 No U.S. price				
❏ 39 No U.S. price				

CAPTAIN BRITAIN (second series, 1985/86)

	ORIG.	GOOD	FINE	N-MINT
❏ 1 ....1.75	1.75	0.35	1.05	1.75
❏ 2 ....1.75	1.75	0.35	1.05	1.75
❏ 3 ....1.75	1.75	0.35	1.05	1.75
❏ 4 ....1.75	1.75	0.35	1.05	1.75
❏ 5 ....1.75	1.75	0.35	1.05	1.75
❏ 6 ....1.75	1.75	0.35	1.05	1.75
❏ 7 ....1.75	1.75	0.35	1.05	1.75
❏ 8 ....1.75	1.75	0.35	1.05	1.75
❏ 9 ....1.75	1.75	0.35	1.05	1.75
❏ 10 ....1.75	1.75	0.35	1.05	1.75
❏ 11 ....1.75	1.75	0.35	1.05	1.75
❏ 12 ....1.75	1.75	0.35	1.05	1.75
❏ 13 ....1.75	1.75	0.35	1.05	1.75
❏ 14 ....1.75	1.75	0.35	1.05	1.75

DAREDEVILS, THE

	ORIG.	GOOD	FINE	N-MINT
❏ 1 no U.S. price				
❏ 2 no U.S. price				
❏ 3 no U.S. price				
❏ 4 no U.S. price				
❏ 5 no U.S. price				
❏ 6 no U.S. price				
❏ 7 no U.S. price				
❏ 8 no U.S. price				
❏ 9 no U.S. price				
❏ 10 no U.S. price				
❏ 11 no U.S. price				

DOCTOR WHO 10TH ANNIVERSARY SPECIAL 1979-1989

	ORIG.	GOOD	FINE	N-MINT
❏	7.95	1.59	4.77	7.95

DOCTOR WHO 25TH ANNIVERSARY SPECIAL
❏ (1988) No U.S. price ....

DOCTOR WHO AUTUMN SPECIAL

	ORIG.	GOOD	FINE	N-MINT
❏ (1987)...............................5.95	5.95	1.19	3.57	5.95

DOCTOR WHO CLASSIC COMICS

	ORIG.	GOOD	FINE	N-MINT
❏ 1 ....4.95	4.95	0.99	2.97	4.95
❏ 2 ....4.95	4.95	0.99	2.97	4.95
❏ 3 ....4.95	4.95	0.99	2.97	4.95
❏ 4 ....4.95	4.95	0.99	2.97	4.95
❏ 5 ....4.95	4.95	0.99	2.97	4.95
❏ 6 ....4.95	4.95	0.99	2.97	4.95
❏ 7 ....4.95	4.95	0.99	2.97	4.95

DOCTOR WHO COLLECTED COMICS

	ORIG.	GOOD	FINE	N-MINT
❏ nn.....................................5.95	5.95	1.19	3.57	5.95

DOCTOR WHO HOLIDAY SPECIAL

	ORIG.	GOOD	FINE	N-MINT
❏ (1992)...............................4.50	4.50	0.90	2.70	4.50

DOCTOR WHO MAGAZINE (was Doctor Who Monthly)
❏ 85 No U.S. price.................

	ORIG.	GOOD	FINE	N-MINT		ORIG.	GOOD	FINE	N-MINT
86 No U.S. price					141	4.75	0.95	2.85	4.75
87 No U.S. price					142	4.75	0.95	2.85	4.75
88 No U.S. price					143	4.75	0.95	2.85	4.75
89 No U.S. price					144	4.75	0.95	2.85	4.75
90 No U.S. price					145	4.75	0.95	2.85	4.75
91 No U.S. price					146	4.75	0.95	2.85	4.75
92 No U.S. price					147	4.75	0.95	2.85	4.75
93 No U.S. price					148	4.75	0.95	2.85	4.75
94 No U.S. price					149	4.75	0.95	2.85	4.75
95 No U.S. price					150	5.95	1.19	3.57	5.95
96	2.00	0.40	1.20	2.00	151	5.95	1.19	3.57	5.95
97	2.00	0.40	1.20	2.00	152	3.25	0.65	1.95	3.25
98	2.00	0.40	1.20	2.00	153	4.95	0.99	2.97	4.95
99	2.00	0.40	1.20	2.00	154	4.95	0.99	2.97	4.95
100	2.00	0.40	1.20	2.00	155	4.95	0.99	2.97	4.95
101	2.00	0.40	1.20	2.00	156	4.95	0.99	2.97	4.95
102	2.00	0.40	1.20	2.00	157	2.95	0.59	1.77	2.95
103	2.00	0.40	1.20	2.00	158	2.95	0.59	1.77	2.95
104	2.25	0.45	1.35	2.25	159	2.95	0.59	1.77	2.95
105	2.25	0.45	1.35	2.25	160				
106	2.25	0.45	1.35	2.25	161	3.95	0.79	2.37	3.95
107	2.25	0.45	1.35	2.25	162	3.95	0.79	2.37	3.95
108	3.00	0.60	1.80	3.00	163				
109	2.25	0.45	1.35	2.25	164	3.95	0.79	2.37	3.95
110	2.25	0.45	1.35	2.25	165	3.95	0.79	2.37	3.95
111	2.25	0.45	1.35	2.25	166	3.95	0.79	2.37	3.95
112	2.25	0.45	1.35	2.25	167 (with record)	5.50	1.10	3.30	5.50
113	2.25	0.45	1.35	2.25	168	3.95	0.79	2.37	3.95
114	3.00	0.60	1.80	3.00	169	3.95	0.79	2.37	3.95
115	2.75	0.55	1.65	2.75	170	3.95	0.79	2.37	3.95
116	2.75	0.55	1.65	2.75	171	3.95	0.79	2.37	3.95
117	2.75	0.55	1.65	2.75	172	3.95	0.79	2.37	3.95
118	2.75	0.55	1.65	2.75	173	3.95	0.79	2.37	3.95
119	2.75	0.55	1.65	2.75	174	4.50	0.90	2.70	4.50
120	3.75	0.75	2.25	3.75	175	3.95	0.79	2.37	3.95
121	2.75	0.55	1.65	2.75	176	3.95	0.79	2.37	3.95
122	2.75	0.55	1.65	2.75	177	3.95	0.79	2.37	3.95
123	2.75	0.55	1.65	2.75	178	3.95	0.79	2.37	3.95
124	2.75	0.55	1.65	2.75	179	3.95	0.79	2.37	3.95
125	2.95	0.59	1.77	2.95	180	4.50	0.90	2.70	4.50
126	2.95	0.59	1.77	2.95	181	4.50	0.90	2.70	4.50
127	4.50	0.90	2.70	4.50	182	4.50	0.90	2.70	4.50
128	2.95	0.59	1.77	2.95	183	4.50	0.90	2.70	4.50
129	2.95	0.59	1.77	2.95	184 (postcards)	4.50	0.90	2.70	4.50
130	2.95	0.59	1.77	2.95	185 (postcards)	4.50	0.90	2.70	4.50
131	3.50	0.70	2.10	3.50	186 (postcards)	4.50	0.90	2.70	4.50
132	3.50	0.70	2.10	3.50	187 (postcards)	4.50	0.90	2.70	4.50
133	3.50	0.70	2.10	3.50	188 (postcards)	4.50	0.90	2.70	4.50
134	3.50	0.70	2.10	3.50	189 (postcards)	4.50	0.90	2.70	4.50
135	3.75	0.75	2.25	3.75	195 (postcards)				
136	3.75	0.75	2.25	3.75	196 (postcards)	4.95	0.99	2.97	4.95
137	3.75	0.75	2.25	3.75	197	4.95	0.99	2.97	4.95
138	3.75	0.75	2.25	3.75	198	4.95	0.99	2.97	4.95
139	4.75	0.95	2.85	4.75	199	4.95	0.99	2.97	4.95
140	4.75	0.95	2.85	4.75	200	4.95	0.99	2.97	4.95

	ORIG.	GOOD	FINE	N-MINT

DOCTOR WHO MARVEL ADVENTURE COMIC
(miniature giveaway comics)

❏ 1 ....
❏ 2 ....
❏ 3 ....
❏ 4 ....
❏ 5 ....
❏ 6 ....

DOCTOR WHO MONTHLY
(was Doctor Who Weekly)

❏ 44 No U.S. price ....
❏ 45 No U.S. price ....
❏ 46 No U.S. price ....
❏ 47 No U.S. price ....
❏ 48 No U.S. price ....
❏ 49 No U.S. price ....
❏ 50 No U.S. price ....
❏ 51 No U.S. price ....
❏ 52 No U.S. price ....
❏ 53 No U.S. price ....
❏ 54 No U.S. price ....
❏ 55 No U.S. price ....
❏ 56 No U.S. price ....
❏ 57 No U.S. price ....
❏ 58 No U.S. price ....
❏ 59 No U.S. price ....
❏ 60 No U.S. price ....
❏ 61 No U.S. price ....
❏ 62 No U.S. price ....
❏ 63 No U.S. price ....
❏ 64 No U.S. price ....
❏ 65 No U.S. price ....
❏ 66 No U.S. price ....
❏ 67 No U.S. price ....
❏ 68 No U.S. price ....
❏ 69 No U.S. price ....
❏ 70 No U.S. price ....
❏ 71 No U.S. price ....
❏ 72 No U.S. price ....
❏ 73 No U.S. price ....
❏ 74 No U.S. price ....
❏ 75 No U.S. price ....
❏ 76 No U.S. price ....
❏ 77 No U.S. price ....
❏ 78 No U.S. price ....
❏ 79 No U.S. price ....
❏ 80 No U.S. price ....
❏ 81 No U.S. price ....
❏ 82 No U.S. price ....
❏ 83 No U.S. price ....
❏ 84 (becomes Doctor Who Magazine) No U.S. price

DOCTOR WHO SUMMER SPECIAL

❏ 1981, No U.S. price ....
❏ 1982, No U.S. price ....
❏ 1983, No U.S. price ....

	ORIG.	GOOD	FINE	N-MINT
❏ 1984, No U.S. price.............				
❏ 1985	3.95	0.79	2.37	3.95
❏ 1986	3.50	0.70	2.10	3.50
❏ 1991	4.50	0.90	2.70	4.50

DOCTOR WHO WEEKLY

❏ 1 No U.S. price....................
❏ 2 No U.S. price....................
❏ 3 No U.S. price....................
❏ 4 No U.S. price....................
❏ 5 No U.S. price....................
❏ 6 No U.S. price....................
❏ 7 No U.S. price....................
❏ 8 No U.S. price....................
❏ 9 No U.S. price....................
❏ 10 No U.S. price...................
❏ 11 No U.S. price...................
❏ 12 No U.S. price...................
❏ 13 No U.S. price...................
❏ 14 No U.S. price...................
❏ 15 No U.S. price...................
❏ 16 No U.S. price...................
❏ 17 No U.S. price...................
❏ 18 No U.S. price...................
❏ 19 No U.S. price...................
❏ 20 No U.S. price...................
❏ 21 No U.S. price...................
❏ 22 No U.S. price...................
❏ 23 No U.S. price...................
❏ 24 No U.S. price...................
❏ 25 No U.S. price...................
❏ 26 No U.S. price...................
❏ 27 No U.S. price...................
❏ 28 No U.S. price...................
❏ 29 No U.S. price...................
❏ 30 No U.S. price...................
❏ 31 No U.S. price...................
❏ 32 No U.S. price...................
❏ 33 No U.S. price...................
❏ 34 No U.S. price...................
❏ 35 No U.S. price...................
❏ 36 No U.S. price...................
❏ 37 No U.S. price...................
❏ 38 No U.S. price...................
❏ 39 No U.S. price................
❏ 40 No U.S. price.................
❏ 41 No U.S. price.................
❏ 42 No U.S. price.................
❏ 43 (becomes Doctor Who Monthly) No U.S. price

DOCTOR WHO WINTER SPECIAL

	ORIG.	GOOD	FINE	N-MINT
❏ 1982 No U.S. price.............				
❏ 1983/1984 No U.S. price.....				
❏ 1985	2.50	0.50	1.50	2.50
❏ 1985	3.00	0.60	1.80	3.00
❏ 1986	3.75	0.75	2.25	3.75

	ORIG.	GOOD	FINE	N-MINT
❑ 1991	4.50	0.90	2.70	4.50
❑ 1992	4.50	0.90	2.70	4.50

DOCTOR WHO YEARBOOK (hardcover)

	ORIG.	GOOD	FINE	N-MINT
❑ 1992	8.95	1.79	5.37	8.95
❑ 1993	8.95	1.79	5.37	8.95

FANTASTIC (reprints of X-Men, Thor, etc)

❑ 1 No U.S. price
❑ 2 No U.S. price
❑ 3 No U.S. price
❑ 4 No U.S. price
❑ 5 No U.S. price
❑ 6 No U.S. price
❑ 7 No U.S. price
❑ 8 No U.S. price
❑ 9 No U.S. price
❑ 10 No U.S. price
❑ 11 No U.S. price
❑ 12 No U.S. price
❑ 13 No U.S. price
❑ 14 No U.S. price
❑ 15 No U.S. price
❑ 16 No U.S. price
❑ 17 No U.S. price
❑ 18 No U.S. price
❑ 19 No U.S. price
❑ 20 No U.S. price
❑ 21 No U.S. price
❑ 22 No U.S. price
❑ 23 No U.S. price
❑ 24 No U.S. price
❑ 25 No U.S. price
❑ 26 No U.S. price
❑ 27 No U.S. price
❑ 28 No U.S. price
❑ 29 No U.S. price
❑ 30 No U.S. price
❑ 31 No U.S. price
❑ 32 No U.S. price
❑ 33 No U.S. price
❑ 34 No U.S. price
❑ 35 No U.S. price
❑ 36 No U.S. price
❑ 37 No U.S. price
❑ 38 No U.S. price
❑ 39 No U.S. price
❑ 40 No U.S. price
❑ 41 No U.S. price
❑ 42 No U.S. price
❑ 43 No U.S. price
❑ 44 No U.S. price
❑ 45 No U.S. price
❑ 46 No U.S. price
❑ 47 No U.S. price
❑ 48 No U.S. price

❑ 49 No U.S. price
❑ 50 No U.S. price
❑ 51 No U.S. price
❑ 52 No U.S. price
❑ 53 No U.S. price
❑ 54 No U.S. price
❑ 55 No U.S. price
❑ 56 No U.S. price
❑ 57 No U.S. price
❑ 58 No U.S. price
❑ 59 No U.S. price
❑ 60 No U.S. price
❑ 61 No U.S. price
❑ 62 No U.S. price
❑ 63 No U.S. price
❑ 64 No U.S. price
❑ 65 No U.S. price
❑ 66 No U.S. price
❑ 67 No U.S. price
❑ 68 No U.S. price
❑ 69 No U.S. price
❑ 70 No U.S. price
❑ 71 No U.S. price
❑ 72 No U.S. price
❑ 73 No U.S. price
❑ 74 No U.S. price
❑ 75 No U.S. price
❑ 76 No U.S. price
❑ 77 No U.S. price
❑ 78 No U.S. price
❑ 79 No U.S. price
❑ 80 No U.S. price
❑ 81 No U.S. price
❑ 82 No U.S. price
❑ 83 No U.S. price
❑ 84 No U.S. price

HULK COMIC

❑ 1 reprints, No U.S. price
❑ 2 reprints, No U.S. price
❑ 3 reprints, No U.S. price
❑ 4 reprints, No U.S. price
❑ 5 reprints, No U.S. price
❑ 6 reprints, No U.S. price
❑ 7 reprints, No U.S. price
❑ 8 reprints, No U.S. price

MARVEL BUMPER COMIC

❑ 1 No U.S. price
❑ 2 No U.S. price
❑ 3 No U.S. price
❑ 4 No U.S. price
❑ 5 No U.S. price
❑ 6 No U.S. price
❑ 7 No U.S. price
❑ 8 No U.S. price

	ORIG.	GOOD	FINE	N-MINT

❑ 9 No U.S. price ....
❑ 10 No U.S. price ....
❑ 11 No U.S. price ....
❑ 12 No U.S. price ....
❑ 13 No U.S. price ....
❑ 14 No U.S. price ....
❑ 15 No U.S. price ....
❑ 16 No U.S. price ....
❑ 17 No U.S. price ....
❑ 18 No U.S. price ....
❑ 19 No U.S. price ....

MARVEL COMIC

❑ 1 No U.S. price ....
❑ 2 No U.S. price ....
❑ 3 No U.S. price ....
❑ 4 No U.S. price ....
❑ 5 No U.S. price ....
❑ 6 No U.S. price ....
❑ 7 No U.S. price ....
❑ 8 No U.S. price ....
❑ 9 No U.S. price ....
❑ 10 No U.S. price ....
❑ 11 No U.S. price ....
❑ 12 No U.S. price ....
❑ 13 No U.S. price ....
❑ 14 No U.S. price ....
❑ 15 No U.S. price ....
❑ 16 No U.S. price ....
❑ 17 No U.S. price ....
❑ 18 No U.S. price ....
❑ 19 No U.S. price ....

MIGHTY WORLD OF MARVEL (1972-1973)

❑ 1 reprints, No U.S. price .....
❑ 2 reprints, No U.S. price .....
❑ 3 reprints, No U.S. price .....
❑ 4 reprints, No U.S. price .....
❑ 5 reprints, No U.S. price .....
❑ 6 reprints, No U.S. price .....
❑ 7 reprints, No U.S. price .....
❑ 8 reprints, No U.S. price .....
❑ 9 reprints, No U.S. price .....
❑ 10 reprints, No U.S. price ...
❑ 11 reprints, No U.S. price ...
❑ 12 reprints, No U.S. price ...
❑ 13 reprints, No U.S. price ...
❑ 14 reprints, No U.S. price ...
❑ 15 reprints, No U.S. price ...
❑ 16 reprints, No U.S. price ...
❑ 17 reprints, No U.S. price ...
❑ 18 reprints, No U.S. price ...
❑ 19 reprints, No U.S. price ...
❑ 20 reprints, No U.S. price ...
❑ 21 reprints, No U.S. price ...
❑ 22 reprints, No U.S. price ...

	ORIG.	GOOD	FINE	N-MINT

❑ 23 reprints, No U.S. price....
❑ 24 reprints, No U.S. price....
❑ 25 reprints, No U.S. price....
❑ 26 reprints, No U.S. price....
❑ 27 reprints, No U.S. price....
❑ 28 reprints, No U.S. price....
❑ 29 reprints, No U.S. price....
❑ 30 reprints, No U.S. price....
❑ 31 reprints, No U.S. price....
❑ 32 reprints, No U.S. price....
❑ 33 reprints, No U.S. price....
❑ 34 reprints, No U.S. price....
❑ 35 reprints, No U.S. price....
❑ 36 reprints, No U.S. price....
❑ 37 reprints, No U.S. price....
❑ 38 reprints, No U.S. price....
❑ 39 reprints, No U.S. price....
❑ 40 reprints, No U.S. price....
❑ 41 reprints, No U.S. price....
❑ 42 reprints, No U.S. price....
❑ 43 reprints, No U.S. price....
❑ 44 reprints, No U.S. price....

MIGHTY WORLD OF MARVEL (1983-1984)

❑ 1 reprints, No U.S. price......
❑ 2 reprints, No U.S. price......
❑ 3 reprints, No U.S. price......
❑ 4 reprints, No U.S. price......
❑ 5 reprints, No U.S. price......
❑ 6 reprints, No U.S. price......
❑ 7 reprints, No U.S. price......
❑ 8 reprints, No U.S. price......
❑ 9 reprints, No U.S. price......
❑ 10 reprints, No U.S. price....
❑ 11 reprints, No U.S. price....
❑ 12 reprints, No U.S. price....
❑ 13 reprints, No U.S. price....
❑ 14 reprints, No U.S. price....
❑ 15 reprints, No U.S. price....
❑ 16 reprints, No U.S. price....
❑ 17 reprints, No U.S. price....

OVERKILL (features stories later reprinted in Hell's Angel/Dark Angel, Pendragon, etc.)

❑ 1 No U.S. price...................
❑ 2 No U.S. price...................
❑ 3 No U.S. price...................
❑ 4 No U.S. price...................
❑ 5 No U.S. price...................
❑ 6 No U.S. price...................
❑ 7 No U.S. price...................
❑ 8 No U.S. price...................
❑ 9 No U.S. price...................
❑ 10 No U.S. price.................
❑ 11 No U.S. price.................
❑ 12 No U.S. price.................
❑ 13 No U.S. price.................

	ORIG.	GOOD	FINE	N-MINT
14 No U.S. price				
15 No U.S. price				
16 No U.S. price				
17 No U.S. price				
18 No U.S. price				
19 No U.S. price				
20 No U.S. price				
21 No U.S. price				
22 No U.S. price				
23 No U.S. price				
24 No U.S. price				
25 No U.S. price				
26 No U.S. price				
27 No U.S. price				
28 No U.S. price				
29 No U.S. price				
30 No U.S. price				
31 No U.S. price				
32 No U.S. price				
33 No U.S. price				
34 No U.S. price				
35 No U.S. price				

SPIDER-MAN COMIC (reprints)

1 No U.S. price				
2 No U.S. price				
3 No U.S. price				
4 No U.S. price				
5 No U.S. price				
6 No U.S. price				
7 No U.S. price				
8 No U.S. price				
9 No U.S. price				
10 No U.S. price				
11 No U.S. price				
12 No U.S. price				
13 No U.S. price				
14 No U.S. price				
15 No U.S. price				
16 No U.S. price				
17 No U.S. price				
18 No U.S. price				
19 No U.S. price				
20 No U.S. price				
21 No U.S. price				
22 No U.S. price				
23 No U.S. price				
24 No U.S. price				
25 No U.S. price				
26 No U.S. price				
27 No U.S. price				
28 No U.S. price				
29 No U.S. price				
30 No U.S. price				
31 No U.S. price				
32 No U.S. price				

	ORIG.	GOOD	FINE	N-MINT
33 No U.S. price				
34 No U.S. price				
35 No U.S. price				
36 No U.S. price				
37 No U.S. price				
38 No U.S. price				
39 No U.S. price				
40 No U.S. price				
41 No U.S. price				
42 No U.S. price				
43 No U.S. price				
44 No U.S. price				
45 No U.S. price				
46 No U.S. price				
47 No U.S. price				
48 No U.S. price				
49 No U.S. price				
50 No U.S. price				
51 No U.S. price				
52 No U.S. price				
53 No U.S. price				
54 No U.S. price				
55 No U.S. price				
56 No U.S. price				
57 No U.S. price				
58 No U.S. price				
59 No U.S. price				
60 No U.S. price				
61 No U.S. price				
62 No U.S. price				
63 No U.S. price				
64 No U.S. price				
65 No U.S. price				
66 No U.S. price				
67 No U.S. price				
68 No U.S. price				
69 No U.S. price				
70 No U.S. price				
71 No U.S. price				
72 No U.S. price				
73 No U.S. price				
74 No U.S. price				
75 No U.S. price				
76 No U.S. price				
77 No U.S. price				
78 No U.S. price				
79 No U.S. price				
80 No U.S. price				
81 No U.S. price				
82 No U.S. price				
83 No U.S. price				
84 No U.S. price				
85 No U.S. price				
86 No U.S. price				
87 No U.S. price				

	ORIG.	GOOD	FINE	N-MINT
❏ 88 No U.S. price				
❏ 89 No U.S. price				
❏ 90 No U.S. price				
❏ 91 No U.S. price				
❏ 92 No U.S. price				
❏ 93 No U.S. price				
❏ 94 No U.S. price				
❏ 95 No U.S. price				
❏ 96 No U.S. price				
❏ 97 No U.S. price				
❏ 98 No U.S. price				
❏ 99 No U.S. price				
❏ 100 No U.S. price				
❏ 101 No U.S. price				
❏ 102 No U.S. price				
❏ 103 No U.S. price				
❏ 104 No U.S. price				
❏ 105 No U.S. price				
❏ 106 No U.S. price				
❏ 107 No U.S. price				
❏ 108 No U.S. price				
❏ 109 No U.S. price				
❏ 110 No U.S. price				
❏ 111 No U.S. price				
❏ 112 No U.S. price				
❏ 113 No U.S. price				
❏ 114 No U.S. price				
❏ 115 No U.S. price				
❏ 116 No U.S. price				
❏ 117 No U.S. price				
❏ 118 No U.S. price				
❏ 119 No U.S. price				
❏ 120 No U.S. price				
❏ 121 No U.S. price				
❏ 122 No U.S. price				
❏ 123 No U.S. price				
❏ 124 No U.S. price				
❏ 125 No U.S. price				
❏ 126 No U.S. price				
❏ 127 No U.S. price				
❏ 128 No U.S. price				
❏ 129 No U.S. price				
❏ 130 No U.S. price				
❏ 131 No U.S. price				
❏ 132 No U.S. price				
❏ 133 No U.S. price				
❏ 134 No U.S. price				
❏ 135 No U.S. price				
❏ 136 No U.S. price				
❏ 137 No U.S. price				
❏ 138 No U.S. price				
❏ 139 No U.S. price				
❏ 140 No U.S. price				
❏ 141 No U.S. price				
❏ 142 No U.S. price				
❏ 143 No U.S. price				
❏ 144 No U.S. price				
❏ 145 No U.S. price				
❏ 146 No U.S. price				
❏ 147 No U.S. price				
❏ 148 No U.S. price				

	ORIG.	GOOD	FINE	N-MINT
❏ 149 No U.S. price				
❏ 150 No U.S. price				
❏ 151 No U.S. price				
❏ 152 No U.S. price				
❏ 153 No U.S. price				
❏ 154 No U.S. price				
❏ 155 No U.S. price				
❏ 156 No U.S. price				
❏ 157 No U.S. price				
❏ 158 No U.S. price				
❏ 159 No U.S. price				
❏ 160 No U.S. price				
❏ 161 No U.S. price				
❏ 162 No U.S. price				
❏ 163 No U.S. price				
❏ 164 No U.S. price				
❏ 165 No U.S. price				
❏ 166 No U.S. price				
❏ 167 No U.S. price				
❏ 168 No U.S. price				
❏ 169 No U.S. price				
❏ 170 No U.S. price				
❏ 171 No U.S. price				
❏ 172 No U.S. price				
❏ 173 No U.S. price				
❏ 174 No U.S. price				
❏ 175 No U.S. price				
❏ 176 No U.S. price				
❏ 177 No U.S. price				
❏ 178 No U.S. price				
❏ 179 No U.S. price				
❏ 180 No U.S. price				
❏ 181 No U.S. price				
❏ 182 No U.S. price				
❏ 183 No U.S. price				
❏ 184 No U.S. price				
❏ 185 No U.S. price				
❏ 186 No U.S. price				
❏ 187 No U.S. price				
❏ 188 No U.S. price				
❏ 189 No U.S. price				
❏ 190 No U.S. price				
❏ 191 No U.S. price				
❏ 192 No U.S. price				
❏ 193 No U.S. price				
❏ 194 No U.S. price				
❏ 195 No U.S. price				
❏ 196 No U.S. price				
❏ 197 No U.S. price				
❏ 198 No U.S. price				
❏ 199 No U.S. price				
❏ 200 No U.S. price				
❏ 201 No U.S. price				
❏ 202 No U.S. price				
❏ 203 No U.S. price				
❏ 204 No U.S. price				
❏ 205 No U.S. price				
❏ 206 No U.S. price				
❏ 207 No U.S. price				
❏ 208 No U.S. price				
❏ 209 No U.S. price				

	ORIG.	GOOD	FINE	N-MINT
☐ 210 No U.S. price				
☐ 211 No U.S. price				
☐ 212 No U.S. price				
☐ 213 No U.S. price				
☐ 214 No U.S. price				
☐ 215 No U.S. price				
☐ 216 No U.S. price				
☐ 217 No U.S. price				
☐ 218 No U.S. price				
☐ 219 No U.S. price				
☐ 220 No U.S. price				
☐ 221 No U.S. price				
☐ 222 No U.S. price				
☐ 223 No U.S. price				
☐ 224 No U.S. price				
☐ 225 No U.S. price				
☐ 226 No U.S. price				
☐ 227 No U.S. price				
☐ 228 No U.S. price				
☐ 229 No U.S. price				
☐ 230 No U.S. price				
☐ 231 No U.S. price				
☐ 232 No U.S. price				
☐ 233 No U.S. price				
☐ 234 No U.S. price				
☐ 235 No U.S. price				
☐ 236 No U.S. price				
☐ 237 No U.S. price				
☐ 238 No U.S. price				
☐ 239 No U.S. price				
☐ 240 No U.S. price				
☐ 241 No U.S. price				
☐ 242 No U.S. price				
☐ 243 No U.S. price				
☐ 244 No U.S. price				
☐ 245 No U.S. price				
☐ 246 No U.S. price				
☐ 247 No U.S. price				
☐ 248 No U.S. price				
☐ 249 No U.S. price				
☐ 250 No U.S. price				
☐ 251 No U.S. price				
☐ 252 No U.S. price				
☐ 253 No U.S. price				
☐ 254 No U.S. price				
☐ 255 No U.S. price				
☐ 256 No U.S. price				
☐ 257 No U.S. price				
☐ 258 No U.S. price				
☐ 259 No U.S. price				
☐ 260 No U.S. price				
☐ 261 No U.S. price				
☐ 262 No U.S. price				
☐ 263 No U.S. price				
☐ 264 No U.S. price				
☐ 265 No U.S. price				
☐ 266 No U.S. price				
☐ 267 No U.S. price				
☐ 268 No U.S. price				
☐ 269 No U.S. price				
☐ 270 No U.S. price				

	ORIG.	GOOD	FINE	N-MINT
☐ 271 No U.S. price...............				
☐ 272 No U.S. price...............				
☐ 273 No U.S. price...............				
☐ 274 No U.S. price...............				
☐ 275 No U.S. price...............				
☐ 276 No U.S. price...............				
☐ 277 No U.S. price...............				
☐ 278 No U.S. price...............				
☐ 279 No U.S. price...............				
☐ 280 No U.S. price...............				
☐ 281 No U.S. price...............				
☐ 282 No U.S. price...............				
☐ 283 No U.S. price...............				
☐ 284 No U.S. price...............				
☐ 285 No U.S. price...............				
☐ 286 No U.S. price...............				
☐ 287 No U.S. price...............				
☐ 288 No U.S. price...............				
☐ 289 No U.S. price...............				
☐ 290 No U.S. price...............				
☐ 291 No U.S. price...............				
☐ 292 No U.S. price...............				
☐ 293 No U.S. price...............				
☐ 294 No U.S. price...............				
☐ 295 No U.S. price...............				
☐ 296 No U.S. price...............				
☐ 297 No U.S. price...............				
☐ 298 No U.S. price...............				
☐ 299 No U.S. price...............				
☐ 300 No U.S. price...............				
☐ 301 No U.S. price...............				
☐ 302 No U.S. price...............				
☐ 303 No U.S. price...............				
☐ 304 No U.S. price...............				
☐ 305 No U.S. price...............				
☐ 306 No U.S. price...............				
☐ 307 No U.S. price...............				
☐ 308 No U.S. price...............				
☐ 309 No U.S. price...............				
☐ 310 No U.S. price...............				
☐ 311 No U.S. price...............				
☐ 312 No U.S. price...............				
☐ 313 No U.S. price...............				
☐ 314 No U.S. price...............				
☐ 315 No U.S. price...............				
☐ 316 No U.S. price...............				
☐ 317 No U.S. price...............				
☐ 318 No U.S. price...............				
☐ 319 No U.S. price...............				
☐ 320 (becomes Super Spider-Man and Captain Britain) No U.S. price.......................				

STAR WARS WEEKLY (reprints)

	ORIG.	GOOD	FINE	N-MINT
☐ 1				
☐ 2				
☐ 3				
☐ 4				
☐ 5				
☐ 6				
☐ 7				
☐ 8				

	ORIG.	GOOD	FINE	N-MINT
❑ 9				
❑ 10				
❑ 11				
❑ 12				
❑ 13				
❑ 14				
❑ 15				
❑ 16				
❑ 17				
❑ 18				
❑ 19				
❑ 20				
❑ 21				
❑ 22				
❑ 23				
❑ 24				
❑ 25				
❑ 26				
❑ 27				
❑ 28				
❑ 29				
❑ 30				
❑ 31				
❑ 32				
❑ 33				
❑ 34				
❑ 35				
❑ 36				
❑ 37				
❑ 38				
❑ 39				
❑ 40				
❑ 41				
❑ 42				
❑ 43				
❑ 44				
❑ 45				
❑ 46				
❑ 47				
❑ 48				
❑ 49				
❑ 50				
❑ 51				
❑ 52				
❑ 53				
❑ 54				
❑ 55				
❑ 56				
❑ 57				
❑ 58				
❑ 59				
❑ 60				
❑ 61				

STRIP (color magazine)

	ORIG.	GOOD	FINE	N-MINT
❑ 1	2.50	0.50	1.50	2.50
❑ 2	2.50	0.50	1.50	2.50
❑ 3	2.50	0.50	1.50	2.50
❑ 4	2.50	0.50	1.50	2.50
❑ 5	2.50	0.50	1.50	2.50
❑ 6	2.50	0.50	1.50	2.50

	ORIG.	GOOD	FINE	N-MINT
❑ 7	2.50	0.50	1.50	2.50
❑ 8	2.50	0.50	1.50	2.50
❑ 9	2.50	0.50	1.50	2.50
❑ 10	2.50	0.50	1.50	2.50
❑ 11	2.50	0.50	1.50	2.50
❑ 12	2.50	0.50	1.50	2.50
❑ 13	2.50	0.50	1.50	2.50
❑ 14	2.50	0.50	1.50	2.50
❑ 15	2.50	0.50	1.50	2.50
❑ 16	2.50	0.50	1.50	2.50
❑ 17	2.50	0.50	1.50	2.50
❑ 18	2.50	0.50	1.50	2.50
❑ 19	2.50	0.50	1.50	2.50
❑ 20	2.50	0.50	1.50	2.50

SUPER SPIDER-MAN AND CAPTAIN BRITAIN
(combined Spider-Man and Captain Britain)

❑ 231	No U.S. price
❑ 232	No U.S. price
❑ 233	No U.S. price
❑ 234	No U.S. price
❑ 235	No U.S. price
❑ 236	No U.S. price
❑ 237	No U.S. price
❑ 238	No U.S. price
❑ 239	No U.S. price
❑ 240	No U.S. price
❑ 241	No U.S. price
❑ 242	No U.S. price
❑ 243	No U.S. price
❑ 244	No U.S. price
❑ 245	No U.S. price
❑ 246	No U.S. price
❑ 247	No U.S. price

MARVEL/NELSON

ILLUMINATOR

	ORIG.	GOOD	FINE	N-MINT
❑ 1	4.99	1.00	2.99	4.99
❑ 2	4.99	1.00	2.99	4.99

LIFE OF CHRIST, THE

	ORIG.	GOOD	FINE	N-MINT
❑ 1	2.99	0.60	1.79	2.99

MARVEL/RAZORLINE

HYPERKIND

	ORIG.	GOOD	FINE	N-MINT
❑ 1 foil cover	2.50	0.50	1.50	2.50
❑ 2	1.75	0.35	1.05	1.75

STAR

AIR RAIDERS

	ORIG.	GOOD	FINE	N-MINT
❑ 1	1.00	0.20	0.60	1.00
❑ 2 (Becomes Marvel Comic)	1.00	0.20	0.60	1.00

ANIMAX

	ORIG.	GOOD	FINE	N-MINT
❑ 1	0.75	0.15	0.45	0.75
❑ 2	0.75	0.15	0.45	0.75

	ORIG.	GOOD	FINE	N-MINT
❑ 3 ....0.75	0.15	0.45	0.75
❑ 4 ....0.75	0.15	0.45	0.75

BULLWINKLE AND ROCKY

	ORIG.	GOOD	FINE	N-MINT
❑ 1 ....1.00	0.20	0.60	1.00
❑ 2 (Becomes Marvel Comic)			
....1.00	0.20	0.60	1.00

CARE BEARS

	ORIG.	GOOD	FINE	N-MINT
❑ 1 ....0.65	0.15	0.45	0.75
❑ 2 ....0.65	0.15	0.45	0.75
❑ 3 ....0.65	0.15	0.45	0.75
❑ 4 ....0.75	0.15	0.45	0.75
❑ 5 ....0.75	0.15	0.45	0.75
❑ 6 ....0.75	0.15	0.45	0.75
❑ 7 ....0.75	0.15	0.45	0.75
❑ 8 ....0.75	0.15	0.45	0.75
❑ 9 ....0.75	0.15	0.45	0.75
❑ 10 ....0.75	0.15	0.45	0.75
❑ 11 ....1.00	0.20	0.60	1.00
❑ 12 ....1.00	0.20	0.60	1.00
❑ 13 A:Madballs...................1.00	0.20	0.60	1.00
❑ 14 (becomes Marvel Comic)			
....1.00	0.20	0.60	1.00

CHUCK NORRIS

	ORIG.	GOOD	FINE	N-MINT
❑ 1 SD...................................0.75	0.15	0.45	0.75
❑ 2 SD...................................0.75	0.15	0.45	0.75
❑ 3 SD...................................0.75	0.15	0.45	0.75
❑ 4 ....0.75	0.20	0.60	1.00

DEFENDERS OF EARTH

	ORIG.	GOOD	FINE	N-MINT
❑ 1 Flash Gordon, Mandrake, Phantom			
....0.75	0.15	0.45	0.75
❑ 2 Flash Gordon, Mandrake, Phantom			
....0.75	0.15	0.45	0.75
❑ 3 Flash Gordon, Mandrake, Phantom			
....0.75	0.15	0.45	0.75

DROIDS

	ORIG.	GOOD	FINE	N-MINT
❑ 1 Star Wars......................0.75	0.15	0.45	0.75
❑ 2 Star Wars......................0.75	0.15	0.45	0.75
❑ 3 Star Wars......................0.75	0.15	0.45	0.75
❑ 4 Star Wars......................0.75	0.15	0.45	0.75
❑ 5 Star Wars......................0.75	0.15	0.45	0.75
❑ 6 Star Wars......................0.75	0.15	0.45	0.75
❑ 7 Star Wars......................0.75	0.15	0.45	0.75
❑ 8 Star Wars......................1.00	0.20	0.60	1.00

EWOKS

	ORIG.	GOOD	FINE	N-MINT
❑ 1 Star Wars......................0.65	0.15	0.45	0.75
❑ 2 Star Wars......................0.65	0.15	0.45	0.75
❑ 3 Star Wars......................0.65	0.15	0.45	0.75
❑ 4 Star Wars......................0.65	0.15	0.45	0.75
❑ 5 Star Wars......................0.65	0.15	0.45	0.75
❑ 6 Star Wars......................0.65	0.15	0.45	0.75
❑ 7 Star Wars......................0.75	0.15	0.45	0.75
❑ 8 Star Wars......................0.75	0.15	0.45	0.75

	ORIG.	GOOD	FINE	N-MINT
❑ 9 Star Wars......................0.75	0.15	0.45	0.75
❑ 10 Star Wars....................0.75	0.15	0.45	0.75
❑ 11 Star Wars....................0.75	0.15	0.45	0.75
❑ 12 Star Wars....................0.75	0.15	0.45	0.75
❑ 13 Star Wars....................0.75	0.15	0.45	0.75
❑ 14 Star Wars....................1.00	0.20	0.60	1.00

FLINTSTONE KIDS, THE

	ORIG.	GOOD	FINE	N-MINT
❑ 1 ....1.00	0.20	0.60	1.00
❑ 2 ....1.00	0.20	0.60	1.00
❑ 3 ....1.00	0.20	0.60	1.00
❑ 4 (Becomes Marvel Comic)			
....1.00	0.20	0.60	1.00

FOOFUR

	ORIG.	GOOD	FINE	N-MINT
❑ 1 ....1.00	0.20	0.60	1.00
❑ 2 ....1.00	0.20	0.60	1.00
❑ 3 ....1.00	0.20	0.60	1.00
❑ 4 (Becomes Marvel Comic)			
....1.00	0.20	0.60	1.00

FRAGGLE ROCK

	ORIG.	GOOD	FINE	N-MINT
❑ 1 ....0.65	0.13	0.39	0.65
❑ 2 ....0.65	0.13	0.39	0.65
❑ 3 ....0.65	0.13	0.39	0.65
❑ 4 ....0.65	0.13	0.39	0.65
❑ 5 ....0.65	0.13	0.39	0.65
❑ 6 ....0.65	0.13	0.39	0.65
❑ 7 ....0.75	0.15	0.45	0.75
❑ 8 ....0.75	0.15	0.45	0.75

GET ALONG GANG

	ORIG.	GOOD	FINE	N-MINT
❑ 1 ....0.65	0.13	0.39	0.65
❑ 2 ....0.65	0.13	0.39	0.65
❑ 3 ....0.65	0.13	0.39	0.65
❑ 4 ....0.65	0.13	0.39	0.65
❑ 5 ....0.65	0.13	0.39	0.65
❑ 6 ....0.65	0.13	0.39	0.65

HEATHCLIFF

	ORIG.	GOOD	FINE	N-MINT
❑ 1 ....0.65	0.13	0.39	0.65
❑ 2 ....0.65	0.13	0.39	0.65
❑ 3 ....0.65	0.13	0.39	0.65
❑ 4 ....0.65	0.13	0.39	0.65
❑ 5 ....0.65	0.13	0.39	0.65
❑ 6 ....0.65	0.13	0.39	0.65
❑ 7 ....0.75	0.15	0.45	0.75
❑ 8 ....0.75	0.15	0.45	0.75
❑ 9 ....0.75	0.15	0.45	0.75
❑ 10 ....0.75	0.15	0.45	0.75
❑ 11 ....0.75	0.15	0.45	0.75
❑ 12 ....0.75	0.15	0.45	0.75
❑ 13 ....0.75	0.15	0.45	0.75
❑ 14 ....0.75	0.15	0.45	0.75
❑ 15 ....0.75	0.15	0.45	0.75
❑ 16 ....1.00	0.20	0.60	1.00
❑ 17 ....1.00	0.20	0.60	1.00

	ORIG.	GOOD	FINE	N-MINT
❏ 18	1.00	0.20	0.60	1.00
❏ 19	1.00	0.20	0.60	1.00
❏ 20	1.00	0.20	0.60	1.00
❏ 21	1.00	0.20	0.60	1.00
❏ 22 (Becomes Marvel Comic)				
	1.00	0.20	0.60	1.00

HEATHCLIFF ANNUAL

	ORIG.	GOOD	FINE	N-MINT
❏ 1 (Becomes Marvel Comic)				
	1.25	0.25	0.75	1.25

HEATHCLIFF'S FUNHOUSE

	ORIG.	GOOD	FINE	N-MINT
❏ 1	1.00	0.20	0.60	1.00
❏ 2	1.00	0.20	0.60	1.00
❏ 3	1.00	0.20	0.60	1.00
❏ 4	1.00	0.20	0.60	1.00
❏ 5 (becomes Marvel Comic)				
	1.00	0.20	0.60	1.00

HUGGA BUNCH

	ORIG.	GOOD	FINE	N-MINT
❏ 1	0.75	0.15	0.45	0.75
❏ 2	0.75	0.15	0.45	0.75
❏ 3	0.75	0.15	0.45	0.75
❏ 4	0.75	0.15	0.45	0.75
❏ 5	1.00	0.20	0.60	1.00
❏ 6	1.00	0.20	0.60	1.00

INHUMANOIDS

	ORIG.	GOOD	FINE	N-MINT
❏ 1	0.75	0.15	0.45	0.75
❏ 2	0.75	0.15	0.45	0.75
❏ 3	0.75	0.15	0.45	0.75
❏ 4	1.00	0.20	0.60	1.00

MADBALLS

	ORIG.	GOOD	FINE	N-MINT
❏ 1	0.75	0.15	0.45	0.75
❏ 2	0.75	0.15	0.45	0.75
❏ 3	0.75	0.15	0.45	0.75
❏ 4	1.00	0.20	0.60	1.00
❏ 5	1.00	0.20	0.60	1.00
❏ 6	1.00	0.20	0.60	1.00
❏ 7	1.00	0.20	0.60	1.00
❏ 8 (becomes Marvel Comic)				
	1.00	0.20	0.60	1.00

MASTERS OF THE UNIVERSE

	ORIG.	GOOD	FINE	N-MINT
❏ 1	0.75	0.15	0.45	0.75
❏ 2	0.75	0.15	0.45	0.75
❏ 3	0.75	0.15	0.45	0.75
❏ 4	0.75	0.15	0.45	0.75
❏ 5	0.75	0.15	0.45	0.75
❏ 6	0.75	0.15	0.45	0.75
❏ 7	1.00	0.20	0.60	1.00
❏ 8	1.00	0.20	0.60	1.00
❏ 9	1.00	0.20	0.60	1.00
❏ 10	1.00	0.20	0.60	1.00
❏ 11	1.00	0.20	0.60	1.00
❏ 12	1.00	0.20	0.60	1.00
❏ 13	1.00	0.20	0.60	1.00

MISTY

	ORIG.	GOOD	FINE	N-MINT
❏ 1	0.65	0.15	0.45	0.75
❏ 2	0.65	0.15	0.45	0.75
❏ 3	0.75	0.15	0.45	0.75
❏ 4	0.75	0.15	0.45	0.75
❏ 5	0.75	0.15	0.45	0.75
❏ 6	0.75	0.15	0.45	0.75

MUPPET BABIES

	ORIG.	GOOD	FINE	N-MINT
❏ 1	0.65	0.15	0.45	0.75
❏ 2	0.65	0.15	0.45	0.75
❏ 3	0.65	0.15	0.45	0.75
❏ 4	0.65	0.15	0.45	0.75
❏ 5	0.65	0.15	0.45	0.75
❏ 6	0.65	0.15	0.45	0.75
❏ 7	0.75	0.15	0.45	0.75
❏ 8	0.75	0.15	0.45	0.75
❏ 9	0.75	0.15	0.45	0.75
❏ 10	0.75	0.15	0.45	0.75
❏ 11	0.75	0.15	0.45	0.75
❏ 12	0.75	0.15	0.45	0.75
❏ 13	0.75	0.15	0.45	0.75
❏ 14	1.00	0.20	0.60	1.00
❏ 15	1.00	0.20	0.60	1.00
❏ 16	1.00	0.20	0.60	1.00
❏ 17 (Becomes Marvel Comic)				
	1.00	0.20	0.60	1.00

MUPPETS TAKE MANHATTAN

	ORIG.	GOOD	FINE	N-MINT
❏ 1 movie adaptation	0.60	0.13	0.39	0.65
❏ 2 movie adaptation	0.60	0.13	0.39	0.65
❏ 3 movie adaptation	0.60	0.13	0.39	0.65

PETER PORKER, THE SPECTACULAR SPIDER-HAM

	ORIG.	GOOD	FINE	N-MINT
❏ 1	0.65	0.20	0.60	1.00
❏ 2	0.65	0.20	0.60	1.00
❏ 3	0.65	0.20	0.60	1.00
❏ 4	0.65	0.20	0.60	1.00
❏ 5	0.65	0.20	0.60	1.00
❏ 6	0.65	0.20	0.60	1.00
❏ 7	0.75	0.15	0.45	0.75
❏ 8	0.75	0.15	0.45	0.75
❏ 9	0.75	0.15	0.45	0.75
❏ 10	0.75	0.15	0.45	0.75
❏ 11	0.75	0.15	0.45	0.75
❏ 12	0.75	0.15	0.45	0.75
❏ 13	0.75	0.15	0.45	0.75
❏ 14	0.75	0.15	0.45	0.75
❏ 15	0.75	0.15	0.45	0.75
❏ 16	1.00	0.20	0.60	1.00
❏ 17	1.00	0.20	0.60	1.00

PLANET TERRY

	ORIG.	GOOD	FINE	N-MINT
❏ 1	0.65	0.13	0.39	0.65
❏ 2	0.65	0.13	0.39	0.65
❏ 3	0.65	0.13	0.39	0.65

	ORIG.	GOOD	FINE	N-MINT
4	0.65	0.13	0.39	0.65
5	0.65	0.13	0.39	0.65
6	0.65	0.13	0.39	0.65
7	0.65	0.13	0.39	0.65
8	0.65	0.13	0.39	0.65
9	0.65	0.13	0.39	0.65
10	0.65	0.13	0.39	0.65
11	0.65	0.13	0.39	0.65
12	0.65	0.13	0.39	0.65

POPPLES, THE

	ORIG.	GOOD	FINE	N-MINT
1	0.75	0.15	0.45	0.75
2	0.75	0.15	0.45	0.75
3	0.75	0.15	0.45	0.75
4	1.00	0.20	0.60	1.00

ROYAL ROY

	ORIG.	GOOD	FINE	N-MINT
1	0.65	0.13	0.39	0.65
2	0.65	0.13	0.39	0.65
3	0.65	0.13	0.39	0.65
4	0.65	0.13	0.39	0.65
5	0.65	0.13	0.39	0.65
6	0.65	0.13	0.39	0.65

SILVER HAWKS

	ORIG.	GOOD	FINE	N-MINT
1	1.00	0.20	0.60	1.00
2	1.00	0.20	0.60	1.00
3	1.00	0.20	0.60	1.00
4	1.00	0.20	0.60	1.00
5 (becomes Marvel comic)	1.00	0.20	0.60	1.00

STAR COMICS MAGAZINE (digest)

	ORIG.	GOOD	FINE	N-MINT
1 reprints	1.50	0.30	0.90	1.50
2 reprints	1.50	0.30	0.90	1.50
3 reprints	1.50	0.30	0.90	1.50
4 reprints	1.50	0.30	0.90	1.50
5 reprints	1.50	0.30	0.90	1.50
6 reprints	1.50	0.30	0.90	1.50
7 reprints	1.50	0.30	0.90	1.50
8 reprints	1.50	0.30	0.90	1.50
9 reprints	1.50	0.30	0.90	1.50
10 reprints	1.50	0.30	0.90	1.50
11 reprints	1.50	0.30	0.90	1.50
12 reprints	1.50	0.30	0.90	1.50
13 reprints	1.50	0.30	0.90	1.50

STRAWBERRY SHORTCAKE

	ORIG.	GOOD	FINE	N-MINT
1	0.65	0.13	0.39	0.65
2	0.65	0.13	0.39	0.65
3	0.65	0.13	0.39	0.65
4	0.65	0.13	0.39	0.65
5	0.65	0.13	0.39	0.65
6	0.65	0.13	0.39	0.65

THUNDERCATS

	ORIG.	GOOD	FINE	N-MINT
1	0.65	1.20	3.60	6.00
2	0.65	0.60	1.80	3.00

	ORIG.	GOOD	FINE	N-MINT
3	0.75	0.20	0.60	1.00
4	0.75	0.15	0.45	0.75
5	0.75	0.15	0.45	0.75
6	0.75	0.15	0.45	0.75
7	0.75	0.15	0.45	0.75
8	0.75	0.15	0.45	0.75
9	0.75	0.15	0.45	0.75
10	0.75	0.15	0.45	0.75
11	1.00	0.20	0.60	1.00
12	1.00	0.20	0.60	1.00
13	1.00	0.20	0.60	1.00
14	1.00	0.20	0.60	1.00
15	1.00	0.20	0.60	1.00
16	1.00	0.20	0.60	1.00
17	1.00	0.20	0.60	1.00
18	1.00	0.20	0.60	1.00
19	1.00	0.20	0.60	1.00
20	1.00	0.20	0.60	1.00
21 (Becomes Marvel Comic)	1.00	0.20	0.60	1.00

TOP DOG

	ORIG.	GOOD	FINE	N-MINT
1	0.65	0.13	0.39	0.65
2	0.65	0.13	0.39	0.65
3	0.65	0.13	0.39	0.65
4	0.65	0.13	0.39	0.65
5	0.65	0.13	0.39	0.65
6	0.65	0.13	0.39	0.65
7	0.75	0.15	0.45	0.75
8	0.75	0.15	0.45	0.75
9	0.75	0.15	0.45	0.75
10	0.75	0.15	0.45	0.75
11	0.75	0.15	0.45	0.75
12	0.75	0.15	0.45	0.75
13	0.75	0.15	0.45	0.75
14	1.00	0.20	0.60	1.00

VISIONARIES

	ORIG.	GOOD	FINE	N-MINT
1	1.50	0.30	0.90	1.50
2 (Becomes Marvel Comic)	1.00	0.20	0.60	1.00

WALLY THE WIZARD

	ORIG.	GOOD	FINE	N-MINT
1	0.65	0.13	0.39	0.65
2	0.65	0.13	0.39	0.65
3	0.65	0.13	0.39	0.65
4	0.65	0.13	0.39	0.65
5	0.65	0.13	0.39	0.65
6	0.65	0.13	0.39	0.65
7	0.65	0.13	0.39	0.65
8	0.65	0.13	0.39	0.65
9	0.65	0.13	0.39	0.65
10	0.65	0.13	0.39	0.65
11	0.65	0.13	0.39	0.65
12	0.65	0.13	0.39	0.65

YOUR MARVEL® HEADQUARTERS

COMICS BUYER'S GUIDE

The "weekly leader" in the comics field for the latest industry news, reviews, and ads for hundreds of great deals on **Marvel** collectibles!

CBG PRICE GUIDE

MORE of the current values than any other price guide...from the comics authorities at **Comics Buyer's Guide**. Plus tips on new hot releases, trading cards and more!

Pick up copies at your local shop, or subscribe today!